Expositions of the Psalms

Augustinian Heritage Institute

Board of Directors
+John E. Rotelle, O.S.A. (1939–2002), founding director
Joseph L. Farrell, O.S.A.   Jane E. Merdinger
David Hunter   Boniface Ramsey
Joseph T. Kelley   James Wetzel
Patricia H. Lo   Jonathan Yates

Translation Advisory Board
Allan D. Fitzgerald, O.S.A.   Edmund Hill, O.P.
Joseph McGowan   Boniface Ramsey

THE WORKS OF SAINT AUGUSTINE
A Translation for the 21st Century

Part III — Books

Volume 20:

Expositions of the Psalms

121-150

The English translation of the works of Saint Augustine has been made possible with contributions from the following:

Order of Saint Augustine
Province of Saint Thomas of Villanova (East)
Province of Our Mother of Good Counsel (Midwest)
Province of Saint Augustine (California)
Province of Saint Joseph (Canada)
Vice Province of Our Mother of Good Counsel
Province of Our Mother of Good Counsel (Ireland)
Province of Saint John Stone (England and Scotland)
Province of Our Mother of Good Counsel (Australia)
The Augustinians of the Assumption (North America)
The Sisters of Saint Thomas of Villanova

Order of Augustinian Recollects
Province of Saint Augustine
Mr. and Mrs. James C. CrouseMr.
and Mrs. Paul Henkels
Mr. and Mrs. Francis E. McGill, Jr.
Mr. and Mrs. Mariano J. Rotelle

THE WORKS OF SAINT AUGUSTINE
A Translation for the 21st Century

Expositions of the Psalms
(Enarrationes in Psalmos)

121-150

III/20

translation and notes by
+ Maria Boulding, O.S.B.

editor
Boniface Ramsey

New City Press
Hyde Park, New York

Published in the United States by New City Press
202 Comforter Blvd., Hyde Park, New York 12538
©2000 Augustinian Heritage Institute

Cover picture (paperback): Saint Augustine in his study, Sandro Botticelli
Uffizi Gallery, Florence, Italy.

Library of Congress Cataloging-in-Publication Data:
Augustine, Saint, Bishop of Hippo.
　The works of Saint Augustine.
　"Augustinian Heritage Institute"
　Includes bibliographical references and indexes.
　Contents: — pt. 3, v .15. Expositions of the Psalms, 1-32
—pt. 3, v. 1. Sermons on the Old Testament, 1-19.
— pt. 3, v. 2. Sermons on the Old Testament, 20-50 — [et al.] — pt. 3,
v. 10 Sermons on various subjects, 341-400.
　1. Theology — Early church, ca. 30-600. I. Hill,
Edmund. II. Rotelle, John E. III. Augustinian
Heritage Institute. IV. Title.
BR65.A5E53 1990 270.2 89-28878
ISBN 1-56548-055-4 (series)
ISBN 1-56548-211-5 (pt. 3, v. 20)
ISBN 1-56548-210-7 (pt. 3, v. 20: pbk.)

4th Printing February 2020

Printed in the United States of America

Contents

Exposition of Psalm 121 1
Introduction: the power of love to lift us to Jerusalem—1; Verse 1. Mutual encouragement along the road—2; Verse 2. Think of yourself as though you were there already—3; Verse 3. The holy city is still being built—4; It participates in the being of God—6; Verse 4. The tribes of the Lord, the true Israel—10; Verse 5. The apostles sit on seats to judge, but they are themselves the Lord's seat—13; Verse 6. The peace of Jerusalem is founded on love—15; Verse 7. Love is the city's strength—17; Verses 8–9. Fraternal charity is the reason for preaching of Jerusalem's peace—19

Exposition of Psalm 122 21
Introduction: Christ ascends, with his body; the two-way link of charity—21; Verse 1. The one Christ prays from the ends of the earth—22; The humble climber; keep your eyes off yourself—23; The spiritual heaven—24; Verse 2. Expectant servants, chastised but watching for mercy—26; Verses 3–4. Those who are affluent in any sense will despise us—30; The true poverty of a Christian—34; Riches, health, and righteousness elude us in this life, but we hope for them in the new Jerusalem—35

Exposition of Psalm 123 37
Verses 1–2. This is a song of triumph; let us join in as though we were part of the triumph already—37; Verse 3. What does the psalm mean about our being swallowed alive?—41; Verses 4–5. Rushing water as a symbol of persecution—44; "Insubstantial water" signifies wealth gained in violation of conscience—46; Verses 6–7. The sparrow's escape—49; Verse 8. Acknowledge that your escape was due solely to God's help—50; Conclusion: plans for tomorrow's sermon—51

Exposition of Psalm 124 53
Verse 1. Rightness of heart; stability in God—53; Verse 2. Some mountains receive light, peace, and righteousness from God and transmit them to his people; other mountains are proud and dangerous—56; Verse 3. Christian submission to lawful authority—60; But the unjust will not dominate in the long run—63; Verses 4–5. Peace is the inheritance of people with upright hearts—64

Exposition of Psalm 125 67
Verse 1. The song of former captives, redeemed by Christ's blood—67; Released from captivity, the redeemed are comforted in hope—70; Verse 2. The difference between the bodily mouth

and the mouth of the heart—72; Verses 3–4. Captivity is canceled and sins forgiven, as ice melts in warm wind—77; Verse 5. Sowing seed means doing good works and helping the poor, but almsgiving is not confined to giving money—79; Verse 6. Sow courageously in harsh conditions—82; Conclusion: we descended disastrously, but our good Samaritan lifted us up; now let us ascend—82

Exposition of Psalm 126 85

Verse 1. Solomon, named in the title, prefigures Christ, whose body is the true temple—85; The vigilance and humility required of a bishop or overseer—87; Verse 2. Do not try to rise before Christ, your light—89; Sitting down before rising signifies humility before exaltation—91; Verse 3. The Church is in labor, but not all the children to be born are "the beloved"—94; Verse 4. Shaking out the prophets, the Lord made the apostles their sons; the apostles are the Lord's far-shot arrows—96; Verse 5. The apostles' preaching: universal, open, and centered in Christ—100; Conclusion: plans for tomorrow—101

Exposition of Psalm 127 103

Verses 1–4. Why we cannot take this psalm as simply a promise of material happiness—103; We have here a prophecy that needs to be shaken out—104; The man pronounced blessed in the psalm must be Christ—106; The martyr Felix found dead in his dungeon—108; Fear and chaste love—109; Test the quality of your fear and love: searching questions—112; How we eat the labors of our fruits—113; Christ's fruitful wife, the Church—116; Members of the Church are both wife and children to Christ, and even mother—117; Verse 5. The blessings and good things that last—119; Verse 6. Peace in Jerusalem—121

Exposition of Psalm 128 125

Introduction: sowing the word for various hearers—125; Verses 1–3. The Church has been under attack all down the ages—126; Against avarice—128; It is no excuse for vicious conduct to say that you earn your living that way—130; The Church carries the unrepentant—131; Verse 4. A warning for the proud who defend their sins—133; Verses 5–7. The fate of grass growing in high places—135; Verse 8. All who have passed along the way have blessed us—136

Exposition of Psalm 129 139

Verses 1–3. A sinner cries from the depths, hoping for God's mercy—139; Verse 4. The law of charity: bear one another's burdens, and forgive if you hope to be forgiven—141; Verses 5–6. Hoping from the morning watch means hoping to share in Christ's resurrection—145; Hoping even until night means hoping until the end of your life or the end of the world—147; The true hope of the true Israel—149; Verses 7–8. Hope only in the redemptive mercy of God—150

Exposition of Psalm 130 153

In Christ's body, the true temple, acceptable prayer is offered—153; The cords of sin—154; Let us hear our own voice in the psalm—155; Verse 1. Humility of heart is a sacrifice offered to God—156; Do not covet the power to work miracles; the story of Simon Magus—157; Diversity of function is necessary within the body—158; The serious danger of pride over graces received: Paul's humiliation—160; The important thing is to be a healthy member whose name is written in heaven—162; Verse 2. Be nourished on milk until you are ready for bread; do not follow the heretics in aspiring to bread too soon—163; A different interpretation: the unweaned child is one who refuses to grow—167; Even those who eat solid food are not yet perfect—170; Go on hoping until hope gives way to the reality—171

Exposition of Psalm 131 173

Introduction—173; Verses 1-2. David's forbearance—174; Verses 3-5. David's vow; he aspires to make a place for the Lord in himself—176; Turning over private property to the common good makes a place for the Lord—177; The perils and illusions of sleep—179; The difference between tent-dwelling and living in a house—180; Verse 6. Ephrathah and the woodland pastures—181; Verse 7. The place for the Lord's house—182; Verses 8-9. Christ's resurrection and the hope of resurrection for his holy ark—184; Verse 10. For David's sake Christ does not withdraw from the remnant of Israel—185; Verse 11. God's promise to David is irrevocable—187; Verse 12. Though the promise to David is expressed conditionally, God's oath secures its fulfillment in his own way—188; Verses 13-15. God's promises to Zion, city of his choice—190; Verses 16-18. Augustine's conclusion roots this messianic psalm explicitly in Christ—194

Exposition of Psalm 132 197

Verse 1. The opening words of this psalm inspired the early community of Jewish Christians and later engendered monasteries—197; Circumcellions—pseudo-monks—199; Three groups mentioned in the gospels typify clerics, religious, and laity—200; Noah, Daniel, and Job are also types of the same three vocations—202; An argument about the scriptural basis for the terms "agonistici" and "monks"—203; Verse 2. Oil flows from head to beard, from Christ to the strong; oil symbolizes the Holy Spirit—204; Unconquered love in Stephen: the effect of the oil—205; The oil flows from the beard to the border of the tunic: monastic life—206; Verse 3. From Hermon, the "exalted light," grace flows to the mature in Zion—207; The circle of blessing—209

Exposition of Psalm 133 211

Verse 1. Blessing God in the spaciousness of love—211; Verse 2. Praising God in the dark night—212; Verse 3. Many bless the Lord, but he blesses his servants as one—213

Exposition of Psalm 134 215

Verse 1. As his servants and his children, we must praise the Lord—215; Verse 2. Praise him out of gratitude for being brought into his house—216; Verse 3. God is essential goodness—217; To contemplate God's goodness in himself is beyond our capacity, but he has given us the mediator—220; Since we cannot grasp Being-Itself, God has named himself the God of Abraham, Isaac, and Jacob—221; Verse 4. The election of Israel—224; Verse 5. God is above all so-called gods—224; Verse 6. The Lord is omnipotent in creation and in the realm of grace—226; Verse 7. Clouds, lightning, wind: the works of the wise creator—229; Verses 8–12. The wonders of the exodus and the appropriation of the land—229; Verse 13. Thanksgiving and praise for God's work in creation and redemption—230; Augustine begins to expound the spiritual sense of the foregoing verses. Verse 6: The creation of the Church—231; Verse 7. Clouds, lightning, rain, and wind signify preaching—232; Verses 8–9. The first-born represent faith, the beginning of our life with God—233; Verses 10–13. The slaying of pagan kings symbolizes God's punishment of the demons who trouble the Church and block our way—235; Verse 14. The Lord makes a distinction within his own people and calls the gentiles—238; Verses 15–18. The folly of idols, their defeat by the Lord, their detrimental effect on their clients—240; Verses 19–20. The work of grace in the new house of Israel—242; Verse 21. The vision of peace—242

Exposition of Psalm 135 245

Verse 1. The primary motive for praise and confession: God's mercy—245; Verses 2–3. How can God be called the "God of gods"?—246; Verses 4–7. Augustine finds that his Latin version obscures the psalm's intention—249; Verses 5–10. God alone creates; the intelligent heavens are his spiritual creation—250; Verses 11–26. A rapid application of the remaining verses to God's continuing activity in the realm of grace—253

Exposition of Psalm 136 255

Verse 1. The two cities—255; Love of Zion colors our whole life—256; What are these rivers of Babylon?—257; False and true sadness, false and true joy—259; Verse 2. Christian harps may have to be hung on Babylonian trees for the present—260; Verse 3. When the devil uses his spokespersons to ask us for songs, it is better to hang up our harps—261; Verses 4–5. Be careful not to forget Zion yourself—266; Zion has songs for both rich and poor—267; Verses 5–6. Zion is your right hand, earthly happiness your left; the songs of Zion are your native tongue—269; Verse 7. The malice of Edom, descended from Esau—271; Verses 8–9. Revenge on Babylon—274; Conclusion: sing the songs of Zion, slay your enemies, and long for the eternal Jerusalem—275

Exposition of Psalm 137 277

> Verse 1. A holocaust of praise—277; Joy in the presence of the angels: Saint Crispina—278; Verse 2. In our hearts, and in the holy company of the angels, God's name is to be glorified—279; Verse 3. An urgent prayer for spiritual fruitfulness—281; Verses 4-5. The confession of earthly rulers—284; Verse 6. Do not imagine that God cannot see you—285; Verse 7. This present life is anguish for homesick pilgrims—287; God's right and left hands: eternal and temporal salvation—288; Verse 8. Leave vengeance to the Lord; he will repay—290; A different interpretation: Christ repays our debt—291; A final prayer: do not disdain your own work, Lord—292

Exposition of Psalm 138 293

> A mistake has been made by the reader, but we can profit from it—293; Christ and the Church, head and members, two in one flesh and one voice—293; Verses 1-2. The form of God and the form of a servant; death and resurrection—295; Verses 3-4. The prodigal son seems to be speaking here—296; Verses 5-6. God's mysterious wisdom in blinding part of Israel, with a view to ultimate mercy—298; Verses 7-10. You cannot get away from God, but let the wings of charity lift you—303; Verse 11. Christ illumines our night—305; Verse 12. Through recognition of God's remedial punishments, and holy indifference to varying fortunes, believers meet light and darkness with equanimity—306; Verses 13-14. The secret of this inner freedom and detachment—309; Verse 15. Strong inner support—312; Verses 16-17. Christ's imperfect members—314; Verses 18-20. The Church is a mixed collection of people—317; Verses 21-22. Love your enemies, and hate their sins—320; Verses 23-24. God reads the Church's heart and leads it in the eternal way, Christ—321; Conclusion—323

Exposition of Psalm 139 325

> Introduction: the head and the body; good and bad people are inextricably mixed—325; Verse 1. The title points to David, which means, to Christ—327; Verse 2. No one sins without harming anyone else—328; Verses 3-4. Smooth talk and malicious hearts—330; Verses 4-5. Active hostility from the proud; the traps set by sinners—331; Verses 7-8. Intimacy with God in the midst of struggle—334; Verse 9. Watch your desires—336; Verse 10. Lying is a laborious business—338; Verse 11. Burning coals can have different effects on different targets—339; Verse 12. Do not talk more than you must; listen to the teacher within you—341; Verse 13. The Lord will champion the poor—343; Verse 14. The face of God, the face of Christ—344

Exposition of Psalm 140 347

> Introduction: pray for the preacher—347; Scripture teaches one thing: charity; the characteristics of true charity—347; The whole Christ speaks in this psalm—349; Verses 1-3. Christ's evening

sacrifice on the cross; he speaks in our name—351; Verse 4. Do not consort with the self-styled elect, and do not make excuses for your sins—353; Do not blame God or the stars or fate for your sins—356; The Manichean elect—357; Verse 5. Just correction is preferable to insincere flattery—362; Be your own just judge, and align yourself with God—363; Yet the inner struggle continues in this life—364; A further warning against being deceived by flattery—366; Everyone needs forgiveness for some kind of sin—366; Verse 6. Christ's prayer, and Christ's words, have vanquished the wisdom of the ancients—369; Verse 7. The death of martyrs and the fertility of the Church—371; Verses 8–9. Christians under persecution prayed in fear—372; Verse 10. Christ was alone in his passion, abandoned and denied by his disciples—373; Christ was alone until his passover because before him no one had died for confessing Christ—376

Exposition of Psalm 141 379

Introduction; take care to ruminate on what you hear—379; Verse 2. The cry of the heart—380; Verse 3. Pray within your heart, with the door shut against the devil—381; The Lord knows our paths—384; Walking in Christ, the way—386; Verse 5. Christ, or the martyr, stands firm and does not flee—389; Verses 6–7. The Church prays under persecution, but its real enemies are superhuman—391; Verse 8. The prospect of ultimate freedom—394

Exposition of Psalm 142 399

Verse 1. David, persecuted by his son, foreshadows Christ—399; Christ, the head of the body—400; The enemies among our nearest and dearest—403; Verse 2. In this life not one of us is just in God's sight—405; Verses 3–4. The downward pull, the upward call—407; Christ, free among the dead—407; We were there—408; Verse 5. All is grace—409; Verses 6–7. Thirsting for God, the psalmist begs for grace and for God's benign regard—411; Verse 8. Mercy in the morning; while night lasts, walk toward the lamp of the divine scriptures—413; Verse 9. Fleeing to God from invisible enemies—414; Verse 10. God is all things to me—416; Verses 10–12. A hurried conclusion—416

Exposition of Psalm 143 419

Verse 1. The title: David and Goliath—419; The whole body of Christ, armed by the Spirit, fights Goliath—422; The interior warfare of each Christian—423; If you are first subject to God, your carnal impulses will be subject to you—424; Verse 2. The condition for God's mercy to us: we must forgive—427; The prospect of peace after strife—429; Verses 3–4. The glory and humiliation of human beings—430; Verses 5–8. The Church prays for deliverance from pride, conspiracy, and foolish talkers—433; Verses 9–10. The new song; the sword of division—435; Verses 12–14. The aliens are known by their desires. What is happiness?—437; Verse 15. God's children know their right hand from their left—440

Exposition of Psalm 144 443

> Introduction: to show us how to praise him rightly, God has praised himself—443; Verse 1. The honor of the Jewish people—443; Verse 2. Praising God in good fortune and in calamity—444; Verse 3. Your praise of God will not be interrupted by your death—447; Verse 4. Praising God for his wonderful works—448; Verses 5-7. Telling the story of God's greatness and his abundant sweetness—451; Verse 7. The sweetness of grace—452; Verses 8 9. The generosity and forbearance of God—454; Verse 10. The very earth confesses to God's glory—457; Verses 11-13. The glorious beauty of the coming kingdom—459; Verse 13. The scriptures are a record of God's promises to us, and nearly all are fulfilled already—460; Verses 14-17. The Lord sustains those who lose worldly status but remain faithful; he gives or withholds favors for our good—462; Verses 18-19. The right way to pray for things, and God's way of answering—465; Verse 20. Gentleness and severity in God—467; Verse 21. Conclusion: universal praise—467

Exposition of Psalm 145 469

> While dwelling on earth, we are called heavenward by God's word—469; Verse 2. Rejoice in hope—469; Who is the speaker, if the soul is addressed? Not the body, for the soul is nobler than the body—470; The soul admonishes itself: the rational mind counsels the lower faculties—473; Imperfect praise on earth will give way to perfect praise in heaven—474; Verses 3-4. Do not trust in powerful men, or regard the minister of baptism as the source of salvation—477; Verse 5. God will be your possession, and you will be his—480; Verse 6. The glory of God in creation—481; God's providential care encompasses all he has made—482; Verse 7. Not all suffering is injury; God sees justice done for those who suffer injustice—484; Verse 8. The Lord's saving work—487; Verse 9. The Church is a foreigner, an orphan, and a widow—489; Verse 10. The prospect of eternity—491

Exposition of Psalm 146 493

> Verse 1. Why praise God?—493; Let the whole of your life be a psalm of praise to God—494; Verse 2. The building of Jerusalem, whose citizens see God—496; Verse 3. Broken, contrite hearts will be healed—498; A badly set fracture may need to be broken and re-set—500; The Church's sacraments and rites are bandages for our temporal condition—501; Verse 4. Being numbered among the stars, through charity—502; Verse 5. God's understanding is infinite, and it baffles us—504; Verse 6. If scripture at first seems obscure, do not be impatient like the Manichees—506; Verse 7. Begin with confession if you wish to attain to the contemplation of wisdom—508; Verse 8. The sky of scripture is providentially obscured so that, when the clouds expound it, we may enjoy rain—509; Almsgiving to the poor and contributions to your pastors are your duty—510; Verse 9. Raven chicks cry to the Lord for food—514; Verses 10-11.

Not human strength, but hope in his mercy, finds favor with the Lord—515

Exposition of Psalm 147 517

Sunday's sermon on the last judgment did not leave time for any exposition of the psalm, which has been deferred until today—517; If some parts of scripture are initially obscure, knock humbly—518; If our faith is wide awake, we shall long for eternal life—520; How to be prepared for the last day—522; Verse 12. The prophets Haggai and Zechariah stir us to love and longing for the holy city—524; We have better things to watch than pagan shows—526; Verse 13. The reinforced gates—528; The whole Church is a virgin—529; Make sure you have the oil of a good conscience in God's sight—530; Merciful generosity toward the needy will secure a merciful judgment on ourselves, in spite of our shortcomings—532; Verse 14. Love for the peace of Jerusalem—535; The law (Genesis), the prophets (Psalm 21), and the gospel foretell the universality of the Church—536; The rich man's request—but someone has risen from the dead to tell us—539; The risen one not only revealed himself as the bridegroom; he also pointed to his bride, the universal Church—542; Another argument: the Church of the Holy Spirit speaks in all languages—544; Hunger for perfect peace—546; Verse 15. The swiftness of the Word—547; Verse 16. We are cold and unresponsive, but God calls us to repentance through his beneficial mist—549; Verse 17. The significance of ice—552; Verse 18. God's word and God's breath melt even ice—553; Verse 19. Only Christ suffered in total innocence—555; Verse 20. The true Israel—557

Exposition of Psalm 148 559

Lent and Eastertime signify our present life and the life to come—559; Praise God with all your thoughts and actions—560; Verse 1. All creatures praise the Lord in their own way—561; The prophets promise future freedom—563; Verses 2–5. The summons addressed to all creation—564; Verse 6. The guarantee of the promise that we shall live for ever—565; Verse 7. Weather systems and dragons praise God—567; Verse 8. God's providence extends to all his works—568; Verses 9–13. The litany concludes—573; Verse 14. Universal confession—573; In winter life is hidden, but summer will reveal it—574; The Israel that is close to God—575

Exposition of Psalm 149 579

Verse 1. The new song of grace, charity, and unity—579; The new song is sung worldwide—581; Verse 2. Israel sees God through charity—583; Christ is our creator, our king, our priest, and our pure sacrifice—584; Verse 3. Christ's worldwide choir—586; Verses 4–5. True and false glory—587; Verse 6. The saints praise God for his gifts—589; The double-edged sword of God's word—589; Verse 7. The sword is wielded—591; Verse 8. The fetters of restraint, of fear, of love, and of marriage—592; Verse 9. The fulfillment of prophecy, the glory of the saints—596

Exposition of Psalm 150 597
> Why are there 150 psalms?—597; Is there only one book of Psalms or five?—599; There is special significance in the conclusion of each set of fifty psalms—601; Verses 1–2. The attributes of God which the psalm bids us praise are found in the saints themselves—602; Verses 3–4. The diversity of musical instruments represents the diversity of holiness—603; Verses 5–6. Every type of sound is included, every spirit invited to praise God—604; Concluding prayer—605

Index of Scripture 607

Index 617

Exposition of Psalm 121

A Sermon to the People[1]

Introduction: the power of love to lift us to Jerusalem

1. Impure love inflames the soul, lures it toward the pursuit of earthly things which are desirable but doomed to perish, and plunges it headlong into the deepest turpitude.[2] Holy love raises the soul to heavenly thoughts and kindles in it a longing for eternal realities, arousing its desire for what neither passes nor dies, and lifting it from the depth of hell to heaven. Every kind of love has its own energy, and in the soul of a lover love cannot be idle; it must lead somewhere. Do you want to discern the character of a person's love? Notice where it leads. We do not admonish you to love nothing, but we do admonish you to withhold your love from the world, so that you may be free to love him who made the world. A soul enmeshed in earthly love has sticky wings and is unable to fly. But once it is cleansed from filthy, mundane attachments its wings can spread freely. The two commandments of love—love of God and love of neighbor[3]—are like a pair of wings, and as soon as they are disentangled from every impediment the soul flies. And whither does it fly? Where else but to God? It mounts to God in flight because it mounts by love. Before it gains the power to do this, it groans on the ground, if the longing to fly is already in it. *Who will give me wings, as though to a dove?*[4] *Then I will fly away and find rest* (Ps 54:7(55:6)), it moans. Whither shall it fly? Away from the hindrances that surround it, the hindrances that evoke the sighs of the psalmist. He longs to fly away from them, from this place where he is mixed up with bad people, from the place

---

1. According to Possidius (*Indiculus* 10,4) Augustine preached two *Expositions* of this psalm, of which the earlier is apparently lost. The one given here is the second. From here to the Exposition of Psalm 133, inclusive, the Latin text used is that of the CSEL.
2. An abrupt opening, but it introduces immediately the theme of the two loves, which will run through the sermon.
3. See Mt 22:40.
4. On the dative here rather than the expected genitive, see Exposition of Psalm 54, 8 and the note there.

where the grains of wheat are mingled with the straw. He longs to fly to a place where he need no longer suffer close contact and association with any impious person but may live in holy fellowship with the angelic citizens of the eternal Jerusalem.

Verse 1. Mutual encouragement along the road

2. The psalm which we have undertaken to study with you today, holy brethren,[5] is a psalm of longing for that Jerusalem. The one who voices the longing is one who in this psalm is ascending, for this is a Song of Steps.[6] As we have often explained to you, beloved, the steps in question are not for going down but for going up. The psalmist is someone who wants to ascend. And whither would he want to ascend if not to heaven? What is there in heaven to attract him? Does he want to climb up there in order to be with the sun and the moon and the stars? No, of course not. In heaven is the eternal Jerusalem, where dwell the angels, our fellow-citizens. For a little while we are absent from those compatriots of ours, while we are journeying on earth. On our pilgrimage we sigh, but in our own city we shall rejoice.

Yet even while we are still on the journey we find companions who have already seen that city and they invite us to run toward it. The speaker in the psalm is happy about the encouragement they offer, and he says, *I rejoiced over those who told me, We are going to the Lord's house.* Dearly beloved brothers and sisters, call to mind a scene familiar to you. When some festival of the martyrs falls due, perhaps, and some holy place is named at which all are to assemble to celebrate the solemn rites, remember how the throngs incite one another, how people encourage each other, saying, "Come on, let's go, let's go!" Others ask, "Where are we going?" And they are told, "To that place, to the holy site." People talk to each other and catch fire with enthusiasm, and all the separate flames unite into a single flame. This one flame that springs up from the conversation of many people who enkindle one another seizes them all and sweeps them along to the holy place. Their devout resolve sanctifies them. If, then, holy love energizes people and tugs them to a material place, what kind of love must it be that tugs persons united in heart toward heaven, as

---

5. *Sanctitati vestrae.*
6. On this group of psalms and the probable dating of Augustine's expositions of them, see his general introduction in Exposition of Psalm 119,1 and the note there.

they say to each other, *We are going to the Lord's house?* Let's run, let's run fast, they say, for *we are going to the Lord's house!* Let's run and not weary, because we shall reach a place where fatigue will never touch us. Let's run to the Lord's house, and let our soul be gladdened by those who tell us these things; for those who cheer us on have seen our homeland before we have, and they shout from afar to us latecomers, "We are going to the Lord's house! Walk! Run!" The apostles have seen it, and they exhort us, "Run, walk, follow: we are going to the Lord's house!" And what do we reply, every one of us? *"I rejoiced over those who told me, We are going to the Lord's house.* I rejoiced over the prophets and I rejoiced over the apostles, for all of them have told us, *We are going to the Lord's house."*

Verse 2. Think of yourself as though you were there already

3. *Our feet were standing in the forecourts of Jerusalem.*[7] If you were wondering what the Lord's house is, you know now. In that house of the Lord the founder of the house is praised. He is the delight of all who dwell in the house; he alone is our hope here, as he will be our fulfillment there.

What should the eager runners keep in mind, then? How should they think of it? As though they were there already and standing within it, for it is a wonderful thing to stand there among the angels and never lose one's place. One there was who did lose his place and fall away, because *he did not stand in the truth* (Jn 8:44). All the others, those who have not fallen away, do stand in the truth. The one who stands fast is the one who finds joy in God.[8] They fall, who try to find their joy in themselves. But who tries to find enjoyment in himself? A proud person. Very different was the hope of one whose ambition was to stand for ever in the courts of Jerusalem; he said to God, *"In your light we will see light,* not in my light. *With you is the fountain of life,* not with me." And did he have anything further to say about this? Yes: *Let not the foot of pride come near me, nor the hands of sinners dislodge me.* There they have fallen, all those who work iniquity; they have been driven out, unable to stand (Ps 35:10.12–13(36:9.11–12)). Well then, if some were unable to stand because they were proud, make sure that you ascend humbly, so that

---

7. Variant: *in your forecourts, O Jerusalem.*
8. *Qui Deo fruitur,* a key idea for Augustine. God is to be enjoyed for his own sake; everything else is to be used as a means.

you may say, *Our feet were standing in the forecourts of Jerusalem.* Think of yourself as you will be when you get there. You are still on the way, but keep your future destiny before your eyes as though you were standing there and already rejoicing with the angels in a joy that can never be taken away from you. Bear yourself as though the prophecy in another psalm were already a reality for you: *Blessed are they who dwell in your house; they will praise you for ever and ever* (Ps 83:5(84:4)).

Our feet were standing in the forecourts of Jerusalem. What Jerusalem does this mean? There is another Jerusalem, an earthly city of which people speak often, but it is no more than a shadow of the real one. Would it be any great matter to stand in the earthly Jerusalem when that city itself could not even stand but was reduced to ruins? If the earthly Jerusalem were envisaged, would the Holy Spirit be suggesting any great thing when he evoked from the burning heart of a lover the cry, *Our feet were standing in the forecourts of Jerusalem?* Is not the terrestrial Jerusalem the city to which the Lord addressed his reproach, *Jerusalem, Jerusalem, you kill the prophets and stone those who are sent to you* (Mt 23:37)? Would our psalmist have been aspiring to any special privilege if he had wanted to stand among those who used to kill the prophets and stone those sent to them? Let any notion of the earthly Jerusalem be banished from the mind of one who is in love, who is afire, who longs to reach that Jerusalem which is our mother,[9] which the apostle calls our *everlasting home in heaven* (2 Cor 5:1).

Verse 3. The holy city is still being built

4. But don't just take my word for it; listen to the next verse, for that indicates to which Jerusalem the psalm means us to direct our minds. It states, *Our feet were standing in the forecourts of Jerusalem,* but then it seems to anticipate a question from someone, "What Jerusalem do you mean? About which Jerusalem are you speaking?" The psalm immediately adds a clarification: *The Jerusalem that is being built like a city.* When David said that, brothers and sisters, the city was already complete; it was not still under construction. The psalm must therefore be speaking of some other city which is being built even now. Living stones are hastening toward it, those of which Peter says, *You too must allow yourselves to be built, like living*

---

9. See Gal 4:26.

stones, into a spiritual house (1 Pt 2:5), into a holy temple for God. What is implied by *allow yourselves to be built, like living stones*? You are alive if you believe; and if you believe you are being made into God's temple, for the apostle Paul teaches, *God's temple is holy, and that temple is yourselves* (1 Cor 3:17). This is the city which is now a-building. Stones are hewn out of the mountains by the hands of those who preach the truth, and squared to fit into an everlasting structure. There are still many stones in the builder's hands; he does not drop them,[10] for he means to shape them to perfection, ready to be built in with the rest into the fabric of the temple. This is *the Jerusalem that is being built like a city.* Christ is its foundation, for Paul the apostle says, *No one can lay any other foundation than that which is laid, which is Christ Jesus* (1 Cor 3:11).

Now, when a foundation is laid in the earth, the walls are built up on top of it. The weight of the walls bears downward, down to the bottom where the foundation has been laid. But if our foundation is in heaven, the weight of our building bears upward, toward heaven.[11] Look at the lofty, spacious basilica all round you. It was raised by physical work and, because it was a matter of bodily labor, the builders laid the foundations underneath. We, on the contrary, are being built spiritually, and so our foundation is established in heaven. Let us run to the place where we are to be built in, for of that Jerusalem the psalm says, *Our feet were standing in the forecourts of Jerusalem.* But what Jerusalem is it? *The Jerusalem that is being built like a city.*

Perhaps, though, the indication is not yet clear enough. The psalm has pointed to the Jerusalem *that is being built like a city*, but that might still be taken in a material sense. Suppose there is someone who argues, "Yes, when these things were said in David's time and these verses were sung, the city was complete: I grant you that. But David foresaw in spirit that it would be destroyed and built up anew. In fact his city was overthrown and the people were taken captive and deported to Babylon. Scripture calls this 'the transmigration to Babylon.'[12] Then Jeremiah prophesied that when seventy years had elapsed the city could be rebuilt,[13] that city which had been destroyed

---

10. Variant: "may they not fall from his hands."
11. Compare his meditation in *Confessions* XIII,9,10 on love as the "weight" that bears things toward their place of rest.
12. See Mt 1:11.
13. See Jer 25:11–12; 29:10.

by the attackers." Someone might argue in this way. "David saw in spirit that the city of Jerusalem would be razed by its enemies," he might say, "and he also saw that it could be rebuilt after seventy years; that was why he said, *Jerusalem, that is being built like a city*. You need not refer the text to the Jerusalem which consists of holy persons, built up like living stones."

Let us clear up this ambiguity by looking at the next lines. The psalmist says, *"Our feet were standing in the forecourts of Jerusalem.* Which Jerusalem do I mean? Not the one that you see to be built of material walls but *the Jerusalem that is being built like a city."* Why *like a city*? Why not just say "a city"? Surely because the edifice with material walls, the earthly Jerusalem, was a visible city; it was a city properly so called, it was what is called a city in common parlance. But the heavenly Jerusalem is being built up *like a city*, just as the living components that are being built into it are *like living stones*, for they are not literally stones. And just as they are not stones, but like stones, so the heavenly Jerusalem is not a literal city but *like a city*.

We should note that by using the word *built* the psalm clearly meant us to think of a growing structure and the interlocking of component parts and walls. Strictly speaking, of course, a city means the people who live there; but the psalmist indicates that he means us to think of an actual place by using the verb *is being built*. The spiritual edifice bears a certain resemblance to a material building, and so he says it *is being built like a city*.

5. But let the psalmist continue and exclude all doubt, because we must not think in a materialistic way about this Jerusalem, the *Jerusalem that is being built like a city*.

It participates in the being of God

It shares in the Selfsame.[14] Now, brothers and sisters, if anyone can apply the keen edge of the mind, if anyone can lay aside the murk of the flesh, if anyone can cleanse the eye of the heart, let him or her look up and see. What is *idipsum*? It is simply *idipsum*, Being-Itself. How can I say anything about it, except that it is Being-Itself? Grasp

---

14. *Cuius participatio eius in idipsum.* The redundant *eius* is a Hebraism. Here, as in *The Confessions* IX,4,11, where he is meditating on Psalm 4:9, Augustine understands the word *idipsum* ("the selfsame") as an echo of the mysterious, ineffable name of God, who is infinite, immutable Being. Compare also Confessions VII,17,23; IX,10,24; XII,7,7.

it if you can, brothers and sisters, for whatever else I may say, I shall not have defined Being-Itself. All the same, let us attempt to direct the gaze of our minds,[15] to steer our feeble intelligence, to thinking about Being-Itself, making use of certain words and meanings that have some affinity with it.

What is Being-Itself? That which always exists unchangingly, which is not now one thing, now another. What is Being-Itself, Absolute Being, the Selfsame? That Which Is. What is That Which Is? The eternal, for anything that is constantly changing does not truly exist, because it does not abide—not that it is entirely nonexistent, but it does not exist in the highest sense. And what is That Which Is if not he who, when he wished to give Moses his mission, said to him, *I AM WHO AM* (Ex 3:14)? What is That Which Is if not he who, when his servant objected, *So you are sending me. But what shall I say to the sons of Israel if they challenge me, Who sent you to us?* (Ex 3:13), refused to give himself any other name than *I AM WHO AM*? He reiterated, *Thus shall you say to the children of Israel, HE WHO IS has sent me to you* (Ex 3:14). This is Being-Itself, the Self-same: *I AM WHO AM. HE WHO IS has sent me to you.*

You cannot take it in, for this is too much to understand, too much to grasp. Hold on instead to what he whom you cannot understand became for you. Hold onto the flesh of Christ, onto which you, sick and helpless, left wounded and half dead by robbers, are hoisted, that you may be taken to the inn and healed there.[16] Let us run to the house of the Lord, run all the way to that city, so that our feet may stand there, in that place which *is being built like a city, which shares in the Selfsame*. To what am I telling you to hold fast? Hold onto what Christ became for you, because Christ himself, even Christ, is rightly understood by this name, *I AM WHO AM*, inasmuch as he is in the form of God. In that nature wherein *he deemed it no robbery to be God's equal* (Ph 2:6), there he is Being-Itself. But that you might participate in Being-Itself, he first of all became a participant in what you are; *the Word was made flesh* (Jn 1:14) so that flesh might participate in the Word.

But God speaks to weak people, telling them that this Word which was made flesh and lived among us came from the stock of Abraham (for the promise was made to Abraham and Isaac and Jacob that

---

15. Some witnesses omit "direct the gaze of our minds."
16. See Lk 10:30–34.

through their seed all nations would be blessed,[17] and that is why we see the Church spread throughout the whole world). God looked for strong hearts when he said, *I AM WHO AM*; he looked for strong hearts and the keen, focused gaze of contemplation when he told Moses to say, *HE WHO IS has sent me to you.* But perhaps you do not yet practice contemplation.[18] Do not be put off, do not despair. HE WHO IS willed to become a human being like you, so he had more to say when Moses was terrified of his name. What name? The name, HE WHO IS. But he said more: *"I am the God of Abraham, the God of Isaac and the God of Jacob; this is my name for ever* (Ex 3:15). Do not despair of your own prospects because I have told you, *I AM WHO AM, and HE WHO IS has sent me to you.* Do not despair, reflecting how you are tossed to and fro, and precluded from sharing in the Selfsame by the mutability of all human things and the inconstant state of mortals. I am coming down to you, because you cannot come up to me. *I am the God of Abraham, the God of Isaac and the God of Jacob.* Put your hope in Abraham's seed, that you may be strengthened to see the one who is coming to you from Abraham's seed."

6. This is the Selfsame to whom another psalm says, *You will discard them like a garment, and so they will be changed, but you are the Selfsame, and your years will not fail* (Ps 101:27–28(102:26–27)). He whose *years will not fail*, he alone is Being-Itself. Do not our years fail every day, brothers and sisters? Do they ever stand still? The years that have come exist no longer; those which are still to come have no existence yet. The years that have passed have already failed us, and the years of our future will fail us in their turn. The same is true, brothers and sisters, even of a single day. Take today: we are talking now, at this moment, but the earlier hours have slipped away and the later hours have not yet arrived. When they have arrived, they too will slip away and fail. Are there any years that fail not? Only the years that stand. There beyond are the years that stand, and there the stable years are but one year, and that one year that abides is one single day, because that one abiding day knows neither sunrise nor sunset; it does not succeed yesterday nor is it chased away by tomorrow, but it abides forever as this one day—if you want to call it a day. If you

---

17. See Gn 12:3; 22:18; 26:4.
18. Variant: "But you do not yet practice strong contemplation."

prefer to think of it as years, call it so; if you want to call it a day, it is a day; but, however you think of it, it stands.

The city that *shares in the Selfsame* shares in that stability, and because it does so the speaker in the psalm, who is running toward the city, cries out, *Our feet were standing in the forecourts of Jerusalem*; for there all things stand, and nothing passes away. Do you too hope to stand there immovably? Run thither. No one has absolute being as of himself. Think hard about this, brothers and sisters. A person has a body, but the body is not absolute being, because it has no stability in itself. It changes with the passing stages of life, it changes as we move from place to place and changes with the seasons, it is changed by disease and the infirmities of the flesh. In itself it cannot stand. Nor do the heavenly bodies stand in themselves, for they too undergo certain mutations, even though some of these are concealed from us. They obviously move from place to place, rising from the east and traveling to the west and then finding their way back to the east once more. They too are powerless to stand, for they are not Being-Itself. Not even the human soul can stand. What a variety of thoughts flit across it! What intense feelings of pleasure[19] sway it! How fiercely it is pulled this way and that and stretched[20] by its desires! The human mind itself, the so-called rational mind, is mutable, for it is not Being-Itself. One moment it wants something, and then it wants it no longer; now it knows something, and then it does not know; now it remembers, now it forgets. No one of himself has absolute being.

One there was who arrogated absolute existence to himself, as of right, one who desired to be his own absolute; and he fell. An angel fell and became a devil. He then offered the fatal drink of pride to humans and in his envy dragged down with him the man and woman who had been standing. They too began to want to be their own selfsame; they tried to be their own rulers, to exercise lordship over their own lives. They refused their real Lord, who truly is the Selfsame, to whom a psalmist said, *You will discard them like a garment, and so they will be changed, but you are the Selfsame* (Ps 101:27–28(102:26–27)). But now at last, after such protracted sickness, after such grievous disease, struggles and toil, let the humbled soul turn back to him who is Absolute Being and find its place in the city that *shares in the Selfsame*.

---

19. Variant: "acts of will."
20. Variant: "cut and torn."

Verse 4. The tribes of the Lord, the true Israel

7. *Thither have the tribes ascended.* We told you earlier that in this psalm we hear the voice of people ascending, the voice of the Church as it makes the ascent, and so we were prompted to inquire where fallen humans are going in their climb. Are we still wondering about their goal? The height they are bound for, the end of their climb, the goal of their ascent, is that place *whither the tribes have ascended*, as our psalm now tells us. But where is that? Where *have the tribes ascended*? Into that city which *shares in Being-Itself.* That is the goal of our ascent—Jerusalem. There was once a man who, instead of mounting to Jerusalem, went down from Jerusalem to Jericho[21] and fell among robbers. If he had not gone down, he would not have fallen foul of them. Anyone who has fallen among robbers on his downward path must change course and climb up instead and encounter angels. Let such a one mount to that place, for *thither have the tribes ascended.*

But what are these tribes? Many know the answer, but many do not. Let those of us who know what the tribes are go down to those who do not know, so that they may ascend with us to the place whither the tribes have gone. "Tribes" can also be called *curiae*, if this word is used loosely. There is no exact synonym for the term "tribe," though *curia* comes somewhere near it.[22] In the strict sense we use *curia* for the council which sits in an individual city, whence are derived the names *curiales* and *decuriones*,[23] so called because they are members of a *curia* or a *decuria.* You know how every city has one *curia* of this kind. But there are also (or formerly were) groups of people in these same cities, each of which could be called a *curia.* When the word is used in this sense we can say that each city has many of them; Rome has thirty-five. These may be styled "tribes." The people of Israel had twelve, corresponding to the number of Jacob's sons.

8. The people of Israel comprised twelve tribes, but among them were both bad people and good. What a bad tribe they were, what

---

21. See Lk 10:30.
22. A *curia* was originally one of the thirty divisions of the Roman people established by Romulus for voting purposes. Thereafter the name came to be used for the meeting place of the Roman Senate or for that of the local senate in other cities. As Augustine points out, the word was often used more widely.
23. The *decuriones* were municipal councillors. A municipal senate was supposed to consist of ten divisions of ten men each.

a wicked party, that crucified the Lord! And what a good fraternity acknowledged the Lord! The clans that crucified the Lord are the tribes of the devil. The psalm says not merely, *Thither have the tribes ascended*; it specifies *the tribes of the Lord* to make it clear that not all the tribes are meant. What, then, are these *tribes of the Lord*? Those who knew the Lord. Among the twelve bad tribes were some good people, members of good clans that acknowledged the architect of the city. They were grains of wheat among the tribes, but they were mixed up with the chaff. They went up, but not in the company of the chaff; they went up as sifted, purified, elect tribes, as *tribes of the Lord. Thither have the tribes ascended, the tribes of the Lord.*

Now what else is said about *the tribes of the Lord*? That they are *the testimony to Israel*.[24] Listen, brothers and sisters, and understand what this *testimony to Israel* is, who these people are in whom the proof of the true Israel may be discerned. What does "Israel" mean? The interpretation of the name has been mentioned before, but it is as well to repeat it frequently, for it may have slipped the minds of some, even though we spoke of it not long ago.[25] By repeating it we make sure that it is not forgotten even by those unable or unwilling to read; let us serve as a book for them. "Israel" is taken to mean "seeing God." Or rather, if we analyze the name more exactly, we can say that "Israel" means "the seeing one is."[26] So when we put these two interpretations together we get "the one who sees God, is." No human being *is* in his or her own right, for we are inconstant and subject to change, unless we participate in him who is the Selfsame. A human being truly *is* when he sees God. He *is* when he sees Him Who Is, for, in seeing Him Who Is, the creature too comes to be in his measure. Thus he becomes Israel, for Israel is the seeing one.

A proud person is not Israel, for, instead of sharing in Being-Itself, the proud person wants to be his own absolute being. Anyone who tries to be the source of his own being is no Israel. No impostor can be Israel, and every proud person is an impostor. What I mean is this, brothers and sisters: any proud person pretends to be something he is not; he cannot do otherwise. It would not be so bad if a proud

---

24. *Testimonium Israel*: "a testimony to Israel," or "a guarantee of Israel," or "a proof that Israel truly exists"; the genuine members who deserve the sacred name "Israel."
25. See, for example, Expositions of Psalms 97,3 and 120,6 (and the note there).
26. *Est videns*.

person tried to appear what he is not in the sense, say, of wanting to be thought a flautist,[27] when he is no such thing. He could soon be proved bogus if people said to him, "Go on, then, sing. Let's hear what you can do." If he could not, he would be shown up as having made false claims when he tried to appear as something he was not. Or again, if someone said he was a fluent orator, we could say to him, "Very well; give us a speech, and prove it." As soon as he began to speak, he would be shown up; he would not be what he claimed to be.[28] But what is much worse is the claim of a proud person to be righteous when he is not. Righteousness is difficult to discern, and hence it is not easy to detect proud persons. Yet the proud want to seem what they are not, and therefore they do not share in Being-Itself, and they do not belong to Israel, "the one who sees God."

Who, then, does belong to Israel? One who *shares in the Selfsame*. And who is that? One who confesses that he is not what God is and that he holds from God whatever good he can claim to have, that of himself he is nothing but sin and that he possesses righteousness only as a gift from God. Such a person is one in whom there is no guile. What did the Lord say on catching sight of Nathanael? *Look, there is a true Israelite, in whom there is no guile* (Jn 1:47). If the true Israelite is one in whom no guile is to be found, we infer that the tribes that have ascended to Jerusalem are those found free of guile. They are the authentic Israel, the ones who give proof of being the real thing, because through them it can be seen that there were grains of wheat among the straw all the time, even though to an onlooker the threshing-floor seemed to contain nothing but chaff. The grains were there among it, but when they have ascended in heavenly splendor and the winnowing is finished, then will the *testimony to Israel* be rendered, for then will all the evildoers say to each other, "When the whole lot looked bad to us, there really were righteous people among the bad. We thought everyone was as bad as we were ourselves." Thus the good are a *testimony to Israel*.

Why do they ascend? *To confess to your name, O Lord.* No more glorious motive could be envisaged. As pride makes one presumptuous, so does humility prompt confession. As a presumptuous person

---

27. *Choraula*, see Exposition of Psalm 96,10; but it is evident from the present passage that the flautist was also expected to sing.
28. The two examples touch on areas where Augustine himself was expert and sensitive.

tries to pose as something he is not, so a confessing person has no wish to appear other than he is but loves what God is. The Israelites in whom there is no guile mount to this confession because they are truly Israelites. In them is the testimony to Israel, and they ascend for this purpose: *to confess to your name, O Lord.*

Verse 5. The apostles sit on seats to judge, but they are themselves the Lord's seat

9. *There the seats sat in judgment.* This is a puzzling expression and likely to raise problems unless it is rightly understood. Our translation renders as *seats* what the Greeks call θρόνοι. The Greeks use the word θρόνοι for benches of honor, or sedilia. There is nothing remarkable, brothers and sisters, about people sitting on seats or judicial benches. But how are we to understand a statement that the seats themselves sit down? It is as strange as though someone were to say, "Let the bishop's chair sit here, and the benches sit there." People sit on benches, on seats, and on chairs. Seats are for sitting on; the seats themselves do not sit.

What can the psalm mean, then, by saying, *There the seats sat to exercise judgment*? Well, you are certainly familiar with a saying of the Lord, *Heaven is my throne, but the earth is my footstool* (Is 66:1; Acts 7:49). This amounts to God telling us that his seat is heaven. But now who are the heavens? Who else but just persons? These heavens are a single heaven, just as the individual churches are the one Church: they are many, but in such a way as to form one; and the same is true in the inverse sense of the just, for they are heaven, but in their separate individuality they are heavens. God has his seat in them, and from them God exercises judgment. A psalm had good reason to say, *The heavens proclaim God's glory* (Ps 18:2(19:1)), for the apostles were made into heaven. How did that come about? By their being justified. As a sinner was made into earth when he was told, *Earth you are, and back to earth you shall go* (Gn 3:19), so were the justified made into heaven. They carried God, and from them God constantly flashed the lightning of his miracles, thundered his terrors, and rained down his consolations. They were heaven; they truly were. And they incessantly proclaimed the glory of God. The psalm left you no room for doubt about the apostles being heaven, for it went on to say, *Their sound went forth throughout the world, their words to the ends of the earth* (Ps 18:5(19:4)). Whose sound, whose words? Those of the heavens.

Well now, if heaven is God's seat, and the apostles are heaven, it follows that they are God's seat, God's throne. Scripture says elsewhere, *The soul of a just person is the throne of wisdom* (Prv 12:23, LXX). That is a tremendous statement: *The soul of a just person is the throne of wisdom*; it implies that in the soul of a righteous person wisdom sits as on a judicial bench, or a throne, and from there judges all things. The apostles were thrones for wisdom and yet the Lord said to them, *You will sit upon twelve thrones, judging the twelve tribes of Israel* (Mt 19:28). It seems, then, that they will themselves sit upon the twelve seats, but at the same time they are seats for God. This is what our present psalm teaches when it speaks of the seats sitting: *There the seats sat.* Who sat? *The seats.* And who are *the seats*? The heavens. Who are the heavens? Heaven. And what is heaven? That of which the Lord said, *Heaven is my seat* (Is 66:1; Acts 7:49).

We are taught three things, therefore. The just are seats, and they have seats, and it is in Jerusalem that the seats will sit. To what purpose? For judgment. The Lord promised, *You will sit upon twelve seats*, you who yourselves are my seats, *judging the twelve tribes of Israel*. Whom will they judge? Those below, on earth. Who will judge? Those who have become heaven.

Those amenable to their judgment will be divided into two groups, one to the right, the other to the left. The saints will join Christ in judging; as Isaiah says, *the Lord will come in judgment, with the elders of his people* (Is 3:14). Those who will collaborate with him are distinct from those subject to his judgment and to theirs. The people facing judgment will be segregated into two groups.[29] One will be placed at his right, and the acts of mercy they have performed will be enumerated to them. The others will be relegated to his left, and they will be reminded of their cruelty and their barrenness where mercy was called for. To those stationed at his right the invitation will be extended, *Come, you who are blessed by my Father, take possession of the kingdom prepared for you since the creation of the world.* And why? *I was hungry, and you fed me*, he will tell them. But they will protest, *When did we see you hungry?* He will reply, *When you did that for even the least of those who are mine, you did it for me* (Mt 25:34-35.37.40).

---

29. The repetition in these sentences may be due to Augustine's having suddenly remembered another text he could adduce, that of Is 3:14.

What is the implication, brothers and sisters? The apostles will judge concerning those people who have been advised to make friends for themselves by using iniquitous mammon, *so that they may welcome you into the tents of eternity* (Lk 16:9). The saints will sit in judgment with the Lord, marking carefully who among those before them have performed acts of mercy; they will take into their company those placed at the Lord's right and welcome them into the kingdom of heaven. And this, even this, is the peace of Jerusalem. In what does the peace of Jerusalem consist? In the conjunction of corporal works of mercy with spiritual works of preaching, so that in both giving and receiving there may be peace. The apostle saw almsdeeds as a matter of due payment and receipts,[30] for he said, *If we have sown spiritual seeds for your benefit, is it too much to ask that we reap a carnal harvest from you?* (1 Cor 9:11) On the same subject he said in another passage, *The one who gathered much had no surplus, and the one who gathered little, no lack* (2 Cor 8:15). Why did the one who had gathered a great deal have nothing left over? Because anyone who had more than enough gave to someone in need. And why did the one who gathered little not go short? Because he received from someone else who had plenty. This was done *that there might be equality* (2 Cor 8:14). And this is the peace for which our psalm prays, *May peace reign in your strength.*

Verse 6. The peace of Jerusalem is founded on love

10. What we have just said is certain, for the psalm makes it clear. It has told us that *there the seats sat in judgment over the house of David*, which means "over Christ's household," to which they conscientiously gave food in due season.[31] But immediately after this the psalm turns to the seats and admonishes them, *"Ask[32] what makes for the peace of Jerusalem.* You are the seats that are sitting to judge. You have become the Lord's seats and so you function as judges. But it is the duty of judges to ask questions, and of those before them to answer when questions are put to them. So then, *ask what makes for the peace of Jerusalem."* What will their interrogation reveal? That some people have been active in works of mercy and others have not.

---

30. See Ph 4:15.
31. See Mt 24:45.
32. *Interrogate.*

They will call into Jerusalem those who have performed works of mercy, for these are the things that *make for the peace of Jerusalem.*

Love[33] is a powerful thing, brothers and sisters; love is a powerful thing. Would you like a proof of how strong it is? Consider, then: if someone is prevented by circumstances from carrying out a duty enjoined by God, let him love someone else who performs that duty, and he fulfils it through that other. Note this carefully, beloved. Suppose, for instance, a man has a wife whom he cannot leave. He must obey the apostle's orders, *Let the husband render his debt to his wife* (1 Cor 7:3), and again, *Are you bound to a wife? Then do not seek to be unbound.* (1 Cor 7:27) It will occur to him that there is a better way of life, concerning which the same apostle says, *I wish everyone were as I am* (1 Cor 7:7). He marks those who have taken this course, he loves them for it, and in them he carries out what he is unable to do himself. Love is a powerful thing. It is our strength, and anything else we may have is useless without it. *If I speak with human tongue or angel's tongue, but have no charity, I have become like a booming gong or a clashing cymbal,* warns the apostle; and then he adds something even weightier: *If I distribute all my resources to feed the poor, and deliver my body to be burnt, yet have no charity, it profits me nothing.* (1 Cor 13:1.3) If charity exists alone and has no goods to distribute to the poor, let it simply love and give only a cup of cold water,[34] and the act will be judged as meritorious as that of Zacchaeus, who gave half his patrimony to the poor.[35] How can that be? The one gave so little, the other so much. How can the one be as highly deserving as the other? Yet he is indeed just as deserving. The material possibilities were not comparable, but charity was equal in the two cases.

11. The judges are questioning you, then, and you must assess what you are. We have been told, *We are going to the Lord's house.* We were certainly gladdened by those who gave us those tidings: *We are going to the Lord's house.* Find out, then, if we are truly going there. We travel not on foot but by our affections. Test whether we are on the way. Each one of you must question himself about his attitude to the holy poor person, the needy brother or sister, the penurious beggar. Let each one check that his compassion is not too narrow,

---

33. *Dilectio,* the love of free choice.
34. See Mt 10:42.
35. See Lk 19:8.

because the seats which will sit in judgment will have to interrogate you, and their duty is to seek out what makes for the peace of Jerusalem. How will they conduct their interrogation? As seats for God. Is God interrogating you, then? Does anything lie hidden from God, and can anything elude those interrogators who are bidden, *Ask what makes for the peace of Jerusalem*?

But what makes for the peace of Jerusalem? *There are abundant riches for those who love you.* The psalmist has now turned to address Jerusalem herself. There are great riches for those who love her—riches after poverty, for here below her lovers are in need, but affluent there; here they are weak, there strong; here in penury, there in wealth. How did they become rich? Here below they gave away what they had received from God for a limited time, and there they receive the reward that God will give them for eternity. Here on earth, brothers and sisters, even the rich are paupers. A rich man is lucky if he recognizes his poverty, for if he thinks himself full, that is no more than puffed-up pride, not plenitude. Let him acknowledge that he is empty so that he may be deserve to be filled. What does he possess? Gold. What does he not yet possess? Eternal life. Let him take stock of what he has and recognize what he has not. Let him give to others from what he has, brothers and sisters, that he may receive what he has not; let him use what he has to buy himself what he does not have, and there will be abundant riches for those who love Jerusalem.

Verse 7. Love is the city's strength

12. *May peace reign in your strength.* O Jerusalem, city being built like a city, city whose share is in Being-Itself, *may peace reign in your strength*. Let there be peace in your love, for your strength lies in your love. Listen to the Song of Songs: *Love is as mighty as death* (Sg 8:6). That is a solemn utterance, brothers and sisters: *Love is as mighty as death*. There could be no more glorious assertion of the strength of charity than *Love is as mighty as death*, for who can stand firm against death? Fire, water, the sword—against all these we can make a stand; we can resist potentates, we can resist kings. But death, death alone, no one can resist. This is why death is used as a comparison to suggest the power of love: *Love is as mighty as death*.[36] Moreover, love itself effects a kind of death in us, for charity slays what we once were so that we may become what we were

---

36. Compare a similar passage in Exposition of Psalm 47,13.

not. The man who said, *The world has been crucified to me, and I to the world* (Gal 6:14), had died that death, and so too had those to whom he said, *You are dead, and your life is hidden with Christ in God* (Col 3:3). *Love is as mighty as death.* If it is mighty, it has great power and force; it is strength itself. Through love weak people are ruled by the strong, earth by heaven, the nations by the seats; and therefore the psalm prays, *May peace reign in your strength*, may peace reign in your love.

What is more, through that strength, through that love, through that peace, may there be *abundance in your towers*, which means in your elevated places. Only a few will sit in judgment, but the great crowds at Christ's right hand make up the population of the city. There are many under the protection of each one of the exalted judges, many who are welcomed by the judges into the tents of eternity;[37] and thus there will be abundance in its towers. God himself is the fullness of delights and our all-sufficient riches. He is Being-Itself, in which the city participates; in this will our abundance consist.[38] But how can this be? Through charity, which is to say, through the city's strength. But who has charity, brothers and sisters? The person who in this life is not self-seeking.[39] The apostle Paul was a man of charity. Listen to what he tells us: *Try to appease everyone in all circumstances, as I too make myself agreeable to all in every respect* (1 Cor 10:33). What has become of the claim you made elsewhere, Paul? You said, *If I were still out to please men, I would not be Christ's servant* (Gal 1:10), yet now you say that you try to mollify others, and you exhort your disciples to do the same! But in denying that he tried to please men he omitted to mention the object some have in making such efforts; they curry favor with others for their own advantage, not for the promotion of charity. The person who is intent on his own reputation is not seeking the salvation of other people. But Paul elaborates: *Try to appease everyone ... as I too make myself agreeable to all in every respect, seeking not my own advantage but the profit of the many, that they may be saved* (1 Cor 10:33).

---

37. See Lk 16:9.
38. Variant: "He himself will be our abundance."
39. See Ph 2:4.21.

Verses 8–9. Fraternal charity is the reason for preaching of Jerusalem's peace

13. The psalmist[40] has been speaking about charity, and in the same vein he continues, *For the sake of my brethren and kin I spoke always of your peace*. O Jerusalem, you are the city that shares in Being-Itself, but I am still in the midst of this life on earth, a pilgrim poor and groaning. I do not yet enjoy your peace, but I preach of your peace to others. I preach it not for my own gain, as do the heretics who seek their own advancement as they say, "Peace be with you," when in truth they do not have the peace they preach to the peoples. If they had, they would not tear apart the unity of the Church.

But I, says the psalmist, *I spoke always of your peace*. From what motive? *For the sake of my brethren and kin*, not to win a reputation for myself, not for money, not even to save my life, for *life to me is Christ, and death is gain* (Ph 1:21). But *I spoke always of your peace for the sake of my brethren and kin*. He was longing[41] *to die and to be with Christ* (Ph 1:23), but this man who preached peace to his brethren and kin knew that it was necessary for them that he remain in the flesh.[42] *For the sake of my brethren and kin I spoke always of your peace*.

14. *For the sake of the house of the Lord my God I have sought your good*. I have sought good things indeed, but not for myself, for then I would have been seeking good not for you but for me, and I would not even have gained any good myself, because I was not seeking it for you. No, it is *for the sake of the house of the Lord my God* that I have preached: for the Church, for the saints, for the pilgrims, for the needy, so that they may make the ascent. To them we say, *We are going to the Lord's house*. It is *for the sake of the house of the Lord my God* that *I have sought your good*.

This exposition has been rather long, brothers and sisters, but it was necessary. Pluck fruit from it, eat, drink, grow strong, and seize the prize.

---

40. *Hic* ("he") apparently refers to the psalmist, but the reference throughout section 13 could be to Paul.
41. Variant: "I was longing."
42. See Ph 1:23–24.

Exposition of Psalm 122

A Sermon to the People

Introduction: Christ ascends, with his body; the two-way link of charity

1. I have undertaken to study the *Songs of Ascent* with you, holy brethren.[1] They are the songs of one who ascends and loves, one who, being a lover, cannot but ascend. All love either descends or ascends, for by good desire we are raised to God, but by bad desire we are plummeted into the depths. Sinful desire has brought us down already; we have fallen, but there is another chance left to us. We must acknowledge who it is who has descended to us—not fallen, but descended—and then we can ascend by clinging to him, for we cannot rise by our own strength. The Lord Jesus Christ himself testified, *No one has gone up to heaven except the one who descended from heaven, the Son of Man who is in heaven* (Jn 3:13). But that could be taken to mean that he ascended alone. Are we to think that the rest of us have been left behind, if only he who came down has ascended? What are the rest to do? We must be united to his body so that there may be only the one Christ who both descended and ascended. The head came down, but he went up with his body; he went up clothed in the Church, whom he made ready for himself, free from spot or wrinkle.[2] Did he ascend alone? Yes, in a way, but not without us, as long as we are so closely united with him that we are members of his body. He is alone, yet he is with us, forming one person, and one for ever. Unity binds us to the one Lord. The only people who do not ascend with him are those who have refused to be one with him.

We must not therefore feel our situation to be hopeless, even though that flesh in which he was for a time mortal has now been raised to immortality, and in this immortal state he has taken his place in heaven. There in heaven he suffers no persecution, no malice or insult, such as he graciously willed to endure for our sake while on earth. Yet though his passion is over he still has compassion for his

---

1. *Cum sanctitate vestra.*
2. See Eph 5:27.

hard-pressed body on earth. *Saul, Saul, why are you persecuting me?* (Acts 9:4) he cried. No one was touching him, yet he cried out from heaven that he was being persecuted! We have no reason to despair, then; rather must we with great confidence take it for granted that, if he is with us on earth through charity, we are, through the same charity, with him in heaven. We have explained to you how he is so truly present with us on earth that he could shout from heaven, *Saul, Saul, why are you persecuting me?* although Saul was not touching him in any way and could not even see him. But what about the other side of it? How can it be proved that we are with him in heaven? The same apostle, Paul, demonstrates it, for he says, *If you have risen with Christ, seek what is above, where Christ is seated at the right hand of God. Have a taste for the things that are above, not the things on earth; for you are dead, and your life is hidden with Christ in God.* (Col 3:1–3) Both things are quite evident, therefore: he is still down here, and we are already up there. He is down here by compassionate charity, and we are on high by hopeful charity, *for in hope we have been saved* (Rom 8:24). But because our hope, even though it bears upon the future, is absolutely certain, Paul's statement is made about us as though it were realized already.

Verse 1. The one Christ prays from the ends of the earth

2. Let the singing psalmist make the ascent; but let him sing from the heart of each one of you like a single person. Indeed, let each of you be this one person. Each one prays the psalm individually, but because you are all one in Christ, it is the voice of a single person that is heard in the psalm. This is why you do not say, "To you, Lord, have we lifted up our eyes," but *To you,* Lord, *have I lifted up my eyes.* Certainly you must think of this as a prayer offered by each of you on his or her own account, but even more should you think of it as the prayer of the one person present throughout the whole world. This same one person is praying who says elsewhere, *From the ends of the earth I have called to you, as my heart was wrung with pain* (Ps 60:3(61:2)). Who is this, crying out from the ends of the earth? How can any one person be present even to earth's bounds? Each individual can cry out from his or her own country, but how is it possible to cry from every extremity of the world? Ah, but Christ's inheritance can. To him a promise is made in another psalm, *I will give you the nations as your heritage, and the ends of the earth for your possession* (Ps 2:8), and it is the voice of this heritage that we

hear in the verse, *From the ends of the earth I have called to you, as my heart was wrung with pain.* Let our heart too be wrung with pain, and let us cry out with him. What should cause our heart anguish? Not any of the woes that afflict the wicked equally—for instance, suffering some loss—for if our heart is tormented over something like that, it is dust and ashes. Or suppose you have by God's decree lost someone dear to you. Is that so exceptional that your heart should be in anguish over it? The hearts of unbelievers anguish over it too. Those who have not yet come to believe in Christ suffer just as much over these things.

What strikes anguish into the heart of a Christian? The fact of not yet living with Christ. Over what is a Christian heart wrung with pain? Over being a pilgrim still, and longing for our homeland. If that is what wrings your heart with anguish, you groan even if you are well off as the world sees it. Even if everything is turning out prosperously for you and the world is smiling upon you in your every enterprise, you groan nonetheless, because you see yourself still in your pilgrim state, and you are aware that though in the eyes of the foolish you enjoy good fortune, you still lack the happiness Christ has promised. Groaning, you seek it; seeking it, you long for it; and as you long, you ascend, singing this *Song of Steps.* You sing, *To you have I lifted up my eyes, you who dwell in heaven.*

The humble climber; keep your eyes off yourself

3. In which direction was this praying climber to lift his eyes? Where else but to the place he was making for, the place to which he longed to ascend? He is ascending from earth to heaven. But look, the earth is below us, our feet tread on it, and the sky is above, the sky we can see. Yet we mean to ascend, and we sing, *To you have I lifted up my eyes, you who dwell in heaven.* Where are the ladders? We observe the enormous distance between heaven and earth, the vast space between, the huge separation; we want to ascend to heaven, but there are no ladders to be seen. Are we not indulging in wishful thinking when we sing a *Song of Steps*, a song of ascending?

No. We ascend to heaven if we think of God, who arranges ascents in our hearts.[3] But what does it mean, to ascend in the heart? To draw closer to God. Anyone who slackens and gives up does not descend but falls; just so does everyone who is making progress ascend, but

---

3. See Ps 83:6(84:5).

only as long as his progress does not make him proud, only if he ascends in such a way as to beware of a fall. If people take pride in their progress, their very ascent will bring them tumbling down again. How are they to conduct themselves in order to avoid pride? Let them lift their eyes to him who dwells in heaven and not focus on themselves. Every proud person is self-absorbed and self-satisfied and thinks himself important. But anyone who is satisfied with himself is feeling pleased with a fool, because when he finds himself pleasing he is foolish. The only man or woman who can be pleasing without risk is the one who is pleasing to God. And who is pleasing to God? A person who finds God pleasing. God cannot be dissatisfied with himself; let him be satisfying to you as well, so that you may be satisfactory to him. But you cannot find God pleasing unless you are displeased with yourself. But then, if you find yourself unpleasant, take your eyes off yourself! Why focus on yourself? If you look at yourself as you truly are, you find unpleasant things, and then you say to God, *My sin confronts me all the time* (Ps 50:5(51:3)). Make sure your sin is before your eyes so that it will not be before the eyes of God; but do not keep yourself before your eyes, if you want to be before the eyes of God. Just as we do *not* want God to turn his face away from us, so we *do* want him to turn it away from our sins. The psalms pray for both. One psalm prays, *Do not turn your face away from me* (Ps 26(27):9), and certainly we recognize our own voice in that plea. But after saying, *Do not turn your face away from me*, the psalmist begs in another place, *Turn your face away from my sins* (Ps 50:11(51:9)). If you want God to turn his face away from your sins, turn your own face away from yourself; but do not turn your face away from your sins, for if you do not avert your eyes from them, you will be angry with your sins. And if you do not turn your face from your sins, then, even as you look at them, God overlooks them.[4]

The spiritual heaven

4. Lift your eyes away from yourself, then, and regard him. Say to him, *To you have I lifted up my eyes, you who dwell in heaven.* Now what is heaven, brothers and sisters? If we take it in a material sense, take it to be the sky we can see with our bodily eyes, we shall certainly go wrong and think that we cannot ascend there except by setting up ladders or some kind of scaffolding. But if our ascent

---

4. *Tu agnoscis, et ille ignoscit.*

is spiritual, we must also understand heaven in a spiritual sense. If our ascent is made by our loving will, heaven consists in righteousness. What, then, is God's heaven? All holy souls, all just souls. The apostles were heaven even while they were still on earth as to their bodies, because the Lord was enthroned in them and through them traversed the whole earth.

God dwells in heaven, then. But how? In the manner indicated by another psalm: *You dwell in your holy place, you who are the praise of Israel* (Ps 21:4(22:3)). God, who dwells in heaven, dwells in his holy place, and what else is his holy place but his temple? But *God's temple is holy, and that temple is yourselves* (1 Cor 3:17). All those who, though still weak, are walking in faith[5] are God's temple now in virtue of their faith; but one day they will be his temple in direct vision. How long do they remain his temple by their faith? As long as through their faith Christ continues to be present in them, according to the apostle's prayer, *May Christ dwell in your hearts through faith* (Eph 3:17). But those in whom God already dwells through direct vision are already heaven. These are the holy angels who see him face to face, all the holy powers, sovereignties, thrones, and dominations;[6] they constitute the heavenly Jerusalem for which we sigh on our pilgrimage, and for which we pray in our longing. This is where God dwells. Thither has the psalmist lifted up his faith, thither is he ascending by love and desire. This very desire makes the soul rid itself of[7] the filth of sin and cleanse itself of every stain, so that it too may become a heaven, for it has raised its eyes to him who dwells in heaven.

If we suppose that God's habitation is the material sky we see with our eyes, we shall be forced to say that God's dwelling is impermanent, because the Lord tells us in the gospel that *heaven and earth will pass away* (Mt 24:35). And then we shall be faced with the question, "Where was God living before he made heaven and earth?"[8] Perhaps someone may pose a variant of this question: "Where was God living before he made his holy ones?" God was dwelling in himself; he dwells with himself; with himself he is God. Moreover, when he

---

5. See 2 Cor 5:7.
6. See Eph 1:21; Col 1:16.
7. Literally "sweat out."
8. Comparable to the question, "What was God doing before he made heaven and earth?" which Augustine shows to be a non-question in his *Confessions* IX,12,14 and the following sections. Time itself is a creature of God.

graciously wills to dwell in the saints, they do not become a kind of supportive house for God in such a way that, if the house disappeared, God would fall. We dwell in a house in our human fashion, but God dwells in the saints in a way entirely different. You live in your house and, if it is swept away, you fall. But God dwells in the saints in such a way that, if he departs, they fall. If anyone is a bearer of God, God's temple, let him not imagine that God relies on him and that he would frighten God by withdrawing his support. Rather, woe betide this God-bearer if God withdraws from him, because then he will be the one who falls. God abides eternally in himself. The places we dwell in contain us, but those in whom God dwells are contained by him.

Now you can see what a wide difference there is between our manner of dwelling and God's. Let the soul say, *To you have I lifted up my eyes, you who dwell in heaven,* and say it in the knowledge that God does not need heaven to live in, but heaven needs God: it needs him to dwell in it in order to be heaven.

Verse 2. Expectant servants, chastised but watching for mercy

5. The psalmist has said, *To you have I lifted up my eyes, you who dwell in heaven.* How does he continue? How did you lift up your eyes, psalmist? *Even as the eyes of servants are on the hands of their masters, and as the eyes of a maid are on the hands of her mistress, so are our eyes on the Lord our God, until he take pity on us.* We are servants, and we are a maid; God is both our master and our mistress. What do these words mean? What is the force of these comparisons? You must concentrate for a little while, beloved.[9] There is nothing strange in our being servants, with God as our master; what is strange is that we should be a maid and God our mistress. Yet there is nothing really incongruous about our being a maid, because we are the Church. And indeed, there is not even anything strange about Christ being our mistress, because he is the power and the wisdom of God.[10] Listen to what the apostle has to say: *We preach Christ crucified, to Jews a stumbling-block and to gentiles folly; but to those who are called, both Jews and Greeks, a Christ who is the power of God and the wisdom of God* (1 Cor 1:23–24). Thus the people are a servant and the Church is a maid. When you hear the name of Christ, lift your eyes to the hands of your master; but when you hear him called

---

9. *Caritas vestra.*
10. *Virtus et sapientia*, both feminine nouns.

the power and the wisdom of God, lift your eyes to the hands of your mistress, because you are both a servant, being his people, and also a maid, being the Church.

This maid has been endowed with great dignity before God, because she has become a wife. But for the present, until she attains the spiritual embrace where she may without fear enjoy him whom she has loved, and for whom she has sighed on her tedious pilgrimage, she is still a bride. Yet she has received a great pledge,[11] the blood of her bridegroom, for whom she sighs with no sense of constraint. There is no need to warn her, "Wait, the time for love has not come yet," as a virgin betrothed but not yet married is sometimes cautioned. People may have good reason to say to a betrothed girl, "Do not love him yet; when you have become his wife you can love him." That is sound advice, because if she loves a man before she is certain of marrying him, her desire for him is premature, precipitous and unchaste. Another suitor may claim her and make her his wife. But there is no one who can take precedence over Christ, and the bride therefore loves him without anxiety. Let her love him before their union and sigh for him while still far off. He alone will wed her at the end of her long journey, because he alone has laid down such an enormous pledge.[12] Who else marries a bride by dying for her? If he wants to die for her, he will not be there to marry her. But Christ unhesitatingly died for his bride, because he was to marry her when he rose from the dead.

All the same, brothers and sisters, we must conduct ourselves in the meantime like servants or like a maid. It is true that the Lord said, *I call you servants no longer; I call you friends* (Jn 15:15), but perhaps he meant this only for the disciples. No; listen to Paul, who says, *You are a servant no longer, but a son; and if a son, an heir too, through God's act* (Gal 4:7); and Paul was speaking to the whole people, to all the faithful. Already we have been redeemed and claimed as the Lord's possession by his blood, we have been washed in the laver of his baptism, we are sons and daughters—or rather we are the one

---

11. *Arrha*, in the Septuagint (see Gn 38:17.18), like ἀρραβών in the Greek New Testament, is a loan-word from Hebrew. The *arrha* was a first installment of the purchase-price, a pledge or deposit or down-payment which made a contract valid and obligated the contracting party to make further payments. God has *deposited the first installment of the Spirit* (or *the Spirit as the first installment*) *in our hearts* (2 Cor 1:22); and the Spirit is *the pledge/first installment of our inheritance* (Eph 1:14). Here the *arrha* is Christ's blood.
12. *Arrham*.

single son, because though many we are one in him. How, then, can we still comport ourselves as servants?

From our servile state we have been raised to be true sons and daughters, to be sure. But do we stand as high in merit in the Church as did the apostle Paul? Hardly. But what does he say in his letter? *From Paul, a servant of Jesus Christ* (Rom 1:1). If the man through whom the gospel was preached to us still calls himself a servant, how much more must we acknowledge our condition, that Christ's grace may increase in us? Initially he claimed those whom he redeemed as his servants, for his blood was a purchase-price for slaves, as well as a pledge[13] for his bride. We must acknowledge our condition: though sons and daughters through grace, we are still servants because we are creatures, and all creation serves God. Let us say, therefore, *Even as the eyes of servants are on the hands of their masters, and as the eyes of a maid are on the hands of her mistress, so are our eyes on the Lord our God, until he take pity on us.*

6. The psalm has explained why *our eyes are on the Lord our God*, after the manner of servants who watch the hands of their masters, or maids who watch the hands of their mistress. Now you may ask, "But to what purpose?" The psalmist accordingly adds, *Until he take pity on us*. What kind of servants[14] watching their masters' hands did he want us to think of, brothers and sisters, what kind of maids eyeing the hands of their mistress, until she take pity on them? Who are these servants and maids, watching so intently? They must be ones who have been condemned to a beating. *Our eyes are on the Lord our God, until he take pity on us.* And how do we keep our eyes focused on him? *Even as the eyes of servants are on the hands of their masters, and as the eyes of a maid are on the hands of her mistress.* It is implied that these servants and maids are also looking for mercy from their master or mistress. Imagine a master who has ordered that his servant be beaten. The servant is whipped and feels the pain of the welts, so he fixes his gaze on his master's hands, longing for the master to signal, "That's enough." The hand symbolizes authority.

---

13. *Pignus.* In his Sermons 23,8.9; 156,16; 378, Augustine explains that a *pignus* is a pledge given as a guarantee, which is returned when that which is guaranteed is fulfilled (e.g. if you lend a book you ask a *pignus* from the borrower, which you return to him when he restores the book). Thus *pignus* differs from *arrha*. In the present exposition the distinction is less clear.
14. Or "slaves"; so throughout this section.

What about ourselves, brothers and sisters? Our Lord has ordered us to be beaten; our mistress, the wisdom of God, has ordered us to be beaten; and the whole of this mortal life is a flogging for us. Listen to what another psalm has to say: *You have chastised human beings for their sin, and brushed my soul away like a spider* (Ps 38:12(39:11)).[15] Think how fragile a spider is, brothers and sisters: a light touch is enough to squash it and kill it. And the psalm did not intend us to think only of our flesh in its fragile, mortal weakness, for it did not say, "You have brushed me away"—a statement that could be referred to the flesh—but *you have brushed my soul away like a spider.* Nothing is weaker than the human soul tossed among the temptations of the world, amid groans and anguish and afflictions; nothing is weaker, until our soul is indissolubly bound to the solid strength of heaven and finds its way into God's temple, never to fall away from there again. Our soul was reduced to this infirmity and subjection to decay, which left it as weak as a spider when it was cast out of paradise. That was when God's servant was ordered to undergo a beating.

Consider when our whipping began, brothers and sisters. Adam has endured a whipping in all those who have been born since the dawn of the human race; Adam is whipped in all who are alive today; and his whipping will continue in all who come after us. Adam is the human race under the whip, and many have so hardened themselves that they do not even feel their lacerations. But those members of the human race who have been made God's children have been given sensitivity to the pain. They feel their lashes, they know who ordered their chastisement, and they keep their eyes fixed on him who dwells in heaven. Their eyes are therefore on the hands of their Lord, longing for him to take pity on them, as servants' eyes are on the hands of their masters, or a maid's eyes on the hands of her mistress. You may see some prosperous people in this world laughing and behaving pretentiously; they are not aware of being under the lash. But in truth they are being whipped much more severely, for their flogging is all the worse in that they have lost all sensitivity to it. Let them wake up and take their whipping; let them feel it and know that they are being thrashed and let them suffer under it; for *the more one knows, the keener the pain* (Qoh 1:18), as scripture teaches. This is why the

---

15. *Aranea* commonly means the spider's web rather than the spider; but in his Exposition of Psalm 38,18 Augustine explicitly says that he is thinking primarily of the animal.

Lord declared in the gospel, *Blessed are those who mourn, for they shall be comforted* (Mt 5:5).

7. As we listen to the cries of the sufferer under the lash, let these cries be our own, echoed by each one of us, even when things are going well. Is there anyone who is unaware of being whipped when he is ill, or in prison, or perhaps in chains, or being attacked by robbers? It is quite unmistakable then. Or when troubles are inflicted on someone by dishonest aggressors, he knows he is under the lash. But it takes great insight to know one is being whipped when one's affairs are prospering. In the Book of Job scripture does not say, "There are plenty of trials in human life." It does say, *Is not human life on earth all temptation?* (Jb 7:1) It calls our entire life one long trial. All your life on earth is your beating. Mourn, then, as long as you live here on earth, whether you are enjoying good fortune or are beset by troubles; cry to God, *To you have I lifted up my eyes, you who dwell in heaven.* Cry out to the hands of your Lord, who has ordered your beating, to whom you lament in another psalm, *You have chastised human beings for their sin, and brushed my soul away like a spider* (Ps 38:12(39:11)). Cry out to the hand that beats you, *Have mercy on us, O Lord, have mercy!* Is not this the plea of someone being whipped: *Have mercy on us, O Lord, have mercy?*

Verses 3–4. Those who are affluent in any sense will despise us

8. *Have mercy on us, O Lord, have mercy, for we are overwhelmed with contempt. Our soul is saturated with it, a disgrace to the affluent and contemptible to the proud.* To be viewed with contempt is to be despised. All those who try to live a godly life according to Christ's teaching[16] will inevitably suffer disgrace; they will of necessity be despised by those who want to live in ungodly fashion and look to find their whole happiness in earthly things. People of a different persuasion, who regard something invisible as their happiness, are taunted: "You fool, what do you believe? Can you see this thing you believe in? Has anyone come back from the underworld to tell you what goes on there? What I love are things I can see and enjoy." You are treated with contempt because you hope for what you do not see, treated with contempt by someone who seems to have a firm grasp of what he can see. But consider how secure his grip is. Do not worry; just watch whether he does truly hold it. Do not take his insults to

---

16. See 2 Tm 3:12.

heart, lest while judging him to be happy in this present life you lose your true happiness in the life to come. Do not worry; just reflect on whether his hold is secure. Does his property slip through his fingers, or does he slip away from his property? Either he will leave his possessions behind or they will leave him; one or the other is bound to happen. Who is abandoned by his possessions? A person who is ruined in his lifetime. And who leaves his possessions behind? The one who dies rich; because when he dies he does not take his wealth with him to the underworld. "I own my house," he boasted. You ask him, "What house would that be?" "The house my father left me." "And where did he get it from?" "Our grandfather bequeathed it to him." Go back to his great-grandfather, and then to his great-great-grandfather, and now he cannot even tell you their names. Do you not find it more frightening than a matter for pride when you reflect that so many have passed through that house and not one of them has taken it with him to be a home for eternity? Your father left it behind here; he went his way, as you too will go your way. If all you have in this house of yours is a temporary occupancy, it is a lodging for passers-by, not an abode for permanent residents. And yet we, for our part, *are overwhelmed with contempt* by those who seek or possess happiness in this world, because we hope for what is still future, because we sigh for a happiness yet to come, and because, although we are God's children already, *what we shall be has not yet appeared* (1 Jn 3:2), for our life *is hidden with Christ in God* (Col 3:3).

9. *Our soul is saturated with it, a disgrace to the affluent, and contemptible to the proud.* We were perhaps wondering who *the affluent* are, and the psalm made it clear to you by calling them *the proud.* Similarly *disgrace* is parallel to *contemptible,* as *the affluent* are parallel to *the proud.* The thought is repeated: *a disgrace to the affluent, and contemptible to the proud.* Why are the proud affluent? Because they want to be happy here. But they are wretched too, surely, so how can they be affluent? Well, perhaps when they are reduced to wretchedness, they will not taunt us any more. But this is not so certain, so pay attention now, beloved. Perhaps they jeer at us when they are enjoying good fortune themselves, when they flaunt their ostentatious wealth, when they make their windy boasts over trumpery privileges. Then they mock us, as though saying, "Look how well off I am! I'm enjoying good things here and now. Away with people who promise what they cannot show me! I hold onto what I see and make the most of what I see. I'm out to have a good time in life." But what

about you? You must be more secure than he is. Christ is risen, and he has taught you what he means to give in another life; be certain that he does indeed give it. The proud mocker insults you because he has his good fortune now. Put up with him and his insults, for you will laugh at him later when he is groaning. The time will come when people like him will say, *These are the people we once held in derision* (Wis 5:3). That text comes from the Book of Wisdom; scripture has made known to us what they will be saying one day, these people who laugh at us now, who despise us and dismiss us as disgraceful and contemptible. We are told what they will be saying then, when they are shamed by the truth. They will see, shining gloriously at Christ's right hand, those whom they despised when living among them, for in those formerly contemptible folk the apostle's prophecy will have been verified: *When Christ appears, Christ who is your life, then you too will appear with him in glory* (Col 3:4). They will say, *These are the people we once held in derision, as a byword and a butt for our mockery! Fools that we were, we thought their life madness and their end a disgrace. How has it happened that now they are reckoned among the children of God, and their lot is among the saints?* (Wis 5:3–5) The text continues to relate their chagrin: *No doubt of it, we strayed from the path of truth. On us the light of righteousness did not shine, nor did the sun rise for us. What good has our pride done us,* and what benefit has come to us from our vaunted wealth? (Wis 5:6–8) There will be no need for you to reproach them then, for they will be reproaching themselves.

Until this comes to pass, brothers and sisters, let us lift our eyes to him who dwells in heaven and never turn our gaze away from him until he take pity on us and set us free from all temptation and reproach and contempt.

10. There is more to be said, though: sometimes even people who are under the lash of temporal misfortune insult us too. You may come across someone who for his sins is thrown into prison and shackled, either as a result of God's secret judgment or because his guilt is manifest. Perhaps someone says to him, "Why did you not live a good life? Look where your wrongdoing has led you." He retorts, "And why do some who do live good lives suffer the same fate?" We may reply that these latter suffer to be proved sound; the trials that come their way serve to put them through their paces; repeated scourging turns out to their advantage, for God *whips every child whom he accepts* (Heb 12:6). If he caused his sinless only-begotten Son to be scourged

and delivered him to death for us all,[17] are we not rightly scourged, we whose deeds have merited a beating? But when we make these points, an answer comes from people who, far from being humbled by their affliction, are proud even of their misfortune: "That is the way those stupid Christians talk. They believe in what they do not see."

If even people in that situation insult us, brothers and sisters, can we suppose that they are not included in the groups envisaged in the psalm, when it says that we are *a disgrace to the affluent, and contemptible to the proud*? We know that insults are hurled at Christians by those also who are not affluent yet never stop railing at us even in their poverty and distress. Is the psalm right, then, to say that we are *a disgrace to the affluent*? Would we find no one in a calamitous situation ever insulting others if we did not know about the robber who insulted Christ, crucified alongside him?[18] If those who are not affluent insult others as much as those who are, why does the psalm say that we are *a disgrace to the affluent*?

If we examine the matter carefully, we find that persons who mock even when in distress are affluent—yes, even they are. Why can they be regarded as affluent? Because if they were not affluent, they would not be proud. One person is affluent in money and is proud about that; another is well off with regard to prestigious offices, and that makes him proud; another thinks himself wealthy in righteousness and is proud on that score, which is worse. Some who do not appear to be wealthy as far as money is concerned think themselves affluent in righteousness in despite of God. When overtaken by disasters they justify themselves and accuse God. "Of what am I guilty? What have I done?" such a person asks. You answer, "Take a good look, recall your sins and ask yourself whether you have really done nothing wrong." His conscience is stirred a little. He returns to himself and reflects on his misdeeds. But even after having thought it over he is unwilling to confess that his punishment is deserved. Instead he says, "Well, yes, I have obviously done many bad things, but I know many others have done worse yet suffer no harm for it." So he sets himself up as just, in opposition to God. He too is therefore affluent, for he has a heart full of self-righteousness, since in his eyes God is doing wrong, while he himself is suffering unjustly. If you were to entrust him with the navigation of a ship, he would wreck it along with

---

17. See Rom 8:32.
18. See Lk 23:39.

himself; yet he wants to wrest the control of this world from God and steer creation himself, distributing to all their pains and joys, their punishments and rewards. Unhappy soul! But is it surprising? He is one of the affluent, but his affluence is in wickedness and malice. And the more affluent he thinks himself to be in righteousness, the more affluent he is in sin.

The true poverty of a Christian

11. A Christian has no business to be affluent but has a duty to recognize that he is poor. Even if he has worldly wealth he must realize that it is not true wealth, and so he must long for wealth of a different kind. Anyone who longs for false riches does not seek true riches; but a person who is in search of true riches knows himself or herself to be still a pauper and rightly admits, *I am poor and sorrowful* (Ps 68:30(69:29)). But what of a person who is materially poor yet full of wickedness? Why can such a one be regarded as affluent? Because he hates his poverty but believes himself richly supplied with justice in his heart, in opposition to the justice of God. What kind of riches does our righteousness amount to? However abundant righteousness may be in us, it is no more than dew in comparison with the fountain of God's justice, no more than a few drops compared with that great feast, drops that only dampen our life and soften the hard surface of our iniquity. Let us in this life long to be fully fed from that plenteous fount of justice; let us yearn to be satisfied with that abundance of which another psalm predicts, *They will be inebriated by the rich abundance of your house, and you will give them the torrent of your delights to drink* (Ps 35:9(36:8)).

But, as long as we live here, let us understand that we are penurious and needy not only in the matter of true riches but even with respect to our health. Even when we are well, let us realize that we are infirm. As long as this body hungers and thirsts, as long as it is tired by keeping vigil, tired by standing, tired by walking, tired by sitting; as long as it gets tired of eating, and finds some new form of fatigue wherever it turns to relieve its tiredness, we do not have perfect health, not even bodily health. This state is not riches but beggary, because the more there is of it, the more our need and avarice increase. It is not bodily health, but infirmity. Every day our condition is alleviated[19] by God's remedies as we eat and drink, for these are medicines prescribed for us. If you want to diagnose the disease that has hold of us, brothers and sisters, think how a person who fasts for a week is consumed by hunger. The hunger is there all the time, but you do not feel it because you cure it every day. Even our bodily health is not perfect.

Riches, health, and righteousness elude us in this life, but we hope for them in the new Jerusalem

12. I want you to be quite clear, beloved, as to how we should understand that we are poor, so that we may lift our eyes to him who dwells in heaven and rejoice unto him. Worldly riches are not true riches, for they only increase cupidity in those who possess them. Nor is what is reckoned bodily health true health, because we carry within us infirmity which lets us down on every side; whichever way we turn, there is deficiency. Even in applying the remedy you will not find stable strength. A person is weary of standing and wants to sit down. But can he bear to remain sitting indefinitely? He adopted a sitting position to relieve his fatigue, but even sitting down is no answer. He was wearied from keeping vigil, and so he is going to sleep awhile. Now he has slept, but does that mean the end of his weakness? By no means. He is fatigued by fasting and goes to take refreshment. If he goes on eating, that too is bad for him. This weak condition of ours cannot bear any activity for long.

What about righteousness? What does our righteousness amount to amid such fierce temptations? We can refrain from murder, from adultery, from theft, from perjury, from fraud. But can we restrain ourselves from evil thoughts? Or from the wicked desires that suggest themselves? What is our righteousness, then?

We must therefore long for wholeness, for true riches and true health and true righteousness. What are true riches? Our heavenly abode in Jerusalem. Who is reckoned rich on earth? When a rich person is the subject of gossip, what do people say? "He is very wealthy, he lacks nothing." That may be genuine praise in the intention of the one who says so; but to assert of someone, "He lacks nothing," is a hollow sort of praise. Look into the statement carefully and find out

---

19. *Paregorizamur*, derived from the Greek παρηγορίζω. This unusual verb has given rise to a crop of variants: *quare curamus; pare gloridiamur; parum ergo rigamur; par ego rideamur*, etc.

whether he is really in want of nothing. If he lacks nothing, he craves nothing; but if he is still craving for more than he has, his accumulation of riches has only increased his need. In that city, though, there will be true riches for us, because we shall need nothing whatever, and our health will be true health. What is true health? That state wherein death has been swallowed up in victory and this corruptible nature has clothed itself with incorruptibility and our mortality is clothed in immortality.[20] Then there will be true health for us; and then also there will be true and perfect righteousness, for not only shall we be incapable of doing wrong: we shall not even be able to think of it.

But now, needy, poor, destitute, and in pain, we sigh and groan and pray and lift our eyes to God; for those who enjoy this world's goods—the affluent, that is—despise us; but so too do the unfortunate. Even those who do not prosper in this world despise us, because they too are affluent in their way, with an abundance of righteousness in their hearts, but a righteousness that is counterfeit. They do not attain true righteousness because they are full of the kind that is false. But you, for your part, be needy, be a beggar for true righteousness, that you may reach it. Listen to the gospel: *Blessed are those who hunger and thirst for righteousness, for they shall be satisfied* (Mt 5:6).

---

20. See 1 Cor 15:54.53.

Exposition of Psalm 123

A Sermon to the People[1]

Verses 1–2. This is a song of triumph; let us join in as though we were part of the triumph already

1. Dearest brothers and sisters, you are well aware that a Song of Steps is a song about our ascent and that the ascent is not made by our bodily feet but by the affections of our hearts. We have pointed this out to you very frequently, and it is not a good idea to repeat it too often, for we need to reserve time for the topics of which we have not yet spoken. The song you have just heard being sung to you is headed, like others in this group, *A Song of Steps*. That is its title; so it is a song chanted by people mounting upwards.[2] Sometimes a single voice is heard and at other times there seems to be a multitude, because, though many, we are one, for Christ is one, and Christ's members are one with Christ, one in Christ. The head of all these members is in heaven. The body is toiling on earth, but it is not separated from its head, for the head looks down from heaven and cares for his body. If he had not been caring for it, he would not have said to the persecutor, Saul (who was not Paul yet), *Saul, Saul, why are you persecuting me?* (Acts 9:4)

You know all this perfectly well; these matters are familiar to you. But I hope it will not be boring for those among you who have not forgotten them to be reminded, so that through your patience the facts may be recalled to the hearts of those who have. These are salutary teachings and need to be reiterated often.

Well then, whether one voice sings or many sing, there are many people, and one individual composed of the many by reason of their unity. As we have explained, there is one Christ, and all Christians are members of Christ.

2. What are they singing, these members of Christ—what are they singing? They are in love, and they sing for love, they sing for

---

1. Possibly preached on Saturday, 22 December 406. See the note at Exposition of Psalm 119,1, and the last section of the present exposition.
2. Variant: "Sing it as you mount upwards."

longing. Sometimes they sing in their troubles and at other times, when they are singing in hope, they sing exultantly. Our troubles are part of our life in the present world, but our hope is fixed on the world to come and, if our hope in that future world does not console us in the troubles of this one, we perish. This means, brothers and sisters, that our joy is not realized yet but is already ours in hope.[3] Our hope is so unshakable that it is as though the reality were here already, for we cannot be anxious about what the truth itself has promised. Truth can neither be deceived nor deceive us. Our good consists in clinging to the truth that sets us free as long as we abide in his word.[4] We believe now, and hereafter we shall see. When we believe, we live in this present world in hope; when we see, we shall enjoy the reality in the world to come. Then we shall see God face to face.[5] But face-to-face vision depends on our having cleansed our hearts, for the Lord tells us, *Blessed are the clean of heart, for they shall see God* (Mt 5:8). How are hearts cleansed? Only through faith. As Peter testifies concerning the gentiles in the Acts of the Apostles, God was *cleansing their hearts by faith* (Acts 15:9). Our hearts too are cleansed by faith until they are fit to be granted vision. We walk now by faith, not yet by sight. The apostle reminds us that *as long as we are in the body we are on pilgrimage and away from the Lord*. And what does it mean to be on pilgrimage? To *walk by faith, not by sight* (2 Cor 5:6.7).

Anyone who is still on pilgrimage, walking by faith, has not yet reached home but is already on the way to it. A person who is not in that homeland, but does not believe, is not even on the way there. Let us walk, then, like people who know they are on the way, because the king of our homeland has made himself our way. The king is the Lord Jesus Christ; there at home he is our truth, but here he is our way.[6] To what are we traveling? To the truth. How shall we get there? Through faith. Whither are we traveling? To Christ. How shall we reach him? Through Christ. He told us himself, *I am the way, the truth and the life* (Jn 14:6). Sometime before this he had assured those who believed in him, *If you abide in my word, you will truly be my disciples; you will know the truth, and the truth will set you free* (Jn

---

3. *Nondum est in re, sed iam in spe,* a recurrent note in Augustine's preaching.
4. See Jn 8:32.31.
5. See 1 Cor 13:12.
6. See Jn 14:6.

8:31–32). He promised them, *You will know the truth*, but he attached a condition: *if you abide in my word.* His word? What word? The apostle answers, *The word of faith which we preach* (Rom 10:8). The word is first of all the word of faith; if we continue in this word of faith we shall know the truth, and the truth will set us free.[7] Truth is immortal, truth is unchangeable, truth is that Word of whom scripture says, *In the beginning was the Word, and the Word was with God; he was God* (Jn 1:1). Who can contemplate this Word except from a purified heart? And how are hearts cleansed? *The Word was made flesh, and dwelt among us* (Jn 1:14). The Word abiding in himself is the truth we are approaching, the truth that sets us free. But the word of faith preached to us, the word in which the Lord bids us abide in order to know the truth, is the Word made flesh who lives among us. You believe[8] in Christ born in the flesh, and you will attain to Christ born of God, God with God.

3. In the psalm we hear the voices of jubilant singers; it is the exulting members of Christ who are chanting.[9] But who exults in this world except people whose joy springs from hope, as I have explained? Let this hope be unhesitating in us, and let us sing for joy. It is not as though these singers were strangers to us or as though our own voice were missing from this psalm. Listen to it as though you were hearing yourselves. Listen as though you were looking at your own reflection in the mirror of the scriptures. When you gaze into the scriptural mirror your own cheerful face looks back at you. When in your exultant hope you observe the likeness between yourself and other members of Christ, the members who first sang these verses, you will be certain that you are among his members, and you too will sing them.

Now why are the singers so happy? Because they have escaped. That must mean that they are singing in hope, for as long as we are on our pilgrimage in this world, we have not escaped yet. But some members of this body to which we also belong have gone on ahead of us, and they can truly sing of their escape. The holy martyrs have sung about it, for they have escaped and are now exulting with Christ, certain that they will be given back their bodies free from corruption, even those same bodies that were formerly subject to decay, in which

---

7. Variant: "We know the truth, and the truth has set us free."
8. Variant: "Believe" (imperative).
9. Variant: "Let the exulting... chant."

they suffered torments. In heaven those torments will be transformed into emblems of honor.

Let us all sing the psalm together—both the saints who rejoice in the reality and we who join them in hope, rejoicing at their garlands of victory and longing to share that life which we do not have here but which we shall never have unless here on earth we have desired it. Let us all sing together and say, *If the Lord had not been in*[10] *us.* The saints have looked down on the afflictions they endured; even in that place of rest, established in beatitude and safety, they have reflected on the way by which they traveled, and where they have arrived. They remember how difficult it would have been to struggle free from their distress had the hand of their liberator not been helping them; and in their joy they say, *If the Lord had not been in us.* Thus do they strike up their song. They have not yet said what it was that they escaped from, so intense is their delight. All they can say is, *If the Lord had not been in us.*

4. *Let Israel now say, If the Lord had not been in us.* Let Israel say this now, because it has escaped. This psalm sets the escapers before our eyes—those, that is, who have escaped already. Let us too set up these triumphant heroes in our hearts and exult as though we were in their company, in the spirit of another psalm that sings, *Our feet were standing in the forecourts of Jerusalem* (Ps 121(122):2). The people who sang that were not yet there, but they were on the way, and so great was their joy as they hastened onward, so strong their hope of arriving, that even while still struggling along the road they felt as though they were already safe at home. The same conviction should be in us. Let us see ourselves included in the triumph[11] to be celebrated in the world to come, when we shall taunt death, defeated now and swallowed up in victory. *What has become of your strife, O death? Where, O death, is your sting?* (1 Cor 15:55) We shall be united with the angels and rejoice with our king, who willed to be the first to rise again, although not the first to die; for many died before

---

10. In the original perspective of the psalm the meaning is: "If the Lord had not been on our side." That is, "in" is equivalent to "among us, and fighting for us," as in Ex 14. But Augustine packs more into the "in." For him it means the indwelling of the Lord in the individual believer, especially when the believer faces martyrdom, and the union of all believers in Christ, who dwells in them.
11. The scene of a Roman triumph is evoked here, with the defeated leaders mocked. See the note at Exposition of Psalm 40,4.

him, but none rose to eternal life before he did. We are there already in hope and in our hearts, so let us rejoice with him and reflect on our escape from the scandals and the distress of this world, from persecutions by all the pagans, from the deceitful ploys of heretics, from the enticements of the devil and our conflicting lusts. Who could ever have escaped from all these *if the Lord had not been in us*? Let Israel ask this question now. Beyond the reach of anxiety, Israel can now sing, *If the Lord had not been in us.*

When was his presence so opportune? *When men rose up against us.* Do not be surprised that they have been routed, for they were only men. The Lord, and no mere man, was among us and in us. Men rose up and attacked us; and they would have defeated us as men defeat other men, had it not been for the Lord, who was more than man, present among us. Because of him we, human though we were, became invincible.

Verse 3. What does the psalm mean about our being swallowed alive?

5. *If the Lord had not been in us, when men rose up against us*—what would they have done to you, poor humans under attack? You who are rejoicing and singing now, you who possess everlasting life with no fear of ever losing it, what would human attackers have done to you, if the Lord had not been within you? If the Lord were not within us,[12] what would they do to us? *Perhaps they would have swallowed us alive.* Notice that phrase: *They would have swallowed us alive.* They would have gulped us down without killing us first. How wicked! That is hideous cruelty. The Church does not devour anyone like that. Peter was commanded, *Slaughter and eat* (Acts 10:13), not, "Gulp them down alive."

How, then, does Peter (the Church, I mean) slay before eating? And why is it said of our attackers that *perhaps they would have swallowed us alive, if the Lord had not been in us*? Because no one is absorbed into the body of the Church unless he or she is first slain. The person's former self is put to death so that he may become something new. Without this death no one is eaten by the Church. Someone may appear to belong to this people of God that is visible to our eyes, but unless he has been eaten he cannot belong to the people that is known to God, the people of which the apostle says,

---

12. Variant: "you."

The Lord knows his own (2 Tm 2:19); and he cannot be eaten unless he has first been slain. Along comes a pagan, still living in idolatry but wanting to be incorporated into the body of Christ. If he is truly eaten he will inevitably be grafted in among Christ's members, but he cannot be eaten by the Church unless he is first put to death. Let him renounce the world: this is his slaughter. Then let him believe in God: then is he eaten.

Now, what about those attackers? How would they have swallowed us alive but for the presence of the Lord among us? In earlier days many persecutors arose; and even now we are not free of them, though they attack us singly nowadays and sometimes still swallow us alive—but only those of us in whom the Lord is not present. This is why the psalm says, *If the Lord had not been in us*, before going on to speak of the persecutors; for although many are indeed gulped down, it is only those from whom the Lord is absent. The ones who are swallowed alive are those who know it is wrong to consent and do so only verbally. Some persecutors arose and ordered their victims, "Offer incense;[13] if you refuse, we will kill you." Some of the victims were in love with this life, and the sweetness of it seduced them. Instead of choosing to set their love on what God had promised, they preferred the good things they saw on earth, for God commanded them to believe in realities they could not yet see, and visible joys appeared more lovable. To these they held fast, shutting the Lord out of their hearts and, because the Lord was not in them, they were swallowed alive. Why "swallowed alive"? Because they burned incense to an idol though aware that an idol is nothing.[14] If they had sacrificed in the belief that the idol was something real, they would have been dead when swallowed, but because they knew that the idol was nothing, and that all the gods of the pagans are meaningless nonentities, they were alive. Yet, when such living persons do what the persecutors demand, they are swallowed alive, but swallowed alive only because the Lord is not in them. People in whom the Lord is present are killed by their persecutors but do not die, whereas those who consent to the persecutors' demands to save their lives are swallowed alive and, being swallowed, they die.

---

13. To the gods. This symbolic act of apostasy was a prominent feature of the persecutions, at least from the time of Cyprian, in the mid-third century.
14. See 1 Cor 8:4.

The others, those who have suffered without giving way under pressure, exultantly proclaim, *If the Lord had not been in us when men rose up against us, perhaps they would have swallowed us alive.* Let Israel sing this now, and sing it exultantly, without fear.

6. *When their fury broke over us.* You know how in one of the earlier psalms, brothers and sisters, at the very beginning of the *Songs of Steps*, someone begged for help against a guileful tongue as he began his ascent. He prayed, *O Lord, rescue my soul from wicked lips and the guileful tongue* (Ps 119(120):2). It always happens. As soon as a person begins to climb and is making some headway he has to endure guileful tongues from the very outset, tongues that speak soothingly only to do him harm, smooth tongues offering bad advice. "What are you about?" they ask. "Why are you attempting this? Is there no other lifestyle? Surely it is possible to serve God in other ways? You are trying to be somebody special, different from everybody else!" Even if there are others with you, it does not silence the guileful tongue. "Well, yes," they say. "Those others do seem to have succeeded, but you may not be equal to it. You will undertake it, and fail. Better not to begin at all than to begin and then drop out." The guileful tongue is still speaking pleasantly, but if you stick to your resolve, the deceitful, soothing tone is abandoned. The words become openly fierce, and the tongue that spoke in friendliness to seduce you now threatens and tries to frighten you. But if the Lord is within you and you do not forsake Christ in your heart, you will overcome those who now menace you in anger because they failed to lead you astray with their suave persuasion. You will overcome your misleading, deceitful advisers as you overcame those others, with sharp arrows and destructive, all-devouring coals,[15] that is to say, with the words of God by which your own heart has been pierced, and with the examples of just men and women brought to life from the dead—sinners transformed and justified, like coals rekindled. As the flatterers were vanquished in their attempts to mislead you, let them now be worsted when they threaten.

But how are they vanquished? They could not have been, *if the Lord had not been in us.* It is quite plain that you yourself are not the victor—only he is, who dwells in you. Can you carry such a commander in you and be defeated? Is not he whom you bear within you he who proclaimed, *I have overcome the world* (Jn 16:33)? Was not he

---

15. See Ps 119(120):4.

the first to defeat the devil by dying, though he was himself sovereign over every creature, being the Word, God-with-God? And why did he so defeat him, if not to teach you how to do battle with the devil? Yet this is what you have been taught by him: that unless he who first of all conquered on your behalf is in you now, you will be overcome. *If the Lord had not been in us, when men rose up against us, perhaps they would have swallowed us alive when their fury broke over us.* They are angry now; this is the time for their naked hostility.

Verses 4–5. Rushing water as a symbol of persecution

The water would perhaps have overwhelmed us. The psalm designates sinful nations as *water*, and what kind of water we shall see in the subsequent lines. If anyone had consented to their demands, he or she would have been drowned in this water and died like the Egyptians, rather than crossing as the Israelites did. You know the story well, brothers and sisters: how the people of Israel crossed the sea, while the Egyptians were overwhelmed.[16] This is why the psalm says, *The water would have overwhelmed us.*

7. Well then, what kind of water is meant here? It is a torrent, flowing with mighty force, but it will pass. Rivers swollen by sudden storms of rain are called torrents. They course along with impetuous energy and anyone who steps into them is swept away. But this is true only of one in whom the Lord does not dwell; if the Lord is present in a person, his soul crosses the torrent. It continues to flow, but the souls of the martyrs have crossed it safely. As long as this world flows on, with its succession of births and deaths, it is a torrent, and from it arise persecutions. Our head drank from it first, he of whom it is said in another psalm, *He drank*[17] *from the torrent beside the way* (Ps 109(110):7). From that cascading water that symbolizes a persecuting nation he drank, he who asked his disciples, *Are you able to drink the cup I am to drink?* (Mt 20:22)

He drank from the torrent beside the way. What does that mean—he drank *beside the way*? It means that he drank but passed on: he did not dally there. He drank while on his way, for the verse of another

---

16. See Ex 14:22–29.
17. Variant: *will drink*. The evocation of Ps 109(110) in the following lines echoes Augustine's remarkable treatment of that psalm. See especially Exposition of Psalm 109,20, where the wayside torrent is "the cascade of human mortality," the torrent of human birth, transience, and death, from which the incarnate Word willed to drink.

psalm can perhaps be applied to him: *He did not stand in the way of sinners* (Ps 1:1). He drank and pressed on. What else is said of him? *Therefore he has raised*[18] *his head*. That psalm tells us that *he drank from the torrent beside the way, and therefore he has raised his head*. Our head has already been lifted up because he drank from the torrent at the wayside, for our Lord chose to suffer. If our head has been exalted, why should his body fear the torrent? With the head exalted already, the body will follow and say, *Our soul has crossed over the torrent; perhaps our soul crossed insubstantial water.* This is the water the psalm referred to when it said, *The water would perhaps have overwhelmed us.* But what kind of water is insubstantial? What does *insubstantial* mean?

8. We had better examine first the expression, *Perhaps our soul crossed.* What does that mean? The Latin translators rendered as best they could the word ἄρα found in the Greek text. The Greek manuscripts wrote ἄρα because this is a way of making a tentative statement; and the Latins likewise used a word conveying doubt: *perhaps*.[19] But in doing so they did not accurately represent the sense. We can suggest it better with a word less at home in Latin but quite accessible to you. When Punic-speakers say *iar* they do not mean "wood" but indicate some hesitation. The Greeks convey the same nuance with ἄρα, and Latin-speakers may sometimes say, "Do you suppose that...?" So, for instance, they might say, "Do you suppose I could have escaped that danger?" You can see now that to render this as "Perhaps I escaped" does not capture the meaning of the colloquial "Do you suppose...?" But this is not good Latin. I can say it when talking with you; I often use non-Latin words to help you understand.[20] But it could not be used in the translation of the scriptures, not being acceptable Latin; and since there was no good Latin equivalent for the Greek, an expression was used which does not exactly correspond to the original in meaning. Never mind: you must understand the line like this: *Do you suppose our soul could have crossed the insubstantial water?* And why this question? Because the gravity of the danger made it scarcely believable that they had escaped. They had faced a great slaughter; they had been in a situation

---

18. Variant: *will raise*; so too in the next sentence.
19. *Forsitan.*
20. These comments indicate how widespread the use of Punic still was in Augustine's day, although many of its users were evidently bilingual.

of grave crisis. The pressure on them had been so intense that they, living men and women, had almost consented and so had all but been swallowed alive. Thus, now that they have escaped at last and find themselves safe, they look back on their fearful peril and say, *Do you suppose our soul could have crossed the insubstantial water?*

"Insubstantial water" signifies wealth gained in violation of conscience

9. What can this *insubstantial water* be, if not the water of insubstantial sins? Sins have no substance. They are a lack, not a substance, a poverty, not a substantial reality. In that insubstantial water the younger son in the parable lost all his substance.[21] You remember how the younger son set out on a journey and, before leaving, said to his father, *Give me the portion of your substance that is due to me* (Lk 15:12). What are you trying to get for yourself? It is safer kept at home with your father. It is coming to you in any case. Do you mean to fritter it away? Do you intend to go far? But no, "Give it to me." All he can say is, "Give it to me." His father gave it to him. Off he went to a distant country. He lived recklessly and squandered his substance on prostitutes. He stayed on and, reduced to want, he fed pigs. In his need he remembered his father's wealth. If he had not felt the pinch of poverty he would not have hungered for that plentiful provision. Let all reflect on their sins and see whether those sins have any substance in them. *To what purpose has the ungodly irritated the Lord?* (Ps 9B(10):13) If you do not see your sin clearly before you commit it, at least take a good look at it afterwards. The delights of this world taste sweet in the mouth for a time, but the aftertaste is very bitter. Now suppose you have sinned and made a profit. What have you gained? In order to make your profit you have offended God. For the sake of gain your good faith[22] has been eroded, while your gold has increased. What have you lost, and what have you acquired? What you have acquired is called gold, what you have lost

---

21. Augustine is playing on two meanings of "substance." In the philosophical sense evil can be viewed as the lack of a due good and thus as "insubstantial"; in the commercial sense, echoed by the parable he is about to quote, substance means property or wealth. For similar word-play see Exposition 1 of Psalm 68,4 and the notes there.
22. *Fides* here and all through the following argument has the sense of good faith, honesty, honor, fair dealing, a good conscience. Compare Exposition 2 of Psalm 33,15.

is called honor. Weigh honor against gold. If honor were a marketable commodity it would be expensive. Can you reckon up your gains and ignore your losses? Can you gloat over your treasure-chest and not bewail the void in your heart? You are well off as regards the contents of your treasure-chest, but look what has been diminished[23] in your heart. When you open the chest you will find gold coins that were not there before. Good for you! You are gratified to see them in that place from which they used to be absent. But look into the treasury of your heart. Good faith used to be there, but now it is empty. If the one change gives you satisfaction, why does the other not make you weep? Your loss outweighs your gain. Do you wish to assess what you have lost? Think, then: not even shipwreck would have taken it from you. Sometimes people lose all their belongings at sea and escape naked. Many were shipwrecked with Paul.[24] Some of these were lovers of this world; they were wrecked but escaped naked, and they not only lost all their external goods but found the house of their heart empty too. Paul, unlike them, carried his inheritance in his heart, his precious faith. That could not be snatched from him by any waves or storms, so, though he too escaped naked, he escaped a rich man.

We must seek riches of that kind. "But I can't see them," you tell me. Foolish soul! You do not see them with your bodily eyes, but open the eye of your heart and you will see them. You protest that you cannot see faith. Why, then, are you aware of it in others? Why do you complain when someone breaks faith with you if you are blind to it? Let someone break faith with you, and you cry out at once. You want another person to show it in dealings with you, and you see it well enough then. How is it that you cannot see it when someone demands it of you? You complain if another fails to act honestly in your regard; be equally grieved, then, if you fail to deal honestly with him.

Moreover, notice that the sin you are committing is something without substance. Ill-gotten gains appear to be substantial, but the loot is not really yours. The only person who truly possesses gold is the one who knows how to use it. One who does not know does not own it but is owned by it; he does not possess it but is himself possessed. Be masters and mistresses of your gold, not its slaves; because, though God also made gold, he made you more precious than gold. He made

---

23. Variant: "violated."
24. See Acts 27:14–44.

gold to be your resource, but he made you in his own image. Look to what is above you, and trample on what is beneath you.

What have you gained? Do you wish to see how lacking in substance it is, like insubstantial water? Alright then: take your gains with you to the underworld! What are you going to do? You have acquired gold and lost your honor; only a few days later you depart this life and find that you cannot take with you the gold you won at the expense of your honor. Empty of good faith, your heart goes off to its punishment, whereas had it been full of faith it would have gone to its reward. Take stock, then: what you did comes to nothing, yet for the sake of this nothingness you offended God. It was water lacking in substance that drowned you. *To what purpose has the ungodly irritated the Lord? Let them be confounded, the unjust whose actions are futile.* (Pss 9B(10):13; 24:4(25:3)) No one who does wrong acts to any purpose, yet no one considers the fact.

10. People go their way; they listen to a certain well-known saying, but the sayings of God are dormant in them.[25] What saying do I mean? "Better in hand than in hope."[26] But what do you hold in your hand, you poor fellow? "Better in hand than in hope," you say. Make sure of your grip on it before you say, "Better in hand." If your grip is not secure, why not hold on instead to what you cannot lose? What do you think you have in your grasp? Gold. Alright, hang onto it. Hold tight, and make sure no one snatches it from you against your will. But if on account of that gold you are dragged where you do not want to go, and a more powerful predator is after you because he has seen in you a lesser predator; if it is on account of the gold that he is on your trail; if the mightier eagle is pursuing you because you seized the hare first, then as the lesser creature was a prey to you, you will be the stronger raptor's prey. People do not seem to see this in their business dealings, so blinded are they by greed. This is a strange fact, brothers and sisters. Those who do consider it are appalled. A strong man seeks out a weaker one and tries to crush him for no other reason than that he has something the stronger one wants to take from him. The strong one sees some weakling put to a great deal of trouble over what he possesses, and yet the stronger wants to add that very thing

---

25. Variant: "They hear the word of God and the sayings of God and go to sleep over them. They hear a certain well-known saying, and they are wide awake over that."
26. Or, as we might say, "A bird in the hand is worth two in the bush."

to his own pile. Pursuing the lesser man, all he could think about was that his victim possessed something; he failed to notice that the weaker man's sufferings—his flight, his tormenting anxiety, his fear, his search for somewhere to hide—were all the consequences of his possessing it. At least learn from watching your victim, you powerful pursuer, that if the wealth caused him such torments when you pursued him and he feared to see it taken from him, it can cause you just as much anguish if someone else pursues you. All you can think of is that your victim is fat and juicy. If you are after him for that reason, because you view him as succulent prey, take care not to grow fat and juicy yourself, in case another predator hunts you.

All this effort is pointless. Look for its results and all you see is darkness. Ask about its purpose and you find nothing at all.

Verses 6–7. The sparrow's escape

11. All the more reason, then, why the people who can say, *Our soul crossed insubstantial water*, should exult and rejoice in Christ and look to receive their substance. They lost it by living extravagantly, but their Father has not been impoverished. Let them return home and there they will find the wealth they wasted on prostitutes during their sojourn in the far country. Let them steer clear of the insubstantial water and say, *Blessed be the Lord, who did not leave us like hunters' prey between their teeth*. The hunters were the persecutors, who baited their traps with food. What food? The sweetness of this present life, to tempt each victim to thrust his head into sin for the sake of that sweetness and so be caught in the trap. The only ones not caught were those in whom the Lord was present, who say, *If the Lord had not been in us*. Let the Lord be in you and you too will avoid being ensnared. Cry out with the just, *Blessed be the Lord, who did not leave us like hunters' prey between their teeth*.

12. *Our soul is like a bird escaped from the fowlers' net*. This soul was plucked from the fowlers' snare like a sparrow, because in it the Lord was present. Why like a sparrow? Because, like a sparrow heedless of where it was flying, it had fallen and later found the strength to say, "God will forgive me."[27] You flighty sparrow! Roost safely on the rock[28] and do not go near the trap; if you do, you will be caught, killed, and crushed. Let the Lord be in you, and he will

---

27. Variant: "Forgive me, O God.
28. On sparrows singing from rocks, compare Exposition 3 of Psalm 103,5–7.

deliver you from even greater dangers that threaten you, as though from the fowlers' net. If you see a bird about to fall into a trap, brothers and sisters, you shout and make a lot of noise to warn it away, and it was the same with the martyrs. It might happen that some of them were beginning to stretch their necks toward the sweet lure of this life; but then the Lord who was in them set up the din of hell, and the sparrow was headed off from the hunters' trap. *Our soul is like a bird escaped from the fowlers' net.* What happened next? Would this trap be a menace for ever? No, because the trap was the sweetness of the present life. The martyrs did not entangle themselves in it, and they were killed. But once they had been put to death the snare was broken as far as they were concerned. No trace of the sweetness of this life remained to entrap them again; it was nothing but a broken snare. Was the sparrow broken too? By no means, for it had not been caught. *The trap is broken, and we have escaped.*

Verse 8. Acknowledge that your escape was due solely to God's help

13. Let them shout for joy at their deliverance, let them fly to God and triumph in God over their rescue, because the Lord was in them and saved them from being captured in the snare. Why can they sing, *The trap is broken, and we have escaped*? You ask why? Because *our help is in the name of the Lord, who made heaven and earth.* If that help had not been to hand, the trap would certainly not have endured for ever, but the sparrow caught in it would have been smashed to pieces. This present life will pass away, and those who have been captivated by its sweetness, and thereby seduced into offending God, will pass away with it, as transient as life itself. There is no doubt at all that the trap will be broken in due course, for the present life with all its attractions will no longer exist once the setting prepared for it[29] has fulfilled its destiny. The important thing is to avoid getting stuck in this life so that, when at last the trap is broken apart, you may shout joyfully, *The trap is broken, and we have escaped.*

But you must never think you can achieve this by your own strength. Be devoutly humble[30] that you may be delivered, for if you

---

29. The earth.
30. *Esto pius.* Variants: *esto pius cuius es*, "Be devoutly filial toward him to whom you belong"; *cuius est opus*, "Be devoutly filial toward him whose work it is."

conduct yourself proudly you fall into the trap. Take care to say, *Our help is in the name of the Lord, who made heaven and earth.*

Conclusion: plans for tomorrow's sermon

14. This psalm has now been studied and, as I think, explained, insofar as the Lord has graciously helped us. You are well aware that we owe you a sermon for tomorrow, beloved. Come along tomorrow, then, and aid us with your prayers. You surely remember our promise; indeed, I would not have told you what I intend to preach about were it not for the need I have to be helped by your eager faith and your prayers. You remember, then, that I promised[31] to study with you that saying in the gospel, *The law was given through Moses, grace and truth came through Jesus Christ* (Jn 1:17). There are some heretics—the Manichees in particular—who habitually belittle the law and deny that it came from God. We therefore need to expound that text to make it clear, first, that God did give the law, and, second, that the law given through Moses was not a law that could bring salvation. There was a good reason for the law's impotence to save us: God intended that the legislator himself, our Lord and ruler, should be the object of longing, as the one who would grant forgiveness to sinners. Thus, while the law had been given through Moses, grace and truth would come through Jesus Christ. I wanted you to concentrate on this. The mercy of the Lord will be present to help us, not in response to any merit on my part but perhaps in response to your desire. Not from our own cleverness, but from the abundance of his own gifts, he will see to it that a question so vital for people living under the New Covenant may be satisfactorily resolved—and resolved in such a way that the enemy may find no nook or cranny where he may hide in order to deceive the faithful.

---

31. He promised it at the end of his Second Homily on the Gospel of John (Hom. 2,16). The Third Homily fulfils the promise and is presumably the sermon he is referring to here.

Exposition of Psalm 124

A Sermon to the People

Verse 1. Rightness of heart; stability in God

1. This psalm belongs to the group called the *Songs of Steps*. We have said a good deal about this title in connection with other psalms, and we do not want to repeat it now, or we might wear you out instead of instructing you. As we make our ascent and lift our souls to the Lord our God with love and devotion, the psalm teaches us to pay no attention to the prosperous folk of this world. Their spurious happiness is often not only hollow but downright dangerous, because it leads them so far astray that all they think of is how to cosset their pride. Their hearts freeze up solid against God and become so hard and impermeable under the showers of his grace that they bear no fruit. An abundance of all things needed for this life—indeed, a superfluity—gives them a pretext for arrogance; though they are no more than human, and in fact less honorable than all others because more sinful, their pride prompts them to consider themselves better than everyone else. If only they would stop there and at least reckon themselves human like the rest of us!

Faithful worshipers of God are apt to be over-impressed by such folk and think too much about them, wavering and tottering in faith as though their own reward for loyal discipleship had been called in question. They may ask themselves why they bother to worship God as they struggle along in hard work and poverty and distress, in illness and pain and various troubles, all the while observing others who not only do not worship God but are also a trial to everybody else, yet enjoy bodily health, wallow in temporal goods, rejoice in the safety of their families, and are honored for their flashy success. Watching these prosperous people, the faithful falter and murmur in their hearts the questions openly posed in another psalm: *How does God know? Is there any knowledge in the Most High? Look, they are sinners, yet they have won abundant wealth in this world.* And it continues, *Is it then to no purpose that I have justified my heart, and washed my hands in innocence?* (Ps 72(73):11–13) Did I perhaps make a big mistake when I resolved to live justly and act towards others in a spirit of innocence, when I know that people who make no attempt to preserve such innocence enjoy good fortune and mock the just by doing wrong and getting away with it?

2. But remember who said these things in the psalm (I mean the psalm I was referring to just now, the one that asks, *How does God know? Is there any knowledge in the Most High? Look, they are sinners, yet they have won abundant wealth in this world. Is it then to no purpose that I have justified my heart, and washed my hands in innocence?* This is the one I mean, not the psalm we have begun to study and expound today). Well now, who said those things in the psalm? Someone who was not yet straightforward of heart. It is a psalm in which you observe a soul in peril and feet on a slippery slope. It opens thus: *How good God is to Israel, to those of straightforward hearts! But as for me, my feet had all but slipped, my steps very nearly slid out of control.* Why was that? *Because I envied sinners, seeing the peace that sinners enjoy.* (Ps 72(73):1–3) He pointed to the reason why his feet were slipping and his steps almost sliding into a catastrophic fall away from God: it was because he saw the prosperity of sinners and focused his attention on it, observing that they enjoyed peace while he himself labored under hardship.

But notice that he recalled all this after he had escaped from the danger, after he had straightened his heart and begun to cling to God.[1] From this new vantage-point he recounted the perils of his past. *How good God is!* But to whom? *To those of straightforward hearts.* Who are the people with straightforward hearts? Those who do not find fault with God. Whose hearts are straight? The people who align their wills with the will of God, not those who attempt to bend God's will to their own. It is such a brief precept laid upon us human beings, to straighten our hearts! Do you aspire to have a straightforward heart? Then do what God wants and stop wanting God to do what you want.

The people with twisted hearts, the ones whose hearts are not straightforward, are those who sit and argue about how God ought to have acted. Instead of praising him for what he has done, they find fault with it. They want to put him right. Not content with simply refusing to be corrected by him, they go further and argue, "God had no business to make people poor. There ought to have been rich people only, and they alone should have been allowed to live. Why

---

1. See Ps 72(73):28.

was any poor person created? What is the point of his existence?" In this they are rebuking the God of the poor. How much better it would be for such a critic to be poor himself, but to be God's property, knowing that his riches flow from God! How much better for him to follow the will of God, view his poverty as temporal and transient, and all the while look forward to spiritual wealth that cannot possibly melt away! Then his riches would consist of faith in the heart, even if there were no gold in his treasure-chest. If he did store gold there he would need to beware of thieves and might lose it against his will; but he never loses faith from his heart unless he has chosen to expel it.

In any case, beloved, the objection raised by such critics can easily be countered. God makes someone poor in order to test him, and he makes someone else rich to test him on his attitude to the poor. Everything that God has done he has done rightly. Even though we cannot see his plan or understand why he has done this in one way and that in another, it is good for us to be submissive to his wisdom and believe that he has acted well even if we do not yet know why he has done so. Then we shall have straightforward hearts and be disposed to rely on the Lord and trust him. Then our feet will not slip, and as we make our ascent the first verse of the psalm we are studying will be verified in us: *Those who trust in the Lord will be like Mount Zion, they*[2] *shall not be moved for ever.*

3. Who are they? *Those who dwell in Jerusalem.* These are the ones who will not be moved for ever, *those who dwell in Jerusalem.* If we take this to refer to the earthly Jerusalem, it seems that all who used to live there have been displaced by wars and the destruction of the city. You may look for a Jew in the city of Jerusalem and you will not find one. Can it be true, then, that *they shall not be moved for ever, those who dwell in Jerusalem*? It can be true only if there is another Jerusalem, one of which you are accustomed to hear a great deal. She is our mother,[3] and we sigh and groan for her on our pilgrimage, longing to return home to her. We had wandered from the way;[4] indeed, we had no way at all. The king of that city came and made himself the way for us[5] so that we could return to her. She is the city of which an earlier psalm in this collection of *Songs of*

---

2. Variant: "it."
3. See Gal 4:26.
4. See Wis 5:6. Variant: "had wandered from her."
5. See Jn 14:6.

Steps chanted, *Our feet were standing in the forecourts of Jerusalem* (Ps 121(122):2). We have already dealt with that earlier psalm and explained it to those of you who were present. Of this same city the singer exclaimed with longing, *Jerusalem that is being built like a city; it shares in the Selfsame* (Ps 121(122):3).[6] Those who dwell in this city *shall not be moved for ever.*

As for the dwellers in the other Jerusalem, the earthly one, they certainly were dislodged, at first in their hearts and subsequently in a bodily way through exile. When they were displaced in their hearts they fell, and then they crucified the king of the heavenly Jerusalem. They were spiritually excluded themselves, and they excluded their king, for they cast him out of their city and crucified him outside its walls.[7] And so he cast them out of his city, out of the eternal Jerusalem that is the mother of us all, the Jerusalem in heaven.[8]

Verse 2. Some mountains receive light, peace, and righteousness from God and transmit them to his people; other mountains are proud and dangerous

4. What is this Jerusalem like? The psalm gives only a brief description: *Mountains stand round about it.* Is it then such a great privilege for us to live in a city surrounded by mountains? Is that the sum of the happiness in store for us, that we shall possess a mountain-girt city? Are we not already familiar with mountains, which, after all, are no more than elevations of land? Clearly the mountains intended by the psalm must be different: mountains worthy of our love, lofty mountains, preachers of the truth, whether they be angels or apostles or prophets. They are all around Jerusalem, encircling it and forming a kind of protective wall. Scripture speaks continually of these lovable, delightful mountains. Notice the many references when you listen to scripture or read it: you will find allusions to delightful mountains in more places than we can count.

All the same, it is a pleasure for us to speak of these mountains, insofar as the Lord reminds us of relevant passages; and indeed many divine testimonies in the holy books do spring to mind. There are the mountains illumined by God; they receive the light first so that from

---

6. On the translation of *idipsum* as "the Selfsame" see Exposition of Psalm 121,5 and the note there.
7. See Jn 19:17–18; Heb 13:12.
8. See Gal 4:26; 2 Cor 5:1.

them it may radiate down to the valleys and to the hills which do not match the mountains in height. To them scripture is initially entrusted so that through them it may reach us, whether in prophecy or in the epistles[9] or in the gospel. They are the mountains of which we sing, *I have lifted my eyes to the mountains, from where comes help for me* (Ps 120(121):1), because in this life we look to the scriptures for help. But these mountains have no power either to protect themselves[10] or to further our interests from any resources of their own; nor should we allow our hope to rest in the mountains, lest we deserve the curse that falls on anyone who puts his trust in human help.[11] That earlier psalm therefore carried the thought further: *I have lifted my eyes to the mountains, from where comes help for me. My help is from the Lord, who made heaven and earth.* (Ps 120(121):1–2) Moreover these are the mountains of which yet another psalm prays, *Let the mountains receive peace for your people, and the hills justice* (Ps 71(72):3). Mountains soar; hills are lower. The mountains see, the hills believe. Those who see have received peace and have transmitted it to those who believe; and believers are said to receive justice because *the one who lives by faith is just* (Hb 2:4; Rom 1:17). The angels see directly and announce what they see; and we believe. John too saw, John who proclaimed, *In the beginning was the Word, and the Word was with God; he was God* (Jn 1:1)—he saw and preached to us, so that we might believe. As the mountains receive peace, so the hills have received justice. For what does scripture say of the mountains themselves? It does not say, "They enjoy peace as from themselves," or "they create peace," or "they generate peace." No, it says, "They receive peace," and the source of the peace they are given is the Lord. Lift your eyes to the mountains to seek peace, then, but do so remembering that your help comes from the Lord, who made heaven and earth.

In a similar passage the Holy Spirit speaks of the same mountains in this way: *You send your wondrous light from the eternal mountains* (Ps 75:5(76:4)). It does not say, "The mountains emit light," but, *You send your light from the eternal mountains.* You preach the gospel to us through those mountains which you have willed should stand for ever; but it is *you* who *send your light*, not the mountains. Such, then, are the *mountains round about* Jerusalem.

---

9. Variant: "apostles."
10. Variant: "protect us."
11. See Jer 17:5.

5. There is a sure way to discern the character of the mountains which are said to stand around Jerusalem. Whenever scripture mentions mountains, meaning good ones, it scarcely ever—perhaps never—fails to mention the Lord immediately in the same context, at least by implication, so that no one's faith may remain with the mountains and stop short of the Lord. Think of the many instances I have quoted: *I have lifted my eyes to the mountains, from where comes help for me*; but you must not stop there, so the psalm continues, *My help is from the Lord, who made heaven and earth*. Then again, when another psalm prays, *Let the mountains receive peace for the people*, it indicates by the use of the verb *receive* that there is a different source[12] from which they derive that peace. Then there is the psalm that speaks of illumination from the mountains, but it says, *You, you, the Lord: you send your wondrous light from the eternal mountains*. This same rule applies in the psalm we are considering today. In the very verse where it speaks of *mountains round about* Jerusalem, it takes care that you do not stay with those mountains. It immediately adds, *And the Lord is round about his people*. You must not settle your hope in the mountains but in him who illumines the mountains. The Lord dwells in the mountains, which represent his saints, and he is thus round about his people. He has walled in his people with a spiritual fortification, that it may not be shaken or dislodged for ever.

The case is different when scripture mentions bad mountains, for then it does not speak of the Lord in connection with them. As we have often pointed out to you, mountains represent some kind of great personalities, but in this case bad ones. You must not suppose, brothers and sisters, that heresies could have come into being through spiritual midgets. It was only persons of considerable stature who instigated heresies, but the height of these mountains was matched by their malice. They were not the kind of mountains to receive peace, so that from them the hills might in turn receive justice; all they received was discord from their father, the devil. They were mountains, to be sure, but be careful not to fly for refuge to mountains like that. People will approach you and say, "So-and-so was a great man! And that other, he was a fine fellow, you must admit. Think of Donatus,[13] and

---

12. Variant: "mountain."
13. On Donatus and his schism, see the notes at Expositions of Psalms 10,1; 64,2; 95,2.11; 119,9.

how remarkable he was! And then Maximianus:[14] there is a splendid character for you! Then there was someone else called Photinus:[15] what a great man! And what about Arius?[16] He was undoubtedly important." I have listed all these mountains, but be wary, for they cause shipwrecks. You see them emitting beams of light in the way of inflammatory exhortations, and some fire is kindled from them. If you are piloting your boat[17] and darkness has overtaken you (the obscurity of this life, I mean), do not let them[18] deceive you into setting your course in their direction. You will hit the rocks. Disastrous wrecks occur there. If you hear people singing the praises of those mountains and almost persuading you to make your way toward them as though to seek help and find a safe haven, you must reply, *I trust in the Lord. How can you say to my soul, Migrate to the mountains*[19] *like a sparrow?* (Ps 10:2(11:1)). Your salvation lies in lifting your eyes to those mountains from which the Lord's help comes to you so that, like a sparrow, you may avoid the fowlers' snare[20] and not migrate to the mountains. A sparrow is an unstable creature; it moves fast, flitting hither and thither. But you, for your part, trust in the Lord and you will be like Mount Zion, unmoved for ever; you will not be flitting off to those mountains. Could you find the Lord's name mentioned anywhere when you were invited to migrate to them? I think not.

6. Love the mountains in which the Lord is present. Yes, love them; but those mountains love you only if you do not fix your hope on them. Observe what God's mountains are like, brothers and sisters; for this is what they are called in another passage: *Your justice is like God's mountains* (Ps 35:7(36:6)). Notice that it does not attribute justice to them: it is God's justice, *your justice*. Well now, listen to what a mountain of this kind has to say, listen to the apostle: *May I be found in him, not having any righteousness of my own, derived from*

---

14. Initiator of a break-away movement within Donatism, a schism within a schism. See Exposition 2 of Psalm 36,19–23 and the notes at Expositions of Psalms 35,9 and 57,15.
15. A heresiarch; see the note at Exposition of Psalm 67,39.
16. On Arius: see the notes at Expositions of Psalms 35,9 and 54,22.
17. *In ligno*: "in your wooden boat." In classical Latin *lignum* is sometimes used for an object made from wood, such as a table or writing-tablet, but Christian usage may possibly be alluded to here.
18. Variant: "it."
19. Variant: *mountain*.
20. See Ps 123(124):7.

the law, but that which comes through faith in Christ (Ph 3:9). Others aspired to tower like mountains with a righteousness of their own. Such were some of the Jews, especially their leaders, the Pharisees, and they are rebuked: *They failed to recognize the righteousness that comes from God and, by seeking to set up a righteousness of their own, they did not submit to God's righteousness* (Rom 10:3). Those, on the contrary, who have subjected themselves to it are high indeed, yet in such a way as to be humble. Being great, they deserve to be called mountains; but, being subject to God, they are valleys. Because their loving devotion gives them great capacity to receive, they welcome God's overflowing peace and flood the hills with it. Now take note and see what mountains you must love.

If you want to be loved yourself, however, by these good mountains, do not rest your hope on them, do not rely on them, good mountains though they are. What a lofty mountain Paul was! Can anyone compare with him? (I am speaking of human greatness, of course.) You will not easily find anyone else so highly graced. And yet he was afraid the sparrow might put its trust in him. What did he say? *"Was Paul crucified for you* (1 Cor 1:13)? Rather lift your eyes to the mountains whence help may come to you, for while *I planted, and Apollos watered*, your help is from the Lord who made heaven and earth, for *it is God who gives the growth"* (1 Cor 3:6).

Mountains stand round about Jerusalem, then. But as the *mountains stand round about it*, so is *the Lord round about his people, from now on and for ever*. If this is so, if *mountains stand round about it, and the Lord is round about his people*, the Lord must be binding his people in a single bond of charity and peace so that those who trust in the Lord may be like Mount Zion and not be moved for ever. This is what is suggested by the psalm's words, *from now on and for ever*.

Verse 3. Christian submission to lawful authority

7. *For he will not leave the rod of sinners in control over the fate of the just, lest the just stretch out their hands to iniquity.* As things are at present the just are rather hard pressed, and the unjust sometimes have dominion over them; this holds under the present dispensation. In what ways do we find this happening? Unjust persons sometimes attain worldly rank, and when they become judges or rulers (for God so disposes matters for the discipline of his ordinary subjects, indeed for the discipline of his whole people) it is necessary that they be paid the honor due to authority. God has so ordered affairs in his Church

that every authority duly constituted in this world should be accorded respect,[21] and this sometimes means by persons better than those to whom it is paid.

I will give one example of this situation, from which you can extend the principle to every case of human rank and dominance. The most obvious example of the authority of one human being over another is one we encounter every day: that of a master's power over his slave. Nearly all households witness the exercise of this kind of power.[22] There are masters, and there are also slaves: these are two different names; but if you remember that both are human beings, there is a name common to both.

Now, reflect why the apostle says that slaves are subordinate to their masters. *Slaves, obey those who are your masters according to the flesh* (Eph 6:5). He puts in that qualification, *according to the flesh*, because there is a different master, one "according to Christ."[23] He is the true and eternal master, whereas those others are masters only for a time. While you are walking in the way, living in this present life,[24] Christ does not want to make you proud. Perhaps it happened that you, having become a Christian, found yourself subject to a human master. That is as it should be: you did not become a Christian in order to throw off your servile status as beneath your dignity. When at Christ's command you serve a human being, it is not he whom you are serving but Christ, who commanded you. So Paul continues, *Obey those who are your masters according to the flesh in fear and trembling, in simplicity of heart. Serve not only where it shows, as though you only wanted to please men, but like slaves of Christ, doing God's will from your hearts, with a good will.* (Eph 6:5-7) So you see, Paul does not try to turn slaves into free men and women, but bad slaves into good slaves.

What a debt of gratitude rich people owe to Christ for bringing peace to their households! If in such a house there were an unbelieving slave and Christ were to convert him, he would not say to him, "Leave your master, for now you have come to know him who is your true master. Your earthly master may be bad and unjust, while you are now

---

21. Compare Rom 13:1-7.
22. Variants: "Nearly all of us have households where this kind of power is exercised"; "Nearly all have masters endowed with this kind of power."
23. Variant: "according to the Spirit" or "the spirit."
24. Possibly "the way" and "the life" may be used in a Christological sense.

a believer and a person of upright life: it is unfitting that a righteous and faithful person should be enslaved to a wicked unbeliever." No, that is not what Christ has said; rather he commands, "Do your duty as his slave." And then, to strengthen the slave, he tells him, "Follow my example in being a slave, for I went before you in submitting to evil men." When the Lord endured such contumely in his passion, under whom did he suffer it? The Lord suffered it under his slaves. And what kind of people were they? Wicked slaves; for if they had been good slaves they would have respected their Lord, whereas, being bad slaves, they treated him disgracefully. But did he retaliate in kind? On the contrary, he rendered love for hatred. He prayed, *Father, forgive them, for they do not know what they are doing* (Lk 23:34). If the Lord of heaven and earth, through whom all things were made,[25] bore himself like a slave to the unworthy, interceded for savage and enraged tormentors, and presented himself to them as their healer (and remember that doctors are superior in skill and in health to those whom they serve), how much less should an ordinary man or woman disdain to serve a master with sincerity, total good will, and love—even if the master is bad? We then have a situation where a better person is serving a worse, but only for a time.

Apply what I have said about a master and a slave to rulers and sovereigns and to all exalted persons in this world. Sometimes these authorities are good and fear God; sometimes they do not. Julian was an unbelieving emperor; he stood out as an apostate, an idolater, and an unjust man.[26] In his reign Christian soldiers served under an unbelieving emperor. If Christ's cause was at stake they acknowledged no one but their Lord in heaven; and if the emperor tried to make them worship idols or burn incense to the gods they set God's authority above his. But if Julian ordered, "Deploy into battle formation! March against the enemy!" they obeyed him at once. They drew a clear distinction between their eternal Lord and their temporal

---

25. See Jn 1:3.
26. Flavius Claudius Iulianus, or "Julian the Apostate," emperor 361–363, attempted to substitute paganism for Christianity by reviving pagan worship throughout the empire, restricting the privileges Christians had enjoyed since Constantine's reign, punishing many persons for Christian practice, and fomenting dissension in the Church. Personally austere, he also attempted to raise moral standards among pagans. The legend that he died with the acknowledgement on his lips, "Thou hast conquered, O Galilean!" is late and unreliable.

master, but they subjected themselves to their temporal master for the sake of their eternal Lord.

But the unjust will not dominate in the long run

8. But will it always be like this, with the wicked having dominion over the just? No, it will not. Consider the witness of the psalm: *The Lord will not leave the rod of sinners in control over the fate of the just.* The rod of sinners lies heavy upon the just now, but it will not be left there; it will not be there for ever. The time will come when one sole God will be acknowledged; the time will come when Christ will appear in radiant glory to gather all nations before him, when he will sort them out as a shepherd separates goats from sheep and place the sheep at his right, the goats at his left.[27] Then you will see many slaves among the sheep and many masters among the goats; but you will also observe plenty of slave-owners among the sheep and of slaves among the goats. We have spoken comforting words to slaves, but this does not imply that all slaves are good; and we have curbed[28] the pride of their masters, but without suggesting that all masters are bad. There are masters who are believers and good people, and there are bad ones; so too there are slaves who are believers and good, and there are bad ones. But as long as good slaves have to serve bad masters, they must endure their lot, knowing that it is temporary, for *the Lord will not leave the rod of sinners in control over the fate of the just.* Why not? *Lest the just stretch out their hands to iniquity.* He wants the just to bear the dominance of the unjust for the time being and to understand that it will not last for ever. In the meantime they should prepare themselves for the possession of their everlasting inheritance, the inheritance that will fall to them when all mighty power has been destroyed, *that God may be all things in all of us* (1 Cor 15:28). As the just save themselves up for this, and contemplate it in their hearts, and hold onto it in faith, and endure whatever comes so that they may one day see it, they do not stretch out their hands to iniquity.

If, on the contrary, they were to regard the sway of sinners over the just as permanent, they would think within themselves, "What do I gain by being just? This unjust master will always rule over me, and I shall always be a slave. Alright, then; I'll commit iniquity

---

27. See Mt 25:32–33.
28. Variant: "rebuked."

too. There's no point in holding fast to righteousness." To ward off such ideas the message of faith is hammered home: though the rod of sinners may lie over the fate of the just for a time, the Lord *will not leave it in control over the fate of the just, lest the just stretch out their hands to iniquity.* Rather will they withhold their hands from iniquity and choose to bear iniquity sooner than commit it. It is better to suffer injustice than to deal unjustly.[29] Why will the supremacy of the unjust not last for ever? Because the Lord *will not leave the rod of sinners in control over the fate of the just.*

Verses 4–5. Peace is the inheritance of people with upright hearts

9. People with straightforward hearts, the kind of people I spoke about earlier,[30] think along these lines. They follow the will of God, not their own; they are the ones who want God to lead them so that they may follow him and do not try to take the lead themselves and make God follow. They find God good in all circumstances, whether he is chastising them or consoling them, whether putting them through their paces or crowning their efforts, whether purifying or illuminating. So the apostle teaches: *We know that for those who love God all things work together for good* (Rom 8:28). This is why the psalm goes on to say, *Deal kindly, O Lord, with the good, and those of straightforward hearts.*

10. A person of straightforward heart turns away from evil and does good.[31] One of this disposition is not jealous of sinners when observing the peace they seem to enjoy.[32] Conversely, anyone with a crooked heart is scandalized at the Lord's ways,[33] turns away from God, and does wrong. Lured on by the attractions of this world, such a person is ensnared and captivated by its sweetness, only to incur bitter punishment. Unwilling to bear the discipline of God, from whom he turns away, he soon finds that what was unreal pleasure becomes by God's judgment a real trap. Accordingly the psalm continues, *But to*

---

29. An echo of Cicero. Compare *Tusc.* 5,56: *Cum accipere quam facere praestat iniuriam*; and *Leg.* 3,34: *Vi opprimi in bona causa est melius quam malae cedere.* Augustine quotes from the *Tusculan Disputations* in *Confessions* I,16,25.
30. See section 2 above.
31. See Ps 36(37):27.
32. See Ps 72(73):1.3.
33. See Hos 14:10.

those who turn aside into tortuous paths[34] *the Lord will allot a place with the workers of iniquity,* whose deeds they have imitated, because they envied the present prosperity of sinners and did not believe in their future punishment.

But what about the people whose hearts are straight and honest, those who do not turn aside? What will their portion be? Let us now consider the question of our inheritance, brothers and sisters, because we are God's children. What will our possession be? What is our heritage? What is our homeland? What is it called? Peace. In the name of peace we greet you, and peace is what we proclaim to you; this is what the mountains receive, in order that through them the hills may receive justice. Peace is the name of Christ himself, for scripture tells us, *He is himself our peace, since he united the two, and has broken down the dividing wall of hostility* (Eph 2:14). Because we are sons and daughters of God we shall receive an inheritance, and what is its name if not peace? Those who are no lovers of peace have been disinherited, as you see.[35] It is those who tear our unity apart who do not love peace. Peace is the possession of dutiful and loving sons and daughters; it is the property of God's heirs. Who are his heirs? His children. And listen to the gospel's word: *Blessed are the peacemakers, for they shall be called God's children* (Mt 5:9).

Listen also to the closing words of this psalm: *Peace upon Israel.* Israel means "one who sees God," and Jerusalem is interpreted "vision of peace." Use your intelligence on these names, beloved. If the name Israel is said to mean "one who sees God," and the name Jerusalem means "vision of peace," what does the comparison of the two suggest? Who are the people who *shall not be moved for ever*? Those who *dwell in Jerusalem*. Those who dwell in the "vision of peace" will not be displaced for ever. And *peace is upon Israel*. Evidently the Israel that sees God sees peace, and this Israel is also Jerusalem, because God's people is the same as God's city. If, then, the people that sees peace thereby also sees God, we are right to infer that God himself is peace.

---

34. *In stranguilationem*, literally "into strangulation." Augustine's Latin version is an over-literal rendering of the Greek εἰς τας στραγγαλιές. The word means primarily something tight and suffocating and, by extension, crooked or twisted.
35. The following remarks obviously envisage the Donatists.

Christ, the Son of God, is peace, and he will therefore come to gather his own and separate them from the unjust. Which of the unjust? Those who hate Jerusalem and hate peace, those who want to rend our unity apart, those who do not believe in peace, who mouth words of false peace among the people and have no peace in themselves. They say, "Peace be with you," and people reply, "With[36] your spirit," but they are listening to falsehood and giving a hollow answer back. To whom are their preachers saying, "Peace be with you"? To disciples whom they are drawing away from the peace that binds the whole world together. As for those to whom the reply, "With[37] your spirit," is given, if peace really were present in their spirits, would they not commit themselves in love to our unity and abhor schism? Of course they would; and so they are mouthing a dishonest greeting and accepting a dishonest response.

Let us, on the contrary, speak truth and listen to truth. Let us be Israel and embrace peace, because Israel is the "vision of peace," and we are Israel. *Peace is upon Israel.*

---

36. Variant: "And with…"
37. Variant: "And with…" as above. Another variant inserts "those who embrace dissensions and hate peace" after "is given."

Exposition of Psalm 125

A Sermon to the People

Verse 1. The song of former captives, redeemed by Christ's blood

1. Since we have been taking this group of psalms in numerical order, you will already be aware that the one we deal with today is the 125th and that it belongs to the collection entitled *Songs of Steps*. You know too that this psalm, like the others, is sung by people who are ascending. And to what other place can they be ascending but to the Jerusalem on high that is the mother of us all, the city in heaven?[1] That city on high is eternal, but the earthly Jerusalem foreshadowed it. The earthly city fell, but the heavenly city abides; the one fulfilled its task relative to the era when salvation was proclaimed, but the other embodies our everlasting restoration as something realized. In this life we are exiles from the heavenly city, and we sigh with longing to return to it; we go on sighing in our wretchedness and toil until we make our way to that city where we shall be at home. But our fellow-citizens, the angels, have not forsaken us during our exile, for they announced to us that our king would come in person. He came to us, but he was despised among us and by us, and since that time he has been despised with us. He taught us how to endure contempt by being himself the object of contempt; he taught us how to endure, because he endured; he taught us how to suffer, because he suffered; and he promised that we shall rise again, because he rose. He showed us in himself what we must hope for.

If the ancient prophets, our forebears, yearned so ardently for that city, even before the Lord Jesus Christ came in the flesh, even before he had died and risen and ascended into heaven, how ardently ought we to desire it, brothers and sisters? What should be our longing for that place whither he has gone ahead of us? Though in truth he never left it, for the Lord did not come to us in such a way as to abandon the angels. He remained with them but came to us as well: he remained with them in majesty and came to us in the flesh. But where were we?

---

1. See Gal 4:26; 2 Cor 5:1.

If he is called our redeemer, we must have been prisoners in need of ransom. Where were we held, that he had to come and redeem us from captivity?[2] Where were we held? Among barbarians, perhaps? No, worse than that: the devil is far more cruel than any barbarian, and so are his angels. Until that time they had held the human race in thrall, but the Lord bought our freedom—not with gold or silver but by offering for us his own blood.

2. Let us question the apostle Paul to find out how the human race had fallen captive, for Paul himself groaned louder than most others in his captivity as he longed for the eternal Jerusalem, and he taught us to groan in the same Spirit that filled him and inspired his groans. He tells us, *Until now all creation has been groaning in its birth-pangs*; and again, *All creation has been subjected to vanity, not by its own choice, but by him who subjected it in hope.* (Rom 8:22.20) All creation is groaning in travail, he says, and he clearly includes people who do not yet believe but who will believe eventually. Does this imply that only those are groaning, only the ones who are not yet believers? By no means! Does creation not groan in travail in those who already believe? Surely it does, for Paul continues, *But not creation only: we ourselves, though we have the first-fruits of the spirit.* He is referring to us who already serve God in spirit, who have already come to believe in God with our minds and so have offered him a kind of first-fruits of our spirit[3] as a pledge that we will follow with the gift of our whole selves. We too, then, Paul continues, *groan inwardly as we await our adoption as God's children, the redemption of our bodies* (Rom 8:23–24).

Paul was groaning himself, and all the faithful groan as they await their final adoption, the redemption of their bodies.[4] Where do they groan? In this mortal state. What kind of redemption are they awaiting? That perfect redemption of their humanity of which we have seen an exemplar in the Lord, who rose from the dead and ascended into heaven. Until our redeemed bodies are restored to us we cannot but groan, even though we are believers and even though we hope. This is why Paul goes on to say.... Just a minute: I want to add something. When Paul said, *We too groan inwardly as we await our*

---

2. Variant: "that he had to come and free the guilty?"
3. Our own spirit, in Augustine's understanding, rather than the Holy Spirit of God, as in Paul. See the note at Exposition 12 of Psalm 118,1.
4. In the sense of "the whole person."

adoption as God's children, the redemption of our bodies, someone might have objected, "If you are still groaning, what good did Christ do you? In what sense did the Savior really save you? Anyone who is groaning must still be unwell." In reply to this, Paul continued, *In hope we have been saved. But if hope is seen, it is hope no longer, for when someone sees what he hopes for, why should he hope for it? But if we hope for what we do not see, we wait for it in patience.* (Rom 8:24-25) This is why we groan, and this is how we groan: we are awaiting what we hope for, but we do not grasp it yet, and until we do lay hold on it we sigh in this in-between time, because we are longing for what we do not yet possess. Why must we wait? Because *in hope we have been saved.* The flesh which the Lord took from us is saved in him, not in hope but in actuality.[5] In him, our head, our flesh rose and ascended, in salvation fully realized; but in his members it is to be saved still. Let the members rejoice without anxiety, for they have not been forsaken by their head. To his toiling members he gave this assurance: *Lo, I am with you even to the end of the ages* (Mt 28:20).

All this was so done that we might be converted to God. We had no hope, except as directed toward the world. Hence we were wretched,[6] and twice-wretched because in this life we not only had our faces turned toward the world but we also had our backs to God.[7] But once the Lord has turned us round so that we begin to face toward God and thrust the world behind our backs, then, although we are still wayfarers, we are tending toward our homeland. We may at times suffer distress, but we hold to our course and are borne along in our boat.[8] The wind may be high, but it is with us; it sweeps us along very swiftly, even if the voyage is rough.

So preoccupied were we with our groaning—even those of us who already believe—that we had forgotten how we came to be captured. Scripture reminds us, however. Let us ask the apostle Paul. *We know that the law is spiritual,* he says. *But I am carnal, sold under sin* (Rom 7:14). That was how we were taken into captivity: we were sold under sin. Who sold us? We sold ourselves by consenting to our seducer. We had the power to sell ourselves but no power to buy

---

5. *Non spe, sed re*, Augustine's familiar distinction.
6. Variant: "wretched slaves."
7. Compare Jer 2:27. Augustine uses this image several times; see, for instance, *Confessions* II,3,6.
8. *Ligno*, "wood." See the note at Exposition of Psalm 124,5.

ourselves back again. We sold ourselves by sinful consent; we are redeemed by justifying faith. Innocent blood was the price paid for our redemption. When the devil shed blood in his persecution of the just, what kind of blood did he spill? He certainly did shed the blood of righteous prophets, our ancestors; he also shed the righteous blood of martyrs;[9] but all these sprang from sinful stock. Once only was the blood shed of a man who needed no justification, because he was just from his birth. By that unique blood-shedding the devil lost those he had in his grasp. They on whose behalf innocent blood was given have been redeemed. As they turn away from their captivity, let them sing this psalm.

Released from captivity, the redeemed are comforted in hope

3. *When the Lord turned Zion's captivity around, we became like people comforted.* This means, "We became joyful." When did the change occur? *When the Lord turned Zion's captivity around.* Which Zion is this? Jerusalem, the eternal Zion. But how can it be the eternal Zion if it was also Zion the captive? It is eternal in the angels, but it was captive in men and women; for not all its citizens were taken prisoner but only those who are on pilgrimage, exiled from their city. The first humans were citizens of Jerusalem, but when sold under sin they became exiles. From their stock our whole race was propagated, and thus a captive Zion filled the whole earth. How can this captive Zion be a shadow of the eternal Jerusalem? The likeness is to be found in the sign granted to the Jews when, after seventy years' captivity in Babylon, the people returned to its own city. Those seventy years represent the whole of time, which revolves in a seven-day rhythm. When the entire stretch of time has passed we shall return to our homeland, as the Jewish people returned after its seventy-year exile in captivity. Clearly Babylon is a symbol of this world, for the name Babylon means "confusion." Is not the whole of human life one long confusion? Think about it. People act at the prompting of their futile hopes and, when they recognize what they are doing, many are ashamed. What are they working for? For whose benefit? "For my children," someone replies. And for whom will they work? "For their children." And they, in their turn? "For their children again." So no one works for himself! But of believers who had already turned away from this confused situation the apostle demanded, *What fruit*

---

9. Variant: "the blood of righteous martyrs."

did you reap then from those things of which you are now ashamed? (Rom 6:21) Human life is all confusion as long as it is not made over to God. Zion is held prisoner in this confusion, in this Babylon; but *the Lord turned Zion's captivity around.*

4. *We became like people comforted*; that is to say, we were as joyful as though we had been given consolation. Comfort is appropriate only for those bewailing their misfortune, for people groaning and in sorrow. Why does the psalm say *like people comforted* and not "because we were comforted"? Surely because we are still groaning. We groan over our situation as it is, but we are comforted by our hope. When the present reality has passed away, eternal joy will take the place of groaning, and then we shall have no need of consolation, because no unhappiness will ever hurt us.

But why *like people comforted*? Why not say simply that we are comforted? The words "like" or "as" can be used either to indicate a comparison or to make a statement relating to the proper quality of the person or thing spoken of. In the present context the word is used in the latter way. Examples from common speech may make the distinction readily intelligible. If we say, "As the father lived, so does the son," we are using "as" to make a comparison. Again, we may say, "As an animal dies, so does a man"; this too is a comparison. But if we say, "He acted like a good man," do we mean that he is not a good man but is only being compared to one? "He behaved as a just man behaves": in this case too the word "as" does not suggest that the person is not just but indicates the quality properly inherent in him. If you said to him, "You acted like a senator," and he replied, "Are you implying that I am not a senator?" you would answer, "On the contrary, because you are a senator you acted in character; because you are a just man you behaved like a just man; because you are good you acted as a good man acts."

So too in the psalm. Because these people[10] had been genuinely comforted, they rejoiced *like people comforted.* Their joy was very great, like that of those who receive real consolation, because he who died was comforting those who were to die. All of us groan at the prospect of death, but he who died comforts us so that we do not fear to die. He rose so that we might have something to hope for. Because he was the first to rise from the dead he gave us hope; distressed though we are at present, this hope has brought us comfort.

---

10. Variant: "the just."

Huge joy is ours, therefore. The Lord has turned our captivity round, so that now we have a way out of it, a way we can hold to, a way back to our homeland. We are already redeemed, so let us not fear enemies lurking by the wayside. He redeemed us so that no enemy may dare to ambush us—provided we do not step off the way. Christ himself has become our way.[11] Do you want to be safe from robbers? He says to you, "I have opened a way for you to your homeland; do not leave it. I have so fortified this way that no robber will dare to approach you. You, for your part, must be careful not to stray from it, and then no robber will come anywhere near you." Walk in Christ, then, walk joyfully and sing, sing like one comforted, because he has gone before you and commands you to follow.

Verse 2. The difference between the bodily mouth and the mouth of the heart

5. *Then was our mouth filled with joy, and our tongue with gladness.* If we think this means our bodily mouth, brothers and sisters, how can it be filled with joy? It is generally filled with food, or drink, or anything else of that kind that we put into our mouths. So our mouths are certainly filled sometimes. And there is something else that we must point out to you, holy brethren:[12] when our mouths are full, we cannot speak.[13]

But we have also an inner mouth in our hearts and, if what comes out of it is bad, it defiles us;[14] but if good, it cleanses us. You heard about this inward mouth when the gospel was being read. The Jews censured the Lord because his disciples were accustomed to eat without first washing their hands. The scoffers cultivated external cleanliness but were full of filth within; they were people whose righteousness extended only as far as the opinion of other people. But the Lord was looking for inner purity; if we have that, everything outside is inevitably clean. *Cleanse the things within,* he advised them, *and then things without will be clean too* (Mt 23:26). In another place the Lord says, *Give alms, and everything will be clean for you* (Lk 11:41). But where does almsgiving spring from? From the heart. So true is this that, if you open your hand but have no compassion in your heart, you

---

11. See Jn 14:6.
12. *Sanctitati vestrae.*
13. A limitation not associated with the mouth of the heart, as he will show later.
14. See Mt 15:11.18–20.

have done nothing, whereas, if you have nothing in your hand to give but have merciful intentions in your heart, God accepts your alms.

The Jews, however, were looking for external purity. One such was the Pharisee who had invited the Lord to a meal.[15] A woman who was a notorious sinner in the town squeezed in, washed the Lord's feet with her tears, dried them with her hair, and anointed them with ointment. The Pharisee who was the Lord's host had no purity in him except outward, bodily cleanliness; at heart he was full of wickedness and acquisitive habits. He said to himself, *If this man were a prophet, he would know who this woman is, who has approached his feet* (Lk 7:39). How did he know whether the Lord knew or not? He assumed that he did not, because the Lord did not repulse the woman. If a woman of that character had accosted the Pharisee, who valued purity as though it were a merely physical thing, he would have blown her away, brushed her off, thrown her out, for fear that this unclean woman might touch his clean person and tarnish his purity. Since the Lord did not do this, the Pharisee inferred that he did not know the character of the woman who had approached his feet. But not only did the Lord know her; he was also listening to the Pharisee's thoughts. Even if bodily contact could produce such an effect, you unclean Pharisee, would the Lord's flesh be contaminated by contact with the woman? Would she not rather be cleansed by contact with the Lord? The physician allowed a sick woman to touch the healing remedy. She had come in because she knew her physician. She was probably used to acting brazenly in her licentious pursuits, but now she was more shameless still in her demand for salvation. She burst into a house where she had not been invited: but, after all, she was wounded, and she had found out where the doctor reclined at table. The host who had invited the physician believed himself to be healthy; that is why he was not cured. You know how the gospel story continues: how the Pharisee was shamed when the Lord proved to him that he had been aware not only of the woman's character but also of the Pharisee's thoughts.

6. Now, beloved, turn your minds to something else read to us in the gospel that throws light on the verse we are considering in our psalm, the one that runs, *Then was our mouth filled with joy, and our tongue with gladness.* We were wondering what mouth and what tongue were meant, you will remember.

---

15. See Lk 7:36–50.

The Lord was criticized because his disciples ate without first washing their hands. He answered as the critics deserved and then called the crowds together to hear his teaching. He bade them, *Listen and understand. It is not what enters your mouth that defiles you, but what comes out; that is what defiles a person.* (Mt 15:10–11) How are we to understand this? When he said, *What enters your mouth,* he must have been referring to the bodily mouth. Various foods enter it, and foods do not defile people, for *to the pure all things are pure* (Ti 1:15), and *everything created by God is good; nothing is to be rejected, provided it is received with thankfulness* (1 Tm 4:4). Certain things were forbidden to the Jews and termed unclean, but this had figurative significance. After the era of figures the light itself came to us and the shadows were dispelled. We are no longer held back by the letter but brought to life in the spirit.[16] The yoke of legal observance that was laid upon the Jews is not imposed on Christians, for the Lord said, *My yoke is kindly and my burden light* (Mt 11:30). *To the pure all things are pure,* says the apostle, *but to the impure and unbelievers nothing is pure; their minds and consciences are polluted* (Ti 1:15). What did he mean us to understand from this? To a pure man or woman both bread and pork are pure; to an impure person neither is pure. *To the impure and unbelievers nothing is pure.* Why is it that for them *nothing is pure*? Why are *their minds and consciences polluted*? Because if what is within a person is impure, nothing external can be pure. It follows, then, that if for people who are impure nothing outside can be pure, you must clean what is inside if you want external things to be pure for you.

There, within you, is the mouth that will be filled with your joy, even when you are silent; for when you are silent but joyful your mouth is shouting to God. But make sure about the source of your joy. If what makes you joyful is your luck in this world, you are yelling to God with unclean joy; but if you are rejoicing over your redemption, in the same vein as the psalm, which sings, *When the Lord turned Zion's captivity around, we became like people made happy*,[17] then your mouth is filled with true joy, and your tongue with gladness. Then it is quite certain that you are rejoicing in hope,[18] and your joy is acceptable in God's presence. In this joy, with this interior mouth

---

16. See 2 Cor 3:6.
17. *Iucundati* here; when verse 1 was quoted above it was *consolati*.
18. See Rom 12:12.

of ours, we also eat and drink, for, as our bodily mouth is used for the refreshment of the body, so is our inner mouth for the refreshment of the heart. For why are they *blessed who hunger and thirst for righteousness*? Because *they shall be satisfied* (Mt 5:6).

7. But the gospel tells us that it is only what comes out of the mouth that makes someone unclean. It would be an absurd position, an exceedingly foolish one, to understand this as referring only to the bodily mouth, for then one would be holding that a person does not become unclean by eating but is unclean if he vomits. The Lord says, *It is not what enters your mouth that defiles you, but what comes out; that is what defiles you* (Mt 15:11). So you do not defile yourself by eating but become unclean if you vomit? You are not rendered unclean by drinking but are defiled if you spit it out? That absurd conclusion would follow, because something emerges from your mouth when you spit and, when you drink, something goes in. What, then, did the Lord mean when he said, *It is not what enters your mouth that defiles you, but what comes out; that is what defiles you*? According to another evangelist[19] he went on to speak in the same place of the things that come out of the mouth, and in so doing made it quite clear that he meant not the bodily mouth but the mouth of the heart. *For, he said, from the heart come forth evil thoughts, impurity, murders, and blasphemies: these are the things that defile a person. But to eat with unwashed hands does not defile anyone.* (Mt 15:19–20)

But tell me, my brothers and sisters, how do these things come out of the mouth unless their source is the heart, as the Lord indicated? We cannot assume that these vicious things pollute us only when we put them into words. Were that the case, someone might say, "When we speak, they come out of our mouth, because words and sounds are produced by the mouth. So when we speak of evil things, we become unclean." That cannot be right. What if someone does not speak evil but only thinks it? Does that keep him clean, the fact that nothing came out of his bodily mouth? God has already heard what the mouth of his heart uttered. I want you to think carefully about what I am saying, brothers and sisters. Suppose I utter the word "theft." There, I have said it: "Theft!" Does that make me guilty of theft? It came out of my mouth, didn't it? Yet it did not make me impure. But what about a thief who rises in the night, saying nothing? His mouth has not made him impure, but his deeds do. Not only does he say nothing

---

19. Compare Mk 7:20–23, though the quotation that follows is closer to Mt.

but he actually conceals his crime by his complete silence; not only does he fear to make his voice heard but he makes sure that not even his footsteps are audible. If he is so totally silent, does it mean he is pure? Obviously not.

I will go even further, brothers and sisters. Think of him still lying in bed. He has not yet risen to commit his theft; he is staying awake until everyone else is asleep. Yet already he is bawling in God's ears. Already he is a thief, already impure. Already the crime has come out of his interior mouth. When does it emerge from the inner mouth? When the will to commit the crime is formed. If you have decided to do it, you have said it; and if you have said it, you have done it. If you have not put your plan into operation, the person from whom you intended to steal has not had the misfortune to lose his goods, yet, though he has lost nothing, you will be condemned for stealing. If you have formed the intention of killing someone, you have spoken the word in your heart; your inner mouth has uttered it: "Murder." Even though your intended victim is still alive, you are punished for murder. What counts is what you are in God's sight. If other people do not yet see you so, it makes no difference.

8. We know for certain that the heart has a mouth and the heart has a tongue. It is our business to know this and to hold onto it firmly. With that interior mouth we pray to God, and even when our lips are closed our conscience lies open. Silence reigns, yet our breast is shouting. In whose ears? Not in any human ears but in God's. Do not worry, then, for he who takes pity on you can hear you. On the other hand, if bad things are coming out of that mouth of yours,[20] do not think you are safe because no human being can hear them, for God hears and condemns. Susanna was not heard by her unjust judges, but she prayed silently.[21] Her mouth uttered no sound audible to other people, but her heart was crying out to God. Did the silence of her bodily voice render her unworthy of a hearing? By no means. She was heard, though when she prayed no man or woman knew it.

It is necessary to take strict account of what we have in our inner mouths, brothers and sisters. If you are careful to say nothing bad within, you will do nothing bad without, for a person can act outwardly only in conformity with what he has said within himself. Keep the mouth of your heart clear of evil and you will be innocent. Your bodily

---

20. Variant: "out of your heart."
21. See Dn 13:35–44.

tongue will be innocent, your hands innocent; your feet too will be innocent, your eyes will be innocent, and your ears innocent. All your members will be fighting on the side of righteousness,[22] because the heart that controls them is a righteous commander.[23]

Verses 3–4. Captivity is canceled and sins forgiven, as ice melts in warm wind

9. *Then will they say among the nations, The Lord has dealt magnificently with them! Indeed, the Lord has dealt magnificently with us, and how happy we are!* Consider, brothers and sisters: Does Zion not say this *among the nations* all over the world? Are people not running toward the Church in every land? Throughout the world our ransom-price is effective and all reply, "Amen." It is true, then, that citizens of Jerusalem are saying this *among the nations*: citizens of Jerusalem captive still, but on their way home, exiles sighing for their homeland. What are they saying? *The Lord has dealt magnificently with us, and how happy we are!* Did they deal so well with themselves? Far from it: they dealt badly by selling themselves as slaves into sin. But the redeemer came and dealt kindly with them. *The Lord has dealt magnificently with them. Indeed, the Lord has dealt magnificently with us, and how happy we are!*

10. *Turn our captivity around, O Lord, like a torrent in the south wind.* Notice what this implies, beloved. Earlier in the psalm we read, *The Lord turned Zion's captivity around.* That seemed to refer to a past event; but it is quite usual for a prophet to foretell what is future by speaking as though it were past. In another psalm he seemed to be speaking of things already accomplished when he said, *They dug holes in my hands and my feet; they numbered all my bones* (Ps 21:17–18(22:16–17)). He did not say, "They will dig holes" or "They will number my bones"; he did not say, "They will share out my garments among them" or "They will cast lots for my tunic."[24] The events were future, yet they were sung about as though they had taken place already, because for God all future things are already accomplished. So here the psalmist said, using the past tense, *When the Lord turned Zion's captivity around, we became like people comforted.* Then was

---

22. See Rom 6:13.19.
23. Or possibly "because a righteous commander controls your heart"; but the translation offered above suits the context better.
24. See Ps 21:19(22:18).

our mouth filled with joy, and our tongue with gladness. But to show that under the guise of past statements he was really indicating what would happen in the future, he continues, *Then will they say among the nations* (*will say*: notice that he is using the future now), *The Lord has dealt magnificently with us, and how happy we are!*

When these events were first celebrated in song they were still future, though for us they are present and plain to see. The psalmist had ostensibly been singing about past happenings but in fact envisaging the future; and in this verse he explicitly prayed with regard to things yet to come. *Turn our captivity around, O Lord,* he begged. Zion had not yet been brought back from captivity because the redeemer had not yet come. But the freedom for which the psalm was praying at the time of its first use is real now.

Turn our captivity around, O Lord, like a torrent in the south wind. As torrents are changed when the wind blows from the south, so change our captive state. Was someone asking what this is about? It will become clear in a minute with the help that I pray the Lord will give us in answer to your prayers. Scripture says somewhere, when giving us commands and admonitions concerning good works, *Your sins will melt away like ice in fair weather* (Sir 3:17). This must mean that sins were formerly binding us. How did they do that? In the same way that cold locks up water and prevents it from running freely. We froze because the cold of our sins locked us in. But the south wind is warm, and when it blows ice melts and torrents are in spate. Winter rivers are called torrents, for they flow with great force when the sudden access of water swells and fills them. We had frozen over during our captivity, and our sins immobilized us, but the Holy Spirit blew upon us like a warm wind from the south. Our sins were forgiven, and we were freed from the frost of iniquity. Our sins melt away like ice in fair weather.

Let us run toward our homeland, run like torrents in the south wind. We have struggled long; indeed we still struggle even now when we live good lives, for this human life on which we have entered is a wretched life, full of hard work and sorrows and dangers, full of distress and temptations. Do not be led astray by pleasant human experiences; rather be aware of all that is to be deplored in them. A new-born child could just as well have laughed. Why does it begin its life by crying? Because it has not yet learned to laugh, you say. But it knew how to cry, didn't it? Why was that? Because of the nature of this life on which it was entering. If it is one of the captives we meet in this psalm, there will be tears and groaning in store for it here. But joy will follow, as the next verse promises.

Verse 5. Sowing seed means doing good works and helping the poor, but almsgiving is not confined to giving money

11. The psalm continues, *Those who sow in tears will reap with joy.* Let us sow[25] in this tear-filled life. What shall we sow? Good works. Works of mercy are seeds for us. Of them the apostle says, *Let us not weary of doing good, for in due time we shall reap without weariness. So while we still have the opportunity, let us do good to all, but especially to members of the household of the faith.* (Gal 6:9–10) And what does he say elsewhere, when speaking directly about almsgiving? *Whoever sows sparingly will also reap sparingly* (2 Cor 9:6). We conclude that a person who sows plentifully will reap plentifully, one who *sows sparingly will reap sparingly*, and one who sows nothing at all will reap nothing. What is the point of coveting wide estates in the hope of sowing plentifully there? No place is vaster than Christ, who willed to be himself the earth ready to welcome our seeds. Your ground is the Church: sow there as much as you can.

Perhaps you lack the resources? Never mind: you have the will. Just as your possessions would count for nothing if your gift were not offered with a good will, so too you must not be grieved if you lack the means, provided that your good will is there. After all, what are you sowing? Mercy. And what will you reap? Peace. But the angels did not sing, did they, "Peace on earth to rich people"? What they sang was, *Peace on earth to people of good will* (Lk 2:14). In Zacchaeus[26] there was a mighty will, in Zacchaeus a powerful charity. He welcomed the Lord as a guest, he received him with joy and promised that he would give half his inheritance to the poor and reimburse fourfold anyone whom he had wronged.[27] This is mentioned to show that he retained half his fortune in order to pay his debts, not because he wanted to keep some possessions. His was a mightily generous will: he gave away a great deal and in so doing sowed a great deal.

What about the widow who put in two tiny coins?[28] Was hers a meager sowing? On the contrary, she sowed as much as did Zacchaeus.

---

25. Variant: "We sow."
26. Variant: "In the widow," anticipating the example to be cited a few lines later.
27. See Lk 19:8.
28. See Lk 21:1–4.

She brought slighter resources but an equally generous will. She gave her two little coins as willingly as Zacchaeus parted with half his fortune. If you concentrate on what they gave, you will find it unequal in the two cases; but if you look at the motive for their giving, you find parity. She gave whatever she had, and he too gave whatever he had.

12. Now imagine that you lack even two small coins. Is there anything even cheaper that we could sow in order to reap a harvest? Yes: *Anyone who gives a cup of cold water to one of my disciples will not miss his reward* (Mt 10:42). A cup of cold water does not cost even two little coins; it comes free. Yet though it is sometimes free for the one who has it, another person does not have it and needs it. If, then, the one who has it gives it to the one who has not and makes the gift with unreserved charity, he or she has given as much as the widow gave with her two small coins and Zacchaeus with half his fortune. The word *cold* is a significant addition, because it suggests poverty. The Lord spoke of *a cup of cold water* lest anyone make excuses, pleading that he had no firewood to heat it. *Anyone who gives a cup of cold water to one of these little ones will not miss his reward* (Mt 10:42). But what if someone has not even that to give? Let such a person be easy in mind, for if he lacks even something so slight there is *peace on earth to people of good will*. The only thing that should make us anxious is having the means and refusing to give; for if anyone who has the means does not give, he is frozen within. His sins are not melted like a torrent in the south wind, because his will is too cold. In that case, what is the value of the wealth we possess? But if an ardent will is present, sins are already melted by the warmth of the wind, and even someone who possesses nothing is accounted unstintingly generous. What great services even beggars can render to one another!

Consider all the ways in which almsgiving can be practiced, beloved. Certainly there are beggars to whom you should give alms, for they are in want. Perhaps you are also aware of some need suffered by your own kin, and then you offer help if Christ is in you; and you offer it to strangers too. And the same holds good for beggars among themselves: professional beggars, I mean. Even they have the means to give help to one another in times of trouble. God has not so abandoned them that they lack the opportunity to prove their worth through almsgiving. One person is disabled and cannot walk; let another who can walk lend his feet to the lame man. Let someone who can see lend her eyes to the blind. And let one who is young and healthy lend his strength to another who is old or ill and carry him. The one is in need; the other is rich.

13. It can happen that even a rich person finds himself poor in some respect, and a poor person may have the opportunity to help him. Imagine some traveler arriving at a river. His rich lifestyle has left him delicate, and he is unable to make the crossing. If he stripped off his clothes to cross he would catch cold and be ill and die. But a poor man comes along. His body is inured to hardship and he carries the rich man over: he is giving an alms to the rich man.

You must not think that people who lack money are the only ones who are poor. Be sensitive to each person's needs, to the particular area in which he or she is poor, because you are perhaps rich in that respect and in a position to lend what you have. You may lend your strong limbs, and that is better than lending money. Or the other may need advice, and you are full of it. He or she is poor in this matter, while you are rich in good counsel. It costs you no labor and you lose nothing by giving it. Give good advice and you have given alms.

Even now while we are talking to you, my brothers and sisters, you are like poor people in relation to us. Because God has graciously given to us, we in turn give to you from our store, and all of us receive from him who alone is rich. This is how the body of Christ holds together. Its members are neighbors to one another, knit together and united by the bond of peace, as each one, rich in some respect, gives to another what he lacks—some good thing in which that other is poor. This is how you must cherish one another. Take this as a pattern for your mutual love.

Do not restrict your concern to yourselves, but have a care for the needs of those around you. This entails hard work and bitter trouble in the present life, but do not flag. You are sowing in tears, but you will reap with joy. Does not your own experience confirm it, my brothers and sisters? A farmer goes out to plough, carrying his seed. Is the wind not cold sometimes? Does the rain not daunt him? He looks at the sky and it is lowering; he shivers with cold; yet he gets on with the job and sows. He cannot afford to pay too much attention to the gloomy weather and wait for a bright day, for time is slipping by and he must not put his harvest at risk. You must not put it off either, brothers and sisters. Sow in winter, sow good works even as you weep, for those who sow in tears will reap with joy. They scatter good will and good works as their seed.

Verse 6. Sow courageously in harsh conditions

14. *They went on their way weeping, as they scattered their seed.* Why were they weeping? Because they lived among the miserable and were miserable themselves. It would be better, brothers and sisters, that no one be miserable than that there be some miserable persons to give you the chance to show mercy. Anyone who hopes to find miserable people so that he can be merciful to them has a cruel notion of mercy. It would be as if a doctor hoped to find crowds of sick people to give him the opportunity to employ his skill: that would be a cruel sort of healing. It is better for everyone to be well than for the doctor's art to be practiced. Similarly it is better for all to reign happily in their homeland than for there to be needy people upon whom mercy should be lavished.

As long as there are people to whom we must show mercy, however, let us not falter in sowing our seed amid bitter hardship. Though we sow weeping, we shall reap with joy. At the resurrection of the dead each one will receive his or her sheaves as the fruit of the sowing: each will receive a crown of joy and delight. Then will exulting people triumph, mocking the death that used to evoke their groans. Then will they taunt death: *Where, O death is your strife? Where is your sting, O death?* (1 Cor 15:55) And why will they be rejoicing? Because they will be *carrying their sheaves.* In this life *they went on their way weeping, as they scattered their seed.* Why did they scatter it? Because *those who sow in tears will reap with joy.*

Conclusion: we descended disastrously, but our good Samaritan lifted us up; now let us ascend

15. Our aim in expounding this psalm has been above all to encourage you to practice kindness, for that is the means whereby you will ascend, and, as you know, only those who are ascending can sing this Song of Steps. Remember this: you must not be content to sink down and not mount upward; you must think hard about ascending, because someone who went down from Jerusalem to Jericho fell among robbers.[29] If he had not descended, he would not have fallen into the robbers' hands. Adam had already descended and fallen among robbers, and Adam is all of us. A priest passed by and scorned us, a Levite passed by and scorned us, because the law could not bring us

---

29. See Lk 10:30–37.

healing. A certain Samaritan passed by: he is our Lord Jesus Christ. We know this, for when he was challenged, *Are we not right to say that you are a Samaritan, and that you have a demon?* he did not reply, "I am no Samaritan," but, *I have no demon* (Jn 8:48.49). The word "Samaritan" is interpreted as "guardian." If he had replied, "I am not a Samaritan," it would have been tantamount to saying, "I am no guardian," and who else would there be to guard us? But the Lord told a significant story in this connection, as you know: *A Samaritan passed by, and took pity on him* (Lk 10:33). The traveler was lying wounded in the road, because he had gone down. The Samaritan who passed by did not spurn us. He tended us, hoisted us onto his beast by uniting himself to us in his flesh, and took us to the inn, which represents the Church. He entrusted us to the innkeeper, who stands for the apostle, and gave two denarii for our cure: charity toward God and charity toward our neighbor, for *on these two commandments depend all the law and the prophets* (Mt 22:40).

But he said to the innkeeper, *If you spend over and above this, I will reimburse you when I return* (Lk 10:35). The apostle certainly spent over and above what was due, for although it was legitimate for all apostles as soldiers of Christ to accept stipends from Christ's civilians,[30] he labored with his hands and gave the proceeds to his civilians.[31] All this has been done for us.[32] If we have descended and been wounded, let us now ascend. Let us sing and make headway, so that we may arrive at our homeland.

---

30. *Provinciales*; see Exposition 1 of Psalm 90,10 and the note there.
31. See 1 Cor 4:12; 9:3–18; 1 Th 2:7–9; 2 Th 3:8–9; Acts 20:33–34.
32. *Omnia facta sunt*. A variant plausibly suggests: *Et omnia omnibus factus est*, referring to Paul's generosity just mentioned; compare 1 Cor 9:22.

Exposition of Psalm 126

A Sermon to the People[1]

Verse 1. Solomon, named in the title, prefigures Christ, whose body is the true temple

1. All the psalms in the group we are studying bear the title *A Song of Steps*, but this one has an addition; it is headed: *A Song of Steps, Solomon's*. This unusual feature catches our attention and prompts us to ask why Solomon's name was added. There is no need for us to delay over the rest of the title, for it is pointless to keep on reminding you what a Song of Steps is. Many things have already been said on this subject: we have told you that in these psalms the voice of a singer making his ascent is to be heard and that he expresses his devotion and love for the heavenly Jerusalem for which we are sighing now as long as we are on pilgrimage, and in which we shall rejoice when our pilgrimage is over and we reach home. Everyone who is making progress is climbing up to this city; anyone who stops trying falls away. You must not attempt to climb with your feet, nor must you think that it is on foot that you will descend, for you ascend by loving God and fall by loving the world. These psalms are therefore the songs of lovers, afire with holy longing. All who sing them from the heart are on fire too, and their burning hearts are revealed in their way of life: in their good conduct, their sincere observance of God's commandments, their refusal to set much store by the fleeting things of time, and their love for things eternal.

But now, in the measure that the Lord inspires me, I will tell you, beloved, why the name of Solomon was added here.

2. In his own day Solomon was that great son of David through whom the Holy Spirit caused to be recorded many holy precepts, much salutary advice, and many divine mysteries;[2] all these are found in

---

1. Tentatively assigned to Saturday, 5 January 407.
2. *Sacramenta*, a word with deep and wide meanings. For Augustine, any reality that pointed beyond itself to some greater event or meaning was a *sacramentum*; it could be a teaching, or an event, or a person such as Solomon, to whom were attributed the books of Proverbs and Ecclesiastes and who by building

the sacred scriptures. However, Solomon was condemned by God because in his personal life he was a womanizer, and his lust so entrapped him that he was even cajoled by his numerous women into offering sacrifices to idols. Scripture bears witness to his activities.[3] All the same, if on account of his fall his sayings were to be cut out of the record, that would be to assume that he had been speaking in his own name, whereas he was in fact no more than the channel of all that had been said. God's mercy and the action of God's Spirit worked with sovereign wisdom in this matter, so that whatever good advice was given through Solomon should be attributed to God but that the human sin should be ascribed to the human instrument. Do you find it surprising that Solomon fell, even from his place among God's people? Did not Adam fall in paradise? Did not an angel fall from heaven and become a devil?[4] It all goes to show that we should put our trust in no human being.

Now this man Solomon had built a temple to the Lord,[5] which was a type and figure of the Church and of the body of the Lord, as we know from the gospel testimony, *Dismantle this temple, and in three days I will raise it up again* (Jn 2:19). In building this temple Solomon prefigured our Lord Jesus Christ, the true Solomon, who built the true temple and was the real man of peace. The name Solomon is interpreted "peacemaker," but the true peacemaker is he of whom the apostle says, *He is himself our peace, since he united the two* (Eph 2:14). He is the true peacemaker because he is the cornerstone[6] who joined in himself the two walls that came from different directions. One was that of the Jews who believed in him, the other was that of the gentiles, believers also. The circumcised and the uncircumcised, two peoples, were united into the Church, and Christ was made the cornerstone. This is why he is the true peacemaker.

---

the temple and earning a reputation as a peacemaker prefigured Christ. See also the notes on *sacramenta* at Expositions of Psalms 67,16 and 73,2 and at Exposition 23 of Psalm 118,2.

3. See 1 Kgs 11:1–10.
4. See Is 14:12. The passage is a taunt-song aimed probably at a King of Babylon but interpreted by Christian tradition of the devil, who therefore was given the name Lucifer.
5. See 1 Kgs 5–8.
6. See Eph 2:20.

Solomon, King of Israel, the son of David, whose wife was Bathsheba,[7] prefigured the true peacemaker when he built the temple; but scripture wants to make sure you do not think that Solomon himself built the house of God. It therefore makes the matter clear at the very beginning of our psalm: *Unless the Lord has been building the house, in vain have its builders labored.* It is the Lord who builds the house, for our Lord Jesus Christ builds his own house. Many people labor in the construction of it, but, unless he has been building, *in vain have its builders labored.*

Who are the workers who labor on it? All those who preach God's word in the Church, all who are ministers of God's mysteries. All of us run, all of us work, all of us build today; and before us others have run,[8] and worked, and built. But *unless the Lord has been building the house, in vain have its builders labored.* The apostles from time to time saw some parts of their work collapsing. Paul is an outstanding example: he chides his converts, *You observe years, and months, and seasons. I am anxious about you, lest I be found to have labored over you to no purpose.* (Gal 4:10–11) He knew that he was himself being built up inwardly by the Lord, but he mourned over them, seeing his work on them go for nothing.

It is like this, you see: we speak to you externally, but the Lord builds within you. We observe how attentively you listen, but what you are thinking is known only to him who sees your thoughts. He it is who builds you up; he warns, he frightens you, he opens your understanding, he guides your minds to faith. We ourselves, like workmen, do the labor, but *unless the Lord has been building the house, in vain have its builders labored.*

The vigilance and humility required of a bishop or overseer

3. What we are calling a house is also a city, for God's house is nothing else but God's people. We know this, because the house of God is the temple of God, and what does the apostle say about God's temple? *God's temple is holy, and that temple is yourselves* (1 Cor 3:17). This house of God is comprised of all the faithful, not only those alive today but also our predecessors in the faith who have fallen asleep and those who will come after us, those to be born into this human life even to the end of the world. All these believers gathered together

---

7. See 2 Sm 12:24. The name appears as *Bersabee* in Augustine's Latin text.
8. See 1 Cor 9:26.

are beyond counting, but their number is known to the Lord, for the apostle assures us that *the Lord knows his own* (2 Tm 2:19). They are the grains of wheat which at present mourn amid the straw, but when the winnowing takes place at the end they will form one solid mass of grain. This entire number of holy, faithful people is drawn from the human race and destined to be changed until its members are equal to the angels of God[9] and fit to be the angels' companions, for the angels are not exiles as we are but await us until we reach home after our pilgrimage. All of us together form one single house of God and one city. And this city is Jerusalem.

Jerusalem has its vigilant guardians. Just as it has its builders, the workers who labor on the edifice, so too does it have its watchmen. The words of the apostle indicate how seriously he took his duty of guarding it: *I am afraid that, just as the serpent seduced Eve by his cunning, so too your minds may be led astray, and fall away from that simplicity which you have in Christ* (2 Cor 11:3). He was guarding it, he was its keeper,[10] he kept watch to the utmost of his ability over those committed to his care. And this is what bishops do still. A higher position[11] is assigned to bishops precisely that they may oversee the people and so guard them.

The name they bear is ἐπίσκοπος in Greek,[12] *episcopus* in Latin. It means a superintendent or overseer, because they look down from a raised position. In a vineyard a watchtower is provided for the worker responsible for the vineyard's safety, so that he may keep an eye on it; and similarly a higher station is accorded to bishops. But the account to be rendered concerning our high station imperils us, unless we stand here with such an intention in our hearts that we place ourselves beneath your feet in humility and pray for you, so that he who knows your thoughts may himself be your guardian. We can watch you come in here and go out again, but we cannot even see what you do in your own homes, much less what you think in your hearts.

How then can we guard you? Only in the measure of our human ability, as best we can, as we have been given the grace. Does that mean that, since we, your guardians, are no more than human and unable to watch over you perfectly, you will be left without a guardian?

---

9. See Lk 20:36.
10. Variant: "He was careful."
11. A higher rank, but also a literally higher place when preaching in the church.
12. Whence, ultimately, the English word "bishop."

Far from it. For where is he of whom the psalm says, *Unless the Lord has been guarding the city, in vain has its guardian*[13] *labored?* We work hard to guard you, but our labor is futile unless he who sees your thoughts guards you himself. He keeps guard over you when you are awake and guards you still when you sleep. He slept once on the cross, but he rose again and sleeps no more. You must be his Israel, for *he will not be drowsy or sleep, the guardian of Israel* (Ps 120(121):4).

In virtue of the duty assigned to us we guard you, brothers and sisters, but our desire is to be guarded by God along with you. We act as your shepherds, but along with you we are sheep under the one shepherd.[14] We stand in this elevated position as your instructors, but we are your fellow-students in this school under our one teacher.[15]

Verse 2. Do not try to rise before Christ, your light

4. If we want to be kept safe under the wings of God,[16] guarded by him who was humbled for our sake and exalted for our protection, let us be humble. Let no one arrogate any praise to himself, for nobody has anything good unless he has received it from God,[17] who alone is good. Anyone who claims wisdom as his own prerogative is a fool. Such a person needs to be humbled so that wisdom may come to him and enlighten him. If he thinks himself wise before wisdom comes to him, he is rising before the light and inevitably walks in darkness.[18] And what has the psalm to say about that? *It is a waste of time for you to rise before the light.* What does that suggest—*It is a waste of time for you to rise before the light*? If you rise before the rising of the light itself, you are wasting your time and effort, because you will be in the dark. Christ our light has risen, and the best thing you can do is to rise after Christ, not before him. What kind of people rise before Christ? Those who want to take precedence of him. But who would want to do that? All those who aspire to high positions here where Christ was humble. They too must be humble here if they want to be exalted where Christ is now exalted, for he prayed for the exaltation of those who had clung to him in faith, and we are among

---

13. Variant: *have its guardians.*
14. See Jn 10:11.14.16; 1 Pt 2:25; 5:4.
15. See Mt 23:10.
16. See Ps 16(17):8; 60:5(61:4); 90(91):4.
17. See 1 Cor 4:7.
18. See Jn 12:35.

them if we believe in him with pure hearts. *Father,* he prayed, *I will that where I am, those also whom you have given me may be with me* (Jn 17:24). What a magnificent gift, my brothers and sisters, what a tremendous grace, what a marvelous promise!

Is there anyone who does not want to be with Christ, there where Christ is? Surely not. But Christ is already on high. Do you want to be there too, on high with him? Be humble, then, here where he too was humble. He who is our light warned his followers, *A disciple is not above his teacher, nor a servant above his master* (Mt 10:24). Any disciples who wanted to be above their teacher, and any servants who aspired to be above their master, were trying to rise before the light. Their attempts were a waste of time, because they were not following the light. The psalm tells them, *It is a waste of time for you to rise before the light.*

The sons of Zebedee made this mistake by choosing the places where they thought they would like to sit, one at the Lord's right, the other at his left, and making these plans before they had been humbled in conformity with the Lord's passion. They wanted to rise before the light, and so they were wasting their time. When the Lord heard of it he recalled them to humility and asked them, *"Are you able to drink the cup I am to drink?* (Mt 20:22) I have come in humility, and do you two seek to be exalted before me? You must follow in the way I shall take. If you try to take a course that is not mine," he implied, *"it is a waste of time for you to rise before the light."*

Peter likewise had risen before the light when he tried to deter the Lord from suffering for us. In speaking of the passion whereby we were to be saved, the Lord had implicitly spoken also of his humility, for nothing could be humbler than the way in which he suffered. Peter was appalled by this talk of suffering and frightened by the prospect of Christ's death although he had, only a moment before, confessed him to be the Son of God. *Far be it from you, Lord, have some pity for yourself,* he protested. *This will not happen!* (Mt 16:22) He wanted to rise before the light and even to give the light good advice! But what did the Lord do? He showed Peter that the proper time to rise was after the light. *Get behind me, Satan* (Mt 16:23), he ordered.[19] You are a Satan because you try to rise before the light. Get behind

---

19. The meaning of "before" and "after" shifts between the temporal and local senses.

me: let me go first, so that you may follow. You must tread the path I tread, not try to lead me in the path of your choosing.

Sitting down before rising signifies humility before exaltation

5. To those who aspired to rise before the light the psalm says, *It is a waste of time for you to rise before the light*. When shall we rise? After being humbled, for it continues, *Rise up after sitting down*. To rise up symbolizes exaltation, and to sit down represents humility. In some contexts sitting down may suggest the honor of judicial office, but in others humility. How can sitting represent the judicial office? Remember the promise, *You will sit upon twelve thrones, judging the twelve tribes of Israel* (Mt 19:28). And how can sitting be a token of humility? *At the sixth hour the Lord, being weary, sat down by the well* (Jn 4:6). The weariness he suffered was the Lord's weakness, the weakness of strength itself, the weakness of wisdom,[20] and this weakness is his humility. Thus, when weakness obliges him to sit down, his very posture betokens humility. Moreover his need to sit down, this humility on his part, was our salvation, for *the weakness of God is stronger than mortals* (1 Cor 1:25). In the same perspective another psalm prays, *O Lord, you know my sitting down and my rising up* (Ps 138(139):2), which means my humility and my exaltation.

What then is the point of your ambition to be exalted before the light, you sons of Zebedee? We may make bold to ask them this and use their name in this way; they are not likely to be angry with us, because the episode was recorded about them so that others might shun the pride for which they were rebuked. Why do you wish *to rise before the light*? You wish in vain. Do you expect to be glorified before being humbled? Listen to Paul's teaching: *Being in the form of God he deemed it no robbery to be God's equal* (Ph 2:6). Why was that no robbery on his part? Because he was equal by nature; he was born equal to the Father who begot him. But then, what did he do? For our sake *he emptied himself and took on the form of a slave. Bearing the human likeness, sharing the human lot, he humbled himself and was made obedient to the point of death, even death on a cross*. This is his act of sitting down. But now hear about his rising up: *Therefore God raised him high and gave him a name above every other name.* (Phil 2:7–9) You are in a hurry, sons of Zebedee, to draw near to that

---

20. See 1 Cor 1:24.

exalted name. *Rise up*, by all means, but only *after sitting down*. You long to rise up, but sit down first.

When you rise up from your lowly state[21] you will attain to the kingdom, but if you try to snatch at the kingdom prematurely you will fall away from it even before you rise. *Are you able to drink the cup I am to drink?* the Lord asked. *We are*, replied the sons of Zebedee. And he promised them, *You shall indeed drink my cup, but to sit at my right or my left is not mine to grant you: it is prepared for others by my Father.* (Mt 20:22-23) Why did he say, *It is not mine to grant you?* He meant, "It is not mine to confer on proud persons." And that was what they still were. Do you really want it? Then cease to be what you are. *It is prepared for others.* If you become "other" it is prepared for you too. What does it mean to become other? Be humbled first, you who aspire to be exalted. Then they understood that humility was in their own interest, and they were corrected. Let us too hear this admonition, which echoes the psalm's words, *Rise up after sitting down*.

6. The psalm adds another phrase to avert a possible misconception, for someone might have taken this command as an invitation to sit down and receive honors, thinking that he or she had been told to[22] sit either to exercise some judicial function or to participate in a banquet or to make merry. Such a misunderstanding would bolster pride even further. To exclude this interpretation and insist that the sitting it enjoins signifies humility, the psalm adds, *You who eat the bread of sorrow*. The people who eat the bread of sorrow are those who mourn during this present pilgrimage, the people who walk in the valley of weeping. God has placed steps in our hearts by which we must ascend. Where does he place them? In our hearts, for another psalm tells us: *God has arranged ascents in the heart* (Ps 83:6(84:5)). Who put them there? God. If these steps are in our hearts—and that is why the *Songs of Steps* are sung—let us be humbled in this world, and let us climb them. But how? In our hearts. This ascent of the heart begins from the valley of weeping; that other psalm specifies: *in the valley of weeping* (Ps 83:7(84:6)). As mountains can be said to have risen up, so we can think of valleys as places that have sat down, for it is sunken regions of the countryside that are called valleys. Regions

---

21. Augustine here switches from the second person plural to the second person singular.
22. Variant: "that it was just for him or her to."

that are higher, though less high than those very lofty places that rank as mountains, are called hills. But scripture was not content to tell us, "Make your ascent from a hill," or even "from a plain." It speaks of something even lower than a plain: a valley. So if you find yourself in the valley of weeping, eating the bread of sorrow, if you can say, *My tears have been bread to me day and night, as every day I hear the taunt, Where is your God?* (Ps 41:4(42:3)) you are climbing well, because you have first sat down.

7. Perhaps you still wanted to ask, "When do we rise up? We are bidden to sit down now; but when will our rising up be?" Ask yourself: When was the Lord's rising up? Wait for him who has gone ahead of you. If you do not wait for him you are wasting your labor in rising up before the light. Think now: when was Christ exalted? After his death. That means that you too must hope for your rising up after death. Hope for the rising up of all the dead, because he has risen and ascended. But where did he sleep? On the cross. When he slept on the cross his sleep was a sign; or, rather, a fulfillment of the sign given in Adam. When Adam slept, a rib was withdrawn from him[23] and Eve was created; so it was with the Lord also when he slept on the cross, for his side was struck with a lance and there flowed out the saving mysteries from which the Church was born.[24] The Church is the bride of the Lord, made from his side, as Eve was made from Adam's; and as Eve could be made from the man's side only when he slept, so was the Church made only from the side of a man who died. And if Christ rose only after he had died, can you hope for exaltation, unless it be after this life? But perhaps you wanted to press the question further: "When shall I rise up?

Couldn't it be before I have sat down?" The psalm takes care to enlighten you: *After I have given*[25] *sleep to his beloved*, it says. God gives this gift after his beloved have fallen asleep, for then his beloved—Christ's beloved, that is—will rise. All will rise, in fact, but not all in the same way as Christ's beloved. There will be a rising

---

23. See Gn 2:21–22.
24. See Jn 19:34. The water and blood that flowed from Christ's side have traditionally been seen as symbols respectively of baptism and the Eucharist, constitutive of the Church in its union with Christ.
25. A well-supported variant is *after he has given*. The difference in Greek between the first and third persons of the verb is very slight. But Augustine, reading the first person, takes God (the Father) to be the subject: he gives sleep to the beloved of Christ.

up for all the dead, but what does the apostle say about it? *Though we shall all indeed rise again, we shall not all be changed* (1 Cor 15:51).[26] Some rise for punishment, but we rise as our Lord rose, provided that we are his members, so that we may follow our head. If we are his members, we are also his beloved, and then the rising which initially was real only in the Lord will be ours also. The light rose before us, and we rise after the light. It is a waste of time for us to rise before the light—to seek exaltation before our death, I mean—for Christ our light was not exalted as to his flesh until after he had died. The same is true for us who are built into him as his members and, being his members, are his beloved. After we have accepted our sleep, we shall rise again at the resurrection of the dead.

One man, and one only, rose never to die again. Lazarus rose,[27] but he was to die again later. The widow's son rose[28] only to die once more. The daughter of the synagogue's president rose,[29] but she too would die again. Christ rose, but he would never die any more. Listen to the apostle: *Rising from the dead, Christ will never die again, nor will death ever again have the mastery over him* (Rom 6:9).

That is the kind of rising you must hope for. Be a Christian with that in view, not with an eye to any happiness in this world. If you try to be a Christian for the sake of this world's happiness, you are trying to rise before the light, and you will inevitably remain in darkness, for he who is your light sought no worldly happiness. Let yourself be changed, then, and follow your light. Rise as he rose. Sit down first, and rise up only after that, *after I have given sleep to his beloved.*

Verse 3. The Church is in labor, but not all the children to be born are "the beloved"

8. If, still unsatisfied, you go on asking questions like, "Who are these beloved ones?" the psalm answers, *Lo, the Lord's inheritance will be children, and the reward will be for the fruit of the womb.* In saying *the fruit of the womb* the psalm implies that these are children already born. There is a certain woman, then, in whom is spiritually

---

26. The sense of the original is different: We shall not all fall asleep, but we shall all be changed. Paul was thinking in terms of some being still alive at the coming of the Lord. The Latin, which Augustine follows, thinks of a general resurrection, at which transformation into glory is reserved for some.
27. See Jn 11:44.
28. See Lk 7:15.
29. See Mk 5:42.

verified the prophecy spoken to Eve: *You shall bear children in pain.* The Church is Christ's bride and bears children to him and, if she bears them, she experiences travail. Eve was called *the mother of the living* (Gn 3:20) because she was a type of the Church. Among the members of this childbearing woman was he who wrote, *My little children, I am in travail with you over again, until Christ be formed in you* (Gal 4:19). But her labor has not been fruitless, nor has she borne her children to no purpose, for at the rising of the dead there will survive a holy seed;[30] they will be very numerous, for even now they are spread abroad throughout the world. The Church anguishes over them; she is in travail with them; but at the rising of the dead the Church's offspring will be revealed, and all pain and sighs will pass away. What will people say then? *Lo, the Lord's inheritance is children, and the reward will be for the fruit of the womb.* The word *fruit* is genitive:[31] the reward will belong to this *fruit of the womb.* What will its reward be? Nothing less than rising from the dead. What reward? To rise up after you have sat down. What kind of reward? To be joyful after you have eaten the bread of sorrow.

But to whose womb is the psalm referring? That of the Church. Rebecca was another type of the Church when twins struggled within her like two contending peoples.[32] One mother held together within her body two brothers already at variance even before their birth. They battered their mother's belly with their antenatal wrangling. She moaned at the violence she was enduring, but when the time came to bring them forth she marked the difference between the twins who had made her pregnancy so difficult.

The same is true today, brothers and sisters, as long as the Church's lot is to moan with pain, as long as she is in labor with her children, for within her are both good and bad people. But it is Jacob who will be recognized as the true fruit of her womb, for he is the one his mother specially loved. *I have loved Jacob, but hated Esau* (Mal 1:2–3; Rom 9:13), God declares. Both came forth from the same womb, but while one deserved to be loved, the other merited rejection. The beloved

---

30. See Is 6:13.
31. *Merces fructus ventris.* Since *fructus* could be nominative, the phrase could in Latin be taken to mean that the fruit of the womb is itself the (Lord's) reward. Augustine rules out this interpretation.
32. See Gen 25:22–23.

ones will be the true fruit of the womb, and to their reward the psalm points: *Lo, the reward will be for the fruit of the womb.*

Verse 4. Shaking out the prophets, the Lord made the apostles their sons; the apostles are the Lord's far-shot arrows

9. *Like arrows in the hand of a mighty archer are the children of those shaken out.*[33] How did the Lord's inheritance come into being, brothers and sisters? Where did that enormous inheritance spring from, the inheritance which will at the end evoke the astonished cry, *Lo, the Lord's inheritance will be children, and the reward will be for the fruit of the womb*? Certain men were fired off from the Lord's hand like arrows; they traveled a long way, and they have filled the whole earth. In the places they reach, saints spring up. This is the same inheritance promised to the Lord in another psalm: *Ask of me, and I will give you the nations as your heritage, and the ends of the earth for your possession* (Ps 2:8). How does the Lord's possession keep pushing on and growing, even to the ends of the earth? Because *like arrows in the hand of a mighty archer are the children of those shaken out.*[34] Arrows are launched from a bow, and the stronger the archer who bends it the further the arrow flies. But what can be stronger than the Lord, who launches his apostles with the bow of his command?[35] There could be no remote backwater of a place where an arrow shot by so mighty an archer did not reach; his arrow traveled to the ends of the earth. The only reason why it did not go any further is that there is no place more distant where the human race could live. So powerful is the Lord that, if there had been any further place for an arrow to go, he would have shot one there too.[36] The children of those shot forth are as widespread as are the flying arrows themselves.

---

33. *Excussorum.* Augustine makes play with the verb *excutere* in this and the following sections. It is not easy to find a single English word to cover the various meanings: to launch, drive, shake off, shake out, drive out, shoot.
34. Variant: *the children of the exalted ones.*
35. *Quid autem fortius excutiente Domino de arcu mandati apostolos suos?.* This is judged by the CSEL editors to be the best reading. An easier variant supported by many witnesses gives *mandat* instead of *mandati*; this, with amended punctuation, would yield the meaning, "But what can be stronger than the Lord who shoots? With his bow he commissions his apostles."
36. For the salvation of whatever extra-terrestrials there may be, Augustine might perhaps say.

A question has been raised about the expression *shot forth* or *shaken out* or *driven out*,[37] which was also raised by those who expounded the psalm before us. Why, it is asked, are some people called *children of those shaken out*? And who are they? It has seemed to some commentators[38] that they are the children of the apostles, as I have just explained.

10. But I want you to listen carefully for a few minutes, beloved friends. The question has been asked, "In what sense were the apostles driven off, or shaken out?" And an answer was proposed: because the Lord commanded them, *On leaving a town where people refuse to listen to you, shake*[39] *the dust from your feet* (Mk 6:11). Then someone[40] objected, "But in that case they ought to be called not children of those driven off, or shaken out, but 'children of those who shake out,' because the Lord made them the shakers, not the shaken, when he ordered them, *Shake the dust from your feet*." The one who spoke thus wished to contradict in a subtle way the opinion just stated and defended. For our part, however, if we seek with the Lord's help to understand how people whom the Lord had commanded, *Shake the dust from your feet*, can also be rightly described as "shaken out" themselves, we find that there is no contradiction involved. Although they shook off the dust, they in a sense shook out themselves. This is what I mean: if someone shakes off, he shakes off either himself or something else. If he shakes off something else, he is a shaker but is not himself shaken. But if he shakes out himself, he is both a shaker and shaken. Think hard: I will explain it more clearly if I can. If someone shakes off something else, he is a shaker but not shaken. If he is shaken out by someone else, he is shaken out but is not a shaker. But if he shakes himself out, he is a shaker because he shakes himself out, but he is also shaken because he is shaken out by his own act.

Well now, whom did the apostles shake out? Themselves, obviously, for they shook the dust from their feet. But someone objects, "No, they didn't shake themselves out, they shook off the dust." That is mere quibbling. We can speak of something being shaken out in two senses: it can refer either to what is shaken out or to the object from which it is shaken. We can say "the dust was shaken out" or "the

---

37. *Excussorum.*
38. For example Jerome; see his Letter 34,3.
39. *Excutite.*
40. Marcella; see Jerome, *ibid.*

garment was shaken out." If someone holds a garment and shakes it and the dust that was sticking to it flies off, what do you say of the dust? "The dust has been shaken out." And what do you say of the garment? "The garment has been shaken out." If, then, it is normal to speak both of what flies out in the shaking and of what it flies out from, as being shaken out, we can rightly say that both the dust and the apostles were shaken out. And if that is so, what is wrong with taking *the children of those shaken out* to be the children of the apostles?

11. There is another opinion, however, which we should not omit to mention. It is possible that the phrase was couched somewhat obscurely on purpose, so that it might be open to numerous understandings. People will go away more enriched if they have come upon a text that lends itself to various interpretations than if it bears one meaning only. Now, we shake something out so that what has perhaps been hidden inside it may come to light. Do you see what I mean? We say that people shake out a garment to get the dust out of it but also that a sack is shaken out so that what was concealed inside may tumble out and be seen.

Well now, brothers and sisters, I will tell you as best I can how in this latter sense I understand the apostles themselves to be *the children of those shaken out* because they are the sons of the prophets. The writings of the prophets contained mysteries that were sealed and hidden;[41] but the prophets were shaken out so that these mysteries might fall out and become manifest. Take an example of something a prophet might have said—or, better, something one of them did say: *The ox knows its owner, and the ass its master's manger; but Israel does not know me* (Is 1:3). That text I have quoted from a prophet is one that comes into my mind at the moment; if some other had occurred to me, I would have quoted that. Now when you hear this text and think of the cattle and other animals with which we are familiar, you will be handling it from the outside as one might feel an object bundled up in wrappings, but you do not know what lies within. The ass and the ox stand for something. So what are we to say to a person anxious to give an opinion about it? Wait and see! What you are handling is concealed at present.

Now shake out its wrappings. The prophet hid something, using the animals' names as veils to conceal his meaning: he meant some unknown ass, some unknown ox. The ass is a symbol of God's people;

---

41. Variant: "mysteries both sealed and open."

it is God's mount, carrying its Lord seated upon its back to guide it, so that it may not miss the way. The ox is a figurative reference to the apostle's injunction, *You shall not muzzle an ox while it is threshing. Now, does God care about oxen? Scripture is talking about us, clearly.* (1 Cor 9:9–10) Everyone who preaches God's word, warning, chiding, terrifying the hearers, is trampling on the threshing-floor and doing the job of an ox. The ox came from the Jewish people, for the apostles, who were the first preachers, were Jews. The ass came from the uncircumcised gentiles, for it came to carry the Lord, and the Lord chose to ride an ass on which no one had previously ridden[42] because neither the law nor the prophets had been sent to the gentiles. Our Lord Jesus Christ wanted to be our food, and therefore as soon as he was born he was laid in a manger, and on this account the prophet could say, *The ox knows its owner, and the ass its master's manger.*

But would these things have emerged if the sack had not been shaken out? If the prophecy had not been taken apart[43] with all due diligence, would those concealed[44] meanings have emerged for us to see? They were all closed to us until the coming of the Lord. He came and shook out those hidden things, and so they were made manifest. The prophets were shaken out, and the apostles were born; and since it was only when the prophets were shaken out that the apostles came to birth, they can be called *the children of those shaken out*. They were like arrows held in the hand of a powerful archer, and they were shot to the very ends of the earth. This is why the psalm goes on to say, *Lo, the Lord's inheritance will be children, and the reward will be for the fruit of the womb*, for that inheritance was gathered from the ends of the earth by the work of the apostles, who were sons of the prophets. *Like arrows in the hand of a mighty archer are the children of those shaken out.* Being mighty, he shot them with immense power and, because he shot so powerfully, the arrows he launched reached the very ends of the earth.

---

42. See Mk 11:2.7; Lk 19:30.35.
43. *Discuteretur*, related to the verb *excutere*, with which Augustine has been concerned. Its primary meaning is "to dash to pieces, scatter, dissipate"; but in post-classical Latin it acquired the sense "to discuss." Both meanings are implied here.
44. Variant: "open."

Verse 5. The apostles' preaching: universal, open, and centered in Christ

12. *Blessed is everyone who has satisfied his longing from them.* Who do you think is meant, brothers and sisters? Who satisfies his longing from the apostles' preaching? Certainly not anyone who is in love with this world. If a person is enamored of the world, there is no room in him or her for the apostles' message to find lodging.[45] Empty out what you are carrying and make space within you for what you do not yet have. What I mean is this: Do you crave wealth? If so, you cannot satisfy your longing from what the apostles offer. Do you crave earthly honors? Do you crave what God has granted even to the beasts—temporal pleasure, bodily health, and suchlike? Then you will not satisfy your longing from anything the apostles preach.[46] But if your longing is like that of *a deer that longs for springs of water* (Ps 41:2(42:1)) and if you can say, *My soul faints with longing for the courts of the Lord* (Ps 83:3(84:2)), then you will satisfy your longing from the apostles' preaching not because they can themselves satisfy such desire but because by imitating people like them you will reach him who has fulfilled all their desire.

13. *He will not be ashamed when he speaks to his enemies at the gate.* Let us too speak at the gate, brothers and sisters, for this symbolizes speaking openly, so that all may know what we say. One who is unwilling to speak at the gate tries to conceal what he is saying, perhaps because he does not want it shown up as evil. But if a speaker is confident, let him or her speak in the gateway, as wisdom is said to do: *She speaks boldly at the city gates* (Prv 8:3, LXX). As long as people are innocent and are holding fast to justice, they will have no reason to be ashamed. This is what it means to preach at the gate.

And who preaches at the gate? One who preaches in Christ, for Christ is the gate whereby we enter that city. If I am not mistaken, he said himself, *I am the door* (Jn 10:9). If he is the door, he is also the gate. We speak of a door as the entrance to a house; a city's door is its gate, and the gate of a house is its door. But perhaps we have no

---

45. Variant: "Such a person is not the kind who can enter into their message."
46. It is possible to understand the foregoing sentences, with the repeated warning, "You cannot satisfy your longing from them," as meaning that the various forms of worldly happiness enumerated cannot satisfy. "Them" is ambiguous, but the translation offered here assumes that it refers to the apostles and their message.

right to speak of a gate in the case of the house we have been considering? Of course we are right, for what we called a house is truly also a city. In fact both words are used of it in the psalm: *Unless the Lord has been building the house, in vain have its builders labored*, it said; but then, in case the word *house* brings to your mind something small, it added, *Unless the Lord has been guarding the city, in vain has its guardian labored.* So the house is also a city. As a house, it has a door; as a city, it has a gate. He who is the door of the house is the same as he who is the city's gate.

If, then, Christ is the gate of the city, no one who takes his stand in Christ and preaches from there has any reason to be ashamed. But if anyone preaches against Christ, the door is closed against him. Who are they who preach against Christ? Those who deny that arrows were shot by the hand of a mighty archer, arrows that reached the ends of the earth, and that this entire earth is the inheritance of which a psalm spoke prophetically: *Ask of me, and I will give you the nations as your heritage, and the ends of the earth for your possession* (Ps 2:8). The worldwide inheritance was preached about, and heard about, before ever it came into being, and yet now that the prophecy is fulfilled they refuse to acknowledge it.[47] Those who argue against Christ are outside the gate, for they are pursuing honors for themselves, not for Christ. Anyone who preaches at the gate is seeking Christ's honor, not his own. The genuine preacher at the gate therefore insists, "Do not rest your confidence in me. You will not get in through me, but only through the gate." The other kind, those who try to attract people's trust to themselves, want to stop their hearers from entering by the gate. It is no wonder that such preachers find the gate shut in their faces. If only they would knock and beg for[48] it to be opened!

Conclusion: plans for tomorrow

I want you to be present, enthusiastic and attentive, at tomorrow's sermon too, brothers and sisters. This will be the one we promised you[49] on the gospel about the dove,[50] and with the Lord's help we

---

47. This seems to be aimed at the Donatists, who contended that the true Church was confined to their own territories. As always, Augustine seizes on any universalizing passage in the psalms to refute them.
48. Variant: "They knock in vain, begging for."
49. See *Homilies on the Gospel of John* 4,16. These homilies were begun during the same period in which Augustine was preaching on the Gradual Psalms.
50. 50. See Jn 1:32–33.

will pay our debt. We made the promise to you in his name, and by his mercy we will keep it. But you must pray for us so that we may be equal to the task and not be proved to have made a rash promise.

Exposition of Psalm 127

A Sermon to the People[1]

Verses 1–4. Why we cannot take this psalm as simply a promise of material happiness

1. Dearly beloved brothers and sisters, there is reason to fear that some carnally-minded persons, insensitive to anything that concerns the Spirit of God, may be tripped up rather than built up by this psalm. The apostle knew of this possibility, for he wrote, *We interpret spiritual truths to people possessed of the Spirit; but the unspiritual person has no perception for the things that belong to the Spirit of God* (1 Cor 2:13–14). Although we did hear the psalm when it was sung, I will just run through it briefly (it is a short psalm, after all), not explaining it[2] but only reading it, and you will see what I mean.

Suppose someone attaches great importance to the kinds of good fortune mentioned in the psalm and fervently hopes to obtain them from God but perhaps does not obtain them—not because he or she has been forsaken by God but rather because this disappointment is a mark of God's special love. Suppose, further, that such a person observes others who do not fear God enjoying a plethora of the good things we hear the psalm promising as rewards for God-fearing people. Will the believer's steps not falter? Will he not begin to lose his footing? He may murmur in his heart that his own God-fearing life has been pointless, for it has not earned him the gifts promised to those who hold God in awe, while others who do not reverence God at all, and even blaspheme against him, have received all these favors. Look at what the psalm says. *Blessed are all who fear the Lord, and walk in his ways. You yourself shall eat the labors of your fruits; you are blessed, and it shall go well with you.* So far we could still refer this, couldn't we, to the happiness of the world to come, and so could any

---

1. Possibly preached on 14 January 407, the feast of Saint Felix of Nola, a few days after the Exposition of Psalm 126, at Hippo. But see the note on dating at section 2 below.
2. It is hard to see what he means by this, as he does in fact explain it at considerable length. Perhaps he meant to be brief but was simply carried away.

carnally-minded person. But look at the next verses: *Your wife shall be like a fruitful vine on the sides of your house, your children like olive seedlings around your table. Lo, this is how anyone who fears the Lord will be blessed.*[3] How will this God-fearer be blessed? By seeing his wife like a fruitful vine against the sides of his house, and his children like young sprouting olives around his table. Does this mean that people who for God's sake have renounced marriage have missed their reward? Perhaps a celibate will say, "God blesses[4] me in other ways." But that will not do: either he blesses you like this or he does not bless you at all, for the psalm plainly says, *Lo, this is how anyone who fears the Lord will be blessed.*[5]

We have here a prophecy that needs to be shaken out

2. What does it mean, then, brothers and sisters? I think the prophet has handed us something like a wrapped-up parcel, so that we do not lose heavenly happiness by pursuing temporal, earthly well-being. This wrapped-up parcel has something important concealed inside it. You remember, dearly beloved, that, when we were studying with you the psalm immediately before this one, we came upon an obscure verse that ran, *Like arrows in the hand of a mighty archer are the children of those shaken out* (Ps 126(127):4). We wondered what *the children of those shaken out* might mean, and at the suggestion of the Lord, I like to think, we decided that the apostles, who are the sons of the prophets, were called *the children of those shaken out*. Why? Because the prophets spoke in riddles, concealing their real meaning within figurative expressions like the wrappings of mysterious parcels. The contents could not be disclosed until the wrappings were shaken out; this is why the apostles were called *the children of those shaken out*. They began their mission from the shaking-out of the prophets. Let us now do some shaking out for ourselves, for we do not want to be put off by the wrappings. If we only feel what is inside without seeing it, we might mistake gold for wood or think that silver was only clay. So please, beloved friends, let us shake all this. The Lord will be helping us so that what is inside may come tumbling out. This is particularly appropriate today, brothers and

---

3. Variant: *is blessed.*
4. Variant: "will bless."
5. Variant: *is blessed.*

sisters, because we are celebrating the birthday of martyrs.[6] How grievously the martyrs suffered! What pain, what appalling tortures, what squalor in prison, chafing of chains, savagery of beasts, searing flames, and stinging insults! Would they have undergone all this if they had not seen something ahead of them, something that is not even hinted at by the happiness this world offers? It would be disgraceful on our part if we were to celebrate the birthdays of martyrs, of those men and women who spurned the world for the sake of everlasting felicity, and yet at the same time were to refer the promises in our psalm to this-worldly happiness. That would be to say of any faithful follower of God, any citizen of the heavenly Jerusalem who, though married, does not happen to have any children, "That man clearly does not fear the Lord. If he did, his wife would be like a fruitful vine in his house, not a barren woman unable to bear him children. If that man reverenced the Lord, his children would be all around his table like young olive trees." If we talk like that, we show ourselves to be carnally-minded, with no sensitivity to anything that concerns the Spirit of God.

Let us begin to do some shaking-out ourselves, so that we too may be children of the shaken ones. If we in our turn are the children of those shaken out, we shall be like arrows in the hand of a mighty archer, who will bend the bow of his command to shoot us into the hearts of people not yet his lovers, so that when pierced by

---

6. In section 6 below Augustine names the martyr Felix. 14 January 407, the date given by La Bonnardière for this sermon, is the day on which the feast of Saint Felix of Nola was kept, and Augustine shared the devotion of his friend and correspondent, Paulinus of Nola, to that saint. But the Felix of Nola made famous by Paulinus, though venerated as a martyr because he had suffered greatly during the persecution of Decius, did not die as a martyr. So he cannot be the Felix mentioned in section 6 of this sermon; and that would seem to work against La Bonnardière's dating, which is also that accepted by the CSEL editors of the text, and by Perler. The Italian editors of the CCL text mention Zarb's dating, which assigns the sermon to 17 December 412; this could mean that it was preached on the festival of a different Saint Felix, also called Felix of Nola, who is said to have been bishop of a small town, martyred in Carthage with thirty companions in A.D. 287. The Maurists, for their part, say that the Felix Augustine is talking about was martyred on 6 November at Thyniss, a small town not far from Hippo Regius. He was said to have been found dead in his prison cell, so this seems to be the most likely identification, but nobody suggests that Augustine's sermon was preached on that date. The problem remains.

the arrows of God's words they may begin to love him. If we preach a false message to them, saying, "My children, my brethren, fear the Lord. Then you will have children and grandchildren and a happy home," we are not effective arrows inducing them to love the eternal Jerusalem. They will remain trapped in the love of earthly things. When they see bad people enjoying plenty of good fortune, they will say in their hearts, even though they dare not say it in our hearing, "How can that be right? Does that fellow with a houseful of children reverence God?" Then perhaps someone else will say to them, "Ah, but you don't know what will happen to him, do you? What if he had to bury them? Perhaps the punishment for his godless life is that many children have been born to him only that he may suffer all the more grief when they die." But if you try that line, one of them will retort, "But I know a godless man, a pagan, sacrilegious, idolatrous"—and indeed he probably does, and is telling the truth; doubtless he knows not one, nor even two or three only. So he continues, "I know a man like that who went to his grave at an advanced age, worn out. He had died in his bed, he had crowds of children and grandchildren. He never showed any sign of reverence for God, yet the swarming progeny who filled his house were there to close his eyes." What are we to reply? No such misfortune as having to bury his children in his own lifetime can befall him, for he has already been carried to his own splendid tomb by his children.

The man pronounced blessed in the psalm must be Christ

3. Let us do some shaking out, then; come on, let us shake the psalm if we want to be children of the shaken ones. Let us see if something comes to light. There is indeed a certain man who is blessed[7] like this; and, what is more, nobody fears the Lord without being among the members of this one man. He is many people yet one individual, many Christians but one Christ. All Christians, in union with their head who has ascended into heaven, form one Christ. It is not as though he were one and we many; no, we who are many are one in him, who is one. Christ, head and body together, is a single individual. What is his body? The Church, for the apostle tells us, *We are members of his body* (Eph 5:30), and again, *You are Christ's body, and his members* (1 Cor 12:27). Let us then listen to the voice of this single individual and understand it, for in his body we ourselves

---

7. Variant: "will be blessed."

are this one man spoken of in the psalm, and in his body we shall see the good things of Jerusalem. This is what the psalm speaks about in a later verse: *May you see the good things that belong to Jerusalem.* If you look for those good things with earthly eyes, you will be expecting hordes of children and grandchildren, and a wife who is fertile and frequently pregnant. But these are not the good things of the eternal Jerusalem; they are the good things that belong to the land of the dying, and Jerusalem is the land of the living.[8] Do not take it too much to heart if you have children who are going to die—if not before you, at any rate after you. Wouldn't you rather have children who will never die but live with you for ever? Then make sure that you are in the body of which the apostle said, *You are Christ's body, and his members.*

4. The psalm hinted at this interpretation by expressing itself so obscurely that it warns us to knock at its door. It has covered its meaning in such a way that it invites us to shake it out. What I mean is this: it began with the plural: *Blessed are all who fear the Lord, and walk in his ways.* It is obviously speaking here of many people but, because all these are one in Christ, it continues in the singular, promising, *You yourself*[9] *shall eat the labors of your fruits.* After saying in the plural, *Blessed are all who fear the Lord, and walk in his ways,* why did it switch to the singular for its promise in the next verse? Why *the labors of your*[10] *fruits,* rather than putting this in the plural? Did the psalmist forget so quickly that he was speaking to many people? Hardly. But, if you shake out his psalm, what will he tell you? "When I address many Christians, I understand them to be one in the one Christ," he will say. "You are many, and you are one single individual." We are many, and we are one individual. How can we be both many people and one individual? Because we cling inseparably to him of whom we are members; our head is in heaven, and he is drawing his members there after him.

5. Let the psalmist go on to tell us about this one individual, now that he has made it plain whom he is describing. Then all the rest of the psalm will be easily understood. Your business is simply to fear the Lord and walk in his ways, the psalm implies; do not envy those who do not walk in his ways when you see them being happy in their

---

8. See Pss 26(27):13; 141:6(142:5).
9. Singular.
10. Singular.

own unhappy fashion. Worldly people are happy in an unhappy way, but the martyrs were happy to be unhappy. They were unhappy for a short time, but they are happy for all eternity; and even during their temporary unhappiness they were not as unhappy as the onlookers thought they were. What does the apostle say about this? *As if sorrowful, we always have cause for joy* (2 Cor 6:10), he says.[11] Why *always*? Because we find joy both here and in the world to come. Yes, I mean it: both here and in the world to come; for what have we to make us joyful here? Our hope. And there? The reality.[12] Anyone who rejoices in hope has intense joy. And if we rejoice in hope, look at the consequence to which the apostle points: we are *patient in anguish* (Rom 12:12). The martyrs were patient in anguish because they were all the while rejoicing in hope. But because the reward promised to them was not yet theirs, what does the apostle say? *If hope is seen, it is hope no longer. But if we hope for what we do not see, we wait for it in patience.* (Rom 8:24–25) As I was saying, because the martyrs could not yet see it, they waited for it patiently, and that was how they were able to endure so much pain. The persecutors who were putting them to death were in love with things they could see; those who were being killed were sighing for things they could not see, were in a hurry to seize those invisible joys, and thought it tiresome if their deaths were hindered.[13]

The martyr Felix found dead in his dungeon

6. This is why the martyr Felix, whose festival we keep today,[14] had the strength to spurn the world, brothers and sisters. And truly Felix was an apt name for him; he was felicitous in his name and felicitous in the crown he won. Does that mean that because he was a God-fearing man he deserved the felicity and blessedness here on earth of a wife like a fertile vine and children all round his table? He certainly does enjoy these blessings to perfection, but within the body we are talking about in this psalm; and because Felix understood this,

---

11. See Augustine's powerful meditation on the "as if" quality of a Christian's sorrow, as contrasted with the reality of joy, in his Exposition 2 of Psalm 48,5.
12. *Spes* and *res*, as frequently in Augustine.
13. This could mean when the killing process was a slow one, or, more probably, when their passion was deferred. Augustine's remarks evoke the impatience of Ignatius of Antioch in his *Letter to the Romans* 2–5, where he begs his friends not to intervene and prevent his martyrdom.
14. On the identification of this Saint Felix, see the note at section 2 above.

he turned away from present joys to gain those still in the future. But as you know, brothers and sisters, he did not endure the same kind of death as other martyrs. He confessed his faith and was imprisoned and kept in reserve to be tortured later; but on another day his body was found lifeless. They had shut up his body in prison, but not his spirit. The executioners were preparing to torture him, but they found that he had gone, and their cruelty was thwarted. He lay there lifeless, unconscious of them and so incapable of being tortured, but fully conscious to God, so that he could receive his crown. We must therefore say that he was truly Felix, the happy one, not only because that is his name but also because he won the prize of eternal life, and he won it because he set his heart on these things.[15]

Fear and chaste love

7. Let us then listen to this psalm in the certainty that it is speaking about Christ. We are grafted into Christ's body; we have been made Christ's members. So let us walk in the Lord's ways and fear him with a chaste fear that abides for ever, for eternity. There is another kind of fear which is excluded by charity, as John tells us: *There is no room for fear in charity, for charity made perfect casts out fear* (1 Jn 4:18). But it cannot be said of every kind of fear that it is excluded by charity, for another psalm declares, *The fear of the Lord is chaste, enduring for ever and ever* (Ps 18:10(19:9)). Evidently there is one kind of fear that abides and another that is cast out. The kind that is cast out is not chaste fear; but the kind that abides is chaste.

What sort of fear is excluded by love? Please give me your full attention now. Some people fear the Lord only because they are afraid they may incur some earthly misfortune if they do not. They are afraid they may be struck down by illness or sustain financial loss; they fear bereavement or the loss of some dear friend, or that they may be banished or condemned and thrown into prison, or that some other kind of distress may overtake them. They are therefore full of dread, but this fear is not chaste. Go on listening, please. Another

---

15. The last three words, *si ista dilexit*, could mean that he set it on the good things of the future, to be experienced within Christ's body; the translation offered here assumes this meaning. If, however, *ista* are the tangible goods here and now, in the "carnal" sense of the psalm which Augustine has mentioned and rejected, the sentence could be understood as a question: "How could we have said that he was happy, Felix both in his name and in the prize of eternal life, if he had set his heart on these [material, this-worldly] things?".

person is not afraid of troubles on earth but does fear hell; and indeed the Lord gave us good reason to be terrified. You heard the gospel speaking of a place *where their worm*[16] *will never die, nor their fire be extinguished* (Mk 9:47). People hear about this prospect and know that this really is what will happen to the wicked, and so they are frightened and keep clear of sin. They are motivated by fear, and it is their fear that deters them from sin, but it does not make them love righteous conduct. As they continue to refrain from sin out of fear, however, they gradually develop good habits of acting justly, and so they begin to love what at first was hard and to find sweetness in God. After a time such a person comes to live righteously not because he or she is afraid of punishment, but out of love for eternal life. One kind of fear has been cast out by charity, but chaste fear has taken its place.

8. Now what is this chaste fear, the fear we must take the psalm to mean when it says, *Blessed are all who fear the Lord, and walk in his ways*? What is it, my brothers and sisters? With the help of the Lord our God I want to speak clearly about chaste fear because, if I can, it may be that many of you will recognize it and be enkindled thereby and catch fire with chaste love. Perhaps the best way to explain it is through a simile. Think of a chaste woman who fears her husband. And now think of an adulteress, who also fears her husband. The chaste woman fears that her husband may go away; the adulteress fears that hers may return. What if both husbands are absent? One is afraid that her husband may come home unexpectedly; the other is afraid that his return may be delayed. Now apply this to ourselves. The bridegroom to whom we have been wedded is absent, in a sense. He gave us his Holy Spirit as his pledge,[17] but he is absent himself; he redeemed us with his blood, but now he has gone away. He is a bridegroom unsurpassed in beauty, yet he appeared ugly in the hands of his persecutors, for of him Isaiah had said not long before,[18] *We saw him, and there was no fair form or comeliness in him* (Is 53:2). Can that really be true, that our bridegroom is hideous? Perish the thought! How could he have been loved by virgins who sought no earthly husbands?

---

16. Variant: *worms*.
17. *Arrha*. See 2 Cor 1:22; 5:5; and also Augustine's Sermons 23,8.9; 156,16; and 378, where he explains the difference between an earnest (*arrha*) and a pledge (*pignus*). Compare also the note at Exposition of Psalm 122,5.
18. It would be surprising if Augustine thought of this as not long before Christ's passion, but it is possible to understand him as meaning that the passage had been read very recently.

He only seemed ugly to his persecutors, for if they had not regarded him as loathsome they would not have pounced on him, scourged him, crowned him with thorns, or dishonored him with spittle. Only because he looked ugly to them could they do these things, for they lacked the eyes to see Christ's beauty. To what kind of eyes would Christ appear beautiful? Those eyes, surely, that Christ himself was seeking when he said to Philip, *Have I been all this time with you, and yet you have not truly seen me?* (Jn 14:9) These eyes[19] first need to be cleansed to enable them to see the light, but even when gently touched by its splendor they are enkindled with love and a longing to be healed, and at last they are illumined. If you are in any doubt that Christ is beautiful, listen to the prophet who sings to him, *Fair are you beyond all humankind* (Ps 44:3(45:2)); his beauty surpasses all other human beauty. Why do we love him? What are we loving when we hear that *he suffered for us* (1 Pt 2:21)? Crucified limbs? A torn side? Or his charity? Yes: charity falls in love with charity! He loved us in order to win our answering love, and to empower us to love him in return he came to us in his Holy Spirit. He is beautiful, but he is absent. His bride must question herself, if she is chaste.[20] We are all among his members, my brothers and sisters, we are among his members, and that is why we form a single individual.

Now let each one of us discern what kind of fear he or she has. Is it the kind that charity casts out or the chaste fear that abides for ever, for eternity? Each of you must test[21] it now. I will spell it out, and you test it. Our bridegroom has gone away. Question your conscience: Do you want him to come back, or would you prefer him to delay his return? Go on, ask yourselves, brothers and sisters! I have knocked at the doors of your hearts, but he alone hears the reply from within. The answers given by all your consciences cannot reach my ears, because I am only a man. But he, who is absent as far as bodily presence goes, is present in all the power and vigor of his majesty, and he has heard you. If we say, "Look, Christ is almost here! Tomorrow will be judgment day!" how few people will reply, "Good! Let him

---

19. According to a note in the CSEL edition of the Latin text Augustine would have tapped himself on the chest at this point to show that he meant the eyes of the heart. But it is clear in any case.
20. Or perhaps: "must ask herself whether she is chaste." This accords better with the following lines, but we might have expected *si casta sit* instead of the *si casta est* of the text.
21. Variant: "has tested."

come!" Those who do react like that are the ones who love much,[22] and if you then tell them, "Oh, no; he has been delayed," they will dread any delay, and their dread is chaste fear. And just as chaste fear dreads any delay in his coming, so, when he has come, will it dread his going away. But this fear is tranquil and unworried, another proof that it is chaste fear. We are not likely to be forsaken by him once he has found us, are we? Not anyone who believes in him.[23] After all, he sought us before ever we began to seek him.

Chaste fear bears this telltale mark, my brothers and sisters: it springs from love. A fear not yet chaste, on the contrary, stands in dread of the Lord's presence and is frightened of being punished. Even when it does some good deed it acts out of fear—not the fear of losing that good but the fear of suffering that evil. In other words, it is not afraid of losing the embrace of a supremely beautiful bridegroom; it is simply frightened of being sent to hell. This is a good fear and a useful one, but it is not yet chaste. It will not abide for ever, because only chaste fear *endures for ever and ever.*

Test the quality of your fear and love: searching questions

9. But in what does this chaste quality consist? Again I am going to ask you a question, but it is one that you must put to yourselves. Suppose God came and spoke to us here in his own voice (he never ceases to speak through his scriptures,[24] of course). But now, imagine that he is here and saying to one of you, "Do you want to sin? All right, go ahead, then: sin. Do anything that gives you pleasure. Anything that you love on earth shall be yours. You are angry with someone? Fine: let him die. You want to lay violent hands on someone? He is yours to seize. If you want to hit someone, you can hit him. If you want someone condemned, condemned he shall be. Whatever you want for yourself, you shall possess it. No one is to oppose you, no one is to say to you, 'What are you doing?' No one will say to you, 'Don't do that.' No one will say, 'Why did you do it?' All the earthly things you crave shall be yours in abundance. You shall live to enjoy

---

22. See Lk 7:47.
23. These last words, which break the flow of Augustine's sentence, are omitted by many witnesses to the text.
24. *Per litteras suas*: the phrase recalls Augustine's idea about scripture being God's letters to his people; see Exposition of Psalm 73,5 and the note there.

them not just for a time but always. But there is just one reservation: you will never see my face."

You groaned when I said that, my brothers and sisters. Why did you groan? Only because chaste fear has been born in you, the fear that *endures for ever and ever*. Why were your hearts stricken? If God were to say to you, "You will never see me face to face; but look: you will have all that earthly prosperity. You will have overflowing wealth and be awash with all kinds of temporal goods. You will not lose them, and you will never be asked to leave them behind. What more do you want?" Chaste fear would weep and groan at that and would answer, "Away with all of it, if only I may see your face." Chaste fear would reply in the words of a psalm, *Convert us, Lord God of hosts, show us your face and we shall be saved* (Ps 79:8(7)). Chaste fear would make another psalm's words its own: *One thing have I begged of the Lord.* Feel how ardent this chaste fear is, this true love, this love that does nor dissemble: *One thing have I begged of the Lord, and that will I seek after.* What is it? *To live in the Lord's house all the days of my life.* But in view of some earthly felicity, perhaps? No, for listen to the next line: *That I may contemplate the Lord's delight, and that I, his temple, may be protected.* (Ps 26(27):4)[25] I want to be his temple, and I want to be protected by him, and these two things together make up the *one thing I have begged from the Lord.* If you beg for this one thing and train[26] your heart to this one thing, and if your only fear is that you could lose it, you will not covet earthly happiness. You will hope for the true happiness and you will belong in the body of Christ, to whom the psalm sings,[27] *Blessed are all who fear the Lord, and walk in his ways.*

How we eat the labors of our fruits

10. *You yourself*[28] *shall eat the labors of your fruits.* You, all of you; you, individually, each of you; you who are many yet form a single individual—*you yourself shall eat the labors of your fruits.* To any of us who do not understand what the psalm is hinting at, this appears to be the wrong way round. It ought to have said, "You

---

25. There are many variants for the last phrase, *et protegi templum eius*. Augustine quotes it in this form in Expositions of Psalms 26 and 143,10.
26. Variant: "lift up."
27. Variants: "they sing," "you sing," "is sung."
28. Singular: hence Augustine's emphasis in the next lines on the many who are one.

yourself shall eat the fruits of your labors." Plenty of people eat the fruits of their own labors. They toil in a vineyard, but they do not eat the work itself; they eat the produce that results from their labor. They work around fruit trees,[29] but who is going to eat that work? They eat what the trees have produced; that is the fruit of their work, and that is what gladdens the farmer.

What can the psalm mean by saying, *You yourself shall eat the labors of your fruits*? We have to work hard now; the fruit will come later. Yet our labors themselves are not without joy because of the hope we cherish, of which we quoted just now the apostle's words, *rejoicing in hope, patient in anguish* (Rom 12:12). Even now our very labors gladden us, making us joyful in our hope.

But if our work has already proved eatable and has already shown its power to give us joy, how happy will the eater be when he or she comes to eat the fruit of the work? If people who *went on their way weeping as they scattered their seed* ate their labors, how much more gladly will they eat the fruit of their labors when *they come back leaping for joy, carrying their sheaves* (Ps 125(126):6)? If you need confirmation that this kind of labor is edible, brothers and sisters, remember that in an earlier psalm you heard the admonition to proud persons who try to rise before the light (before Christ, that is) and do not seek to rise through humility, which was the way Christ came to his resurrection. *Rise up after sitting down*, they were told: be humbled first and then rise up from a base of humility, because he too came to be humbled, he who has now been exalted for your sake. And that same psalm continued, *You who eat the bread of sorrow* (Ps 126(127):2). Why did it say that? This is what the labor of our fruits is: the bread of sorrow. If it were not edible it would not be called bread; but if this bread did not contain some sweet relish, no one would eat it. A praying person weeps and sighs, but with what sweetness! The tears of those who pray are more delicious than the pleasures offered by theatrical shows. And listen to the burning desire that arises when this bread is eaten.

Whom did that psalm mean, then, when it said, *You who eat the bread of sorrow*? In another passage the lover whose voice we often recognize in the psalms complains, *My tears have been bread to*

---

29. *Circa arbores pomiferas*. If we give the preposition *circa* its full weight, Augustine could be thinking of putting manure around them, as in Lk 13:8, in which case he is emphasizing the absurdity of eating the work itself.

me day and night. Why did tears become his bread? Because *every day I hear the taunt, Where is your God?* (Ps 41:4(42:3)) During this time before we see him who has loved us, him who has given us his pledge,[30] him to whom we have been wedded, the pagans mock us. "Where is the god those Christians worship?" they ask. "Let them show him to us. Look, I can show him[31] my god, so let him show me his."[32] When a pagan challenges you like this you cannot find anything to show him, because he is not the kind of person to whom it could be shown. You turn away, then, and go back to God and moan in his ears, for he is the one you are sighing for until you come to see him. You groan with longing for him and weep with desire; and, because it is desire that moves you to weep, your very tears are sweet and are like food to you. He himself has[33] become for you *bread by day and night*, while you hear the daily taunt, *Where is your God?*

But your God will come, even he of whom they ask, "Where is he?" He will wipe away your tears.[34] He will himself take the place of the bread of tears you used to eat, and he will be your rich satisfaction for ever, because he, the Word of God on whom the angels are fed, will be with us.

But in the meantime you must eat the labors of your fruits, as you hope hereafter to eat the fruits of your labor. *You yourself shall eat the labors of your fruits; you are blessed, and it shall go well with you.* The psalm speaks of the present in reminding you that *you are blessed*, and it promises the future: *It shall go well with you.* While you eat the labors of your fruits *you are blessed*; and when you attain to the fruits of your labors *it shall go well with you.* What has the psalm said? It seems to repeat the thought for, if things are to go well with you, of course you will be blessed; and if you are to be blessed, obviously things will go well with you. But there is a difference between hope and realization.[35] If the hope is so delicious, how much more delicious will the realization be!

---

30. *Pignus*: see the note at section 8, above.
31. Variant: "them."
32. Variant: "let them show me theirs."
33. Variant: "they themselves have."
34. See Rv 21:4.
35. *Inter spem et rem.*

Christ's fruitful wife, the Church

11. To that we must now turn. *Your wife*: this is addressed to Christ, so his wife is his Church. And his wife, his Church, is ourselves. *Your wife shall be like a fruitful vine*. But in whom is this vine fruitful? We see many barren people within these walls; we see many come within them drunk, many who are moneylenders or slave-dealers, others who consult soothsayers, and those who run to enchanters or enchantresses when they have a headache. Is this the vine's fertility? Is this the ample progeny of Christ's wife? It is not. These are the thorns, but the thorns are not rampant everywhere. The vine is indeed fertile and bears its own generous crop, but in whom? In those who grow *on the sides of your house*. It is not all Christians who can be called the sides of the house. I wonder what these sides are? What am I to say about them? Does it mean stone walls?[36] Perhaps, if we were talking about this material dwelling, we should assume that its sides must be its walls. But in our present context it is people who hold fast to Christ who are the sides of the house. In everyday speech we rightly say of someone who behaves badly and is influenced by bad companions, "He sides with them."[37] What does it mean, to side with them? The bad friends stick closely to him, and he to them. Of another person we may say, "He sides with good causes,"[38] because he lives by good advice. And what does that mean? That he is ruled by good counsel. The sides of the house, then, are people who cling tightly to Christ. It was significant that a wife was created from a man's side: when Adam slept Eve was created,[39] and when Christ died the Church was born—the one from her husband's side when his rib was extracted, the other from her husband's side when it was pierced with a lance and the sacraments flowed out.[40] *Your wife shall*, on this account, *be like a fruitful vine*. But in whom will she be fruitful? In those who are *the sides of your house*. In others, who do not cling closely to Christ, she is barren. But then I do not count them as belonging to the vine at all.

---

36. The variant, "strong stones" came about by the attachment of the first word of the next sentence, *forte*, to the preceding sentence.
37. Literally, "He has bad sides."
38. Literally, "He has good sides." Perhaps it would not be far from the mark to think of someone who is "on the side of the angels."
39. See Gn 2:21–24.
40. See Jn 19:34 and Exposition of Psalm 126,7 with the note there.

Members of the Church are both wife and children to Christ, and even mother

12. *Your children.* Who is the wife? And who are the children? In carnal marriage and relationships the wife and the children are distinct, but in the Church's case wife and children are identical. The apostles belonged to the Church and were among the Church's members. This means that they were within Christ's consort, but at the same time they were his consort, with regard to the share they had among his members. Why else did the gospel say of them, *When the bridegroom has left them, then his children will fast* (Mt 9:15)? So, you see, they are both the Lord's consort and his children. This is a wonderful thing that I am telling you, my brothers and sisters. From the Lord's own words we learn that the Church is his brothers, and the Church is his sisters, and the Church is his mother, for when a message was passed to him that his mother and his brothers were standing there, a symbolic fact was mentioned: they were outside.[41] Who was his mother, in a typical sense? The synagogue. And whom were his brothers according to the flesh representing? The Jews who stood outside. The synagogue stands outside too, even today. This must be the meaning, because Mary was not personally outside: she was on the sides of his house; and those of his kinsfolk who believed in him, who were related to him by blood through his mother, were also on the sides of his house not in virtue of their physical consanguinity but inasmuch as they heard the word of God and acted on it.[42] The Lord made this plain when he replied, *Who is my mother, who are my brothers?* (Mt 12:48) Some people have seized on this and tried to make out that Christ cannot have had a mother, since he asked, *Who is my mother?*[43] But how does that follow? Would they say that Peter, John, James, and the other apostles had no earthly fathers? Of course not. Yet what did Christ say to them? *Call no one on earth your father, for you have only one Father, and he is in heaven* (Mt 23:9). He demonstrated with regard to his mother what he taught his disciples with regard to their fathers: namely, that the Lord wants us to give God preference over earthly kin. Defer to your father because he is your father, and defer to God because he is God. Your father

---

41. See Mt 12:46; Mk 3:31.
42. See Lk 8:21.
43. Presumably he means the Manichees and also other heretics such as the Docetists, who denied the reality of the incarnation.

procreated you by making proper use of his flesh; God created you by the exercise of his power. A father must not be annoyed when God is given a higher place; rather he should be glad that he has been shown so much honor that nobody except God can been found who deserves greater honor still.

Well now, what am I to say about the Lord's relatives? What did the Lord himself say? *Who is my mother, who are my brothers? And he stretched out his hands over his disciples, saying, These are my mother and my brothers.* They were his brothers, that is plain enough. But in what sense were they his mother? He added, *Anyone who does the will of my Father is to me brother and sister and mother.* (Mt 12:48–50) You can take Christ's brother to represent those of the male sex who belong to the Church, the men whom Christ has here among his members.[44] But how can we understand Christians to be his mother? Surely because Christ is inside Christians, whom the Church brings to birth every day.[45] In all those whom you understand to be Christ's consort you must therefore recognize also his mother and his children.

13. Now let the psalm tell us what these children ought to be like. What kind of people are they? Peacemakers. Why is that? Because the gospel promises, *Blessed are the peacemakers, for they shall be called God's children* (Mt 5:9). Now the psalm mentions olives in this connection, and I will explain why. The olive is the fruit that signifies peace, because oil represents charity, and there is no peace without charity. It is plain for all to see that those who have torn our peace apart have no charity.[46] I have already explained to you, beloved,[47] why a dove brought a branch bearing leaves and fruit to the ark;[48] it

---

44. The translation offered follows the CSEL text, which omits a variant accepted by the CCL editors and inserted after "belong to the Church": *soror propter feminas quas*. This, if correct, would mean, "Christ's brother to represent those of the male sex who belong to the Church and his sister to be the women whom Christ has here among his members." Which suggests that whoever was responsible for this reading had some doubt about the permanence of women in this happy state beyond "here."
45. A variant adds "through baptism."
46. The Donatists.
47. *Caritati vestrae*, Augustine's customary mode of address to his people; but perhaps it has a special point here, just after his allegation that the schismatics lack charity. The explanation he refers to occurs in his *Homilies on the Gospel of John* 6,19.
48. See Gn 8:11.

was intended as a sign. When people who have been baptized outside the Church, like trees baptized outside the ark, have nonetheless borne not only leaves but also fruit—for the leaves represent words alone, but the fruit is charity—such people are brought to the ark by the dove. They come into unity with us.[49] People of this sort are the children who take their rightful places around the Lord's table, like olive seedlings. This is a scene of perfect tranquillity and great happiness; surely everyone would wish to be part of it. But when you see some blasphemer with a wife, children, and grandchildren, while you perhaps have none of these, do not be jealous. Believe rather that the same promises are fulfilled in yourself, but spiritually. Unless, that is, you are not among Christ's members. If you are not, you have reason to mourn, for these blessings will not be yours either here or hereafter. But if you are to have them only there, in the next life, do not worry because, even if they are to be yours there only, and not here, remember that you will enjoy them more fruitfully there than you could here.

14. If this is to be our possession, what is our title to it? *Lo, this is how anyone who fears the Lord will be blessed.* Many individuals are this one individual, and the one is many, for the many form a unity because Christ is one.

Verse 5. The blessings and good things that last

15. *May the Lord bless you from Zion.* You began to take notice, didn't you, when the psalm said, *Lo, this is how anyone who fears the Lord will be blessed*? Your eyes were beginning to rove, perhaps, over people you know who do not fear the Lord, and you observed their fertile wives and the swarms of children encircling their fathers' tables. I don't know where your imagination was wandering.[50] *May the Lord bless you*, certainly, but only if it is *from Zion*. Beware of running after blessings that are not from Zion.

But wait a minute, my brothers and sisters. Has the Lord not blessed those other people? Yes, these temporal things truly are blessings from the Lord. If they did not come from him, would anyone marry, in defiance of the Lord's will? Could anyone be healthy if the Lord did not wish it? Could anyone be rich if it were not the Lord's

---

49. In the preceding lines the Church has implicitly been called peace (which the schismatics tear apart), unity, and the ark.
50. Variants expand this: "wandering after blessings that are not from Zion."

will? He gives these gifts, but do you not see that he has given them to animals as well? That blessing cannot originate *from Zion*. But, as for you, *may the Lord bless you from Zion, and may you see the good things that belong to Jerusalem*. Those temporal blessings do not belong to Jerusalem. Do you want me to prove this to you? Remember how even the birds were bidden, *Increase and multiply* (Gn 1:22). Can you rate so highly a gift conferred equally on birds? It was certainly God's word that granted it to them; we all know that.

If you are given these temporal blessings, make good use of them; but give more thought to how you are going to bring up the children already born than to having even more. Happiness lies not in merely having children but in having good ones. If they are already born to you, work hard on their upbringing; if they are not born, give thanks to God, because you will perhaps have fewer worries. All the same, it does not mean that you have remained sterile—not in your union with such a mother. It may be that some of those young olive saplings crowding round the Lord's table are your spiritual children, borne to you by mother Church. May the Lord console you, then, and grant you to see the good things of Jerusalem. Good things they *are*, indeed. Why do we say they *are*? Because they are eternal. Why do we say of them that they *are*?[51] Because in that country the King is he who says, *I AM WHO AM* (Ex 3:14). The other goods, the earthly ones, both are and are not; for they cannot stand. They slide away and dissolve.

Your children are little; you cuddle them[52] and they cuddle you back. But do they stay small? You hope they will grow; you look forward to the next stage. But notice how, as each stage arrives, another dies. When childhood comes, infancy dies;[53] when adolescence is gained, childhood dies; when youth arrives, adolescence dies; when old age comes on, youth dies; and when death comes, every one of life's stages dies. Even as you enjoy their growing up, you are hoping for these successive deaths. Clearly none of these happy experiences has being in the full sense. And consider this: Have your children been born to you in order to live with you on earth? Or to supplant you and oust you? Can you rejoice over the birth of those who are born only to push you aside? All new-born children tacitly say to

---

51. The verb "to be" has full force here.
52. Variant: "When you are little, you are cuddled."
53. Compare *Confessions* I,8,13, where Augustine wonders what happened to his infancy when boyhood caught up with him.

their parents, "Get out of the way, it's our show now." The whole life of the human race, a life of trial and temptation, is no more than a show played out on stage; as a psalm says, *All things are empty, and everyone who lives* (Ps 38:6(39:5)).

Yet if, in spite of all, we still enjoy the children who will displace us, how much more should we rejoice in the children with whom we shall live for ever, and how intense should be our joy in the Father who, having given us life, will never die but destines us to live with him for all eternity! These are *the good things of Jerusalem*, good because they truly exist. So *may the Lord bless you from Zion, and may you see the good things that belong to Jerusalem.* Those earthly good things you hope for, you see only with blind eyes. *May you see* the truly good things that are seen only with the heart.

And for how long will I see the good things that belong to Jerusalem? *All the days of your life.* But if your life is going to be eternal life, you will see the good things of Jerusalem for all eternity. Earthly blessings are good indeed, my brothers and sisters, but you do not go on seeing them *all the days of your life*, for your life does not end when you leave your body behind. Your life goes on: the body dies, but the life of your spirit endures. The bodily eyes do not see any more because the one who used to see through those eyes has departed. But wherever their former user is now, he or she sees something. This must be true, because the rich man who on earth used to dress in purple and fine linen had not entirely died; if he had been completely dead, he could not have been tormented in hell.[54] He may well have wished that he could die, but unfortunately for him he was alive and was suffering hell's anguish. He was in terrible pain and could no longer see the good things he had left behind on earth. He still had life, such as it was, but he did not see those former goods of his. As for you, make sure you desire the kind of goods that you will be able to see *all the days of your life*; desire to live with those good things eternally.

Verse 6. Peace in Jerusalem

16. Finally, brothers and sisters, consider what those good things are. Can they be put into words? Is it gold? Or silver? Or a pleasant estate? Or marble walls? Or a paneled ceiling? No, nothing like that; far from it! Even poor people have these things in richer abundance,

---

54. See Lk 16:19–31.

even in the present life; for it is more glorious for a poor person to look up at a star-studded sky than for a rich man to gaze at his gilded ceiling. What is it, then, brothers and sisters, this good thing that kindles our desire, the thing for which we sigh, the reality that sets us afire, the good thing for which we endure such arduous labors, if only we may win it and behold it? For labor we do, as you were reminded when the apostle's words were being read: *All who want to live devoted to God in Christ suffer persecution* (2 Tm 3:12). Do you suppose that, because the devil no longer does his savage work through pagan kings, Christians no longer endure persecution? If the devil is dead, then we have indeed seen the last of persecution. But if our adversary[55] is alive, how can he not still be insinuating temptations, how not rampaging, how not contriving threats or schemes to trip us up? If only you would begin to *live devoted to God*! Once you begin, you will discover that everyone who purposes *to live devoted to God in Christ will suffer persecution*. What motivates us, that we are prepared to endure such intensely hostile opposition? *If our hope in Christ is a matter for this present life only, we are in a more wretched state than all the rest of humankind* (1 Cor 15:19), the apostle reflects. What motivated the martyrs who were condemned to face wild beasts? Can it be uttered, that good thing on which they set their hope? How can we know it? What tongue can express it? What ears hear it? None, for scripture tells us it is something that *ear has not heard nor human heart conceived* (1 Cor 2:9; Is 64:4). Yet let us love it, and make progress toward it.

You are well aware that warfare never ceases, for we must fight our unruly desires. We wage outward battles with unbelievers and rebels and inward battles against the urges and tumults of the flesh. We still must keep up the fight on every front, for *the corruptible body weighs down the soul* (Wis 9:15). We cannot slacken in the conflict, because even though *the spirit is life, the body is a dead thing by reason of sin*. But what is in store for us in the future? *If the Spirit of him who raised Christ from the dead lives in you, he will bring life to your mortal bodies too, through his Spirit who dwells in you*. (Rom 8:10–11) When these death-doomed members of ours have been given immortal life, nothing will fight against our spirit. There will be no hunger, no thirst, for these arise from our perishable bodies. You need

---

55. See 1 Pt 5:8.

refreshment because something in you is failing.[56] Craving for carnal pleasures attacks us. We carry death within us because our bodies are so weak, but when death itself has been changed into indefectible life, and this perishable nature has clothed itself in imperishability, and this mortal frame has put on immortality, what will death be made to hear? *O death, where is your striving? Where, O death, is your sting?* (1 Cor 15:55) But even if death itself dies, perhaps someone will say, "But there may still be other enemies left!" No, there will not, for scripture has an answer to that: death is *the last enemy* (1 Cor 15:26). When death has been destroyed, immortality will take its place unchallenged. If no enemy remains, it will truly be the destruction of *the last enemy* when death is vanquished.

The good for which we sigh, our true good, will be peace. This is our good, brothers and sisters, a great good, and its name is peace. Were you not trying to find a name for our good just now, and thinking it might be called gold, or silver, or a large farm, or fine raiment? No, its name is peace—not peace like that which people sometimes agree on among themselves: a treacherous, unstable, precarious, unreliable peace. Nor is it such peace as a single individual may have within himself, for we have pointed out to you that each of us must fight even with himself. Until he has subdued all his unruly desires he must go on fighting. What kind of peace will it be, then? A peace that *eye has not seen nor ear heard* (1 Cor 2:9). What will that peace be like? A peace that arises in Jerusalem, for the name Jerusalem is interpreted as "vision of peace." Thus may *the Lord bless you from Zion; may you see the good things that belong to Jerusalem,* and see them *all the days of your life.*

And may you see not your children only but *your children's children.* What do your children represent? The works you perform here. Who then are your children's children? The fruits of those works. If you give alms, they are your children; but because you gave alms you receive eternal life, and that is what your children's children stand for. *May you see your children's children,* and, when you do, there will be an inevitable result: there will be *peace upon Israel.* This peace is what we preach to you, what we love, and what we want you to love. Those who even here are peacemakers attain this peace. Those who are at peace there beyond are the ones who have been peacemakers here, the ones who surround the Lord's table like a nursery of young

---

56. Neater in Latin: *Ideo reficis, quia aliquid deficit.*

olive trees. They are not barren, like the fig tree on which the hungry Lord found no fruit.[57] Look what happened to that! It had leaves but no fruit, like people who are full of words but have no deeds to show. The Lord comes in his hunger and finds nothing he can eat, because the Lord is hungry for our faith and good works. Let us feed him by living good lives and he will feed us by granting us life for all eternity.

---

57. See Mk 11:13.

Exposition of Psalm 128

A Sermon to the People

Introduction: sowing the word for various hearers

1. The psalm we have sung today is a short one. But we are told in the gospel that Zacchaeus was short of stature but great in his generosity[1] and that the widow who dropped two small coins into the treasury was short of money but great in charity.[2] Something similar might be said of this psalm: if you count its words it is short, but if you weigh its contents it is great. However, being short, it will not detain us too long, so there is no danger that anyone will be bored.

All the same, your own prudent self-interest should warn you to listen and to use the resources of your Christian understanding. Let God's word resound for those who want to hear it and those who do not, in season and out of season.[3] It finds a place for itself; it finds a heart where it may be at home; it finds soil where it may germinate and bear a crop. Everyone knows that there are many bad people, people of wicked lives, whom the Church carries even to the end. These are the hearers who have no interest in the word of God: either it falls upon them like seed by the wayside,[4] where it is trodden on and pecked up by birds, or it falls on them like seed into rocky places where there is little soil and then shoots up quickly but dries up as soon as the sun grows hot because it has no roots. Or again, the word falls on them like seed sown among thorns because, although it sprouts and tries to fight its way upward into the light, the thorns choke it. The hearers who despise God's word from the outset are like the road where some seed fell and could not germinate at all; others who are initially pleased with it but lose interest when troubles overtake them are like growth that withers and shrivels in hot sun; others again smother what has begun to grow within them under the distractions and cares and anxieties of this world, as though under

---

1. See Lk 19:2–9.
2. See Mk 12:42–44.
3. See 2 Tm 4:2.
4. See Mk 4:3–9 and parallels.

a thorny tangle of avarice. But there is also good soil and, when the seed falls there, it bears a crop: in some places thirty-fold, in others sixty-fold, in others a hundredfold. But whether the yield is small or large, all these will be found in the barn.

There are people here of this kind, and it is for their sake that we speak. For their sake scripture speaks, and for their sake the gospel is never silent. But let the others listen too: it is possible that, though they are unreceptive today, they will be different tomorrow. Perhaps they will be changed as they listen and plough up the roadway or clear away the stones or root out the thorns.

Let the Spirit of God speak. Let him speak to us, let him sing to us. Whether we are willing to dance or not, let him sing. A dancer moves his limbs in response to the music, and those who dance to the music of God's commandment show their response by their deeds. What does the Lord say in the gospel to those who refuse to dance? *We sang to you, but you did not dance. We played a lament, but you did not mourn.* (Mt 11:17) Let him sing then, for by the mercy of God we believe there will be some from whom we can take comfort. As for the contumacious ones, who persist in their ill-will even though they hear the word of God, they are a daily source of trouble and scandal to the Church. The psalm describes their activities, for it begins like this:

Verses 1–3. The Church has been under attack all down the ages

2. *Very often have they attacked me, ever since I was young.* The Church is speaking of the tormentors it has to endure. But perhaps someone will ask, "Does this mean now?" and the psalm answers. The Church has been here for a very long time; ever since there have been people who could be called holy, the Church has been present on earth. Time was when it existed only in Abel,[5] and he was slain by his wicked, reckless brother. At another time the Church was present only in Enoch, and he was taken away from bad people.[6] Then, later, the Church consisted only of Noah and his family, who at first had to endure the company of all those who were to perish in the flood, while the ark alone floated over the waves and reached dry land safely.[7] In another age the Church was present in Abraham alone, and we all

---

5. See Gn 4:8.
6. See Gn 5:24.
7. See Gn 6:8–8:18.

know how much he had to put up with from unjust people.[8] In Sodom the Church existed only in Lot, the son of Abraham's brother, and in his household; Lot had to endure the sins and perverted conduct of the Sodomites until God plucked him away from them into freedom.[9] Then the Church came to be among the people of Israel, but it had to endure harsh treatment from Pharaoh and the Egyptians. Even among this Church, which at the time consisted of the whole people of Israel, there was a group of saints, for Moses and the other holy ones had to bear with the unfaithful Jews, even though these were themselves Israelites.

Then, in the time of our Lord Jesus Christ and the preaching of the gospel, the verse of another psalm was verified: *I announced the news and spoke the message,* but *they were multiplied, in numbers beyond reckoning* (Ps 39:6(40:5)). What does *beyond reckoning* suggest? Innumerable people surged into the Church, not only true believers whose place is in the number of the saints but others too. Many of them were just, but even more were unjust people, and the just have been sorely tried by the unjust ever since. When is this state of affairs found in the Church? Only now, during the period that can be recalled, only within living memory? By no means.

Now we can see why our psalm opens as it does: it wants to make sure that neither the Church itself nor anyone in the Church shall be dismayed or surprised. Everyone who wants to be a good member should listen to the Church itself, his mother, telling him, "Do not be surprised that you have to endure these things, my son, for *very often have they attacked me, ever since I was young.*"

3. A spirited declaration it is that opens the psalm: *Very often have they attacked me, ever since I was young.* It sounds as though a discussion were under way already and the Church not initiating it but replying. But replying to whom? To those who think and loudly complain, "What a lot we have to put up with! What grievous scandals are all about us, multiplying by the day, as bad people flock into the Church and we have to bear with them!" So the Church has to respond in the persons of certain of its members—that is, with the voice of its stronger adherents. With their voices let the Church reply to the complaints of the weak, so that the steady ones may strengthen the unsteady and those of greater stature support the little ones. Let

---

8. See Gn 12ff.
9. See Gn 19:1–23.

the Church answer, *Very often have they attacked me, ever since I was young. Let Israel testify, Very often have they attacked me, ever since I was young.* Let the Church say it and not cringe to say it, for what is the force of those last words? After declaring, *Very often have they attacked me,* it adds, *ever since I was young.* Why the addition? In our days the Church is ancient and still under attack, but let it not fear; let it remember that *very often have they attacked me, ever since I was young.* Do their unrelenting attacks mean that it never reached[10] old age? Did they ever manage to destroy the Church? No, and therefore *let Israel testify,* let Israel take comfort, let the Church itself take comfort from past examples, and say, *Very often have they attacked me, ever since I was young.*

Against avarice

4. Why have they attacked? *Indeed they could not prevail against me: sinners have wrought upon my back, they have removed their wickedness to a distance.* Why did they attack? Because *they could not prevail against me.* What does that mean? They could not achieve anything.[11] What does it mean, *they could not prevail against me*? I did not consent when they tried to make me do wrong.

Every evil-doer harasses a good person who will not consent to follow him into bad conduct. If some rascal commits a bad deed and the bishop does not rebuke him, he regards the bishop as a good fellow; but if he is rebuked, he thinks the bishop a spoilsport. If he robs someone and the victim keeps quiet about it, that person is thought to be a good sort, but if he so much as remonstrates and denounces the thief, then he is bad, even if he does not try to get his property back. So the one who blames the robber is bad, and the robber himself is good! Great! *Let us eat and drink, for tomorrow we die* (Is 22:13; 1 Cor 15:32). But the apostle censures this attitude: *Evil conversations corrupt good morals. Be sober and live justly,*[12] *and do not sin.* (1 Cor 15:33–34) The word rings out, the word that denounces his depravity, but he regards his vice as his friend and the word that rebukes him as his enemy, and so he is aggressive and hates the word of God. Avarice has become his friend, and God his foe, because God forbids avarice and does not wish us to be lured into it. "I want to be your

---

10. Variant: "I never reached"; the Church would still be speaking.
11. These last words are omitted by some witnesses to the text.
12. Variant: *Be sober, you just ones.*

possession," [13] God says. "Why seek to be possessed by avarice? Its demands will be very hard on you, but mine are gentle. Its burden is heavy, but my load is light. Its yoke is rough, mine smooth. Do not aim to be the slave of avarice. It orders you to cross the seas, and you obey; it orders you to risk your life in winds and storms. All I order you is that you give something of what you have to the poor person who stands at your gate. You are too lazy to do this good work that is under your nose, but you are energetic when asked to cross the sea." Because avarice issues the order you are a slave eager to do its bidding, but because it is God's order you hate it.

And when the sinner begins to hate it, he begins also to hope that those from whom he receives good admonitions may themselves become targets of denunciation; he hopes by spying on them to ferret out the misdeeds of God's servants. "They point out our wrongdoing," he will say, "but they do the same themselves, don't they?" He will make the accusation whether it has any basis in fact or not. Things that do not occur at all are alleged to occur, what is done innocently is presented as ill done, and the evils we have to endure in others are charged to us. What are we to say in reply?

Take no notice of me, you rascal; listen to the word itself. The word is addressing you through someone else, whoever he or she may be, the word that you have made your enemy. *Come to terms with your adversary while you are with him on the road* (Mt 5:25), we are warned; and you have made God's word your adversary. Never mind who its mouthpiece may be. The person who speaks to you is bad, perhaps, but the one who speaks to you through that person is not bad. Accuse God's word, accuse God himself, if you can!

5. Can you believe, brothers and sisters, that the persons referred to in the psalm, the ones who *have very often attacked me, ever since I was young*, have sunk so low that they do not hesitate to accuse God himself? You rebuke a miser, and he blames God for making gold! "Don't be so greedy," you say to him, and he retorts, "It's God's fault. He shouldn't have created gold." The only excuse left to you when you cannot restrain yourself from evil works is to blame the good works of God; the creator and maker of the world is at fault, according to you. He had no business to make the sun either, by your account, because so many stand at their open windows arguing about the luminaries in the sky and drag each other off to court. If only we could curb

---

13. Variant: "I want to possess [you]."

our vices! All these things are good because God who made them is good, and all of them praise him when studied in the right spirit, the spirit of piety and wisdom. God is praised by his works from every corner of creation, as they praised him through the tongues of the three young men.[14] Is anything left out of their song? The sky praises God, the angels praise him, the stars praise him, sun and moon praise him, days and nights praise him, everything that grows in the earth praises him, everything that swims in the sea praises him, everything that flies in the air praises him, all mountains and hills praise him, cold and heat[15] praise him, and so do all the other things God has made. You hear how they praise God. But do you hear anything in the song about avarice praising him? Or self-indulgence? I don't think so. These things do not praise him, because he did not make them. Men and women praise God in the song, for God is the creator of men and women. Avarice is the creation of a bad human being, but the human being is the work of God. And what does God want? To kill in you your own handiwork and to save what he wrought himself.

It is no excuse for vicious conduct to say that you earn your living that way

6. Do not be a moneylender.[16] You find fault with scripture when it speaks of a good man who *has not put his money out to usury* (Ps 14(15):5). It was not I who wrote that, nor did it come originally from my mouth. Listen to God. But he retorts, "It only means that clerics must not be moneylenders." Very likely the person who takes you to task is not a moneylender himself. But if by chance he is—let us suppose he is, for the sake of argument—then is God, who speaks through him, a moneylender? If the speaker lives himself as he urges you to live, and you refuse, you will go to the fire and he to the kingdom. If he does not live in the way he tells you to live but does the same bad things that you do and recommends good conduct that he does not observe himself, he will go with you into the fire. The grass will burn, but the word of the Lord abides for ever.[17] Will the word that speaks to you through that other person be destroyed by fire? Certainly not. Either Moses is speaking to you—and he is a

---

14. A variant adds, "in the fiery furnace." See Dn 3:57–90, Vulgate.
15. Variant: "summer."
16. On the traditional view of usury see the note at Exposition 3 of Psalm 36,6.
17. See Is 40:8.

good, just servant of God—or else a Pharisee is speaking, one who sits in the chair of Moses. But even of the latter kind of teacher you have heard the warning, *Do what they tell you, but do not imitate what they do* (Mt 23:3). You have no excuse, when it is God's word that addresses you. But, being unable to kill God's word, you try to discredit those through whom it is spoken to you. Try as hard as you like, make whatever allegations you like, blaspheme as much as you like, still the Church will say, *Very often have they attacked me, ever since I was young. Let Israel testify, Very often have they attacked me, ever since I was young.*

Yet moneylenders have the effrontery to argue, "I have no other means of supporting myself." A robber caught in the act of murder[18] might say the same; so might a burglar caught climbing into someone's property; so might a pimp selling girls into prostitution; so might a sorcerer weaving evil spells and selling his wickedness. If we ever tried to forbid any of these professions their practitioners would all reply that they had no other livelihood, that they must engage in such business to feed themselves—as though they were not especially deserving of punishment for choosing to earn their living[19] in a wicked profession and to feed themselves in a way that offends God, by whom all are fed.

The Church carries the unrepentant

7. You may shout these warnings to them, and all they will say is, "Alright, then, we won't come any more. If this is how it is, we won't enter the church." Let them come, though, let them enter and hear the psalm proclaiming, *Very often have they attacked me, ever since I was young. For indeed they could not prevail against me: sinners have wrought upon my back.* When they could not persuade me to consent to their evil designs, they made me carry them. How well that is expressed, how elegant and telling is this verse! *Indeed they could not prevail against me: sinners have wrought upon my back.* Their first ploy is to ingratiate themselves in the hope of extorting our consent to their evil courses. If we do not consent, they say,

---

18. *Deprehensus in fauce,* literally "seized in the [act of cutting someone's] throat." A similar expression occurs in Exposition of Psalm 55,12 where, speaking of the robber crucified beside the Lord, Augustine says, "He went from murder (*de fauce*) to judgment." See the note there. But in the present context a variant reads *in furto,* "in the act of theft."
19. Variant: "spend their lives."

"Very well, carry us." You could not prevail against me, says the Church, so climb onto my back; I must carry you to the end, for so was I commanded, that I may bear fruit through long endurance.[20] If I cannot correct you, I will bear with you; or perhaps, if I bear with you, you will correct yourself before the end. I will bear with you until the end, and even to the very end you will be a load upon my back. But only to the end of time. Will you be on my back for ever? No, for someone will come to knock you off; the time for harvest will come. The world will come to its end and God will send in his harvesters. *The harvesters are the angels* (Mt 13:39) who separate the wicked from the just like tares from wheat. The grain they will store in the barn, but the straw they will burn *in unquenchable fire* (Mt 3:12). I have carried you to the very limit of my strength. Now I can pass joyfully into God's barn, freed from care and singing, *Very often have they attacked me, ever since I was young.*

8. What effect did they manage to have on me, when they *attacked me,* all that time since I was young? They put me to the test, but they did not overpower me. They even did me good, as fire does to gold, not as fire does to grass. Fire applied to gold purges it of dross, but applied to grass it reduces it to ashes. *They could not prevail against me,* for I did not consent; they could not make me like themselves.

Sinners have wrought upon my back, they have removed their wickedness to a distance. They made for me a load I have to carry but not a plan to which I would consent; and this is why their unjust behavior is far away from me. Bad people commingle with good people not only in the world but even within the Church: even here the wicked are mixed up with the good. You know this, you have plenty of experience of it, and if you are good yourselves you will be all the more keenly aware of it, for *when the shoots had grown up and come into ear, then the tares became apparent* (Mt 13:26). The bad people within the Church are obvious only to one who is good. But you know that they are mingled with the rest, always and everywhere, and scripture testifies that they will not be sorted out until the end. Yet they are mingled with good people in such a way that the Church can say, "They are far from me." The psalm wants to make it clear to us that no one who observes the intermingling of bad people with good should conclude that iniquity and righteousness are near neighbors. No, they are not; and so the Church declares in

---

20. See Lk 8:15.

the psalm, *They could not prevail against me*. They talked in their wicked way and suggested, *Let us eat and drink, for tomorrow we die* (Is 22:13; 1 Cor 15:32); but their bad conversations did not corrupt my good morals.[21] I had been listening to what God had to say and did not yield to human persuasion. Sinners wrought for me a load I had to shoulder, not a proposal with which I was willing to align myself, and thus their wickedness was far removed from me. What is closer, as appearances go, than two people side by side in one church? Yet what is further apart than iniquity from justice? It is consent that makes propinquity. Suppose two men are bound and committed to judgment, a robber and his fellow-prisoner, the one guilty and the other innocent. One single chain binds the two of them, yet they are far apart. How far? As far as crime is distant from innocence. There is a vast space between them. But another robber who commits his crime in Spain is near neighbor to the robber who commits his in Africa. How close is he? As close as robbery is to robbery.

No one should be worried, then, about the present confusion and afraid to be physically mixed up with bad people. Each one of us must be far removed from them in heart, and then he or she will carry without anxiety the wrongdoers who cannot frighten us, for *they have removed their wickedness to a distance*.

Verse 4. A warning for the proud who defend their sins

9. But what tells against this? The wicked prosper and flourish. They sound off, as the colloquial expression has it; they are loud and proud and arrogant in their malice. What are we to make of it? Will it be like this always? No. Listen to the next verse. *The Lord who is just will break the necks of sinners*. Your close attention is needed here, beloved. The psalm foretells that *the Lord who is just will break the necks of sinners*. Who would not shudder on hearing this? Is there anyone who has not sinned? Yet *the Lord who is just will break the necks of sinners*. All who hear this verse must feel fear creeping into their hearts, if they believe in God's scripture. For it seems to apply to everyone, you see: if just people beat their breasts insincerely, their sham penitence is a lie to God, and so they become sinners. But if they have reason to beat their breasts, they are sinners already. And is there anyone among us who does not beat his breast? Or anyone of us who does not cast his eyes down like the tax collector, saying, *Lord,*

---

21. See 1 Cor 15:33.

be merciful to me, a sinner (Lk 18:13)? If then all of us are sinners, and no one is found without sin, we all need to be afraid of the sword falling upon our necks, because *the Lord who is just will break the necks of sinners.* But I suspect, my brothers and sisters, that it does not mean all sinners, because in specifying the place where the sword will strike, the psalm also indicates which sinners will be struck. It did not say, you notice, "The Lord who is just will break the hands of sinners" or "The Lord who is just will break the feet of sinners." It did not say either of these, because it wanted to point to proud sinners in particular, the arrogant, stiff-necked kind. All proud persons are stiff-necked and obstinate. Not only do they do wrong, but they refuse to acknowledge it, and when rebuked they justify themselves. You did it, didn't you? At least admit what you did. God hates the sinner, does he? You must do the same. Make common cause with God![22] Hunt down your sin, in partnership with God. "No!" one of them will say. "I have been in the right; it is God who has done wrong." What do you mean? "I have done nothing wrong," he maintains. "Saturn did it, or Mars did it, or Venus did it. It wasn't my fault; the stars were responsible." So you justify yourself by accusing God, who made the stars and all the heavenly array.

Well now, let us look at this. You defend your sin and argue proudly against God; you exculpate yourself and blame God. You have stiffened your neck and tossed your head; you have pitted yourself against God in the way described in the Book of Job, where it is said of an impious sinner that he pitted himself against God with his grossly fat neck for a shield.[23] Notice that the neck is mentioned! You stand up haughtily, you do not cast your eyes to the ground or beat your breast or pray, *Lord, be merciful to me, a sinner* (Lk 18:13), but flaunt your merits instead. "You are presuming to take me to court," says God. "You want to put your case against me," when you ought to be making amends to God in your guilt. You should be crying out to him in the words of another psalm, *If you take account of our lawbreaking, O Lord, Lord, who will hold up his head?* (Ps 129(130):3)

---

22. Until the words above, "they justify themselves," Augustine was talking generally. The next passage, "You did it... cause with God!" is in the singular and could be taken either as an illustration of an argument with one of the proud, obstinate persons he has mentioned or as an appeal to any individual among his hearers.
23. *Currens adversus Deum in crassa cervice scuti sui.* This appears to be based on Jb 15:26, which is somewhat different in both the Hebrew and the LXX.

You ought to cry out to him as another psalm cries, *I said it myself, Lord: Lord, have mercy on me; heal my soul, for I have sinned against you* (Ps 40:5(41:4)). But, because you refuse to say this and persist in justifying your deeds in opposition to the word of God, the sentence recorded in scripture will fall upon you: *The Lord who is just will break the necks of sinners.*

Verses 5–7. The fate of grass growing in high places

10. *Let them be confounded and thrust away,*[24] *all who hate Zion.* Those who hate Zion hate the Church, for the Church is Zion. And those who enter the Church insincerely hate the Church. Those who will not heed the word of God hate the Church; but all these have wrought upon the Church's back. What is the Church to do except carry them to the very end?

11. But the psalm goes on to suggest what will happen to them: *Let them become like grass on the rooftops that has withered before it is plucked out.* Grass on the rooftops is the kind that sprouts on the top of a house, on an untiled roof exposed to the sun. It is conspicuous on its high place, but it has no roots. How much better off it would have been if it had grown more humbly in the earth[25] and flourished there green and happy! In its lofty site it dries up all the more quickly. It has withered even before anyone pulls it out. So with the proud: they have not yet been finally dealt with[26] at God's judgment, but already they lack the sap needed for any green growth. Only look at their deeds and you will see how withered they are. Yet they are still alive, still here with us; they have not yet been plucked out. They have dried up but are not yet pulled up; they have become *like grass on the rooftops that has withered before it is plucked out.*

12. The harvesters will set to work, but not from such withered grass will they make up their full sheaves. They will come, those harvesters, and gather the wheat into the barn, but they will bind the weeds and throw them onto the bonfire. Grass on the roof is similarly disposed of: whatever is pulled out from there is thrown on the fire, because even before being plucked out it has withered. The harvester does not bother to fill his hand with that. The psalm

---

24. Variant: *and be afraid.*
25. *Humilius*: the word "humility" derives from *humus*, the earth, and here the connection is evident.
26. Variant: "punished."

goes on to say so: *Never has the harvester taken a handful of it, nor the gatherer an armful.* And, as the Lord says, *The harvesters are the angels* (Mt 13:39).

Verse 8. All who have passed along the way have blessed us

And those who pass by along the way have not said, May the blessing of the Lord be upon you; we have blessed you in the name of the Lord. You know well, brothers and sisters, that when people pass by others who are at work, it is customary to greet them by saying, *May the blessing of the Lord be upon you.* This was a very well-established custom among the Jewish people. No one would think of walking past others laboring at some task in a field, or in a vineyard, or at the harvest, or at any such project, without invoking a blessing on them; to omit it was bad manners. Now in the psalm we have two groups of people: the ones gathering sheaves and the ones passing on their way. The sheave-gatherers do not take handfuls of the grass that grows on the rooftops, because it is not collected for storage in the barn. But who are these collectors? The harvesters. And who are the harvesters? The Lord told us: *The harvesters are the angels* (Mt 13:39). And who are the passers-by? Those who have passed along this way: in other words, those who have passed through this life to their homeland. The apostles were passers-by in this life, the prophets too were passers-by. On whom did the prophets and apostles call down a blessing? On those in whom they discerned a root of charity. But when they saw others waving high up on the rooftops, arrogant with their grossly fat necks for shields,[27] they predicted the outcome for such people but invoked no blessing upon them. Accordingly those of you who read the scriptures[28] find all the bad people whom the Church is carrying designated as accursed and as disciples of Antichrist,[29] or as belonging to the devil, or as lumped together with the weeds or the chaff: many things are said about them in figurative language, things beyond counting. It is said of them, for instance, that *not everyone who says, Lord, Lord, will enter*[30] *the kingdom of heaven* (Mt 7:21). You find no passage in scripture that speaks well

---

27. See Jb 15:26.
28. Not all his hearers were literate.
29. See 1 Jn 4:3.
30. Variant: *has entered.*

of them, because those who passed by along the way did not bless them. The prophets passed by and said all kinds of bad things about them. And even David, you see, the writer whom we are studying, he too passed by along the way, and you have heard what he says about them: *The Lord who is just will break the necks of sinners. Let them be confounded and thrust away,*[31] *all who hate Zion. Let them become like grass on the rooftops that has withered before it is plucked out. Never has the harvester taken a handful of it, nor the gatherer an armful.* The psalmist said all this about such people, so it is clear that he himself in his passage through this life did not bless them, and equally clear that he fulfilled his own prophecy by withholding his blessing. *Those who pass by along the way have not said, We have blessed you in the name of the Lord.*

But all these passers-by, brothers and sisters, whether prophets or patriarchs or apostles, or whoever they were who passed along the way, have blessed us in the name of the Lord, if we live as we should. "What?" you ask. "When did Paul bless me? When did Peter bless me?" Look closely into the scriptures and find out there whether your life is what it ought to be, and then you will see that you have been blessed. All who live good lives were blessed by the passers-by. How did they bless us? *In the name of the Lord*, not in their own names, as the heretics do. Those who say, "What we give is holy," are trying to give blessings in their own name, not *in the name of the Lord*. But people who admit that God alone sanctifies, and that no one is good except by God's gift, impart blessings *in the name of the Lord*, not in their own names. The friends of the bridegroom[32] have no wish to seduce his bride.

To the bridegroom let us now turn.[33]

---

31. Variant: *and be afraid.*
32. See Jn 3:29.
33. *Conversi ad sponsum*; probably a phrase inviting the congregation to prayer. Compare *Conversi ad Deum* at Exposition of Psalm 80,22, and *Conversi ad Dominum* at Exposition of Psalm 86,9. Some witnesses omit it in the present context.

Exposition of Psalm 129

A Sermon to the People

Verses 1–3. A sinner cries from the depths, hoping for God's mercy

1. We are taking it for granted that you are fully alert, not only with your bodily eyes open but also with vigilant hearts. It is therefore appropriate that we sing with understanding, *Out of the depths I have cried to you, Lord; O Lord, hear my voice,* for this is the plea of one who is beginning to ascend, and so a Song of Steps is the right place for it. Each one of us must assess what a deep place he or she is in; we must take stock of the depth from which we have to cry to the Lord. Jonah cried out from a very deep place indeed, from the belly of a whale.[1] He was not only submerged under the waves but even hidden in the stomach of a sea monster, yet neither that vast body nor the water blocked his prayer or prevented it from reaching God. Not even the beast's vitals could smother the voice of a man who prayed. It broke down all obstacles, burst its way through, and arrived at God's ears—though perhaps we should not say that it attained God's ears only when all intervening barriers had been broken down, for God's ears were attentive within the heart of him who was praying. Is the voice of any believer raised in prayer if God is not already present?

But in our own case we must be fully aware of the depth from which we need to cry to the Lord. Our depth is our present life, over which death looms menacingly. If we all understand how deep we are, we cry out, groan, and sigh, until we are rescued from our deep place and make our way to him who from his throne above the cherubim beholds all depths.[2] He is seated on high over all he has made, not only above his material creation but even above his spiritual creatures. Our soul groans until it reaches him, until the image of God stamped upon human beings is released by God himself. In these deep places God's image, imprinted upon men and women at their creation, is so roughly tossed about and worn away by the onslaughts of the waves that, unless it is rescued by God and renewed and restored by him, it

---

1. See Jon 2:2 ff.
2. See Dn 3:55, Vg.

remains sunk in the depths for ever, because though men and women were able to effect their own downfall, they cannot bring about their own resurrection. Yet even as they cry out from their deep place they begin to rise from it, for their very plea saves them from the most abysmal place of all. One who does not cry from the depth is very deep indeed.

Scripture tells us that *a person devoid of reverence goes deep into sin and is defiant* (Prv 18:3). Mark well, brothers and sisters, what a depth that is from which a sinner defies God. Someone knows himself to be overwhelmed by daily sins, crushed beneath heaped-up loads of iniquity, and he is urged to offer supplication to God. He ridicules the idea. How does he reply? First he says, "If my villainies were offensive to God, would I be left alive? If God concerned himself with human actions, would I, with all the crimes I have committed, not only be still alive but even prospering?" This is what happens to people deeply sunk in sin: they are successful in their wrongdoing, and plunge yet deeper in the measure that they regard themselves as lucky. Illusory fortune is in truth a greater misfortune. Then such persons proceed to another argument: "I have already committed innumerable sins, and damnation awaits me. So why should I let slip the chance to do all the bad things in my power?"[3] This is the attitude adopted by desperate robbers: "If the judge is going to execute me for ten murders in exactly the same way as for five, or even for one, why shouldn't I do whatever I like?" This is what scripture means by the words, *A person devoid of reverence goes deep into sin and is defiant.*

But our Lord Jesus Christ did not despise us in our depths. He graciously willed to come down into this life of ours, promising us the forgiveness of all our sins, and he aroused human beings to cry out to him even from those deep places where their sins weighed them down, so that the voice of every sinner might reach God. From where else should a sinner cry to him, if not from the depths of misery?

2. Listen now to these voices of sinners shouting from the deep: *Out of the depths I have cried to you, Lord; O Lord, hear my voice. Let your ears be attentive to the voice of my pleading.* Where does this cry come from? From the deep. Who utters it? The sinner. Why can he hope to be heard? Because Christ, who came to do away with sin, has given hope even to a sinner sunk in the deep.

---

3. In other words, "I may as well be hanged for a sheep as for a lamb." A variant adds, "And since I am ruined anyway, why shouldn't I do whatever I can?"

This is why, after his first plea, the sinner continues, *If you take account of our law-breaking, O Lord, Lord, who will stand?* With these words he states plainly the nature of the depths from which he is praying: he is crying out from beneath the massive bulk and surging billows of his own iniquities. He has looked around him and reviewed his life, and on every side he has seen it smothered under disgrace and squalor. Look where he will, he finds nothing good in himself; no reassuring prospect of goodness meets his eye. When he sees such a multitude of grievous sins and the accumulated mass of his misdeeds, he is terrified and cries out, *If you take account of our law-breaking, O Lord, Lord, who will stand?* Notice that he does not say, "I cannot remain standing" but, "Will anyone remain standing?" He has seen the life of almost all humanity beset by sins, as though by dogs barking at it on every side; he has seen the consciences of all men and women accusing them; he has seen that nowhere is there a pure heart that can depend on its own righteousness. If no pure heart can be found, not one that can rely on its own virtue, let the hearts of all of us rely rather on the mercy of God and say to him, *If you take account of our law-breaking, O Lord, Lord, who will stand?*

Verse 4. The law of charity: bear one another's burdens, and forgive if you hope to be forgiven

3. Why is there any hope for us? *Because with you there is propitiation.* What is this propitiation? Surely a propitiatory sacrifice.[4] And what sacrifice is meant if not that which was offered on our behalf? Innocent blood was spilt to efface the sins of all the guilty; an immense price was paid to ransom all captives from the power of the enemy who had imprisoned them. That is why the psalm can say, *With you there is propitiation*, for if no propitiation of you were possible, if you willed to be our judge only and did not will to be merciful, if you took account of our iniquities and sought them out, who could remain standing before you? Who would be able to hold up his head in your presence and say, "I am innocent"? Who could stand his ground at your tribunal? There is but one hope for us, that *with you there is propitiation.*

---

4. See Rom 3:25; compare 1 Jn 2:2; 4:10.

I have held out[5] for you, with your law in view, O Lord. What law is this? The law that only showed us up as guilty? A holy law was given to the Jews, a law that was just and good,[6] but all it could do was convict them. No law was given them that *was capable of giving life* (Gal 3:21), only a law that revealed the sinner to himself.[7] The sinner had forgotten himself and no longer kept his sins in view; he was therefore given a law to help him see himself. The law declared him guilty; only the lawgiver could set him free, for the lawgiver is the sovereign ruler of all. A law was given that can terrify us and lock us into our guilt; it does not free us but merely exposes our sins.

Perhaps it was someone bound by that law, and aware in his deep place how grievous were his transgressions of the law, who cried out in the psalm, *If you take account of our law-breaking, O Lord, Lord, who will stand?* Evidently, then, there is another law, a law of God's mercy, a law whereby God is propitiated. The old law dealt in fear; this new law is a law of charity. The law of charity grants pardon for sins, blots out the past, and cautions us with regard to the future. It keeps us company along the road and never deserts us; it makes itself our companion and leads us along the way. But, remember, we are told to come to terms with our opponent while we are with him on the road,[8] and God's word is your opponent as long as you have not come to terms with it. You reach an agreement with it from the point where you begin to take delight in doing what the word commands you; from that moment the word that was your adversary becomes your friend. If this is how things stand with you, there will be no one to hand you over to the judge at journey's end.

This is why *I have held out for you, with your law in view, O Lord*, for you have graciously appointed for me your law of mercy, forgiven all my sins, and provided me with guidance for the future so that I may not offend you again. If I should falter in any particular as I try to heed your admonitions, you have indicated a remedy for me: I can still pray to you, saying, *Forgive us our debts, as we forgive our debtors* (Mt 6:12). This is the law you have laid upon me, that I shall be forgiven in the measure that I forgive. With this law in view,

---

5. *Sustinui* in Latin is stronger than the English "I have waited for." *Sustinere* implies to "hold out," "hold on," "endure," "maintain," "withstand." Compare Exposition 1 of Psalm 26,14 and the note and Exposition 2 of Psalm 26,23.
6. See Rom 7:12.
7. Variant: "that revealed his sins to the sinner."
8. See Mt 5:25.

I have held out for you, O Lord. I have waited for you to come and rescue me from every predicament, for even in my extreme plight you have not abrogated your law of mercy.

4. Listen now to a plain statement that this is the law in question. If you are not yet convinced that the psalmist envisaged the law of charity, listen to the apostle: *Bear one another's burdens, and so you will fulfil the law of Christ* (Gal 6:2). Who are they who carry each other's burdens? Only those who live in charity. People who have no charity are a heavy burden to each other, but those who have charity carry one another. Suppose someone has injured you and asks pardon: if you do not forgive that person, you are not carrying the burden of your brother or sister; but if you do forgive, you are carrying your weak companion. Then if it happens that you yourself, weak human that you are, fall into some infirmity, it will be your neighbor's turn to carry you, as you did him. This is indicated in the verse that precedes the one we quoted: *My brothers and sisters, if someone is involved in some wrongdoing, you who are spiritual must instruct such a person in a spirit of gentleness* (Gal 6:1). But the apostle was aware that, when addressed as spiritual persons, his hearers might think themselves beyond the reach of temptation, so he immediately added, *But take heed to yourself, lest you be tempted as well* (Gal 6:1). Then he went on to give them the instruction I have already recalled: *Bear one another's burdens, and so you will fulfil the law of Christ.* This is why the psalm too declares, *I have held out for you, with your law in view, O Lord.* It is said that when deer cross a strait to a neighboring island in search of pasture they rest their heads on one another, each on the one in front. Only the deer in the leading position carries the weight of his own head and has no other to rest it on; but when he gets tired he leaves his position and goes around to the rear of the line, where he can rest on another.[9] Thus they carry one another's burdens and reach the place they desire without mishap, because their mutual charity serves them as a sturdy ship.

Charity, then, is a bearer of burdens, but it has no need to fear that the loads will crush it. Rather let each one take care not to be overwhelmed by the weight of his or her own sins. When you bear the infirmity of your brother or sister, his or her sins are not a heavy weight on you—unless, of course, you acquiesce in those sins, but

---

9. Augustine describes this friendly arrangement also in Exposition of Psalm 41,4, and there he quotes the same Pauline text.

then it will be your own sins that weigh you down, not someone else's. If anyone consents to the doings of a sinner, he is burdened not by the other's sins but by his own, for by consenting to another's sin you commit sin yourself, and then you have no reason to complain that other people's sins are onerous to you. It will be said to you, with good reason, "Onerous they are, but they are yours. You saw a thief, and went along with him."[10] What does that mean? With your feet you walked to the scene of the crime, but with your mind you associated yourself with the theft. The deed that was originally his alone has become yours as well, because you approved it.

But if you disapprove of it, pray for the thief, and grant pardon when you are asked to, you will be in a position to stand unashamed before God and make with him in your prayer the bargain dictated to you by one skilled in the law of heaven: *Forgive us our debts as we forgive our debtors* (Mt 6:12). You will have learned to bear the burdens of your brother or sister, so that someone else may bear yours, if any there be. Then the apostle's injunction will be obeyed, *Bear one another's burdens, and so you will fulfil the law of Christ* (Gal 6:2). And then too you will be able to sing with confidence what has been said in the psalm, *I have held out for you, with your law in view, O Lord*.

5. If anyone does not obey this law, he either does not hold out for the Lord at all or, if he wishes to hold out hopefully, he has no ground for doing so. His hopeful expectation has no basis. The Lord will come and will uncover your sins. What he will not find is any perfectly righteous living on your part. It may be that he will not discover in you any grave or very heinous sins: perhaps he will not find you guilty of murder, or adultery, or theft, or robbery, or sorcery, or idolatry. No, he will not convict you of any of these. Does that mean he will find nothing to condemn? Listen to the gospel: *If anyone says to his brother, You fool!* Does anyone avoid even these tiny sins[11] of the tongue? Perhaps you will say, "But they are only slight." Yet scripture continues, *He will be liable to hell fire* (Mt 5:22). If saying "you fool" to your brother seems to you a slight and trivial thing, let hell fire convince you of its gravity. If you scorned it as a little sin, at least be deterred from it by the magnitude of the punishment. But still you argue, "These are inconsequential, unimportant faults. Human

---

10. See Ps 49(50):16.
11. Variant: "very savage sins."

life cannot be entirely free of them." Heap together many tiny objects and they form a great pile. Grains of wheat are individually tiny, but they add up to an enormous harvest; drops of water are tiny, but they fill the rivers and sweep away huge rocks.

The psalmist must have been thinking how many of these small daily sins a person commits, at least in thought and with the tongue, if in no other way. He reflects on how numerous they are, and if he regards them as individually slight he is also aware that these innumerable small sins form a mighty heap. He is thinking not only of his own past sins but of the fragility of all human beings, and so as he begins his ascent he sends forth his prayer, *Out of the depths I have cried to you, Lord; O Lord, hear my voice. Let your ears be attentive to the voice of my pleading. If you take account of our law-breaking, O Lord, Lord, who will stand?* I can keep clear of murder, adultery, robbery, perjury, sorcery, idolatry. But can I also avoid sins of the tongue? Or sins committed in the heart? No. It is written, *Sin is breaking God's law* (1 Jn 3:4). *Who*, then, *will stand, if you take account of our law-breaking?* If you decide to deal with us as a severe judge, instead of acting as a merciful father, who will stand his ground in your sight? Yet *with you there is propitiation, and I have held out for you, with your law in view, O Lord.* What law is in question here? *Bear one another's burdens, and so you will fulfil the law of Christ.* Who are they, these bearers of each other's burdens? Those who pray with sincerity, *Forgive us our debts as we forgive our debtors.*

6. *My soul has held out in hope for your word.* The only person who holds out hopefully for something is one who has not yet received what was promised. If one has received it already, why hold out further in expectation? We have received forgiveness for our sins, but we have been promised the kingdom of heaven. Our debts have been canceled, but our reward is still delayed. Pardon is ours already, but we do not yet possess eternal life. If our hope were grounded in any word of our own we would rightly be anxious, but the word is God's, and it cannot deceive. In unshakable hope we wait for the word of him who cannot play us false.

Verses 5–6. Hoping from the morning watch means hoping to share in Christ's resurrection

From the morning watch even until night, my soul has hoped in the Lord. What is he saying? That he hoped in God for the space of one day only, and that was the sum total of his hope? That he hoped in the Lord only from the morning watch until nightfall? The morning watch marks the end of night. Did he hope in the Lord only from that point until night came again? This verse certainly needs to be understood correctly, for we must not suppose that our hope in the Lord should endure for one day only, *from the morning watch even until night*. What do you think it means, brothers and sisters?

The psalm says, *From the morning watch even until night, my soul has hoped in the Lord*, because at the morning watch the Lord, through whom our sins have been forgiven, rose from the dead. So we must hope that what has taken place in the Lord first of all may be realized also in ourselves. Our sins are forgiven already, but we have not yet risen from the dead. And since this is so, what took place in our head has not yet come to pass in us. What was it that first happened in our head? His own flesh, the flesh that belonged to our head, rose again. His spirit never died, but that part of him that did die rose again. He arose on the third day; and now the Lord seems to be saying to us, "What you have seen accomplished in me, hope for in yourselves." That is to say, "There will be a resurrection for you:[12] you too will arise."

7. But some people say, "Well, yes, the Lord rose again, but is that any reason for me to hope that I can rise too?" Yes, that is precisely the reason. The Lord rose in the nature which he received from you. He could not have risen unless he had first died, and he could not have died unless he had borne your flesh. What did the Lord take from you? Flesh. What was he in himself, he who came to us? The Word of God, which existed before all beings, through which all beings were made.[13] But in order to receive something from you, *the Word was made flesh, and dwelt among us* (Jn 1:14). He took from you something that he could offer for you, just as a priest takes from you something which he will offer on your behalf when you want to appease God for your sins. That was what happened with Christ, exactly that. Our priest took from us what he was to offer for our sake. He received flesh from us, and in that flesh he became a victim, he became a holocaust, he was made into a sacrifice. In his passion he became our sacrifice, but in his resurrection he restored to newness the flesh that had been slain and gave it back to God as the first-fruits of your humanity. He says to you, "See now, everything that is yours is consecrated, because

---

12. Variant: "I have risen."
13. See Jn 1:3.

these first-fruits of your nature have been dedicated to God. Hope, therefore, that what has been done in advance with respect to your first-fruits will come to completion in yourself one day."

Hoping even until night means hoping until the end of your life or the end of the world

8. Since Christ arose at the *morning watch*, our soul begins to hope in him from that moment. But how long must we continue? *Even until night*, which means until we die, for the death of every carnal creature is like a falling asleep. You began to hope from the moment when the Lord rose; do not stop hoping until you leave this life. If you do not go on hoping until night comes, all that you earlier hoped for will be lost. There are people who begin to hope but give up before nightfall. They begin to experience various kinds of trouble, temptations beset them, and they observe bad, unjust people radiant with temporal good fortune. They themselves entertained similar hopes, believing that the Lord would make them happy and successful in this world. Yet now they observe others who have committed flagrant sins enjoying the good things they hoped to have, and therefore they lose their footing and give up hope.

Why does this happen? Because their hope did not really spring *from the morning watch*. What do I mean by that? What they began to hope for from the Lord was not the destiny that first of all shone forth in the Lord himself at the time of that morning watch. On the contrary, what they hoped to gain from him was something different: that as a reward for their being Christians their homes would be full of grain, wine, oil, silver, and gold; that no one in their families would die prematurely; that any who were childless would have children; that anyone not yet married would find a wife; that not only would no woman in their households miscarry but that not even any one of their cattle would lose its young; that the wine in no one's cask would turn sour; and that no one's vineyard would be battered by hail. If these are the kinds of things a Christian hopes to gain from the Lord, he will notice that other people, who do not worship the Lord, have plenty of such goods. Then his feet will begin to slip.[14] He has failed to go on hoping *even until night* because he did not begin *from the morning watch*.

---

14. See Ps 72(73):2.

9. Who, then, are the ones who begin to hope *from the morning watch*? Those who hope to obtain from the Lord what he first displayed in himself *from the morning watch*, when he rose from the dead. Before that day, remember, no one had ever risen from the dead to live for ever. Pay careful attention to this point, beloved. Dead people had sometimes been raised even before the Lord's coming, for Elijah raised a dead child[15] and so did Elisha,[16] but these children arose only to die again later. Even those dead persons brought back to life by the Lord himself arose only to die again. Whether we think of the young man who was the son of a widow,[17] or of the twelve-year-old daughter of the president of the synagogue,[18] or of Lazarus,[19] the same is true: the circumstances were different in each of these cases, but they were all brought back to life only to die again later. They were born once but died twice. One, and one only, rose never to die again,[20] and that was the Lord. But when did the Lord rise from the dead, never to die? In the *morning watch*. And this is what you must hope to win from the Lord for yourself too: that you will rise again, but not as Lazarus rose, nor as the widow's son rose, nor as the daughter of the president of the synagogue rose, nor as those children rose who were brought back to life by the ancient prophets. You must hope to rise again as the Lord rose, so that after your resurrection you need never again fear death. If you hope like that, you have begun to hope *from the morning watch*.

10. But go on hoping *even until night*, until this life ends, until night falls upon the whole human race at the sunset of this world. Why must our hope last until then? Because after that nightfall there will be no place for hope any longer, only for the reality. *If hope is seen, it is not hope*, the apostle teaches, *for when someone sees what he hopes for, why should he hope for it? But if we hope for what we do not see, we wait for it in patience.* (Rom 8:24–25) If then our job is to wait in patience for what we do not see, let us hope *even until night*, even to the end of our lives or the end of the world. But when that night has passed, what we were hoping for will come, and then we shall hope no more. But that does not mean we shall be hopeless people!

---

15. See 1 Kgs 17:19–23.
16. See 2 Kgs 4:32–36.
17. See Lk 7:11–15.
18. See Mk 5:38–43.
19. See Jn 11:38–44.
20. See Rom 6:9.

To call someone hopeless is a way of insulting him; we sometimes curse somebody by saying he is hopeless. But it is not always a bad thing to be without hope. In this present life it is, certainly: it is bad to have no hope now, for anyone who has no hope here will not have the reality hereafter. We must have hope during this present life. But when the reality has come, there will be no place for hope, will there? *When someone sees what he hopes for, why should he hope for it?* The Lord our God will come, and what he will first of all display to the human race is the human form in which he was crucified and in which he rose again, so that he may be seen by both devout believers and godless unbelievers. Let the former see and be joyfully thankful that they have found at last what they believed in before they saw it; but let the others be shamed because they did not believe in what they now see. The unbelievers will to their chagrin be condemned, the joyful will be crowned. To the former in their shame the Lord will say, *Depart from me into the eternal fire which was prepared for the devil and his angels.* To the rejoicing he will say, *Come, you who are blessed by my Father, take possession of the kingdom prepared for you since the creation of the world* (Mt 25:41.34), and once they have taken possession of that kingdom there will be nothing left to hope for, because they will grasp the reality. When hope has become obsolete, the night will be over too; but until this happens, let our souls hope in the Lord *from the morning watch* onward.

The true hope of the true Israel

11. Now the psalm takes up the same words again: *From the morning watch*[21] *let Israel hope in the Lord*, as the psalmist has already testified in his own case that *from the morning watch even until night, my soul has hoped in the Lord.* But what did it hope for? Now the psalm prays, *From the morning watch let Israel hope in the Lord.* Israel is not only to hope in the Lord but specifically to hope in him *from the morning watch.* Am I condemning hope for worldly advantages, if God is besought to grant them? No, but there is another kind of hope proper to Israel. It is not Israel's true calling to hope for riches or bodily health or an abundance of earthly assets, as though such things were its supreme good; on the contrary, it may well experience distress on earth if its lot is to undergo persecution for the truth. The martyrs cannot be accused of any lack of hope in

---

21. A variant inserts *even until night.*

God, can they? Yet they suffered the same fate as robbers and other criminals. They were made to confront wild beasts, they were burnt, put to the sword, lacerated with hooks, chained and fettered, and killed by the conditions of their imprisonment. They endured all such torments. Does that mean they had not been hoping in the Lord? Or that they had hoped in him only to be freed from their ill-treatment and allowed to enjoy this present life? Certainly not. It means that they did indeed hope but that their hope sprang *from the morning watch*. In other words, they turned their eyes toward that dawn watch when their Lord rose, and they saw that before his resurrection he had endured the same kind of torments that they were undergoing. Therefore they did not give up hope that after their sufferings they would rise again to eternal life. *From the morning watch even until night has Israel hoped in the Lord.*

Verses 7–8. Hope only in the redemptive mercy of God

12. *Because with the Lord there is mercy, and with him is plenteous redemption.* A magnificent saying! Nothing more appropriate could have been said in this context, where we have just heard the words, *From the morning watch*[22] *let Israel hope in the Lord.* Why? Because the Lord rose at *the morning watch*, and the body must hope to participate in the resurrection accomplished first in its head. Yet to some the thought may occur, "It was all very well for the head to rise again, for he was burdened by no sins at all; there was no sin in him. But what about us? Can we hope for a resurrection like the Lord's, weighed down as we are by our sins?"

Look what the next verse has to say to that. *With the Lord there is mercy, and with him is plenteous redemption. He will redeem*[23] *Israel from all its iniquities.* If Israel's sins seemed like a crushing load, the mercy of God is ready to hand. Our sinless Lord went ahead of us in order to blot out the sins of those who follow. Do not trust in yourselves, but trust *from the morning watch*. Behold your head, who has risen and ascended into heaven. He was faultless, but through him your faults will be effaced, for *he will redeem*[24] *Israel from all its iniquities.* Israel had the power to sell itself, to deliver itself into

---

22. A variant adds *even until night*.
23. Variant: *has redeemed*.
24. Variant: *has redeemed*, and so in the repetition of this verse in the following lines.

slavery under sin, but it had no power to buy itself back from its iniquities. He alone, who could not sell himself, had the power to ransom us. He who committed no sin is our redeemer from sin. *He will redeem Israel*. From what? From this or that particular iniquity? No: *from all its iniquities*.

Anyone who aspires to draw near to God need therefore have no fear concerning any of his iniquities; all he need do is approach wholeheartedly and stop committing those sins. He must not say, "That special iniquity of mine is not forgiven." If he says that, he proves that he is not fully converted, and then he will go on committing other sins and will forfeit the pardon he could have had even for those in respect of which he did not doubt forgiveness. "I have committed so grave a sin that forgiveness is impossible in my case," he will say. "So why should I not go on and commit others? Why should I waste those opportunities?"[25]

Do not be afraid. You are in the deep, but do not be ashamed to call out to the Lord from your depths and say to him, *If you take account of our law-breaking, O Lord, Lord, who will stand?* Keep your eyes on him, wait for him, hold out and hold on, because of his law. What was the law he laid down for you? *Forgive us our debts as we forgive our debtors*. Hold onto the hope that you will rise again and that you will then be free from sin because he who was the first to be without sin has risen from the dead. Draw hope *from the morning watch*. Do not say, "I am unworthy to rise again because of my sins." Unworthy you certainly are, but *with him is plenteous redemption. He will redeem Israel from all its iniquities.*

---

25. A portrait of despair, like the one sketched earlier in section 1.

Exposition of Psalm 130

A Sermon to the People

In Christ's body, the true temple, acceptable prayer is offered

1. This psalm brings to our attention the humility of a servant of God, a faithful servant whose voice rings out here and who stands for the entire body of Christ. We have often pointed out to you, beloved, that a psalm must not be understood as the prayer of a lone singer but as the prayer of all who are within Christ's body. Being members of his body, they all speak like a single individual; the many are one in him who is one. This body is also God's temple, of which the apostle says, *God's temple is holy, and that temple is yourselves* (1 Cor 3:17). All who believe in Christ form the temple—at least, all who believe in him in such a way as to love him. Truly to believe in Christ means to love Christ. The demons believed quite differently,[1] for their belief implied no love for him, and therefore in spite of their belief they demanded, *What have we in common with you, Son of God?* (Mt 8:29) Let us so believe in him that our faith is full of love for him. It is not for us to cry, *What have we in common with you?* Rather let us confess, "We belong to you. You have redeemed us."

All who believe in this way are like the living stones from which God's temple is built.[2] They are like the rot-proof wood used in the construction of the ark,[3] to prevent it from sinking in the flood. Believers form the temple in which prayer is offered to God and heard by him. If a person prays anywhere else than in this temple, he is not heard in a way that would bring him to the heavenly peace of Jerusalem,[4] even if he is heard when he prays for various temporal goods, which God

---

1. See Jas 2:19.
2. See 1 Pt 2:5.
3. See Gn 6:14 for the coating of Noah's ark with pitch, which is apparently what Augustine is thinking of here. Tradition also suggested that another ark, the ark of the covenant (see Ex 25:10), was made from rot-proof wood; this latter belief was applied symbolically to Christ and the Blessed Virgin Mary. Augustine refers to this idea in Exposition of Psalm 131, 15.
4. Variant: "the peace of the heavenly Jerusalem."

has given[5] even to pagans. After all, even the petition of the demons was granted when they begged to go into the pigs.[6] To be heard in a way conducive to eternal life is something quite different, and it is granted only to one who prays in the temple of God. But the only petitioner who prays in God's temple is the one who prays within the peace of the Church, within the unity of Christ's body. The body consists of a vast number of believers all over the world; and only a person who prays in this temple is heard by God. Prayer offered in the ancient temple, which was no more than a type, was not necessarily prayer in spirit and truth. The one who worships in spirit and truth[7] is the person who prays within the peace of the Church.

The cords of sin

2. The Lord performed a symbolic action in throwing certain people out of the temple,[8] those who went there to seek their own ends, to use the temple for buying and selling. That temple was only a figure, yet it is quite clear that even the real temple which it signified, the body of Christ, contains buyers and sellers mingling with the rest, people who pursue their own ends, not those of Jesus Christ.[9] But they are excluded[10] with a scourge made of cords. Cords symbolize sins, as the prophet suggests: *Woe to those who drag out their sins into a long cord* (Is 5:18). The people who drag out their sins into a long cord are they who add sins to sins: having committed one sin they commit another to cover it up. A cord is made by adding fiber to fiber, but no strand goes in straight: it is twisted into the cord. So too, when all those disgraceful, sinful actions are combined, and sin added to sin, sin twisted with further sin, the result is a long cord for people whose paths are tortuous and whose steps are crooked.[11] What is such a cord good for except to bind them hand and foot, ready to be cast out into the darkness? You remember how this was said to be the fate of a certain sinner in the gospel: *Bind his hands and feet, and throw him into the darkness outside, where there will be weeping and gnashing of teeth* (Mt 22:13). There would not have been any

---

5. Variant: "has made and given."
6. See Mt 8:31–32.
7. See Jn 4:23.
8. See Jn 2:15–16.
9. See Ph 2:21.
10. Variant: "will be excluded."
11. See Jb 6:18.

cord to bind his hands and feet, had he not made it for himself. This is why scripture says explicitly in another passage, *Each one of us is bound by the fine hairs of his own sins* (Prv 5:22). It was to show that people are scourged by their own sins that the Lord made a whip out of cords and used it to cast out of the temple all who were pursuing their own ends, not those of Jesus Christ.

Let us hear our own voice in the psalm

3. The voice of the true temple resounds in the psalm. As I have explained already, it is in this temple, not in the one that prefigured it, that prayer is offered to God in spirit and in truth,[12] and here that prayer is heard. The former temple was only a shadowy representation, designed to show what was to come, and now it has crumbled. Does this mean that our house of prayer has crumbled? No, of course not. That old temple, now ruined, was not the real house of prayer of which a prophet foretold, *My house shall be called a house of prayer for all nations* (Is 56:7). Now you heard the Lord Jesus Christ declaring, *It is written, My house shall be called a house of prayer for all nations; but you have turned it into a den of robbers* (Mk 11:17). But did those who tried to turn God's house into a robbers' den bring about its collapse? By no means. Nor do those who lead unworthy lives in the Catholic Church, and do their level best to make it a robbers' den, overthrow our temple. The time will come when they will be thrown out of it, bound by the cords of their sins.

But this temple of God, this body of Christ, this assembly of the faithful, has but one voice and sings like one individual in the psalm. We have heard its voice in many psalms; now let us hear it again in this one. If only we want it to be so, it is our own voice; if we are willing we can hear the singer's voice with our ears and sing along with it in our hearts. If we refuse, we shall be like the buyers and sellers in that temple of old, seeking our own selfish ends: we may come into this church, but not for any purpose that is pleasing in the sight of God. Let each one of you, then, consider how he or she is listening. Are you listening in order to ridicule that voice or to hear the message only to thrust it behind your back? Or are you listening in order to attune your own voice to that of the singer, and know the singer's voice as your own, and let the voice of your heart chime in with the voice of the psalm? Whichever way it is for you, the voice

---

12. See Jn 4:23.

of the psalm will not fall silent. Let those who can—or, rather, those who choose to—be instructed by it; and let those who are unwilling not hinder the others. Let us learn from it about humility. It begins:

Verse 1. Humility of heart is a sacrifice offered to God

4. *O Lord, my heart is not exalted.* The psalmist has offered a sacrifice. How can we prove that? Because humility of heart is a sacrifice. In another psalm the speaker testifies, *If you had wanted a sacrifice I would certainly have offered it.* He wanted to make satisfaction to God for his sins; he wanted to propitiate God so as to win pardon. Looking around for a means of propitiating God, he declared, *If you had wanted a sacrifice I would certainly have offered it; but you take no pleasure in holocausts* (Ps 50:18(51:16)). It was no use looking for rams or goats or any such victims if he wanted to appease God. What was he to do? If God takes no pleasure in holocausts, does that mean that no sacrifice is acceptable to him? No, for if there is no sacrifice there can be no priest; but we know we have a priest in heaven who intercedes for us[13] with the Father. He has entered into the holy of holies, beyond the veil, where in the liturgy of the figurative temple[14] the high priest entered only once a year, as our Lord also was offered once only, at one moment in history. He offered himself, he who was both priest and victim, and entered once for all into the holy of holies. He can never die again, *nor will death ever again have mastery over him* (Rom 6:9). Let us then be without anxiety,[15] for we have our priest. The place where we must offer our sacrifice is where he is.

We must find out what kind of sacrifice is expected of us, since our God takes no pleasure in holocausts, as you heard in the other psalm. But its next words indicated what kind of sacrifice was to be offered: *A sacrifice to God is a troubled spirit. A contrite and humbled heart God does not scorn* (Ps 50:19(51:17)). We conclude then that if a humbled heart is a sacrifice to God, the psalmist who said, *O Lord, my heart is not exalted,* offered a true sacrifice. He offers himself in the same way in another psalm, where he says to God, *Look upon my humility and my toil, and forgive all my sins* (Ps 24(25):18).

---

13. See Rom 8:34; Heb 7:25.
14. See Heb 9:11–12; 6:19.
15. Variant: "We are without anxiety."

Do not covet the power to work miracles; the story of Simon Magus

5. *O Lord, my heart is not exalted, nor my eyes raised high. Never have I walked in great matters, or in wonders above me.* We had better express this more simply, to make sure everyone understands. It means, "I have not been proud, I have not tried to make a name for myself among other people by pretending to understand wonders above me; nor have I sought to do anything beyond my powers in order to show off to the ignorant." Pay careful attention here, beloved, for an important point is being made. We are reminded of the magician, Simon,[16] who certainly did aspire to walk in wonders above him. He was keener to acquire the power of the apostles than to imitate the holy lifestyle of the Christians. Seeing that God conferred the Holy Spirit upon believers when the apostles laid hands on them and prayed, and that the coming of the Holy Spirit was manifested by their all speaking in tongues they had never learned, Simon wanted to wield the same power as did the apostles; but he did not want to be like them. (We should notice, by the way, that although believers no longer speak in strange tongues, this does not mean that the Holy Spirit is not given nowadays. Speaking in tongues was necessary then as a prophetic sign that peoples of all languages would believe in Christ; but this prophecy has now been fulfilled, so the miracle no longer occurs.) Simon envied the power of the apostles and, as you know, he tried to buy the Holy Spirit with money.[17] He was one of the band who enter the temple for the purpose of buying and selling: he wanted to buy something he planned to sell later. Indeed, brothers and sisters, because he was that sort of person and had come in with that intention, all the more clear is it why the Lord cast out[18] of the temple those who sold doves, for the dove is a symbol of the Holy Spirit. Simon was hoping to buy and sell that dove, but the Lord Jesus Christ, who dwelt in Peter,[19] broke in with his whip of cords and ejected that dishonest trader.

---

16. See Acts 8:18-24.
17. Whence the name of the sin of simony.
18. *Adeo Dominus illos expulit.* Variants: *ideo* ("therefore the Lord"); *ad eum/eos* ("the Lord cast out to him/them").
19. Variant: "dwelt in the temple of Peter."

Diversity of function is necessary within the body

6. There are people like that, you see, people who hanker after the power to work miracles and demand miraculous powers from those who are more advanced in the Church.[20] By making such demands they show that they have a favorable estimate of the spiritual progress they have made themselves; but they want to match the achievements of others in this sphere, and they imagine that if they cannot do so it must mean that they do not belong to God. But the Lord our God well knows what gifts he wills to give to each, and he is careful to maintain the organic unity of the body in peace. He therefore reminds us through the apostle, *The eye cannot say to the hand, I do not need you, or the head to the feet, I do not need you. If the body were all eye, how would it hear? If it were all hearing, how would it smell?* (1 Cor 12:21.17) You know how true this is of our bodily members, brothers and sisters: you observe how each has its own function. The eye sees but cannot hear; the ear hears but does not see; the hand works but neither hears nor sees; the foot walks, but it neither hears nor sees nor performs the tasks at which the hand is adept. But within a single body, provided that its health is good and its members are not fighting each other, the ear sees through the agency of the eye, and the eye hears through the ear. You cannot reproach the ear for its inability to see; you cannot say to it, "You are nothing, you are quite unimportant. You can't see or distinguish colors as the eye does, can you?" The ear will reply from its secure place within the peace of the body, "I am in the same body, part of the same organism, as the eye. By myself I do not see, but I see in the eye, with whom I am part of the whole." Just as the ear can say, "The eye sees for me," so can the eye say, "The ear hears for me." Eyes and ears together say, "The hands work for us," and the hands say, "Eyes and ears see and hear for us." Eyes and ears and hands say, "The feet walk for us." When all of them work together within the one body, and there is health and good coordination, the members rejoice individually and rejoice in each other.[21] If some injury is sustained by one member, they do not abandon the injured part but suffer together. In our bodies the foot seems to be very distant from the eyes, for the eyes are in the highest position and the feet low down. Yet if it happens that the foot treads

---

20. Variant: "to work miracles; you find some who are more advanced in the Church demanding miraculous powers."
21. See 1 Cor 12:26.

on a thorn,[22] do the eyes ignore it and regard it as none of their business? Do we not rather watch the whole body shudder? The sufferer sits down, and the spine in his back bends over as he looks for the spiny object that has lodged in the sole of his foot. All the members collaborate and make the best contribution they can, so that from that lowly, inconspicuous place the thorn may be extracted.

Now apply this to the body of Christ, brothers and sisters. If someone within the body has no power to raise the dead, let him not seek that power lest he cause dissension in the body, as the ear might if it tried to see. If a member has not been given a particular faculty, it cannot perform that operation. But suppose it is reproached for its lack of ability and someone says to a member of Christ's body, "If you were holy you would be able to raise the dead, as Peter did."[23] After all, it looks as though the apostles, by abiding in Christ, worked greater miracles than the Lord himself.[24] But how is it possible for the twigs to do better than the root? How did it happen that they seemed to have performed greater wonders than he did? Dead people rose at the Lord's command, but a dead person rose when Peter's passing shadow fell upon him.[25] This looks like the mightier miracle. But Christ could work his without Peter, whereas Peter could not have done it if he had not been living in Christ. As the Lord told them, *Without me you can do nothing* (Jn 15:5). Well now, suppose, as we have said, a member of Christ's body is taunted for his or her inability to raise the dead. If this person is one well advanced in spiritual understanding, the reproach will be recognized for what it is: a calumny urged by uninstructed pagans, by people who do not know what they are talking about. The Christian so addressed will reply from within the unity of Christ's body, "What do you mean by saying, 'You can't be holy because you don't work miracles'? Would you say to the ear, 'You aren't part of the body because you can't see'?" The accuser persists, "But you should be able to do what Peter did." "But Peter did it on my behalf, because I am within the same body as Peter, the body in which he did it. In this body I can do whatever he can do. I am not separated from him. If my power is slighter, he has compassion for my weakness; if he is more powerful, I am delighted for him."

---

22. *Spina* in Latin. Augustine is about to make a pun on two kinds of spine.
23. See Acts 9:40–41.
24. See Jn 14:12.
25. See Acts 5:15.

The Lord himself, the very Lord in heaven, cried out from on high on behalf of his body, *Saul, Saul why are you persecuting me?* (Acts 9:4) No one was touching him, but the head shouted from heaven for his body struggling on earth.

The serious danger of pride over graces received: Paul's humiliation

7. We can see now, brothers and sisters, that if each of us honestly does what he can, not envying anyone else who can do more but rejoicing with that other member inasmuch as both of them are united in the same body, he can claim as his own the opening words of this psalm, *O Lord, my heart is not exalted, nor my eyes raised high. Never have I walked in great matters, or in wonders above me.* "Some things exceed my powers," he says. "I have not sought them or overreached myself to achieve them. I have not tried to enhance my reputation in that way." To glorify ourselves over the abundant graces we have received is a danger of which we must be extremely wary. No one must be proud over any gift of God, but rather preserve humility[26] and obey the injunction given by scripture, *The greater you are, the more deeply you are to humble yourself; then you will find favor with God* (Sir 3:20). I cannot emphasize enough to you, beloved, how perilous it is to be proud about any gift received from God. I need to remind you of this again and again, and now a very short psalm like the present one gives me the chance to speak more fully on the subject.

The apostle Paul had been a persecutor before he became a preacher, yet he received more abundant grace for the work of the apostolate than did the other apostles, because God wished to demonstrate that the gifts were from him, not derived from any human source. Doctors like to prove their healing skills by treating desperate cases, and so did our physician and savior, the Lord Jesus Christ. He demonstrated the magnitude of his healing power in the desperate case of a man who had been a persecutor of the Church, for he made him not only a Christian but an apostle too, and not just an apostle like the others but one who worked harder than any of them, as he says himself.[27] Paul was evidently endowed with outstanding grace. You notice, brothers and sisters, that Paul's letters are still

---

26. Variant: "preserve it with humility."
27. See 1 Cor 15:10.

fresh and seasonable in the Church today, more so than those of his fellow apostles, for the others did not so much write as speak to the Church. (There are some works masquerading under the names of other apostles, which persons deceived by error bring forward, but these are apocryphal and the Church does not accept them.) Others among the apostles did write letters, but they did not write as much as Paul or with such great grace. Paul, then, was a man of extraordinary grace who had been found worthy to receive great gifts from God. And what does he tell us in one of his letters? *To make sure that I would not grow conceited over these great revelations.* Did you hear that? It is something awe-inspiring that I am recalling to you. *To make sure that I would not grow conceited over these great revelations, a sting of the flesh was sent to me, a messenger of Satan to buffet me* (2 Cor 12:7). What is this about, brothers and sisters? In order to prevent Paul from growing conceited, as a young man might, he was beaten like a child! And by whom? By Satan's envoy. What was done to him? He is said to have been intensely afflicted by some bodily pain.[28] Physical suffering is often inflicted by Satan's messengers, but they cannot do it unless permitted by God. Holy Job was tested in this way. Satan was given leave to try him and struck him with a disease that caused corruption and worms.[29] The unclean spirit was given free rein, but the holy man was being proved. The devil fails to realize how much good results from his savage attacks. He savagely entered the heart of Judas,[30] savagely handed Christ over to his enemies, and savagely caused him to be crucified. But through Christ's crucifixion the whole wide world was redeemed. The devil's savagery led to the devil's own loss but to our gain, for his captives were lost to him, ransomed by the blood of the Lord which the devil had savagely spilt. If he had understood how immense a loss he was to sustain, would he have poured out onto the earth the ransom-price of the human race?

There is an analogy here with Paul's case. An envoy of Satan was given leave to knock the apostle about and to enjoy himself in doing so, it seems. Yet the apostle was healed thereby. The remedy applied by the doctor was painful to the patient, and he begged the doctor to

---

28. There are other theories about the nature of Paul's "sting of the flesh." Some refer it to the hostility to which he was exposed by some of his own kin.
29. See Jb 2:7.
30. See Jn 13:2.

remove it. You know how a doctor sometimes applies to the patient's vital parts a painful, scalding poultice in an effort to reduce swelling. As soon as the patient begins to feel the heat and to suffer agony from the application, he begs and implores the doctor to remove it. But the physician comforts him and counsels patience,[31] because he knows how efficacious the poultice will be. It was like this with the apostle. *A sting of the flesh was sent to me, a messenger of Satan to buffet me,* he says, and you remember he had told us why he needed it: *To make sure that I would not grow conceited over these great revelations, a sting of the flesh was sent to me, a messenger of Satan to buffet me.* But then he continued, *Three times I begged the Lord to take it away from me.* This is like saying, "I begged the doctor to take off the painful poultice he had put on me." But listen to the physician's reply: *He said to me, My grace is sufficient for you, for my power is fully deployed in weakness.* (2 Cor 12:7-9) "I know what I have put on you; I know the nature of your sickness; I know how you will be cured."

The important thing is to be a healthy member whose name is written in heaven

8. Consider this, dearly beloved: If in the absence of any messenger from Satan sent to buffet him, the apostle Paul could have been in danger of getting above himself owing to his sublime revelations, who can feel secure about his or her own situation? It seems as though a person who has been given less treads a safer path. But even if such a person does not misguidedly hanker after what has, for good reasons, been denied him, he must certainly seek a gift without which he cannot be within Christ's body, or at any rate cannot be there in the right way. It is safer to be a healthy finger than a watering eye. A finger is an insignificant member, while an eye is wonderful and has splendid powers; but it is better to be only a finger and healthy than to be an eye that is inflamed, discharging, or going blind. No one should seek anything in Christ's body except health, and in order to be healthy we need faith. Each of us needs faith, for by faith the heart is purified,[32] and only through the purification of our hearts shall we see the face of God. As scripture tells us, *Blessed are the pure of heart, for they shall see God* (Mt 5:8). There is only one

---

31. Variant: "and patiently advises him."
32. See Acts 15:9.

cause for joy, common to those in Christ's body who work miracles and to those who do not: namely, the prospect of seeing God face to face. After the apostles had been sent on a mission by the Lord they came back to him and reported, *Lord, even demons submitted to us in your name!* (Lk 10:17) The Lord saw that pride in their power to work miracles could be a temptation to them. He had come as a physician to cure our swollen pride[33] and to carry our infirmities,[34] and so he promptly warned them, *Do not rejoice over the demons' subjection to you; rejoice because your names have been written in heaven* (Lk 10:20). Not all good Christians cast out demons, but the names of all of them are written in heaven. Christ did not want the apostles to rejoice over something they had which distinguished them from others but rather over the salvation that was theirs in common with the rest. The apostle wanted to be joyful[35] over the same thing that gives you joy. Make sure you grasp this, beloved: there is no hope for any believer unless his or her name is written in heaven. All the faithful who love Christ and walk humbly in the way that he, our humble Lord, taught us, have their names inscribed in heaven. The name of every abject member of the Church, who believes in Christ and holds Christ dear and loves Christ's peace, is written in heaven; this is true of everyone, even though you think him or her beneath your notice. What resemblance is there between this lowly person and the apostles who worked such dazzling miracles? Yet the apostles are chided for making a gift proper to themselves a matter for joy and are bidden to be glad about what inspires joy equally in this lowly believer whom they disdain.

Verse 2. Be nourished on milk until you are ready for bread; do not follow the heretics in aspiring to bread too soon

9. You see then, brothers and sisters, that the psalmist had good reason to say, *O Lord, my heart is not exalted, nor my eyes raised high. Never have I walked in great matters, or in wonders above me. If I was not lowly in mind, but spiritually high-flown, may retribution come upon my soul as on a baby in its mother's arms that is torn away from its milk*. He has bound himself, you see, by an imprecation. This is the same idiom that we find in another psalm: *Lord my God, if I*

---

33. *Tumores nostros*. A variant has *mores nostros* ("our behavior/morals").
34. See Is 53:4; Mt 8:17.
35. Paul. A variant has: "He [Christ] wanted the apostles to be joyful."

have done this, if there is any iniquity on my hands, if I have repaid those who have paid me back with evil, let me fall deservedly before my enemies (Ps 7:4–5(3–4)), and so on. The speaker in the present psalm seems to make the same kind of bargain with God: *If I was not lowly in mind, but spiritually high-flown*, then, he seems to say, let the following fate overtake me. In the earlier psalm the speaker did the same: *If I have repaid those who have paid me back with evil*, let this happen to me. What fate did he envisage? *Let me fall deservedly before my enemies*. So too here. *If I was not lowly in mind, but spiritually high-flown, may retribution come upon my soul as on a baby in its mother's arms that is torn away from its milk*. Pay careful attention to the simile he uses. You know that the apostle said to certain shaky disciples, *I gave you milk to drink, rather than solid food. You were not capable of it then, nor are you even now*. (1 Cor 3:2) There are weak persons, incapable of digesting solid food, who want to stretch out and seize what they cannot eat. Or, if they do somehow manage to eat some of it or think they have, they are pretentious and proud about the matter, believing themselves to be persons of advanced taste. This is what has happened to all heretics. Gross and carnal in their outlook, and defending their distorted opinions—which were false, though they could not see it—they have been shut out of the Catholic Church.

I will explain this verse of the psalm to you as well as I can, beloved. Our Lord Jesus Christ is the Word of God, as John tells us: *In the beginning was the Word, and the Word was with God; he was God. He was with God in the beginning. Everything was made through him; without him was made nothing that was made*. (Jn 1:1–3) This means that he is like bread, the bread on which angels live. This bread has been prepared for you too, but you have to grow up by getting your nourishment from milk until you are ready for bread. "How am I to grow up on milk?" you ask. First of all believe in what Christ became to accommodate your weakness, and hold on firmly to that. When a mother sees that her child is not yet capable of eating solid food, she gives him solids, but only through the medium of her own flesh. What nourishes the baby is the same bread that nourishes the mother, but because the baby cannot cope with an adult meal, the bread from the table is transformed and reaches the child through the mother's breast, which is adapted to his capacity. Thus the same food that she eats reaches the tiny child too. Now think of the analogy. Our Lord Jesus Christ was the Word dwelling with the Father, the Word through whom all things were made. He was *in the form of God, and deemed it no robbery to be God's equal* (Ph 2:6); he was in that divine nature which the angels were able to receive in their own way, on which the intellectual spirits in heaven—all powers and dominions—had the capacity to be nourished. But human beings were weak and engrossed in flesh, lying helplessly on earth. There was only one way for heavenly bread to be made available to them so that men and women might eat the bread of angels[36] and manna fall upon a more richly privileged[37] people of Israel: *The Word was made flesh, and dwelt among us* (Jn 1:14).

10. For this very reason Paul demanded of those shaky disciples of his, the ones he reproached for being gross and carnally-minded, *Did I ever claim to know anything among you, save Jesus Christ and him crucified?* (1 Cor 2:2) He emphasized those last words because Christ had existed before ever he was crucified: *In the beginning was the Word, and the Word was with God; he was God* (Jn 1:1). Because the Word was made flesh it was the very Word himself who was crucified, but the Word was not changed into humanity; rather, humanity was changed by its union with him. Human nature was changed in him to become nobler than it had been before, but it was not changed into the substance of the Word.[38] God died inasmuch as he was man, and man was raised up inasmuch as this man was God. He arose and ascended into heaven. Whatever he suffered as a man, we can say that God suffered, because God assumed that humanity, though he was not changed into humanity. Think of it through a comparison: you cannot deny that you have suffered an injury if someone tears your garment. You may complain about it to your friends or, if you complain before a tribunal, you say to the judge, "That fellow attacked me." You do not say, "He attacked my cloak," but, "He attacked me."[39] If it is possible and right to regard the garment as an extension of yourself, even though it is not really you but only your clothing, how

---

36. See Ps 77(78):25.
37. Variant: "truer."
38. Some decades before the Council of Chalcedon in 451, here is Augustine making careful, clear statements about the hypostatic union that the council will endorse.
39. Literally "He tore me," in all three occurrences, but this sounds unnatural in English. The analogy with the two natures in Christ is obviously far from perfect; his humanity was much more than a cloak that could be taken off at will, as Augustine goes on to say.

much more justified are we in understanding that God himself suffered whatever Christ suffered in the flesh, since that flesh of Christ was the temple of the Word and united with the Word? This does not mean that the Word was capable of dying or undergoing corruption or being changed or being killed but that, whatever the Word suffered, he suffered in the flesh.

You need not think it so strange that in all this the Word as Word suffered nothing, for even with ordinary human beings it is possible for the soul to suffer nothing when the flesh is killed. Our Lord himself bids us, *Do not be afraid of those who kill the body, but cannot kill the soul* (Mt 10:28). If the soul cannot be killed, is it conceivable that the Word of God could be killed? Yet what does he say? "They scourged me, they punched me, they struck me, they lacerated me." None of this touches the soul, yet he says "me" because of the unity between him and the body to which he was wedded.

11. Our Lord Jesus Christ made the bread that was himself into milk for us by becoming incarnate and appearing as a mortal man,[40] so that in him death might be abolished and we, by believing in the flesh which the Word took to himself, might not wander away from the Word. Let us use this means to grow; let us get our nourishment from this milk. During this time when we are not yet strong enough to feed on the Word, let us not abandon our milky diet of faith. There have been heretics who wanted to argue about food beyond their capacities, saying that the Son is inferior to the Father and that the Holy Spirit is inferior to the Son. They postulated differences of rank within the Godhead. The result was that they tried to foist on the Church belief in three gods, for they cannot deny that the Father is God and the Son is God and the Holy Spirit is God; but if God the Father and God the Son and God the Holy Spirit are unequal and not of the same substance, there is not one God but three gods. These heretics were arguing about matters beyond their comprehension—food to which they were unsuited—and so they exalted themselves proudly and met the fate called down by the psalmist: *If I was not lowly in mind, but spiritually high-flown, may retribution come upon my soul as on a baby in its mother's arms that is torn away from its milk.* Their mother is God's Church, from which they separated. They ought to have stayed with her, being fed on milk that would have helped them

---

40. Variant: "appearing to mortals."

to grow until they were ready to feed on the Word who is God with God, in the form of God and equal to the Father.

A different interpretation: the unweaned child is one who refuses to grow

12. There is another interpretation, a different way of understanding these words, which commended itself to some who expounded the psalm before us,[41] and I must not pass over it in silence, dearly beloved. They explained it thus: every proud person is displeasing to God, and so the soul must humble itself in order not to offend him. It must take thoroughly to heart the advice of scripture: *The greater you are, the more deeply you are to humble yourself in every situation; then you will find favor with God* (Sir 3:20). But there are certain people who, on hearing that they must be humble, make this an excuse for refusing to learn anything, thinking that if they learn they will become proud. They therefore stay on a diet of milk alone and earn the rebuke of scripture, *You have continued in your infantile state, still needing milk, not solid food* (Heb 5:12). They are wrong, because God means us to be nourished on milk for a time only, not to remain on it indefinitely. He wants us to grow strong on milk and then graduate to solid food. We must not exalt our hearts in pride, but we must lift them up to the teaching offered by God's word. If it were not right for us to lift up our souls, another psalm would not have prayed, *To you, Lord, have I lifted up my soul* (Ps 24(25):1). Moreover, if the soul does not pour itself out above itself, it cannot attain to the vision of God or to knowledge of God's unchangeable reality. In our present state, still in the flesh, we are challenged, *Where is your God?* (Ps 41:4(42:3)) God is within, spiritually within, but also spiritually on high, though not in a spatial sense, as high places are distant from us. If God's loftiness were to be sought in that sense, the birds would reach God before we could! No, God who is within us is most high, spiritually exalted, and the soul cannot reach him unless it transcends itself. If you think of God in carnal terms you go seriously astray. And you are being very childish even if you think of God in terms appropriate to the human soul: if, for instance, you think that God forgets, or has the wrong idea about something and has to change his mind, or does something and then regrets it. All

---

41. Compare Hilary of Poitiers, *Tractate on Psalm 130*, 4–5; Ambrose, *On Psalm 38*, 12,1.

these things are indeed said of him in scripture, but only to make us milk-nourished infants feel at home with God, not to encourage us to take them literally. We must not imagine that God could regret his actions, or learn something of which he was previously ignorant, or understand something he did not understand before, or remember something he had forgotten. These changes are found in the human soul but not in God. Unless the soul, therefore, transcends even its own experience of itself, it will not see that God is Absolute Being. As he said, *I AM WHO AM* (Ex 3:14).

What, then, was the reply of the person who was challenged, *Where is your God?* He answered, *My tears have been bread to me day and night, as every day I hear the taunt, Where is your God?* But what did he do to find his God? *I reflected on these things*, he said, *and poured out my soul above myself.* (Ps 41:4–5(42:3–4)) To find God he poured out his soul above himself. From this it is clear that, when you are bidden to be humble, it does not mean that you must remain a stranger to wisdom. Be lowly where pride is a temptation, but raise your mind high to wisdom. Scripture gives unambiguous guidance on this: *Do not be childish in your outlook; be babes in your innocence of evil,* but so as to be mature in mind (1 Cor 14:20). This has made it quite clear when God wants us to be humble and when he wants us to aspire to the heights, my brothers and sisters: we must be humble to avoid pride but high-minded in pursuit of wisdom. Suck your milk to gain nourishment; gain nourishment in order to grow; grow to gain the strength you need to eat bread. When you are ready to eat bread you will be weaned, for then you will need not milk but solid food.

This seems to be what the psalmist had in mind. The words, *If I was not lowly in mind, but spiritually high-flown*, must mean, according to this interpretation, "If I was a child with regard to wickedness, but not in intelligence." And the same meaning must be conveyed by the preceding words, *O Lord, my heart is not exalted, nor my eyes raised high. Never have I walked in great matters, or in wonders above me.* He would be saying, "Look, I am a child as far as wickedness is concerned. But with regard to intelligence I have been no child. *If I was not lowly in mind, but spiritually high-flown*, let me be rewarded as a young child is rewarded when it is weaned from its mother's milk. It is judged ready then to eat bread."

13. I find this interpretation acceptable, brothers and sisters, because it is not opposed to the faith. All the same, I am not fully persuaded, because the psalm says not simply, *May retribution come*

upon my soul as on a baby that is torn away from its milk, but, *May retribution come upon my soul as on a baby in its mother's arms that is torn away from its milk.* The extra words, *in its mother's arms,* are included. This suggests to me that what the psalmist had in mind was a disaster. It is not a tiny baby that is weaned, but a growing child. A nursling in early infancy (real infancy, I mean) rests in its mother's arms. If it is deprived of its milk, it perishes. So I think the words, *in its mother's arms,* were included in the psalm for good reasons. All children can be weaned as they grow. When a child is growing well and is weaned, that is good for it, but if this is done when it is still a baby in arms, it is harmful. We therefore need to be careful, brothers and sisters, and very cautious lest anyone be weaned prematurely. Every growing child is weaned from milk, but no one should be deprived of milk while still in his mother's arms. A baby is first carried in its mother's womb until it is ready to be born and then carried in her arms until it is grown. While still in her arms it needs milk.

So for the soul: it must not be high-minded at this stage, when it is probably incapable of eating solid food; it must observe the command to be humble. There is work for it to do: it must believe in Christ, in order to gain some understanding of Christ. It cannot see the Word; it cannot yet see the equality between the Word and the Father or how the Holy Spirit is equal to the Father and the Son. Let it simply believe this and go on sucking. It is quite safe, because when it has grown it will eat food that it could not when it was still sucking in order to grow. There are good prospects ahead. Scripture warns us, *Seek not what is above you, and do not scrutinize loftier matters*—that means things of which you are not capable. "What shall I do, then?" you ask. "Am I to remain stuck at this level?" Scripture continues, *But let your mind run constantly on what the Lord has entrusted to you.* (Sir 3:22) What has the Lord entrusted to you? Practice works of mercy, do not depart from the peace of the Church, do not put your hope in human beings, do not tempt God by desiring to work miracles. If there is already some fruit of holiness apparent in you, know that you, together with other good people, must put up with the weeds until harvest time,[42] and that you will be in the company of bad people for a while, but not for ever. During the present era the chaff is mixed up with you on the threshing floor, but it will not be with you in the

---

42. See Mt 13:30.

barn.⁴³ *Let your mind run constantly on what the Lord has entrusted to you.* Do not allow yourself to be separated from your milk as long as you are still in your mother's arms, lest you die of starvation before you are strong enough to eat bread. Grow up first; then your strength will increase, and you will see what you were unable to see and take in what you previously could not.

Even those who eat solid food are not yet perfect

14. What then? When I see what at first I could not see and eat what I was at first unequal to eating, shall I be secure? Shall I be perfect? No, not as long as you are still in this life. True perfection for us is humility. Can you remember how the reading from the apostle ended? He had to undergo buffetings lest he be made proud by the revelations he had received—and what amazing things were revealed to him! So great were they that he might have been vain without that chastisement from Satan's envoy. And yet, what does he say, this man to whom such profound mysteries were revealed? *Brethren, I do not judge myself to have taken hold of the prize already* (Phil 3:13). It is Paul who says this, Paul who needed Satan's messenger precisely so that he would not get above himself after experiencing such tremendous revelations; yet he can say, *Brethren, I do not judge myself to have taken hold of the prize already*! Can anyone else dare to say that he has arrived? Paul does not think he has, for he says plainly, *I do not judge myself to have taken hold of the prize already.* What are you doing⁴⁴ then, Paul? "I am running hard to grasp it," he says. If Paul is still on the way, do you think you have reached home? "*But,* he says, *one thing only I do: forgetting what lies behind* (as you must too: forget your bad early life; if any empty pleasure attracted you then, do not let it lure you now)—*forgetting what lies behind,* he says, *and straining to what lies ahead, I bend my whole effort to follow after the prize of God's call*⁴⁵ *in Christ Jesus* (Phil 3:13–14). I hear the voice of God from heaven, and I keep running to grasp the prize. He has not left me to stick fast on the road, for he never ceases to address me." Notice this, brothers and sisters. God never tires of addressing us. If he speaks to us no longer, what are we doing? What is the point of our holy readings, our sacred songs? But he continues

---

43. See Mt 3:12.
44. Variant: "saying."
45. Variant: *heavenly call.*

to speak to us, so forget what lies behind and stretch out to what is ahead of you. Suck your milk, that you may grow toward solid food. When you reach your homeland, you will rejoice there.

As he presses on toward the palm of his heavenly vocation the apostle has something else to tell us. *Let those of us who are perfect be wise about this.* "I am not talking to the imperfect," he says, "to beginners with whom I cannot speak of wisdom,⁴⁶ or to those who still drink milk and cannot be fed on solids. I am speaking to those who eat solid food already." They seem to be already perfect because they understand the Word's equality with the Father. Yet they still do not see him as we are destined to see him, *face to face* (1 Cor 13:12); they see him only partially, in puzzling riddles. Let them keep running, then, for when our course is finished we shall be at home in our own country. Let them run, let them stretch to the uttermost. *Let those of us who are perfect be wise about this; if any of you think differently, God will reveal this also to you* (Phil 3:15). If you are somehow in error, why not go back to your mother's milk? If you do not exalt yourselves, if you are not spiritually high-flown, if you do not walk in wonders above you but guard humility, God will reveal the truth to you on any point where you differ. But if you try to argue and defend your opinion, asserting your own wisdom in a way that threatens the peace of the Church, the curse implied in the psalm will fall upon you: "You are in your mother's arms, yet you push away her milk; you will therefore be pushed away from your mother's embrace and you will die of hunger." But if you persevere in Catholic peace, any mistaken ideas you may have will be put right, because God will reveal the truth to you who are humble. Why? Because *God thwarts the proud, but gives grace to the humble* (Jas 4:6; 1Pt 5:5).

Go on hoping until hope gives way to the reality

15. The psalm accordingly concludes, *Let Israel hope in the Lord, from now on and for ever.*⁴⁷ This is how the Latin renders the Greek text, which has ἀπὸ τοῦ νῦν καὶ ἕως τοῦ αἰῶνος. When Latin uses *saeculum* it does not always refer to this world; sometimes it signifies eternity. Thus *usque in saeculum* is ambiguous; it could mean either "for ever, without end," or "until we reach eternity." Which way should we take it here? I think it must mean, "Let us hope in the

---

46. See 1 Cor 2:6.
47. *Et usque in saeculum.*

Lord our God until we reach eternity," because when we arrive in eternity there will be no occasion for hope. That will be the reality.

Exposition of Psalm 131

A Sermon to the People[1]

Introduction

1. Dearly beloved, it would have been more fitting for us to listen to an address from my colleague and brother who is here with us all.[2] He has not absolutely refused to preach to us but wishes to put it off. I mention this to you, dear friends, so that, together with me, you may remember his promise. Still, it was in keeping with the charity that binds us together that I should fall in with his wishes. He wanted first to hear what I had to say, and he extracted from me my consent to this arrangement, but I agreed only on condition that I would afterwards listen to him. Within the one charity we are all listeners to our one teacher in heaven.[3]

So now apply your minds to the psalm which we must study today, the one that comes next in the sequence with which you are familiar. This psalm is headed *A Song of Steps*, and it is somewhat longer than others that bear the same title. Let us therefore proceed briskly, not delaying except where it is necessary, in the hope that we may expound the whole of it in one sermon, if the Lord permits. You are not like uninstructed people, who need to have everything explained. You must help us to some extent by remembering what you heard in earlier sermons, so that we need not repeat it all as though it were all new to you.

Yet we must be new ourselves, not allowing any dregs of the old nature to creep stealthily up on us[4] but continually growing and moving onward. The apostle reminds us about this process: *Though our*

---

1. Apparently preached on the day after Augustine's Exposition of Psalm 95; see 95,1 and the note there, as well as 95,5.
2. Probably Severus, Bishop of Milevis. It seems that he refused to preach to this congregation until after Augustine himself had done so. On the day after the present sermon, when Augustine preached on Psalm 95, they were still waiting to hear the reluctant Severus.
3. See Mt 23:10.
4. *Vetustas nobis obrepere non debet.*

outer self is decaying, our inner self is being renewed daily (2 Cor 4:16). Our development must not be a process of growing older and losing the newness we once had; it is our new selves that must grow.[5]

Verses 1–2. David's forbearance

2. *O Lord, remember David, and all his gentleness;*[6] *and how he swore to the Lord, how he vowed to the God of Jacob.* In historical terms David was an individual person, king of Israel and son of Jesse. He certainly was gentle, as divine scripture records of him, for so forbearing and merciful was he that he did not repay even his persecutor, Saul, with evil.[7] To Saul David accorded such humble respect that he acknowledged him as king and referred to himself as a dog.[8] In God's designs David was to be the more powerful, yet he did not reply to the king impudently or with arrogance; he preferred to soothe him by his humble demeanor rather than inflame him further by pride. Saul had, moreover, been delivered into David's power, and this by the Lord God, so that David could do with him whatever he pleased. David had been given the opportunity to kill Saul, and it is legitimate to use power granted to us; but he had not been ordered to kill him, and he steered his God-given power into more merciful courses. If instead he had chosen to kill Saul, he would have been rid of an enemy. But then how could he have prayed, "Forgive me my debts, as I forgive those indebted to me"? This is what happened. Saul entered the cave where David was hidden; he went in to defecate, unaware of David's presence. David softly, slowly, arose behind him and cut a strip off Saul's cloak, intending to show it to him later as proof that he had had Saul in his power but had spared him of his own accord, not of necessity, and had declined to kill him. Perhaps it was this merciful forbearance that the psalm recalls in praying, *O Lord, remember David, and all his gentleness.*

Sacred scripture, in relating all this, gives us a trustworthy account of historical events, as we have said. Our custom in studying the

---

5. A theme common in the liturgical prayers for Advent and Lent; e.g., *Praesta nobis, ita in novitatem a vetustate transire, ut regni caelestis gloriae praeparemur* (Monday of Fifth Week of Lent).
6. *Mansuetudo* includes the ideas of meekness, humility, gentleness, patience, forbearance. The translation below uses these words variously, according to context.
7. See 1 Sm 24:4–23.
8. See 1 Sm 24:15.

psalms, however, is not to stop short at the literal meaning but, as with all prophecy, to pass through the letter and search for the mysteries it conceals. And you will remember, beloved, whose voice we are accustomed to hear in all the psalms: the voice of one who comprises both head and body. The head is in heaven, the body on earth, but where the head has gone the body is to follow. I am not going to tell you who the head is and who they are who form the body, because I am talking to people who know already.

3. David's humility and gentleness are recalled when the psalm prays, *O Lord, remember David, and all his gentleness.* But to what end, in particular, is the Lord asked to remember him? *Remember how he swore to the Lord, how he vowed to the God of Jacob.* Remember him to this end: that he may fulfil his promise.[9] David made the vow himself, as though its implementation were within his power, but he also begs of God to fulfil what he, David, has vowed.[10] He manifests both the devotion of the one who makes a vow and the humility of a suppliant. No one should assume that he can carry out his vows by his own strength. God who encourages you to make your vow also helps you to keep it. Let us see what David vowed, and then we shall discover in what sense David was a representative figure.

The name David means "strong of hand," and indeed he was a mighty warrior. Relying on his Lord he waged all his wars, and with the Lord's help he laid low all his enemies in accordance with the orders he had been given. But he prefigured another who would be strong of hand in defeating other enemies: namely, the devil and his angels. These are the enemies against which the Church wages victorious warfare. How does the Church defeat them? By patient endurance,[11] for it was also by patient endurance that our king himself vanquished the devil. The devil raged, Christ suffered. The raging enemy was defeated, the suffering Christ conquered. By the same patient endurance Christ's body, the Church, vanquishes its enemies. The Church needs to be strong of hand in order to conquer, but Christ's body is his

---

9. Augustine is, as usual, thinking of David as the author of the psalm.
10. The psalm has traditionally been recognized as messianic. According to 2 Sm 7, the occasion of God's explicit promise to David concerning the permanence of his line was David's idea of building a "house" for the Lord. The present psalm gives prominence to this idea, portraying David's resolve as a vow. Augustine's remarks here on human will and divine grace capture something of the dual character of the biblical narrative.
11. *Mansuetudine.*

temple and his house and his city, and he who is head of the body is the dweller in the house and the sanctifier of the temple and the king of the city. As all the former—body, temple, house, city—are truly what the Church is, so is Christ head, sanctifier, dweller, and king: all these. What, then, can we vow to God, except to be God's temple? We can offer nothing more pleasing to him than the prayer found in Isaiah: *Take possession of us* (Is 25:13, LXX). In the transference of earthly properties a householder gains something when he acquires rights of ownership, but with the Church it is different. The property itself gains by being possessed by such an owner.

Verses 3–5. David's vow; he aspires to make a place for the Lord in himself

4. What does he mean by the words, *how he swore to the Lord, how he vowed to the God of Jacob*? Let us see what this vow was. Now to swear is to promise faithfully. Pay careful attention to this vow of David: notice what he vowed and with what ardor, what love, what desire. And yet he besought the Lord that it might be fulfilled, praying, *O Lord, remember David, and all his gentleness*. In this spirit of gentle humility he makes his vow and prays that there may be a house for God: *If I enter the tent[12] where I dwell, if I climb onto the bed they have spread for me, if I allow sleep to my eyes.* But then he finds it insufficient to speak of sleep for his eyes, so he reinforces it: *If I allow slumber to my eyelids or rest for my temples, until I find a place for the Lord, a tabernacle[13] for the God of Jacob.* Where was he seeking a place for the Lord? If he was humble, he must have been seeking it in himself. Why do I say that? How could he be a place for the Lord? A prophet tells us: *Upon whom shall my spirit rest*, asks the Lord, *but upon the humble, peaceable person, the one who trembles at my words?* (Is 66:1–2) Do you want to be a house for God? Then be humble and peaceable and tremble at God's words and you will yourself become what you are seeking. If what you are looking for does not come about in yourself, is it going to be any use to you in anyone else? Admittedly, God does sometimes use the words of one who preaches the gospel to effect the salvation of another person even though the speaker does not practice what he preaches; in that case

---

12. *Tabernaculum* means both "tent" and "tabernacle." The choice varies in the translation offered here, according to context.
13. Or *tent*.

a place is prepared for the Lord through his tongue, but he himself does not become a place for the Lord. But if a teacher honestly lives in accordance with his message and teaches others to do the same, he becomes a place for the Lord and so does his pupil, because all believers together form a single place for the Lord. The Lord establishes his place in the heart, for there is but one heart among all who are united in charity.

Turning over private property to the common good makes a place for the Lord

5. How many thousands came to believe, brothers and sisters, when Christians laid the price of the property they had sold at the feet of the apostles![14] What does scripture say of them? Undoubtedly they became a temple of the Lord; and I do not mean only a lot of individual temples but one single temple, comprised of all of them together. So they became a *place for the Lord*. Scripture makes it quite clear that there was but one place for the Lord, even though they who formed it were many, for it says, *The multitude of believers had but one mind and one heart fixed on God* (Acts 4:32).

Many people, however, have no interest in making a place for the Lord; they seek their own interests, love their own possessions, rejoice in their own power, and are greedy for private property. Anyone who wants to make a place for the Lord must take the opposite line. He or she should rejoice not in what is privately owned but in what is common to all. That is what the first Christians did by making their private goods common. But did they thereby lose what they had owned? No, and I will tell you why not. If all things had remained private property, each person would have owned only what belonged to him or her individually; but when each person turned over his personal things to common ownership, he came to own what had belonged to others as well.

Make sure you understand this, beloved. It is on account of what we own individually that litigation is instituted and enmity, quarrels, and fights break out. Uproar, dissensions, scandals, sins, unjust actions, and even homicide are all the result of private ownership. What are we fighting over? Over the things we call our own. We do not go to law about things we possess in common, do we? We all breathe in the air that belongs to all of us, and we all enjoy the sunshine that is

---

14. See Acts 4:34–35; 2:45.

common to all. Blessed are those who are so intent on making a place for the Lord that they take no pleasure in their private possessions. A person of this disposition was described in the psalm: *If I enter the tent where I dwell,* he said. That was a private place. He knew that private property was an obstacle to him in his search to prepare a place for the Lord, and he mentioned the items he could call his own. I will not enter *the tent where I dwell,* he said, *until I find.* Find what? When you find a place for the Lord, will you then go into your own tent? Or would it be truer to say that the place you have found for the Lord will become your tent? How can that be? Because you will yourself be the Lord's place, and you will be one with all the others who have become the Lord's place.

6. Let us keep clear of private possessions, brothers and sisters; or, if we cannot renounce possessions, let us at least beware of attachment to them. Then we shall make a place for the Lord. "That is too much for me to attempt," someone objects. But consider what it is that you are asked to make: *a place for the Lord.* Suppose some senator asked for hospitality in your home—or not even a senator, but any important secular official—and he were to say, "Something[15] in your house is offensive to me." Now, even if you were fond of that thing, would you not remove it in order to avoid giving offence to this visitor, whose friendship you were trying to secure? And of what use to you will his friendship be anyway? Quite possibly you will find in it not only no help at all but danger instead. There have been plenty of people who were in no danger before they curried favor with the mighty but, being greedy for friendship with persons greater than themselves, they only ran into greater perils.

Long for Christ's friendship and you will be safe. He wants to be your guest. Make a place for him. What do I mean by telling you to make a place for him? Do not love yourself, but love him. If you are in love with yourself, you shut the door in his face; but if you are in love with him, you open it to him. If you open it and he comes in, you will no longer be in danger of being lost through self-love; when he loves you, you will be found.

7. *If I enter the tent where I dwell, if I climb onto the bed they have spread for me.* When people are complacent about privately-owned goods, it makes them proud. This is why he says, *If I enter,* meaning that he will not do so. A person can hardly avoid becoming proud

---

15. Variant: "someone."

about something that is his own exclusive property. The owner makes it an excuse for looking down on his neighbor, though both of them are beings of flesh. What is this human being, brothers and sisters? Flesh. And the other? Flesh too. And yet the flesh-and-blood rich man thinks he towers over the flesh-and-blood poor man, as though he had brought anything into the world when he was born or will take anything with him when he dies. All his ampler property did for him was to swell his pride. But the one who is intent on finding a place for the Lord says, *If I climb onto the bed they have spread for me.*

The perils and illusions of sleep

8. *If I allow sleep to my eyes.* There are many people who make no place for the Lord because they are asleep. The apostle rouses such people: *Arise, sleeper, rise from the dead: Christ will enlighten you* (Eph 5:14); and in another place he urges, *As for us who belong to the day, let us keep awake and be sober, for those who sleep, sleep at night, and those who get drunk, get drunk at night* (1 Th 5:6–7). By *night* he means iniquity; the children of the night fall asleep by coveting earthly things. All the seeming pleasures of this world are like dreams. In his dreams a person sees treasures, and as long as he sleeps he is a rich man, but he will wake up to find himself poor. It is the same with all the empty things of this world to which people look for pleasure: the pleasure is there only as long as the dream lasts. Unless they wake up now, while wakefulness can still be to their profit, they will awaken when they have no wish to and discover that all those pleasant things were only dreams, dreams that are fading away, no more than *the dream of one who awakens* (Ps 72(73):20), as scripture says; and in another passage, *they sank into their native slumber, and no remnant of riches did any of them find in their hands* (Ps 75:6(76:5)). *They sank into their native slumber,* but now their sleep is over and *no remnant of riches* is found in their hands, because what they have been seeing in their dreams is transient. This is why the man who aspires to find a place for the Lord goes on to say, *If I allow sleep to my eyes.*

There are some people who do not sink into deep sleep, but they are drowsy. They restrain themselves to some degree, tempering their love for material goods, but then they fall back into it again, as though frequently nodding off. Wake up, shake off your slumber! Your drowsiness will cause you to fall. The psalmist does not want anyone who means to find a place for the Lord to allow sleep to his eyes or slumber to his eyelids.

9. *Or rest for my temples.* If rest is allowed to the temples, sleep overtakes the eyes, for the temples are close to the eyes. Heaviness in the head, around the temples, is the prelude to sleep. When people are sleepy their heads begin to feel heavy, and when they become aware of this heaviness sleep is very near. If they intend to allow their eyes to close they position their heads comfortably, giving rest to their temples, and sleep soon follows. But if no rest is granted to the temples, sleep does not come. Well then, when some secular pleasure begins to lure you toward sin, your head is growing heavy. Do you want to be fully awake, not sleepy or drowsy? Then do not yield to the pleasure: it will bring you more pain than sweetness. If you use this thought to rub your forehead with you will shake off sleep and prepare a place for the Lord.

The difference between tent-dwelling and living in a house

10. Do this until you *find a place for the Lord, a tabernacle for the God of Jacob.* Sometimes God's house is called God's tabernacle, and in other texts God's tabernacle is called his house, but, though the terms are used interchangeably, dearest brothers and sisters, we should distinguish their meanings. "Tabernacle" indicates the Church in the present era; "house" means the Church of the heavenly Jerusalem to which we are journeying. The word *tabernaculum* is used of the tents of soldiers and all fighters. They live in tents[16] while on campaign and ready for action. This is why soldiers are called "tent-companions."[17] As long as we have enemies to fight, we pitch[18] a tent for God. But the time will come when our warfare will be over and that peace will reign which the apostle calls *the peace of Christ, which outshines every understanding* (Ph 4:7). It will be more glorious than our minds can compass for, however high may be your thoughts about that peace, no mind still hindered by the weight of the body can grasp it. When that peace comes, our homeland will be our house, our home. No adversary will attack it, and so there will be no need to call it a tent any longer. We shall not go out to battle but shall stay at home to praise God. What are we told about that house? *Blessed are*

---

16. *Tabernacula.*
17. *Contubernales;* see Exposition of Psalm 26,6.
18. Variant: "let us pitch."

they who dwell in your house; they will praise you for ever and ever (Ps 83:5(84:4)). Here in God's tent we are still groaning; there in his house we shall be singing his praise. Why the difference? Because groaning is characteristic of pilgrims, and praise of people permanently settled in their homeland. Here on earth is the place where we must first seek a tabernacle for the God of Jacob.

Verse 6. Ephrathah and the woodland pastures

11. *Lo, we heard of it in Ephrathah. It?* What is *it*?[19] We heard of the Lord's throne in Ephrathah. *We found it in the woodland pastures.* The psalm says *We heard of it in Ephrathah, we found it in the woodland pastures.* Does it mean that they found it in the place where they heard of it, or are two different places envisaged? To settle the question we need to ask what Ephrathah is, where the speaker heard about it, and what the *woodland pastures* are, where he found it. Ephrathah is a Hebrew word meaning "mirror," according to those who have translated Hebrew names occurring in scripture into other tongues, so that their meaning may come through to us. They translated from Hebrew into Greek, and then from Greek into Latin for our benefit, for there have been students very alert about the scriptures.

If Ephrathah means "mirror," the psalm is telling us that the house which was found in the woodland pastures was first heard about in a mirror. Now a mirror provides a reflection or image, and all prophecy yields an image of things to come. The house of God which was to exist in the future was foretold in the images of prophecy; and, as the psalm says, *We heard of it in Ephrathah*, which is to say, "We heard about it in a mirror." But *we found it in the woodland pastures.* What are these woodland pastures? Areas in the forests where animals can graze. It does not mean the kind of land of which we might say colloquially, "That rough pasture measures so many acres." Woodland pasture, properly so called, is land still uncultivated, forest land. Some codices even have *in the pastures of the forest.* What, then, were these

---

19. The Ark of the Covenant, captured by the Philistines and lodged for some years in Philistine territory, was conveyed to Beth-shemesh, and thence to Kiriath-jearim; see 1 Sm 6:21–7:2. The *woodland pastures* mentioned in this verse of the psalm may be the name of a place (perhaps "Forest-Fields") which, like Kiriath-jearim, was in the neighborhood of Bethlehem, "Ephrathah." Later David brought the Ark to Zion, see 2 Sm 6. This section of the psalm is concerned with the story of the Ark. From verse 11 onward the perspective will again be that of God's promise to David, recalled in the opening verses.

woodland pastures? What else but the uncultivated gentiles? What were the woodland grazing sites but those nations among which the briers of idolatry were still rank? Yet it was there, where the brambles of idolatry were thickly growing, that we found a place for the Lord, a tabernacle for the God of Jacob. What *we heard of in Ephrathah, we found in the woodland pastures.* What was preached to the Jews through images was manifested in the faith of the gentiles.

Verse 7. The place for the Lord's house

12. *We have entered*[20] *his tabernacles.*[21] *His*? Whose? The tabernacle of the Lord, the God of Jacob. Those who enter it in order to dwell there are the ones who are themselves entered in order that they may be indwelt by God. You enter your own house in order to dwell there, but you enter God's house in order that he may dwell in you, for the Lord is nobler, and when he begins to live in you he will make you happy, whereas if you are not indwelt by him, you will be wretched. The son who said to his father, *Give me the portion of the property that is due to me* (Lk 15:12), wanted to have it under his own control, but it was being kept in his father's hands for the good reason that there it would not be wasted on harlots. But the son took it, and it passed into his control. He set out for a distant country, and there on his harlots he squandered it all. Nonetheless he felt the pinch of hunger, remembered his father, and went home in order to get plenty of bread. You, then, must enter the house in order to be indwelt by God. Regard yourself not as your own property but as his. *We have entered*[22] *his tabernacles.*

13. *We have worshiped*[23] *in the place where his feet have stood.*[24] Whose feet? The Lord's, or the feet of the Lord's house, the Church? The Lord's feet, surely, because his house is the place where the Lord must be worshiped. *We have worshiped*[25] *in the place where his feet have stood.* In no place other than his own house does God hear our prayer—hear it, that is, in a way conducive to eternal life. The person

---

20. Variant: *will enter.*
21. Plural here, according to the best reading.
22. Variant: *will enter.*
23. Variant: *will worship.*
24. *Pedes eius* is not gender-specific in Latin, but a choice must be made in English translation between his, her, or its feet. In the present section 13 Augustine refers it to the Lord's feet, in section 14 to the feet of the Church.
25. Variant: *will worship.*

who belongs to God's house is the one who is bonded to other living stones[26] in the solidity of charity. One who has no charity is a wrecker but, even if he or she falls into ruins, the house stands firm. If someone has once been a stone within the building and decides to fall out of it, he should not threaten the house with possible harm that may come to it when he does. The Jewish race, God's first people, made that mistake. "God gave wonderful promises to our father Abraham concerning the future of his descendants," they said, "and he will never break his promise to Abraham." They therefore committed all kinds of wicked deeds, secure in their illusions about God's promise and telling themselves that they would be spared in view of Abraham's merits rather than their own record. They thought that God would gather into his house to enjoy eternal life all Abraham's children, irrespective of their personal lives. Yet what did John the Baptist have to say to that? *Brood of vipers*, he called them. Some of Abraham's descendants came to John to be baptized in the waters of repentance, but he welcomed them not as "brood of Abraham" but as *brood of vipers*. They were like those whose lives they were accustomed to imitate, not children of Abraham but children of the Amorites, the Canaanites, the Girgashites, the Jebusites, and of all who offended God. They were truly the children of those pagan peoples whose deeds they imitated. *You brood of vipers*, John said to them. *Who has taught you to flee from the wrath that is coming? Bring forth fruit that befits repentance and do not say to yourselves, We have Abraham for our father, for God is able to raise up children to Abraham even from these stones.* (Mt 3:7–9) Probably he had his eye on certain stones *in the woodland pastures*, for it was from these that new children were raised up to Abraham, children who imitated Abraham's faith better than did those who were his children by physical descent. Let no one, then, presume to threaten God's house by saying, "I am going to withdraw, and then the house will collapse." He would do much better to stay and allow himself to be built in with the rest and preserve charity for, even if he crumbles and falls out of his place, the house will still stand.

It is clear then, brothers and sisters, that God's house is comprised of those whom he has predestined, those who, as he sees in his divine foreknowledge, will persevere. They are the ones whom the psalm envisaged when it spoke of the place *where his feet have stood*. God's

---

26. See 1 Pt 2:5.

feet do not stand in those who do not persevere, for these are not the Church. They do not form part of God's tabernacle now, nor will they of his house hereafter. Where have his feet been standing? *With iniquity increasing mightily, the love of many will grow cold* (Mt 24:12). His feet do not stand in people whose charity is cooling off. But what does the Lord say next? *Whoever perseveres to the end will be saved* (Mt 24:13). These are the ones in whom his feet are standing. That is the place where you must worship him: be one of them yourself.

14. If you prefer to take the words about feet to refer to "the feet of his house," make sure your own feet stand fast in Christ. Stand they will, if you persevere in Christ. What is said to the contrary about the devil? *He was a murderer from the beginning, and he did not stand in the truth* (Jn 8:44). The devil's feet did not stand fast. Something similar is said about the proud: *Let not the foot of pride come near me, nor the hands of sinners dislodge me. There they have fallen, all those who work iniquity; they have been driven out, unable to stand.* (Ps 35:12–13(36:11–12)) Contrast this with the feet of God's house, which do stand. John the Baptist, full of joy, testified, *The bride is for the bridegroom; but the bridegroom's friend, who stands and hears him* (he needs to stand, if he is to hear him), *rejoices intensely at the bridegroom's voice* (Jn 3:29). It is because he thrills with joy at the bridegroom's voice that he stands; if he found his joy in the sound of his own voice, he would fall. Now you can see why those who rejoice at the sound of their own voices have fallen.

The friend of the bridegroom insisted, *It is he, Christ, who baptizes* (Jn 1:33). How different those who claim, "It is we who baptize."[27] They have been unable to stand because they found their joy in their own uplifted voices, and they do not belong to the house of which the psalm says, *There his feet have stood.*

Verses 8–9. Christ's resurrection and the hope of resurrection for his holy ark

15. *Arise, O Lord, into your rest.* The exhortation, *Arise,* is spoken to the Lord while he sleeps. You know who it was who slept and then rose again. It was he who in another psalm recalled, *Though disturbed, I lay down to sleep* (Ps 56:5(57:4)). The psalm's exhorta-

---

27. The Donatists, whose practice was to re-baptize any Catholics who joined them. Augustine steadily opposed their policy: it is always Christ who baptizes. Compare Exposition of Psalm 39,1.

tion to him, *Arise into your rest*, is full of meaning. It seems to say, "You will never be disturbed again," for *rising from the dead, Christ will never die again, nor will death ever again have the mastery over him* (Rom 6:9). His voice is heard in another psalm proclaiming the same truth: *I rested, and fell asleep, and I arose because the Lord will uphold me* (Ps 3:6(5)). Christ slept, and to him our psalm says, *Arise, O Lord, into your rest, you and your ark of holiness*. He is urged to arise himself, and his ark of holiness—the ark he has made holy—is associated with his resurrection. He is our head, and his ark is his Church. He rose first, and after him the Church too will rise. The body would not have dared to promise itself resurrection unless the head had risen first. *Arise, O Lord, into your rest, you and your ark of holiness*.

Another interpretation proposed by some[28] identifies the ark of holiness with the body of Christ born from Mary.[29] Thus the verse, *Arise, O Lord, into your rest, you and your ark of holiness*, would mean, "Rise up in your human body, so that those who do not believe in your resurrection may handle you."[30] *Arise, O Lord, into your rest, you and your ark of holiness*.

16. *May your priests be clothed in holiness, and your saints rejoice.* With your resurrection from the dead and your return to the Father, may your royal priesthood[31] be clothed in faith: this is what it means, because *the one who lives by faith is just* (Hb 2:4; Rom 1:17). And may the saints who are your members, who have received the pledge of the Holy Spirit, rejoice in the hope of their own resurrection, on the pattern of the resurrection already accomplished in their head. To them the apostle says, *Rejoice in hope* (Rom 12:12).

Verse 10. For David's sake Christ does not withdraw from the remnant of Israel

17. *For the sake of your servant David, do not turn away the face of your anointed.* This plea is addressed to God the Father: *For the sake of your servant David, do not turn away the face of your anointed.* The Lord was crucified in Judea and crucified by the Jews. Disturbed by them, his own people, he lay down to sleep. He lay down to sleep

---

28. Compare Hilary of Poitiers, *Tractate on Psalm 131*, 16.
29. Compare Exposition of Psalm 130,1 and the note there.
30. See Jn 20:27.
31. See 1 Pt 2:9.

after suffering at their cruel hands, and he arose to judge them: as he says in another passage, *Raise me up; then I will requite them* (Ps 40:11(41:10)). He did requite them, and he will requite them, for the Jews themselves know how much they suffered after killing the Lord. They were all driven out from the very city where they slew him. Does this mean that all David's descendants have died out? And everyone from the tribe of Judah? Far from it. Some of them believed; indeed, many thousands of them believed, and this very soon after the Lord's resurrection. The cruelty of the Jews had led them to crucify him, but later they began to witness miracles performed in the name of the crucified one. They were overcome with awe at the power of his name, the name of a man who, when he was in their hands, had seemed quite powerless. Pierced to the heart,[32] they believed that in him, whom they had taken to be like other men, divinity had been present. They begged the apostles' advice and were told, *Repent, and let every one of you be baptized in the name of the Lord Jesus Christ* (Acts 2:38).

It was evident, then, that Christ had risen to judge those who had crucified him and that he had turned his face away from the Jews and toward the gentiles. And so this verse of the psalm sounds like a prayer addressed to God on behalf of the remnant of Israel: *"For the sake of your servant David, do not turn away the face of your anointed.* If the chaff has been condemned, at least the grains are collected.[33] *Let a remnant be saved*, as Isaiah says." (Rom 9:27; see Is 10:22) And clearly a remnant was saved, from which emerged the twelve apostles, the more than five hundred brethren to whom the Lord showed himself after his resurrection,[34] and the many thousands who were baptized,[35] who sold their possessions and laid the proceeds at the feet of the apostles.[36] The prayer offered to God in this psalm was obviously answered: *For the sake of your servant David, do not turn away the face of your anointed.*

---

32. See Acts 2:37.
33. Variant: "let the grains be collected."
34. See 1 Cor 15:6.
35. See Acts 2:41.
36. See Acts 4:34–35.

Verse 11. God's promise to David is irrevocable

18. *The Lord swore truthfully to David, and he will not revoke his oath.* What does it mean by saying that he swore? He affirmed the promise by pledging himself. And what about the words, *He will not revoke his oath*? This means that he will not change, for God does not suffer the anguish of repentance, nor does he make any mistake that would require him to go back and put right something he had done wrong. But, when a human being repents, he wants to change what he did; and there is this much similarity with God, that when he is said to repent you are right to hope for a change in the effects of his action. However, even though the word "repent" is used of both God and yourself, you must not think that God repents in the way you do. You repent because you have gone wrong, but God repents when he punishes or sets someone free. He revoked his gift of the kingdom to Saul, and in this sense he repented of making him king: scripture says exactly this. Yet in the same context, where the Lord says that he repents,[37] the contrary is stated: the Lord *is not like a man, to have any regret* (1 Sm 15:29). When in virtue of his unchangeable purpose God changes his practical dispositions, he is said to repent, but only because of the change in his practical dispositions, not of any change in his purpose, which stands firm and irrevocable, like the promise recalled in another psalm: *The Lord has sworn, and will not revoke it: You are a priest for ever after the order of Melchizedek* (Ps 109(110):4). The same is true of what he promised in our present psalm. His promise could not be changed but would necessarily be fulfilled and would stand for ever. *The Lord swore truthfully to David, and he will not revoke his oath.*

From the fruit of your womb will I put a man upon your throne. He might have said, "From the fruit of your loins." Why did he prefer to say, *From the fruit of your womb*? It would still have been true if God had said to David, "From the fruit of your loins," but he chose the more significant expression, *From the fruit of your womb*, because Christ was born from a woman without male intervention.

---

37. See 1 Sm 15:11.

Verse 12. Though the promise to David is expressed conditionally, God's oath secures its fulfillment in his own way

19. So, *the Lord swore truthfully to David: From the fruit of your womb will I put a man upon your throne.* What else did he say? *If your sons observe my covenant and these testimonies of mine which I will teach them, their sons too shall sit upon your throne for ever.* He is saying, If *your* sons observe these injunctions, *their* sons shall sit there *for ever.* It looks as though the merits of the parents are to be transferred to the children. But what if David's own sons were to observe them but their sons did not? How can the children be promised prosperity in response to their fathers' merits? Why does he say, *If your sons observe* them, *their sons shall sit* there *for ever*? Why not say, "If your own sons observe my testimonies, they shall sit upon your throne, and if their sons in turn observe them, they too shall sit upon your throne"? But he does not say that; he says, *If your sons observe* them, *their sons too shall sit upon your throne.* Why? Surely because he meant us to understand by *sons* the fruit they will reap as their reward. He means, "If your sons obey my law, if your sons keep these commandments of mine which I will teach them, *their sons shall sit upon your throne,*" which is to say, "This will be their fruit, their reward: to sit upon your throne."

Think of our own lives now, brothers and sisters, as we all struggle along in Christ, as we all tremble with awe at his words, as we do our very best to conform to his will and beg him with groans to help us fulfil his commands. Are we already seated upon those blissful thrones promised to us? No, but as we hold fast to his commandments we hope that some day we shall be. Now this hope of ours can be called our children, because children are the hope of every living person while this life lasts, as children are also each one's fruit. When people try to justify their stinginess, they say they are saving up for their children. Unwilling to give anything to a person in need, they excuse themselves on the pretext of family loyalty, because their hope is embodied in their children. All who live in accordance with this world's standards agree that their hope lies in having children and leaving descendants. This is why the psalm gave the name *sons* to the future hope itself, saying, *If your sons observe my covenant and these testimonies of mine which I will teach them, their sons too shall sit upon your throne for ever.* It means, "Such fruit shall be theirs that their hope may be guaranteed against disappointment, the hope that they will reach the place where they long to be." People who even now are inspired by hope of the future are like fathers; but when they have gained what they are now hoping for they will be sons, because they will possess what by their good lives they have borne and begotten. At present their reward is held in reserve for them, as something that will accrue to them in the future,[38] just as in ordinary speech we call someone's future prospects[39] his sons.

20. If you prefer to take *sons* literally, you must understand that the words, *If your sons observe my covenant and these testimonies of mine which I will teach them*, refer equally to succeeding generations. Thus the sense will be as follows: *If your sons observe my covenant and these testimonies of mine which I will teach them, and their sons too*, and here you must insert a punctuation mark, then go on to the promise, *they shall sit upon your throne for ever.* That is to say, all of them will sit there, both *your sons* and *their sons*, but only if they keep the covenant.

But what if in the future they have not kept it? Has God's promise been nullified? No. It was stated in this way and expressed as a conditional promise because God was proclaiming something. Proclaiming what? That some would believe. But to exclude the possibility that someone might belittle God's promises and attribute to human power what God pledged himself to effect, the psalm stated that God *swore*, thus indicating that the fulfillment would come without fail.

In that case, why insert the condition, *If they observe*? Because you are not to be complacent and boastful about the promise and let yourself down lightly in the matter of observance. You will be David's son if you keep the covenant, but if you do not, you are no son of David. God made his promise to David's sons, but do not claim, "I am his son," if you are degenerate. Even the Jews do not say that, even though they were born from his stock—or rather, they do say something like it, but they deceive themselves, for the Lord plainly told them, *If you are Abraham's children, act as Abraham did* (Jn 8:39), denying them the dignity of sons because they did not imitate their ancestor's way of life. If, then, even the Jews cannot claim it, how can we presume to call ourselves David's children? We are not of his stock by physical descent. The only way that remains for us to

---

38. *In posterum.*
39. *Posteritas.*

be his children is to prove ourselves such by imitating his faith and worshiping God as he did.

But as for you, if you refuse to obtain by your good works the privilege you cannot hope for by descent, how can the promise that you will sit upon David's throne be fulfilled in your case? If it is not fulfilled in you, do you imagine it will not be fulfilled at all? But then what of the psalmist's assertion that he found God's abode *in the woodland pastures*? How did *his feet* find somewhere to stand? Whatever you are like, that house will stand firm.

Verses 13–15. God's promises to Zion, city of his choice

21. *For the Lord has chosen Zion; he has preferred it for his dwelling.* Zion is the Church, and Zion is also the heavenly Jerusalem toward whose peace we are running. Not in the angels, but in ourselves, is Zion still on pilgrimage, and the nobler part of it awaits the part which has still to find its way home. From there letters reach us, the letters we read every day.[40] This is the city, this is the Zion, on which God has set his preferential love.

22. *This is my rest for ever and ever.* God is speaking here. *My rest*, he says, the place where I shall find my rest. How greatly must God love us, brothers and sisters, if he can say he finds rest because we find rest! It is not as though he were ever disturbed or needing rest in that sense, but he says that he takes his rest in Zion because we shall there find rest in him. *Here will I live, because I have made it my choice.*

23. *I will abundantly bless the widow within it, and I will satisfy its poor with bread.* Every soul that knows itself to be bereft of all help save that of God alone is a widow; for what did the apostle say about this? *One who is truly a widow, and desolate, hopes in the Lord* (1 Tm 5:5). He was talking about the kind whom all of us in the Church are accustomed to call widows, as opposed to those of whom he went on to say, *But a woman who lives in luxury is as good as dead even while she lives* (1 Tm 5:6). This latter he would not enroll among the widows. Describing true widows and holy women, however, he says, *One who is truly a widow, and desolate, hopes in the Lord, and perseveres in prayer and entreaty night and day* (1 Tm 5:5). Then he added the caution already quoted: *But a woman who lives in luxury is*

---

40. On the scriptures as letters from God, or from the heavenly Jerusalem, see Exposition of Psalm 73, 5 and the note there.

as good as dead even while she lives. What makes someone a widow, then? Having no help from any other source but God. Women who have husbands may give themselves airs because they have men to help them, but those who are left alone are true widows, and the help they can expect is all the more powerful for that.

From this we can see that the whole Church is one single widow, whether in men or in women, in those who are married, in the young or the old, or in virgins: the whole Church is one single widow, left alone in this world, insofar as she is conscious of her desolation and acknowledges her widowed state; for then her help is near at hand. Do you not recognize this widow in the gospel, brothers and sisters, in the parable by which the Lord taught us that we must pray always and never give up?[41] *There was a certain judge in a city,* he said. *This man neither feared God nor respected other people. But a widow appealed to him daily, demanding, Do justice for me against my opponent.* (Lk 18:3) By insisting, the widow broke down his resistance. *The judge had neither reverence for God nor respect for anyone else, but he said to himself, Even though I do not fear God or respect other people, I will see justice done for this widow, if only because of all the harassment she is causing me.* (Lk 18:4–5) If the unprincipled judge listened to the widow for no better reason than to rid himself of the annoyance, does not God listen to the Church, whom he urges to pray to him?

24. What is meant by the next promise, brothers and sisters—*I will satisfy its poor with bread*? Let us be poor, and then we shall be satisfied. Many people pin their hopes on this world; though Christians, they are proud; they worship Christ, yet they are not satisfied. The trouble is that they are already filled up with other things and wallow in their proud affluence. These were the kind another psalm referred to when it spoke of the contempt in which we are held, *a disgrace to the affluent, and contemptible to the proud* (Ps 122(123):4). They are well off and therefore have plenty to eat, but they are not satisfied. Again, another psalm said of them, *All the rich of the world have eaten, and worshiped* (Ps 21:30(22:29)). They worship Christ, they hold him in reverence, they say their prayers to Christ, but they are never filled to their satisfaction with his wisdom and justice. Why not? Because they are not poor. The truly poor, on the other hand—that is, the humble of heart—eat all the more as their hunger grows keener, and the more empty they are of what the world enjoys, the

---

41. See Lk 18:1–6.

hungrier they become. If someone is full, you may offer him anything you choose and he will reject it. But give me a hungry person, give me the people of whom the Lord said, *Blessed are those who hunger and thirst for righteousness, for they shall be satisfied* (Mt 5:6), and they will be the poor of whom our present psalm promises, *I will satisfy its poor with bread.* This is certain, for in the other psalm just quoted—the one where it is said, *All the rich of the world have eaten, and worshiped*—mention is also made of the poor, and in almost the same terms as in the psalm we are studying: *The poor shall eat and be satisfied, and those who seek the Lord will praise him* (Ps 21:27(22:28)). Notice the contrast: before telling us that *all the rich of the world have eaten, and worshiped,* it has told us that *the poor shall eat and be satisfied.* Why the difference? If the rich are said to have worshiped, why are they not said to have been satisfied, whereas the poor, also named, are said to have eaten their fill? What was it that satisfied them? In what does this satisfaction consist, brothers and sisters? God himself is bread. This bread came down from heaven in order to be transformed into milk for us,[42] as he said to his followers: *I am the living bread which has come down from heaven* (Jn 6:41). This is why the psalm promises, *The poor shall eat and be satisfied.* With what will they be satisfied? The next words give us a hint: *And those who seek the Lord will praise him.*

25. Be poor, then; let your place be among the members of the widow;[43] look for help in God alone. Money counts for nothing; you will find no help there. Many have stumbled headlong into ruin for the sake of money; many have perished pursuing it. Many have been the target of robbers on account of their money—people who would have been safe if they had not possessed the wealth that made thieves hunt them down. Many again have put their trust in powerful friends; and when these fell, they dragged down with them the clients who had relied on them. Look around you: human experience is full of such examples. Are we telling you anything extraordinary? We are not speaking only of these scriptural passages: you can read the same in the world around you. Be wary of putting your trust in money, or human friendship, or rank and celebrity as the world sees them. Get rid of all these. You possess them, do you? Then be thankful to God

---

42. See Augustine's reflections on this adaptation of diet in Exposition of Psalm 130, 9.
43. See section 23 above.

if you can spurn them. But if you are conceited about them, there is no need to wait until you fall prey to rapacious humans; you are a prey to the devil already. If, however, you put no reliance on these things, you will be among the members of the widow-Church, of whom the Lord says, *I will abundantly bless the widow* in Zion; and you will also be one of the poor, of whom he promises, *I will satisfy her poor with bread*.

26. There is another aspect of poverty and riches which we should not omit to mention. You sometimes find a poor person who is proud and a rich one who is humble. This is a matter of daily and painful experience for us. You hear a poor man apparently groaning under the domination of the rich and, as long as the powerful rich man is oppressing him, you regard the poor man as humble. But it may be that even then he is not really humble; even in that condition you can detect that he is proud. From this you discern what he would have been like if he had been an owner of property. God's poor are poor in their minds, not in their purses.[44]

But then you come across another person who has an ample household, lush lands, many estates, and plenty of gold and silver, yet he knows that these are not to be relied upon. He humbles himself before God and uses his wealth to do good. His heart is so sincerely raised to God that he realizes not only the uselessness of his riches but even their power to trip him up unless God guides and helps him and unless he finds a place among the poor who are full fed with bread.

Then you find another person who is a beggar, yet puffed up with pride—or at any rate, if not puffed up, since he has nothing, then looking for something to get puffed up about. God is not concerned about our resources but about our greed. He judges a person on the cupidity that drives him to lust for temporal things, not on the resources he has not managed to get his hands on.

The apostle gives this advice concerning the well-off: *Instruct the rich of this world not to be high-minded, nor to put their trust in unreliable wealth, but in the living God, who gives us everything to enjoy in abundance.* He goes on to tell them what to do with their wealth: *Let them be rich in good works, give readily, and share what they have.* And notice, they are to be regarded as poor in the present life, for he recommends, *Let them use their wealth to lay a good foundation for the future, and so attain true life.* (1 Tm 6:17–19) When

---

44. *In sacculo*; but many witnesses read *in saeculo* ("in the world").

they have attained it they will be truly rich, but as long as they do not possess it they must recognize that they are poor.

So it comes about that all the humble of heart, all who are established in twofold charity,[45] whatever they may own in this world, are counted by God as his poor, the poor whom he satisfies with bread.

Verses 16–18. Augustine's conclusion roots this messianic psalm explicitly in Christ

27. *I will clothe its priests with salvation, and its holy ones will rejoice with great joy.* We have reached the end of the psalm. Concentrate just a little longer, beloved. *I will clothe its priests with salvation, and its holy ones will rejoice with great joy.* Who is our salvation? Who else but our Christ? What does it mean, then, to say, *I will clothe its priests with salvation*? Remember Paul's words: *As many of you as have been baptized in Christ have clothed yourselves in Christ* (Gal 3:27). *And its holy ones will rejoice with great joy.* Why will they rejoice? Why their great joy? Because they have been clothed with salvation. Once they were darkness but now they are light, though not from any source in themselves; they have been made light in the Lord.[46] Accordingly the psalm adds, *There I will raise up a horn for David.* The true exaltation of David is that we rely on Christ, for Christ is the exaltation of David, and a horn symbolizes something high and uplifted. But what kind of exaltation? Not carnal, certainly. The symbolism makes this clear, for while all the bones of an animal are covered with flesh, the horns stand clear of the flesh. Thus a horn signifies spiritual exaltation. What sort of spiritual exaltation is meant here? That which trusts in Christ and declines to say, "This is my doing," or, "I baptize." Instead it confesses, *He it is who baptizes* (Jn 1:33). That is where David's horn is seen.

If you want confirmation that this is David's horn, notice how the psalm continues: *I have prepared a lamp for my anointed.* What lamp is this? You know the answer, because you have heard what the Lord said about John: *He was a burning, shining lamp* (Jn 5:35). And what did John say? *He it is who baptizes.* This is what will make the saints rejoice, this is why the priests will exult: their certainty that any good in them is not theirs but his. And because it is Christ who

---

45. *In caritate gemina,* toward God and neighbor; compare *Teaching Christianity* 1,36,40. But some witnesses read *in caritate germana* ("in genuine charity").
46. See Eph 5:8.

has the power to baptize, everyone who has received baptism comes calmly to Christ's temple, knowing that it originates not from any human source but from him in whom David's horn has been raised up.

28. *Upon him my sanctifying power shall flourish.* Upon whom? Upon my anointed.[47] This phrase, *my anointed,* is spoken by God the Father, like the preceding words, *I will abundantly bless the widow in Zion, and I will satisfy its poor with bread. I will clothe its priests with salvation, and its holy ones will rejoice with great joy.* And again it is God who says, *There I will raise up a horn for David.* He says, *I have prepared a lamp for my anointed* because Christ is ours, and Christ is also the Father's. He is our Christ because he saves us and rules us as our Lord; and he is the Father's Son. But as Christ, the anointed, he is our anointed and the Father's anointed. If he did not belong to the Father, the psalm would not have prayed earlier, *For the sake of your servant David, do not turn away the face of your anointed.*

Upon him my sanctifying power shall flourish. It flourishes upon Christ. Let no one else arrogate to himself the power to sanctify. If others could claim it, the declaration would not be true that *upon him,* Christ, *my sanctifying power shall flourish.* The glory of this sanctifying power will indeed flourish, because Christ's sanctifying power resides in Christ himself, and this power is the sanctifying power of God in him. He says, *It shall flourish,* because he wants to suggest its beauty and glory, just as trees are beautiful when they flower. How does the sanctifying power of baptism flower and shine out gloriously? How has the world been conquered by its beauty? Because it flourishes in Christ. If it depended on the power of ordinary human beings, how could it flourish? *All flesh is but grass, and human glory like the flower of grass* (Is 40:6).

---

47. Or "my Christ."

Exposition of Psalm 132

A Sermon to the People

Verse 1. The opening words of this psalm inspired the early community of Jewish Christians and later engendered monasteries

1. This is a short psalm, very well known and frequently quoted. *See how good and how pleasant it is for brothers to dwell together in unity!* So delightful a sentiment is this that the verse is sung even by people unfamiliar with the psalter. The sound of it is as agreeable as charity itself, the delightful charity that makes brothers dwell together in unity. There is no need for us to spell out or to explain to you, brothers and sisters, how pleasant and lovely it is for people to live together in unity; but the subsequent verses contain further meaning, which may be opened to those who knock.

However, some understanding of the whole text of the psalm will be more likely to flow down to us from this first verse if we begin by considering the following question very carefully: Is it of all Christians that the psalm says, *How good and how pleasant it is for brothers to dwell together in unity,* or are the ones who dwell in unity certain particular individuals, who have reached maturity and enjoy a blessing granted to them but not to all, even though it does distil from them to the rest?[1]

2. These words of the psalm, this lovely sound, this song equally sweet as a melody sung or a message understood, has given birth to monasteries. Brothers and sisters who longed to live as one were awakened by the song; this verse roused them like a trumpet. It rang all around the world, and those who were dispersed came together into one sheepfold. God had shouted, the Holy Spirit had shouted, the prophets had shouted; they were not heard in Judea, yet their shouting was heard throughout the world. The people among whom the song

---

1. "Blessing" in this first verse is the downward movement of God's grace to believers. In the last verse of the psalm this is seen as part of a circular movement, whereby the gifts of God evoke an answering blessing of God in praise and thanksgiving.

was constantly sung of old were deaf to the sound of it, but others came forward, peoples with open ears, of whom a prophet said, *Those who heard no tidings of him will see,*[2] *and those who have never heard of him will understand* (Is 52:15). All the same, dearly beloved, if we think carefully about the matter, it will be evident that this blessing did originally derive from the wall that represents the Jewish people.[3] It was not all the Jews who perished. Where did the apostles come from, the apostles who were the sons of the prophets, *the children of those shaken out* (Ps 126 (127):4)? We are speaking like this to people well informed already. And what about the five hundred who saw the Lord after his resurrection, whom the apostle Paul mentions:[4] Where did they come from? And the hundred and twenty who were together in one place[5] after the Lord's resurrection and ascension into heaven, upon whom the Holy Spirit came on the day of Pentecost?[6] Gathered together in one place they were, and on them descended the Spirit sent from heaven, just as had been promised. All of these were from the Jewish race. The first people to live together in unity were those who sold all their possessions and laid the proceeds at the feet of the apostles.[7] As we are told, *Goods were distributed to all, as each one needed,* and *no one claimed anything as private property, but all things were held by them in common* (Acts 2:45; 4:32).

What does the psalm imply by the words, *in unity*? The same passages tell us: *They had but one mind and one heart* (Acts 4:32) intent on God. These, then, were the first to hear effectively the psalm's words, *See how good and how pleasant it is for brothers to dwell together in unity!* They were the first but not the only ones, for this love and fraternal unity did not reach them only to end there. The intense joy of charity came upon their descendants too, and with it the practice of vowing to God. Vows are promises made to God, and another psalm encourages us, *Make your vows to the Lord your God and carry them out* (Ps 75:12(76:11)). It is better to abstain from making a vow than to make one and not keep it. All the same, a soul ought to be energetic in this matter, ready both to make a vow and to see it through, rather than hanging back from vowing anything

---

2. Variant: "have seen."
3. See Eph 2:14–22.
4. See 1 Cor 15:6.
5. See Acts 1:15.
6. See Acts 2:1–4.
7. See Acts 4:34–35.

because it believes itself incapable. It certainly will be incapable if it thinks it can fulfil its vow by its own strength.

Circumcellions—pseudo-monks

3. In case you hear anyone insulting you, Catholics,[8] about our monks, we should point out that it is from the words of this psalm that their name is derived. As soon as you begin to revile the heretics, and with justification, about their Circellions,[9] in the hope that their very shame may lead to their amendment, they fling back at you similar insults about monks. But consider first whether the two groups are comparable. If you need to resort to your own arguments you will have a hard time; but there is no need for verbal argument. All you need to do is to advise each of your opponents to look—simply look, that's all—and make the comparison. And what need is there of any words from us either? Only let drunkards be compared with the temperate, the reckless with the circumspect, fanatics with open and straightforward people, vagrants with those who live in communities. Yet the heretics come with their customary challenge, "What does the name 'monks' mean?" And when we reply, with much better reason, "What does the name 'Circellions' mean?" they say, "That is not their name, 'Circellions'!" Perhaps we have, indeed, corrupted the form of the name, but will they tell us the proper name for these ruffians?

---

8. Variant supported by one witness: "hear any Catholic insulting you."
9. *Circellio* appears, from Augustine's ensuing remarks, to be a popular abbreviated form of *Circumcellio*, itself a derogatory term. Augustine refers to them several times, and always unflatteringly, in his anti-Donatist writings, where they appear as bands of fanatical extremists, given to violence, drunkenness, and assaults on the persons and property of Catholics. They may have originated as groups of ascetics trekking from place to place and therefore as pseudo-monks, in Augustine's view. Though Donatist bishops seem to have used Circumcellions at times to harass Catholics, the link between Donatism and the Circumcellions is obscure. Since Roman imperial authority was invoked by Catholics against violence and disorder, and also (eventually) to refute Donatist claims (see the note at Exposition 2 of Psalm 101, 9), it is possible that anti-Roman sentiment may have been the link between them. The real name of the roving ascetics was *Agonistici*, "Warriors" (see section 6 below), but the name "Circumcellions," coined by Catholics, may have meant "those who dwell near the chapels" [of martyrs]. But such chapels usually had stores of food nearby, and Augustine sometimes means by *cellae* "storehouses" rather than "chapels." It may be, therefore, that the notion of "pillaging storehouses" was added by Catholics to the Circumcellions' crime sheet. See also the note at Exposition of Psalm 10,5.

They may indeed be called Circumcellions, not Circellions, and if that is what they are called, let them manifest[10] what they are. They are called Circumcellions because they wander around storehouses;[11] this is their custom, always to be roaming about, with no fixed abode. What they do you well know; and they too[12] know it, whether they approve or not.

Three groups mentioned in the gospels typify clerics, religious, and laity

4. Nonetheless, dearest friends, there are spurious monks too. We know some of them, yet the dedicated brotherhood of real monks is not discredited by those who profess to be what they are not. Just as there are spurious clerics, and some among believers who do not deserve the name, so too there are bogus monks. All these three classes of people, of which I have just reminded you, brothers and sisters, have good and bad among them; and I think this is not the only time I have mentioned them.[13] These three are mentioned in the gospel: *Two men will be in the field: one will be taken, the other left. Two men will be in bed: one will be taken, the other left. Two women will be at the mill: one will be taken, the other left.* (Mt 24:40–41; Lk 17:34) The ones in the field represent those who rule the Church; this is why the apostle says, *I planted, Apollos watered, but God gave the growth* (1 Cor 3:6). That shows he was a worker in the field, doesn't it? By the people in bed the Lord meant us to understand those who love a quiet life—for a bed symbolizes restful quiet—those who do not mingle with the crowds or involve themselves in the general human hubbub but serve God in leisure.[14] Yet even from these one will be taken, another left. There are worthy practitioners among them, but there are also unworthy ones. Do not be shocked when some are shown up as false; there are others lying hidden who will not be shown up until the end. Then again, we are told that *there will be two women at the mill*. This is put into the feminine because the Lord meant ordinary

---

10. Variant: "they manifest."
11. Or possibly "chapels": *circum cellas vagantur.*
12. The Donatist authorities, presumably.
13. Compare Exposition of Psalm 99, 13.
14. *In otio.* A richer and more positive notion for the ancients; see the note at Exposition 1 of Psalm 36, 2.

laity.[15] But why are they said to be at the mill? Because their business is in the world, a world continually revolving like a millstone—and woe betide anyone crushed by it! Good, faithful lay people involve themselves in the world, but in such a way that, while one is ground to powder by it, another is plucked free, for the world's activities turn some into lovers of secular things, frauds, impostors. Others, though engaged in the same business, conduct themselves as the apostle recommends: *Those who use the world should do so as though they made no use of it; for the form of this world is passing away, and I want you to be free from preoccupation* (1 Cor 7:31–32). Do you not gather from that passage who will be freed from the mill?

It is quite obvious that rich people are liable to commit many sins. They are busier, they have more affairs to attend to, and a larger income is at their disposal; it is therefore difficult for them to avoid committing all the more sins. The gospel says of them that *it is easier for a camel to squeeze through the eye of a needle than for a rich person to enter the kingdom of heaven* (Mt 19:24). But when the apostles were saddened by this saying, assuming that there was no further hope for the rich, the Lord consoled them: *Things that are impossible for human beings are easy for God* (Lk 18:27). But how does God accomplish this so easily? Listen to the apostle, and do not take his instructions lightly: *Instruct the rich of this world not to be high-minded* (1 Tm 6:17). You may find a poor person who is proud, but you also find rich people who are humble, Christians well aware that all these things pass and flow away and that they brought nothing with them into this world and will take nothing out of it. They ponder the fate of another rich man who, while burning in hell-fire, longed for a drop of water to trickle down to him from the finger of the pauper who had formerly hungered for crumbs from his table.[16] Mindful of this example, sensible rich persons follow the apostle's guidance: *Let them not put their trust in unreliable wealth, but in the living God, who gives us everything to enjoy in abundance. Let them be rich in good works, give readily, and share what they have.* And how will this profit them? *Let them use their wealth to lay a good foundation*

---

15. In the gospel passages quoted it appears that women are mentioned specifically to make the point that judgment will overtake all, without distinction of sex or age. But Augustine seems to think that women are mentioned because they are subordinate and therefore represent the laity, as ruled by their prelates. This idea is explicit in his Exposition 1 of Psalm 36, 2.
16. See Lk 16:19–31.

for the future, and so attain true life. (1 Tm 6:17–19) This is a description of the woman who will be freed from the mill. But what about anyone who resembles the rich man who *was clothed in purple and fine linen, and feasted sumptuously every day* (Lk 16:19), despising the poor man who lay outside his gate? Such a person will be left, for, of the two working at the mill, *one will be taken, the other left*.

Noah, Daniel, and Job are also types of the same three vocations

5. Ezekiel speaks in a similar way about three typical persons, whom we can reasonably understand to represent the same three groups. *When the Lord unleashes a sword over the land,* he says, *even if Noah, Daniel and Job are among the people, they will not save their sons or daughters. Only they themselves will be saved* (Ezk 14:17.14.16). Those three individuals were indeed saved long ago, but under their three names three classes of people are typified. Noah stands for the rulers of the Church, because he steered the ark through the flood. But Daniel chose a quiet life, in which he might serve God in celibacy; he did not seek a wife. He was a holy man who conducted his life by heavenly desires; through many trials he was proved to be pure gold. What a peaceful person he must have been, if he could be calm even among lions![17] Daniel is called *a man of desires* (Dn 10:11.19)—chaste and holy desires, of course—and he stands for those servants of God of whom the psalm speaks: *See how good and how pleasant it is for brothers to dwell together in unity!*

Job corresponds to the one woman who is taken and freed from toiling at the mill. He had a wife, he had children, he had a vast fortune; in fact he had so plentiful a supply of worldly goods that the devil was able to accuse him of worshiping God not disinterestedly but because of all he had been given.[18] The adversary brought that charge against the holy man, but in the course of his testing it was proved that he did indeed worship God disinterestedly, not because of all he had received but out of love for the giver. When sudden calamities and trials overtook him he lost all his possessions; he lost his inheritance and he lost his heirs. All that was left to him was his wife—left not as a comforter but to tempt him further. Yet you know what he said: *The Lord gave, and the Lord has taken away. This has happened as the Lord willed: may the Lord's name be blessed.* (Jb 1:21)

---

17. See Dn 6:22; 14:39.
18. See Jb 1:9–10.

Another declaration was verified in him, one that we sing every day (and let us hope our way of life is attuned to it): *I will bless the Lord at all times; his praise shall be in my mouth always* (Ps 33:2(34:1)).

Under these three names, then, three types of people are represented, just as they are by the three groups in the gospel, as I have explained.

An argument about the scriptural basis for the terms "agonistici" and "monks"

6. Now what about those who ridicule us for the use of the term "monks"? What do they object to? Perhaps they will say, "Our people aren't called Circumcellions; it is you who give them that abusive name. We don't call them that." Let them tell us what they do call them, and you will be better informed. They call them *agonistici* or "warriors," and we agree that it would be an honorable name—if only the reality matched it! Before we go on to that, holy brothers and sisters, notice in passing how they challenge us: "Show us where the name 'monks' occurs in scripture." Well, come to that, let them show us where scripture uses the term *agonistici*. "Oh, but it does," they say. "We give them that name because it derives from *agon*.[19] They engage in a contest, and the apostle says, *I have fought the good fight* (2 Tm 4:7). They are the warriors who fight against the devil and prevail. Therefore these soldiers of Christ are called *agonistici*." If only they were soldiers of Christ and not soldiers of the devil! Their war-cry, *Deo laudes,* is more frightening than a lion's roar. They presume to rail at us because our brethren, on meeting people, say, *Deo gratias!* "What's that—*Deo gratias*?" the heretics ask. Are you so dull that you don't know what *Deo gratias* means? Anyone who says *Deo gratias* is giving thanks to God. Ask yourself: Is it not right for a brother to give thanks to God when he meets his brother? Is it not a matter for thanksgiving when two people who dwell in Christ see each other? You find in our *Deo gratias* an excuse for derision, but people find in your *Deo laudes* a cause for weeping.

However, you certainly have given a reason for calling them *agonistici*. All right, call them that; it's fine as far as we are concerned. May the Lord grant that they do fight against the devil and not against Christ, whose Church they persecute. But tell me this: you call them *agonistici*, and you find justification for the name in the apostle's

---

19. Conflict.

words, *I have fought a good contest.*[20] Why then should we not use the term "monks" when the psalm says, *See how good and how pleasant it is for brothers to dwell together in unity*? Μόνος means "one," but not any kind of "one." One person may be present in a crowd; he is "one," but one with many others. He can be called "one" but not μόνος, because μόνος means "one alone."[21] But where people live together in such unity that they form a single individual, where it is true of them, as scripture says, that they have but *one mind and one heart* (Acts 4:32)—many bodies but not many minds, many bodies but not many hearts—then they are rightly called μόνος, "one alone."

Why was one man alone healed at the pool? Let those who deride the term "monks" reply and explain to us why the man who *had been ill for thirty-eight years* replied to the Lord's question, *When the water is disturbed I have no one to take me down into it; someone else gets down there before me* (Jn 5:5.7). If one had gone down, no other person could. One alone was healed, symbolizing the unity of the Church. People who have cut themselves off from this unity understandably mock the name that signifies it. Of course the term "monks" irritates them, because they refuse to live as one with their brothers and sisters. They have abandoned Christ to follow Donatus.[22]

Beloved, you have heard this explanation about "one" and about "one alone";[23] now you must rejoice in the psalm. Let us see what comes next. The psalm is short, and we can run through it quickly if the Lord allows us. I think that the following verses, obscure though they may seem, will be clear in the light of what has been said already.

Verse 2. Oil flows from head to beard, from Christ to the strong; oil symbolizes the Holy Spirit

7. *See how good and how pleasant it is for brothers to dwell together in unity!* The psalmist who bade us, *See!* wanted us to see, and see we do, brothers and sisters, and we bless God and pray that we too may be able to invite others, "See!"

Now let the psalm tell us what these brothers are like.[24] *Like fragrant oil upon the head, flowing down upon the beard, Aaron's*

---

20. *Agonem* in this occurrence.
21. In other words, a crowd is not a community.
22. See the notes at Expositions of Psalms 10,1 and 85,14.
23. *Hoc de uno, et de uno solo.* Variant: *hoc denuo, et de uno solo*: "you have heard this afresh, and heard about one alone."
24. Variant: "and let us too run to join them."

beard, the oil that flowed down to the border of his tunic. What was Aaron? A priest. But who is the true priest if not the one priest who has entered once for all into the holy of holies?[25] Who is the real priest if not he who was both priest and victim? Who if not he who could find nothing pure in the world to offer and therefore offered himself?[26] The fragrant oil is upon the head because Christ is one whole with the Church, and the oil flows from the head. Our head is Christ. crucified and buried, who was raised from the dead and ascended into heaven. And the Holy Spirit came from our head.[27] To what did he come? To the beard. A beard is the sign of strong men; a beard is typical of young, vigorous, energetic, eager people. That is why we say, "He's a bearded fellow," when we describe someone of this character. The fragrant oil therefore fell first upon the apostles, upon those who withstood the first attacks from the world: the Holy Spirit came down on them[28] for this reason. Those who first began to live together in unity suffered persecution. Yet, because the oil had flowed down onto the beard, they suffered but were not overcome. Their head had preceded them on the path of suffering, and from him the oil flowed. Who could conquer the beard when such an example had gone before?

Unconquered love in Stephen: the effect of the oil

8. Saint Stephen was part of the beard. This is what being unconquered means: that charity is not conquered by one's enemies. Those who persecuted the saints believed that they had conquered: they beat the saints, and the saints suffered the beatings; the one group was doing the killing, the other being killed. Would not anyone have said that the former were conquerors, the latter conquered? But because charity was not conquered, fragrant oil flowed down onto the beard. Look at Stephen. Charity raged in him: it raged against them while they were listening to him, but while they were stoning him he interceded for them. What did he say while they were listening? *You stiff-necked*

---

25. See Heb 9:12. The mention of oil immediately recalls Christ, the anointed. Augustine thinks of Christ's anointing not as an exclusive privilege but as a dynamic process, spreading out to more and more of his members: the apostles first, then the early Christian community at Jerusalem, then the martyrs, and then monks.
26. See Heb 9:14.
27. Compare the title *Spiritalis unctio* in the hymn *Veni Creator*.
28. Variant: "the Spirit came down on those holy men."

people, uncircumcised in heart and ears, you are for ever resisting the Holy Spirit! (Acts 7:51) Look at that beard! Was he mollifying them? Was he afraid? No, but when they heard his accusations against them they grew enraged too. Stephen raged: he raged with his tongue but loved with his heart, and the charity in him was not overcome. They shrank in horror from his words, like darkness fleeing from light, and rushed for stones to execute Stephen. As Stephen had pelted them with words, they now pelted him with stones. Which do you think ought to have made Stephen angrier—being stoned or being listened to? But watch him: he is gentle and forbearing when stoned and savage when they listen to him. Why was he savage while they listened?[29] Because he wanted them to change their outlook. But when the stones rained upon him his charity was not conquered, because fragrant oil had run down from head to beard, and he had heard the head saying, *Love your enemies, and pray for those who persecute you* (Mt 5:44). From that same head he had heard something else; from Christ hanging on the cross he had heard the prayer, *Father, forgive them, for they do not know what they are doing* (Lk 23:34). The oil that had flowed from the head to the beard produced a similar effect, for as Stephen was being stoned he knelt and prayed, *Lord, do not hold this sin against them* (Acts 7:60).

The oil flows from the beard to the border of the tunic: monastic life

9. The martyrs were thus like the beard; they were many and brave, and they endured multiple persecutions. But if the oil had not descended further, from the beard, we would have had no monasteries today. It flowed down, however, even to the border of the garment, for that is what the psalm says: *It flowed down to the border of his tunic.* That is why the Church could follow the martyrs, and oil from the Lord's garment engendered monasteries, for the priestly garment symbolizes the Church. Of this tunic the apostle says that Christ willed *to present the Church to himself as his bride, free from stain or wrinkle* (Eph 5:27). The Church is cleansed so that no stain may mar it, and stretched so that it may have no wrinkle. Where does a fuller stretch his cloth? On a wooden frame. Every day we see tunics being crucified, as it were: the fullers crucify them to make sure they have no wrinkles.

---

29. This sentence is omitted by many witnesses.

Now what is the border of the tunic? What are we meant to understand by the border of the garment, brothers and sisters? The border is the edge of a garment, so does it mean that even at the end of time the Church will have brothers dwelling in unity? Or should we rather think of the border as a symbol of perfection, since it is at the border that a garment is finished and perfect? They surely are mature persons who have mastered the art of living in unity; they are perfect, for they fulfil the law. How is Christ's law fulfilled by those who dwell as brothers in unity? The apostle gives us the answer: *Bear one another's burdens, and so you will fulfil the law of Christ* (Gal 6:2). This is the border of the tunic. But now, my brothers and sisters, how are we to know which border it is onto which the fragrant oil trickles? There are borders at the sides, but I do not think the psalm meant these. The oil could trickle down, though, from the beard to the border at the top, where an opening is made for the head. Now, just as, when someone is dressing, his head enters through those borders at the top, so too in the case of brothers who dwell in unity. Christ, our head, enters through the borders of fraternal charity that he may be clothed: that is to say, so that he may have the Church clinging closely to him.

Verse 3. From Hermon, the "exalted light," grace flows to the mature in Zion

10. What else does the psalm say? *Like the dew of Hermon, which flows down to the mountains*[30] *of Zion.* The psalmist wanted us to understand, brothers and sisters, that those who live as brothers in unity do so only through the grace of God. They do not achieve it by their own efforts, nor is it the result of their own merits; it is God's gift and comes to us by his grace like dew from heaven. The earth does not rain on itself, does it? Does not everything the earth brings forth dry up if no rain falls on it from above? In another passage of the psalms it is said, *You allotted gratuitous rain to your inheritance, O God* (Ps 67:10(68:9)). Why was it called *gratuitous*? Because it came not in response to human merits but by God's gracious will. Sinners that we are, what good have we deserved? Have we, iniquitous folk, merited any good at all? From Adam is born only another Adam, and Adam is weighed down by many sins. When someone is born, Adam is born, a condemned person from the already condemned, and the

---

30. Plural, according to the best readings here and in the following lines. Many variants read the singular.

new-born will by his or her sinful life augment Adam's score.[31] What good has Adam deserved, then? And yet our merciful Lord loves us. The bridegroom has loved not a beautiful bride but one whom he can make beautiful. This is why God's grace is called *the dew of Hermon*.

11. But you ought to know more about Hermon. It is a mountain far distant from Zion, which is another name for Jerusalem. It is therefore strange that the psalm says, *Like the dew of Hermon, which flows down to the mountains of Zion*, when Mount Hermon is so far from Jerusalem. It is even said to be beyond the Jordan. We had better look for the meaning through some interpretation of Hermon. The name is Hebrew, and a translation has been provided for us by those who know the language. Hermon is said to mean "exalted light." Evidently, then, the dew flows from Christ, for there is no exalted light other than Christ. How was he exalted? At first on the cross when he was humiliated, but such humiliation as his could be nothing but exaltation. The part played by men and women was shrinking and was typified by John the Baptist, while God's action was growing greater and greater and became effective in our Lord Jesus Christ. This is symbolized by the respective birthdays of John and the Lord. According to the Church's tradition, John was born on June 24, at the season when the days begin to grow shorter; but the Lord was born on December 25, as they begin to lengthen. Listen to John himself making the point: *He must grow greater, I must dwindle* (Jn 3:30). The manner of their suffering teaches the same lesson. The Lord was lifted up on the cross, but John was diminished by being beheaded.

The exalted light is Christ, and from him flows the dew of Hermon. Any of you who aspire to live in unity must hope for this dew. Let it soak you, all of you together. Otherwise you will not have the strength to keep to what you profess, nor will you have the strength and daring to make your vows in the first place, unless the Lord has thundered.[32] Nor will you abide by your promises unless his nourishing richness is constantly available to you, the nourishment that falls upon the mountains of Zion.

---

31. Augustine's doctrine of original sin is taken for granted rather than stated here. See Exposition of Psalm 50, 10 and Exposition 1 of Psalm 101, 11 and the notes at both places.
32. In the immediate context he thinks of thunder heralding rain. But there is an echo of the resounding call sent forth by the psalm. See his remarks in section 2.

12. Now *the mountains of Zion* represent great persons in Zion. What is Zion? The Church. And what are mountains in the Church? Our great ones, for those symbolized by mountains are the same people as those suggested by the beard and by the border of the tunic. A beard is not found in anyone except the mature. None are therefore found really living together in unity except those in whom the charity of Christ has come to perfection. If Christ's charity is not present in people, then even if they live together they are disagreeable, offensive, and turbulent; they upset others by their anxieties and look for gossip about their neighbors. It is like what happens when draught-horses are yoked together and one of them is restless: not only does he not do his share of the pulling but he breaks up the cart with his hooves. But a person on whom the dew of Hermon falls, the dew that *flows down to the mountains of Zion*, is quiet, peaceable, humble, and tolerant, and instead of murmuring he devotes himself to prayer. There is a scriptural text that magnificently describes murmurers: *The innermost heart of a fool is like a cartwheel* (Sir 33:5). What does that mean? Why a cartwheel? Because a cartwheel carries a load of grass and creaks. It cannot help creaking. Plenty of brothers are like that. They live together, but only in a physical sense.

But what of the others? Who are the ones who really live in unity? *The multitude of believers had but one mind and one heart intent on God. No one claimed anything as private property, but all things were held by them in common.* (Acts 4:32) This is what has marked them out; this is a description of the ones who belong to the beard, who are found on the border of the tunic, who are counted among the mountains of Zion. And if a few murmurers are found there as well, let them remember the Lord's word: *One will be taken, the other left* (Mt 24:40).

The circle of blessing

13. *For there has the Lord ordained blessing.* Where? Among the brothers who live in unity. There he has ordained that blessing be bestowed, and there do the people who live in concord themselves bless the Lord,[33] for you do not bless him by discord. It is pointless to protest that your tongue is singing the Lord's praise if your heart

---

33. The circular movement of blessing noted in section 1 is explicit in this section. The divine grace that enables frail humans to live together united in mind and heart comes to them as a blessing from God; they in turn praise, thank,

is singing a different tune, for then you will be blessing him with your mouth but cursing with your heart. *With their mouths they were blessing, but cursing in their hearts all the while* (Ps 61:5(62:4)), says another psalm. Are those our own words? Certain people are marked out by them. You bless the Lord and then you continue your prayer by cursing your enemy.[34] Is that what you heard from the Lord himself, when he bade you, *Love your enemies* (Mt 5:44)?

But if you heed his command and love your enemy and pray for him or her, then it will be true in your case that *there has the Lord ordained blessing*, and there you will have *life for ever*, for all eternity. Many people curse their enemies because they are in love with the present life. Why is this? Because they hold this passing life to be all-important and have an eye to the advantages it offers. Where has your enemy pushed you around, provoking you to curse him? Is it here on earth that you feel you are being crowded and trodden on? Then emigrate! Live in heaven! "How can I live in heaven?" you will say. "I am a human being of flesh and blood, given over to the flesh." Let your heart race ahead to where you will follow in body. Do not be deaf to the invitation, "Lift up your hearts."[35] No one will tread on you in heaven.

The next psalm is a good sequel to this.

---

and bless God for his goodness, but their communal life in charity is itself praise and blessing rendered to him.
34. An idea that recurs elsewhere in Augustine's preaching: compare Sermons 56, 2,2 and 211, 7,6; Exposition of Psalm 39, 4. Prayer is not to be viewed as a means of coercing God into harming one's enemies.
35. On this liturgical phrase see the note at Exposition of Psalm 10, 3.

Exposition of Psalm 133

A Continuation of the Preceding Sermon

Verse 1. Blessing God in the spaciousness of love

1. *Come now, bless the Lord, all you servants of the Lord, you who stand in the Lord's house, in the courts of the house of our God.* Why are the words, *in the courts*, added? Courts are wide, spacious areas in a house. Anyone standing in such courts is not cramped or crowded or squeezed but has plenty of room.[1] Remain in this wide space and you will have strength to love your enemy, because you are not in love with those things in which you might have felt that your enemy was cramping your style. How are you to understand this standing in the Lord's courts? Stand in charity; then you will stand in his courts. There is wide space in charity but cramped quarters where there is hatred. Listen to the apostle's words: *May anger, wrath, and tribulation press hard upon every human soul whose deeds are evil* (Rom 2:8–9). But what does he say about the breadth of charity? *The charity of God has been poured abroad into our hearts through the Holy Spirit who has been given us* (Rom 5:5). When you hear *poured abroad*, think of wide space, and when you hear "wide space," think of the courts of the Lord. You will truly enjoy the Lord's blessing when you do not curse your enemies.

The Spirit is urging those who suffer tribulation to view their troubles even as matter for glad thanksgiving, for he says, *Come now, bless the Lord, all you servants of the Lord.* What does *Come now* suggest? Now, in the present era, bless him, for it goes without saying that when our tribulations are over we shall be free to bless the Lord unhindered, as we have been assured elsewhere: *Blessed are they who dwell in your house; they will praise you for ever and ever* (Ps 83:5(84:4)). But those who are destined to bless the Lord unceasingly hereafter begin to bless him now, here amid tribulations and trials and vexations and all the adversity they meet in this world, amid the stealthy attacks of the enemy, amid the devil's trickery and

---

1. Variant: "enjoys it."

open assaults. This is what the psalm means by its invitation, *Come now, bless the Lord, all you servants of the Lord, you who stand in the Lord's house.*

And what does standing indicate? In means that you persevere. Of one who used to be an archangel it was said, *He did not stand in the truth* (Jn 8:44). Of the bridegroom's friend, on the contrary, scripture says, *But the bridegroom's friend, who stands and hears him, rejoices intensely at the bridegroom's voice* (Jn 3:29).

Verse 2. Praising God in the dark night

2. *You who stand in the Lord's house, in the courts of the house of our God, lift up your hands to the holy place at night, and bless the Lord.* It is easy enough to bless him in daytime. What does daytime signify? Favorable conditions, for the night is a sad time, but daylight is cheerful. When your enterprises prosper, you bless the Lord. You want a son, and one is born to you, so you bless the Lord. Your wife has come safely through childbirth, and you bless the Lord. Your child was ill but has recovered, so you bless the Lord. But perhaps when your child was ill you went looking for an astrologer[2] or a fortune-teller. Then you were launching a curse against the Lord, if not with your tongue, at least by your conduct. A curse has emerged from your behavior and your life. Do not pride yourself on praising him with your tongue if by your way of life you are cursing him. "But how do I curse him by my life?" you will ask. Because people notice how you live, and they say, "Look at him: he's a Christian! That's what Christians are like!" And so Christ is blasphemed on your account. If your life curses him, what is the point of the blessings uttered by your tongue?

So then, *bless the Lord.* When? *At night.* When Job blessed God, how gloomy a night had fallen upon him! All his former possessions had been taken away, as were the children for whom he had been keeping them. What a woeful night! But let us see whether he did not bless God *at night.* He said, *The Lord gave, and the Lord has taken away. This has happened as the Lord willed: may the Lord's name*

---

2. *Mathematicum.* From an earlier application to scholars who made mathematical calculations about the stars, the term had become debased and now meant those who superstitiously tried to predict the fate of human beings, or sought the causes of human actions, in the stars. Astrologers and those who consulted them were declared liable to the death penalty under Valentinian I.

be blessed. (Jb 1:21) How black was his night! Stricken with disease from head to foot, he oozed rottenness. And then Eve[3] made bold to tempt him: *Curse God, and die.* But listen to him responding out of his night: *You have spoken like the silly woman you are. If we have received good things from the Lord's hands, should we not endure the bad too?* (Jb 2:9–10) Now you see what the injunction means, *Lift up your hands to the holy place at night, and bless the Lord.* What did Job say? *You have spoken like the silly woman you are.* Stinking though he was, Adam fended off Eve, as though telling her, "Surely it's enough that through your action I've become mortal! You got the better of me in paradise, but you are worsted here on my dungheap."

This was a powerful grace from God. Where could it have come from, had *the dew of Hermon* (Ps 132 (133):3) not drenched his soul and had the Lord not rained down his sweetness, so that our earth might yield its fruit?[4] *Lift up your hands to the holy place at night, and bless the Lord.*

Verse 3. Many bless the Lord, but he blesses his servants as one

3. *May the Lord bless you*[5] *from Zion, he who made heaven and earth.* The exhortation to bless the Lord was addressed to many, but his blessing descends upon only one, because he has made one out of the many, as we heard: *How good and how pleasant it is for brothers to dwell together in unity!* (Ps 132(133):1) We find the many in the word *brothers*, but the one because they dwell *in unity.* Therefore, *may the Lord bless you*[6] *from Zion, he who made heaven and earth.* Let no one among you complain, "The blessing doesn't reach me, it doesn't include me." Who do you think it is that he blessed[7] when he said, *May the Lord bless you from Zion?* He blessed one only. Make sure you belong within that unity, and then the blessing has reached you as well.

---

3. Augustine hears in the dialogue between Job and his wife a replay of the story in Gn 3:6–12. The idea occurs elsewhere in his treatment of the psalms; compare Expositions of Psalms 93,19 and Psalm 97,6.
4. See Ps 84:13(85:12).
5. Singular.
6. Singular.
7. Variants: "Think who it is that he blessed"; "Whom do you think he was speaking about."

Exposition of Psalm 134

A Sermon to the People

Verse 1. As his servants and his children, we must praise the Lord

1. It should be very delightful for us—and a matter for rejoicing that it is so delightful—to do what this psalm urges us: *Praise the name of the Lord.* It immediately indicates the reason why it is right for us to praise the name of the Lord, for it continues, *Praise the Lord, you who are his servants.* What could be more just than that? What more fitting? What more delightful? If the Lord's servants do not praise him, they are proud, ungrateful, and impious. In any case, what will they gain by not praising him except to feel their Lord's severity? An ungrateful servant who has refused to praise his Lord does not thereby escape from his servile status. Whether you praise him or not you are his servant, but if you praise him you appease him, whereas if you do not praise him you offend him. The psalm's exhortation is therefore a good one and expedient for us, for we need to concentrate on how God is to be praised rather than on questioning whether praising him is the right thing to do.

So then, *praise the name of the Lord.* The psalm urges us, the prophet urges us, the Spirit of God urges us, to praise the Lord. *He* does not grow greater through our praise, but we do. God is none the better if you praise him, nor any the worse if you rail against him, but you will be the better for giving him praise and much the worse if you find fault with him. In either case he remains good, as he ever is. Think about it: he teaches the servants who deserve well of him, and the preachers of his word, and the rulers of his Church, and those who reverence his name, and those who obey his commands, that they must guard within their own consciences the sweetness they draw from their good lives and so avoid being either corrupted by human approval or disheartened by human blame. How much more, then, must he who teaches us this lesson himself abide unchangeably above all things? How much more true must it be that he is no greater if you praise him and no less if you denounce him?

But to praise the Lord is beneficial for us, and this is why he commands us to do so; he does not order it out of arrogance. Let us, then, hearken to his command: *Praise the name of the Lord, praise the Lord, you who are his servants.* As his servants, you are not doing anything incongruous in praising the Lord, and it would still be right for you to go on praising him even if you were to remain no more than servants for ever. How much more, then, should you so praise him as his servants that you may deserve to be his children too?

Verse 2. Praise him out of gratitude for being brought into his house

2. It should be noted, however, that another psalm reminds us, *Praise befits the upright* (Ps 32(33):1), and that we are warned elsewhere, *Praise is not seemly in a sinner's mouth* (Sir 15:9). And again in another passage it is said, *By a sacrifice of praise I shall be honored, and there is the way where I will show him the salvation of God*, and therefore *to the sinner the Lord says, What right have you to expound my just judgments, and take my covenant on your lips? You hate instruction, and have thrown my words behind you.* (Ps 49(50):23.16–17) It is evident that, if in this great house[1] there is a bad servant, he or she has no right to seize on the exhortation in our present psalm, *Praise the Lord, you who are his servants*, and suppose that offering praise to the Lord will excuse bad conduct. It will not. The psalm goes on immediately to indicate the character of people who praise the Lord, addressing them thus: *You who stand in the Lord's house, in the courts of the house of our God.* It says, *You who stand*, not, "You who collapse." The people who are described as standing are those who persevere in his commandments, who serve God in sincere faith, in firm hope, and in unfeigned charity; they honor his Church and do not, by unworthy lives, obstruct others who wish to enter it but find stumbling-blocks in their way. And so the psalm invites you, *who stand in the Lord's house: praise the name of the Lord.* Be grateful, for once you were outside it, but now you stand within. And since you now have this firm standing-place, is it not important to you to acknowledge him and praise him who raised you up when you were lying prone, and made you stand in his house? Is it not important to you to praise him here, where he deserves our praise? Do you regard it as insignificant that we stand in the Lord's

---

1. See 2 Tm 2:20.

house? Even in this temporary stage, while we are still wayfarers, while we stand in this house which is also called a tent for travelers, does it not even now evoke our most profound gratitude that we stand here? Should we not reflect on what a privilege this is? Should we not ponder on the status we have been given? Must we not think back to where we lay helpless, and contrast that place with this house where we have been assembled now? Should we not remember how godless, heedless folk were not seeking the Lord, and how he sought out those who did not seek him, how he found them and awakened them, called those whom he had awakened, brought those whom he had called into his house, and made them stand there? Whoever reflects on these things with due gratitude thoroughly belittles himself when faced with the love of his Lord, from whom he has received such immense gifts. He can find no sufficient recompense to offer to the Lord for such great favors. So what is left but to offer him thanks, though this is no adequate requital? The best expression of thanksgiving is to take the chalice of the Lord and call upon his name, for what return can a servant make to the Lord for all he has given?[2] Let us heed the psalm, then: *You who stand in the Lord's house, in the courts of the house of our God, praise the Lord.*

Verse 3. God is essential goodness

3. Why shall we praise him? *Because the Lord is good.* So briefly, in this short phrase, is the motive for praising the Lord our God proposed to us: we must do it because *the Lord is good.* But he is not good in the manner of the good things he has made. God made all things exceedingly good[3]—not just good, but exceedingly good. He made heaven and earth and all that is in them good, exceedingly good. But if he made all these good things, what must he who made them be like? And yet, although he made these things good, and he who made them is vastly better than all he has made, you still find no better way to speak of him than to say, *The Lord is good,* as long as you understand that only he, from whom all other things proceed, is himself good in the proper sense. He made all things that are good, but he is himself the Good whom no one made. He is good by his own goodness, not by participating in some good thing outside himself; he is good by his own good self, not by cleaving to some other good. For

---

2. See Ps 115(116):12–13.
3. See Gn 1:31.

me, it is good to cleave to my God[4], who needs no one else to make him good, though all things need him to become good. Do you want a gospel text to indicate his unique goodness? *None is good except one, God alone* (Mk 10:18).

I do not want to skim quickly over this unique character of his goodness, yet I lack the power to state it as it deserves. I am afraid that if I pass over it hastily I may be convicted of ingratitude; yet I fear equally that if I undertake to expound it I may sink under the mighty weight of the Lord's praise. I ask you, then, brothers and sisters, to accept me as I am—praising him and falling short—so that even if my explanation of the praise I offer is insufficient, at least the devotion of the one who offers it may be acceptable. May he approve me for having tried and forgive me for my shortcomings.

4. When I hear those words, *The Lord is good*, an indescribable sweetness takes hold of me. I study and minutely survey all the things around me; I see that all of them are from him, and so, even though they delight me, I return to him who is their source, longing to understand better that *the Lord is good*. Then, entering again into his presence within myself, as far as I am able, I find him more interior than myself and far above me, because the Lord is so good that he needs nothing else to make him good. Plainly I cannot praise these other things apart from him, but I find him to be perfect without them, needing nothing, unchangeable, seeking no kind of good to enhance his own happiness and fearing no manner of evil whereby he could be diminished. What more can I say? In creation I discover a good sky, a good sun, and good stars; I regard the good earth and find all things that come to birth upon it to be good and all of them dependent on the earth and rooted there. The creatures that walk and crawl upon it are good, and those that fly in the air and swim in the waters are good. Humankind too I know to be good, for the gospel says, *A good man brings out good things from the good treasury of his heart* (Lk 6:45). I recognize as good every angel who has not fallen through pride and become a devil but is united by obedience to the Lord who created him. All these I call good, but good only as specified by their name: a good sky, a good angel, a good man. When I turn to God, I think it better to attach no other word but to say simply that he is good. Our Lord Jesus Christ himself, who spoke of *a good man*, also said, *None is good except one, God alone* (Mk

---

4. See Ps 72(73):28.

10:18). Did he not thereby prompt us to seek further and distinguish a good which is good by derivation from some other good, from a good that is good of itself? How good then must he be from whom all good things derive? You will find no good thing anywhere that does not depend for its goodness upon him. Being good himself, he makes other things good because that is his nature,[5] and so we know him to be essential goodness.

We must not on this account deny true existence to the things he has made, for to deny real existence to his creatures would be to insult their maker. Why did he make them, if anything he has made does not exist? And what did he make, if anything he made has no being? The things he has made do exist; yet, when we compare them with him, we know that he alone is true being. Thus he said, *I AM WHO AM*, and, *Thus shall you say to the children of Israel, HE WHO IS has sent me to you* (Ex 3:14). He did not say, "I am the Lord, the omnipotent, the merciful, the just one," though, if he had said that, he would have spoken truly. Instead he set aside all those names that could be applied to God and answered that he was called Being-Itself, as though that were his name. *Thus shall you say*, he ordered, *HE WHO IS has sent me*. His very nature is to be, and so true is this that, when compared with him, all created things are as though they had no being. When not compared with him they do exist, for they derive their being from him, but compared with him they do not exist, because he is true being, unchangeable being, and this can be said of him alone. He is being, as he is also goodness, the good of all good things.

If you think about this you will realize that, whenever you admire anything, you admire it because it is good. Anyone who commends what is not good is crazy. If you praise a wicked person for his very wickedness, will you not be wicked yourself? If you commend a thief precisely for being a thief, will you not participate in his dishonesty? But if you commend a righteous person precisely because he is righteous, will you not by your commendation share his righteousness with him? Surely you will, for you would not commend a just man unless you loved him, and you would not love him if you had no justice in yourself.

---

5. The scholastics would express this idea by the axiom, *Bonitas est diffusiva sui*.

Whatever else we praise, we praise because it is good, and no greater reason, no better or stronger motive, can be given for praising God than that he is good. *Praise the Lord*, then, *because he is good.*

To contemplate God's goodness in himself is beyond our capacity, but he has given us the mediator

5. How long shall we go on singing of God's goodness? Is anyone able to conceive in his heart or embrace with his mind how good the Lord is? But let us turn our gaze back upon ourselves, recognize him in our own being, and praise the artist in his works, because we lack the capacity to contemplate him in himself. One day, perhaps, we shall be able to contemplate him, when our hearts have been so purified by faith[6] that they can at last rejoice in the truth.[7] But now, while we cannot see him, let us gaze upon his works, so that we may not fall silent in our praise. That is why it is said, *Praise the Lord because the Lord is good; sing psalms to his name, because he is sweet*. He might perhaps have been good, but not sweet, if he had not given you the power to taste him.[8] But God gave himself to men and women in such wise that he even sent us bread from heaven[9] and gave the Son who is his equal, who is everything that God himself is, to be made man and to be slain for us so that, through a humanity that is yours as well as his, you may taste what you are not. It would have been impossible for you to taste the sweetness of God, for it is far beyond you and exceedingly high, whereas you were abased and lying in the depths. But into this vast gulf of separation was sent the Mediator. You were human and could not reach God; God became human so that you, a human being who could reach another human but could not reach God, might attain to God through a man; and thus the man, Christ Jesus, became the mediator between God and humanity.[10] If he had been no more than a man, you could never have reached God by following what you are; if he had been God only, you would never have reached him because you could not have understood what you are not. But God was made a man so that by following a human being, which is within your power, you may attain to God, which is beyond

---

6. See Acts 15:9.
7. See 1 Cor 13:6.
8. See Ps 33:9(34:8).
9. See Jn 6:51.
10. See 1 Tm 2:5.

your power. He is the mediator, and this is what makes him sweet to us. What could be sweeter than angels' bread? How could the Lord fail to be sweet to us, when mortals have eaten the bread of angels?[11] Humanity is fed, as the angels are fed, on the same nourishment. He is the very truth, the very wisdom, the very power of God,[12] but you cannot enjoy his reality in the way the angels do. How do they enjoy him? As he is: *In the beginning was the Word, and the Word was with God; he was God. Everything was made through him.* But what about you? How do you touch upon him? *The Word was made flesh, and dwelt among us.* (Jn 1:1.3.14) To enable men and women to eat angels' bread, the creator of angels became a man. *Sing psalms to his name*, then, *because he is sweet.* If you have tasted, sing psalms; if you have tasted and discovered how sweet the Lord is, sing psalms; if you relish what you have tasted, praise him. If a guest has found some food delicious, would he be so ungrateful to the provider or the cook as not to express his appreciation by praising what he relishes? And if in those circumstances we ought not to be silent, shall we be silent about him who gave us everything? *Sing psalms to his name, because he is sweet.*

Since we cannot grasp Being-Itself, God has named himself the God of Abraham, Isaac, and Jacob

6. Attend now to his works. Perhaps you were straining to see the good of all good things, the good from which all things derive their goodness, the good without which nothing is good, yet which is itself good without any of them. You were straining to see him and perhaps, as you stretched the highest part of your mind, you fell back through weakness. I am guessing, from my own painful experience. But there may be someone—indeed, it is more than likely that there is someone—whose fine intelligence is stronger than mine, who has fixed the contemplation of his heart for a long time on HIM WHO IS. Let such a person praise the Lord as he can, praise him as we cannot. All the same, thanks be to God who has so tempered the expression of his praise in this psalm that both strong and weak can make it theirs. When God gave a mission to his servant Moses, he said, *I AM WHO AM*, and, *Thus shall you say to the children of Israel, HE WHO IS has sent me to you* (Ex 3:14). But because it was difficult

---

11. See Ps 77(78):25.
12. See 1 Cor 1:24.

for the human mind to take in the concept of absolute being, and a man was being sent to other men and women (though not by a man), God immediately tempered his glory and spoke gently of himself in a way that could easily be understood. He did not will to remain isolated in a majesty which demanded to be praised but was out of reach of anyone who praised him. So he continued, *Go and tell the children of Israel, the God of Abraham, the God of Isaac, and the God of Jacob has sent me to you. This is my name for ever.* (Ex 3:15) But, Lord, that other name certainly belongs to you, for you yourself said, *I AM. Tell them, HE WHO IS has sent me to you.* Why have you now changed your name, calling yourself *the God of Abraham, the God of Isaac, and the God of Jacob*?

Do you not think he would reply, giving you his reason like this? "When I said, *I AM WHO AM*, it was true, but you could not understand it. Yet when I say, *I am the God of Abraham, the God of Isaac, and the God of Jacob*, that too is true, but you can take it in. The name *I AM WHO AM* is suitable to me, but the name *the God of Abraham, the God of Isaac, and the God of Jacob* is adjusted to your comprehension. If you fall back defeated from what I am to myself, understand what I am for you."

Someone might possibly have thought that only God's declarations, *I AM WHO AM* and *HE WHO IS has sent me to you*, gave us his eternal name but that his other statement, *I am the God of Abraham, the God of Isaac, and the God of Jacob*, indicated no more than his temporal name. God made sure, however, that we would not misunderstand in this way. When he said, *I AM WHO AM*, and *HE WHO IS has sent me to you*, he did not trouble to add that this was his name for ever; whether he said so or not, it would be plainly understood. He is, he truly is, and, because he is true being, he has no beginning and no end. But for our sake he said, *I am the God of Abraham, the God of Isaac, and the God of Jacob*, and to exclude any human anxiety that this might possibly be his temporal name, but not his eternal name, he reassured us that he is leading us from temporal realities to eternal life. *This is my name for ever*, he said—not because Abraham is eternal or Isaac eternal or Jacob eternal but because God subsequently confers on them eternal life, life without end. They certainly had a beginning, but they will have no end.

7. In Abraham and Isaac and Jacob you must understand that the whole Church is personified, the whole race of Israel. But the race of Israel comprises not only the descendants of the patriarchs accord-

ing to the flesh but also those who are their progeny through faith. The apostle was addressing gentiles when he said, *If you belong to Christ, you are the descendants of Abraham, his heirs according to the promise* (Gal 3:29), and so we are all blessed in the God of Abraham and Isaac and Jacob. God did indeed bless a particular tree; he made the holy patriarchs his olive, as the apostle says, and it flowered into the people of God. This olive tree was pruned but not cut down. The proud branches were broken off: these were the blasphemous, wicked Jews. But good, productive branches remained, for the apostles grew on the olive. When the tree had been trimmed and only healthy branches were left, the wild olive of the gentiles was grafted in by the mercy of God. To this new graft the apostle says, *You, who were a wild olive, have been engrafted into them, and you have come to share in the richness of the olive tree. Do not boast at the expense of the branches. If you are tempted to boast, remember that it is not you who support the root, but the root you.* (Rom 11:17–18) This single tree stems from Abraham and Isaac and Jacob, and, what is more, the engrafted oleaster is more closely related to Abraham, Isaac, and Jacob than are the branches broken off. Since their severance they are no longer in the tree, whereas the oleaster used not to be there but is now. They deserved by their pride to be broken away, but the oleaster deserved by its humility to be grafted in. They have lost their hold on the root, but the oleaster grasps it firmly.

When, therefore, you hear about God's Israel, the Israel that truly belongs to God, do not consider yourselves alien to it. Yes, you were once the oleaster, but now you are the olive and sharers in its succulent richness. Do you want to know how it came about that the wild olive was engrafted into Abraham and Isaac and Jacob? Do you want some proof that the fact of not being related by birth to Abraham's race does not make you foreign to the olive tree? Then remember how the Lord marveled at the faith of the centurion, who belonged not to the race of Israel but to the gentiles: *Therefore I tell you*, he said, *that many will come from east and west*—there you see the oleaster in the gardener's hand. *Many will come from east and west*—we can see what he is carrying, with a view to grafting; now let us see where he inserts it: *and will sit down with Abraham and Isaac and Jacob in the kingdom of heaven.* Now we can see what he has grafted in, and where. But what does the Lord say about the natural branches? *But the children of the kingdom will be thrown into the outer darkness. In that place there will be weeping and gnashing of teeth.* (Mt 8:11–12) The event was prophesied, and the prophecy has been fulfilled.

Verse 4. The election of Israel

8. Well, then, *sing psalms to the Lord, because he is sweet,* and consider what he has done in our regard. *For the Lord chose Jacob for himself, Israel for his own possession.* Praise him and sing him psalms, because he did this. I am putting it in simple terms so that you can easily understand: he assigned other nations to the custody of angels,[13] but *the Lord chose Jacob for himself, Israel for his own possession.* He made his own people a field that he himself would cultivate, that he in person would sow. He created all peoples, of course, but he entrusted the others to angels while reserving this one people, this Jacob, to himself, to own and care for. Was that in consequence of its merits or of his own grace? The apostle tells us the answer: of two brothers not yet born God said, *The elder will serve the younger* (Gn 25:23; Rom 9:12). What merit could unborn children possibly have had before either of them had done anything, good or ill? Let not Jacob be arrogant, let him not boast, let him not attribute his privilege to his own merits. He was foreknown, predestined, and chosen in advance: not chosen for his merits but found by God's grace and given life.[14] But the same is true of all the gentiles. How did the oleaster merit its engrafting? With its bitter berries or its wild, sterile condition? It was a forest tree with no place in the Lord's field, yet in his mercy he grafted the oleaster into the olive. But, at the time when *the Lord chose Jacob for himself, Israel for his own possession,* the wild olive had not yet been grafted in.

Verse 5. God is above all so-called gods

9. How does the prophet continue? *I have known that the Lord is great.* His mind took flight to heavenly things, shaking itself free from the flesh and transcending all creatures, and there it knew that the Lord is great. It is not everyone who can know it by seeing, but all

---

13. See Exposition 1 of Psalm 88,3 and *The Literal Meaning of Genesis* 8,44–47.
14. Later theologians were to dispute hotly as to how predestination *ante praevisa merita* could be reconciled with the exercise of human free will. But both Augustine and Paul plainly consider predestination to be a fact. See also the note at Exposition 1 of Psalm 30,16.

must praise him for what he has done, for *he is sweet; and the Lord chose Jacob for himself, Israel for his own possession.*

But praise him also for this, that the psalmist could say, *I have known that the Lord is great.* This was a prophet speaking, one who had been into God's sanctuary and perhaps heard there ineffable words that human tongue may not utter.[15] What could be told to human beings he told us, but he kept within himself what could not be told. Let us then hear what he has to say with respect to things that we can understand and believe him with respect to what we cannot. Let us listen to him on a matter within our grasp — *The Lord chose Jacob for himself, Israel for his own possession* — and let us believe him concerning matters beyond our ken, his own experience that *the the Lord is great.* If we were to say to him, "Explain his greatness, please," would he not perhaps reply, "If what I see could be explained, it would not be very great, would it?" Let him then turn back to the works of God and tell us about those instead. Let him keep within his own consciousness that greatness of God which he has seen and has committed to us as an object of faith, that greatness to which he was not able to lead our eyes. Let him recount some of the Lord's actions among us so that, although we cannot see his greatness as the prophet saw it, the Lord may grow sweet for us as we contemplate his works, which we can apprehend.

I have known that the Lord is great, and that our God is higher than all gods, he says. *Gods?* Who are they? The apostle teaches that, *even if there are beings called gods in the sky or on earth (as in fact there are gods and lords aplenty), still, for us there is one God from whom all things come, and in whom we exist; and one Lord, our Lord Jesus Christ, through whom all things come, and through whom we exist* (1 Cor 8:5–6). Even to ordinary humans the term "gods" can be applied, as in another psalm: *God has taken his stand in the synagogue of the gods,* and, further on, *This is my sentence: you are gods, sons of the Most High, all of you.* (Ps 81(82):1.6) Is not God higher than human beings? And are we saying anything remarkable about him if we say that he is higher than human beings? He is higher than angels too, for angels did not make God; God made angels. He who made all things must necessarily be above all things. When the prophet came to recognize the greatness of the Lord and saw him to be above every creature, spiritual no less than corporeal, he

---

15. See 2 Cor 12:4.

acknowledged that the Lord is a great king over all gods. He is God most high, above whom no other god exists. Let his works proclaim it, for those we can understand.

Verse 6. The Lord is omnipotent in creation and in the realm of grace

10. *The Lord made whatever he wanted in heaven and on earth, in the sea and in all the places of the deep.* Who can comprehend all these? Who could make a tally of the Lord's works in heaven and on earth, in the sea and in all the places of the deep? But even if we lack the power to comprehend them all, we must firmly believe that any and every creature in the heavens, every creature on earth, every creature in the sea or in all the places of the deep, was made by the Lord, for *he made whatever he wanted in heaven and on earth, in the sea and in all the places of the deep*, as we have said already. He was not coerced into making anything that he made; rather did he make *whatever he wanted*. His will is the cause of everything he made. You make yourself a house because, if you did not, you would be homeless; it is necessity that forces you to build the house, not free will. Or you make a coat because, if you did not make it, you would walk naked; so you are led to make the coat by necessity, not free choice. Or you plant a mountain slope with vines; you sow the seed because, if you did not, you would go hungry. All these things you do under necessity. But God worked out of goodness. He did not need any of the things he made, and so we say, *The Lord made whatever he wanted*.

11. Do you think that we too have scope to act from our free will? The kinds of work we have mentioned are not done freely; we are driven by necessity because, if we omitted them, we should remain needy and unsupported. Can we find any occupation that we engage in of our free will? Yes, we certainly can. We find it when we praise God out of love for him. You act freely when you love what you praise, giving him glory not under compulsion but because you delight to praise him. God's righteous and holy subjects delighted in God, even when he chastised them. Even when all the wicked hated him, the saints delighted in him. Even under his scourge, amid suffering, labors, and wounds, and beset by poverty and need, they praised God. Even their torturers they viewed kindly. This is to love freely, gratis, not with an eye to the reward set before you, because your highest reward will be God himself, whom you love in disinterested freedom. You must so love him that you never cease to long for him as your reward, for

him who alone will satisfy you. Philip was longing like that when he said, *Show us the Father, and that is enough for us* (Jn 14:8). This is exactly the point, that we praise him with our free will, and must do so with our free will, because we praise him with delight and out of love. Even though we are rebuked by him we must never resent him, because he is always just. One who praised him declared, *The good things I have vowed to give you, and the praise I will render you, are within me, O God* (Ps 55(56):12). And in another place it is said, *Of my own free will I will offer sacrifice to you* (Ps 53:8(54:6)). What does *Of my own free will I will offer sacrifice* mean? I will praise you of my own free will, because God declares, *By a sacrifice of praise I shall be honored* (Ps 49(50):23). If you were compelled to offer to your Lord a sacrifice pleasing and acceptable to him, as sacrifices used to be dedicated[16] of old, foreshadowing what was to come, perhaps you would not have found a worthy bull in your herd, or among your goats a buck fit for the Lord's altar, or in your sheepfold a ram good enough to be offered to your Lord. And when you failed to find one you would have been concerned and wondered what to do, and perhaps you would have said to God, "I wanted to, but I had nothing to offer." But you can never say of praise, "I wanted to, but I had nothing to offer," can you? Simply having wanted to is already to have offered him praise, for what God seeks from you is not words but your heart. It will still be no excuse if you say, "But I had no tongue!" If someone is unable to speak on account of his state of health, it is true that he had no tongue, but he still had the power to praise God. If God had bodily ears and needed the bodily sounds you might make, then if you lacked the power of speech you would be forced to remain silent from his praise. But in fact he seeks your heart and sees into your heart; he is the inner witness, the judge, the one who approves your offering, your helper,[17] and the one who crowns you. It is enough if you offer him your will. When you have the health, you confess with your lips and it leads you to salvation; when you lack the health, you believe in your heart with the faith that justifies.[18] With your heart you praise him, with your heart you bless him, with your heart you place sacred victims on the altar of your conscience. And he will reply to you, *Peace on earth to people of good will* (Lk 2:14).

---

16. Variant: "as sacrifice used to be commanded."
17. Variant: "the one who hears you."
18. See Rom 10:10.

12. God is all-powerful, and he *has done*[19] *whatever he wanted in heaven and on earth*. But even in your own house you cannot do everything you want. *In heaven and on earth he has done whatever he wanted*, but you just try to do everything you want, even in your own field! You want many things, but even in your own house you cannot do all you want to do, for perhaps your wife opposes you, or your children disobey you, or sometimes even your slave-boy is rebellious and obstructive, and so what you want does not get done. "But I *do* do what I want," you object, "because I punish anyone who disobeys or opposes me." But you don't necessarily do even that when you want to. Sometimes you may want to punish someone, but you may be unable to; sometimes you threaten, but you may die before you have carried out your threats.

And are we to pretend that you can do all you want to within yourself? Do you curb all your unruly desires? Which ones do you curb, then? You certainly want to. You long to be free from the troublesome titillations of your lust, and yet *the flesh lusts against the spirit, and the spirit against the flesh, so that you do not act as you want to* (Gal 5:17). You cannot do what you want even within yourself, but our God *has done whatever he wanted, in heaven and on earth*. May he grant you his grace, so that you may do what you want to in yourself, for without his help you cannot do what you want even there. Someone who knew his impotence to do what he wanted to in himself made that observation just quoted: *The flesh lusts against the spirit, and the spirit against the flesh, so that you do not act as you want to*. He groaned over his experience of his weakness: *I take great delight in God's law as far as my inner self is concerned, but I am aware of a different law in my members that opposes the law of my mind, and imprisons me under the law of sin inherent in my members* (Rom 7:22–23). He found himself powerless to achieve what he wanted not only in his own house, not only in his own field, but even in his flesh and his spirit, and so he cried out to God, who *has done whatever he wanted, in heaven and on earth*, and pleaded, *Who will deliver me from this death-ridden body, wretch that I am?* (Rom 7:24) And then it seemed that our good God, our sweet God, replied to him, for the answer came swiftly: *Only the grace of God, through Jesus Christ our Lord* (Rom 7:25).

---

19. The Latin *facere* can mean "make" or "do." In section 10 it meant "make." Here the sense shifts to "do."

You must love this divine sweetness, you must praise this sweetness. Try to understand more deeply the God who *has done whatever he wanted, in heaven and on earth*, and he will bring about even in you what you want. With his help you will fulfill your desires. As long as you know yourself impotent to do so, confess your weakness and, when you are given power, thank him. While you lie prone, cry to him; when he has raised you up, do not be proud. He *has done whatever he wanted, in heaven and on earth, in the sea and in all the places of the deep.*

Verse 7. Clouds, lightning, wind: the works of the wise creator

13. *He brings up clouds from the end of the earth.* We see the Lord at work when we turn our eyes to his creation. Clouds come from the edge of the earth and move toward its center and drop their rain, but you do not know whence they come. The prophet suggests their mysterious provenance by saying, *From the end of the earth.* Perhaps the Lord brings them from below, perhaps from the fringes around the earth. The Lord raises clouds from wherever he wishes, but we know it must be from the earth.

He has made lightning to produce rain. If flashes of lightning came without rain they would frighten you and yield you nothing,[20] but he *has made lightning to produce rain.* Lightning flashes and you tremble, but he who has struck fear into you has himself given you reason to rejoice.[21]

He draws forth winds from his treasure-house, from hidden causes, unknown to you. When the wind blows you feel it, but why it blows, or from what treasury of wisdom it is drawn, you do not know.[22] Yet you must have enough reverence for God to believe that the wind would not blow unless its maker had told it to and unless its creator had drawn it forth.

Verses 8–12. The wonders of the exodus and the appropriation of the land

14. We see, then, what God does in his inanimate creation; we praise him for it, we stand amazed, and we bless God. Now let us see what he has done in the human sphere for the sake of his people.

---

20. Variant: "yield no food."
21. Variant: "has re-created you, that you may rejoice."
22. Compare Jn 3:8.

He struck Egypt's first-born. We have recounted divine acts that evoke your love, but nothing has been said so far about those you should fear. Listen now and observe that he does whatever he wants when he is angry too. *He struck Egypt's first-born, man and beast. He launched signs and prodigies into your midst, O Egypt.* You know about these events, for you have read what mighty exploits were performed by the Lord's hand through Moses in Egypt to terrify, smash, and overthrow the proud Egyptians: he sent plagues *on Pharaoh and on all his servants.* But what happened in Egypt was not enough. What else occurred after the chosen people had been led out from there? *He smote many tribes,* the ones who owned the land God intended to give to his people. *He slew mighty kings: Sihon, king of the Amorites, and Og, king of Bashan, and all the kingdoms of Canaan.* The psalm relates these events briefly, but its account is confirmed by what we read in other divine books; certainly the Lord's hand was there in power.

When you see what disasters were inflicted on the impious, beware lest the same things befall you. These punishments were visited upon them so that you might avoid a similar fate: you are not to imitate their wicked conduct or deserve to suffer as they did. All the same, you must notice that the Lord's scourge is used upon all flesh. Do not imagine that you go unseen when you sin; do not think your behavior is overlooked; do not suppose that the Lord is asleep. Let your mind dwell on instances of God's kindness when you recall them, but, when you remember his punishments, be afraid. He is almighty both to console and to chastise. This is why it is good for us to read about such events. When a God-fearing person sees what a godless one has suffered, he must purify himself of godless irreverence, lest he too fall into like calamity and undergo the same punishment. You have learned this lesson well already.

What did God do next? He threw out the godless, *and he gave their land as an inheritance to Israel, his servant.*

Verse 13. Thanksgiving and praise for God's work in creation and redemption

15. Now we come to the moment of exultant praise. *Your name endures for all eternity, O Lord,* after all the things that you have done. What do I see that you have done? I gaze upon your creation in heaven, I gaze upon your creatures in this lowly region where we live, and my mind passes in review your kindly provision of clouds,

winds, and rain. Then I turn my eyes to your people and remember how you led them out of the house of slavery, how you worked signs and wonders among their enemies, how you punished those under whom they had suffered hardship, how you drove the godless out of their land, slew their kings, and gave that land to your people. All these things I see and, filled with praise, I exclaim, *Your name endures for all eternity, O Lord.*

Augustine begins to expound the spiritual sense of the foregoing verses. Verse 6: The creation of the Church

16. We can see now what these verses mean when interpreted literally; we know the sense of them and we praise God. But it may be that they signify something further, and I hope I shall not tire you out if I explain this as well as I can. I see a sense in which the verse, *The Lord has made whatever he wanted, in heaven and on earth*, is applicable also to men and women. The heaven or sky above us I take to represent spiritual persons, and the earth those of carnal disposition, and of these two types the Church consists, as though of heaven and earth. The job of the spiritual element is preaching; of the carnal, compliance. This is why another psalm says, *The heavens proclaim God's glory, and the firmament tells of his handiwork* (Ps 18:2(19:1)). But if it were not true that God's earth represents God's people, the apostle would hardly have said, *You are God's building, and God's cultivated field. I laid the foundation like a skilled master-builder, and another imposes the superstructure.* (1 Cor 3:9–10) So we are both God's building and his field, and the apostle continues the metaphor by asking, *Who plants a vineyard, and receives no fruit from it? I planted, Apollos watered, but God gave the growth.* (1 Cor 9:7; 3:6) Thus God has made whatever he wanted in his Church, both in its preachers and in its laity, as though in heaven and on earth.

But that is not all. *The Lord has done whatever he wanted* also *in the sea and in all the places of the deep*. The sea represents all those who have no faith, all who do not yet believe, and in them too he *has done whatever he wanted*. For they no longer savagely attack us unless God allows them, but neither is punishment inflicted on them for their perverted behavior except at the command of him who made all nations. You do not think, surely, that because the sea is not dry land, it is outside the jurisdiction of almighty God? *He has done whatever he wanted in the sea* as well *and in all the places of the deep.*

What are these deep places? The hidden hearts of mortals, the deep thoughts of human beings. Why can it be said that God does what he wants to there? Because *the Lord questions the righteous and the ungodly, but whoever loves iniquity hates his own soul* (Ps 10:6(11:5)). Where does the Lord conduct this interrogation? We are told where in another passage of scripture: *An inquiry will be instituted in the thoughts of a godless person* (Wis 1:9). It is true, then, that even *in all the places of the deep he has done whatever he wanted*. A good heart is hidden, and a bad heart is hidden; there is an abyss in the good heart and in the bad heart too, but both are naked to the eyes of God, from whom nothing is hidden. He comforts a good heart and torments a bad heart. *He has done whatever he wanted, in heaven and on earth, in the sea and in all the places of the deep.*

Verse 7. Clouds, lightning, rain, and wind signify preaching

17. *He brings up clouds from the end of the earth.* What clouds? Preachers of the word of truth. In another text the Lord expresses his anger with his vineyard by saying, *I will forbid my clouds to send rain upon it* (Is 5:6). But it would not have sufficed to bring up clouds from Jerusalem, or even from Israel, if they were to be sent to preach the gospel throughout the world; for of these clouds it is prophesied, *Their sound went forth throughout the world, their words to the ends of the earth* (Ps 18:5(19:4)). No, that would not have sufficed. But the Lord himself promised, *This gospel will be preached throughout the world, as a testimony to all nations; and after that the end will come* (Mt 24:14), and he therefore brings up clouds *from the end of the earth*. It had to be so, for, as the gospel spread more and more widely, whence would have sprung the preachers who would take it to the uttermost parts of the world if the Lord had not brought up clouds even in those remote places?

And what does he do through the agency of these clouds? *He has made lightning, to produce rain*; he tempered his threats so that they issued in mercy, he sent refreshing rain through his terrors. How did he use his menaces to irrigate us? When God threatens you through a prophet or an apostle, you are afraid. Is it not the flashes of lightning that terrify you? But when you repent and correct your life and acknowledge that this has come about through his mercy, the terrors of his lightning have changed into rain.

He draws forth winds from his treasure-house. I think both clouds and winds stand for the same people, the preachers. They are clouds because they are beings of flesh, but winds because of their spirits; for clouds are visible, whereas winds are felt but not seen. Moreover the psalm says that the Lord *brings up clouds from the end of the earth*, and flesh, as we know, derives from earth. So the psalm makes it clear whence the Lord raises the clouds; but since no one knows where the human spirit comes from, the psalm says of the winds only that the Lord *draws forth winds from his treasure-house*.

Keep on concentrating for a little longer and let us see what else we can find.

Verses 8–9. The first-born represent faith, the beginning of our life with God

18. *He struck Egypt's first-born, man and beast*. May our first-born children be kept safe for the Lord, since it was he who gave them to us. It is a grievous punishment, an exceedingly dreadful plague, this death of the first-born. What are our first-born children? Our present way of life, by which we now serve God. This is our first-born, for the faith we have is our spiritual first-fruits, the point from which we begin. The Church was told, *You will come and pass through, beginning from faith* (Sg 4:8, LXX), and no one begins to lead a good life except from the starting-point of faith.

Our faith therefore plays the part of our first-born. When our faith is guarded and kept safe, further growth is possible. Believers can be purified and make progress every day, as they live better lives and their inner selves are daily renewed. As the apostle says, *Though our outer self is decaying, our inner self is being renewed daily* (2 Cor 4:16). Our first-born faith thrives. On this subject the apostle also says, *Not creation only, but we ourselves, though we have the first-fruits of the spirit*[23]—he means that we are offering to God as first-fruits our faith itself, our first-born—*we ourselves groan inwardly as we await our redemption as God's children, the redemption of our bodies* (Rom 8:23). If, then, it is by a great grace from God that our faith is kept safe, it is conversely a great crime to kill our first-born, as sometimes happens when the Church is afflicted and faith is lost. People afflict the Church in such a way that they destroy their own faith; indeed, the name Egypt means "affliction." Whenever they afflict

---

23. The offering made to God of the highest part of the human spirit, as Augustine understands it. The sense is different in the Pauline context: see Exposition 12 of Psalm 118,1 and the note, and Expositions of Psalms 114,8 and 125,2.

the Church or introduce scandals into the Church, then, even though those responsible bear the name of Christians, their first-born die. They will turn into unbelievers, they will be impostors flaunting the name and sign of Christians while in their hearts they have buried their dead first-born. So true is this that, if you try to say anything to such a person about the good life or the hope of life eternal or the dread of everlasting fire, he will mock you within himself. Or, if he is the type who dares to defy you to your face, he will grimace and say, "Has anyone come back from there to tell us about it? People just say what they fancy." Yet the speaker is a Christian! But, because he is also one who afflicts us, his first-born has been slain; his faith is dead.

The first-born of Egypt were struck down, *man and beast alike*. I will tell you how I understand this, brothers and sisters. I take *man* to have a spiritual significance here and to mean well-instructed persons; this is suitable because a rational mind is proper to human beings. The *beasts* here stand for persons who are poorly instructed; but they do have faith, otherwise they would have no first-born children. It is the learned, well-instructed ones who afflict the Church by initiating schisms and heresies. You will therefore find no faith in them, because they have become "Egypt," the affliction of God's people. Their first-born have been killed, and now they drag along after them crowds of unlearned persons, represented by the beasts. This is an affliction for the Church, and faith dies in those who afflict it, but the first-born of both the learned and the simple die, for God slew *Egypt's first-born, man and beast*.

19. *He launched signs and prodigies into your midst, O Egypt, on Pharaoh and on all his servants*. Pharaoh was the king of the Egyptians. Note the name carefully, and see how God acts. In any nation the king is the leader, and as Egypt stands for "affliction," so Pharaoh's name means "disintegration."[24] Affliction therefore has disintegration as its ruler, because the people who afflict the Church are themselves in a state of disintegration; that is why they behave so. They become disintegrated and the result is that they afflict us, for, where the king leads, the people follow: disintegration comes first and affliction ensues. Listen to those two names, listen to them attentively, for when interpreted they have symbolic meaning, heavy

---

24. *Dissipatio*. The English "dissipation" suggests something a little less destructive. The Latin verb *dissipare* can mean simply "scatter, disperse," but Augustine uses it with the consciousness of its negation of wisdom, *sapientia*.

with wisdom.[25] You cannot find even one element in these names susceptible of a good interpretation, for in them God unleashed his anger.

Verses 10–13. The slaying of pagan kings symbolizes God's punishment of the demons who trouble the Church and block our way

20. *He smote many tribes, he slew mighty kings.* Tell us, then: Which kings, which tribes? *Sihon, king of the Amorites.* Take note of these names too, for they are pregnant with mysteries. The Lord slew *Sihon, king of the Amorites.* He slew them then, and may he slay them now in the hearts of his servants: slay them, so that the Church may no longer be tried by them. May his hand not slacken in the slaughter of such kings and such peoples, for Sihon means "temptation of the eyes," and Amorites signify "those who stir up bitterness." Consider now whether we can understand how those who stir up bitterness can have a temptation of the eyes as their king. A temptation of the eyes is a deceit, for, though it has attractive plausibility, it lacks truth. What is strange, then, if people who stir up bitterness have a king like that, a king who deceives them? If lying and pretence do not come first, there will be no troublemakers in the Church; the troublemakers stir up bitterness because they are not honest. So a temptation of the eyes takes the lead and bitterness follows. The temptation of the eyes has begun with the devil himself, for it is a deceptive temptation of the eyes when he *disguises himself as an angel of light* (2 Cor 11:14). May the hand of the Lord slay both him and those whom he deceives: the devil, so that he may not lead them astray, and his victims, by correcting them. In each of us this king is put to death when we repudiate the pretence and love the truth. The hand of the Lord never tires of effecting this. As he once performed these exploits literally, so now he performs them spiritually, thus fulfilling the prophecies he made long ago.

There was another king and another tribe slain in those early days — *Og, the king of Bashan*, and what an evil king he was! Og means "blockage"; Bashan means "confusion." It is an evil king who blocks the path to God. This is what the devil does. By continually putting his delusions in our way, by blocking our path with his idols, and by getting in the way himself as allegedly necessary through inspired

---

25. The interpretation is full of the wisdom denied by the reality interpreted, *dissipatio*.

ravers,[26] fortune tellers, soothsayers, diviners, magicians, and the sacred rites of demons, he shuts the way against us. Whereas God acts in Christ to open the way that had been blocked—as one who had been redeemed by him put it, *In my God I shall leap over the wall* (Ps 17:30(18:29))—so the devil is unceasingly intent on nothing else but blocking it, in order to stop us from believing in God. If a person believes in God the way lies open, and Christ himself is the way;[27] but where there is no faith in God the way is closed. But then, if it is shut because people do not believe in Christ, what possible outcome is there, except that when he comes, he in whom they did not believe, they will be thrown into confusion? Why? Because first the way was blocked, and then confusion ensued; "blockage" takes the lead as king and "confusion" follows as his people. All those in whose way he stands now, to stop them believing in Christ, will be put to confusion when Christ appears, and their iniquities will rise up against them to betray them. In their confusion the godless will ask, *What good did our pride do us?* (Wis 5:8)

These are profound mysteries, my brothers and sisters. "Disintegration" is the king of "affliction," for some lapse into disintegration and are accordingly afflicted. All this is very mysterious. "Temptation of the eyes," which implies deception, is the king of "those who stir up bitterness," for it deceives them in order to incite them to their bitter work. "Blockage" is the king of "confusion," for people's passage into faith is blocked and, when he in whom we believe comes, they will be put to confusion.

And God *slew all the kingdoms of Canaan.* The name Canaan is interpreted as "ready for humiliation." Humility, the useful kind, signifies something good, but the wrong kind of humility, better called humiliation, is a punishment. If it were not, the gospel would not have said, *Anyone who exalts himself will be humbled* (Lk 14:11; 18:14), for, when someone is punished by being humbled, it is not a reward that he is being given. "Canaan" is therefore someone who is proud now: every impious person, every unbeliever, exalts his heart in arrogance, unwilling to believe in God. But this exaltation is ready for humiliation on the day of judgment; on that day the proud one will be humbled against his will. Such persons are vessels of wrath,

---

26. *Arreptitios*, see the note at Exposition 2 of Psalm 88,14.
27. See Jn 14:6.

completely shaped for destruction.[28] Let them swagger for a while, let them chatter and throw their weight about at the expense of the faithful, let them mock believers, blaspheme against Christians, and say, "What they tell us about the day of judgment is no more than old wives' tales." Arrogance like this is all ready for humiliation. The coming of the judge is announced now, in advance, and he is laughed at. But when he comes, everyone who is proud now will be humiliated, not in a profitable way but as a punishment. He or she is not truly humbled now but is being made ready for humiliation, or, in other words, is being made ready for condemnation, prepared as a victim for sacrifice is prepared.

21. God overthrew all these. At the time when our fathers were led out of the land of Egypt he acted in bodily fashion, but now he acts spiritually, and his hand is at work unceasingly until the end. The psalmist does not want you to think that God's power was exhausted by his exploits at that early time, so as to work no more, and so he says, *Your name endures for all eternity, O Lord.* Your mercy never ceases, he means. Your hand never tires of performing these mighty works in every age, these works which you announced beforehand in figures. *All these things happened to them, but with symbolic import, for they are written down as a rebuke to us, upon whom the climax of the ages has come* (1 Cor 10:11).

The psalm continues, *Your memory,*[29] *O Lord, is constant from generation to generation*: this generation and another still to come, this generation in which we become believers and are reborn through baptism, and another generation in which we shall rise from the dead and live for ever in fellowship with the angels. Your memory, O Lord, extends both to this generation and to that other. He has not forgotten us now but called us, nor will he forget us then, to crown us. *Your memory, O Lord, is constant from generation to generation.*

---

28. See Rom 9:22.
29. *Memoriale*, a word of rich associations. See Exposition 1 of Psalm 101,13.19 and the notes there. But in the present context it seems to mean simply God's remembrance of us.

Verse 14. The Lord makes a distinction within his own people and calls the gentiles

22. *For the Lord has judged his people.* All the mighty deeds we have considered the Lord certainly worked among his people, the Jews, and he brought them all to completion. But that did not mean, did it, that no more divine works remained to be done after he had brought his people into the promised land? No, for he would still judge them. *The Lord has judged his people, and among his servants he will be open to their prayers.* He has already judged his people, for the Jewish people stands under judgment now, though the final judgment is still to come. What does "judged" mean in this context? It means that the just among them have been drawn out, and the unjust have been left there. If I am lying, or anyone thinks I am lying, when I say that the Jewish people has already been judged, listen to the Lord's words: *I came into this world for judgment, so that they who do not see may see, and those who see may become blind* (Jn 9:39). The proud were struck blind, the humble were given light, and so it was that *the Lord judged his people.* Isaiah described the process of judgment: *And now, you house of Jacob, come; let us walk in the light of the Lord.* But that proves little. What follows? *For he has forsaken his people, the house of Israel.* (Is 2:5.6) The house of Jacob and the house of Israel are the same thing, for Jacob and Israel are one and the same. You know the holy scriptures, and I think you will recall that, when Jacob perceived it was an angel who wrestled with him, he was given the new name of Israel.[30] There was but one man, a single person, whether he was called Jacob or Israel, and so the house of Jacob and the house of Israel were one race, one people. And this one people is both invited and forsaken, according to Isaiah's words.

And now, house of Jacob, you have unquestionably killed Christ. You killed Christ, you wagged your heads before the cross, you mocked him who hung there, you taunted him, *Let him come down from the cross, if he is the Son of God* (Mt 27:40.42). Yet the physician prayed for the delirious patients: *Father, forgive them, for they do not know what they are doing* (Lk 23:34). Yes, you did all these things, house of Jacob. But now believe in him whom you killed, and drink the blood you shed.

And now, O house of Jacob, I want to expound with the help of Isaiah's testimony this verse of the psalm, *The Lord has judged his*

---

30. See Gn 32:28.

people, and among his servants he will be open to their prayers. We can understand how he has judged his people, because there among them he has drawn a distinction, separating good from bad, believers from unbelievers, apostles from lying Jews. This was what the prophet's words suggested, as I began to explain. Even after all your wrongdoing, he seemed to say, even now, *You house of Jacob, come; let us walk in the light of the Lord.* Why do I invite you, *Come; let us walk in the light of the Lord*? Lest by remaining stuck in Judaism you fail to reach Christ. But why should that be so? Was Christ not constantly prophesied among the Jews? Certainly he was, yet now *he has forsaken his people, the house of Israel.* Come, O house of Jacob, because God has forsaken his people, the house of Jacob! Come, O house of Israel, because God had forsaken his people, the house of Israel! Who is invited to come, and who is forsaken? What can it mean, except that the judgment passed is *that they who do not see may see, and those who see may become blind* (Jn 9:39)?

So then, *the Lord has judged his people.* He has made a separation, and will he not find some whom he can restore to his kingdom? Indeed he will find some, and *among his servants he will be open to their prayers*, for, as the apostle says, *God has not cast off his own people, whom he foreknew.* And how does he prove this? *For I am myself sprung from the race of Israel* (Rom 11:2.1). The Lord has judged his people by separating the good from the wicked, and so *among his servants he will be open to their prayers.* Whose prayers? Those of the gentiles, for what enormous numbers of gentiles have come to believe! From how many cultivated estates, from how many wild and barren places are they joining us! I cannot count them all. They long to believe. We say to them, "What do you want?" They reply, "To know the glory of God." Believe me, brothers and sisters, we are amazed and overjoyed at hearing these pleas from simple country folk. They come from I know not where, aroused by I know not whom. Or, rather, I do know very well who attracted them, for Christ said, *No one can come to me unless drawn to me by the Father* (Jn 6:44). They come all unexpectedly from forest, from desert, from the remotest and steepest mountains to the Church, and from the lips of many or almost all of these unsophisticated people we hear the same thing, which proves to us that God is truly teaching them within their hearts. The prophecy of scripture is fulfilled: *They will all be taught by God* (Is 54:13; Jn 6:45). "What do you want?" we ask them. "To see the glory of God," they reply, for *all have sinned, and are in need of the glory of God* (Rom 3:23). They believe, they are consecrated to God, they beg to have priests ordained for them. Is the psalm's prophecy not being fulfilled, *Among his servants he will be open to their prayers?*

Verses 15–18. The folly of idols, their defeat by the Lord, their detrimental effect on their clients

23. Finally, after considering the wonderful ordering of events under the whole divine plan, the Spirit of God turns to another matter and begins to rebuke and ridicule the worship of idols, which indeed are today ridiculed even by those who used to worship them. *The idols of the gentiles are fashioned of silver and gold.* God made all that we see; he has made whatever he wanted to in heaven and on earth, he has judged his people and made himself available to the petitions of his servants. After all this, what are we to think of objects shaped by human hands? They deserve mockery, not worship. The Spirit wants to inculcate in us contempt for all these idols of the pagans. Will he then point out that they are no more than stone or wood, plaster or clay? "No," he says, "I will not speak of those; they are all made of base materials. I prefer to speak of what the pagans love and prize most highly." *The idols of the gentiles are fashioned of silver and gold.* Yes, it is certainly gold, it is certainly silver, and they are bright, shiny substances, gold and silver. But does their reflection of the light mean that they have eyes and can see? By no means. Perhaps, being gold and silver, they are useful to a person with an eye to profit but not to one who is bound to God. Or, to put it more accurately, they are not useful even to one who is avaricious but only to one who makes good use of them and by charitable donations gains a title to treasure in heaven. But in any case, these things lack all sensation. So how can you, who are human, make them your gods? Can you not see that those whom you make gods cannot see?[31] *They have eyes, but will not see; ears, but will hear nothing; nostrils, but no sense of smell; mouths, but will never speak; hands that will never work; and feet that will never walk.* A carpenter could have fashioned all these; a silversmith or a goldsmith could have shaped eyes, ears, nose, mouth, hands, and feet; but he could not endow the eyes with sight, the ears with hearing, the mouth with speech, the nose with power to smell, the hand with movement, or the feet with power to walk.

---

31. See Wis 15:15; Ps 113B(115):4–8.

24. If you, human creature, have come to know him by whom you were made, you will doubtless be laughing already at those gods you made yourself. But what does the psalm say about other people, who do not recognize their maker? *May all those who fashion them become like them, and all who put their trust in them.* And believe me, brothers and sisters, they do take on a certain resemblance to their idols, not a bodily likeness but one that affects their inner selves. They have ears but do not hear, although God shouts to them, *Let anyone who has ears for hearing, listen!* (Mt 11:15) They have eyes but do not see, for, though they have bodily sight, they lack the eyes of faith.

In the end we must acknowledge a prophecy that is verified among all nations. Consider how a prophet uttered it. I am not referring to any allegorical or metaphorical statement but to a literal, express, plain, clear prophecy, spoken long ago and now fulfilled before our eyes. The prophet Zephaniah said, *The Lord has prevailed against them.* (Zep 2:11)[32] Against those who resisted him, against all who rebelled, against those who by killing believers created martyrs unwittingly, the Lord has prevailed. How has he prevailed? We see his victory over them in his Church. They sought to snuff out and kill a small band of Christians; they shed Christian blood; but from the blood of the slain so mighty a host arose[33] that it defeated those who killed the martyrs. The pagans who once slaughtered Christians are now looking for safe places to hide their idols. Has the Lord not prevailed against them? Let us see whether he is doing what the prophecy declares he will do. *The Lord has prevailed against them.* And how did he do it? *He has exterminated all the gods of the gentiles throughout the earth. They will worship him from their own homes, every one of them, all the islands of the nations.* (Zep 2:11) What is that about? Was it not foretold? And has it not happened? Can we not see it today, just as scripture describes it? Some there are who have persisted in unbelief; they have eyes but do not see and noses but do not smell. They do not perceive the fragrance, even though, as the apostle says, *We are the fragrance of Christ in every place* (2 Cor 2:15). What use are their noses to them if they are impervious to the sweet scent of Christ? It

---

32. Augustine's reading for this part of the verse does not match either the Hebrew or the Septuagint or the Vulgate.
33. Surely a conscious echo of Tertullian: *Semen est sanguis Christianorum* (*Apol.* 50).

has come true in them, as it was truly said of them, that *all those who fashion idols become like them, and all who put their trust in them.*

Verses 19–20. The work of grace in the new house of Israel

25. Yet every day there are others who come to faith through the miraculous deeds of Christ our Lord. Every day blind eyes and deaf ears are opened; breath is blown into the nostrils of the unperceiving; the tongues of the dumb are released; the muscles of paralyzed hands are toned up; crippled feet are straightened; and from these stones children are raised up for Abraham.[34] To all of these let the invitation now be extended, *House of Israel, bless the Lord.* All of them are Abraham's children and, if children are raised up for Abraham from the stones, it is evident that those who belong to the house of Israel and the race of Abraham by faith, not carnal descent, are more entitled to the name, *house of Israel.* But even if you want to take the invitation as addressed to the original house of Israel and think that Israel as a people is being called, it still makes good sense, because the apostles and thousands of others from the circumcised sprang from that race and became believers. *House of Israel, bless the Lord; house of Aaron, bless the Lord; house of Levi, bless the Lord.* All peoples, bless the Lord, you who in any sense are the *house of Israel.* Bless him, all you who are set over the rest as prelates, who are the *house of Aaron.* Bless him, you his ministers, who are the *house of Levi.* And what about all the other nations? *You who fear him, bless the Lord.*

Verse 21. The vision of peace

26. Let us all therefore say with one voice, *Blessed be the Lord from Zion, he who dwells in Jerusalem.* From Zion and in Jerusalem. Zion means "look-out post" or "watchtower"; Jerusalem means "vision of peace." Which Jerusalem is it where the Lord lives now? The city that fell? No. Rather does he live in that Jerusalem in heaven that is our mother, of which it was said, *She who has been deserted bears many children, more than the wedded wife* (Is 54:1; Gal 4:27). For the present the Lord is invoked from Zion, because we are on the lookout from here until he comes; for the present, as long as we live in hope, we are in Zion. When our journey is ended we shall live in that city which will never crumble into ruin, because the Lord himself lives in it and guards it. This is the eternal Jerusalem, the vision

---

34. See Mt 3:9.

of peace, a peace which no tongue has power to praise sufficiently, my brothers and sisters, for there we shall be exposed to no enemy either within the Church or outside it, either in our own flesh or in our thoughts. Death will be swallowed up in victory,[35] and we shall be free to contemplate God in eternal peace, for we shall be citizens of Jerusalem, the city of God.

---

35. See 1 Cor 15:54.

Exposition of Psalm 135

Verse 1. The primary motive for praise and confession: God's mercy

1. *Confess to the Lord because he is good, because his mercy endures to the end of the age.*[1] This psalm is full of God's praise, and every one of its verses ends with the same significant words. Unmistakably, therefore, it is God's mercy that is above all celebrated here, even though many different things are said in praise of him. The man through whom the Holy Spirit composed the psalm made sure that not one of its verses should close without a most express mention of the mercy of God.

When we were dealing with Psalm 105, which opens with the same phrase as this one, I found that the codex I was using has not *his mercy endures for ever*[2] but *his mercy endures to the end of the age,*[3] and I remember that I sought how best to understand this. The Greek has εἰς τὸν αἰῶνα, which can be translated as either "to the end of the age" or "for ever." But it would take too long to repeat here the explanation which I provided as best I could in that place. In the present psalm, however, this same codex does not read *in saeculum*, as do most others, but *in aeternum misericordia eius*. How are we to understand this assertion? After the judgment that will take place at the end of the age, at which the living and the dead will be amenable, the righteous will have been welcomed into eternal life and the wicked dispatched to everlasting fire,[4] and there will not be anyone thereafter upon whom God can exercise his mercy. All the same, there is a way in which we can speak correctly of God pouring out his mercy for all eternity on his holy, faithful servants, not in the sense that they will be miserable for ever and therefore eternally in need of his mercy but because there will never be an end to the

---

1. *In saeculum* here, though Augustine goes on to say that this is not the reading in his codex.
2. *In aeternum.*
3. *In saeculum.* See Exposition of Psalm 105,2, where Augustine discusses the possibly different interpretations of the two expressions.
4. See Mt 25:41.46.

happiness he mercifully grants to the miserable, thus changing their misery into beatitude. In that sense *his mercy endures for ever*. It is thanks to his mercy that we who were unjust will be righteous, we who were sick will be whole, we who were dead will live, we who were mortal will be immortal, and we who were miserable will be blessed. This new state that we are to enjoy will last for all eternity, and therefore *his mercy endures for ever*.

With this in mind, *confess to the Lord*—in other words, praise him by your confession—*because he is good*. You will get no temporal reward for your confession, *because his mercy endures for ever*; the reward he mercifully bestows on you is eternal. As to the phrase, *because he is good*, our Greek text here has ἀγαθός, unlike the corresponding phrase in Psalm 105, where we read χρηστός. Some translators therefore rendered it as *because he is kind*[5] in that psalm, and others as *because he is good*.[6] But here, in this present psalm, we have ἀγαθός, which can only mean *good*: not good in any general sense but supremely good.

Verses 2–3. How can God be called the "God of gods"?

2. The psalm continues, *Confess to the God of gods, because his mercy endures for ever. Confess to the Lord of lords, because his mercy endures for ever*. It is often asked, and with good reason, who these gods and lords are over whom the true God is God and Lord. In another psalm we find it written that even human beings are called gods: *God has taken his stand in the synagogue of the gods, to make a distinction among them*. And a little further on the same idea recurs: *This is my sentence: you are gods, sons of the Most High, all of you; yet you shall die as mortals die, and fall as any lordly ruler falls.* (Ps 81(82):1.6–7) The Lord himself recalls these texts when he asks in the gospel, *Is it not written in your law, This is my sentence, you are gods? If it called gods those to whom the word of God was addressed, and scripture cannot be disregarded, can you say of him whom the Father has consecrated and sent into the world, You are blaspheming, because I said, I am the Son of God?* (Jn 10:34–35) This saying makes it clear that they were not called gods because they were all good but because the word of God had come to them, for if it had been because they were all good people, he would not have

---

5. *Suavis.*
6. *Bonus.*

passed the judgment that distinguished among them. After saying, *God has taken his stand in the synagogue of the gods*, it does not go on to say that he drew a distinction between gods and men, as though demonstrating the essential difference between them. It says that he took his stand there to make a distinction among the gods themselves. Then it continues, *How long will you judge unjustly?* (Ps 81(82):2), and so on. Evidently this question is addressed not to all of them but only to some, because it is part of the discrimination. Yet the psalm says that to make it he took his stand *in the synagogue of the gods*.

3. Another question arises from this. If human beings to whom God's word was addressed are called gods, should angels also be called gods? After all, the highest reward promised to just and holy men and women is equality with the angels. I do not know whether any instance of angels being plainly called gods can easily be found in the scriptures. But there is a text which says of the Lord God, *He is more to be feared than all the gods*, and this passage immediately goes on to clarify the statement by adding, *for all the gods of the heathen are demons*, and then it continues, *but the Lord made the heavens* (Ps 95(96):4–5). These are the sort of gods to whom the Lord is fearful, and his terrible aspect is seen through his saints, whom he made "heavens" in order to terrify the demons, which is why it adds, *But the Lord made the heavens*. It does not precisely assert that all gods are demons but only that the gods of the heathen are. Yet in the preceding verse it has stated that God is *more to be feared than all the gods*, and by immediately going on to say, *for all the gods of the heathen are demons*, it obviously means to imply that this is true of all of them.

People tell me that this is not exactly what the Hebrew says; the phrase there is: *The gods of the heathen are graven images*.[7] If this is true, we have all the more reason to trust the Septuagint translators, who interpreted the word of God under the influence of the same Holy Spirit,[8] who inspired what is found in the Hebrew text. What I mean is this: it was necessary that through the action of the Holy Spirit the other expression, *All the gods of the heathen are demons*, should also be used. This made it easier for us to understand that the Hebrew statement, *The gods of the heathen are graven images*, implied that

---

7. *Simulacra.*
8. On the possibility that the Septuagint should be regarded as inspired, see Expositions of Psalms 67,16 and 87,10 and the notes at both places.

demons were present in these images. As far as the images themselves are concerned, or the idols, as they are called in Greek (and in our language too, where we have taken over the Greek word), they have eyes but see nothing; they lack all perception, as other psalms point out.[9] They are therefore incapable of experiencing fear, since only sentient beings are capable of emotions. How, then, can it be said of the Lord, *He is more to be feared than all the gods, for all the gods of the heathen are graven images*, unless we understand that by these idols demons are meant, demons who can indeed be terrified? The apostle confirms such an interpretation. *We know that an idol is nothing* (1 Cor 8:4), he says, referring to the insensate earthly material. But in case anyone should doubt that there are living and perceptive beings who take pleasure in pagan sacrifices, he qualifies his statement later: *But the sacrifices offered by pagans are offered to demons, not to God; and I do not want you to have any truck with demons* (1 Cor 10:20).

If, therefore, we find no passage in the word of God where the holy angels are called gods, the principal reason seems to me to be this: had the name been given to angels, men and women might have felt compelled to offer to the holy angels those marks of religious reverence and service which the Greeks call liturgy or latria.[10] The angels themselves do not want human beings to offer such worship to anyone but God, who is their God as well as ours. It is thus much more fitting that they be called angels, a name which means "messengers," so that when we hear them designated by a name which denotes their office, not their essence, we may realize that they want us to worship the God whom they proclaim.

The apostle deals with this whole question clearly and succinctly by reminding us, *Even if there are beings called gods in the sky or on earth (as in fact there are gods and lords aplenty), still, for us there is one God, the Father, from whom all things come, and for whom we exist; and one Lord, Jesus Christ, through whom all things come, and through whom we exist* (1 Cor 8:5–6).

---

9. See Pss 113B(115):5–7; 134(135):16–17.
10. Supreme worship, proper for God alone.

Verses 4–7. Augustine finds that his Latin version obscures the psalm's intention

4. Let us then *confess to the God of gods* and to *the Lord of lords, because his mercy endures for ever. He alone does*[11] *great and wonderful deeds.* As in the second half of every verse the psalm has *because his mercy endures for ever*, so in the first half of these verses we are meant to understand "confess," even though it is not written. This is clearer in the Greek. It would be evident also in Latin if our translators had been able to take over the Greek idiom. As a matter of fact they could have done so in this verse if they had given us *to him who alone does*[12] *wonderful deeds.* Where we have the simple factual statement, *He alone does wonderful deeds*, the Greek has *to him who alone does wonderful deeds*, which requires the verb *confess* at the beginning. I wish the Latin translators had at least given us a pronoun at the beginning to bring out the sense; they could have written "to him who does" or "to him who did" or "to him who established," and so on, because then we would easily have understood that the verb "confess" is implied and that the concluding phrase, *because his mercy*, is the motive for our confession.[13] But, as it is, the translators have made it so obscure that anyone who cannot examine the Greek codex, or has neglected to do so, would think that the psalm is saying, "He made the heavens, he established the earth, he made the great lights, because his mercy endures for ever." So the reader would be misled and think that the psalm is telling us that God created all these things *because his mercy endures for ever.* But this is not so. The people whom he delivers from misery are the ones concerned to confess his mercy. We are not being told that the creation of heaven and earth and the sky's luminous bodies are works of his mercy; they are, rather, manifestations of the goodness of him who made them all exceedingly good.[14] He created all things that they might have being;[15] but it is the work of his mercy to cleanse us from our sins and free us from our misery for ever. That is why the psalm urges us, *Confess to the God of gods, confess to the Lord of*

---

11. Variant: *did* or *has done*.
12. *Facienti mirabilia*, instead of *qui facit mirabilia*.
13. The meaning for which Augustine is arguing is present in both the Hebrew and the Septuagint but is not clear in all modern English versions.
14. See Gn 1:31.
15. See Wis 1:14.

lords; confess to him who *alone does great and wonderful deeds*; confess to him who *made the intelligent heavens*;[16] confess to him who *established the earth upon the waters*; confess to him who *alone made the great lights*. And the reason why we must confess to him is stated at the end of each verse: *because his mercy endures for ever.*

Verses 5–10. God alone creates; the intelligent heavens are his spiritual creation

5. What point is being made when the psalm declares, *He alone does*[17] *great and wonderful deeds*? Does it mean that, although he performs many wonderful deeds through angels or human agents, there are certain great deeds that God alone performs? This seems likely, because it goes on to say, *He made the intelligent heavens, he established the earth upon the waters, he alone made the great lights.* The psalm stressed the word *alone* here, because it will proceed in the following verses to recount other wonderful exploits which God performed through human agency. This must be the explanation, for, after saying, *He alone made the great lights*, it goes on to specify these luminous bodies: *the sun to be the power in daytime, the moon and the stars as powers in the night*. Only after this does it begin to relate what God did through angels or human beings: *He smote Egypt and its first-born*, and so forth. But creation itself, the entire creation, is the work of God alone; for that he used no intermediary. The psalm has mentioned certain very splendid elements in creation, from which we are to understand all the rest: the spiritual heavens and the visible earth. But there are also visible heavens, the sky, and by mentioning the luminous bodies in the sky the psalm has taught us to believe that the entire material heaven also was made by God.

6. A question now arises about the verse, *He made the intelligent heavens*. Others have translated this, *He made the heavens by his intelligence*. Which way should we take it — that the psalm refers to the intellectual or spiritual creation as *intelligent heavens*[18] or that it means that he made the heavens *by his intelligence*? If the latter, it would mean that he made them in his wisdom. As another text

---

16. That is, his spiritual creation. The phrase could also mean *he made the heavens by his intelligence*. Augustine discusses the two possible ways of translating it in sections 6 and 8 below.
17. Variant: *did* or *has done*.
18. Compare *Confessions* 12,2,2, where Augustine discusses *heaven's heaven*.

acknowledges, *In wisdom you have created all things* (Ps 103(104):24), which hints at the only-begotten divine Word.

But if this latter interpretation is correct, and we take our psalm to mean that God made the heavens by his own understanding, why should this be asserted of the heavens alone? Did he not make all the rest in his wisdom too? Was it mentioned only in connection with the heavens because we are expected to understand that it is tacitly implied in all the other creative acts enumerated, so that we should read the passage like this: *He made the heavens by his intelligence; he established the earth upon the waters (by his intelligence); he alone made the great lights (by his intelligence), the sun to be the power in the daytime, the moon and the stars as powers in the night (by his intelligence)*? But this interpretation raises a further difficulty, because if God created these things *by his intelligence*, which is another way of saying "in his wisdom," in his only-begotten Word, how can it be said that *he alone* made them? Well, perhaps because the Trinity is not three gods but one God, and the statement that God did these things *alone* means simply that he did not make use of any creature in his creative act.

7. Now what about the verse, *He established the earth upon the waters*? This is a baffling matter because the earth seems too heavy to be supported by the waters but seems rather to support the waters. We have no intention of appearing to defend our scriptures argumentatively against those who believe that they have acquired exact knowledge of these matters by rational investigation. Whichever account is the true one, there is one point on which we can reach immediate certainty. The earth which is inhabited by human beings, the earth which contains other living creatures, the earth which elsewhere in scripture is called *dry land*—as in the text, *Let dry land appear. And God called the dry land earth* (Gn 1:9–10)—is founded upon the waters in the sense that it rises above the waters that surround it. Think of idioms in our common speech. When we call a coastal city "Somewhere-on-Sea," we do not mean that the sea is literally underneath it, as water flows beneath caverns and galleries in marine caves, or as the sea is beneath ships that sail upon it. We say that a city is "on the sea" simply because it towers above the sea. So too Pharaoh is said to have gone out *onto the water* (Ex 7:15) because he was on the bank above it (which is what the Greek has, though some Latin translators render it "to the water") Similarly, the Lord *sat on the* well (Jn 4:6). In each

case the person was simply in a higher position—the one above the river, the other above the well.

8. It may be that the words, *God made the intelligent heavens*, signify something else which is more to our purpose. They perhaps refer to God's holy spiritual servants, on whom he has bestowed the grace not only to believe in but also to understand the things of God. These people are *the intelligent heavens*, but others, who are not yet capable of such insight but cling most firmly to faith alone, are represented by the earth below the heavens. These latter stand unshakably in faith through the baptism they have received, and it is therefore said of them that God *established the earth upon the waters*.

Moreover, scripture says of the Lord Jesus Christ that *in him are hidden all the treasures of God's wisdom and knowledge* (Col 2:3). Other scriptural teaching suggests that there is a difference between these two, wisdom and knowledge. Especially clear is the explanation of holy Job, who defines them like this: *He has said to us, Reverence for God—that is wisdom; but to avoid evil—that is knowledge* (Jb 28:28). From this we may reliably infer that wisdom resides in knowing and loving him who abides eternally beyond all change, God. The Greek word used in the phrase, *Reverence for God—that is wisdom*, is θεοσέβεια, which can be translated "reverent worship of God." Knowledge, by contrast, is defined as "avoiding evil." What else is that but to conduct oneself prudently and with circumspection in the night of this world, amid a twisted and perverted race?[19] If we avoid iniquity we are not engulfed in darkness but stand out clearly from it, enlightened by the gift of grace proper to each of us. In one of his letters the apostle wished to show us that the great variety of God's graces in men and women all make for a harmonious unity, and he listed these two gifts before all the others. *To one is given wise utterance through the Spirit*, he says, and I take this to be symbolized by *the sun*, which is *the power in the daytime*. Paul continues, *To another knowledgeable speech according to the same Spirit*, and this is suggested by *the moon*. Then he seems to be thinking of the stars when he says, *To another faith in the same Spirit, to another gifts of healing in one and the same Spirit, to another the power to work miracles, to another prophecy, to another the discernment of spirits, to another various tongues, to another the power to interpret them.* (1 Cor 12:8–10) Not one of these gifts is superfluous during the

---

19. See Phil 2:15.

night of this world, but when the night is past they will be needed no longer; that is why they are called *powers in the night*.

We should notice, however, that whether by day or by night these gifts are *powers*, able to shine either in the daytime or in darkness; and so when we take them as symbols of spiritual gifts they recall the *power* given to us to become children of God.[20]

He smote Egypt and its first-born, for he has smitten the world too, along with those who pretended to worldly eminence.

Verses 11–26. A rapid application of the remaining verses to God's continuing activity in the realm of grace

9. *He led Israel out from the midst of them*, as he has also led out his holy and faithful ones from the midst of their evil surroundings. *With powerful hand and majestic arm.* What could be more powerful, more majestic, than he of whom it was asked, *To whom has the arm of the Lord been revealed?* (Is 53:1) *He divided the Red Sea in half,* as he has also caused a division today, such that one and the same baptism shall be a means of life for some and a death sentence for others. *And he led Israel through the middle of it*, as he still leads his renewed people through the laver of rebirth. *He killed Pharaoh and his forces in the Red Sea*, and just as swiftly does he slaughter the sin and guilt of his own servants through baptism. *He guided his people all through the desert*, and he guides us too in the arid, barren stretches of this world, that we may not meet our death there. *He smote mighty rulers, and slew powerful kings*, for he has smitten and slain the diabolical powers too, freeing us from the molestation of those who were harming us. *Sihon, king of the Amorites*: "a useless plant," or "a smoldering temptation," either of which is what the name Sihon means;[21] he was king of "those who stir up bitterness," as the name Amorites is interpreted. *And Og, king of Bashan.* Og's name means "one who heaps up,"[22] and he was king of "confusion," which is said to be the meaning of *Bashan*. What else does the devil heap up but confusion? *And he gave their land as an inheritance, an inheritance for Israel his servant.* Those who used to be the property of the devil

---

20. See Jn 1:12.
21. In his Exposition of Psalm 134,20, Augustine took Sihon to mean "temptation of the eyes."
22. Which is not far removed from "blockage," as he took it to mean in his Exposition of Psalm 134,20.

he made over as an inheritance for the offspring of Abraham, that is to say, for Christ.[23] *For he remembered us in our degradation, and ransomed us from our foes*, with the blood of his only-begotten Son. *He gives food to all flesh*, which means all humanity, not only Israel but also the gentiles. Of this food Christ says, *My flesh truly is food* (Jn 6:56).

Confess to the God of heaven, because his mercy endures for ever. Confess to the Lord of lords, because his mercy endures for ever. When the psalm says here, *to the God of heaven*, I think this is simply another way of saying what it said in verse 2, namely, *to the God of gods*, since in both places the psalm follows it with the same invitation, *Confess to the Lord of lords*. But let us remember the apostle's warning, *Even if there are beings called gods in the sky or on earth (as in fact there are gods and lords aplenty), still, for us there is one God, the Father, from whom all things come, and for whom we exist; and one Lord, Jesus Christ, through whom all things come, and through whom we exist* (1 Cor 8:5–6). To him do we confess, *because his mercy endures for ever.*

---

23. See Gal 3:16.

Exposition of Psalm 136

A Sermon to the People

Verse 1. The two cities

1. Every well-instructed member of holy Church ought to be familiar with the city to which we belong and of which we are citizens. We have often taught you about it, or rather reminded you, and I cannot think you have forgotten. You will be aware that at present we are exiled from our city, away from it on pilgrimage, and that the reason for our exile is sin. But there is a free gift which ensures our return to our homeland, and that is the forgiveness of sins, whereby through God's grace we are justified.[1] You know all this.

You have also heard and know very well that while the centuries roll on to their end there are two cities, intermingled as to physical presence but distinct in heart. One is called Jerusalem and its goal is eternal peace; the other is Babylon, whose ambition is to enjoy a peace that is only temporal.[2] You have grasped and remembered the interpretation of their respective names, unless I am much mistaken: Jerusalem means "vision of peace"; Babylon means "confusion."

Jerusalem has been held captive in Babylon. Not the whole of Jerusalem, because the angels too are numbered among its citizens; but men and women are in a state of captivity. They are predestined to behold the glory of God and entitled by their adoption to be coheirs with Christ, because they have been ransomed from their captivity by his blood. On account of sin, however, they are the portion of the city of Jerusalem which is held prisoner in Babylon: you will remember that we explained this to you before. But these captives are beginning to make their escape, at first in heart only, through confession of their iniquity and the charity that justifies, and eventually, at the end of time, by quitting it in body as well. We drew your attention to these

---

1. See Rom 5:15–16.
2. See Exposition of Psalm 64,1–2, with which sermon the present one has some affinities. His favorite theme of the two cities, to be fully worked out in *The City of God*, runs all through the present Exposition.

facts when studying another psalm here with you, beloved, the one that begins, *A hymn to you in Zion is fitting, O God* (Ps 64:2(65:1)).

Yet today we have been singing, *Above the rivers of Babylon we sat and wept, as we remembered Zion.* Notice the contrast. In one psalm it is said, *A hymn to you in Zion is fitting, O God,* but in the other, *Above the rivers of Babylon we sat and wept, as we remembered Zion,* that very Zion where a hymn is fittingly sung to God.

Love of Zion colors our whole life

2. What are these rivers of Babylon, then, and what is this about our sitting above them to weep as we remember Zion? If we truly are citizens of Jerusalem, the memory of our city is more than something to sing about; it affects the whole way in which we live our lives. In our present condition, in the confusion of this world, we do not live in Babylon as though we were citizens of it, for we are only held here as captives. Our job is not just to sing about this fact but to make it real to ourselves by the love in our hearts and our spiritual longing for our true, eternal city. Even the city called Babylon has its lovers: men and women who exert themselves to promote its temporal peace. Their hopes extend no further; this is the sum total of their joy and they cannot look beyond it. We see how hard they work for the good of their earthly country. Yet God will not let them perish in Babylon if they live good, faithful lives, shunning self-aggrandizement, fickle fame, and the ostentation which can earn them only hatred. If such people bear witness to the true faith[3] as far as they can, as long as they can, wherever the opportunity occurs, then, insofar as they have a sound judgment of the earthly things they can see and an apprehension of the beauty of the eternal city, God will not allow them to perish in Babylon, for he has predestined them to be citizens of Jerusalem. God understands their captive status, and he reveals to them a different city which must be the true goal of their longing, a city for which they must strive to the utmost. On them lies the duty to encourage their fellow-citizens as best they can and to strive along with them to gain that city, for their fellow-citizens are also fellow-pilgrims. With such people in mind the Lord Jesus Christ says, *One who is faithful in lesser matters is faithful also in greater,* and again, *If you have not been trustworthy over what belongs to another, who will give you anything of your own?* (Lk 16:10.12)

---

3. Or, possibly, "show good faith" by acting honorably.

What are these rivers of Babylon?

3. Nonetheless you should be very attentive to these Babylonian rivers, dearest friends. The rivers of Babylon are all the things which people love in this world but which flow away from us.[4] Imagine, for instance, someone who is very keen on farming. To work at it, to grow rich on it, to give his whole mind to it and to gain pleasure from it are all he cares about. But let him consider where it is ultimately leading, and see that this work he has been so enthusiastic about does not belong to the foundations of Jerusalem but is only a river of Babylon. Another man says, "It's a fine thing to be a soldier. All the farming people are afraid of the military; they obey them and cringe before them. If I become a farmer, I'll be afraid of soldiers, but if I'm a military man myself, every farmer will fear me." You stupid fellow! You have thrown yourself into another Babylonian river, and a rougher, more dangerous one at that. You want to be respected by someone weaker than yourself, do you? Then show respect to the person who is over you. The man who fears you today may quite suddenly become more powerful than you are, but it is unlikely that the one to whom you are bound to show respect will ever become your subordinate.[5] A third person says, "To be an advocate is a splendid career. Eloquence is enormously powerful. I would always have clients hanging on every word that falls from the lips of their fluent counsel, expecting from his mouth either loss or gain, death or life, disaster or well-being." You don't realize where you are putting yourself! That is just another river of Babylon, and it makes such a noise only because its waters roar as they crash against rocks. Watch it flowing, look how it slides away from you and, as you see it slip away, take care lest it drag you with it. Someone else says, "To sail the seas and trade, that's a fine thing to do. To get to know many foreign countries and make a profit in all of them, not to truckle to any powerful civic authority but to be always on the move, to broaden my mind through a variety of business affairs and acquaintance with different nations, and to

---

4. The river is an ancient symbol of the transience of human life and human preoccupations, one of which Augustine is fond. Compare, for example, Exposition of Psalm 109,20.
5. It would be possible to understand this the other way round: "Then show respect to the one who is stronger than you are. This stronger man may suddenly become your subordinate and have cause to fear you, and, if he is weaker than you are, you will certainly have no reason to fear him then."

come home a rich man after making a fortune—that's what I want." And this too is a Babylonian river. Are your gains ever going to be stable? When will you ever feel sure of yourself? Will your assets bring you any freedom from anxiety? On the contrary: the richer you are, the more fearful you will be. One shipwreck, and you will come out of it stripped of the lot, and then you will have reason to lament in that river of Babylon, because you refused to sit and weep above the rivers of Babylon.

4. There are others, though, citizens of holy Jerusalem keenly aware of their captivity, who take stock of human strivings and the manifold desires that on every side snatch people, drag them along, and push them into the sea. These prudent citizens watch it happening and do not fling themselves into any Babylonian river. They sit above the rivers of Babylon and weep over the rivers of Babylon. They weep over the unfortunate people snatched away or over themselves because they have deserved their Babylonian exile. They weep sitting, which means that they have been humiliated. *Above the rivers of Babylon we sat and wept, as we remembered Zion.*

O holy Zion, where all is stable and nothing slides away! Who flung us into our present plight? Why did we abandon him who founded you and forsake the fellowship within you? Look upon us, as all things swirl and slide around us. Scarcely one of us will escape from the river except by laying hold of the wood.[6] Humbled in our captivity, let us sit above the rivers of Babylon and not dare to throw ourselves into them, nor let us ever be so bold as to stand up straight and proud amid the evil and woe of our captivity; but let us sit down and weep thus. But let us sit above the rivers of Babylon, not under them; let our humility be such that it does not submerge us.

Sit above the river. Not in the river and not under it; but all the same, sit humbly. Do not talk as you would in Jerusalem. One day you will be there, and then you will be standing, for another psalm sings of that hope, *Our feet were standing in the forecourts of Jerusalem* (Ps 121(122):2). There you will stand tall, if you have humbled yourself in repentance and confession here. *In the forecourts of Jerusalem were our feet standing,* but, for the present, *above the rivers of Babylon we sat and wept, as we remembered Zion.* This is what must draw forth your tears: your memory of Zion.

---

6. A natural image for an escape from drowning, but Augustine is obviously thinking of the cross.

False and true sadness, false and true joy

5. There are many people who weep, you see, but they weep with the tears of Babylon because they also rejoice with the joy of Babylon. If people rejoice over their gains and weep over their losses, both joy and tears are inspired by Babylon. But if you weep because you remember Zion, even though in Babylon's eyes you are prosperous, you are right to weep.

This is why another psalm says, *I found anguish and sorrow, and I called on the name of the Lord* (Ps 114(116):3–4). Why does the psalmist say that he found them? I do not know why any sort of anguish should be sought, yet he says he found it, as though he had been looking for it. And when he had found it, how did that help him? He called on the name of the Lord. There is a considerable difference between your finding tribulation and tribulation finding you. Think of another passage: *Pains from the underworld found me* (Ps 17:6(18:5)). What is the difference between these two statements: *Pains from the underworld found me*, and, *I found anguish and sorrow*? When sadness suddenly sweeps over you because your worldly affairs, which used to comfort you,[7] have gone awry, when such sudden sadness overtakes you from a quarter whence you never thought to be saddened, and you feel distressed, then it is pain from the underworld that has found you. You thought you were above it, but in truth you were underneath. When this pain from the world below found you, you found yourself below it, not above, as you liked to think. You found yourself severely affected by this pain, this sadness over some misfortune, though you had hitherto believed yourself beyond the possibility of being saddened by such a thing. If this has happened to you, pain from the world below has found you.

But what about the times when things are going well for you? All your worldly enterprises are prospering; none of your relatives has died; no plant in your vineyard has withered or been battered by hail or proved barren; the wine in your vat has not turned sour; not one of your livestock has miscarried; you have not been disgraced in any secular position you have attained; you are surrounded by friends who are still alive and maintain amicable relations with you; you have plenty of clients; your children obey you; your servants tremble at your commands; your wife is compliant. So your household is accounted

---

7. A variant adds, "and in which you used to take pleasure."

happy. This is exactly where you must find tribulation if you can, because when you find it you will call upon the name of the Lord.

Perhaps the word of the Lord seems to be teaching us a perverse sort of lesson: to weep in joyful circumstances and to rejoice in distress. But listen to someone who did live like that, someone who rejoiced when things were going badly: *We rejoice in our sufferings* (Rom 5:3), said the apostle. And then think of someone weeping in joyful circumstances and see whether he or she found tribulation. To think of that, each one of us needs to examine his own happiness, the joy that made his heart leap, the swelling elation that filled him, the good fortune that exalted him and prompted him to say, "How lucky I am!" Let him consider whether that good luck is not flowing away from him, whether he can be certain that it will last for ever. And if he is not certain, if he sees the cause of his joy slipping away, he can be sure that it is a river of Babylon, and the best thing he can do is sit above it and weep. He will indeed sit and mourn, if he remembers Zion.

O what peace shall we know in God's presence! O holy, equal fellowship with the angels! O vision of perfect beauty! There is beauty in Babylon too, but a beauty that holds us captive. Let it not detain us nor deceive us. A sop to prisoners is one thing, the joy of free men and women something else. *Above the rivers of Babylon we sat and wept, as we remembered Zion.*

Verse 2. Christian harps may have to be hung on Babylonian trees for the present

6. *On the willows that grew in the midst of that city we hung up our harps.* The citizens of Jerusalem have their harps—God's scriptures, God's commandments, God's promises, the habit of pondering on the world to come—but when they live in the middle of Babylon they hang up their harps on Babylon's willows. Now willows are trees that bear no fruit. When they are mentioned in this context, it is to suggest that nothing good can be expected from them, though this would not necessarily be the case in other passages. In our psalm, picture to yourselves sterile trees springing up above the rivers of Babylon. They are watered by Babylon's rivers, and they bear no fruit. The people who live there are greedy, miserly, and barren with respect to good works, and so they are like the trees of their region, for the citizens of Babylon feed on the pleasures derived from transient things, like trees irrigated by Babylon's rivers. You look for fruit and there is none anywhere.

When we find people like this difficult to put up with, we know we are dealing with those who live in the center of Babylon. But there is a wide difference between this city and its suburbs.[8] Some there are who do not live in the city center, not being so completely overwhelmed by the lusts and pleasures of the world. Others, who are very bad indeed—if I may put it so bluntly and briefly—live in the center of Babylon, and they are barren trees, just like the local willows. When we encounter them we find them so sterile that it is difficult to discern in them any starting-point from which they could be led toward true faith, or good works, or hope in the world to come, or any desire to be freed from the captivity of their mortal condition. We know the scriptures and try to speak to these people about them but, on finding no fruit there which could at least have offered us a place to begin from, we turn away, despairing. "These people simply have no perception of such things," we complain. "They cannot take anything in. Whatever we say to them, they will have some perverse, obstinate retort."

We are therefore left with no choice but to withhold our scriptures from them for a time: we hang up our harps on the willows because we do not consider such persons worthy to handle them. That is not to say that we fasten our harps to these people in any intimate way; we merely hang them up there and await a more favorable time. People of this type are willows in Babylon, barren trees drawing nourishment from transitory pleasures, as though from Babylonian rivers.

Verse 3. When the devil uses his spokespersons to ask us for songs, it is better to hang up our harps

7. See whether the next verses of the psalm do not bear this out. *On the willows that grew in the midst of that city we hung up our harps, for those who had led us into captivity asked us for songs; our captors requested a hymn.* They had led us away into captivity, and now they were asking us about the words of our songs, demanding that we sing them a hymn. Who led us into captivity, brothers and sisters?

Certainly the earthly city of Jerusalem suffered under Babylonians, Persians, Chaldeans, and all the other invaders in that part of the world, all of whom captured its citizens. But all this happened later,

---

8. In *Confessions* II,3,8 Augustine says that in adolescence he was roaming the streets of Babylon and that his mother had at that period fled from its center but was still lingering in its suburbs.

not at the time when the psalms were first sung.[9] We have already explained to you, beloved,[10] that the disasters which befell that city in a literal sense were types of what was to happen to us; it can easily be demonstrated that we are captives. We do not yet breathe the sweet air of freedom, we do not yet enjoy the truth in all its purity or contemplate that wisdom which, abiding unchanged in herself, makes all things new.[11] We are tempted by the lure of temporal things and struggle every day against the forbidden delights that entice us. Even in prayer we scarcely find relief. We cannot but admit that we are captives. But who led us into captivity? Which powerful men, what nation, what king? If we are redeemed, we must have been captives. Who redeemed us? Christ. From whom did he redeem us? From the devil. It was the devil and his angels who led us into captivity, but they could not have done so without our consent.

So we were led away as prisoners, and I have told you who our captors were. They were the violent robbers who wounded a traveler going down from Jerusalem to Jericho and left him half dead from his injuries.[12] But the good Samaritan was our guardian (the name Samaritan means "guardian"). When the Jews flung at Christ the challenge, *Are we not right to say that you are a Samaritan, and that you have a demon?* (Jn 8:48) he rebutted half the accusation but tacitly accepted the other half. *I have no demon* (Jn 8:49), he said. Notice that he did not say, "I am not a Samaritan." If this Samaritan of ours does not guard us, we perish. The Samaritan was on his journey when he saw an injured man, left lying wounded, and he took him to shelter: you know the story. Sometimes those who have inflicted the wounds of sin on us are called robbers (though they could not have hurt us unless we were already their willing captives); and in other passages they are called our jailers.

8. Now the psalm recalls that *those who had led us into captivity asked us for songs*; they are the devil and his angels, as we have seen. When did they *ask us for songs*? How are we to understand this? It must mean that when we are solicited by people through whom the devil is at work, it is he himself who is soliciting. The apostle reminds us, *Once you were dead in your trespasses and sins, while you lived*

---

9. Augustine assumes that all the psalms were composed by David.
10. See Exposition of Psalm 64,1–2.
11. See Wis 7:27. 12.
12. See Lk 10:30–35.

in them in obedience to this world, and to the prince of the power of the air, who is now at work in the children of unbelief. We too once lived in the same way. (Eph 2:1-3) He makes it clear that he has now been ransomed from Babylon and has begun to move away from it, yet what is this that he is still saying? That we are struggling against our enemies. But the apostle would not have us direct our wrath against human persecutors, so he turns our gaze away from human beings and from any hatred we might feel for them. He directs our attention elsewhere, to a conflict waged against spirits we cannot see, although we are fighting them. *It is not against flesh and blood that you have to struggle*, he warns us: not against the visible human beings at whose hands you seem to be suffering ill-treatment, not against your persecutors. After all, we are commanded to pray for such as these.[13] No, he says, *It is not against flesh and blood that you have to struggle, but against principalities and powers and the rulers of this world of darkness* (Eph 6:12). What does *this world* mean here? The lovers of this world. He also calls these people *darkness*; in other words, the wicked and vicious, unbelievers and sinners, are contrasted with those who have come to believe, whom he congratulates by reminding them that *you were darkness once, but now you are light in the Lord* (Eph 5:8). Against the commanders of such wicked people is our warfare waged, he says, and these are the ones who have led us into captivity.

9. Remember how the devil entered the heart of Judas, prompting him to betray the Lord.[14] The devil would not have been able to get in had opportunity not been offered him. The same thing happens when many bad people, living in the center of Babylon, make their carnal and unlawful lusts the entrée into their hearts for the devil and his angels, who thus gain the power to work in and through them. Such people sometimes interrogate us. "Explain to us," many pagans ask, "Explain to us why Christ came and what benefit he has conferred on humanity. Since his coming things have only got worse, haven't they? Were human affairs not in a happier state before his arrival than they are now? Let the Christians demonstrate what good Christ has done us. What makes them think human society is in any way better since Christ came?"

You see what they are getting at, don't you? If the theaters and the amphitheaters and the circuses stood firm and undamaged, if nothing

---

13. See Mt 5:44. 14.
14. See Jn 13:2.27.

ever fell into ruins in Babylon, if people who want to sing and dance to lewd songs were awash with pleasures all the time, if the lusts of fornicators and whores were given free rein, if anyone who clamors for pantomime performers to be decked out never needed to fear hunger in his own home, if all such forms of indulgence were flowing along without hindrance and frivolity enjoyed complete license—then, they think, our times would be happy, and Christ would have brought great good fortune to human existence. But things are not like that, are they? In fact sinful behavior is in decline so that with the uprooting of greed the charity of Jerusalem may be planted. Bitter experiences besprinkle our temporal life so that we may long for life eternal. People are educated by the chastisements they suffer and accept a Father's discipline lest they later incur a judicial sentence. And because this is how human affairs have developed, the pagans think that Christ has brought us no good but plenty of hardship. You try to tell the challenger how much good Christ has done us, but he cannot take it in. You draw his attention to people who follow the counsel you heard just now in the gospel, people who sell all their possessions and give the proceeds to the poor, so that they may have treasure in heaven, and then follow the Lord.[15] You say to your questioner, "Look! That is what Christ has done for us! Think how many hear the invitation to distribute their goods to the needy and become poor themselves, not of necessity but by choice, because they want to follow God and hope for the kingdom of heaven." But it is no use, they only deride us as fools. "So that is the good Christ has done for us, is it, that a person must lose his belongings and, by giving to the needy, become permanently needy himself?"

What are you to do? "You cannot comprehend the good things of Christ," you will tell him. "You are full of someone else, someone who is Christ's opponent, someone to whom you have given a place in your heart. You look back at earlier ages and you think those days happier because people were like olives hanging on a tree, free to swing at will in every breeze, experiencing a kind of liberty in the indulgence of their capricious desires. But the time came for the olive to be thrown into the press. It could not remain hanging on the tree for ever, for the year was closing in. With good reason are certain psalms entitled *For the presses*,[16] for there is liberty on the tree but crushing

---

15. See Mt 19:21.
16. See Pss 8; 80(81); 83(84).

in the olive-press. When human experience is full of grinding down and pressing out, all you can think of is that this is a sign of increasing avarice. Can you not see that self-control is on the increase too? Why are you so blind that you see only the dregs running into the streets and fail to see the oil in the storing vessels?"[17]

But perhaps such blindness is understandable, because those who live wicked lives are always in the news, whereas those who have turned to God and are being purged of the stains of their evil desires are hidden. In the press, and from the press, the dregs flow in view of everyone, but the oil trickles down unseen.

10. When I tell you these things, brothers and sisters, you shout out joyfully, which proves that you are already strong enough to sit above the rivers of Babylon and weep. But those who led us into captivity still invade people's hearts and use the tongues of those who are their possession to *ask us for songs*. "Explain the reason for Christ's coming," they demand, "and the nature of that other life you talk about. I want to believe.[18] Explain why you are ordering me to believe."

My reply to him will go like this. "Why do you not want me to command you to believe, my friend? I will tell you: you are full of evil cravings. If I tell you about the good things of Jerusalem you will not understand. You need first to be emptied of the things that fill you to make room for what you lack."

Do not be too ready to answer a person of this type: he is a willow, a sterile tree, so do not try to strike your harp for him; just hang it up. He may insist, "Tell me, sing to me, explain to me. Don't you want me to learn?"[19] "But you are not listening in good faith, you are not knocking in a way that makes you fit to have the door opened. The devil who once took me prisoner has taken full possession of you, and he it is who is putting his carping questions through you. He is very wily and his enquiries are full of guile. He does not ask in order to learn but only to find something he can sneer at. So I am not going to talk to you. I will simply hang up my harp."

---

17. *Gemellaria*, a rare word. See Augustine's Exposition of Psalm 80,1 for ideas very similar to the ones he proposes in the present section, and a note there on pagans who harked back to the allegedly good old days.
18. Variant: "I don't want to believe."
19. A variant would attach these last words to the following sentence: "explain to me." "But you don't really want me to tell you. You aren't listening."

Verses 4–5. Be careful not to forget Zion yourself

11. He persists, however. What will he say next? *Sing songs to us, sing us a hymn, sing us one of the songs of Zion.* How shall we respond? "Babylon is carrying you, Babylon is hugging you, Babylon supplies your nourishment, Babylon speaks through your voice. All you can grasp are things that glitter for a short time; you have no idea how to meditate on the things of eternity. You do not even understand what you are asking." *How can we sing a song of the Lord in a foreign land?*

Truly, brothers and sisters, that is how the case stands with them. Begin to try to preach even the tiny portion of truth that you have understood and you will find out for yourselves how we are forced to bear with such mockers, who demand truth but are full of falsehood. Have an answer ready for those folk who pester you for what they are incapable of grasping. Confident in the worth of your holy song, ask them, *How can we sing a song of the Lord in a foreign land?*

12. But be careful how you bear yourself among them, O people of God, O body of Christ, O noble caravan of pilgrims, for you do not spring from Babylon; your homeland is elsewhere. When they say to you, *Sing songs to us, sing us a hymn, sing us one of the songs of Zion*, as though they knew you loved them and sought their friendship and feared to offend them—when they say this to you, be careful lest Babylon begin to attract you and you forget Jerusalem. The singer in the psalm knew this danger. Look at what he says next, read the next verse. Our singer braved this danger, and we are all this one man, if we consent to be. He endured such pressures from every side: people questioning him and flattering him, bitterly reproaching and insincerely praising him, demanding what they could not take in and refusing to void themselves of the evil that filled them. Hemmed in by crowds of such people he seemed to sense the peril, so he raised his mind to the memory of Zion. His noble soul bound itself by an oath: "*If ever I forget you, Jerusalem,*" he said, "amid the talk of my captors, the talk of the cunning, the prating of sly questioners who ask but have no mind to learn."

Zion has songs for both rich and poor

13. There was a rich man[20] who was one of these. He questioned the Lord: *Good teacher, what must I do to gain eternal life?* (Mt 19:16) By his enquiry about eternal life, was he not asking for a song of Zion? *Keep the commandments* (Mt 19:17), the Lord told him. But on hearing this he haughtily replied, *I have kept them all since my youth* (Mt 19:20). Then the Lord said something to him which he knew the questioner would not accept. Yet he said it all the same, because he wished to give us an example, knowing that many people pretend to ask us about eternal life and continue in their sycophancy as long as we keep on answering them. He used the situation to give a lesson to us, who would often be faced with the need to put off inquirers of this sort by asking, *How can we sing a song of the Lord in a foreign land?* So look what the Lord said: *If you want to be perfect, go and sell all you possess and give the money to the poor: you will have treasure in heaven. Then come, follow me.* (Mt 19:21) If he was to learn the rich repertoire of Zion's songs he needed first to throw away all that hindered him and walk unencumbered,[21] free from any burdens that could weigh him down. Only then would he learn anything about the songs of Zion. But no, he departed sadly. Let us shout after him, *How can we sing a song of the Lord in a foreign land?*

That man departed, to be sure, but the Lord gave hope to the rich nonetheless. The disciples were dismayed too and asked him, *Who then can be saved?* He answered, *What is humanly impossible is easy for God.* (Mk 10:26–27) The rich have their own way to salvation, and some of them have caught the strains of a song from Zion and made it their own. The apostle left them directions on how to sing it: *Instruct the rich of this world not to be high-minded, nor to put their trust in unreliable wealth, but in the living God, who gives us everything to enjoy in abundance* (1 Tm 6:17). When he goes on to spell this out for them he seems to be touching his harp, not hanging it up: *Let them be rich in good works, give readily, and share what they have. Let them use their wealth to lay a good foundation for the future, and so attain true life.* (1 Tm 6:18–19) This is one of the songs of Zion, and rich people have learned from it first of all *not to be high-minded*, for riches are apt to make their owners overbearing, and then the rivers

---

20. Variant: "a citizen, and a rich one."
21. *Expeditus*, the term used in the Roman army for a soldier who had shed his baggage and was ready for action.

of Babylon bear them away.[22] So what instructions does the apostle leave them? Above all, *not to be high-minded*. The rich must be aware of the effect of riches and avoid pride even though riches are their lot, for in careless persons pride is the paramount danger posed by wealth. Gold in itself is not evil, for God created it, but a miser is evil if he abandons his creator and turns to a created thing instead. Every rich person must make it his primary concern to eschew pride and to sit above the rivers of Babylon. He is admonished *not to be high-minded*, and that means he must humbly sit down. Nor must he *put his trust in unreliable wealth*, and therefore it is above the rivers of Babylon that he must take his seat, for if he has trusted in his wealth the Babylonian river will sweep him away. If, however, he has humbled himself and not behaved arrogantly, nor put his trust in his wealth, he is sitting above that river, remembering Zion and sighing for the eternal Jerusalem. And, in order to reach Zion, he gives alms.

There you have it: this is the song of Zion which rich people have made their own. Let them work hard, play their harps, and not be idle. Perhaps, though, they may encounter someone who says to them, "What ever are you doing? You are squandering your property by your lavish almsgiving. Save it up for your children." If they see that the objector is a sterile willow who misses the point and is incapable of learning what they do and why they do it, they must hang up their harps on these Babylonian willows. But apart from encounters with the willows they should go on singing tirelessly and work hard. They do not lose what they give away. If they entrust something valuable to a slave, they know it is safe. Are they likely to lose what they entrust to Christ?

14. You have heard the song of Zion that belongs to the rich. Now listen to the song that concerns the poor. The same Paul is singing it: *We have brought nothing into this world, and we can certainly take nothing away with us; if we have food and clothing, let us be content with that. Those who want to get rich succumb to temptation and to many foolish and harmful desires, which plunge a person into destruction and disaster*—in other words, into the rivers of Babylon. *Covetousness is the root of all evils. Many who have chased after it have made shipwreck of their faith, and entangled themselves in manifold troubles.* (1 Tm 6:7–10)

---

22. A pun in Latin: *Extollunt enim divitiae, et quos extollunt, flumina illa tollunt.*

Do these two songs contradict each other? Not at all. Look what the rich were told: *not to be high-minded, nor to put their trust in unreliable wealth,* to employ themselves in good works, to give generously, and to lay down a good foundation for themselves for the future. And what have the poor been told? *Those who want to get rich succumb to temptation.* Notice that the text does not say, "Those who are rich," but, *Those who want to get rich,* for if they were rich already they would be listening to the other song. A rich person hears that he must give his wealth away, a poor one that he must not hanker after it.

Verses 5–6. Zion is your right hand, earthly happiness your left; the songs of Zion are your native tongue

15. As long as you are living among people deaf to any song of Zion, hang up your harps there, in the center of Babylon, as I have advised you. Save up what you were going to say for a more opportune time, for the trees can change and begin to be fruitful and eventually yield a good crop. But when you find yourselves among those who shout you down with their arguments, or question you with dishonest intent, or resist the truth, bind yourselves by oath so that you will not try to align yourselves with their wishes, for fear you may forget Jerusalem. May you say with one mind, one single mind formed out of many in the peace of Christ, and may Jerusalem itself, captive here on earth, say it: *If ever I forget you, Jerusalem, let my right hand forget me.* The singer has bound himself very emphatically, brothers and sisters. *Let my right hand forget me*: that is an appalling oath to take upon oneself. Our right hand represents eternal life, our left hand temporal life. When you do anything for the sake of eternal life, your right hand is working. If you act out of love for eternal life, but allow some other motive to mix itself up with your intention—a desire to enhance your temporal life, or to win human admiration, or to secure some worldly advantage, for instance—your left hand has found out what your right hand is doing. And you know the gospel precept: *Do not let your left hand know what your right hand is doing* (Mt 6:3). The psalm prays, *If ever I forget you, Jerusalem, let my right hand forget me*; and truly that is what happens. The singer foresaw it, though he did not hope for it. Those who forget Jerusalem suffer the fate he mentioned: their right hand forgets them. Eternal life abides unchanged in itself, but they remain stuck in temporal enjoyment, and they turn what belongs to their left hand into their right.

16. Focus your attention on these matters, brothers and sisters. I want to instill this idea into your minds, insofar as the Lord enables me, for the salvation of all of you. You may remember that I preached here on an earlier occasion about people who treat what belongs to the left hand as though it were the right.[23] In other words, some people who have more in the way of temporal goods seek happiness in these things, unaware of what constitutes real joy and what is truly their right hand. Scripture calls these people foreigners, implying that they are citizens not of Jerusalem but of Babylon, for in another psalm we find this: *Deliver me from the hands of foreigners, whose mouths have spoken empty words, and whose right hand is a hand that deals unjustly.* It goes on to explain why: *Their sons are like well-set saplings, their daughters are adorned and gathered round them like the pillars of the temple, their storerooms are full to overflowing, their ewes fruitful, increasing at every lambing time, and their oxen are sturdy. Never is their hedge broken down or their property invaded, nor is there rioting in their streets.* (Ps 143(144):11–14) Is it sinful to have such good fortune? No, certainly not; but to regard it as your right hand when in fact it is only your left, that is sinful. And this sinful attitude is what the psalm just quoted goes on to suggest. What does it say? *They have called blessed people who have these things* (Ps 143(144):15). That is why they were accused of speaking empty words, for it certainly is an empty opinion to count others blessed merely for having all that wealth. But as for you, you are a citizen of Jerusalem, one who is careful not to forget Jerusalem lest your right hand forget you. The foolish people you just heard about, the ones who spoke empty words, held that the possessors of such wealth are blessed on that account. What about you? You sing me a song of Zion: *Blessed rather is the people whose God is the Lord* (Ps 143(144):15).

Question your own hearts, brothers and sisters. Do you long for the good things of God, do you long for the city of Jerusalem, do you yearn for eternal life? Whatever good fortune you may have on earth, regard it as your left hand, and be sure that your right hand is the happiness you will enjoy for ever. Even if that left-hand happiness is available to you, do not trust your left hand. Do you not censure anyone who uses the left hand to eat? Well then, if you think it bad manners when someone at table with you uses the left hand, how can it be acceptable at God's table to treat your right hand as though it were

---

23. See Exposition of Psalm 120,8.

your left and to use your left as your right? What are we to conclude, then? *If ever I forget you, Jerusalem, let my right hand forget me.*

17. *May my tongue stick to the roof of my mouth if I do not remember you.* May I be struck dumb, he means, if I do not keep you in mind, for what is the point of speaking, what is the point of singing, if one does not sing Zion's songs? The song of Jerusalem is our own language. The song that tells of love for this world is a foreign tongue, a barbaric language we have picked up in our captivity. Anyone who has forgotten Jerusalem will therefore be dumb before God. Yet it is not enough merely to remember Jerusalem, for its enemies remember it too, plotting to overthrow it. "What kind of city is that?" they ask. "Who are these Christians? What sort of people are they? Let's get rid of the lot of them." In our day the crowd of captives has conquered its captors, yet still they fume and try to destroy the holy wayfaring city in their midst, as once Pharaoh tried to slaughter a whole people by killing its new-born boys, while allowing its baby girls to live. He was strangling virtues, you see, and fostering sensual desires! So it is not enough simply to remember Jerusalem; take care *how* you remember it, for we remember some things with hatred and others with love.

Accordingly the psalm first says, *if ever I forget you, Jerusalem, let my right hand forget me. May my tongue stick to the roof of my mouth if I do not remember you,* but then it promptly adds, *if I do not make Jerusalem the height of my joy.* Supreme joy is found where we delight in God, where, free from all anxiety, we live in united fellowship with our brothers and sisters and our true companions in that city. No tempter will molest us there, no one will be able to force us toward any seductive pleasure, nothing will attract us except what is good. All pressure of need will fade away, and supreme happiness will dawn upon us. *I will make Jerusalem the height of my joy.*

Verse 7. The malice of Edom, descended from Esau

18. Now the singer turns to the Lord to pray for help against the enemies of his city. *Remember the sons of Edom, O Lord.*[24] The race here called Edom is the same as Esau; and you heard just now in the reading from the apostle, *I have loved Jacob, but hated Esau* (Rom 9:13; Ml 1:2–3). Scripture is recalling two children in one womb. The twins in Rebecca's womb were children of Isaac and grandsons

---

24. It seems that when the Babylonian armies were besieging Jerusalem the Edomites allied themselves with the besiegers.

of Abraham. They were born, the one to an inheritance, the other to disinherited status. But Esau was at odds with his brother, because the younger had usurped his blessing; and the prediction was later confirmed, *The elder will serve the younger* (Rom 9:12; Gn 25:23).

We can now see clearly who is the elder and who the younger and how it came true that the elder was to serve the younger. For a long time it was obvious that the Jewish people was the elder, and the Christian people was the younger, chronologically speaking. And then look what happened and how the elder has come to be the servant of the younger now. They carry our books for us, and we draw life from books that once were theirs.[25]

But this contrast between elder and younger has a more general relevance, brothers and sisters, for carnal humanity can be regarded as the first-born, and the spiritual as a later arrival. The apostle says explicitly, *The first man was from the earth, earthly, but the second man is from heaven, heavenly. As the earthly man was, so too are the earthlings; as the heavenly man is, so too are the heavenly ones. As we have borne the image of the man of earth, so too let us bear the image of him who is of heaven.* (1 Cor 15:47–49) But just before this he said, *It is not the spiritual that comes first. The animal body comes first, and what is spiritual afterwards.* (1 Cor 15:46) Here he calls what is demonstrably carnal an *animal body*. As soon as a human being is born he begins to be animal and carnal.

If he turns away from captivity in Babylon and sets his course to return to Jerusalem he is made new. A transformation takes place that renews him in his inner self and, though younger in time, he becomes like a more powerful elder sibling. Esau therefore represents all carnal men and women, Jacob all those who are spiritual. The younger are chosen, the first-born rejected.

Does Esau want to be chosen too? Let him become small and humble, like a younger child. But no, for Edom's name derives from red lentils and from a stew that was red in color;[26] the lentils had been pounded and well cooked. Esau begged for some of the stew from his brother Jacob and, being overcome by his hunger for the lentils, he

---

25. Fuller developments of this idea that the Jews serve as book-bearers for Christians are to be found in Expositions of Psalms 40,14 and 56,9 and the notes in both places.
26. In Hebrew the words "Esau" and "red" (or "blood") are akin. See Exposition of Psalm 46,6 and the note there on Augustine's treatment of the story of Jacob and Esau. Israelites regarded Esau as the ancestor of the Edomites.

ceded his birthright to his younger brother.[27] Jacob, on the contrary, gave up the delicious food to win an honorable privilege. It was therefore in a sense agreed between them that they should change places and that the first-born become the servant of the younger. This story also explains why Esau was called Edom, for those who know the language interpret the name Edom as "blood." Even in Punic blood is called *edom*. There is nothing strange about this, for all carnal persons are, as it were, bloodstained, and, as scripture says, *Flesh and blood will not possess the kingdom of God* (1 Cor 15:50). Edom has no kinship with that realm, but Jacob belongs there, for he went without carnal food and gained spiritual honor. On this account Esau became Jacob's enemy. All carnally-minded people are at odds with the spiritually-minded, for the former crave only present satisfaction and harass those whom they perceive to be focused on eternity.

The psalmist has turned his eyes to Jerusalem, but he prays against these enemies, begging the Lord for deliverance from captivity. *Remember the sons of Edom, O Lord*, he says. Deliver us from carnal people, from those who imitate Edom, from those who, though our elder brothers, have made themselves our enemies. They were born first, but their younger siblings have overcome them and seized the honors of primogeniture; for while carnal desire brought down the elder sons, contempt for greed raised up the younger. So it comes about that the elder sons survive[28] and are jealous and persecute.

19. *Remember the sons of Edom, O Lord, remember against them the day of Jerusalem*. Which *day of Jerusalem* is meant? The day of Jerusalem's distress, the day on which it was captured? Or the day of Jerusalem's happiness, when it is set free, when it reaches journey's end, when it enters eternity? *Remember the sons of Edom, O Lord*, prays the psalm; do not forget what they did. Who are they? *Those who shouted, Destroy it, destroy it, right down to its foundations!* Remember the day when they wanted to overthrow Jerusalem.

What fierce persecutions the Church has endured! The sons of Edom are carnally-minded men and women, dominated by the devil and his angels, worshiping stones and wooden idols and pursuing the lusts of the flesh. How often have they shouted, "Stamp out those Christians! Get rid of them, don't let even one remain! Lay waste their city, even to its foundations!" This is what was said, isn't it? But the

---

27. See Gn 25:29–34; compare Gn 27:1–40.
28. Variant: "see it."

persecutors were proved impotent, and the martyrs were crowned. The persecuting powers shouted, *Destroy it! Destroy it right down to its foundations!* The sons of Edom clamor, *Destroy it, destroy it!* but God says, "No, you serve the younger." Which will prevail? Surely God, who foretold, *The elder will serve the younger.* Yet still the cry goes up, *Destroy it! Destroy it right down to its foundations!*

Verses 8–9. Revenge on Babylon

20. Now the psalm addresses Babylon: *Ill-fated daughter of Babylon!* You are ill-fated despite your triumphant jubilation, your presumption, and your hostility, O *ill-fated Daughter of Babylon!* That city is called both Babylon and daughter of Babylon. The same usage is found when we speak of Jerusalem and the daughter of Jerusalem, of Zion and the daughter of Zion and, indeed, of the Church and the daughter of the Church.[29] Babylon is regarded as a mother because of its seniority, but as a daughter because it had successors. There was an ancient city of Babylon, but did its original populace survive there? No, but that city had its heirs and successors, rightly called the daughter of Babylon.[30] *Ill-fated* are you, daughter of Babylon! Yet *blessed is he who requites you in accordance with your treatment of us.* Wretched and ill-fated are you, blessed he.

21. What did you do to us, and what will be your punishment? *Blessed is he who requites you in accordance with your treatment of us.* What retribution is envisaged? The last words of the psalm spell it out: *Blessed is the one who shall seize your infants and dash them against the rock.* It calls Babylon ill-fated, but it calls blessed anyone who shall visit upon it the same punishment it visited upon us. What is that? *Blessed is the one who shall seize your infants and dash them against the rock.* That is the retribution.

What did Babylon do to us? Well, think: in another psalm we sang, *The words of sinners had power over us* (Ps 64:4(65:3)). As soon as we were born the confusion[31] of this world took hold of us, and even before we learned to speak it choked us with the futile opinions spawned by a host of errors. The newborn child is potentially

---

29. This last expression seems to have struck some copyists as odd; many corrected *filia* to *filii*. But the thought is clear.
30. The city of iniquity, which in every age continues to oppose the city of God. See, among other examples, Exposition of Psalm 64,2.
31. Augustine took "confusion" to be the interpretation of the name Babylon; see section 1 above.

a citizen of Jerusalem—indeed, by God's predestination a citizen already—but for the time being he or she is a prisoner. What can a child learn to love except what his parents whisper to him? They form his mind, teaching him avarice, plunder, habitual lying, all kinds of idolatry and devil-worship, and unlawful recourse to spells and amulets. What is the child to do? He is an infant still, a tender, delicate little creature. He watches his elders to see how they behave, and what can he do but follow their example? In this sense Babylon persecuted us when we were still tiny children, but as we grew up God gave us some knowledge of himself, and so we learned not to copy the mistakes of our parents. I remember preaching about this matter on another occasion,[32] and I quoted then a prophetic saying, *Gentiles will come to you from the furthest parts of the earth, and they will say, Truly our ancestors worshiped a lie,*[33] *a futile thing that could not help them* (Jer 16:19). It is young people who say this. They were exposed to death as little children by following those futile things, but they have thrown away futility and come back to life; now they can grow up toward God and requite Babylon. How will they repay it? With the same punishment it inflicted on us. It will be the turn of Babylon's little ones to be choked now; or, rather, its infants will in their turn be dashed to pieces and killed. Who are these little ones in Babylon? Evil desires newly come to birth. Some people have to fight against inveterate desires, but you can do better than that. When evil desire is born, before your bad habits reinforce it, while it is still in its infancy and has not yet fortified itself by alliance with depraved custom, dash it to pieces. It is only a baby still. But make sure it does not survive your violent treatment: dash it on the rock. *And the rock is Christ* (1 Cor 10:4).

Conclusion: sing the songs of Zion, slay your enemies, and long for the eternal Jerusalem

22. Let our harps not fall silent, brothers and sisters; let them play constantly as you sing to each other the songs of Zion. You have listened eagerly. Be just as eager to put into practice what you have heard, if you do not want to be Babylonian willows, nourished only by Babylon's rivers and bearing no fruit. Let your ardent sighs be for the eternal Jerusalem. Your hope has gone ahead of you and your

---

32. See Exposition of Psalm 64,6.
33. Variant: *made a lie their own.*

life follows,[34] for there we shall be with Christ. Christ is our head even now, for he guides us from on high, but then he will take us into his embrace in that city, and we shall be equal to the angels of God. We would not have dreamed of such a destiny for ourselves had not the truth promised it. Long for it, then, brothers and sisters. Think about it night and day. If this world smiles favorably on you in some matter, put no reliance on that, and do not consent to any dalliance with your lusts. If your enemy is fully grown, slay him on the rock. If your enemy is still small, dash him against the rock. Either way, great or small, let them be killed on the rock. Let the rock win the day.

Allow yourselves to be built on the rock if you do not want to be swept away by the river or the wind or the rain.[35] If you want to be armed against temptations in this world, let desire for the eternal Jerusalem increase and grow strong in your hearts. Our captivity will pass, happiness will come, the last enemy[36] will be condemned, and we shall triumph with our king, freed from death for ever.

---

34. Variants: "will follow"; "let your life follow."
35. See Mt 7:24–25.
36. See 1 Cor 15:26.

Exposition of Psalm 137

A Sermon to the People[1]

Verse 1. A holocaust of praise

1. The title of this psalm is short and simple. It need not detain us, because we know whom David symbolizes: the one in whom we recognize ourselves, since we are members of his body. Let us therefore hear in this psalm the voice of the Church, to which we rejoice to belong; it was truly the voice of the Church that we heard as it was sung. The title consists simply of the words, *For David himself.* So let us see what there is here for David.

2. *I will confess to you, O Lord, with my whole heart.* Ordinarily we expect the title of a psalm to give an indication of its content, but in this case the title says nothing of what is to come but only names the one for whom it is sung. It is left for the first verse to proclaim the business of the rest of the psalm, which it does by the words, *I will confess to you, O Lord, with my whole heart.* Let us now listen to this confession. But first of all I want to remind you that, when scripture speaks of confession to God, the word may be understood in two ways: confession of sins or confession as praise. Everyone knows about confession of sins, but few are aware of the other meaning, confession as praise. So well known is the confession of sins that whenever some passage of scripture says, *I will confess to you, O Lord,* or, *We will confess to you,* people all begin to strike their breasts from force of habit, because that is how they usually understand the word. This suggests how accustomed they are to taking it in one sense alone, that of the confession of sins. But our Lord Jesus Christ was no sinner, was he? Yet he said in the gospel, *I confess to you, Father, Lord of heaven and earth.* And he went on to articulate the reason for his confession, so that we might understand it as praise, not admission of iniquity. *I confess to you, Father, Lord of heaven and earth,* he said, *because you have hidden these matters from the wise and knowing, and have revealed them to little ones* (Mt 11:25).

---

1. Probably preached at Hippo on 5 December, the feast of Saint Crispina. The year is disputed.

He praised his Father, he praised God, for not despising the humble but despising the proud.

This is the kind of confession that we are about to hear, a confession of praise and thanksgiving to God. *I will confess to you, O Lord, with my whole heart.* I place my whole heart on the altar in confession to you, I offer you a holocaust of praise. The word "holocaust" denotes a sacrifice in which everything is burnt up, for the Greek ὅλον means "whole." Observe how the singer who declares, *I will confess to you, O Lord, with my whole heart,* offers a spiritual holocaust. "May my entire heart burn with love for you," he implies. "Let nothing of myself be left to me, nothing that could turn my eyes back to myself again. Let me be totally afire for you, wholly burning with love for you. Let me love you with my entire self, as though you had set me on fire. *I will confess to you, O Lord, with my whole heart, because you have heard the words my mouth has spoken.* And what *mouth* do I mean but the mouth of my heart?"

From that mouth of our hearts comes the voice that God hears, though no human ear can catch it. Susanna's accusers certainly shouted loudly enough but did not raise their eyes to heaven; she was silent but cried to heaven in her heart. From heaven she was deservedly heard, and they were punished.[2] We have an interior mouth, you see; with it we frame our petitions, and from it we plead. If we have prepared within ourselves a guest-chamber or house for God, we talk with him there, and there our prayer is heard, for *he is not far from any one of us, he in whom* we live and move and have our being (Acts 17:27–28). Nothing sets you far from God except iniquity. Break down the dividing wall of sin and you are with him to whom you are praying. So the psalm proclaims, *You have heard the words my mouth has spoken; I will confess to you.*

Joy in the presence of the angels: Saint Crispina

3. *And before the angels I will sing psalms to you.* Not in the presence of men and women will I sing psalms, but before the angels. My psaltery is my joy. When I find joy in things here below, my joy is obvious to other people, but when I find my joy in things on high, I sing in the presence of the angels. A godless person knows nothing of the joy of the just, for *there is no joy for the wicked, says the Lord* (Is 48:22, LXX; 57:21, LXX). The ungodly may find joy in a cook-

---

2. See Dn 13:35–62.

shop;³ the martyr finds joy in his chain. Think how Saint Crispina rejoiced, the martyr whose festival we keep today:⁴ she rejoiced when arrested, rejoiced when haled before the judge, rejoiced when thrown into prison, rejoiced when bound and led forth, rejoiced when hoisted onto the scaffold,⁵ rejoiced when the people listened to what she had to say, and rejoiced on being condemned. In all these trials she rejoiced. Wretched onlookers deemed her wretched, yet she was rejoicing in the sight of the angels.

Verse 2. In our hearts, and in the holy company of the angels, God's name is to be glorified

4. *I will worship at your holy temple.* What holy temple is this? The temple where we shall live⁶ and where we shall worship you; for we are running toward it to offer you our worship. Our heart is pregnant, on the point of giving birth, and searching for a place to bring forth its adoration. Where is the right place for God to be worshiped? What world is a fit place for his worship, what building? What throne, even in the sky or among the stars, is fit for him? If we search the holy scripture, we find an answer, for there wisdom says, *I was with him, I was the one in whom he delighted daily* (Prv 8:30, LXX). Then she describes his works and explains to us where he placed his throne: *When he made the mighty clouds above, when he set apart a throne for himself upon the winds* (Prv 8:27–28, LXX). But his throne is not different from his temple. Where are we to go, then? Must we mount above the winds to worship him? If he is to be adored above the winds, the birds have the advantage over us. But perhaps *winds* here means souls. Sometimes souls are called winds in scripture, as in the text which says of God, *He flew upon the wings of the wind* (Ps 17:11(18:10)); this means upon the powers of souls. Similarly the soul is said to be God's breath,⁷ which evokes the idea of wind: not the kind of wind which we feel as a physical force when it blows but something invisible which can neither be discerned with our eyes nor heard with our ears nor perceived as a fragrance nor tasted with the palate nor felt with the hand. Yet it is something alive

---

3. *Popina.* A few witnesses read *pompa* ("ostentation," "pomp"), perhaps rightly.
4. See Exposition of Psalm 120,13 and the note there. That Exposition was also preached on the feast of Saint Crispina, 5 December, in another year.
5. Or stage, or platform, *catasta*; see the note at Exposition of Psalm 96,16.
6. Variant: "where you [God] live."
7. See Gn 2:7.

and something which causes us to live. It is called the soul. Now if by *winds* we understand the psalm to mean souls, we have no need to seek material wings wherewith to fly up with the birds in order to worship at God's temple, for we shall discover that we ourselves are God's throne, as long as we have the will to be faithful to him. Scripture bears out this interpretation, for the apostle says, *God's temple is holy, and that temple is yourselves* (1 Cor 3:17).

Yet it is certain and quite obvious that God dwells in the angels. When, therefore, our joy springs not from earthly good fortune but from spiritual causes, and we are inspired to strike up a song to God and sing to him in the presence of the angels, this very concourse of angels is God's temple, and we worship in it. The Church is both here below and on high: the Church below consists of all the faithful, the Church above of all the angels. Yet the Lord of the angels came down to the Church below, and on earth angels served him[8] who had come to serve us, as he said himself: *I did not come to be served, but to serve* (Mt 20:28). And what did he serve to us if not what we eat[9] and drink today?[10] If, then, the Lord of the angels has made himself our servant, we should not give up hope of one day being equal to the angels. He who is greater than the angels came down to the human level, the creator of the angels took upon himself our humanity, and the Lord of angels died for us humans. *I will worship at your holy temple*, for I understand your temple to be not a building fashioned by human hands but the place you have made for yourself.

5. *And I will confess to your name about your mercy and your truth.* About these two qualities we confess to him, as in another psalm scripture declares, *All the Lord's ways are mercy and truth* (Ps 24(25):10). About these two things, *your mercy and your truth*, we confess. In your mercy you have looked upon the sinner, and in your truth you have shown yourself faithful to your promise. *About your mercy and your truth*, then, I will confess to you.

But these are also gifts with which you have endowed me, and in my small measure I too will show mercy and truth: mercy in helping others and truth in judgment. In these virtues we are helped by God, and through them we come to deserve God as our reward. Truly,

---

8. See Mk 1:13; Lk 22:43.
9. Variant: "have eaten."
10. Probably an allusion to the Eucharist.

then, are *all the Lord's ways mercy and truth*. By no other ways did he come to us, and by no other ways do we come to him.

6. *Because you have glorified your holy name above all else.* How should we understand this joyful reason for thanksgiving, brothers and sisters? He glorified his holy name in Abraham, for Abraham believed God, and it was accounted to him as righteousness.[11] All the other nations were sacrificing to idols at this time and worshiping demons. From Abraham was born Isaac, and God was glorified in his family too. From Isaac came Jacob, and again God was glorified, God who said, *I am the God of Abraham, and the God of Isaac, and the God of Jacob* (Ex 3:6). From Jacob sprang twelve sons, and from them the people of Israel which was rescued from Egypt, led through the Red Sea, tested in the wilderness, and established in the promised land when its gentile inhabitants had been displaced. Surely, then, the Lord's name was magnified in Israel; but there was more, for thence came the Virgin Mary, and from her Christ the Lord, who died for our sins and rose for our justification.[12] He filled believers with the Holy Spirit and sent them to preach among the nations. *Repent*, they were to say, *for the kingdom of heaven is near* (Mt 3:2). This is how he glorified his holy name, glorified it above all else.

Verse 3. An urgent prayer for spiritual fruitfulness

7. *On whatever day I call upon you, hear me quickly.* Why *quickly*? Perhaps because you, Lord, have assured us, *While you are yet speaking, I shall say, Lo, here I am* (Is 58:9, LXX; 65:24). But still, why *quickly*? Because, answers the psalmist, I no longer pray for earthly happiness; I have learned holy desire from the New Testament. I do not ask for this earth, or for a brood of children, or temporal well-being, or the submission of my enemies, or riches or rank. None of these do I seek, and therefore I pray, *Hear me quickly.* Since you have taught me what to ask for, give me what I ask.

Let us question the psalmist: Is it really nothing of this kind that you are pleading for? Then let us listen while he blurts out his petition, and let us see for ourselves what he prays for and learn to pray through him, so that we may deserve to obtain what we ask.

You there, you came to church today intending to pray for something or other, didn't you? What are we to suppose you had in mind

---

11. See Gn 15:6; Rom 4:3.
12. See Rom 4:25.

when you came to offer your petition? You certainly brought your desire with you. I don't know what it was: innocent, I hope, even if concerned with material things. But now, banish iniquity and banish carnal thoughts; learn how to present your requests to God, and remember what you are commemorating today. You are celebrating the birthday[13] of a holy, blessed woman, and are you by any chance entertaining desires for earthly prosperity?[14] Such was the strength of her holy desire that she gave up the prosperity she had enjoyed on earth. She gave up even her weeping children who mourned her, heartless mother as she seemed to them. It looked as though she had lost all human pity in her hurry to reach a divine reward. Must we conclude that she had no sense of what was worth longing for and what was best trampled underfoot? On the contrary, she knew how to sing psalms in the presence of God's angels and how to long for their friendship, for a holy, pure society where she would never die again, where she would meet a judge with whom no lie could prevail.[15] What are we to make of her decision? Must we suppose that in the life beyond there are no good things to enjoy? Far from it. Only there are truly good things to be found, things purely good without taint of evil, secure happiness in which you can rejoice as intensely as you wish, with no one to say to you, "Be careful, restrain yourself." Here below it is harmful and very dangerous to exult with such abandon in earthly delights, lest your pleasure keep you stuck fast in them and your unwise indulgence bring you to ruin. Why does God temper our earthly joys by infecting them with troubles? Surely so that, when we experience pain and bitterness, we may learn to long for eternal sweetness.

8. Let us see, then, what the psalmist is asking for and what prompted him to beg, *Hear me quickly*. What are you praying for, psalmist, that you need to beg for a speedy hearing? *You will grant me increase*: this is his prayer. Now *increase* can be variously understood. Earthly procreation is an increase, part of the primal blessing conferred on our nature when God told us, *Increase and multiply, and fill the earth, and have lordship over it* (Gn 1:28). Was that the kind of increase the psalmist hoped for when he prayed, *Hear me quickly*? Such fruitfulness is undoubtedly a gift, only possible if the

---

13. *Natalitium*, see the note at Exposition of Psalm 63,15.
14. Variant: "earthly celebrity."
15. In contrast to the human judge who condemned her.

Lord's blessing is its source. What about other modes of increase? One man increases in gold, another in silver, another in livestock, another in household servants, another in personal possessions, and another again in all these things. Earthly increase can take many forms. The happiest of them is a growing family of children, yet to stingy people this fecundity is itself a grief, for they are afraid of being left penniless if many children are born to them.[16] Such worries have driven many to denial of their family responsibility, so that, forgetting their duty as parents and divesting themselves of all human tenderness, they have exposed their children and treated them as strangers. The woman who bore the child casts it away, and another woman who was not its mother picks it up. The one despises the child, the other loves it; the first was physically a mother, but to no purpose, the second is more truly a mother because she wants to be.

There are many kinds, many modes of increase. For what sort of increase is the psalmist praying when he says, *Hear me quickly*? We know he has it in mind, for he explicitly says, *You will grant me increase*. We must wait to hear in what respect he hopes for it. Listen then: he continues, *in my soul*. Not in my flesh but *in my soul*, he says. *You will grant me increase in my soul*. But does he still need to add something else in case even increase in his soul does not immediately and without more ado signify happiness? After all, people may suffer a multiplication of cares in their souls; and even someone in whom vices are multiplying could be thought to have a certain increase in his soul, could he not? If you think of one person who is greedy but free from other vices, another who is proud only, another who is only licentious, and then you picture someone else who is greedy and proud and licentious, you could regard the last one as spiritually increased, but only in his own vicious characteristics. That is an increase of need, not an increase of wealth.

Well then, you who prayed, *Hear me quickly*, what did you want? You have distanced yourself from bodily preoccupations, from earthly goods, and from all worldly desires, to the point where you could say to God, *You will grant me increase in my soul*. Explain to us what you still desire. *You will grant me increase in my soul*, he replies, *with respect to virtue*. There you have it, an explicit prayer, an express desire, with all ambiguity sheared away. If he had said no more than *You will grant me increase*, one might have thought he meant increase

---

16. Conjecturally amending *qui* to *quia*.

in some sort of earthly commodities, so he added, *in my soul*. But this is still open to misinterpretation, for one could think of vices multiplying in his e added, *with respect to virtue*. There is nothing more that you can desire from God, if you want to face him honestly and sincerely and beg, *Hear me quickly*.

Verses 4–5. The confession of earthly rulers

9. *May all earth's kings confess to you, O Lord*. Thus will it be, thus is it happening now and happening daily. It is plain that these words were not spoken pointlessly; they were prophetic and were uttered only because they were to be proved true in the future. *May all earth's kings confess to you, O Lord*. But it is important that even they do not seek earthly benefits from you when they confess to you and praise you. What are earthly kings likely to desire? They have supreme sovereignty, have they not? Whatever else a person may desire in this world, his desire cannot mount higher than imperial power. What more is there for him to covet? It would have to be some status higher still, but perhaps the higher it was the more dangerous it would be. The greater kings are in earthly eminence, the more deeply they must humble themselves before God.

Why so? *Because they have heard all the words of your mouth.* O Lord, *all the words of your mouth*! Within a certain nation were hidden the law and the prophetic writings, *all the words of your mouth*. In the Jewish nation alone *all the words of your mouth* were treasured, and the apostle singled out this privilege as the nation's glory: *Is there any advantage in being a Jew? Or is circumcision of any value? Of great value, in every respect. To begin with, because to the Jews God's words were entrusted.* (Rom 3:1–2) Among them, and only among them, resided the words of God.

But there is a significant story about a holy man who lived in the era of the Judges. His name was Gideon. Notice what sort of sign he asked from the Lord: *I will place this fleece on the threshing floor*, he said. *Let the fleece be rained upon, but all the threshing floor be dry* (Jgs 6:37). And that is what happened: the fleece alone was soaked, and the floor around it was dry. Then he asked for another sign: *Let all the threshing floor be wet and the fleece alone be found dry* (Jgs 6:39). This again happened as he asked, for the threshing floor was soaked with rain, the fleece dry. At first the fleece was rained on and the ground was dry; then the ground was wet and the fleece was dry. What do you think the threshing floor represents, brothers and sisters?

The whole world, I think, don't you? And the fleece? It was like the Jewish race in the center of the world, possessing the mystery of grace not in an open, manifest way but clouded, veiled and secret, like rain hidden in the fleece. The time came for the hidden moisture to be revealed all over the floor; thereafter it was plain for all to see, not concealed as it had been in earlier times. In this way the prophecy in the psalm came to be fulfilled: *May all earth's kings confess to you, O Lord, because they have heard all the words of your mouth.* What is it, Israel, that you were hiding? How long did you go on hiding it? The fleece was wrung out, and the rain flowed forth from you. Christ alone is the sweetness in this rain, yet although the scriptures came into being to reveal him, you do not recognize him in your scriptures. Nonetheless, *may all earth's kings confess to you, O Lord, because they have heard all the words of your mouth.*

10. *And let them sing in the ways of the Lord, Great is the glory of the Lord.* Let the kings of the earth sing in the ways of the Lord. What ways? Those ways of which we spoke earlier: *your mercy and your truth,*[17] because *all the Lord's ways are mercy and truth* (Ps 24(25):10). Let earth's kings not be proud; their business is to be humble. Then, if they are humble, let them sing in the ways of the Lord; let them love him, and then they will sing. We have all seen traveling singers; they sing and are in a hurry to arrive at the place they are making for. But theirs are bad songs, the songs of the old humanity. Our new self demands a new song. Let the kings of the earth walk in your ways, Lord; let them walk and sing in your ways. What are they to sing? *Great is the glory of the Lord*, not the glory of kings.

Verse 6. Do not imagine that God cannot see you

11. Now consider how the psalmist wanted these kings to sing in the Lord's ways. He would have them humbly bearing the Lord, not exalting themselves against the Lord. If they do exalt themselves, what will the consequences be? The psalm affirms, *The Lord is most high, and he looks on the lowly.* Do the kings want him to look upon them, to have regard for them? Very well, let them be humble. Why should they? Well, think: If they exalt themselves proudly, is it possible for them to be hidden from his eyes? No, do not make that mistake. Suppose you heard the psalm say that *he looks on the lowly,* and you want to be proud. Perhaps you whisper to yourself, "If God looks

---

17. See section 5 above.

on the humble, he doesn't look on me, so I will do what I like. No one can see me—no human eye, anyway. And God does not want to see me, because I'm not humble, and he only looks on the lowly. So I may as well do whatever I want to." Would you talk like that, you unmannerly fellow, if you knew what you ought to love? And, even supposing it were true that God is unwilling to see you, do you not think that in itself a reason to be afraid? If you greet some important person who is your patron, and he is preoccupied with some other matter and fails to see you, are you not upset about it? Well then, do you think you are safe if God does not see you? If your savior does not see you, your despoiler will!

But in any case God himself does see you. Do not assume you are unseen; rather, pray to be worthy of his gaze, for he does indeed see you. It is written, *The eyes of the Lord are upon the righteous.* But does that mean the unrighteous can do as they please, since the eyes of the Lord are not on them? After all, it does say, *The eyes of the Lord are upon the righteous.* But listen to the next words: *And his ears are open to their prayers* (Ps 33:16(34:15)). Are the unjust as safe as they thought in assuming that the eyes of the Lord are not on them? Should they not be afraid when they find out that his ears are not open to them either, not open to their prayers? Are we not better off if we have both—his eyes on us and his ears attentive to our prayers? If you do things on which you do not want the Lord's gaze to rest, you certainly do not deserve to have his ears open to your prayers, and yet when you do wrong you do not succeed in turning his gaze away from you. For what does that psalm say next? *But the Lord frowns on evildoers.* To what purpose? *To blot out their memory from the earth* (Ps 33:17(34:16)). You are seen, you see! Can you not see that you will not escape detection? If, then, you are seen by him, whatever you do, why not behave in such a way as to be pleasing in his sight?

How does our psalm continue this thought? *Great is the glory of the Lord, because the Lord is most high, and he looks on the lowly.* It seems to be saying that he has no regard for what is lofty but regards the lowly. What about those lofty things? *Whatever is exalted he knows from afar.* If that is so, what good does a proud person do for himself? He does not avoid being seen but only ensures that he is seen *from afar.* Do not comfort yourself with the delusion that, if you are seen only from afar, you are seen less accurately. In your own case it is true that you cannot see clearly what you see only from a distance, but God sees you perfectly, even though you are far away and he is not with you. When you commit some shameful deed, you are not seen any less well, but you are not with him who sees you.

So much for the proud person. What does the humble one achieve? *The Lord is close to those who have bruised their hearts* (Ps 33:19(34:18)). Let the proud person lift himself as high as he likes; he will not draw nearer to God. God is in heaven, certainly. Do you want him to come close to you? Then humble yourself. The more high and mighty you are, the more he will tower above you, and *whatever is exalted he knows from afar.*

Verse 7. This present life is anguish for homesick pilgrims

12. *If I walk amid anguish you will give me life.* This is true. In whatever anguish you may be, confess to God and call upon him. He sets you free and gives you new life.

However, there is another point here which we need to understand better if we are to cling to God in such close intimacy that we can say to him, *Hear me quickly!* Remember how the psalm said just now, *Whatever is exalted he knows from afar.* The arrogant, the high and mighty, the proud, do not experience anguish. Well, what I mean is this: they do not know the kind of anguish of which another passage says, *I have found anguish and sorrow, and I called on the name of the Lord* (Ps 114(116):3–4). Have you done anything remarkable, if anguish finds you? But if you have the courage, go and find anguish.[18] Why would anyone go and find anguish? you ask. Who would ever go looking for it? But you are beset by anguish, without even realizing it, aren't you? Isn't this present life a considerable anguish in itself? If it is not an anguish, it is no pilgrimage. But if it is a pilgrimage, either you do not love your homeland or you are suffering keenly, for could anyone not suffer as long as he is absent from the one he longs to be with? If you do not experience your present life as anguish, you are not in love. Love that other life and you will see that our present life is tribulation. However it may glitter with prosperity, however much it may abound and overflow with luxuries, this life is undeniably a source of anguish as long as we have not reached the joy that is utterly safe against all temptation, the joy that God is reserving for us at the end.

Let us look honestly at the anguish of our present life, brothers and sisters. When the psalmist says, *If I walk amid anguish you will*

---

18. Augustine explains his ideas on this more fully in Exposition of Psalm 136,5.

give me life, he does not mean, "If some affliction chance to overtake me, you will deliver me from it." What does he mean, then? *If I walk amid anguish you will give me life*, or, in other words, you will give me life only if I walk amid anguish, not otherwise. *If I walk amid anguish you will give me life*, because, as the gospel says, *Woe to you who laugh now, but happy are those who weep* (Lk 6:25.21). *If I walk amid anguish you will give me life.*

God's right and left hands: eternal and temporal salvation

13. *You have stretched out your hand, and that is worse than the anger of my enemies; your right hand has saved me.* Let my enemies rampage. What can they do? They may take away my money, seize my goods, make me an outlaw, exile me, cruelly torture me, and eventually, if given permission, kill me. Can they go any further? But as for you, Lord, *you have stretched out your hand, and that is worse than the anger of my enemies*, worse than all they can do to me. My enemies have no power to separate me from you; but by keeping me waiting you inflict a heavier punishment. *You have stretched out your hand, and that is worse than the anger of my enemies*; for, rage as he will, no enemy sunders me from God. But as for you, Lord, you still do not call me home, you wear me out in this exile of mine, you still withhold your joy and your sweetness, you have not yet inebriated me with the rich abundance of your house nor have you given me the torrent of your delight to drink.[19] Yet *with you is the fount of life, and in your light we will see light* (Ps 35:10(36:9)). I have already consecrated to you, Lord, the first-fruits of my spirit;[20] I have believed in you, and with my mind I am submissive to the law of God.[21] All the same, we are still groaning within ourselves, awaiting our perfect adoption as God's children in the redemption of our bodies.[22] This is the life God has assigned to us, sinners that we are, a life in which Adam must be worn down by hard work and the sweat of his brow, as the earth yields him thistles and thorns.[23] Could any of our foes contrive a more grievous torment? *You have stretched out your hand, and that is worse than the anger of my enemies*, but this does

---

19. See Ps 35:9(36:10).
20. In the act of faith; see Exposition 12 of Psalm 118,1 and the note there; Exposition of Psalm 134,18.
21. See Rom 7:25.
22. See Rom 8:23. 23.
23. See Gn 3:18–19.

not drive me to despair, for, as the psalm goes on to say, *your right hand has saved me.*

14. There is another possible way of understanding this verse. *You stretched out your hand over the anger of my enemies.*[24] This could equally well mean, "My enemies raged, but you vindicated me against them." In another psalm it was predicted, *The sinner will be enraged at the sight; he will gnash his teeth and pine away* (Ps 111(112):10), and the prediction has been proved true. Where are they who used to say, "May the Christian name disappear from the earth"? Where are they now? They are either dead or converted. At the time when the words of another psalm were all too apposite: *My enemies reviled me, saying, When will he die, and his name disappear?* (Ps 40:6(41:5)) at the time when they echoed those words, demanding, "When will the Christians' name be blotted out from the earth?"—at that very time you stretched out your hand over their anger. Even as they mouthed their threats some of them came to believe, some perished, and a timid few remained undecided. How the rage of our enemies mounted when they shed the martyrs' blood! How sure they were that they would stamp out the Christian name from the earth! Yet *you stretched out your hand over the anger of my enemies; your right hand saved me.* The people who formerly persecuted the martyrs now flock to the martyrs' shrines. They may seek to worship there or they may hope to get drunk there,[25] but in either case it is to the shrines of their one-time victims that they go. *You stretched out your hand over the anger of my enemies; your right hand saved me.*

In accordance with my true desire, *your right hand saved me*, for there is one kind of salvation pertinent to the right hand and a different kind to the left. Temporal salvation, the well-being of the body, is the work of the left hand, but eternal salvation in the company of the angels belongs to the right. This is why Christ, now raised to immortality, is said to sit at the right hand of God[26]—not because God has a right hand or a left but because a happiness beyond the power of human eyes to see is called by that symbolic name. And so

---

24. *Super iram inimicorum meorum.* In section 13 Augustine took *super* to mean "more than," "more grievous than," "worse than." Here he takes it as a simple preposition, "over."
25. Because it was customary to celebrate feasts at the tombs of the martyrs, and drunkenness was not unknown. See Exposition of Psalm 59,15 and the note there.
26. See Mk 16:19.

the Church confesses in our psalm, "With this right hand of yours, Lord, you saved me; it was no temporal salvation that you conferred on me." Think again about Crispina: she was slain, but did that mean God had abandoned her? By no means. He did not save her with his left hand, to be sure, but he did save her with his right. Remember what terrible torments the Maccabees endured.[27] But how different was the fate of the three youths amid the flames! They walked about in the furnace, praising God.[28] The Maccabees were saved with the right hand, the three youths with the left as well as the right. It seems that God does not always save his holy ones with his left hand, but he always does with his right. The case of the impious is different: there he often saves with his left hand but not with his right, for those who persecuted Crispina were healthy enough in body; they survived, while she was killed. But their "salvation" was only of the kind granted by the left hand, whereas hers came from the right. *Your right hand saved me.*

Verse 8. Leave vengeance to the Lord; he will repay

15. *You will vindicate me,*[29] *Lord.* I take no revenge myself; you will avenge me. Let my enemies rage as much as they like; it is for you to exact the vengeance that I cannot. *You will vindicate me, Lord.* Study the conduct of our head, for he left us an example and means us to follow in his footsteps.[30] *He committed no sin, nor was any guile found on his lips. When he was reviled, he did not answer by reviling,* for he said, *You will vindicate me, Lord.* Moreover, *when he was judged, he uttered no threats, but entrusted himself to the one who judges justly.* (1 Pt 2:22–23) What does this mean: *You will vindicate me, Lord*? As he says: *I do not seek my own glory; there is one who seeks it and will judge* (Jn 8:50). And as the apostle says: *Do not seek revenge yourselves, dearly beloved, but leave space for God's wrath, for it is written, Revenge is for me; I will see justice done, says the Lord* (Rom 12:19; Dt 32:35). *You will vindicate me, Lord.*

---

27. See 2 Mac 7.
28. See Dn 3:24.
29. *Retribues pro me.* In section 16 Augustine will see a different meaning in these words.
30. See 1 Pt 2:21.

A different interpretation: Christ repays our debt

16. There is another interpretation which should not be ignored and which may perhaps be preferable.[31] *You will repay my debt*, Lord Christ. If I undertake to make restitution, it is because I have stolen. But you repaid a debt you had not incurred, and so I can say, *You will repay my debt, Lord.* Consider an episode in the gospel where he paid our debt. The collectors of the tribute approached him, demanding the didrachma,[32] for each person was liable to pay this. Or, more accurately, they approached his disciples and asked them, *Does your teacher not pay tribute?* They referred the matter to him. He asked in reply, *From whom do earthly kings exact tribute? From their own sons, or from others?*[33] They replied, *From others. In that case*, said Jesus, *the sons are free of the obligation. But so that we may not scandalize them* (here he spoke to Peter), *go and cast a hook into the sea. Open the mouth of the first fish that rises, and you will find a shekel*, which equals two didrachmas. A stater or shekel is a coin equal to four drachmas. *You will find it there*, he said; *give it to them for me and for yourself.* (Mt 17:23–26) *You will repay my debt, Lord.* Ours is indeed the first fish to be hooked, the first fish caught with a hook,[34] the first to rise from the sea, the first-born from the dead.[35] In the fish's mouth we find a shekel or two didrachmas, which make four drachmas. In Christ's mouth we find the four gospels. With these four drachmas we are freed from the demands of this world; thanks to the four gospels we shall not remain debtors, for through

---

31. The meaning of *retribuere* shifts in this section from "avenge" to "pay a debt" or "make restitution."
32. Or half-shekel, a temple tax levied on adult males.
33. It could mean, "From their subjects, or from foreigners?" but Jesus took advantage of the Aramaic idiom which called a ruler's subjects his children to suggest his own filial relationship to the God whose temple tribute was in question, and to imply that his disciples were by adoption sons also.
34. Variant: "with love."
35. See Col 1:18; Rv 1:5. The use of the fish symbol to represent Christ was already old by Augustine's time. It is found in the second century in *The Shepherd* of Hermas, in Tertullian's *De Baptismo*, and in Clement of Alexandria. It became common in Christian iconography. The symbol is said to have derived from the acrostic ΙΧΘΥΣ, the first five letters of the phrase "Jesus Christ, Son of God, Saviour" in Greek; when read as a single word these five letters mean "fish." But it is possible that the idea of the fish as rising from the deep, as suggested by Augustine here, came first and that the acrostic explanation came later.

them all our sins are canceled. Thus Christ has paid the debt for us. Let us give thanks to him for his mercy. He owed nothing; he had no debt to pay on his own account. But he paid ours. *Now the prince of this world is coming,* he said, *and he will find nothing in me.* What does that mean—*He will find nothing in me?* He will find no sin in me, no pretext for killing me. *But so that the world may know that I am doing my Father's will, rise, let us leave here* (Jn 14:30.31). Why did he say, *Rise, let us leave here?* He meant, "Not of necessity, but of my own free will do I suffer, to pay a debt I do not owe." But *you will repay my debt, Lord.*

17. *O Lord, your mercy endures for eternity.* What should I desire? Not the human light of day, as Jeremiah put it: *Not under duress do I follow you, Lord. I have never craved the human light of day, as you know.* (Jer 17:16) If our martyr Saint Crispina had desired the human light of day she would have denied Christ. Then she would have lived longer here on earth, but she would not have lived for eternity. She chose to live for ever rather than to prolong her earthly life for a brief span. *Your mercy endures for eternity,* and in your mercy you freed the martyrs, snatching them quickly from this life. *O Lord, your mercy endures for eternity.*

A final prayer: do not disdain your own work, Lord

18. *Do not despise the works of your hands.* I am not saying, "O Lord, do not despise the works of *my* hands," for about those I do not boast. It is true that *with outstretched hands I sought God in the night, and I was not disappointed* (Ps 76:3(77:2)), but still I do not extol any activities of my own hands, because I fear that if you examine them you may find more sins than merits. One thing only do I ask, one thing I beg, one thing I long to obtain from you: that you will not despise the works of your own hands. Contemplate in me not my work but yours, for if you take account of mine, you must condemn it, but if you regard your own, you will crown it. Whatever good works I may have done are your gift to me, and therefore they are more yours than mine. Ringing in my ears are the words of your apostle, *By grace you have been saved, through faith, and this is not your own doing but the grace of God. It does not come from works, lest anyone boast. We are his own handiwork, created in Christ Jesus for good works.* (Eph 2:8–10) Whether we think only of our creation as human beings or also of being changed from our godless state and justified, in either case, Lord, *do not despise the works of your hands.*

Exposition of Psalm 138

A Sermon to the People

A mistake has been made by the reader, but we can profit from it

1. We had prepared a short psalm for our consideration today[1] and indicated to the reader that this was the psalm to be recited. But at the last minute he apparently became flustered and read this one instead. We have deemed it preferable to see in the reader's mistake a sign of the will of God and to follow that rather than to do our own will by sticking to our original plan. If, therefore, it turns out that we have detained you for a long time on account of the length of this psalm, you must not blame us but believe that God has willed us to work in such a way as to be fruitful. There was good reason for the punishment imposed on us at the time of the first sin: that we must eat our bread in the sweat of our brow.[2] Only be sure that what you eat is really bread. It is true bread if it is Christ; as he said of himself, *I am the living bread which has come down from heaven* (Jn 6:51). We find him manifested in the gospel; let us look for him also in the prophets. The people over whose hearts a veil still lies[3] cannot see him there, but you heard something about that veil yesterday, beloved. For us the situation has changed, because the evening sacrifice of the Lord's cross tore the veil apart, laying bare the secret recesses of the temple.[4] Whenever Christ is preached to us there is bread for us to eat, even though it be at the cost of labor and sweat.

Christ and the Church, head and members, two in one flesh and one voice

2. Now our Lord Jesus Christ sometimes speaks through the prophets in his identity as our head, for he is Christ, our savior. He is seated at the right hand of the Father,[5] but for our sake he was also

---

1. Possibly Psalm 137(138); see the note at section 18 below.
2. See Gn 3:19.
3. See 2 Cor 3:15.
4. See Mt 27:51.
5. See Mk 16:19.

born of the Virgin and suffered under Pontius Pilate. You know how he suffered: his innocent blood was poured out as our ransom. He redeemed us, guilty prisoners that we were in the devil's clutches, and forgave us our transgressions, using his own blood, our ransom price, to blot out the record of our debt.[6] He is the ruler, the bridegroom, and the redeemer of the Church, and he is our head.

Now, if he is the head, obviously he must have a body. His body is holy Church, and she, to whom the apostle says, *You are Christ's body, and his members* (1 Cor 12:27), is also his bride. The whole Christ, head and body together, constitute a perfect man.[7] Women are included in this, for woman was formed from man and belongs with him. Of the first marriage it was written, *They will be two in one flesh* (Gn 2:24), and the apostle interprets this saying in the light of the mystery, for the statement was made about those two original humans only because in them the marriage of Christ and the Church was prefigured. This is how the apostle explains it: *They will be two in one flesh. This is a great mystery, but I am referring it to Christ and the Church.* (Eph 5:31–32) He tells us elsewhere that Adam foreshadowed Christ: *Adam was a type of the one who was to come* (Rom 5:14). And, as Adam was a type of Christ, so too was the creation of Eve from the sleeping Adam a prefiguration of the creation of the Church from the side of the Lord as he slept, for as he suffered and died on the cross and was struck by a lance, the sacraments which formed the Church flowed forth from him.[8] By Christ's sleeping we are to understand his passion. This image is used in another psalm, which says in his name, *I rested, and fell asleep, and I arose because the Lord will uphold me* (Ps 3:6(5)). As Eve came from the side of the sleeping Adam, so the Church was born from the side of the suffering Christ.

As you know, our Lord Jesus Christ speaks through the prophets sometimes with his own voice and at other times with ours, because he makes himself one with us; as scripture says, *They will be two in one flesh* (Gn 2:24). Indeed, the Lord referred to this himself when, speaking about marriage in the gospel, he emphasized, *So they are two no longer, but one flesh* (Mt 19:6). One flesh, because Christ

---

6. See Col 2:13–14.
7. *Vir.*
8. See Jn 19:34. On this doctrine, compare Expositions of Psalms 56,11; 65,7; 126,7 and the notes at all these places.

took flesh from our mortal stock, but not one godhead, because he is the creator and we are creatures. Yet because of our union with him, whatever the Lord says in virtue of the fleshly nature he assumed can be taken as said both by the head who has now ascended into heaven and by the members who still struggle along on their earthly pilgrimage. When Saul was persecuting Christ's earthly members, Christ cried out from heaven in the person of those suffering members, *Saul, Saul, why are you persecuting me?* (Acts 9:4)

Let us now listen to the Lord Jesus Christ speaking in our psalm's prophetic words and remember that, though the psalms were sung long before the Lord was born from Mary, they were not sung before he was the Lord. From the beginning of time he is the creator of all that is, but at a certain point in time he was born from a creature. Let us believe in his Godhead and understand, to the best of our ability, that he is equal to the Father. But that divine person, equal to the Father, became a sharer in our mortality, a mortality that belonged not to him but to us, so that we might share the divine nature that belongs not to us but to him.

Verses 1–2. The form of God and the form of a servant; death and resurrection

3. *O Lord, you have tested me and you know me.* It is quite possible for the Lord Jesus Christ himself to say this: even he can rightly say *Lord* to the Father. His Father would not be his Lord had he not graciously willed to be born according to the flesh. In his divine nature God is his Father; in his humanity God is his Lord. Shall I tell you to whom God stands as Father? To the Son who is his equal. So the apostle says, *Being in the form of God he deemed it no robbery to be God's equal* (Ph 2:6). God is Father to Christ in this coequal *form*, Father to his only-begotten Son who is born from his own substance. But the only-begotten Son became a participant in our mortality, as I have reminded you, in order that we might be created anew and be made participants in his divinity, being restored to eternal life. After saying of him, *Being in the form of God he deemed it no robbery to be God's equal*, what else does the apostle say? *Yet he emptied himself and took on the form of a slave; and, bearing the human likeness, he was revealed as man* (Ph 2:7). In the form of God he is equal to the Father, but he took the form of a servant whereby he is less than the Father. He states both these truths in the gospel. *I and the Father are one* (Jn 10:30), he says, and also, *the Father is greater than I* (Jn

14:28). He can say, *I and the Father are one*, when he speaks in the form of God, and *the Father is greater than I*, when he speaks from his servile nature. God is therefore both his Father and his Lord: Father to him in his divine nature and Lord to him as servant. Let him say, then, *O Lord, you have tested me and you know me*, and let us not be surprised or shocked to hear the only-begotten Son of God saying this.

You have tested me and you know me. This does not mean that God did not know him already; it means that he made him known to others through the testing. *You have tested me*, he acknowledges, *and you know me*.

4. *You know my sitting down and my rising up*. What is this sitting? And this rising up? To sit is to humble oneself. Thus the Lord sat down in his passion and rose up in his resurrection. *You know this*, he says to God: you willed it, you approved it, it was done according to your purpose.

Alternatively, you may prefer to hear the voice of the body speaking in these words of its head. In this case we ourselves can say, *You know my sitting down and my rising up*. We sit down when we humble ourselves in repentance, and we rise up when our sins have been forgiven, for then we rise up toward the hope of eternal life. This is why another psalm advises, *Rise up after sitting down, you who eat the bread of sorrow* (Ps 126(127):2). In yet another psalm penitents are eating the bread of sorrow when they sing, *My tears have been bread to me day and night* (Ps 41:4(42:3)). What does the admonition mean, then, *Rise up after sitting down*? Take care that you are not exalted unless you have first been humbled. Plenty of people aspire to rise up before they have sat down: they want to be thought holy before they have confessed that they are sinners.

You can take the verse either way, then. If you hear in it the head speaking in his own name, the words, *You know my sitting down and my rising up*, will mean "my passion and my resurrection." If you prefer to hear the body speaking, the same words will mean, "In your sight I have both confessed my sins and been justified by your grace."

Verses 3–4. The prodigal son seems to be speaking here

5. *You have understood my thoughts from afar; you have traced my path and my boundary, and foreseen all my ways*. What do the words *from afar* suggest? While I am still on pilgrimage, before I reach my homeland, my mind is already an open book to you. Refer this to the younger son in the parable, for he too became part of Christ's body.

He represents the Church gathered from the gentiles, this younger son who had departed for a distant country. A certain man, the head of a family, had two sons.[9] The elder did not go far away; he used to work on the estate, and he represents the holy people of the Old Testament who carried out the duties imposed by the law and kept its commandments. But the rest of the human race had strayed away into the worship of idols, which was like wandering off into a far country. For what is more distant from him who made you than an artifact that you made for yourself? So this younger son set off for a far-off region, taking his money with him, and, as we know from the gospel, he squandered it by reckless living in the company of prostitutes. Then he began to feel hungry, and he applied to a leading citizen in the district, who gave him a job feeding pigs. He longed to satisfy his hunger with the pods thrown to the pigs, but he could not. Laboring, miserable, ground down by want, he remembered his father and wanted to go home. *I will rise up and return to my father* (Lk 15:18), he resolved. *I will rise up*, he said, for he had been sitting. Catch the sound of his voice in the words of the psalm, *You know my sitting down and my rising up.* I sat down in my poverty, I rose up by longing for your bread. *You have understood my thoughts from afar* for, although I had wandered far off, is there any place where you are not present, you whom I had abandoned? *You have understood my thoughts from afar*: this is why the Lord says in the gospel, *While he was still on his way his father ran to meet him* (Lk 15:20), for he had understood the boy's thoughts even when he was far away. *You have traced my path and my boundary.* He mentions his *path*, and what path can he mean except the bad path he had taken in abandoning his father—as though he could ever be hidden from the eyes of the one who would see justice done?

But we could understand it in another way. Would he ever have been crushed by poverty, or set to feed pigs, if his father had not willed to chastise him while he was far off in order to welcome him when he came back? He was caught like a fugitive, pursued by the righteous punishment of God. Wherever we flee, however far we may have gone, God punishes our willfulness. Like a recaptured fugitive the errant son declares, *You have traced my path and my boundary.* What does *my path* mean? The way on which I first set out. And what is *my boundary*? The very limit of my wandering. *You have traced*

---

9. See Lk 15:11–32.

my path and my boundary. The most distant place I reached was not too far away for you to see; I had traveled many miles, but you were there. *You have traced my path and my boundary.*

6. *You have foreseen all my ways.* Notice that he says not "seen" but *foreseen*. Before I went along those ways, before ever I began to walk in them, you foresaw them, and you allowed me to weary myself in my own ways so that, when I could endure the weariness no longer, I would return to your ways.

For there is no guile on my tongue. Why did he say that? "See, Lord, I am making this confession to you: I went away from you, in whose company all was well with me; and when I was away from you everything went badly. But this was for my good, for, if I had been happy without you, perhaps I would never have wanted to return." This is Christ's body speaking, confessing its sins, and justified not of itself but by his grace. Therefore it can say, *There is no guile on my tongue.*

Verses 5–6. God's mysterious wisdom in blinding part of Israel, with a view to ultimate mercy

7. *Now, Lord, you know everything about me, most recent things and things of long ago.* You know all about my most recent plight, when I was reduced to feeding pigs, and you know my ancient sin, when I demanded from you my share of your wealth. My ancient deeds were the root of my most recent woes. With our ancient sin we fell, and we suffered our later punishment when we were born into this wearisome, perilous, mortal life. Please God this may be our final punishment! It will be, provided we are now willing to return to him,, but there is a still later punishment, a final one, reserved for certain godless people who will hear the sentence, *Depart from me into the eternal fire which was prepared for the devil and his angels* (Mt 25:41).

What about ourselves, brothers and sisters? Even if we have hitherto turned our backs on God, let our toil be limited to this mortal life. Let us remember the bread offered to us by our Father, let us recall the happiness of our Father's house, and let us not hanker for the pigs' husks, the doctrines of demons. *Now, Lord, you know everything about me, most recent things and things of long ago*: the latest state to which I am reduced and the most ancient sin whereby I offended you.

You fashioned me, and you have laid your hand upon me. Where did you fashion me? In this mortal condition, destined for hard labor, to which all of us were born. Everyone who is born has been fashioned by God in the womb of his mother, for there is no creature that is not shaped by him. But *you fashioned me* in this toilsome existence, *and you have laid your hand upon me,* a punishing hand that lies heavy on the proud. It has thrown down all the self-important for their own good, so that it may raise them up humbled. *You fashioned me, and you have laid your hand upon me.*

8. *Your knowledge is too wonderful for me; mighty it is, beyond my reach.* Now, brothers and sisters, it is time for you to listen to something that is admittedly somewhat obscure but most rewarding in its sweetness once it is understood.

Moses was a holy servant of God. With him God spoke through a cloud, because, when God chose to communicate with any of his servants in time, he customarily did so through some created medium; that is to say, he did not speak through his own substance but by employing some material, created thing, through which his words might be transmitted and made audible to human, mortal ears. That was God's ordinary way of speaking to people; he did not speak to them as he speaks through his own substance. How does he speak in his own substance? The speaking of God is the Word of God, and Christ is the Word of God. That divine Word does not sound forth and then fade away. The Word through whom all things came into being[10] abides immutably for ever. This Word is also the wisdom of God, and to the Word a psalm says concerning created things, *You will discard them, and so they will be changed, but you are the selfsame* (Ps 101:27–28(102:26–27)). Similarly in another passage scripture says of divine wisdom, *Abiding in herself, she renews all things* (Wis 7:27). Wisdom stands firm—if we can properly say that she stands; the expression connotes immutability, not immobility—and stands in total self-consistency, varying in no place nor at any time. Nowhere is she other than she is here or there, never is she different from what she is now or was formerly. This is what God's utterance is.

But the communication of God with Moses was a form of speech addressed to a human being, making use of transitory sounds. It could not have taken this form if God had not pressed into service some created, corporeal medium, through which his words could be made

---

10. See Jn 1:3.

intelligible. Moses desired and earnestly longed to see God's very form, and as God spoke to him he pleaded, *If I have found favor in your sight, show me yourself* (Ex 33:13). He longed intensely for this, and tried to cajole God by alleging the friendly intimacy of which he, Moses, had been found worthy. So he entreated God to allow him to see his majestic glory and his face—insofar as we can speak about the face of God. But God's answer was, *You cannot see my face, for no one has seen my face and lived. But I will place you in this crevice in the rock, and I will cover you with my hand. When I pass by, you shall see my back.* (Ex 33:20.22-23) These words in their turn give rise to a further riddle, or rather they are an obscure figure of the way things are. *When I pass by, you shall see my back*, says God, as though his face were in front, and his back behind him. Yet far be it from us to think of his majestic reality in this way. If anyone does think of God in those terms, how has he profited from the closing of the temples? He is fashioning an idol in his own heart.

Evidently these words conceal great mysteries. The Lord was speaking to his servant through some created medium, as I have indicated—speaking in a way of his own choosing, and some intimation is given here of the person of our Lord and savior Jesus Christ. Inasmuch as he is in the form of God, and thus equal to the Father,[11] he is invisible to human eyes, just as the Father too is invisible. For if not even human wisdom can be perceived with our eyes, can the power and wisdom of God[12] be seen with the eyes of the body? But in the fullness of time our Lord was to assume human flesh and make himself visible even to fleshly eyes, so that our inward minds, so sorely in need of healing, might be cured. Therefore God enigmatically foretold that future manifestation to Moses, promising him, *You cannot see my face. You shall see my back*, but only *when I pass by*. To ensure that you do not see my face, my hand will shade you. What does it mean by suggesting that the Lord would *pass by*? Surely nothing else but what the evangelist meant by saying, *When the hour had come, Jesus was to pass from this world to the Father* (Jn 13:1). This is what the Pasch signifies, for the word "Pasch" means "Passover." "Pasch" is a Hebrew word, and the Latin equivalent is *transitus*. What, then, is meant when God promises, *You cannot see my face* but *you shall see my back*? Whom did Moses represent when he was told, *You cannot*

---

11. See Ph 2:6.
12. See 1 Cor 1:24.

see my face but *you shall see my back*, and that only *when I pass by*, and also warned that, in order that he not see God's face, *I will cover you with my hand*?

The Lord called his early deeds his *face*, but his passing from this world in the passion was in a sense his *back*. He appeared to the Jews and they did not recognize him. Moses represented them at this time when he was told, *You cannot see my face*. Why was it that they could not see God when he was present to them in the flesh? Because the hand of the Lord lay heavy upon them. Isaiah had said concerning them, *Blind this people's heart, O Lord, and make their eyes heavy* (Is 6:10), and the voice of this same Jewish people is heard in another psalm acknowledging that *your hand lay heavy upon me* (Ps 31(32):4). But this heaviness was God's doing, designed to make sure they would not recognize Christ's divinity for, if they had known it, they would never have crucified the Lord of glory,[13] and, if the Lord had not been crucified, his blood would not have redeemed the whole world. What, then, did God's action mean? Surely it was a manifestation of the rich depths of his wisdom and knowledge, of which the apostle exclaims, *O how deep are God's wisdom and knowledge, how unfathomable his decisions and inscrutable his ways! Who has understood the mind of the Lord, or been his counsellor? Who ever forestalled him in giving, and so deserved a recompense? From him are all things, through him are all things, in him are all things. To him be the glory for ever and ever.* (Rom 11:33–36) The apostle utters this cry after pointing out that *blindness has fallen upon part of Israel so that the full tally of the gentiles may come in, and so all Israel may be saved* (Rom 11:25–26). As a punishment for their pride, some of the Jewish people were blinded, for they had declared themselves righteous, and in their blindness they crucified the Lord. He laid his hand upon them to prevent them from seeing him until he had passed from this world to the Father.

But did they not see his back after his passing? The Lord arose and appeared to his disciples and to all who had believed in him. He did not appear to others, to those who had crucified him, because he had covered them with his hand until his passover. After spending forty days with his disciples, however, he ascended into heaven and, when in the fullness of time the day of Pentecost arrived, he sent the Holy Spirit to them. Filled with the Holy Spirit, these men, who had

---

13. See 1 Cor 2:8.

all been born into one mother tongue and had learned no other, began to speak in the languages of all nations.[14] The thousands of hearers who had crucified the Lord were terrified and pierced to the heart at such a wondrous sign. After listening to the apostles preaching Christ to them and marveling that such unlearned people could speak in all tongues, they sought advice from the apostles as to what they should do. Peter proclaimed Christ to them, Christ whom they had despised as he hung on the cross, whom they had mocked as no more than a mortal man, whom they had jeered at because he did not come down from the cross, though in fact he did something much greater than coming down from the cross: he rose from the grave. Hearing Christ so proclaimed, the crowds asked, *What shall we do?* (Acts 2:37) These people who raged against the Lord when they could see him were now asking advice about their salvation! They were told, *Repent, and let every one of you be baptized in the name of the Lord Jesus Christ, that your sins may be forgiven* (Acts 2:38). So they did see his back, though they had not managed to see his face. His hand had been covering their eyes, not permanently, but until his passover. After he had passed from this world he took his hand away from their eyes and, once it had been removed, they asked the disciples, *What shall we do?* At first they were enraged but later devout, at first angry but later fearful, at first blind but afterwards illuminated.

9. I think that in our psalm too we should hear the voices of such people recalling their unbelief, for *God imprisoned all in unbelief, that he might have mercy upon all* (Rom 11:32). The psalm recalls his act: *You fashioned me, and you laid your hand upon me. Your knowledge is too wonderful for me; mighty it is, beyond my reach.* It seems to imply, "It was when you laid your hand upon me that you became wonderful to me." I do not understand you. Yet I used to live with you. How easily accessible to me was my father's face when I said, *Give me the portion of the property that is due to me* (Lk 15:12). But, now that I have departed to a distant country and find myself worn down by hunger, it is beyond my perception; *it is too hard for me* (Ps 72(73):16), and I can no longer see what I left behind. *Your knowledge is too wonderful for me,* the psalmist confesses. As a consequence of my sin it became too wonderful, and to me incomprehensible. It was easy for me to contemplate you before I abandoned you in my pride. But now *your knowledge is too wonderful for me; mighty it*

---

14. See Acts 2:4 ff.

is, beyond my reach. I cannot reach it by my own efforts, he means. When I do reach it, I shall reach it by your grace.

Verses 7–10. You cannot get away from God, but let the wings of charity lift you

10. By now you realize that this runaway, however far his flight has carried him, cannot be hidden from the eyes of God, from whom he is trying to escape. Where is he to turn now, when even his boundary has been traced? Listen to his question: *Whither shall I go from your spirit?* If the Spirit of the Lord fills the whole earth,[15] where can anyone go to escape this all-pervading Spirit? *Whither shall I go from your spirit, and whither flee from your face?* He is looking for a place to which he can run to escape God's anger. But what place is going to give sanctuary to one who is a fugitive from God? People do sometimes take in fugitives, but only after enquiring from whom they have escaped. If they ascertain that a runaway slave belongs to a master who is not very powerful, they are not so anxious, reassuring themselves that the poor wretch is not likely to be discovered by a master like that. But, if they find out that he belongs to a powerful owner, they either refuse to take him in or do so only in great fear, comforting themselves that a man, even a powerful one, can after all be deceived. But is there any place from which God is absent? Can anyone deceive God? Is anyone invisible to him? If someone runs away from him, will he not demand his fleeing servant back from anyone who harbors him? Where, then, can a fugitive go from God's face? He scurries hither and thither, looking for a refuge.

11. *If I mount to heaven, you are there; if I sink down to hell, even there you are present*, he says. So you have understood at last, have you, poor runaway, that you cannot possibly put any distance between yourself and him from whom you tried to flee so far? Now you see that he is everywhere. Where do you plan to go?

The fugitive has stumbled upon sound advice, inspired by God, who in his mercy has deigned to call him back. *If I mount to heaven, you are there; if I sink down to hell, even there you are present.* If I exalt myself, I find you there in my high station ready to push me down. If I hide, I know you are searching for me, and not only searching me out but subjecting me to your scrutiny; for, if I am proud on the score of my own pretended righteousness, you are there, you who

---

15. See Wis 1:7.

alone are truly righteous. If my sins plunge me into the depths of evil, and I refuse to confess,[16] saying, *Who will see me? Who will confess to you in hell?* (Sir 23:25; Ps 6:6(5)) still you are there to punish me. Where am I to go in order to escape from your face? Is there any place where I shall not feel you present and angry?

But he has hit upon a good plan. "I know how to flee from your face," he says. "I know how I can get away from your Spirit. I will flee from your avenging Spirit, from your stern, menacing countenance." And how will you do that? *If I take once more the wings that will carry me straightforward, and dwell at the uttermost parts of the sea*, then I shall be able to escape from your face.

Is he right? He thinks he can hide from God's face in the uttermost regions of the sea. But will God not be there too, since of him the fugitive has already admitted, *If I sink down to hell, even there you are present*? It would be strange if he who is not absent even from the world below were not present also at the furthest bounds of the sea.

12. But the runaway insists, "I know how to escape from your anger. I need to get back my wings, wings that will take me straight ahead, not off course: wings that will neither allow me to mount in proud presumption nor sink me into despair and ruin." What are these wings he means to take? Surely the paired wings of the twin commands of charity, the paired commandments on which both the law and the prophets depend.[17] "If I take these wings," he says, "if I equip myself with these two pinions, and make my dwelling at the uttermost edge of the sea, I can flee from your face to your face, from the frown of your anger to the smiling countenance of your appeasement." For what does the uttermost edge of the sea signify if not the end of the world? Let us fly thither even now in hope and desire, borne upon the paired wings of twofold charity; and let us seek no rest except that which awaits us at the furthest bounds of the sea. If we seek rest anywhere else, into the sea we shall plunge. Let us fly toward that boundary where the sea ends. Let us keep ourselves aloft on the two wings of love. Let us fly to God in hope, even now, in this in-between time, and through faithful hope fix our thoughts in advance on that final shore.

13. Observe now who is to be our guide. He it is, and no other, from whose angry presence we are trying to escape; for how does the

---

16. See Prv 18:3.
17. See Mt 22:40.

psalm continue? *If I sink down to hell, even there you are present. If I take once more the wings that will carry me straightforward* (notice that he speaks of taking them once more, so we know he has lost them) *and dwell at the uttermost parts of the sea, even there your hand will lead me, your right hand bring me through.* Let us ponder this truth, beloved brothers and sisters; let it be our hope and our comfort. Let us recover through charity the wings we lost by indulging inordinate desires. These self-indulgent desires have become like sticky birdlime hampering our wings and dashing us down from our free flight in our native air, in the free breezes of God's Spirit. Struck down from this air we lost our wings and fell into the clutches of the fowler. But Christ bought us back by his blood, though it was our attempt to escape from him that led to our captivity. With his commandments he nourishes the new growth of our wings so that now we can soar again, free from our sticky impediment. Let us not be enamored of the sea, then, but fly beyond it, even to its furthest end. Let no one be afraid, but neither let anyone trust in the power of his wings because, even though we are winged creatures once more, we shall plunge into the depths of the ocean, exhausted and weary, if we rely on our own strength rather than allowing him to lead us. Both things are needful: that we have wings and that he lead us on, for he is our helper. We have free will, but how much can our free will achieve if he who commands us does not also help us? *Even there your hand will lead me, your right hand bring me through.*

Verse 11. Christ illumines our night

14. He has come a long way. He looks back, and how does he reflect on the journey? *I said, Perhaps the darkness will overwhelm me.* I have already put my faith in Christ, certainly, and already I am borne aloft on the wings of twofold charity. But iniquity is rampant in this world and, as it increases, the charity of many people cools down. The Lord warned that it would be so: *With iniquity increasing mightily, the love of many will grow cold* (Mt 24:12). And here I am, in this life, beset by such great scandals, so many sins, such hordes of temptations and evil suggestions with every passing day. What am I to do? How will I ever reach those distant limits of the sea? I hear the Lord's dreadful warning, *With iniquity increasing mightily, the love of many will grow cold,* and then the promise that he attached to it: *Whoever perseveres to the end will be saved* (Mt 24:13). But I

quail at the length of the journey, and I say to myself, *Perhaps the darkness will overwhelm me.*

Yet the very night was my illumination in my delight. The night itself proved to be light for me, because in the night of my despair—despair of ever having the strength to cross the vast sea, or to sustain so long a flight, or to reach the furthest shore by persevering to the end—he sought me out and found me as I fled. Thanks be to him who struck at my fleeing back with his whip, and called me, and pulled me away from disaster, and so made my night radiant.

As long as we are in this life, it is night for us. How was our night illumined? By Christ's descent into the night. Christ took flesh from this world and lit up the night for us. A woman in the gospel had lost a drachma,[18] and she lighted a lamp. The wisdom of God had also lost a drachma. What is a drachma? A coin, but on it is stamped the image of our emperor himself, for men and women were made in the image of God,[19] and they were lost. What did that wise woman do? She lighted a lamp. A lamp is made from clay, but it carries a light by which the drachma can be found. Wisdom's lamp was the flesh of Christ; it was made from earth's clay, but it shone with the light of the Word and found those who were lost. *The very night was my illumination in my delight*; night itself held delight for us, because Christ is our delight. Think how we should rejoice in him. These shouts of yours, this evidence of your joy[20]—what prompts them? Your delight, obviously. But where does your delight spring from? Surely from a night that has become radiant with light because Christ the Lord is preached to us? He sought you before you began to seek him, and he found you so that you might find him. *The very night was my illumination in my delight.*

Verse 12. Through recognition of God's remedial punishments, and holy indifference to varying fortunes, believers meet light and darkness with equanimity

15. *For the darkness will not be further darkened by you, Lord.* But make sure that you yourself do not make your darkness darker. God will not do so: he enlightens our darkness. This is why another psalm says, *You, Lord, will light my lamp; my God, you will enlighten*

---

18. See Lk 15:8–9.
19. See Gn 1:26–27.
20. Evidently Augustine's congregation was signifying its assent noisily.

my darkness (Ps 17:29(18:28)). Are there any people who do deepen their own darkness, which God never does? Yes, there are. Bad people, perverted people, are obviously darkness when they sin, but if they refuse to confess the sins they have committed, and even go so far as to defend them, they are making their darkness darker still. If you have sinned, you are in darkness, but if you confess your darkness, you will deserve to have your darkness turned into light. If, however, you defend your darkness, you are making your darkness darker than ever. And when will you ever get out of this doubly dark darkness, when even in simple darkness you were blundering about?

How can we say that the Lord does not further darken our darkness? He does not allow us to go unpunished when we sin; he chastises us through the very confusion and unhappiness we create for ourselves, and he teaches us through the experience. You must understand, brothers and sisters, that all the misery of the human race, all the woe in which the world groans, is a medicinal pain, not a penal sentence. You observe pain on all sides, everywhere fear, everywhere deprivation, everywhere hardship. Avarice increases, certainly, but only in bad people. If God is educating us by means of such chastisements[21] to prevent our darkness from growing deeper still, we should acknowledge that we are under his disciplinary scourge. Let us bless God, who mingles bitterness into the sweetness we find in our temporal life lest we become so desensitized by immersion in temporal pleasures that we lose our desire for eternal joys, no longer wanting the sea to end for us so that we may dwell beyond its utmost bounds. Let the ocean's waves roar as they will. The more they rage and foam, the more surely does the dove[22] soar above them on its outspread wings. God does not darken our darkness. He ensures that our sins entail their own suffering, and he sprinkles bitterness over our depraved pleasures. Let us, then, not darken our own darkness by defending our sins, and then night itself will be our illumination in our delight, *for the darkness will not be further darkened by you.*

16. *And the night will be as bright as the day.* The psalm speaks of a night that is like day. By *day* it means here worldly good fortune, and by *night* the adversity we encounter in this life. If we acknowledge

---

21. Variant: "delivers us from such chastisements."
22. This dove is not mentioned in the present psalm in either the Hebrew or the Septuagint. It seems to have flown in from Augustine's Exposition of Psalm 54,8–9, of which there are several echoes here.

that the adversity we endure is the just punishment for our sins, the chastisement laid upon us by our Father will even seem sweet to us, since we thereby avoid the bitter sentence of a judge. Thus we shall regard the darkness of our night as all one with the light of this night.

But if it is a night, how can there be any light in it? It is night because the human race has gone astray in this world; it is night because we have not yet reached that day which is not hemmed in by either yesterday or tomorrow, that everlasting day which knows no sunrise because its sun never sets. It is therefore still night for us in this world, but a night that has a kind of light of its own, as well as its own darkness. We have already explained why it is called night in a general, overall sense. But what is there within it that can be called light? Worldly prosperity and happiness, temporal enjoyment, temporal honor and renown—these are a kind of luminosity in the night. But adversity, bitter troubles, and disgrace are like this night's darkness. During this night, during this mortal life, human beings experience both light and darkness: the light of prosperity and the darkness of misfortune. But when Christ has come and made the soul his own dwelling through its faith, when he has promised a different light, when he has inspired and granted patience, when he has counseled men and women not to be too happy over prosperity lest they be crushed by adversity—then believers begin to treat the present world with detached indifference. No longer are they elated when things chance to go well with them, nor are they shattered when things turn out badly. They bless the Lord in all circumstances, not only in abundance but also in loss, not only in health but also in sickness. The promise sung of in another psalm is kept in their lives: *I will bless the Lord at all times; his praise shall be in my mouth always* (Ps 33:2(34:1)). If it is to be *always*, his praise must be on your lips when this present night is enlightened and when it is dark, when prosperity smiles upon you and when misfortune brings sadness. Then will the promise of our present psalm come true for you: *Its darkness will be all one with its light.* Its darkness does not crush me underfoot, because its light does not elate me.

17. Job was an example of one who lived in this world's light, for initially he possessed ample wealth. At first we are given a description of the light that shone on him during the night, the light of his riches. So abundant were his goods and resources that they seemed like light for him, even while he dwelt in the night. The enemy therefore concluded that such a man must be a worshiper of God simply

because so much had been given to him, and he begged that it be taken away. Thus Job's night, formerly so well lighted, became deep darkness. But whether it was luminous or dark, Job knew that it was night in either case, a night in which he was still a wayfarer, not yet at home with his God. This God of his was his inner light, and in its radiance he treated the light and the darkness of this night with calm indifference. When the night was enlightened for him by his abundant wealth, he worshiped God. When all these things were taken away and the darkness was total, what did he say? *The Lord gave, and the Lord has taken away. This has happened as the Lord willed: may the Lord's name be blessed.* (Jb 1:21) Throughout this life I am in the night, he seems to say. But my Lord dwells within my heart. When he lavished temporal wealth on me he enlightened the night with comforts of a sort, and when he withdrew that temporal light it seemed that the night grew darker. But I know that *its darkness is all one with its light*, and so I can say, *The Lord gave, and the Lord has taken away. This has happened as the Lord willed: may the Lord's name be blessed.* I am not sad in this night, because *its darkness is all one with its light*. Both of them are passing, and therefore let the joyful be as though they did not rejoice and mourners as though they were not weeping,[23] for *its darkness is all one with its light*.

Verses 13–14. The secret of this inner freedom and detachment

18. *For you have taken possession of my inmost parts,*[24] *O Lord.* I am well able to say, "The night's *darkness is all one with its light*," because I am the property of him who dwells within me. He is the owner not of my heart alone but of my inmost parts too, not only of my thoughts but also of my passions. He therefore possesses that part of me which could be tempted to take pleasure in some glimmer of light in the night. He controls the source of my feelings and affections, and I cannot take delight in anything but the inner light of his wisdom.

What are you saying, psalmist? Can you not feel pleasure in the success of your business, in seasons of happiness, honors, riches, or a contented household? No, he replies. Why not? Because *its darkness is all one with its light*. But what is the source of this indifference of yours, this detached attitude that makes you regard this night's

---

23. See 1 Cor 7:30.
24. Literally *kidneys*, regarded by the ancients as the seat of the passions and affections, as the heart represented the locus of thoughts.

darkness and this night's light as all one? Where does it spring from? He answers, *You have taken possession of my inmost parts, O Lord; you took me to yourself*[25] *even from the womb of my mother.* While I was in my mother's womb, I could not regard the darkness of this night as all one with its light, for my mother's womb symbolizes the standards of the city to which I then belonged. What city is that? The city that brought us to birth in captivity. We know all about that city, Babylon, of which we spoke yesterday.[26] Believers leave that city and set their course for the heavenly light of Jerusalem.[27] This is why I said that from my mother's womb I was taken up by the Lord; this is why there is now for me no difference between the darkness of the present night and its light. Those who are still in the womb of Babylon, their mother, rejoice over this world's successes and are shattered by its calamities. They know no rejoicing except that which comes to them when some temporal affair turns out well, and they are strangers to sadness except when their temporal enterprises go wrong.

But you, for your part, leave Babylon. Strike up a hymn to the Lord. Come forth and be born! The Lord will take you up even as you leave your mother's womb. Who is God? None other than the God of the apostle Paul, who testified, *It pleased God, who set me apart from my mother's womb, to reveal his Son in me* (Gal 1:15–16). Who was Paul's mother? The synagogue. And what had he learned there except what the Jews, all the Jewish people, had held and learned[28] there? They professed to praise God, but no corresponding deeds were to be found in them. The words of God, though cherished among them, were only like leaves; there was no fruit anywhere. As you know, when the Lord came across a tree like that, he cursed it and made it wither.[29] He found leaves on it, but no fruit. Now this episode was recounted to turn our minds toward a different tree, for in the natural

---

25. *Suscepisti me.* On the nuances of the verb *suscipere* see the note at Expositions of Psalms 3,3; 45,11, 83,9. In the present context the idea of a father picking up his newborn child seems to be present.
26. If he is referring to his Exposition of Psalm 136, which treats extensively of Babylon, it may be that the "short psalm" he had intended to preach on today was Psalm 137(138), inadvertently skipped by the reader. See section 1 of the present Exposition.
27. Variant: "the light of the heavenly Jerusalem."
28. Many codices omit "and learned."
29. See Mt 21:19.

order it was not yet the season for fruit,[30] and, if everyone knew that, is it possible that the designer of heaven and earth did not?

Well then, he who set Paul apart from his mother's womb has likewise set us apart from our mother's womb. Who was our mother? The city of Babylon. Taken up and acknowledged by him, we are already beginning[31] to cherish a different hope. Brothers and sisters, his promise has given you cause for joy; take root in that different hope and produce fruit. From now on we know no disaster except to offend God and to refuse to let him lead us to the reward he has promised, and we know no happiness except to deserve God and to be led to the fulfillment of his promise. What do this world's goods, or this world's woes, mean to us? Let them be all one to us, for now that we have been taken up by God from the womb of that mother who bore us, we can view both with detachment, saying, *Its darkness will be all one with its light*. Successes in this world do not make us happy, nor do its troubles make us miserable. All we need is to hold fast to righteous conduct, love the faith, hope in God, love God, and also love our neighbor. After all our efforts we shall have unquenchable light, we shall enjoy a day that knows no sunset. Whatever has been a glimmer of light in our night, along with its darkness, will have passed away, for *you have taken possession of my inmost parts, O Lord; you took me to yourself even from the womb of my mother*.

19. *I will confess to you, O Lord, for you have revealed yourself as wonderful and terrible*. The psalm says that in his wonderful being God shows himself as terrible. Even as we marvel at you, Lord, you are terrible in our eyes, and we rejoice with fear. We are afraid that, if we bear ourselves proudly on account of the gifts you have given, we may lose through pride what we gained by humility. *I will confess to you, O Lord, for you have revealed yourself as wonderful and terrible; wonderful are your works, and my soul knows it*. My soul has reached this keen perception now, because you took me to yourself from the womb of my mother, but even before that your knowledge of me was wonderful. It had become so powerful that I could not reach it. I mean that it had become so powerful, as far as I and my understanding were concerned: so powerful as to be beyond my grasp.

Why has my soul attained to this keen awareness? Because the night has itself become my enlightenment in my delight, and your

---

30. See Mk 11:13.
31. Variant: "let us now begin."

grace came to me to enlighten my darkness. It could have happened only because you took possession of my inmost parts and embraced me even from the womb of my mother.

Verse 15. Strong inner support

20. *My bone is not hidden from you, for it was you who created it in that secret place.* He speaks of his bone, *os*, another form of which in popular Latin is *ossum*. This meaning is clear in the Greek. If we had no access to the Greek we might have thought he meant *os* ("mouth"), of which the plural is *ora*, rather that *os* ("bone").[32] *My bone is not hidden from you*, he says, *for it was you who created it in that secret place.* I have a certain *ossum* hidden within me (we prefer to use the word *ossum*; better that linguistic experts should find fault with us than that people should not understand). This *ossum* of mine is hidden inside me; you made it for me secretly within, and therefore it is not hidden from you. Though you made it secretly, it is no secret from you, is it? Other people do not see this interior *ossum*; they know nothing about it. But you know it because you made it. Now what is this bone that he is talking about, brothers and sisters? Since it is not immediately visible, we must look for it. But because we are Christians speaking in the name of the Lord to other Christians, we have already had experience of this special kind of bone. It is an inner firmness or strength, suitably called a bone because firmness and strength are what we expect in bones. Similarly there is an inner firmness in the soul, which saves it from breaking down.[33] Whatever sufferings come our way, whatever distress, whatever the misfortunes of this world that seethe around us, the inner structure that God has made firm in us cannot break or even bend under pressure. The steady strength of our endurance is the Lord's creation. As another psalm says, *To God will my soul be subject, for my patience comes from him* (Ps 61:6(62:5)). Think of the apostle Paul and how he manifested the firmness that was within him. *As if sorrowful, we always have*

---

32. The two words are *os, ossis* (" bone") and *os, oris* ("mouth" or "face"). They coincide only in the nominative and accusative singular, and only there if the length of the vowel is disregarded. Augustine goes on to say that he will use the collateral form *ossum* ("bone") to avoid ambiguity. He says this is a popular form, though it is found in ancient classical examples.
33. Variant: "an inner strength in the soul, a firmness that does not break down."

cause for joy (2 Cor 6:10), he says. Why did he say, *As if sorrowful?*[34] Because the apostles had to withstand abuse, reproaches, persecutions, beatings, blows, stoning, prison, and chains. Would anyone have thought them anything other than wretched then? The persecutors themselves would not have bothered to treat them so badly if they had not been confident of reducing the apostles to misery by their onslaughts. But the persecutors based that judgment on their own weakness, for they did not have the hidden bone within them. The victims, who did possess it, appeared outwardly wretched to onlookers, but they were rejoicing inwardly to God, from whom their inner bony structure was not concealed, because he had built it in secret.

But the same apostle, Paul, gives us a glimpse of that bone which God had secretly made, when he says, *What is more, we even glory in our sufferings* (Rom 5:3). If you are simply saying that you are not sad, Paul, that does not amount to much. But do you even glory in your sufferings? Surely it would be enough if you warded off sadness? No, he replies, that would not be enough for Christians. God has made such a strong bone, and hidden it inside me, that I would not be satisfied with not breaking. I must also glory! And what are you glorying about? *Our sufferings, knowing that suffering fosters endurance.* Then he describes the process whereby this inner firmness is established in the heart: we know that *suffering fosters endurance, and endurance constancy, and constancy hope; but hope does not disappoint us, because the charity of God has been poured out into our hearts through the Holy Spirit who has been given us* (Rom 5:3–5). So well formed, so firmly set, is the hidden bone that it causes us to glory in our sufferings. Yet we appear wretched to other people, because what we have within us is hidden from them.

But *my bone is not hidden from you, for it was you who created it in that secret place, as you also formed my nature in the lower regions of the earth.* My nature is endued with flesh and is therefore at home in the lower regions of the earth. Yet I have within me the bone you formed, thanks to which I do not collapse under any persecutions I meet in this lower region where my natural self lives.

Would it be surprising if an angel proved strong? No, but it is a great achievement if flesh is strong. And whence would flesh derive

---

34. See the powerful meditation on the "as if" quality of Christian sadness in Exposition 2 of Psalm 48,5. Christian life may be "as if" sad, but it is joy without qualification.

its strength, where would the strength of a fragile vessel come from, if that bone had not been fashioned in secret? *You formed my nature in the lower regions of the earth.*

Verses 16–17. Christ's imperfect members

21. What about those who are less firm? As I have already reminded you, Christ speaks in this psalm. Many things have been said in the name of his body, but the head is speaking too, though not in the sense that they are distinct from each other like two persons: now the head and now the body. To distinguish them like that would be to divide them, and then they would not be two in one flesh.[35] But if they are two in one flesh, do not be surprised if the two speak with one voice.

Now when our Lord Jesus Christ suffered, his disciples did not yet have that bone within them. The strength to suffer had not yet been firmly established in them, and so they hid. They had no realistic idea of their own strength or weakness. Thus Peter made bold to promise the Lord that he would stay with him in his passion, even to death. He did not realize that he was a sick man, but his physician knew it. What happened? *I will go with you even to death* (Lk 22:33), promised Peter. And the Lord replied, *Truly I tell you, before cockcrow you will deny me three times* (Mt 26:34). The doctor's assessment proved truer than the sick man's presumptuous assertion.

When, therefore, the psalm says, *My bone is not hidden from you, for it was you who created it in that secret place*, it is speaking of those in whom strong, firm bone has developed within. But this is true above all of the steady courage of our Lord and Savior Jesus Christ himself in confronting his passion. When he willed, he sat down; and when he willed, he rose up.[36] When he willed, he slept, and when he willed, he awoke; as he said, *I have the power to lay down my life, and I have the power to take it up again* (Jn 10:18). But what of those in whom such fortitude had not been formed or firmly established? What has the psalm to say about them? Observe what Christ says to God, his Father: *Your eyes beheld my imperfection.* "My imperfection includes my Peter, making promises and then denying me, presumptuous and then failing through fear. Yet your eyes have seen him." It was when the Lord himself had looked at Peter after his third denial that Peter was reminded of the Lord's prediction to him,

---

35. See Eph 5:31–32.
36. See section 4 above.

and then, as the gospel relates, *he went outside, and wept bitterly* (Lk 22:62). Those tears were evoked by God's gaze upon him, for *your eyes beheld my imperfection*, as the psalm says.

That imperfect man who tottered during the Lord's passion would undoubtedly have perished, but your eyes saw him and, along with him, all those who had been imperfect until they were made firm by Christ's resurrection. Then it was made plain before their eyes that the Lord's mortal body—that body in which he had died—had not perished. Strong bone was then secretly formed within them, so that they too might have no fear of dying.

Your eyes beheld my imperfection, and in your book all shall be written: not only the perfect, but *all*, and therefore the imperfect as well. Let the imperfect not be afraid but make progress. They must not take my injunction not to be afraid as an excuse for being complacent about their imperfection and remaining stuck where they were when grace found them. Let them simply make as much progress as they can. They must grow daily, and daily draw closer to Christ. What matters above all is that they do not leave the body of the Lord. Provided that they are part of this one body, conjoined with all its other members, they will deserve to hear this voice and know that it applies to them: *Your eyes beheld my imperfection, and in your book all shall be written*.

22. *They will go wrong concerning the day, and not one of them will be there*. Before the passion, our Lord Jesus Christ was the "day" still with them, as he indicated himself by telling them, *Walk, while you have daylight* (Jn 12:35). But his imperfect members *will go wrong concerning the day*. They, even they, thought that our Lord Jesus Christ was nothing more than a man, that there was no hidden Godhead in him, that he was not in his invisible nature God, and that there was no more to him than what could be seen. Even they held this opinion—even Peter. We shall speak of Peter in particular, because in him we are given an example to encourage us not to despair of our own weakness.[37] Earlier the Lord had questioned his disciples as to what people thought about him, and Peter answered, *You are the Christ, the Son of the living God*. The Lord said to him in reply, *Blessed are you, Simon, son of Jonah. It is not flesh and blood that revealed this to you, but my Father, who is in heaven.* (Mt 16:16–17) Why did the Lord say that? Because Peter had called him the Son

---

37. Variant: "our own strength," in a potential sense, presumably.

of God. But immediately after this, in the same context, we hear the Lord beginning to speak of his approaching passion. Then this same Peter, the one who had confessed Jesus to be the Son of God, was afraid that he might die like any son of man. He was certainly the Son of God, but he was also a son of man: the Son of God because he was in the form of God and equal to the Father, and a son of man because he had taken the form of a servant, in which he is less than the Father.[38] He was confronting his passion in the form of a servant, but what grounds had Peter for fearing that the form of God would perish along with the form of a servant, rather than taking it for granted that from the form of God the servant-form would come to life again? Yet Peter was afraid and said to him, *Far be it from you, Lord, have some pity for yourself* (Mt 16:22). And the Lord, who a moment before had declared Peter blessed, now said, *Get behind me, Satan. You have no taste for the things of God, but only for human things.* (Mt 16:23) Directly after Peter had confessed, *You are the Christ, the Son of the living God*, he heard the words, *It is not flesh and blood that revealed this to you, but my Father, who is in heaven*: he was the rock, he was blessed, on account of his confession. But now he was called *Satan* because he had spoken not at the prompting of any revelation from the Father but out of the weakness of his flesh. *You have no taste for the things of God, but only for human things*, Christ told him.

Think of it, brothers and sisters: Christ was there with them. This was the Christ who had gone about among them, who had commanded the waves and walked on the waters before their eyes,[39] who had raised up a man dead for four days as they looked on,[40] who had performed other mighty miracles before their eyes;[41] and yet they were terrified during his passion, as though they had lost someone in whom they had hoped in vain. *They will go wrong concerning the day, and not one of them will be there.* Not a single one of them, not even he who had said, *I will go with you even to death* (Lk 22:33). Jesus had foretold it, saying, *The hour is coming when each of you will go his own way, leaving me alone. Yet I am not alone, for the Father is with me* (Jn 16:32). The Father was with him, and he was

---

38. See Ph 2:6–7; Jn 14:28.
39. See Mk 4:39; Mt 14:25.
40. See Jn 11:39–44.
41. See Jn 11:47.

with the Father; the Father was in him, and he was in the Father.[42] He and the Father are one,[43] yet the disciples were frightened when he died. Why? Because they went wrong concerning the day, and so not one of them was there. The psalm foresaw it: *They will go wrong concerning the day, and not one of them will be there.*

23. What else is implied in that prophecy, *They will go wrong concerning the day*? Does it mean they will be lost? Surely not, for then what would become of the promise, *Your eyes beheld my imperfection, and in your book all shall be written*? When did they go wrong about the day? When they failed to understand the Lord dwelling among them on earth. Yet how does the psalm continue? *But your friends have become for me exceedingly honorable, O God.* These same disciples who went wrong concerning the day, these same men of whom not a single one was to be found when Christ suffered, became your friends and were made exceedingly honorable in my eyes. After the Lord's resurrection that firm bone was secretly built within them, and they themselves suffered for the name of Christ, at whose passion they had been terrified. *Your friends have become for me exceedingly honorable, O God; their pre-eminence has been most firmly established.* They were made apostles, they became leaders of the Church, they took their places as rams leading the flock;[44] *their pre-eminence has been most firmly established.*

Verses 18–20. The Church is a mixed collection of people

24. *I will count them, and they will be more numerous than grains of sand.* Through those disciples who went wrong concerning the day, through those of whom not one was there, so great a multitude has come to birth that, like grains of sand, they are beyond counting, except by God. He said, *They will be more numerous than grains of sand*, yet he also said, *I will count them.* Counted they have been, even though more in number than grains of sand, for grains of sand have themselves been counted by him who knows the number of the hairs on our heads.[45] *I will count them, and they will be more numerous than grains of sand.*

---

42. See Jn 14:10.
43. See Jn 10:30.
44. See Exposition of Psalm 64,18.
45. See Mt 10:30.

25. *I have risen, and I am still with you.* What does he mean by this: *I have risen, and I am still with you*? I have undergone my passion, he is saying; I was buried, and now I have arisen, and they do not yet understand that I am with them. *I am still with you*,[46] but not yet with them, for they do not yet recognize me. This is attested by the gospel, where we read that after the resurrection of our Lord Jesus Christ the disciples did not immediately recognize him when he appeared to them.

Another interpretation is possible. *I have risen, and I am still with you* could refer to the present era, when he is still hidden at the right hand of the Father, before being revealed in his glory when he comes to judge the living and the dead.

26. Now he tells us what he is suffering in his body, the Church, throughout this whole long period when he is risen and still with the Father. These sufferings are caused by the presence of sinners in the midst of the Church and by the heretics who separate themselves from it. Thus the psalm continues, *If you slay sinners, O God, then, men of blood, depart from me; because you will say in your thoughts, They will capture their cities in vain.* I think the sequence of ideas here is as follows: *If you slay sinners, O God, they will capture their cities in vain.* The psalmist wishes us to understand that these sinners are slain because, when they become puffed up with pride, they lose the grace which was their true life. *The holy spirit of discipline rejects falsehood, and withdraws from stupid thinking* (Wis 1:5). This is how sinners are slain: darkened in their understanding, they are alienated from the life of God.[47] Through self-exaltation they lose hold of their confession, and so they are killed, and the warning of scripture is exemplified in them: *No confession can be made by a dead person: he is as though nonexistent* (Sir 17:26).

Thus it happens that they *capture their cities in vain*, for *cities* represent the empty-headed people whom these sinners persuade to follow their own empty-headed errors. Inflated by their reputation for holiness, the leaders persuade blind and ill-educated folk to follow them as though they were more trustworthy, tearing apart the Church's bond of unity. They often find an excuse for separating themselves from our unity in Christ by accusing some among us of evil lives and pretending to shun communion with such persons. It may be that in

---

46. The Father.
47. See Eph 4:18.

so doing they not only defame the innocent, whom they pretend to avoid as evil-doers, but also make true allegations about others as bad as themselves. There are such bad persons among us, and the true wheat of Christ[48] groans in their company but still keeps the bond of unity intact.[49] In the voice of those who suffer in this mixed company, the psalm cries, *Men of blood, depart from me; because you will say in your thoughts, They will capture their cities in vain.* It means this: the reason why the heretics will lure their disciples away into their own sects, there to be corrupted by their stupid notions, is that *you will say in your thoughts, Men of blood, depart from me.* Heretical leaders, spiritually slain as a punishment for their pride, capture their cities in vain, which is a figurative way of saying that they seduce their followers in vain, luring them into vain errors, tearing apart the Church's unity and deserting the good wheat on the pretext of taking offence at the straw mixed with it. But the psalm has a warning also for the wheat itself, the good, faithful people: they must not openly separate themselves from the wicked before the final winnowing, which will sort them out at the end. If they did so prematurely, they might also distance themselves from the good who are still mingled with the bad. Rather should good people, through their praiseworthy conduct and plainly different way of life, tacitly say every day, *Men of blood, depart from me.* This is said to the wicked by God's voice, but his voice speaks in the thoughts of holy people, as the psalm indicates. Who are the *men of blood*? Who else but those who hate their brothers and sisters? John says, *Everyone who hates his brother is a murderer* (1 Jn 3:15). But sinners, spiritually slain, do not understand how God says to the wicked, using the thoughts of his good followers as his medium, *Men of blood, depart from me.* They therefore rebuke the faithful for maintaining communion with bad people, and, using this reproach as an excuse for separating themselves from the Church, they *capture their cities in vain.* This dismissal is spoken to the wicked only in the thoughts of good people at the present time, but one day it will be spoken to them aloud and openly, when they

---

48. See Mt 3:12; 13:30.
49. As he often does, Augustine defends the idea of the Church found in the gospels: a mixture of wheat and weeds, good fish and bad, during this time before the judgment. His target in this section is obviously the different notion of the Donatists, that the Church is the society of the pure.

hear from our head himself, *I never knew you; depart from me, all you who act unjustly* (Mt 7:23).

Verses 21–22. Love your enemies, and hate their sins

27. But now Christ's body, the Church, protests, "How can the proud slander me, alleging that the sins of others defile me? How can they make that a pretext for separating from me and so capturing *their cities in vain*? *Do I not hate those who hate you, O Lord?* How can they demand that I separate physically from bad people, when they who make the demand are worse themselves? Were I to do as they ask, the wheat would be uprooted with the weeds before harvest-time,[50] and I would lose the patience that enables me to bear with my straw until the final winnowing.[51] I would tear apart the nets of unity before the mixed catch of fish is hauled ashore for sorting at the end of the world.[52] Do the sacraments I receive belong to those evil-doers? Do I, by consent, communicate with their way of life or their deeds? *Do I not hate those who hate you, O Lord? Have I not been consumed with indignation over your enemies?* Was I not furious, did not zeal for your house devour me,[53] when I saw how senseless they were? Did not disgust always possess me at the sinners who abandon your law?[54] And who are your enemies, if not those who prove by their lies that they hate your law? If, then, I have hated them, how can people who *capture their cities in vain* impute to me the sins of those I have hated, the sins of those over whom I have been filled with disgust out of zeal for your house?"

But what has become of the Lord's injunction, *Love your enemies*? Do you think that, because he mentioned only yours, God's enemies fall outside its scope? It is true that he said, *Do good to those who hate you* (Mt 5:44), not "to those who hate God." The psalm too asks, *Do I not hate those who hate you, O Lord?* It does not say, "Those who hate me." And it continues, *Have I not been consumed*

---

50. See Mt 13:29.
51. See Mt 3:12.
52. See Mt 13:47–48; Lk 5:6. Elsewhere Augustine thinks of the fishing episode in Lk 5 as a symbol of the Church's mixed catch in the present age, where the nets are in danger of tearing. In the other fishing episode, in Jn 21:1–8, the catch represents for him the netful of the elect, who do not tear the nets. See Exposition 3 of Psalm 30,2 and the note, and also Exposition of Psalm 49,9.
53. See Ps 68:10(69:9).
54. See Ps 118(119):53.

with indignation over your enemies? Not "over mine." But if people hate us and are enemies to us because we serve God, are they not hating him and making themselves his enemies? It cannot be right, then, can it, for us to withhold our love from enemies such as these? When the Lord went on to say, *Pray for those who persecute you* (Mt 5:44), surely he implied that those to whom he spoke would suffer persecution on God's account. We need to seek clarification from the psalm's next verse.

28. *With a perfect hatred I have hated them.* What is *perfect hatred*? It means, I hated the sins in them but I always loved your creation. To hate with perfect hatred implies that you neither hate the persons because of their vices nor love the vices because of the persons. This interpretation is confirmed by the next words, *They have become foes to me*; the psalmist shows that they are not only God's enemies but his own as well. How, then, is he to do justice both to his own declaration, *Do I not hate those who hate you?* and to the Lord's command, *Love your enemies*? How is he to do justice to both, except through a *perfect hatred*, whereby he hates everything in them that makes them sinful and at the same time loves them because they are human beings? Even in the period covered by the Old Covenant, when a carnal people was customarily kept in line by visible punishments, there was a man whose insight gave him kinship with the New Covenant. This was God's servant, Moses. How could he have hated sinners when he prayed for them?[55] But, equally, how could he not have hated them when he killed them?[56] The answer must be that he hated them with a perfect hatred. In the perfection of this hatred he hated the iniquity he was punishing, but in such a way that he loved the human beings for whom he habitually prayed.

Verses 23–24. God reads the Church's heart and leads it in the eternal way, Christ

29. This, then, is our situation. Although at the end Christ's body will be separated from godless and wicked folk even physically, for this time in between it must still sigh among them. The sinners who have been spiritually slain denounce good people in the Church for maintaining communion with bad members and make the presence of these bad members a pretext for separating themselves from the

---

55. See Ex 32:11–13.
56. See Ex 32:26–28.

good and innocent ones. Thus the schismatic leaders *capture their cities*, but *in vain*. Meanwhile plenty of bad people refuse to follow the breakaway movements and remain in the Church, mixed inextricably with its good members, so that the good will have to tolerate them to the end.

What does the body of Christ do amid these trials? What must it do, in order to bring forth fruit in patience,[57] a harvest of a hundred-, sixty-, or thirty-fold?[58] Christ's beloved is among maidens like a lily amid thorns.[59] What is she to do? What does she ask? How does she understand herself? What is the beauty of the king's daughter like, that beauty which she hides within?[60]

Listen to the Church's prayer. *Test me, O God, and know my heart*. It is for you to test me, O God; I pray that you will know me—not any heretic who cannot test or know my heart, for there in my heart you test me and know that I do not consent to the deeds of the wicked, though they believe that I am contaminated by sins that are not mine. As I persevere in my long pilgrimage I am mindful of the groan I uttered in another psalm, that I must deal peaceably with those who hate peace,[61] until I reach that vision of peace which is the name of Jerusalem, the mother of us all, our eternal city in heaven. By their quarrelsome calumnies and by their separation from me my enemies may capture cities for themselves, but not cities that will last for eternity. *They will capture their cities in vain*.

Test me, then, *O God, and know my heart; examine me, and take cognizance of my ways*. To what end? Listen to the remaining verse.

30. *See whether there is any way of sin in me, and lead me in the eternal way*. The psalmist prays, *Take cognizance of my ways*—that is, of my plans and thoughts—*and see whether there is any way of sin in me*, through action or through consent. Then *lead me in the eternal way*. What else does this mean but "Lead me in Christ"? Who is the *eternal way* if not he who is eternal life? He is eternal, he who said, *I am the way, the truth, and the life* (Jn 14:6). Perhaps you may find something in the way I am walking that is displeasing in your eyes, for my way is mortal. *Lead me*, then, *in the eternal way*,

---

57. See Lk 8:15.
58. See Mt 13:23.
59. See Sg 2:2.
60. See Ps 44:14(45:13).
61. See Ps 119:7(120:6–7).

where there is no sin, for *if anyone has sinned, we have an advocate with the Father, Jesus Christ the righteous one, and he himself is the expiation for our sins* (1 Jn 2:1-2). He is our *eternal way* beyond sin, and he is eternal life beyond all punishment.

Conclusion

31. These are profound and holy signs, brothers and sisters. How wonderfully does the Spirit of God speak to us! And what delights he prepares for us in this our night! But how does it happen, brothers and sisters? How is it that these truths are all the sweeter to us for being more obscure?[62] With marvelous skill he mixes a love-potion for us. He has made his own words so wonderful that when we tell you things you already know, the fact that we draw them forth from what seemed to be obscure passages makes them like a fresh discovery for you. You see what I mean? You already knew, didn't you, that bad people must be borne with in the Church of God and that schisms are to be avoided? And you surely knew before now that we have to hold out and persevere in these nets which hold both good and bad fish until we reach the final shore. You knew that in the meantime the nets are not to be torn, because when they are brought ashore the good will be put into containers and the bad thrown away.[63] You knew all this, didn't you? But you did not understand the corresponding verses in this psalm. So now what you did not understand has been explained, and what you already understood has been made new.

---

62. Variant: "These truths are sweeter to us for their very obscurity."
63. See Mt 13:47-48.

Exposition of Psalm 139

A Sermon to the People

Introduction: the head and the body; good and bad people are inextricably mixed

1. Those of my brethren whom I regard as my lords have ordered me to bring this psalm to your notice,[1] so that you may understand it better, to the degree that the Lord of us all gives us his grace. In my brethren's order I hear his command, and I pray that he may help us in response to your prayers, so that I may say what I ought to say and what you need to hear. Only thus will the word of God be profitable to us all. It is not everyone who can profit from his words, because *not everyone has faith* (2 Thes 3:2). Faith acts in a soul like a healthy root which draws moisture downwards, so that the plant may bear fruit. Faithlessness, diabolical error, and love of money are the root of all evils;[2] they are more like the root of a thorn bush, which turns even the sweet, wholesome rain into piercing spikes.

2. I feel sure that you absorbed the principal content of this psalm when it was sung. The body of Christ, destined to live among bad people, complains and groans and pours out its prayer to God. In every prophecy of this type its prayer can be heard, the prayer of a poor suppliant, needy, not yet satisfied, hungering and thirsting for what is right,[3] and looking forward to a satiety promised, to be sure, but deferred until the end of time. Meanwhile Christ's body has to hunger and thirst here on earth, sighing, knocking at the door, and imploring.[4] It does not wallow in any unlawful pleasures that solicit it here in exile, nor does it settle down in this world as though in its

---

1. Augustine was often asked to preach when bishops gathered. This sermon may have been preached on such an occasion. If *fratres* is regarded as a vocative the first sentence would mean "My lords have ordered me, brethren, to bring...." But it seems better to take it as a nominative.
2. See 1 Tm 6:10.
3. See Mt 5:6.
4. These same ideas and phrases recur in section 17 of the sermon, forming an *inclusio*.

homeland. It knows that Christ came to set us free from the world's tyranny, for Christ has willed to be our head, and a head implies a body. If there is a head, there must be a body that belongs to it, and therefore, if Christ is a head, there must also be a body that is Christ's body. Holy Church is the body joined to him, and we are numbered among its limbs, provided that we love our head.

Let us listen to all that Christ's body has to say, and, if we are within that body, hear our own voices there. If anyone has no place in the body, he or she will be among those who cause the body to sigh and groan. Either you will be part of the body, which means that you will have to suffer amid evil-doers, or you will have no place in the body but will find yourself among the bad people who evoke its moans and groans. You have to be one or the other: either a member of Christ or an enemy of the body of Christ.

The enemies and opponents of Christ's body come in many guises and adopt many different tactics, for he who rules them and uses them as his tools is a master of dissimulation.[5] All the time, however, many people are being freed from him and passing over into the body of Christ. Who they are, and how many there will be in the future, is known only to him who redeemed them with his blood, though they knew it not. But there are others who do not belong to Christ's body who will remain obstinately set in their wickedness, and these too are certainly known to him, for there is nothing he does not know.

In this present era those who are united with his members do not yet enjoy the resurrection that is to come. In that future bliss all sighs will pass away and praise will take their place; all distress will be done away with and there will be exultant joy without end. Christ's members do not yet possess this beatitude as a reality, but they hold fast to it in hope, groaning with desire and praying to be delivered from the bad people among whom the good are obliged to live. No one can safely draw a distinction between them at this stage. To sort them out is the prerogative of him who can make no mistake. What do I mean by that? Why do I say he is incapable of getting it wrong? Because he will never usher a bad person to a place at his right hand, or a good person to his left. We, though, find it difficult enough in this life to know ourselves. How much less qualified are we to pass premature judgment on anyone else! We may know that someone is wicked today, but we never know what he will be like tomorrow. It

---

5. *Versipellis*, one who changes his shape or skin.

may be that someone whom we hate intensely is our brother or sister, and we do not realize it.[6] The only safe course for us it to hate the bad attitudes of bad people but love God's creation in them. Let us love what God made and hate only the handiwork of men and women themselves, for God made human beings, but men and women made the sin. Love God's work and hate the botched work of men and women; then you will be an enemy of perverse human doings, but in such a way as to contribute to the freeing of God's creation.[7]

Verse 1. The title points to David, which means, to Christ

3. *To the end, a psalm for David himself.* When you hear this phrase, *the end*, always direct your thoughts to that end which the apostle has predetermined for us: *Christ is the end of the law, bringing justification to everyone who believes* (Rom 10:4). When the psalm says, *To the end*, let all hearts turn to Christ. The title of the psalm serves as a herald for the whole psalm, shouting, "Look, he is coming! It is of him that I am going to tell you! I am going to sing about Christ!"

What I have just told you is certain, because I cannot recognize anyone in the words, *for David himself,* except him who *was made for God from David's line, according to the flesh* (Rom 1:3). The name is appropriate for him in consideration of the human stock from which he sprang, for he was descended from David according to the flesh, though his spiritual generation was far above David. He was not only before David but before Abraham also,[8] and not only before Abraham but even before Adam, and not only before Adam but before heaven and earth, before all angels, all sovereignties and heavenly hosts, before all things, visible and invisible. Why can we say that? Because, in order that they might have existence, *everything was made through him; no part of created being was made without him* (Jn 1:3). Clearly he is not of David's line with respect to his divinity, for he is David's creator. But according to the flesh he is descended from David, and this is why he deigned to be called David in prophecy.

So now look to *the end*, for the psalm is sung *for David himself.* Hear the voice of his body in the psalm, and make sure you are in

---

6. A recurrent idea in Augustine. See, for example, Exposition of Psalm 54,4.
7. Compare Augustine's reflections on *perfect hatred* in his Exposition of Psalm 138,27–28.
8. See Jn 8:58.

the body yourself. May the voice you hear be your own voice. Make the following words your own.

Verse 2. No one sins without harming anyone else

4. *Rescue me, O Lord, from the malicious man*: not from one only but from the whole tribe of them, not from the underlings only but from their leader, the devil himself. But why does the psalm mention a man if it means the devil? Because in a parable even he was represented as human: *A malicious man came and over-sowed the field with tares.* The hired men said to the landowner, *Was it not clean seed that you sowed? Where have the tares come from?* He answered, *Some man who hates me has done this.* (Mt 13:25.26–27) Pray with all your might to be delivered from this *malicious man*, for *it is not against flesh and blood that you have to struggle, but against principalities and powers and the rulers of this world of darkness* (Eph 6:12), which is to say, the rulers who have dominion over sinners. We ourselves were once among their number, for now we hear the apostle reminding us, *You were darkness once, but now you are light in the Lord* (Eph 5:8). Having been transformed into light not by our own doing but by the Lord, let us pray for protection not only against darkness, which represents sinners who are still in the devil's grasp, but also against their sovereign, the devil, who is at work in rebellious unbelievers.[9]

Deliver me from the unrighteous fellow. This is a repetition of the previous phrase: *from the unrighteous fellow* means the same as *from the malicious man*. The psalm declares him malicious because he is unrighteous, and it does not want you to think that any unrighteous person could be anything other than malicious. It is true that there are many unrighteous persons who appear to will no harm to others;[10] they are not aggressive or harsh in their demeanor; they are not unkind nor do they harass others. Yet they are unrighteous, and their unrighteousness consists in some kind of dissolute living or intemperance or addiction to carnal pleasures. How is it possible for one who so harms himself to do no harm to others? An innocent person is one who is altogether innocuous,[11] and one who harms

---

9. Literally "sons of unbelief." See Eph 2:2.
10. *Quasi non nocentes.*
11. Augustine is drawing attention to the etymology of the word "innocent": non-harming or harmless.

himself is therefore not innocent. Moreover, how can a person who harms himself fail to harm you? You may object, "But how is he doing any harm to me? He has not laid hands on my property or attacked me personally. He thrives on his licentious lifestyle and indulges in his own pleasures. If they are polluted pleasures, the foulness sticks to him. What does it matter to me? He does not bother me."

But he does harm you by his example if not in any other way. He lives alongside you and invites you to share in his conduct. When you see him flourishing in those filthy activities, are you not enticed to behave likewise? Even if you do not consent, you have at least found something within yourself with which you must do battle. How, then, can you say he has done you no harm when you have to struggle hard to conquer something he occasioned in your heart? Every unrighteous person is malicious. He cannot avoid being a danger to others, whether he is charming or repellent. Anyone who becomes involved with him, anyone who is caught in his toils, will find out that what seemed smooth and pleasant was very noxious.

After all, brothers and sisters, it is not the roots of thorny plants that prick you. Dig the bush up out of the ground and handle the roots. Do you feel any pain? No. Yet the plant that hurts you above ground has grown up from this root. So do not trust people who seem to be smooth and pleasant but are enamored of carnal pleasures and addicted to foul self-indulgence. Do not trust them. Even if they seem still gentle, they are the roots from which thorns grow. By their actions and their licentious behavior they often sprout forth what was in them from the first. And, having sprouted so, will they not bring those shoots to full growth? They will not refrain now, will they, from robbery or deceitful fraud, or from planning any kind of malevolent act? Now you see how bad he is, this person you used to think mild and gentle. When you saw him regularly getting drunk, you thought him a good fellow; now that you detect him in theft, or fear him as a robber, you realize that thorns have sprung up from those roots. When you were running your hands over the smooth roots of the thorn bushes, that was the time when you might have burned them, and then there would have been no spiky growth to stab you now. Learn the lesson, my brothers and sisters, you who are Christ's body and individually his members and groan among evil-doers of this type. Whenever you come across people with a propensity for sinful lust or dangerous debauchery, rebuke them straight away, castigate them at once, burn them on the spot! Let the root burn, and then there will be nowhere for any thorn to spring from.

If you are unable to do this, be sure that you will find these people to be your enemies. They may be silent, and they may conceal their animosity, but they certainly will not love you. And if they are incapable of loving you they will hate you, and if they hate you they will sooner or later seek to do you harm. Take care, then, that your tongue and your heart never cease to say to God, *Rescue me, O Lord, from the malicious man; deliver me from the unrighteous fellow.*

Verses 3–4. Smooth talk and malicious hearts

5. *They have harbored unrighteous thoughts in their hearts.* To whom does this refer? Surely to people who do not dare to take unjust words on their lips but cherish unjust thoughts in their hearts. The psalmist makes this prayer because such people often speak pleasantly. What you hear sounds like the voice of a just person, but the words do not come from a just person's heart. If this were not the meaning intended, why add the phrase, *They have harbored unrighteous thoughts in their hearts*? Free me from these smooth talkers, the psalm implies; may your almighty hand be there to deliver me. It is easy to get away from the openly hostile, easy to dodge a visible, manifest enemy whose iniquity is obvious even from his speech. The one who is difficult to avoid is the secret enemy who has fair words on his lips but hidden malice in his heart. So the psalmist prays to be delivered from all who *have harbored unrighteous thoughts in their hearts.*

They contrived warfare against me all day long. What is this warfare? He means all those things that the enemy has thrown in his way, which he must struggle against daily, for all that a Christian has to contend with arises from such perfidious hearts. If sedition breaks out, or schism or heresy, or if violent dissension bursts forth, its source is always those evil thoughts that were harbored secretly. Even when the words spoken were reassuring, *they contrived warfare against me all day long.* You hear their peaceable words, but belligerent designs are never absent from their hearts. When the psalm says *all day long,* it means incessantly, all the time.

6. *They have sharpened their tongues like snakes.* If you are still trying to identify the duplicitous person that the psalm has in view, take note of the simile it uses here. The snake is the creature that harms us with more craft and cunning than any other. Its slithering motion is a sign of its guile, for it does not even have feet that would

make a sound we could hear as it approaches. It glides along smoothly, quietly, and not even in a straight line. Just so do our cunning enemies creep and slither along, armed with hidden venom that can hurt us at the slightest contact. Accordingly the psalm continues, *Vipers' venom is under their tongues.* It says *under* because what is under their tongues is quite different from what is on their tongues for us to hear. Another psalm delineates them clearly: *They speak peaceably with their neighbors, but wickedly in their hearts* (Ps 27(28):3).

Verses 4–5. Active hostility from the proud; the traps set by sinners

7. *Preserve me, O Lord, from the sinner's hand; deliver me from the unrighteous.* Who these people are we know already. It is not further insight that we need now, but action; our job is to pray, not to go on trying to identify them. But the next lines of the psalm show you how you ought to pray against people of this stamp, for although many pray against them, not all do so with discernment.

The psalm therefore continues, *They have plotted to trip me up.* This could still be taken in a material sense. Suppose a person has an enemy who, in some business they are conducting together, tries to cheat him and defraud him of some money. Or again, suppose someone has a neighbor who is at odds with him, who plans to make mischief in his family or to bring about some diminution of his goods. Undoubtedly the thoughts of such an enemy are full of guile and dishonesty, and he goes about his evil work with the contrivances of the devil. All the same, that is not why they should be shunned. The real danger is that by their deceitful stratagems they may lure you over to themselves, sundering you from the body of Christ and making you part of their body, for, as Christ is the head of good people, so is the devil the head of the wicked.

They have plotted to trip me up, the psalmist complains. What does he mean by *to trip me up*? Not to make you go wrong in the business you are conducting with him, nor to cheat you over a case you and he are disputing in court. No, he will have tripped you up if he sets up a road-block for you in the way of God, if some good enterprise you meant to pursue falters, or slips out of the way, or falls flat on the way, or veers right off the way, or remains stuck in the way, or even turns right around and goes back where it came from. If the enemy has done anything like this to you, he has tripped you up and deceived you.

Pray against all such insidious attacks, so that you may not forfeit your heavenly inheritance or lose Christ, your fellow-heir.[12] You are called to live for ever with him who made you an heir, but he is not a testator who causes you to inherit on his death; rather, you will live with him for all eternity.

8. *The proud have hidden a trap for me.* The psalm has summed up the whole body of the devil[13] in that brief phrase, *the proud*. It is pride that most often drives the devil's followers to proclaim themselves righteous when they are sinful. It is also because of this pride that they hate nothing more than confessing their sins. Bogus pretenders to justice as they are, they envy the truly just, for no one envies any quality in another unless he wants to possess it himself or at least to be thought to possess it. If another person envies you because you are rich, his envy springs from his desire to be rich himself or to be regarded as rich. If someone else envies you because you are famous and nobly born, he either wishes he were so himself or he longs to make people believe he is. The same is true of everything in this world which either is good or is regarded as good. Whatever a person wants to have, in whatever respect he longs to excel, whatever kind of reputation he aspires to, that is what he will envy in you. The sham pretenders to righteousness want to appear righteous and holy, whereas they are not; and when they see someone who is truly righteous they necessarily envy him and deal with him in such a way as to make him lose the very endowment that is his glory, if they can. Hence arise all the attempts to lead the just astray and trip them up.

The first one to attempt such a seduction was the devil himself. He had fallen, but human beings were still on their feet. He had lost the kingdom of heaven and therefore did not want us to gain it, nor does he want us to now. He still exerts himself to prevent men and women from reaching the place from which he was cast out. He is proud, and his envy springs from pride, and so all those adherents of his who form his body are proud like him. Let us pray against him who cannot be corrected and pray for those who can. In this spirit let us demand of any unjust person, "Why envy the just, you unjust fellow? Is it because you want to appear just yourself? Be quick and take a better course and you will more easily become what you want people to think you are. Be just yourself and then you will love the

---

12. See Rom 8:17.
13. That is, his adherents, as in section 7.

one you now envy. At present his goodness irritates you, but then you will be good yourself, and you will love yourself in him and him in yourself. Think carefully about this. If a rich person were the target of your envy, it would not be within your power to grow rich. If you were envious of some honorable, nobly born senator, it would not be possible for you to become noble or of high repute yourself. If you envied a beautiful person, you would never thereby make yourself beautiful. If you felt envy for a brave, strong individual, you could never gain like strength by envying his. But if you envy a just person, the matter is in your own hands: you can be what that other person is, what he now is to your chagrin. Be just yourself. You will not have to buy that quality which he possesses and you do not, for it costs nothing and is obtained instantly. *Peace on earth to men of good will* (Lk 2:14)." [14]

9. *The proud have hidden a trap for me*, the psalmist has said; they have done their best to trip me up.[15] What did they do? *They stretched out cords as a snare for my feet*. What cords does he mean us to think of? This image of cords occurs elsewhere in the scriptures, and we can discover its meaning from other texts. The Lord made a whip of little cords and used it to drive out of the temple those who were behaving there in unseemly ways.[16] Another passage shows us how to understand the word when it warns, *Each one of us is bound by the fine hairs of our own sins* (Prv 5:22). Isaiah speaks even more plainly: *Woe to those who drag out their sins into a long cord* (Is 5:18). But why are sins called a cord? The reason, I think, is this: when a sinner continues obstinately in his way, he adds sins to sins. Instead of allowing himself to be corrected by accusing himself of his sin, he doubles it by defending what he could have been rid of by confession. Moreover, a sinner often tries to protect himself against the consequences of his actions by committing further sins. Suppose he has committed adultery. To avoid capital punishment, he plans to

---

14. To our ears this text evokes the Christmas story and the alternative translation, *good will toward men*. But for Augustine the stress was on the last words, *men of good will*. Compare his reflections in *Confessions* VIII, 8,19–9,21 on the difference between wanting some external object, which may be obtained only with difficulty if at all, and wanting the good, "for in this sole instance the faculty to act and the will to act precisely coincide, and the willing is already the doing" (VIII,8,20).
15. Variant: "to make well-directed steps stumble."
16. See Jn 2:15.

kill someone; so he has added another sin to his first sin. If he carries out his plan and kills, he who until now had only one crime to be fearful about now has two. But on realizing that his situation is more frightening than before, he does not seek to diminish his guilt but rather adds another sin, one he has not yet committed, perhaps by resorting to sorcery. So now he has three sins. Who can foresee where this will lead? Who can find the end of this rope of sins?

To call it a cord is an apt metaphor, because it is by adding strand to strand that a cord is made. And the strands that are added are not straight but twisted. Human crookedness becomes more and more involved in itself and stretches out into a long, tangled yarn. Instead of determining to cut through the muddle he has made, a depraved person only adds to it, carries it further, and stretches it out into such a long cord that it finally binds his hands and feet, and he is cast into the outer darkness.[17]

But malevolent people use their own sins to stretch out an ensnaring cord for the just when they persuade good people to commit the same iniquities. This is why the psalm says, *They stretched out cords as a snare for my feet*: they tried to throw me down by using their own sins to trip me. And where did they place the snare? *They set their traps near the paths, to make me stumble.* Not on the paths, but *near the paths.* Your paths are God's commandments. They have set their trip-cords close to the paths, but if you take care not to leave the paths, you will not blunder into them. I don't want you to say, "God ought to forbid them to lay snares for me close to the paths, and then they would not put any there." It is much more likely that God allowed them to place traps close to the paths to deter you from straying off them. *They set their traps near the paths, to make me stumble.*

Verses 7–8. Intimacy with God in the midst of struggle

10. What is left for us? What can our recourse be amid such great evils, beset as we are by all these temptations and dangers? *I have said to the Lord, You are my God.* Those enemies are only men, and they are not "mine"; you are God, and you are mine. *I have said to the Lord, You are my God.* A mighty voice raised in prayer is heard here, and it gives us confidence. But is God not the God of our enemies too? If he is the true God, is there anyone of whom we could say, "He is not their God"? No, but he is more properly called the God

---

17. See Mt 22:13.

of those who enjoy him and serve him and willingly submit to him. It is true that bad people are subject to him too, but unwillingly. His willing subjects call upon God, by whom they hope to be crowned; the others are under him and attempt to flee from him by whom they are in danger of being damned. If a wicked person does not want to have the Lord as his God, where is he to take refuge from the God of all things? Better for him to be converted to the God of all things and make God his God by conversion. Though still surrounded by sinners, seducers, hypocrites, and arrogant companions, he will then be in a state to say to God, whom by his conversion he has accepted as his own God, *I have said to the Lord, You are my God.*

Let your ears receive the voice of my entreaty, O Lord. This is a simple petition, and easy to understand, yet perhaps it is pleasant for us to consider why he did not say, "Let your ears receive my entreaty, O Lord," but expressed what was in his mind more plainly by expanding the petition to *the voice of my entreaty.* He means, "My whole life is my entreaty, my soul is my entreaty—not just what is audible in my words but myself, whence the words draw their life." Other sounds, in which no soul is present, can be called noise but cannot be called voices, because a voice belongs properly to animated creatures; it is a sign that they are alive. How many people are there who mouth entreaties to God but are not conscious of God and do not think rightly of him? The noise of entreaty is heard from them, but it can hardly be called a voice, for there is no life in it. Very different was the prayer of the psalmist. This was the voice of someone who was truly alive because he understood that God was his God, contemplated the God by whom he hoped to be set free, and was aware of the snares from which he needed deliverance. This was the voice of his entreaty.

11. Urging this entreaty in God's ears, let him now continue, *Lord, Lord.* You, Lord, are the Lord; that is to say, you are the Lord in all reality, not like human lords, not like the kind of lords who acquire their subjects with their purses, but the Lord who bought his with his blood. *Lord, Lord, you are the strength of my salvation,* you grant me strength that I may be saved. What is the meaning of the phrase, *the strength of my salvation*? The psalmist has been complaining about the obstacles put in his way by sinners, about the ambushes they lay for him, about malicious people, tools of the devil, who yap all around him and set traps on every side, and about the proud persons who envy the just. Among all these we must live, as long as we are still on our pilgrim road here. The Lord foretold all these manifold obstacles

that we would meet in the future, saying, *With iniquity increasing mightily, the love of many will grow cold.* But he immediately added a comforting promise, *Whoever perseveres to the end will be saved.* (Mt 24:12.13) The psalmist listened to the warning and was afraid and troubled by the mounting tide of iniquities, but he turned his eyes toward the hope offered him, that *whoever perseveres to the end will be saved.* He braced himself to persevere, he saw the length of the way, he knew that perseverance is a great matter and very difficult, and then, since it was God who had ordered him to persevere, he prayed to God to perfect his perseverance.[18] I know for certain that I shall be saved if I persevere to the end, he seems to say, but perseverance demands strength if I am to merit salvation. You are *the strength of my salvation*, for you make me persevere so that I may reach it. *Lord, Lord, you are the strength of my salvation.*

What is it that gives me this hope, assuring me that you are yourself the strength that will enable me to reach salvation? *You have shaded my head on the day of battle.* Look at me and see how I am still fighting. I fight outwardly against people who feign goodness and I fight within myself against my lusts, for *I am aware of a different law in my members that opposes the law of my mind, and imprisons me under the law of sin inherent in my members. Who will deliver me from this death-ridden body, wretch that I am? Only the grace of God, through Jesus Christ our Lord.* (Rom 7:23–25) Hard pressed in his warfare, he looked to the grace of God. He had already begun to suffer from heat and lack of water, but in God's grace he seemed to find a shady covering under which he could survive. *You have shaded my head on the day of battle*, when I was stricken by the heat, so that I would neither weary nor faint with thirst.

Verse 9. Watch your desires

12. *Do not let me be betrayed by my desire, Lord, and delivered to the sinner.* The shady canopy you have spread over me will ensure that I do not suffer from heat generated by myself. And if that is so, what can any sinner, however ferocious, do to hurt me? Wicked people raged furiously against the martyrs: they dragged them away, bound them with chains, shut them up in prison, slew some with the sword, exposed others to wild beasts, and burned others to death. Persecutors

---

18. *Ipsum oravit ad perfectionem perseverantiae suae*, a pregnant phrase suggesting the mysterious marriage of grace and human free will.

did all this to them, yet God did not hand the martyrs over to sinners, because they were not handed over by their own will.

Pray, then, with all your might, pray that God will not hand you over to a sinner by your own desire. When you let desire lead you, you give the devil his chance. Imagine that the devil has dangled before you an opportunity to make money and invited you to commit fraud. You can't have the money unless you consent to the fraud too. Now the money is a bait, and the fraud is a snare. Take a good look at the bait, so good that you detect the snare as well, because you cannot reach the food unless you deal dishonestly, and, if you commit the fraud, you will be caught. When I say that you will be caught, I do not mean that you will necessarily be found out. Sometimes you will get away with it and not be found out, as far as human beings are concerned. But will you not be caught by God? You will certainly be caught and dragged to judgment and put to death. Anyone who acts like this destroys himself. Well, then, there is the bait, and there is the snare too. Curb your desire and you will not fall into the snare. But if your desire for the food gets the better of you, the diabolical fowler, hunter of souls, thrusts your neck into his trap and captures you.

Do not let me be betrayed by my desire, and delivered to the sinner. It is from these dangers that we are protected on the day of battle by the shady covering the Lord spreads over us, for our desire inflames us, but the Lord's shade cools our desire, giving us strength to curb the force that threatens to snatch us away and saving us from the fierce heat that might lead us into the snare.

They have plotted against me; do not forsake me, lest they be exalted. In another passage you find a similar fear: *Those who harass me will make merry when I am shaken* (Ps 12:5(13:4)). Our oppressors are like this because that is what the devil is like. When he has seduced a person, he is glad and shouts in triumph over his victim: the devil is exalted because someone has been brought low. Why was the human sinner brought low? Because he had first been exalted in the wrong way; but the one who is shouting over him now will be humbled in his turn. The same is true of all those who rejoice over evil. For a time they think they are victorious and triumphant, and they proudly toss their heads. Do not let their merrymaking[19] bring you any joy; they have the bait between their teeth, but the hook too. The thing that gives them pleasure is in their jaws, and along with

---

19. Variant: "their exaltation."

it the line that will drag them away. *Do not forsake me, lest they be exalted*; let them not triumph over me, and let them never rejoice at my fate.

Verse 10. Lying is a laborious business

13. *The principle of their gyration, the fabrication of their lips, will cover them.* For my part, he implies, the shade of your wings will cover me, for you have sheltered me on the day of battle. But what about those others? What will their covering be? *The principle of their gyration* is pride. What is meant by *their gyration*? They go round and round and never stand still, they tread a winding path of error to which there is no end. If someone goes on a long journey he begins from a certain point and ends at a certain point, but one who walks round and round in circles ends nowhere. This pointless activity is the occupation of the impious, as another psalm states more clearly: *The wicked walk around in a circle* (Ps 11:9(12:8)). But the beginning of their gyration is pride, because pride is the starting-point of every sin.[20]

But why is pride *the fabrication of their lips*? Every proud person is a sham, and everyone who is a sham is a liar. People who tell lies have to work hard at elaborating them, whereas they could have told the truth quite easily. One who is making up what he says has to work at fabricating his story, but one who speaks truthfully need not go to such trouble, because truth itself speaks without effort. The psalmist is thinking of people like this when he says to God, "Your shady canopy will protect me, and their lies will cover them. But this lying tale of theirs is wearisome for their lips to fabricate." *That person has been giving birth to injustice. Just look at him! He has conceived toil and has brought forth iniquity.* (Ps 7:15(14))

All wrongdoing is laborious, and lying is at the root of every bad action that is ever planned, for truth is to be found only in good actions. All men and women toil away at fabricating lies, yet what does truth himself cry out to them? *Come to me, all you who labor and are heavily burdened, and I will give you relief* (Mt 11:28). The same voice cries to laborers in another psalm, *How long will you be heavy-hearted, human creatures? Why love emptiness and chase falsehood?* (Ps 4:3(2)) Again, the hard work entailed in lying is plainly indicated in a prophetic text: *They have schooled their tongues to tell*

---

20. See Sir 10:15.

lies; they have exerted themselves to deal unjustly (Jer 9:5). *The principle of their gyration, the fabrication of their lips, will cover them.*

Verse 11. Burning coals can have different effects on different targets

14. *Burning coals will fall upon them on earth, and you will cast them down.* What do the words, *on earth*, signify? Here, while they are still in this life, *burning coals will fall upon them on earth, and you will cast them down.* We have met these coals before.[21] Or are the coals we thought about before different from those we must discuss now? The former were a symbol of punishment, whereas those I am going to speak of now seem rather to concern salvation. In the earlier case, someone was seeking help against a deceitful tongue, and the psalm asked, *What is to be given to you, what provided for you, that you may withstand the deceitful tongue?* And it answered its own question, *Sharp arrows of the mighty one, with destructive, all-devouring coals.* (Ps 119(120):3-4) The weapons are, first, the words of God[22] with their power to transfix the heart, to destroy all that is old, and to generate love, and then the examples[23] of people who used to be dead and came to life, who used to be very dark but were made to glow brightly. Coals represent darkness, as their color suggests. But the flame of charity is applied to them, and they burst into life after being dead. Then let them hear the apostle reminding them, *You were darkness once, but now you are light in the Lord* (Eph 5:8).

Brothers and sisters, these are the coals we can see at work when we have been transfixed by God's arrow, and are determined to change our lives but hindered by the malicious tongues of those who try to stop us—those same tongues that were mentioned just now. They want to divert us from the way of truth and lead us instead into their own errors, and so they tell us that, if we dedicate ourselves to our good enterprises, we shall not be able to stay the course. But then we look to the coals. Someone we know was a drunkard yesterday, but today he is temperate. Someone else was an adulterer yesterday but today is chaste. Another was a robber yesterday but today is open-

---

21. See Exposition of Psalm 119,5, with which the present section shares some ideas.
22. Arrows.
23. Coals.

handed in giving away his goods. All these are burning coals. These examples, these coals, are applied to the wound inflicted by God's arrows—I must not shrink from speaking of a wound, for the bride herself cries, *I am wounded with love* (Sg 2:5, LXX)—and the result is the destruction of all the hay it finds in us. That is why they are called all-devouring coals. Hay is burnt up, but gold is refined. A man or woman is changed from a corpse into a living being and becomes yet one more burning coal, one such as was the apostle. He had at first been a blasphemer who inflicted much harm on people,[24] like a black coal with no spark in it, but he received God's mercy and was set on fire from heaven. The voice of Christ enkindled him, all the blackness in him was destroyed, his spirit caught fire, and he began to spread to others the flame that was burning in himself.

What of the passage in our present psalm? Are we to take the coals mentioned here in the same sense, these coals that fall upon the wicked, who are cast down? Certainly nothing precludes this sense. I can see an interpretation beginning to dawn, one that is probable and unobjectionable. I think the psalm means that these coals fall upon such persons in order to throw them down. They fall upon some people, you see, to set them on fire, but on others to overthrow them. That special coal we mentioned just now indicated as much: *For some we are the stench of death unto death, but for others the scent of life, leading to life* (2 Cor 2:16). Unbelievers observe the just afire in spirit, glowing with light, and are so envious that they are made to fall, thus verifying the psalm's prediction that burning coals will fall upon them on earth, and they will be cast down. Why *on earth*? Even while they are here, in this present life, before eternal fire has reached them, these coals knock them over, and there is further punishment reserved for the godless at the end. *Burning coals will fall upon them on earth, and will cast them down.*

In their wretchedness they will not keep their footing. When a wretched fate overtakes them they cannot bear it, unlike Paul, who kept his footing and claimed, *We even glory in our sufferings, knowing that suffering fosters endurance, and endurance constancy, and constancy hope; but hope does not disappoint us, because the charity of God has been poured out into our hearts through the Holy Spirit who has been given us* (Rom 5:3–5). As for the others, only a little distress, some misery overtaking them, is enough to make them lose

---

24. See 1 Tm 1:13.

their footing and fall over. When such people find themselves under any pressure of this kind they cannot endure it; they fall down into heinous sins, because they are delivered into a sinner's hand by their own desire.

Verse 12. Do not talk more than you must; listen to the teacher within you

15. *The talkative man will not be guided on earth.* A talkative man loves lies. What gives him pleasure? Only talking. He does not even listen to what he is saying; all that matters is to keep talking. It is not possible for a person like that to be guided aright.

What about a servant of God who has been set on fire by the coals we have been discussing and has become a salutary coal himself? What should he be like? He, or she, should prefer to listen rather than to speak; as scripture says, *Let everyone be quick to hear, but slow to speak* (Jas 1:19). God's servant should, as far as possible, desire not to be obliged to speak or preach or teach. To put it plainly to you, beloved: we are talking to you now in order to teach you something. But how much better it would be if we all knew it, so that no one would need to teach anyone else. Then we would not need to have one person speaking and another listening, but all of us would be listening to God, to whom another psalm says, *As I listen you will give me delight and gladness* (Ps 50:10(51:8)). Think of John the Baptist. He was joyful, but not because he was preaching or teaching; he was joyful because he was constantly listening; as he said: *The bridegroom's friend, who stands and hears him, rejoices intensely at the bridegroom's voice* (Jn 3:29).

Well, then, beloved brothers and sisters, let me tell you briefly how each one can test himself in this matter. It is not that one should never speak but that one should speak only if it is a duty demanded by one's office. Even then we should be glad to keep silence, as far as we have any choice, and use our voice in teaching only when there is need. After all, when is your teaching voice required? When you encounter some ignorant person or someone poorly educated. It follows, then, that if you find pleasure in teaching all the time, what you would really like is to have ignorant persons permanently available, so that you can teach them! But if you are so kindly disposed that you want everyone to be well instructed, you will prefer that there should not be any in need of your teaching. And then you will exercise and demonstrate your teaching skills not because you want to but only when it is necessary. Let your enjoyment be in listening to God and your speaking be prompted only by necessity; then you will not be a chatterbox at risk of not being guided aright.

Anyway, why do you want to speak and not want to listen? You are always rushing out of doors but are unwilling to return into your own house. Your teacher is within. When you teach, you go out to those who are outside. It is inside that we listen to the truth, and after listening we speak to people who are outside our own heart. Yes, outside; for, though it is sometimes said that when we are thinking of other people we "have them in our hearts," what we really have is a kind of image which they have impressed upon us. If they were inside us in the fullest sense they would obviously know what was in our heart, and so we would not need to speak to them. If, then, you take pleasure in what you do outside yourself, take care that you do not become so swollen with pride out there that you cannot make your way back through the narrow door[25] and God cannot invite you, *Enter into the joy of your Lord* (Mt 25:21.23). Rather will he have to say to you, since you were so fond of what was outside, *Bind his hands and feet, and throw him into the outer darkness* (Mt 22:13). In this text, where the Lord suggests that it is a bad thing to be outside, he also shows that to enter within is good for us; for what did he say to his faithful servant? *Enter into the joy of your Lord.* But of the bad servant he said, *Cast him into outer darkness* (Mt 25:30). Let us not love external things too much, but rather what is within. Let us enjoy interior realities and engage in external affairs out of necessity, not by choice. *The talkative man will not be guided on earth.*

16. *Troubles will hunt the unrighteous man to perdition.* When troubles come, the unrighteous loses his footing; this is why the psalm says that they *will hunt him to perdition.* Troubles have befallen many good, just people, and it has sometimes seemed as though troubles were hunting them down. The word *hunt* is aptly used by the psalm, because everyone wants to hide from disaster, but, when trouble catches up with someone who is fleeing from it, he is like its prey. Is it only bad people who flee from bad things, when those evils are looking for them? Were not the good also advised, *If they have persecuted you in one city, flee to another* (Mt 10:23)? When wicked people persecuted the good—our martyrs, I mean—and arrested them, they hunted them, certainly, but not to perdition. The flesh was tortured but the

---

25. See Mt 7:13.

soul was crowned; the soul was released from the flesh and nothing that was done to the flesh could be to its disadvantage in the long run. Flesh was burned or scourged or mangled. But did its delivery into the hand of the persecutor mean that it was put beyond the reach of its creator? If he created it from nothingness and non-being, will he not create it anew, better than before? Whenever just people were arrested, evil people did indeed hunt them, but not *to perdition*. But as for those others, the ones who will not be guided aright and are always talking, calamities will hunt them down *to perdition*. Why? Because *in their wretchedness they will not keep their footing*.

Verse 13. The Lord will champion the poor

17. *I know that the Lord will see justice done for the needy*. This needy person is not talkative, for anyone who is talkative aspires to wealth and is a stranger to hunger. The needy are those to whom the Lord says, *Knock, and the door will be opened to you; seek, and you will find; ask, and you will obtain* (Mt 7:7). It is to a needy person that the promise applies, *Blessed are those who hunger and thirst for righteousness, for they shall be satisfied* (Mt 5:6). These needy people groan amid the obstacles put in their path by the wicked, and they pray to their head to be delivered from the unrighteous, rescued from the malicious,[26] and plucked free from the hands of unjust foes. These needy folk are the ones whose cause the Lord will not ignore. They may suffer hardships in this present era but, when their head is revealed, their glory will be revealed with him, for it is to people suffering now that scripture says, *You are dead, and your life is hidden with Christ in God* (Col 3:3). So we are poor, and our life is hidden; let us then cry out for bread, the living bread that came down from heaven.[27] On our journey it refreshes us, and when we reach our homeland it will satisfy us wholly. We need refreshment now to keep us going, but it is essential that we hunger until we are satisfied.

I know that the Lord will see justice done for the needy. The psalmist was quite certain that *the Lord will see justice done for the needy and will avenge the poor*. He will prove to the wicked how much he loves his just ones; he will prove to the rich how much he loves his poor. He has called the proud "rich" and the humble folk "poor." The former are rich because they are so well off they seek nothing, and

---

26. See verse 2.
27. See Jn 6:41.

God's holy ones are poor because they sigh with ardent desire. The Lord will see justice done for them.

Verse 14. The face of God, the face of Christ

18. *The just will indeed confess to your name.* When you take up their cause, and when you see justice done for them, they will confess to your name. They will attribute nothing to their own merits but give the entire credit to your mercy alone. *The just will indeed confess to your name.* And since they will confess so wholeheartedly to your name that, however righteous they may have been, they will claim nothing of their own and take no credit for themselves, how are they to direct their hearts? When they turn to themselves, their hearts feel only anguish, but when they look to the Lord they direct their hearts aright. Where are they to find pleasure, where rest, where joy, where beatitude? In themselves? By no means, but in the Lord, in whom they have been transformed into light. Now they *are light in the Lord* (Eph 5:8), says scripture.

Look at the consequences of this and meditate on the psalm's closing words. *Straightforward people*—those who are rightly directed—*shall live with your face*. Bad things happened to them in respect to their own faces, but with your face all shall be well with them. Betrayed by self-regarding love, they were condemned to eat their bread with sweat on their faces.[28] But now let them come back and wipe off the sweat. With hard toil finished and groaning silenced, your face will be there for them to be their overflowing satisfaction. They will seek nothing else, because there cannot be anything better. They will never abandon you[29] again, nor will they ever be abandoned by you. This is quite certain, for what is said about the Lord after his resurrection? *You will fill me with joy in beholding your face* (Ps 15(16):11; Acts 2:28). If he hid his face from us, he would not be giving us joy. Let us cleanse our own faces, that we may rejoice at the sight of his face. *We are children of God already, but what we shall be has not yet appeared. We* know that when he appears, we shall be like him, for we shall see him as he is (1 Jn 3:2), because *straightforward people shall live with your face.* Are we to think that this means with the face of the Father but not with the face of the Son? Or with the face of the Son but not with the face of the Father? Or is

---

28. See Gn 3:19.
29. Variant: "May they never abandon you."

there, in some mysterious way, one single face of the Father and the Son and the Holy Spirit?

Let us see whether the Son himself does not promise to make us joyful with the sight of his own face. The Lord God inspired us just now to read the very chapter of the gospel that confirms our psalm. In that chapter the Lord promises, *Anyone who cherishes my commandments and keeps them, that is the one who loves me; and whoever loves me will be loved by my Father, and I will love him, and will show myself to him* (Jn 14:21). What kind of reward was it that he promised, dearly beloved? Surely the apostles were looking at him already, so how could he promise to show himself to them? Was he not there before them? Was not his human face there before their eyes? What could he have meant to show to people who saw him already?

We must remember that the Christ whom the disciples were looking at was not different from Christ as he was when the Jews crucified him. Yet within the flesh that met their eyes, God was hidden. Human disciples could see only his humanity; they could not see God, even though God was in this man. Because this was their limitation, and because, as he said, *Blessed are the pure of heart, for they shall see God* (Mt 5:8), he offered himself in his humanity to both the devout and the impious, but he reserved the reality of his Godhead for the pure-hearted and the devout, so that we may be glad in him and find our joy for ever in seeing his face.

Exposition of Psalm 140

A Sermon to the People[1]

Introduction: pray for the preacher

1. When a letter from the apostle was read just now, brothers and sisters, you heard in it an admonition and a request that could just as well have come from us. He said, *Be assiduous in prayer, and keep watch prayerfully. Pray also for us, that God may open to us a door for the word, whereby we may speak of his mystery and make it known, as it is my duty to speak.* (Col 4:2–4) I ask you, please, to regard these words as my own. In the holy scriptures there are profound mysteries which are hidden so that no one may approach them disrespectfully. But we must search for them and allow them to exercise our minds, knowing that when they are opened they will nourish us. The psalm we have just sung is an example, for its meaning is somewhat obscure in many places. But, as with the Lord's help its message begins to be teased out and explained, you will see that what you are hearing is something you knew already. Nonetheless, this teaching was communicated in different ways so that the variety of expression might guard against any boredom with the truth itself.

Scripture teaches one thing: charity; the characteristics of true charity

2. Think of it this way, brothers and sisters. Are you ever likely to hear or understand anything vaster in scope, or more important for salvation, than the command, *You shall love the Lord your God with all your heart and all your soul and all your mind* (Mk 12:30), and again, *You shall love your neighbor as yourself* (Mk 12:31)? And in case you are tempted to underrate the importance of these two precepts, remember that *on these two commandments depend all the law and the prophets* (Mt 22:40). Whatever salutary idea anyone may conceive or formulate in words, whatever truth may be dug out

---

1. Probably preached during the vigil of a martyrs' feast at Hippo, between 397 and 405. See the note at section 13 below.

from any page of the divine scriptures, it tends toward one end only, and that is charity.

But this does not mean any kind of relationship that goes under the name of charity, for even persons of evil life are entangled with one another in a fellowship of ruined consciences. It is said that they love each other, are unwilling to leave the group, and are united in friendly discussion; they are said to miss those of their members who are away and to be glad when they return. But love like this is born from the infernal regions. It generates a sticky substance that plunges people into the depths instead of equipping them with wings to lift them to the sky. What is true charity, then, and what qualities mark it off from spurious forms that claim to be charity?

The true charity proper to Christians has been described by Paul and so clearly demarcated within its own boundaries that it is entirely distinct from all pseudo-charity—although, inasmuch as it is divine in origin, we should not speak of its having any bounds at all. *The end of the commandment is charity* (1 Tm 1:5), he says. He was able to leave it at that, just as in other passages, where he was speaking to well-instructed hearers, he could simply say, *The fullness of the law is charity* (Rom 13:10), without stating what kind of charity he meant. He had explained this elsewhere,[2] and it is neither possible nor desirable to repeat everything in every context. So too here: *The fullness of the law is charity.* Were you perhaps wondering what charity or what kind of charity? You find the answer in the other text I quoted: *The end of the commandment is charity from a pure heart* (1 Tm 1:5). Now consider whether robbers exercise charity from a pure heart when they hatch their plots together. To love with a pure heart means to love another person in accordance with God's will. This is how you are bound to love yourself, if the criterion that *you shall love your neighbor as yourself* (Mk 12:31) is to make sense. For if you love yourself in the wrong way you are doing yourself no good, and then, if you love your neighbor as yourself, you are not doing him much good either, are you?

But how is it possible to love yourself in the wrong way? Scripture, which flatters no one, gives us a hint. It proves that you do not truly love yourself—indeed, that you even hate yourself—by pointing out, *Whoever loves iniquity hates his own soul* (Ps 10:6(11:5)). So, if you love iniquity, can you pretend to love yourself? You are mistaken.

---

2. For example, in 1 Cor 13.

And, if you love your neighbor in the same fashion, you will lead him or her into sin, and your friendship will entrap your friend. *Charity from a pure heart* is therefore charity exercised according to the will of God, from *a good conscience, and unfeigned faith* (1 Tm 1:5).

Charity thus defined by the apostle comprises two commandments: love of God and love of neighbor. You need look for nothing else in scripture, and let no one lay upon you any other command. Wherever there is any obscure passage in scripture, charity is concealed in it, and wherever the sense is plain, charity is proclaimed. If it were nowhere plain to see, it would not nourish you; if it were nowhere concealed, it would not exercise you. This same charity cries out from a pure heart in the words of the psalm and from hearts like his who prays here. And who this is, I can tell you in a word: it is Christ.

The whole Christ speaks in this psalm

3. But you will hear some words which cannot fittingly be attributed to our Lord Jesus Christ, and so anyone who lacks understanding will think I spoke rashly in identifying the "I" in the psalm as Christ. How can the speaker be Christ? He is the spotless lamb[3] in whom alone no sin was found, who alone could say with perfect truth, *Now the prince of this world is coming, and he will find nothing in me* (Jn 14:30), for he was blameless and entirely free from guilt. He alone made restitution, though he had committed no robbery.[4] He, the only-begotten Son of God who took flesh, not diminishing himself by his incarnation but ennobling us, he alone poured out innocent blood. How, then, could these words of the psalm be correctly understood as spoken by him: *Set a guard over my mouth, O Lord, and a door to restrain my lips, that my heart may not turn aside into dishonest words, to seek excuses in its sins* (verses 3–4)? The meaning is perfectly clear: Guard my mouth, O Lord, with a gate, and with the strong door of your commandment, so that my heart may not turn away to wicked words. What kind of wicked words? Those by which excuses are sought for sins. I pray, says the psalmist, that I may never choose to defend my sins instead of accusing myself of them. Such words obviously have no relevance at all to our Lord Jesus Christ himself, for what sins did he commit, that he had a duty to confess rather than defend?

---

3. See 1 Pt 1:19.
4. See Ps 68:5(69:4).

No, these words are for us. "But Christ is speaking, isn't he?" Most certainly he is. "But if the words are ours, how can Christ be speaking?" If you ask that, I must ask you a question. Where is the charity of which I was speaking a moment ago? Do you not understand that it is charity that makes us one in Christ? Charity cries out to Christ from our hearts, and charity cries out from Christ on our behalf. How does charity cry out from our hearts to Christ? *It shall come to pass that whoever calls on the name of the Lord will be saved* (Jl 2:32; Acts 2:21; Rom 10:13). And how does charity cry out from Christ on our behalf? *Saul, Saul, why are you persecuting me?* (Acts 9:4) The apostle tells us, *You are Christ's body, and his members* (1 Cor 12:27). If then he is the head and we are the members, one single individual is speaking. Whether the head speaks or the members speak, the one Christ speaks. Moreover it is perfectly proper for the head to speak on behalf of the members; this is something we are accustomed to. Consider first how it is the head, and only the head, that is able to speak for the limbs. Think of how this happens in your own experience, how the head speaks up for the rest of you. If you are in a crowded place and someone treads on your toes, your head protests, "You're treading on me!" No one touched your head, but the organic unity of the body speaks. Your tongue, which resides in your head, has spoken in the name of all your members. It discharges the duty of speech on behalf of them all.

This is how we should hear Christ speaking. Yet each one of us should at the same time hear his or her own voice, since we are all organically parts of Christ's body. Sometimes he will speak words that none of us can recognize as our own, for they belong only to the head, but even then Christ does not divorce himself from our words and withdraw into his own, nor does he go so far away as not to return from his own words to ours. Of him and of the Church it was prophesied, *They will be two in one flesh* (Gn 2:24); and Christ himself, speaking about the same mystery in the gospel, reasserted, *So they are two no longer, but one flesh* (Mt 19:6).

These things are not new to you, for you are always hearing them from us. But it is necessary that they be recalled from time to time, partly because the scriptures on which we preach are so closely connected among themselves that many truths recur in many different passages, and partly also because it is profitable for you to hear these things again. Preoccupation with worldly matters can cause thorns to spring up and choke the seed.⁵ You need therefore to be reminded by the Lord fairly often of things which the world tries to make you forget.

Verses 1–3. Christ's evening sacrifice on the cross; he speaks in our name

4. *I have cried to you, O Lord; hear me.* We can all say this. Yet, if I say it, it is not I but the whole Christ. He says it primarily in the name of his body, just as when he was on earth he prayed in the name of his body to the Father. While he was praying drops of blood were forced from all over his body; this is what the gospel says: *Jesus prayed vehemently, and he sweated blood* (Lk 22:44). What was the meaning of this bleeding from his whole body if not that the whole Church would bleed in the suffering of the martyrs?

I have cried to you, O Lord; hear me. Listen to the voice of my entreaty whenever I cry to you. You thought, perhaps, that the business of crying out to him was finished when you had said, *I have cried to you.* Yes, you have cried to him, but do not be complacent. The need to cry to him is past only if the tribulation is past. But if tribulation remains the lot of the Church, Christ's body, until the end of the world, it must say not only, *I have cried to you; hear me,* but also, *Listen to the voice of my entreaty whenever I cry to you.*

5. *Let my prayer rise like incense before you, and the raising of my hands be an evening sacrifice.* Every Christian knows that this verse is customarily understood of Christ the head, for as the day drew on toward evening the Lord laid down his life on the cross in order to take it up again.⁶ It was not snatched from him against his will. All the same, we too were prefigured there, for what was it that hung on the cross? The body Christ had taken from us. Moreover, how could it ever happen that God the Father should forsake and abandon his only Son, who most certainly is one God with him? Yet when he fastened our weak nature to the cross, *our old humanity was nailed to the cross with him* (Rom 6:6), as the apostle teaches, and he cried out in the voice of that old humanity of ours, *O God, my God, why have you forsaken me?* (Ps 21:2(22:1)) The evening sacrifice is the Lord's passion, the Lord's cross, the offering of the saving victim in a holocaust acceptable to God. Through his resurrection his evening sacrifice was transformed into a morning oblation. Because of him,

---

5. See Mk 4:18–19 and parallels.
6. See Jn 10:17.

every prayer purely directed from the heart of a believer rises like incense, as from a holy altar. Nothing is more delightful than this fragrance of the Lord. May all who believe send forth the same fragrance.

6. *Our old humanity was nailed to the cross with him*, the apostle teaches, and he goes on to say why: *so that our sinful self may be nullified, and we may be slaves of sin no longer* (Rom 6:6). Similarly in that earlier psalm, after crying, *O God, my God, why have you forsaken me?* the speaker immediately added, *The tale of my sins leaves me far from salvation* (Ps 21:2(22:1)).[7] If you think only of the head, what sins could these be? Yet the head himself testified on the cross that it is indeed his voice we hear in the psalm for he spoke these very words, he recited this verse.[8] No room is left for human guesswork, nor is denial of the attribution of the verse to Christ possible for anyone who claims to be Christian. What I read in the psalm I hear spoken by Christ. Furthermore, in the same psalm I recognize actions of which I read also in the gospel: *They dug holes in my hands and my feet, and numbered all my bones. These same people looked on and watched me, they shared out my garments among them, and cast lots for my tunic.* (Ps 21:17–19(22:16–18)) All these things were prophesied, and they happened just as foretold. As we heard of them, so did we see them.[9]

We can say, then, that our Lord Jesus represented us, in the charity of his body, and that although he was personally without sin, he spoke in the name of his body of *the tale of my sins*. But if this is so, can anyone among his members pretend to have no sin? Only someone who is so bold as to flaunt himself and claim a spurious holiness and accuse Christ of falsehood. Confess, then, you who are a member of Christ, that your head spoke there for you.

In the next words he has shown us how we may make this confession and do it effectively and avoid the temptation of trying to justify ourselves in the sight of God, who alone is just and justifies the godless.[10] Still speaking with the voice of his body, he continues, *Set a guard over my mouth, O Lord, and a door to restrain my lips.* He does not say "a barrier to keep them closed" but *a door*. A door

---

7. Augustine accepted this sense in Exposition 2 of Psalm 21, though in Exposition 1 he had preferred the sense resulting from an alternative punctuation: *Why have you forsaken me, and left me far from my salvation?*
8. See Mk 15:34.
9. See Ps 47:9 (48:8).
10. See Rom 4:5.

can be both opened and closed, so, if there is a door at our lips, let it be opened and closed: opened to confess our sins and closed to any excuses for them. Then the door will be a restraint for us, not our ruin.

Verse 4. Do not consort with the self-styled elect, and do not make excuses for your sins

7. How will the restraining door be useful to us? What is Christ praying for in the person of his body? *Turn not my heart aside to dishonest words*, he says. But what is *my heart*? The heart of my Church, which is the very heart of my body. Call to mind other texts of scripture where this rule of identification is established for us: *Saul, Saul, why are you persecuting me?* (Acts 9:4) he asked, though no one had touched him. And again, *I was hungry, and you fed me; I was thirsty, and you gave me a drink*, and the rest. And the just will ask him, *When did we see you hungry or thirsty?* He will answer, *When you did that for even the least of those who are mine, you did it for me.* (Mt 25:35.37.40) These truths should not be unfamiliar to Christians, especially not to those who have taken them to heart as a norm for understanding other passages as well. Such discerning Christians will either not be disconcerted by similar texts or at any rate will be quickly reassured.

Well then, as in the gospel passage we found the just asking, "Lord, why did you say, *I was hungry, and you fed me? When did we see you hungry?*" and we heard what his reply will be: *When you did that for even the least of those who are mine, you did it for me*, so must we question Christ within us, where he graciously dwells in our inmost selves through faith.[11] It is not as though he were absent from us, and we had no one to ask. On the contrary, he promised, *Lo, I am with you throughout all days, even to the end of the ages* (Mt 28:20). Now we have already ascertained that his voice is to be heard in the psalm, for no one can possibly deny that the words, *Let the raising of my hands be an evening sacrifice*, are his. Accordingly you must say to him, "What of these words, Lord? *Set a guard over my mouth, O Lord, and a door to restrain my lips, that my heart may not turn aside into dishonest words, to seek excuses in its sins*? Why do you pray in these terms, Lord? What sins have you, for which you would need to seek excuses?" He will answer, "When one of my members

---

11. See Eph 3:17.

prays so, I pray so," just as he told us, *When you did that for even the least of those who are mine, you did it for me.*

8. But if your heart has not turned aside, you who are a member of Christ—if your heart has not turned aside *into dishonest words, to seek excuses in its sins with people who commit iniquity*—you *will have no part with the elect among them*. That is how the psalm continues: *And I will have no part with the elect among them.* Who are their so-called elect? People who seek to justify themselves. Who are their elect? Those who regard themselves as righteous and condemn others, like the Pharisee in the temple who said, *O God, I thank you that I am not like other people* (Lk 18:11). Who are their elect? One such was he who thought, *If this man were a prophet, he would know who this woman is, who has approached his feet* (Lk 7:39). Do you not hear the voice of another Pharisee, the one who had invited the Lord to his table? When a sinful woman from the city came in and approached the Lord's feet, that was the host's reaction. She was unchaste, and she had been forward and brazen about fornication, but she was more brazen still in seeking salvation, and so she burst into a stranger's house. Yet the guest who was there at table was no stranger. She was no gatecrasher pursuing some ordinary guest but a servant following her Lord. She drew near to his feet because she was longing to follow in his footsteps; she bathed them in her tears and wiped them with her hair. Who are Christ's feet? The people through whose ministry he has traversed the whole world. *How beautiful are the feet of those who announce peace, who announce good news!* (Is 52:7; Rom 10:15) How many people there are who have given hospitality to the Lord's feet! By giving hospitality to a just person inasmuch as he or she was just, they received a just person's reward, and by giving hospitality to a prophet inasmuch as he was a prophet, they received a prophet's reward;[12] for the Lord promised, *Anyone who gives a cup of cold water to one of my little ones simply because he is a disciple, I tell you, he will not miss his reward* (Mt 10:42). But when someone has shown this kindness in welcoming the Lord's feet, what has he spent on hospitality? Only superfluities that he had in his house. I am sure this is implied by the woman's action in drying the Lord's feet with her hair, for hair is superfluous to the body. Your superfluous goods become vitally necessary to you if they are the means whereby you follow obediently in the footsteps of the Lord.

---

12. See Mt 10:41.

The woman in the gospel story sought to be healed, for she knew she was gravely wounded. Hers was a great wound, but he was no slight physician, was he? The Pharisees, however, shrank from being touched by unclean persons and shunned all physical contact with sinners. If any unavoidable contact occurred, they washed afterwards. They were for ever dipping and sprinkling not only themselves but also their vessels, beds, cups and dishes, as the Lord remarks in the gospel.[13] If the woman had approached the Pharisee's feet, he, knowing her, would have pushed her away, fearing that his holiness might be smirched. His supposed holiness resided only in his body, not in his heart, and, because he had no holiness in his heart, what he had in his body was meaningless. He would have repulsed the woman, and when the Lord did not do so the Pharisee thought it must be because he did not know who she was. He therefore said to himself, *If this man were a prophet, he would know who this woman is, who has approached his feet* (Lk 7:39). He did not say, "If he were a prophet, he would have pushed her away"; he only said, *If he were a prophet he would know who she is*, as though the inevitable consequence of knowing would have been to repulse her; and so he took the fact that the Lord did not do so as clear proof that he was ignorant of her character.

But while the Lord's eyes were fixed on the woman his ears were alert to the Pharisee's heart and, as soon as he had heard the man's thoughts, he propounded a parable, one that you know well: *There was a certain creditor to whom two people were in debt. One owed him five hundred denarii, the other fifty. Since neither had the means to pay, he let them both off. I ask you, then, which of them will love him more? He replied, I suppose, sir, the one to whom he remitted the larger debt*—for he was cornered, you see, and forced to pronounce judgment against himself. *Then, turning to the woman, Jesus said to Simon, You see this woman? I entered your house, and you gave me no kiss, but she has not ceased to kiss my feet; you offered me no water for my feet, but she has washed my feet with her tears. You gave me no oil, but she has anointed my feet with ointment. Therefore, I tell you, many sins have been forgiven her, because she has loved so much.* (Lk 7:41–47) How did she show her love? By confessing and weeping, by not letting her heart turn aside into dishonest words in order to seek excuses in her sins, and by not making common cause with their so-called elect by defending herself.

---

13. See Mt 23:25; Mk 7:3-4.

Do not blame God or the stars or fate for your sins

9. If this woman's heart had turned aside into dishonest words, she would not have needed to look far to find excuses. Do we not hear excuses every day from women who are her peers in disgraceful conduct but not her peers in confession: from prostitutes, adulterers, and all kinds of dissolute women? If they have sinned in secret, they deny it; if they have been caught and convicted or sinned in public, they defend their deeds. And how glibly, how quickly, they present their defense! Yet how dangerous their excuses are, how trite from daily repetition, and how sacrilegious! "If God hadn't made me do it, I wouldn't have done it, would I? God willed it, it was just my luck, it was my destiny."[14] Such a sinner never confesses, *I said, Lord, have mercy on me*, never comes to the physician's feet like the sinful woman in the gospel, pleading, *Heal my soul, for I have sinned against you* (Ps 40:5(41:4)).

I ask you, brothers and sisters, what sort of people have recourse to a defense like this? Not only the uneducated but the learned too. They sit down and base their calculations on the stars; they study, describe, and guess the distances, the courses, the rapid whirling, the fixed states, and the motions of the celestial bodies. So far, so good: they are regarded as scholars and eminent men. But all this learned, pretentious discourse is used to defend sins. "You will be an adulterer because Venus will influence you in this way," or, "You will be a murderer because of the position of Mars." So it is Mars that will be the murderer, not you, and Venus that will be the adulterer, not you. Take care, then, that you are not condemned for the sins of Mars and Venus! God will condemn you, for he knows that it is you who commit these sins, you who have the effrontery to say to the judge who knows everything, "It was not my sin."[15]

Now, what about the astrologer[16] who sells you these fables to entrap you? (And notice that he sells them, so you do not even get your death free. You disdain to get life free from Christ, but you buy

---

14. In section 8 above Augustine considered self-righteous Pharisees as typical of persons who make excuses for their sins. In the present section it is those who blame God or fortune or fate, and then the astrologers who held the stars responsible for the misdeeds of human beings.
15. Similar thoughts on the folly of blaming the stars are expressed in the Exposition of Psalm 40,6, where Augustine is considering the verse of Psalm 40(41) which he has just quoted here.
16. *Mathematicus*. See the note on this term at Exposition 2 of Psalm 33,25.

death from an astrologer out of your own pocket.) Well now, if this astrologer catches his own wife in even slightly saucy behavior, or sees her looking impudently at other men, or notices that she is rather too often at the window, does he not seize her and beat her and enforce discipline in his own house? And suppose the woman protests, "Hit Venus, if you can, not me!" will he not retort, "You stupid woman! Can't you understand that I have to take one approach when I am dealing with my customers and quite another when I am ruling my household?"

Who, then, are *the elect among them*? They are the elect among bad people, the "chosen" among the godless, those with whom we must never throw in our lot, with whom we must not associate. But who are they? Can we identify them? Yes, they are people who consider themselves righteous and condemn others as sinners, like the Pharisee in the gospel. Or again, they are people whose sins are unmistakably shown up, or committed in public, who defend their actions and insist that no fault attaches to themselves. In order to escape blame they declare that it is all God's fault, either because he created human beings with such propensities or because he ordered the stars in a certain way or because he has simply neglected human affairs. These are the excuses proffered by the "elect" of this world.

A member of Christ, or the whole body of Christ, or Christ speaking in the name of his body, must make a different plea: *Turn not my heart aside into dishonest words, to seek excuses in its sins, with people who commit iniquity; I will have no part with the elect among them.*

The Manichean elect

10. There is another point here which we should not omit to notice, brothers and sisters. Among the Manichees there are certain people who are thought to be especially holy and to have reached the highest rung of holiness, and these are called the elect.[17] Those of you who

---

17. In sections 8 and 9 Augustine has considered in turn various groups who excuse their sins: the Pharisees, the notorious sinners who blame God or fortune or destiny, and the *mathematici* who hold that the stars are responsible. In sections 10–12 he attacks another group, the elect among the Manichees, who have a more complicated theory to exculpate themselves. The radically dualistic Manichean system postulated two warring kingdoms: the kingdom of light and the kingdom of darkness. The latter had attacked the kingdom of light and, though unable to defeat it, had captured certain particles of light from among its defenders. These light-particles were thereafter imprisoned

know about all this can recognize what I am referring to, and let those who do not know, listen.

All the saints are truly God's elect, as the scriptures tell us. But the Manichees have usurped the title and applied it to themselves, as though they alone had the right to be called elect in the proper sense. Now who are these self-styled elect? The people who, when you say to them, "You have sinned," at once come out with an impious defense, an excuse which is worse and more sacrilegious than all the others. "It is not I who have sinned," they say, "but the race of darkness." But what is this race of darkness? The horde that fought against God. "So when you sin, it is really the dark power that sins?" "Yes, the dark power, because I am mixed with it," they reply. But if God caused this mingling, what was he afraid of? They say, you see, that the realm of darkness rebelled against God before the world was made, and that God was fearful lest his domain be partially laid waste by a hostile incursion. To guard against this he dispatched certain portions of himself, his own substance, his very being—gold, if gold is what we are thinking about, or light, if light is what we consider, and anything else that exists—these things he sent and mixed into the bowels of the kingdom of darkness. And that, they say, was how God fashioned the world. As for ourselves, they continue, insofar as we are souls we belong to these members of God, but we are confined and oppressed by the bowels of the dark realm, and so, whenever we are accused of sinning, it is really the dark realm that sins.

---

in the universe, in stars, trees, plants, and the earth, and in men and women. Thus each human being was inhabited by two souls: a dark, evil soul that animated the body and a light-soul that was a particle of divinity, and moral life consisted in the effort to liberate the light-soul. The sun and moon were apparently vehicles for conveying elements of light, purified and released from their imprisonment in the world, back to the kingdom of light. Human beings were bound to avoid any actions which might increase the mastery of the powers of darkness over any elements of light still held prisoner, including the plucking and eating of fruit from trees. Augustine ridicules these beliefs in his *Confessions*; see especially III,10,18. The practical difficulties raised by these forms of asceticism were overcome by the division of the sect into the elect (considered in the present Exposition) and the hearers who, content with a lower grade of sanctity, performed the proscribed actions and provided food for the elect. Augustine was himself a Manichee for about nine years (see *Confessions*, Books IV and V), but probably never advanced beyond the rank of hearer. Sections 10–12 are the only passage in his *Expositions of the Psalms* which he devotes to the Manichees.

They think that by this theory they exonerate themselves from sin, but they do not exonerate their God from the charge of cowardice, nor the very substance of God from liability to corruption. For, if God is incorruptible, immutable, and invulnerable, and beyond all possibility of being contaminated or defiled, what could that hostile race ever do to him? Whatever kind of attack it had chosen to mount against him, how could it have intimidated one who was impenetrable, inviolable, immune to contamination, unchangeable, and incorruptible? And if God had really done what you say he did, it would have been cruel of him, because he would have put you into that state unnecessarily, since he himself was immune to all harm. Why did he send you there? The dark powers could not hurt him, but he hurt you seriously. That means that God was even more your enemy than was the race of darkness, although that has hurt you too. Moreover, if you could be oppressed, imprisoned, defiled, and corrupted, so too could God, for a morsel or tiny part of his nature in some sense brings the whole into disrepute. If the portion he sent into the dark realm is guilty, so is that which remained with him. But this is the Manichees' doctrine. They confess that there are two primal substances, the one and the other. Their books record this belief. If they deny it, a study of their books is enough to refute them.

11. What are we to think of all this? I do not mean to speak more fully about this basic premise of theirs; I do not intend to speak of the more shameful, more disgraceful implications of it. But notice how even in this introductory thesis, where they postulate a primordial war, they are themselves overcome in warfare. By asserting that the realm of darkness fought against God, they are captured by their own belligerent words. There is no answer that they can make, no loophole of escape for them. You attempt to excuse your sin, you impious fellow, you false "elect," by saying that, when you have done something wrong, you should not be thought to have done it. You look for someone whom you can blame for your sin, and you shift the blame onto the race of darkness.[18] But think about God: Are you

---

18. Compare *Confessions* V,10,18, where Augustine describes his having joined some Manichees in Rome and being half-persuaded by their teaching: "It still seemed to me that it is not we who sin but some other nature within us that is responsible. My pride was gratified at being exculpated by this theory: when I had done something wrong it was pleasant to avoid having to confess that I had done it, a confession that would have given you [God] a chance to heal this soul of mine that had sinned against you. On the contrary, I liked

not shifting the blame onto him? What if that realm of darkness you have invented were to challenge you like this: "Why accuse me? Did I have the power to harm your God, or didn't I? If I did, I am stronger than he. If I didn't, why was he afraid of me? And if he were not afraid, why did he send you here where you would suffer so much, if you were a member of him, made from his own substance? If he were not afraid, it must have been spite that motivated him; if he did not act out of fear, he acted from cruelty. How wicked he must be if, though nothing could hurt him, he caused his members to be so badly hurt here! If, on the other hand, he were in danger of being hurt, he couldn't be incorruptible."

You see, then, that if you try to defend yourself over your sin, you cannot praise God. You would not have experienced praising God as a captivity if you had not been so busy boasting in praise of yourself. Change course and censure yourself, and then you will praise God. Turn back to those words in a psalm that are so loathsome to you, and make them your own: *I said it myself, Lord, have mercy on me; heal my soul, for I have sinned against you* (Ps 40:5(41:4)). I have said it: it is I who have sinned, not bad luck or fate or the race of darkness. If you have sinned, look at the wide road that lies open before you, the road of praising God, that praise which you used to find cramping as long as you were trying to defend yourself. It is better for you to find your sins stifling and to find praising God an experience of broad freedom. Now that you have confessed your sin, see how God is to be praised, for he is both just when he punishes you in your obstinacy and merciful in freeing you when you confess. And so the psalm prays, *Turn not my heart aside into dishonest words, to seek excuses in its sins*, and to claim that the races of darkness did what I did myself.

12. *With people who commit iniquity.* Is any particular sort of iniquity meant here? Let us consider a detestable form of it prevalent

---

to excuse myself and lay the blame on some other force that was with me but was not myself…. It was a detestable wrong, almighty God, to prefer the lie that you were suffering defeat in me for my destruction to the truth that I was being mastered by you for my salvation. You had not yet set a guard over my mouth or a chaste gate at my lips to keep my heart from straying into evil talk, and from making excuses for itself in its sins as it consorted with evildoers; and so I continued to associate with their elect." In this passage the same constellation of ideas and allusions is found as in the present Exposition: the references to Psalm 40:5(41:4) (see section 9 above); the reference to verses 3–4 of the present Psalm 140(141); the shifting of blame; the Manichean elect.

among them. Listen to a vile Manichean iniquity, one they commit publicly and admit. They say that it is better for a person to be a moneylender than to be a farmer.[19] You ask why, and they state the reason, or what they call a reason: see whether madness would not be a more apt name. "Someone who lends money at interest," they say, "does not damage the cross of light." (Many people here will not understand this, but I will explain it.) "But," they continue, "a farmer seriously damages the cross of light." You ask what this cross of light is, and they tell you, "The members of God that were captured during the battle have been mingled into the whole of this world. They are trapped in trees, in plants, in fruits, and in other crops. Therefore anyone who breaks up the soil into furrows disturbs God's members. Anyone who plucks a plant from the earth disturbs God's members; anyone who picks fruit from a tree disturbs God's members."[20]

In order to avoid committing imaginary homicide in a field, the Manichee commits real homicide through usury! Moreover, he refuses to give bread to a beggar. Can there be any greater iniquity than this so-called righteousness? He refuses to give bread to a beggar, and, if you ask him why, he explains that the life in the bread is a member of God, a particle of the divine substance, and if the beggar eats it he will be binding it into flesh. So what about yourselves, you Manichees? Why do you eat? Are you not flesh too? "Ah," they say, "we have been purified by our faith in Mani. We, who are the elect, purge the life that is in the bread by our prayers and psalms and send it to the treasure-houses of heaven." So very elect are they that they do not need to be saved by God; rather they are saviors of God! And Christ himself, they hold, is crucified all over the world. I have accepted Christ, whom I find in the gospels, as my savior, but you, according to your books, are the saviors of Christ. It is quite plain, on the contrary, that you are blasphemers of Christ and therefore not on the way to being saved by him. You think that a beggar should not be given a mouthful in case a member of God that is present in the mouthful should be grieved, though the beggar is on the point of

---

19. A startling assertion, in view of the low opinion of usury common in Augustine's day. On the ancients' idea that usury was immoral, see the note at Exposition 3 of Psalm 36,6.
20. This passage is thought to be the only mention of the cross of light (*crux luminis*) in Augustine's extant works.

dying from hunger! The Manichee shows meaningless mercy to the mouthful while committing real homicide against a human being.

Who, in the end, are these elect among them? *Turn not my heart aside into dishonest words. I will have no part with the elect among them.*

Verse 5. Just correction is preferable to insincere flattery

13. *A just man will correct me with mercy, and will rebuke me.* Read this as coming from a sinner confessing his sin. He wants to be corrected and chastised mercifully rather than praised insincerely. If he is just and merciful, *a just man will correct me with mercy* when he sees me committing a sin. These are the authentic words of certain members of Christ, spoken about certain other members, and always within the one body. Our gracious Lord speaks in his own name as one who gives correction, but he does not disdain to speak also in the name of one who has received it, or needs it; for all the members of the body are in Christ, and speaking for them he can say, *A just man will correct me.* Who is the just one who will correct or chastise you? The head corrects all the members. *The just man will correct me with mercy, and will rebuke me.* He will rebuke me, but mercifully; he will rebuke me, but he does not hate me. Indeed, he will be the more zealous in correcting me because he does not hate me. The sinner surely finds that a reason for thanksgiving. Why? Because, as scripture reminds us, *Offer correction to a wise man, and he will love you for it* (Prv 9:8). Is it because he wants to hound you that a just man corrects you? By no means. If his correction were motivated by hatred, he would need correction himself. Why does he offer correction? Out of mercy. *He will correct me.* How? *With mercy.*

But let a sinner's oil never be nourishment for my head. What ever does that mean: *Let a sinner's oil never be nourishment for my head*? It means that my head will never be swollen by flattery. Flattery is hollow, insincere praise; and the duplicitous flattery offered by a sycophant is sinner's oil. When people have made a mockery of someone by disingenuous praise, they say, "I buttered him up!"[21] Be eager for the rebuke offered in mercy by a just person, but do not seek to be praised derisively by a sinner. Make sure you have the oil in your own keeping, and do not look for a sinner's oil. The wise maidens

---

21. Literally, "I anointed his head!"

in the gospel carried oil with them;[22] because their consciences bore them witness, they were said to take their own oil with them. Oil is a symbol of bright glory, for it shines and glistens on any surface, but the true glory, the glory that is worth having, must be stored within, safe in its own containers. Scripture suggests what these containers might be: *Let each of us examine our own work, and then it is only within ourselves that we will have credit, not in the eyes of others* (Gal 6:4). But if you are still unsure what the containers are, listen to the apostle: *Our boast is this: the witness of our own conscience* (2 Cor 1:12).[23]

Be your own just judge, and align yourself with God

14. One last point should be made on this matter of correction. You are within Christ's body, but you still carry the weight of your mortality. Be just toward yourself and just against yourself. You are a sinner, so punish yourself; go to the tribunal of your conscience, sentence yourself, and subject yourself to painful retribution. In so doing you are offering a sacrifice to God. *If you had wanted a sacrifice I would certainly have offered it*, declares a sinner, *but you take no pleasure in holocausts*. Does that mean that no sacrifice is acceptable to him? Far from it: *A sacrifice to God is a troubled spirit. A contrite and humbled heart God does not scorn.* (Ps 50:18–19(51:16–17)) Humble your heart, bruise your heart, make your heart feel the pain, and then you will be correcting yourself with mercy, for when you deal severely with yourself you are not hating yourself. In assuming the role of corrector you are just, even though in the role of one who needs correction you are still a sinner. Certain things in yourself

---

22. See Mt 25:4.
23. A.M. La Bonnardière notes that verse 5b of this psalm, *oleum peccatoris non impinguet caput meum*, was used by the Donatists as an excuse for keeping their distance from Catholics, whom they regarded as sinners. She finds it noteworthy, therefore, that Augustine does not mention the Donatists when dealing with the verse in the present Exposition but simply warns his hearers about the perils of flattery. This latter interpretation is in accord with Augustine's use of the parable in his early writings (e.g. *Confessions* X,37,62; Letter 27,6 to Paulinus of Nola and Letter 28,4(6) to Jerome, dated 394–395). La Bonnardière uses these facts as an argument for dating Augustine's Exposition of Psalm 140 to a period earlier than the major Donatist controversies. See A.M. La Bonnardière, "Les *Enarrationes in Psalmos* prêchées par saint Augustin à l'occasion de fêtes de martyrs" in *Recherches augustiniennes* 7 (1971) pp. 93–94.

displease you and their presence in you renders you unjust, but the displeasure they cause you proves that you are just. Do you want me to demonstrate how just you are? Well now, if what you find displeasing in yourself is displeasing to God also, you have already aligned yourself with the will of God. What you hate in yourself is not what he created but something that he hates. When you hate those things in yourself that are of your own making—things which he did not make, things hateful to him—you begin to treat yourself severely, but he will be merciful and spare you because you have not spared yourself. So from the moment when you take his point of view, find delight in his law, censure whatever in yourself his law censures, and find offensive those things in you that are offensive in God's sight, see how just you are! But since you are a fallen creature and have acted in a way that displeases God, since you lapse into bad deeds through weak, fragile human nature, since you are still carrying about with you the infirmity of your flesh, and since you are woefully aware of a certain struggle, you are to that extent unrighteous and a sinner.

Yet the inner struggle continues in this life

15. "But," you object, "how is it possible to be a good person under one aspect and a sinner under another? What are you talking about?" This is difficult, and we would seem to be contradicting ourselves, were it not that the authority of the apostle comes to our aid. Listen to his teaching and then you will not accuse me of misrepresentation. *I take great delight in God's law as far as my inner self is concerned* (Rom 7:22), he says. That means he is a just man. Is not anyone who is delighted with God's law just? How then can he also be a sinner? *I am aware of a different law in my members that opposes the law of my mind, and imprisons me under the law of sin* (Rom 7:23). I am still waging war against myself, he implies. I have not yet been fully restored to the likeness of him who fashioned me. The process of fashioning me anew has begun and, when I judge from the part of me where I have been reshaped, what is still misshapen is offensive to me. As long as I am in this condition, what can I hope for? *Who will deliver me from this death-ridden body, wretch that I am? Only the grace of God, through Jesus Christ our Lord.* (Rom 7:24–25) The grace of God which has already begun to fashion you anew, the grace of God which infuses such sweetness that you are already delighted with God's law in your inner self—this is what has already healed you in part, and it will heal the rest. But for the present, go

on groaning in your wounded condition, punish yourself, and find yourself less than pleasing.

16. *I do not deal blows like someone merely flailing at the air, but I chastise my body and bring it under control, lest while preaching to others I be disqualified myself* (1 Cor 9:26-27), says the apostle. If someone chastises his body, does that mean that he hates his body? Does a master who disciplines his slave hate his slave? Does someone who beats his child hate his child? But let us look at an even more intimate relationship: your flesh is like a wife to you. This is what the apostle tells us. *No one ever hated his own flesh; he nourishes it and takes good care of it, as Christ does of the Church* (Eph 5:29). This is the firm truth: your flesh is like your wife, and so no one hates his own flesh. Yet what does the apostle say elsewhere? *The flesh lusts against the spirit, and the spirit against the flesh* (Gal 5:17). Your flesh lusts against you like a wife opposing your wishes, so you must both love it and discipline it until undivided concord reigns, through the reformation of your whole self. But when will that be? You cry in distress, *Who will deliver me from this death-ridden body, wretch that I am?* (Rom 7:24) but you do not really think, do you, that you will get rid of your body and find peace that way? There is another scriptural passage to set alongside that one. What about the words, *We groan inwardly as we await our adoption as God's children, the redemption of our bodies* (Rom 8:23)? Your body will be re-created and will make its passage from mortality to immortality, and then it will no longer give trouble, because the mortality that resists you now will no longer exist. This is why you must discipline your body. Gain the mastery now over what you hope to receive back later; give it a hard time now so that it may be happy then.[24] It cannot be fully re-created in this life as long as you carry your mortal burden. Do not let it pull you down or throw off your restraint, but carry it, educate it, subject it to discipline, and it will be re-created in the end. Because *no one ever hated his own flesh*, even our flesh will rise again.[25] What will this risen body be like? Will I have to struggle even then? No,

---

24. Variant: "For the present it is enough if your body does not faint from weakness."
25. The thought here seems to move on from the Christian's restraint of his individual body to Christ's love for his body/bride the Church, the love that will raise it up at the end.

for *this corruptible body must put on incorruptibility, and this mortal body be clothed in immortality* (1 Cor 15:53).

A further warning against being deceived by flattery

17. When the psalm says, *He will correct me, and will rebuke me*, it means that whether the correction comes from your brother, or your nearest and dearest, or your neighbor, or yourself, you must be rebuked and corrected with mercy. But remember, *Let a sinner's oil never be nourishment for my head.* That's all very well, you say, but what am I to do? I have to put up with flatterers all the time; they never cease their hubbub. Anything about me that I would prefer not to have, they praise. Anything about me that to me is unimportant, they make much of. But anything I hold dear, they belittle. They are sycophants, liars, deceivers. They say, for instance, "Gaius Seius is a great man, a fine man, learned and wise, but why on earth is he a Christian?[26] His teaching, his writings, and his wisdom are outstanding." You might reply that, if he is a man of great wisdom, give him credit for wisely becoming a Christian. And, if he is learned, can you not believe he made a well-informed choice? But the point is that what you censure is estimable to the person you praise.

How are we to react? Praise such as theirs does not seem sweet to you, for it is a sinner's oil. "But the flatterer never stops!" Perhaps not, but do not let his oil nourish and fatten your head. This means that you should not take pleasure in their flattery or agree with what they say; do not consent, do not bask in it. Then, even if someone has brought you the oil of adulation, your head has remained untouched. It has not become inflated or swollen. If it became inflated, if you suffered from a swelled head, it would become too heavy and throw you off balance. *Let a sinner's oil never be nourishment for my head.*

Everyone needs forgiveness for some kind of sin

18. *Wait a little, and my prayer will be very popular among them.* At present they do censure me, says Christ, but wait a little. In the earliest days of the faith Christians were denounced as blameworthy by all. But wait a little. Soon *my prayer will be very popular among them.* The time will come when there will be thousands of people

---

26. This passage resembles a mention of Gaius Seius in Tertullian (*Apol.* 3). Compare Exposition of Psalm 39,26 and the note there, and Exposition 1 of Psalm 70,14 and the note there.

beating their breasts and saying, *Forgive us our trespasses, as we forgive those who trespass against us* (Mt 6:12). Even today, how few are left who are too ashamed to beat their breasts! Let these few find fault with us; we can bear with them. Let them find fault, hate us, accuse us, and defame us: *Wait a little, and my prayer will be very popular among them.* The time will come when they will eagerly have recourse to my prayer. At first they will arrogantly pretend to be righteous by their own efforts, but they will be worsted in the struggle, and then, because they reared up in their pride, they will be thrown down and dragged along by their sins. They will recognize their sinfulness, and the warnings of the prophets will be plainly verified. Sinners will begin to fear judgment. The keenest insight of their minds will be directed to their guilt, and they will seize with relief on the prayer, *Forgive us our trespasses, as we forgive those who trespass against us.*

So much for their long-winded defense of their iniquity! No one can deny that already crowds of people are saying this prayer, and the thunderous noise of nations beating their breasts never grows quiet. Those clouds have good cause to thunder, for they are God's habitation. What has become of that wordy bluster, that boastful claim, "I am righteous, I have done nothing wrong"? If you study the norm of righteousness set forth in the holy scriptures, you will find that you are a sinner, however advanced you may be. You have made progress, have you? You worship the one God? Splendid! You do not go a-whoring away from him after idols or astrologers or soothsayers or diviners or augurs or enchanters. All such pursuits are adultery against the Lord God, for you are now numbered among the members of Christ. All right, but take a look at the sins generally committed in the human family. You don't share them, do you? You do not kill anyone; you do not have adulterous relations with anyone else's wife or wrong your own wife by consorting with any other woman; you do not dishonor yourself by any kind of detestable corruption; you keep your hands from theft, your tongue from perjury, and your heart from coveting your neighbor's possessions. You are a righteous person, then. So far, so good.

But you haven't finished yet. Don't be proud too soon. Are you quite sure you commit no sins of the tongue—none at all? You never slip into any harsh word? "Oh, well," you say, "that is no great matter, is it?" No great matter? *If anyone says to his brother, You fool! he will be liable to hell fire* (Mt 5:22). All that pride of yours is beginning to quiver now, isn't it? Yes, it is true that a righteous person does not go to such extremes that God is obviously blasphemed by his impious conduct: he does not violently assail anyone so as to cause bodily harm, he does not treat anyone in a way he would not want to be treated himself. But what about the tongue? Does anyone succeed in controlling it?

You have now gained control of yours, you say? I wonder if anyone is able to do so perfectly, in every respect. Still, you think you have controlled your tongue. All right, but how do you manage with your thoughts? What do you do with the tumultuous rabble of rebellious desires? No, I am not saying you yield to them bodily; I am quite prepared to believe you do not, and in fact I can see you don't. But surely your thoughts sometimes throw you off course and bear you away, and often while you are kneeling in prayer? You prostrate yourself or bow your head, you confess your sins and you worship God. I can see your body lying there, but I wonder where the mind is flying. I see the limbs lying still, but is the attention standing still? Is it concentrated on him whom it is worshipping? Is it not more often torn away by thoughts like a stormy sea and tossed hither and thither by the blasts? If you were talking with me now and suddenly you turned away to talk to your slave instead, ignoring me, would I not think you had been rude to me? And this even though you were not a suppliant begging a favor from me but someone conversing with me as an equal. Yet this is how you behave to God every day!

What kind of person have I been describing, brothers and sisters? One who already worships the sole God, who confesses Christ, who knows the Father and the Son and the Holy Spirit to be one undivided God, who does not go a-whoring away from him or worship demons or seek help from the devil,[27] one who holds fast to the Catholic Church. Nobody complains of any dishonesty on his part; no weak neighbor groans under oppression from him. He makes no advances to any other man's wife but is content to enjoy his own—and even practices abstinence with her insofar as this is lawful, as the apostle's ruling allows, where both consent[28] or while they are not yet married. The person I have been describing has already attained this degree of righteous living, yet even he can be charged with the faults aforementioned.

---

27. Variant: "who seeks help only from the Lord."
28. See 1 Cor 7:5.

19. The time has now come when the prophecy is verified, *Wait a little, and my prayer will be very popular among them*. This could be referred either to the prayer Christ taught us or to the prayer he himself offers as he intercedes for us.[29] In all these daily sins that we commit, what hope have we? Only to say with humble hearts, not excusing our sins but confessing them, that petition of the Lord's prayer which is indeed popular and dearly loved among us, *Forgive us our trespasses, as we forgive those who trespass against us*, and to know that we have an advocate with the Father, Jesus Christ the just one, who is the propitiation for our sins.[30]

Verse 6. Christ's prayer, and Christ's words, have vanquished the wisdom of the ancients

Let the proud protest. They are refuted by our numbers and refuted by the mix of nations as the whole earth, from the sun's rising to its setting, praises the name of the Lord.[31] What power is left to the few who try to argue? They are like judges of the ungodly. What do they matter to you? Look at what the psalm says next: *Their judges have foundered beside the rock*. And remember, *The rock was Christ* (1 Cor 10:4). They *have foundered beside the rock*. The psalm uses the word *beside* to suggest a comparison with the rock, with Christ. Great men, powerful men, learned men: these were all reputed *their judges* because they pronounced on moral matters, handing down judicious opinions. "Aristotle said this." But stand him close to the rock and clearly he has foundered. Who is Aristotle? Let him rather choose to listen. "Christ said this," and Aristotle trembles in the underworld. "Pythagoras said this...Plato said that...." Stand them beside the rock, compare their authority with the authority of the gospel, compare those inflated talkers with Christ crucified. Let us say to them, "You wrote your treatises in the hearts[32] of the proud, but Christ has planted his cross in the hearts of kings. Furthermore, he died and rose again. You have stayed dead, and I do not wish to inquire about your prospects at the resurrection."

We can confidently assert, then, that *their judges have foundered beside the rock*. They seem to be saying something valuable only

---

29. See Rom 8:34; Heb 7:25.
30. See 1 Jn 2:1–2. .
31. See Ps 112(113):3
32. Variant: "on the foreheads."

until they are compared with the rock. If we find that one of them said something that Christ too said, we congratulate him, but we do not follow him. Someone protests, "But he was earlier than Christ." If somebody says something true, does that give him priority over truth itself? Think of Christ, you objector, not at the time when he came to you but when he created you. A sick man might as well say, "I took to my bed before the doctor had come to me." Of course he only came later, because you fell ill first.

20. Recall the psalm's prediction, *Wait a little, and my prayer will be very popular among them*. "But," someone might have said, "there will also be many to gainsay it." Indeed, but *their judges have foundered beside the rock*. Then what will happen? *They will hear my words, for my words have prevailed*. My words will prevail over theirs. They spoke learnedly, but I spoke the truth. It is one thing to commend an eloquent speaker but quite another to commend a truthful one. *They will hear my words, for my words have prevailed*. How can we say they have prevailed? Here is a proof: Is there any unbeliever who, on being caught out offering sacrifice in contravention of our laws, has not denied it? Has anyone among them been caught worshipping an idol and not cried out, "I didn't do it!" in terror of being convicted? The devil used to have[33] servants of that caliber. But in what sense have the words of the Lord prevailed? *See, I am sending you out like sheep among wolves. Do not be afraid of those who kill the body, but cannot kill the soul. Fear him rather who has the power to kill both soul and body in hell.* (Mt 10:16.28) He enjoined fear, but he added hope and enkindled charity. "Do not fear death," he told them. "Are you afraid to die? I will die first. Are you anxious lest even a hair of your head perish? I will rise up first, with my flesh intact." You have indeed heard his words, for his words have prevailed. The martyrs spoke and were killed; they fell, yet they stood firm.

What has resulted from the slaughter of so many martyrs? Christ's words have prevailed and, as the earth was irrigated by the blood of his witnesses, the rich crop of the Church sprang up.[34] *They will hear my words, for my words have prevailed*. How did they prevail? We have indicated this already: because they were spoken by witnesses who were not afraid. What were they not afraid of? Not of exile,

---

33. Variant: "The devil is welcome to have."
34. An echo of Tertullian's famous words, "The blood of Christians is a seed" (*Apol* 50).

not of loss of their property, not of death, not even of crucifixion. It was not just death that they faced without fear but the cross as well, a death more horrible than any other that could be imagined. The Lord accepted it so that his disciples might not only be unafraid of death itself but would shrink from no manner of death. This is why we can say that, because Christ's words are spoken by those who are not afraid, they have prevailed.

Verse 7. The death of martyrs and the fertility of the Church

21. *Like earthy dregs*[35] *spread on the ground, so have our bones been scattered around the grave.* The bones of the martyrs—that is, the bones of Christ's witnesses—were scattered around the grave because the martyrs were put to death. Those who killed them had, to all appearances, prevailed. They prevailed by persecuting so that Christ's words might prevail through preaching. What resulted from the death of his saints? *Like earthy dregs spread on the ground, so have our bones been scattered around the grave.* What does this mean: *Like earthy dregs spread on the ground*? We understand *earthy dregs* to mean any waste products, things that are regarded as rubbish but help to fertilize the earth. Another psalm tells us that the bodies of the saints lay around because there was no one to bury them.[36] But all those deaths acted like dung on the earth. As the ground receives rich nourishment from things people despise and throw away, so did the earth receive material which the world despised, so that the rich crop of the Church might spring up. You know, brothers and sisters, what this despised material is: I do not want to name it for reasons of taste, but the earth receives it as nutritious and becomes fertile and productive. What people think of as disgusting and dirty, what they dispose of, enriches the soil.

But what did our psalmist do? Let us return to his words. God raised up *the needy from the earth, and* exalted *the pauper from the dungheap, to give him a place among princes, with the princes of his people* (Ps 112(113):7–8). The pauper lay prostrate on the ground, spread-eagled, like fertilizing material, like Lazarus who lay covered with sores yet was transported to Abraham's embrace.[37] *Precious in*

---

35. *Crassitudo* ("thickness," "density," or any thickened substance). Augustine takes it as waste material.
36. See Ps 78(79):2–3.
37. See Lk 16:20–22.

the sight of the Lord is the death of his saints (Ps 115(116):15). Their death is ignominious in the world's eyes but precious to the farmer. He can see its potential value and the rich moisture it can generate; he knows what he should look for and select to make sure that a rich harvest will follow. The world has nothing but contempt for such deaths, but do you not remember that *it is the lowly and contemptible things of the world that God has chosen, even the nonentities, along with what matters, to bring to nothing things that are* (1 Cor 1:28; Rom 4:17)? Peter was lifted up from the dunghill, and so was Paul, and when they were slain the world scorned them. But now that the earth has been richly nourished by their deaths and the harvest of the Church is increasing, look at what is held noble and princely in the world. When the emperor comes to Rome, he hastens—where? To the imperial temple or to the memorial of the fisherman?[38] For *like earthy dregs spread on the ground, so have our bones been scattered around the grave.*

Verses 8–9. Christians under persecution prayed in fear

22. *To you, O Lord, my eyes are turned; in you have I hoped, do not take away my life.* Christians were subjected to great cruelty during the persecutions, and many apostatized. The psalmist has just said, in the name of those taken captive, *Like earthy dregs spread on the ground, so have our bones been scattered around the grave*; but now it occurs to him that many defected, and many were in danger of defecting. As though from the heart of these troubles under persecution a voice rises in prayer: *To you, O Lord, my eyes are turned.* I fix my gaze more firmly on your promises than on their threats. I know what you suffered for me and what you promised me, and so *to you, O Lord, my eyes are turned; in you have I hoped, do not take away my life.*

23. *Guard me from the snare they have laid for me.* What was their snare? It went like this: "If you consent, I will spare you." The bait they placed in the snare was this earthly life. If the bird is attracted by the bait, it falls into the snare; but if it is the kind of bird that can say, *I have never craved the human light of day, as you know* (Jr 17:16), its eyes will not stray from God, and he will pluck its feet clear of the snare.[39]

---

38. Compare Exposition of Psalm 86,8.
39. See Ps 24(25):15.

Guard me from the snare they have laid for me, and from the stumbling blocks set by those who sin. He has mentioned two perils, quite distinct from each other: the persecutors have laid a trap, and those who have yielded and apostatized have put stumbling-blocks in the way of others. The psalmist prays to be kept safe from both. On the one hand men rage and threaten, on the other, those who consent are falling. I am afraid lest the former make me afraid or the latter draw me to imitate them. "This is what I will do to you, if you do not consent," they say, so *guard me from the snare they have laid for me.* But look, your brother has already consented, so *guard me* also *from the stumbling blocks set by those who sin.*

Verse 10. Christ was alone in his passion, abandoned and denied by his disciples

24. *Sinners will fall into his nets.* Now what is this about, brothers and sisters: *Sinners will fall into his nets?* It does not mean all sinners; it is saying that those who sin by being so much in love with this present life that they give it precedence over eternal life will fall into the persecutor's snare. But what are you saying, psalmist? You cannot mean that people of that type are the only ones who fall into his snare? What about your own disciples, O Christ? What about that time when persecution grew hot and they all left you alone, each to take his own way?[40] It is true that you had foreseen and foretold that they would, but you did not make them run away by announcing it in advance, nor did you deny yourself through the voice of a disciple. All those who had been continuously your close companions abandoned you in your time of trial and persecution, when your enemies were hunting for you to crucify you. One of them was that daring man who had promised to stand by you even to death, though he proved to be a sick man who needed to hear from the physician what was going on in him. Like a delirious patient he had declared himself healthy, but Christ listened to his heartbeat. The time came for temptations, for the searching test, for accusations, and the disciple was interrogated not by some important person in authority but by an insignificant slave—and a woman at that! Interrogated by a slave-girl, he collapsed. He denied Christ three times. He denied him once, and then, when someone took notice of him again, he denied a second time. After two denials attention was drawn to him once more, and he denied

---

40. See Mk 14:50; Jn 16:32.

a third time. The Lord had foretold this, but he had not ordered it or coerced his disciple. If anyone tries to argue that Peter acted rightly because he fulfilled the Lord's prediction, we would have to conclude that Judas also did the right thing in betraying him, since the Lord had foretold this too. Far be it from us to say so, brothers and sisters; that sounds more like the voice of *the elect among them*, who defend their sins rather than confessing them.[41] We can interpret the episode better by concentrating on Peter himself. If what he did was no sin, why did he weep? Let us not ask questions of Peter but rather take Peter's tears as evidence; we shall find no more reliable witnesses concerning him than his tears. *He wept bitterly* (Lk 22:62), says the gospel. He was not yet ready for suffering. The Lord had promised him, *You will follow me later* (Jn 13:36). He would stand firm later, when the Lord's resurrection had confirmed him.

25. The time had not yet come for those bones to be scattered around the grave. Think how many people fell away. Even those who had been the first to hang on his words, even they failed. Why? *I am all alone, until my passover.* That is the next line in the psalm. He had prayed, *Guard me from the snare they have laid for me, and from the stumbling blocks set by those who sin.* Guard me against both, the snare and the scandals, those who terrify me and those who have lapsed.[42] But during the Lord's passion even his first followers, the men who were to be leaders of the Church and pillars of the earth, failed and fell. The prophecy spoken in another psalm had not yet been fulfilled: *I strengthened its pillars* (Ps 74:4(75:3)).

Why does he say, *I am all alone, until my passover*? He is speaking here in his own person as the head: *I am all alone, until my passover.* All alone, in what sense? In your passion, Lord, you will suffer alone; you alone will be killed by your enemies. *I am all alone, until my passover.* What does he mean by *until my passover*? An evangelist explains this: *When the hour had come, at which Jesus was to pass over from this world to the Father* (Jn 13:1). What else can *until my passover* signify if not his passage *from this world to the Father*? "Then it was that I strengthened the pillars, those pillars that were to

---

41. See sections 7–9 above.
42. *A lapsis.* The word probably awakened echoes for Augustine and his hearers. The problem of the *lapsi* who apostatized under persecution, and repented when it had ceased, had preoccupied Cyprian, bishop of Carthage, in the middle of the third century. The controversy had important consequences for the development of the Church's penitential discipline.

support the earth," he says, "because at my resurrection they learned beyond a doubt that death was not to be feared. So although *I am all alone, until my passover*, once I have made my passover I shall be solitary no longer but multiplied, because many people will imitate me, many will suffer for my name. Until my passover I am one, one alone, but when I have accomplished it many will form one person in me." *I am all alone, until my passover.*

I want to point out to you that there is something mysterious about the word used. The word *pasch* sounds like "suffering" in Greek, since the Greek for "to suffer" is πάσχειν. But in Hebrew the word *pasch* means "passing over," according to those who know the language. If you question Greeks carefully they will tell you that *pasch* is not a Greek word. It does sound rather like the Greek πάσχειν, "to suffer," but the verb is not conjugated like that, and the noun "suffering" is πάθος in Greek, not *pasch*. Those who know Hebrew and have translated for us what we should read have interpreted *pasch* as "passing over." Accordingly, as the Lord's passion drew near, the evangelist took care to use this apposite word: *When the hour had come, at which Jesus was to pass over from this world to the Father*; and this same *pasch* of the Lord is mentioned in the verse of our psalm: *I am all alone, until my passover*. After my *pasch* I shall no longer be all alone; once I have accomplished my passover I shall be solitary no more. Many others will imitate me, many will follow me. And if they do follow me later, what can I say? *I am all alone, until my passover.*

What then does the Lord mean in this psalm when he says, *I am all alone, until my passover*? What has our explanation clarified? If we have understood rightly, compare this with our Lord's own words in the gospel: *Truly, truly I tell you, unless the grain of wheat falls into the earth to die there, it will bear no fruit, but if it dies, it bears much fruit* (Jn 12:24–25). He said this on the same occasion when he promised, *When I am lifted up from the earth, I will draw all things to myself* (Jn 12:32). But *unless the grain of wheat falls into the earth to die there, it will bear no fruit, whereas if it dies, it bears much fruit*. This grain had the right to expect an abundant crop; but wait awhile, for it must be put to death first. Unless it falls into the soil and dies, it will remain alone.

Christ was alone until his passover because before him no one had died for confessing Christ

26. Clearly, then, Christ was alone until he was put to death. This had to be; and therefore not even Peter had the strength to stay with him. Peter would later be given the fortitude to follow Christ, but he could not go ahead of him.[43] Before Christ's death no one died for the sake of Christ: for the confession of his name, I mean, that name on account of which we are called Christians. You can't think of anyone, can you? It is true that many died as martyrs before Christ; many prophets suffered a similar fate. But they did not die because they had foretold Christ; they died because they had openly denounced people's sins and freely opposed the injustices prevalent in society. They are rightly regarded as martyrs, for, although they did not die for confessing Christ's name, they were slain in the cause of truth. But before the wheat-grain fell into the earth, before the death of him who said, *I am all alone, until my passover,* no one died for confessing the name of Christ. You can see how true this is by reflecting that not even John, killed so recently by a wicked king as a reward for a dancing girl,[44] was put to death for confessing Christ. He might well have been: there would have been no lack of people keen to kill him, for if he could be slain by one person for a different reason, how much more might he have been killed by those who were plotting to kill Christ? After all, John had been bearing witness to Christ. Some of those who heard Christ preaching wanted to kill him, yet they did not kill the man who was Christ's witness.

Why was that? Because, I think, if they had attacked John on account of Christ, John would not have denied him, for he was a man of extraordinary strength, which was why he was called the bridegroom's friend.[45] He was endowed with great grace and splendor of character, to which the Lord testified by saying, *There has never arisen a mother's son greater than John the Baptist* (Mt 11:11). The attack was therefore mounted not against John the Baptist but against Peter, who did not possess such fortitude. He was to receive it later,

---

43. Augustine returns several times to the dialogue in Mt 16:22–23, and Jesus' command to Peter, *Get behind me, Satan.* Peter was ordered to follow Christ, not precede him. Compare Exposition 1 of Psalm 34,8 and Expositions of Psalms 62,17 and 126,4.
44. See Mk 6:22–28.
45. See Jn 3:29.

but at the time of the Lord's passion he was still weak. So we see the man who lacked strength being interrogated about the name of Christ; but the one who has the strength does not suffer persecution for Christ's sake, because it would not be fitting that anyone suffer for the name of Christ before Christ himself. John freely bore witness to Christ, whom the Jews killed, yet John himself was not killed by the Jews but by Herod, whom he had warned, *It is not lawful for you to take your brother's wife* (Mk 6:18). (Herod's brother had not died without issue, you see.)[46] John died for the law of truth, for equity, and for justice, and therefore he was a saint and a martyr. But he did not die for that name after which we are called Christians. Why not? Because the prophecy was to be fulfilled, that *I am all alone, until my passover.*

---

46. See Dt 25:5; Mk 12:19.

Exposition of Psalm 141

A Sermon to the People[1]

Introduction; take care to ruminate on what you hear

1. Today's solemn festival of our martyrs demands devout celebration on your part and the ministry of preaching on ours. But you ought to remember, beloved, what a long discourse you heard yesterday. It is true that throughout that sermon you were as eager as though you had only just arrived, so hungry were your spiritual mouths; but all the same we must not make that an excuse for forgetting our weakness, both yours and mine. This is especially the case because we need to pay due honor to beautiful and noble words. As it is written, "The wise words of the Lord God are exceedingly noble."[2] These precious words are conveyed to you through little vessels like ourselves, but, even though the vessels are earthen, they contain heavenly bread. The apostle acknowledges: *We carry this treasure in earthen vessels, so that the sublime power may plainly belong to God* (2 Cor 4:7). He mentions *treasure*, but this means the same as bread; for if a treasure were not also like bread, scripture would not say elsewhere, *A desirable treasure lingers in the wise person's mouth, but the foolish gulps it down* (Prv 21:20, LXX). With this warning in mind we wish to give you some advice, beloved. After you have heard God's words and stored them in the stomach of your memory, bring them up again and turn them over in your thoughts, as though ruminating.[3] What else but this can the text just quoted suggest, *A desirable treasure lingers in the wise person's mouth, but the foolish gulps it down*? It briefly expresses the idea that a wise person ruminates but

---

1. This sermon, for a martyrs' festival, was preached on the day following the preceding Exposition; see the closing lines. Both were probably preached at Hippo during the years 397–407.
2. Apparently a biblical quotation, but unidentified. There are textual variants which perhaps indicate perplexity on the part of copyists. Augustine may have been referring to the general sense of such passages as Jer 15:16 or various statements in the Wisdom literature.
3. This gastronomic metaphor for meditating on scriptural words became very common in mediaeval writings.

a fool does not. If we put that more plainly, in our own terms, what does it mean? A wise person ponders on what he or she has heard, but a fool consigns it to oblivion.

For this reason, and no other, ruminating animals are classed as clean in the law, but those which do not ruminate as unclean,[4] although everything created by God is clean. To God, their maker, a pig is as clean as a lamb, for he created all things to be exceedingly good.[5] *Everything created by God is good* (1 Tm 4:4), says the apostle, and *to the pure all things are pure* (Tit 1:15).[6] According to their nature, therefore, both lamb and pig are clean, but for purposes of signification the lamb stands for what is clean and the pig for what is unclean. The lamb represents the innocence of wise rumination, but the pig represents the impurity of foolish forgetfulness.

A short psalm is appointed for today's solemnity; let us see whether we can discuss it with similar brevity.

Verse 2. The cry of the heart

2. *I cried to the Lord with my own voice.* It might have seemed sufficient to say, "I cried aloud to the Lord," without specifying, *with my own voice*;[7] but perhaps this precision was deliberate, for there are many people who cry to the Lord not with their real voices but only with the voice produced by their physical organs. A person of interior life, one in whom Christ has begun to dwell through faith,[8] must cry to the Lord with his own true voice, not with the noise of the lips but with the affection of the heart. God does not hear where humans hear. Your neighbor will not hear you unless you use your lungs and ribs and tongue to produce a noisy clamor, but your inner thoughts are your clamor in the Lord's hearing.

I cried to the Lord with my own voice; with my own voice I besought the Lord. The psalmist has clarified his statement, *I cried*, by repeating it in the form, *I besought*, for blasphemers too call upon the Lord. In the first line he mentioned a cry to the Lord, and in the second line he clarified the meaning of his cry. It is as though someone had demanded, "What sort of cry did you address to the Lord?" He

---

4. See Lv 11:1–8, and Exposition 3 of Psalm 36, with the note there.
5. See Gn 1:31.
6. Compare the Exposition of Psalm 125,6 and the *Answer to Faustus, a Manichean* VI.
7. Sufficient to say, *Voce clamavi*, without specifying, *voce mea*.
8. See Eph 3:17.

replies, *I besought the Lord.* My cry is a prayer, a prayer of supplication, not a cry of abuse or complaint or blasphemy.

Verse 3. Pray within your heart, with the door shut against the devil

3. *I will pour out my prayer before him.* What does *before him* suggest? It means in his sight, where he can see. But if we say, "Where he can see," do we imply that there is somewhere where he cannot? Well, it might seem so, but consider this: in all the multitude of bodily creatures, human beings can see, and animals can see, but God sees in places where humans do not. No man or woman sees what you are thinking, but God sees it. Take care, then, to pour out your prayer where no one sees except the one who rewards you, for our Lord Jesus Christ ordered you to pray in secret. You need to understand what he meant by *your private room* and ensure that it is clean, and there present your petitions to God. *When you pray,* he told us, *you must not be like the hypocrites who love to stand praying in synagogues and at street corners, to make sure of being seen. When you pray, go into your private room, shut your door, and pray to your God in secret, and he who sees in secret will give you your reward.* (Mt 6:5–6) If you hope for your recompense from other people, go ahead and pour out your petition before them, but, if God is to reward you, pour out your prayer before him. Shut the door, so that the tempter may not enter; he is for ever knocking and trying to burst in, but if he finds the door shut against him he will move on. The apostle knew that it lies with us to close the door (the door of our heart, of course, not some part of a building, for our private room is in our heart). And so, knowing this, he warned us, *Do not give the devil an opening* (Eph 4:27). If the devil does enter and take up residence, examine yourself: you must have closed the door negligently or neglected to close it at all.[9]

4. What does it mean "to close the door"? There are two leaves to this door: that of desire and that of fear. You crave for some earthly thing and the devil enters by that opening, or you are afraid of some earthly misfortune and he gains entry that way. Close both halves against the devil—the leaf of desire and the leaf of fear—and open them to Christ.

How are you to open these leaves to Christ? By desiring the kingdom of heaven and fearing the fire of hell. The devil enters through

---

9. A neat phrase: *Neglegenter clausisti aut claudere neglexisti.*

greed for worldly things; Christ enters through desire for eternal life. The devil enters through fear of temporal troubles; Christ enters through fear of eternal fire. Think how the martyrs shut their gate against the devil but opened it to Christ. This world promised them many a reward, but they laughed and shut the leaf of greedy desire against the devil. Then the world threatened them with wild beasts, fire, and the cross, but they were not afraid; they closed the leaf of fear and shut the devil out once more. Now let us see whether they opened both leaves to Christ. He said, *Whoever acknowledges me in the presence of men, I will acknowledge in the presence of my Father in heaven* (Mt 10:32), and they were in love with the kingdom of heaven, where Christ will acknowledge them as his. How will he do that? *Come, you who are blessed by my Father*, he will invite them. *Take possession of the kingdom prepared for you since the creation of the world* (Mt 25:34). He will acknowledge as his own those who are placed at his right hand. Now let us see whether they also opened the leaf of fear to Christ, after closing it against the devil. In one and the same passage in the gospel Christ ordered that it be shut against the devil and opened to himself. *Do not be afraid of those who kill the body, but cannot kill the soul* (Mt 10:28), he warned: the leaf of fear was to be slammed in the devil's face. Does that mean we should not fear anything? Far from it. After the entrance of fear has been closed to the devil, is it not to be opened to Christ? To be sure it is, for Christ immediately added a further admonition, as though saying, "You have shut it against him; now open it to me." *Fear him rather who has the power to kill both soul and body in hell* (Mt 10:28).[10]

Now that you have come to believe and have opened the door to Christ, shut it against the devil. Christ is within you, he has made his home there. Pour out your prayer before him. There is no need to shout, as though he were far away. The wisdom of God, which *reaches strongly from end to end, disposing all things sweetly* (Wis 8:1), is not distant. Pour out your prayer before him in that inner place within you, for that is where his ears are open to you. *Neither from the east, nor from the west, nor from the deserted mountains* does he hear you, *for the judge is God* (Ps 74:7–8(75:6–7)); but if he is your judge, consider carefully what kind of case you are presenting to him in your heart.

---

10. Quotations from Chapter 10 of Matthew, frequent in this Exposition, were characteristic of the liturgy on festivals of martyrs.

5. I will pour out my prayer before him; I will proclaim my distress in his presence. Notice the repetitions here, both in the two lines that preceded and in these two that follow. There are two sentences, and in each the same statement is made twice. The first is, *I cried to the Lord with my own voice; with my own voice I besought the Lord.* The second is, *I will pour out my prayer before him; I will proclaim my distress in his presence. Before him* corresponds to *in his presence*, and *I will pour out my prayer* matches *I will proclaim my distress.*[11]

Verse 4. When your spirit fails, the Spirit of God takes over

When do you articulate your distress, psalmist? Subjected to persecution, he replies, *When my spirit fails*[12] *within me.* So you are a martyr, suffering under persecution. Why does your spirit fail? "To make sure that I do not ascribe my strength to myself but realize that another is at work in me to create my strength." The Lord gave instructions to those whom he intended to make his martyrs: *When they deliver you up to the magistrates, do not wonder what you are to say, for it is not you who are speaking, but the Spirit of your Father who speaks in you* (Mt 10:19–20). Let your own spirit fail and let the Spirit of God speak. With good reason did he want to make them poor in spirit. *Blessed are the poor in spirit, for the kingdom of heaven is theirs* (Mt 5:3): those who are poor in their own spirit are rich with the Spirit of God.

Anyone who follows his own spirit is proud. Let him subdue his own spirit, so that he[13] may be open to receive the Spirit of God. He was trying to climb to the summit, but he must turn back and find his place in the valley. If he mounts to the summit the water will run down away from him, but if he has stationed himself in the valley he will be filled with it. In him will the prophecy be verified, *Rivers of living water shall flow from within him* (Jn 7:38). Then he can say, "*When my spirit fails within me* I proclaim my distress in your presence. I have been humbled and, as my own spirit fails, I confess to you, for I am filled with your Spirit."

---

11. Augustine frequently draws the attention of his hearers to this characteristic feature of Hebrew poetry, synonymous parallelism.
12. Variant: *has failed.*
13. Variant: "Subdue your own spirit, so that it..."

The Lord knows our paths

6. "Perhaps," he continues, "people will hear that my spirit has failed within me, and they will think there is no hope for me. Perhaps they will say to themselves, 'We have him now, we have worn down his resistance.' *But you know my paths.* They were thinking that I had been overthrown, but all the time you could see that I was still standing. They thought my feet were entangled, but it was their own feet that were tied and they fell, whereas we arose and stood erect,[14] for my eyes are always on the Lord, since he will pluck my feet clear of the snare.[15] Persevering, I have walked on, for *whoever perseveres to the end will be saved* (Mt 10:22). They thought they had pinned me down, but I went on walking. Where was I walking? In paths which they who believed me to be their prisoner could not see, in the paths of your justice, the paths of your commandments. *You know my paths.* The persecutor does not know them, for, if he did, he would not be hating me on their account but would be walking them with me."

What are these *paths*? They must be the "ways" of which another psalm says, *The Lord knows the way of the just, but the way of the ungodly will perish* (Ps 1:6). Observe that it does not say, "The Lord does not know the way of the godless," but, *He knows the way of the just, but the way of the ungodly will perish*, for anything the Lord does not know is bound to perish. In many passages of scripture we find this teaching, that for God to know something is for him to preserve it, and for God to know it is for him to guard it, but for God not to know it is for him to condemn it. If this is not the right meaning, how will it be possible for him to say at the end, *I never knew you* (Mt 7:23)? The wicked would be foolish to find in this an excuse for jubilation, telling themselves, "We won't be punished, the judge doesn't know us." They are punished already if the judge does not know them.

The ways that are said to be known to the Lord in that other psalm are here called *paths*, for our present psalm says to God, *You know my paths.* Every path is a way, but not every way is a path. Why are the "ways" mentioned elsewhere called *paths* here? Surely because they are narrow. The way of the godless is a broad one, but narrow is the way trodden by the just.[16]

---

14. See Ps 19:9(20:8).
15. See Ps 24(25):15.
16. See Mt 7:13–14.

7. This "way" is the same as "ways" in the plural, just as we can speak of the Church and the churches, or heaven and the heavens. Singular and plural can both be used. Because of the unity of the Church we speak of one Church: *One only is my dove, her mother's only child* (Sg 6:8).[17] But because of the many fraternal communities in a variety of places, the churches are many, and so the apostle could write, *Christ's churches in Judea rejoiced to hear that the man who was formerly persecuting us is now spreading the good news of the faith he earlier sought to stamp out; and they glorified the Lord for me* (Gal 1:22–24). In that passage he spoke of *churches*, but in another place he says *Church* in the singular: *Give no offence to Jews, or to Greeks, or to the Church of God* (1 Cor 10:32). Similarly we can speak of ways or the way, paths or the path. Why this differentiation, then, between paths and path? As we gave a reason a moment ago for speaking of churches and the Church, so must we give a reason here. God's paths are spoken of in the plural because there are many commandments. But these many commandments can be reduced to one, for the fullness of the law is charity.[18] These many ways, mapped out in many precepts, can be gathered into one and called a single way, because our way is charity.

Now let us test this assertion and see whether charity is truly the way. Let us listen to the apostle. *Now I will point out to you a supremely excellent way* (1 Cor 12:31), he says. What is this *supremely excellent way* you mean to propose to us, holy apostle? "Listen," he replies, "and I will tell you." *If I speak with human tongue or angel's tongue, but have no charity, I have become like a booming gong or a clashing cymbal. And if I have the gift of prophecy, and have cognizance of all mysteries and all knowledge; if I have such perfect faith that I can move mountains, but have no charity, I am nothing. If I distribute all my resources to feed the poor, and deliver my body to be burnt, yet have no charity, it profits me nothing.* (1 Cor 13:1–3) This is why he called charity the *supremely excellent way*. It is a magnificent way, brothers and sisters, and it works wonders. This is undoubtedly the

---

17. This verse from the Song of Songs, and the theme of the dove, recur frequently in Augustine's *Homilies on the Gospel of John* 5–6, and in the anti-Donatist treatise *Baptism* in connection with the unity of the Church. These works are thought to belong to the years 400–408, which may be a clue to the date of this Exposition of Psalm 141. The verse is not quoted elsewhere in the *Expositions*, except for Exposition of Psalm 67,17, where it is used differently.
18. See Rom 13:10.

way *par excellence*, for what is highest excels all others, and nothing is higher than the way of charity. But only humble people walk in it.

The psalmist refers to the precepts of charity when he speaks of his *paths. You know my paths*, he says. You know that whatever I suffer for you, I suffer for love; you know that charity in me endures all things; you know that even if I hand over my body to be burnt, I have charity, for, without it, such a sacrifice would be pointless.

8. But who truly knows the ways of any man or woman, my brothers and sisters, except the one to whom the psalmist says, *You know my paths*? Any actions a person performs are open to the scrutiny of others, but we cannot know for certain what goes on in people's hearts. How many critics are there who measure us by their own standards and, using that criterion, declare that what we seek in the Church are reputation, praise, and temporal advantages? How many allege that I speak to you only to win your admiration and acclaim, that this is my purpose when I address you? And how am I to prove to them that such is not my intention in speaking? The only thing left to me is to pray to God, *You know my paths*. How do these critics know what even you do not know? *I do not even judge myself, for it is the Lord who judges me* (1 Cor 4:3-4). Even Peter did not know himself but believed himself capable of great deeds. The physician assessed Peter's condition differently.

Let us then cry to the Lord devoutly and with pure intention what is only the simple truth: *You know my paths*. But do you want him to lead you through these same paths? Be gentle, be humble, do not be aggressive, do not be proud, do not be overbearing or headstrong *like a horse or a mule, devoid of understanding* (Ps 31(32):9). For if you are gentle and humble the Lord dwells in you, and he will lead you through his own paths. *He will guide the meek in judgment, he will teach his ways to the gentle* (Ps 24(25):9). You, Lord, *know my paths*.

Walking in Christ, the way

9. *In the way where I was walking they hid a snare for me*. The way in which I was walking is Christ. It is there, in Christ, that the persecutors hid their snare;[19] they persecute me because of Christ's

---

19. *Ibi illi absconderunt muscipulam qui persequuntur in Christo*. The meaning can vary according to punctuation. The CCL edition puts a comma after *muscipulam* but no comma after *persequuntur*. This leaves us with the awkward phrase, *qui persequuntur in Christo*. By supplying an object for the verb

name. There *they hid a snare for me*. Why this animosity toward me? Why do they persecute me? Because I am a Christian. If, then, they persecute me precisely because I am a Christian, I can say that *in the way where I was walking they hid a snare for me*. As far as they possibly can they have hidden it there, in the way where I have been walking. Their greed, their best efforts, their determination, were all directed to this: that there should be a trap laid to catch me in the very way where I was walking. But *the Lord knows the way of the just* (Ps 1:6), and *you know my paths*. That was what they tried to do, but you do not let them place their snare in yourself, for you are my way. The heretics want to set a stumbling-block for us in the name of Christ, but they are misled. What they think they are placing in the way they are really placing wide of the way, because they are wide of the way themselves. They cannot lay any snare in a place where they are not present. So the statement, *In the way where I was walking they hid a snare for me*, was made from their point of view; it expresses their desire, their intention, and their opinion of what they have done. In fact, though, a truer statement was made elsewhere: *They set their traps near the paths, to make me stumble* (Ps 139:6(140:5)). Our present psalm says *in the way* to indicate their wicked desire and purpose, but that other psalm says *near the paths* to indicate the true facts of the case. In reality they do not place their traps in the path; they do not set them in the way itself, for Christ is the way.[20] All they can do is to put them *near the paths*. Christ does not allow them to set snares in the way or we would have nowhere to walk, but he does let them put their snares near the way in order to deter us from straying from it.

A pagan who says to me, "You worship a crucified God!" thinks he is placing a stumbling-block for me right in the way. He insults the cross of Christ because he does not understand it. He thinks he is laying a snare in Christ, but all he is really doing is placing it near the way. I shall not depart from Christ, and so I shall not stray from

---

we could translate: "There they hid their snare, those who persecute [me] in Christ," and the order of words may support this. But in the light of what Augustine says in the rest of this section about setting a trap "in Christ" (that is, making Christ himself the stumbling-block), it seems preferable to omit the comma after *muscipulam* and put it after *persequuntur*. This gives the meaning adopted here.

20. See Jn 14:6. The preceding argument has been building up toward this identification.

the way or fall into the snare. Let him mock Christ crucified; for my part, I prefer to see Christ's cross on the foreheads of kings.[21] What the pagan ridicules is my salvation. Nothing is prouder than a sick man who scorns his means of healing. If the pagan did not mock it, he too would take his medicine and be healed. That cross is a sign of humility, but he in his overweening pride does not recognize the remedy that could cure the tumor in his soul.

But if I recognize it, I am walking in the way. So far am I from being ashamed of the cross that I carry it not in a hidden place but on my forehead. We receive various sacraments in different places: some, as you know, in our mouths,[22] some over our whole body.[23] But it is on our foreheads that we blush.[24] This is why he who said, *If anyone is ashamed of me in the presence of other people, I will be ashamed of him in the presence of my Father in heaven* (Lk 9:26; Mt 10:33), has in a sense placed that sign of ignominy which the pagans mock in the very place where we manifest our shame. When you hear someone denouncing a person who is thoroughly impudent, he says, "That fellow is shameless." What does it mean to say that a person is shameless?[25] That he is incapable of registering embarrassment. But neither do I want to blush, so let the cross of my Lord cover my brow.[26]

In the way where I was walking they hid a snare for me, or they tried their best to do so, though in fact they laid it near the way.[27] But I shall be safe if I do not depart from the way. Scripture warns us, *Do you not know that you are walking midway between traps?* (Sir 9:20) What does it mean by *midway between traps*? When you walk in Christ, the way, there are traps on every side: traps to your right,

---

21. Compare Exposition of Psalm 54,12.
22. A reference to the eucharist in the slightly veiled terms still customary.
23. Baptism was commonly administered by total immersion.
24. Compare Exposition 1 of Psalm 68,12 and the note there. The whole passage throws light on the present section.
25. Literally, "He has no forehead"; see the next note.
26. *Non habeam nudam frontem; tegat eam crux Domini mei.* The thought seems to circle around (1) the forehead (*frons*) as the place where a person's shame is obvious (as we might say, "He blushed to the roots of his hair."); (2) a person who "has no forehead," who is shameless or immune to embarrassment, whence our word "effrontery"; (3) a Christian who would be quite prone to embarrassment in other circumstances, but has his forehead covered by (4) the cross of Christ, considered shameful and ignominious by the pagans but regarded by Christians as their glory.
27. Variant: "they did not lay it near the way."

and traps to your left. The traps on your right are all kinds of worldly prosperity; those on your left are worldly misfortunes. So the traps on your right are promises, and those on your left are the things that frighten you. But you, for your part, walk through the middle of these traps and do not leave the way. Do not let their promises entice you or their terror beat you down. *In the way where I was walking they hid a snare for me.*

Verse 5. Christ, or the martyr, stands firm and does not flee

10. *I looked to the right, and I saw.* The speaker turned his gaze to the right and saw something, but anyone who looks to the left is blinded. What does it mean to turn your eyes to the right? It means to look toward the place where the blessed will stand, those to whom the Lord will say, *Come, you who are blessed by my Father, take possession of the kingdom* (Mt 25:34). Some others will be standing at his left, and to them he will say, *Depart from me into the eternal fire, which was prepared for the devil and his angels* (Mt 25:41). The psalmist found himself in a world all astir with anger and menacing persecutions, with people insulting him and terrors on every side. But he made light of present conditions and looked to the future; he focused his gaze on the place at the Lord's right hand where he himself would stand one day. He was there already in his thoughts. He directed his eyes thither and he saw, and therefore he endured all that happened to him. His persecutors did not see what he saw, and this is why the psalmist, after declaring, *I looked to the right, and I saw,* continues, *but there was no one who knew me.* You may endure all that comes your way, but who knows in which direction your eyes are turned? To the right or to the left? If you are enduring it all because you are looking for human commendation, you are turned toward the left, but if you are suffering for the sake of God's promises, you are turned toward the right. If you have turned toward the right, you will see; if you have turned toward the left, you will be struck blind. But even when you look to the right, there will be no one to recognize you, for who will console you except the Lord, to whom you say, *You know my paths*? And so the psalmist laments, *There was no one who knew me.*

11. *No chance of flight is open to me.* He speaks as though he is hemmed in when he says, *No chance of flight is open to me.* Let the persecutors mock him: "We have him now, he is captured, surrounded, defeated; all possibility of flight has gone from him." When a person

does not flee, he or she loses the chance of doing so. Those who do not flee are the ones who consent to suffer all that their strength can bear for the sake of Christ. That is to say, they do not run away spiritually, although it may be quite legitimate to flee in a bodily sense. The Lord granted this; he allowed for physical escape when he advised his apostles, *If they have persecuted you in one city, flee to another* (Mt 10:23). Well then, if someone does not run away spiritually, the possibility of flight is no longer open as far as he or she is concerned. There can of course be different reasons for this: a person may not flee because he or she is surrounded or captured, or from brave choice. Flight is denied both to a captive and to a brave person.

What kind of flight should we fear and avoid? What kind of flight should we pray to be delivered from? That flight of which the Lord spoke in the gospel when he said, *The good shepherd lays down his life for his sheep. But the hired man, who is not the shepherd, flees when he sees a wolf coming.* (Jn 10:11–12) Why does he flee at the sight of the predator? *Because he does not care about the sheep* (Jn 10:13). That sort of flight had certainly been ruled out by the psalmist, whether we take this voice in the psalm to be that of the head speaking in his own name, the voice of Christ the Lord who died for us all, or that of his members, our brothers and sisters, the martyrs, who also suffered for their brethren. Listen to John when he says: *He laid down his life for us, and so we too must lay down our lives for our brethren* (1 Jn 3:16). But when they lay down their lives it is Christ who does so. While his members are suffering persecution he cries out, *Why are you persecuting me?* (Acts 9:4)

No chance of flight is open to me, and there is no one to seek my life. Can it really be said that no one is seeking his life?[28] He sees people savagely intent on compassing his death, determined to shed his blood. How can he say that no one is seeking his life? We need to take "life"[29] in two senses. Just as we saw that the impossibility of flight could be understood in the case of either a captive or a brave person who chooses not to flee, so too we can think of a person's life[30] being sought by either persecutors or lovers. When the psalmist says, *There is no one to seek my soul,* he is referring to the former, to the

---

28. In the following sentences Augustine plays on the double meaning of *anima*: "life" or "soul."
29. *Animam.*
30. *Anima.*

persecutors. "They certainly seek my life," he says,[31] "but they are not looking for my soul. If they do look for my soul they will find it clinging to you, Lord;[32] and if they have the wit to seek it, they will also have the wit to imitate it."

But a person's soul or life can also be sought malevolently by persecutors, and to make this clear scripture says elsewhere, *Let them be confounded and filled with awe, who seek my soul* (Ps 39:15(40:14)).

Verses 6–7. The Church prays under persecution, but its real enemies are superhuman

12. *To you, O Lord, have I cried. I said, You are my hope.* When I was enduring persecution, when I was deeply distressed, *I said, You are my hope.* You are my hope here, and that is why I endure it all. But you are *my portion* not here but *in the land of the living.* God will give us our portion in the land of the living, but it is not something apart from himself. What will he give to one who loves him? What else but himself?

13. *Give heed to my prayer, for I am deeply humbled.* He has been humiliated by his persecutors,[33] but humbled in his confession.[34] He humbles himself where no eye can see, but he has been humiliated by his enemies in the sight of all. He is therefore raised up both visibly and invisibly. The martyrs have already been invisibly raised up, but they will be raised visibly when our perishable nature has been clothed with imperishability[35] at the resurrection of the dead. The only part of them which the persecutors were able to torture will then be fully restored. *Do not be afraid of those who kill the body, but cannot kill the soul* (Mt 10:28), the Lord bade us. What perishes? What do their enemies kill? Are they even allowed to destroy completely what they have killed? No, not even that. Listen to the Lord's promise: *Truly I tell you, not a hair of your head will perish* (Lk 21:18). Why be anxious about the rest of your body if not even a hair will be lost?

14. *Free me from those who persecute me.* From whom do you think he is praying to be delivered? From human persecutors? Are

---

31. Variant: "he is certainly referring to the former, to the persecutors. They seek my life."
32. See Ps 72(73):28.
33. Variant: "by sinners."
34. The verb *humiliare* can mean either to be humiliated by others or to humble oneself.
35. See 1 Cor 15:53.

human beings our enemies, then? No, we have other foes, invisible enemies who persecute us with other ends in view. A human persecutor aims to kill the body; a spiritual agent persecutes to ensnare the soul. He works through his instruments, as scripture says of him: *He is now at work through the children of unbelief* (Eph 2:2). Through these human instruments he incites persecution against people's bodies in order to bring about inner ruin in their hearts. If the soul stands firm when the body succumbs, the snare has been broken open, and we have escaped.[36]

Our real enemies are not our human persecutors but very different beings. We must pray to God to deliver us from them, lest they seduce us either by breaking us down through worldly calamities or by leading us into temptations. Who are these enemies? Let us see if we can find any clear description of them given by a servant of the Lord—indeed, by a veteran soldier who engaged them in battle. Yes, we can; listen to the apostle: *It is not against flesh and blood that you have to struggle.* Don't go turning your hatred against men and women, he implies. Don't regard them as your enemies or think that you will be broken by their attacks. Those men and women of whom you are afraid are only flesh and blood. *It is not against flesh and blood that you have to struggle.* His words are quite dismissive of mortal human nature. Against whom, then, must we fight? *Against principalities and powers and the rulers of this world of darkness* (Eph 6:12). You shook with fear, didn't you, when you heard him speak of *the rulers of this world*? If they are the rulers of this world, will you have to leave the world in order to be freed from them? No. You must not understand *world* and *the rulers of this world of darkness* to mean that they rule heaven and earth. Far from it. The whole fabric of heaven and earth was created by God. Heaven and earth can be called "the world," but wicked men and women can also be called "the world." Why are they called that? Because they love this world. And, because they are impious and wicked, they are darkness. From their ranks very many people have come to believe, and what does the apostle say to these? *You were darkness once, but now you are light in the Lord* (Eph 5:8). Cast your minds back. Before you became light, while you were still in darkness, who was your ruler? Whom do the wicked have as their ruler if not the devil, even as devout believers have Christ as theirs? This is why the apostle called the devil and his angels *rulers of this*

---

36. See Ps 123(124):7.

world, that is, rulers of those who love the world, rulers of sinners, who are darkness. These are our true enemies, and from these must we beg the Lord to deliver us.[37]

15. There is a text in scripture—in the gospel, to be precise—where we find a clear mention of "the world" in both senses: the world that God made and that other world which consists of this world's lovers, who are ruled by the devil. We must remember that God made men and women, but he did not make them lovers of the world. To love the world is sin, and God did not make sin. Well then, as I began to remark, there is a text which uses "world" in both senses. Listen to it: *He was there in the world.* Of whom was it said that *he was there in the world*? Of the wisdom of God, who is none other than Christ Jesus. A passage I recalled just now said of wisdom, *God's wisdom reaches strongly from end to end, disposing all things sweetly* (Wis 8:1). And again, *Wisdom pervades everything because she is so pure, and nothing defiled enters into her* (Wis 7:24–25). Thus the gospel could say, *He was there in the world, a world made by him, but the world did not know him* (Jn 1:10). There you heard about two worlds: *a world made by him* and a world that *did not know him*. It is not the world made through Jesus that is ruled by the principalities and powers of darkness but the world that did not know Jesus: that is, the lovers of the world, sinful, wicked, proud, unbelieving people. Why do I call sinners "the world"? Because they love the world, and by loving it they make it their home. In a similar way we can use the word "house" to mean either the building or the people who live in it. When we say that a house is good we generally mean that it is well designed and constructed, but we can also call it a good house because good people live their lives there. Conversely, we might say, "Beware of that house: it's dangerous," in either of two senses. We might mean that it is unsafe, because something might fall off it and crush you; or we might mean, "Beware of that bad house. You could fall into the hunters' traps; or you, poor wretch, could be taken advantage of by some rich villain; or you may be cheated somehow."

Now, just as we speak of "house" and "house," so does scripture speak of "world" and "world." But then why are the righteous not also called "the world," when they too dwell in it? Because, as the apostle says, *Though we live in the flesh, our fighting does not rely on the flesh, for our way of life is in heaven* (2 Cor 10:3; Ph 3:20). The

---

37. Compare a fuller development of these ideas in Exposition of Psalm 54,4.

just person lives here in the flesh, but in heart he or she is with God. Yet even the righteous deserve to be called "the world" if they hear the exhortation, "Lift up your hearts,"[38] to no purpose. But you who hear it and act on it must live on high, for *you are dead, and your life is hidden with Christ in God* (Col 3:3).

All those who look to find their life here, all whose love and longing stick fast in this world to be battered and entangled here, are rightly called dwellers in the world. And those who are dwellers in it are rightly called "the world," just as we can say "that house" when we mean the people who live there. And so scripture speaks of "the world" and "the world": *the world made by him* and the world that *did not know him*. You see the difference? On the one hand, you have the world that was made by the Lord, on the other, the world that did not know the Lord. You, for your part, must love the building and love the builder. But do not love to live in the building. Rather, live in him who built it.

16. *Free me from those who persecute me, for they have been strengthened against me.* Who says that *they have been strengthened against me*? Christ's body is crying out. This is the voice of the Church. The members of Christ are lamenting, "Sinners are becoming so very numerous!" *With iniquity increasing mightily, the love of many will grow cold* (Mt 24:12). *Free me from those who persecute me, for they have been strengthened against me.*

Verse 8. The prospect of ultimate freedom

17. *Lead my soul out of prison, that it may confess to your name.* The prison referred to here has been interpreted in various ways by earlier commentators. It is possibly the cave mentioned in the title of the psalm, which runs like this: *Understanding for David himself, when he was in the cave. A prayer.* In that case, cave and prison would be the same thing. We put two things before you for your consideration, but when we have understood one of them it serves for both.

What makes a prison is the status of those in it, and what they deserve, for one and the same residence can be a home for one person and a prison for another. When people hold others in close confinement, the jailers themselves cannot be said to be in prison, can they, if it is in their own house that they are holding them? Yet the house is a prison to those closely confined. So two men can be living under

---

38. See the note at Exposition of Psalm 10,3.

the same roof; for one it is a home because he is free there, but for the other a prison because of his servitude.

Some interpreters have taken the view that the cave or prison is a symbol of the present world. The Church would then be praying to be led forth from prison, that is, from this world, this world under the sun where all is vanity. As scripture says, *All things are vanity and delusion of spirit in a person's toil, all his labor under the sun* (Qoh 1:2–3; 6:9). God promises us that we shall one day find rest beyond our power to imagine in some place other than this world; and perhaps that prospect is what evokes the cry from our present place, *Lead my soul out of prison*. Our soul even now dwells in Christ by faith and hope. As I reminded you just now, *your life is hidden with Christ in God* (Col 3:3), but our body is still in the prison of this world. If the psalm had said, "Lead my body out of prison," we would be more confident in asserting that the prison is this world. But we could also understand that prison to be earthly desires that fetter us, against which we struggle and contend, for, as the apostle says, *I am aware of a different law in my members that opposes the law of my mind* (Rom 7:23). We have good reason to plead, "Lead my soul out of this world," if we mean out of the labors and afflictions of this world. It is not the flesh which you created, Lord, but the corruption of the flesh and the distress and temptations that result from it, that are my prison.

18. Some commentators have asserted that the prison (or the cave) is our body, so that the prayer, *Lead my soul out of prison*, is a prayer for the soul's release from the body. But this interpretation is rather lame. What kind of a prayer would that be, to ask, *Lead my soul out of prison*, if all it means is, "Lead my soul out of my body"? Do not the souls of robbers and criminals leave their bodies, only to go into more severe punishments than they have undergone here? If this is the right interpretation, would we be asking any great favor by praying, *Lead my soul out of prison*, if this is going to happen inevitably, sooner or later?

Perhaps, though, a righteous person might pray, "Let me die soon. Lead my soul out of this prison of the body." Perhaps. But, if he is in too much of a hurry, he lacks charity. Certainly he may desire death and long for it, as the apostle did when he said, *I long to die and to be with Christ, for that is much the best* (Ph 1:23). But what did charity have to say? *It is necessary for you that I remain in the flesh* (Ph 1:24). Let God lead us forth from our bodies at the time he chooses.

The body could be called our prison not because God made it a prison but because it is mortal and bears the marks of our punishment. We have to consider two aspects of it: God fashioned it, but we have deserved punishment. The whole form of the human body—its erect stance, its power to walk, the coordination of the limbs, the interplay of the senses, the faculties of sight, hearing, smell, taste, and touch—all this harmonious unity and beautifully designed differentiation of function could not have come about except as the work of God, who shaped all things, heavenly and earthly, highest and lowest, visible and invisible. What can there be in it, then, that represents punishment? The corruptibility of our flesh, its fragility and mortality, and its manifold needs. These features will not be there when the body finds its reward. I am not saying that when the body rises again it will no longer be a body. But certain characteristics will be absent. Which ones? Corruptibility, for this corruptible nature must be clothed with incorruptibility.[39]

You should remember, then, that, if the flesh seems a prison to you, it is not your body as such that is your prison but the corruptibility of your body. God made your body good because God himself is good; but, because he is a just judge, he introduced corruptibility into it. The former quality belongs to you as a mark of his kindness, the latter as a penalty you deserve. We could perhaps interpret the psalmist's prayer, *Lead my soul out of prison*, as a plea, "Lead my soul forth from corruption." If we take it that way there is no blasphemy involved; such an understanding is sound.

19. In the end, brothers and sisters, what *lead my soul out of prison* really means is, "Lead me out from my cramping, confining condition." Or so I think. To a person who is happy, even a prison seems spacious, whereas a sad person feels cramped even in a field. The psalmist is praying to be led forth from all that confines him. He already enjoys spacious freedom in hope, but the reality of his present condition seems narrow. Consider how cramped the apostle felt. *I had no peace of mind*, he said, *because I did not find my brother Titus* (2 Cor 2:13). And in another passage, *Is anyone weak, and I am not weak too? Is anyone tripped up, without my being afire with indignation?* (2 Cor 11:29) If he was weak and on fire, does it not prove that he was undergoing punishment and felt himself to be in prison? And again, he says elsewhere, *All that remains for me now is the crown of*

---

39. See 1 Cor 15:53.

righteousness which the Lord, as a just judge, will award me on that day (2 Tm 4:8). This amounts to the same thing as *Lead my soul out of prison, that it may confess to your name.*

But if it has been led forth from corruptibility, what has it to confess? There are no sins in that future state, but only praise. We must distinguish two senses of confession, however: confession of our sins and confession of praise to God. Confession of sins is widely understood—so well known to all, in fact, that whenever the word "confession" occurs in the readings, whether it refers to praise or to sins, fists fly toward breasts. Confession of sins is familiar to you, then, but let us inquire what confession as praise can mean. Where can we find out? You read in scripture, *This is how you must confess to him: All the Lord's works are exceedingly good* (Sir 39:15–16(20–21)). This is confession as praise. In another place the Lord himself says, *I confess to you, Father, Lord of heaven and earth.* What was he confessing? Certainly not sins. For Christ, to confess meant to praise. Listen to his praise of the Father, as he continues, *because you have hidden these matters from the wise and knowing, and have revealed them to little ones* (Mt 11:25).

Once freed from the narrow confinement of this corruptible state we shall dwell in God's house, and our whole life will be nothing but praise of God. We have often pointed out to you that when our present needs cease, all the business generated by those needs will become obsolete. We shall not have the trouble of attending to them any more. There will be nothing for us to do all day long—I will not say "day or night" because there will be no night there,[40] but one unending day—nothing to do except to praise him whom we love, whom then at last we shall see. Without having seen him now, we long for him and praise him. How shall we praise him then, when we see him whom we love? Praise will never end because love will never end. This will be our activity then, and so we pray now, *Lead my soul out of prison, that it may confess to your name.* Another psalm cries, *Blessed are they who dwell in your house; they will praise you for ever and ever* (Ps 83:5(84:4)). We are hampered now by our prison, for *the corruptible body weighs down the soul* (Wis 9:15). It is not the body as such that weighs down the soul, for we shall have a body in that future life, but *the corruptible body.* It is not the body itself, but

---

40. See Rv 21:25.

its corruptible condition, that makes our prison. *Lead my soul out of prison, that it may confess to your name.*

In the last line we hear the voice of the head, the voice of our Lord Jesus Christ. And it is the same voice that we heard in the last line of yesterday's psalm, which, if you remember, concluded with the words, *I am all alone, until my passover* (Ps 140(141):10).[41] And what is the last line of today's? *The just are waiting for me, until you give me my reward.*

---

41. The Exposition of Psalm 140 was preached on the day before this one, on the vigil of today's festival.

Exposition of Psalm 142

A Sermon to the People[1]

Verse 1. David, persecuted by his son, foreshadows Christ

1. In the measure that the Lord grants me I am going to speak to you, beloved, about the psalm we have just sung. Yesterday we dealt with a short psalm,[2] but since we had plenty of time we were able to speak on it at some length, brief though it was. Today's psalm is somewhat longer, so we must not linger over individual verses, or the Lord may not make it possible for us to treat of the whole.

2. The psalm's title is *For David himself, when his own son was hunting him down.* We know about these events from the Books of the Kingdoms.[3] Absalom[4] arose as an enemy to his father, stirring up not only civil war against him but domestic strife as well. Yet David was not cast down in any spirit of impious resentment. Humbled and reverent, he accepted his misfortunes as a discipline imposed by the Lord, endured the healing pain, refused to meet iniquity with corresponding iniquity, and prepared his heart to follow the will of the Lord. David behaved in a praiseworthy manner, but we must recognize in him another David, another strong-handed man (that is what the name means), our Lord Jesus Christ. Those events of long ago prefigured what was to happen later, and there is no need for us to spend much time reminding you about them; you have heard the stories many times and remember them well. Let us rather look for our Lord and savior Jesus Christ in this psalm. The psalm is a

---

1. Apparently preached at Carthage on 15 September, the day after the feast of Saint Cyprian. According to Perler, the most likely year is 416. But P.-M. Hombert prefers the year 412. In section 1 Augustine says that he preached on a short psalm the previous day; according to Hombert, this would have been Psalm 86. Thus the Expositions of Psalms 85, 86, and 142 would have been preached on 13, 14, and 15 September 412. See Pierre-Marie Hombert, *Nouvelles recherches de chronologie augustinienne* (Paris 2000).
2. Possibly Ps 86; see preceding note.
3. In our usage, 1–2 Sam and 1–2 Kgs. The events to which Augustine is referring are narrated in 2 Sam 15–18.
4. This name, as usual in the Expositions, is given as Abessalon.

prophecy, and in it he foretells himself. Through the medium of what happened long ago he proclaims what was to occur in our time. In the prophets he was proclaiming himself, for he is the Word of God, and everything they said was full of the Word of God. The prophets were full of Christ, and Christ it was whom they announced. They went ahead of him who was to come, but he did not desert his forerunners.

Let us try to understand how Christ too was persecuted by his own son. Yes, he did have children. He spoke of them when he declared, *The bridegroom's children cannot fast as long as the bridegroom is with them,* but when the bridegroom has left them, then his children will fast (Mt 9:15). From this we gather that the bridegroom's children were the apostles, and among them was a devil,[5] the persecutor, Judas. So Christ is going to preach to us in this psalm about his passion. Now let us listen to it.

Christ, the head of the body

3. We want you to focus your attention on a vital point, beloved. We are not teaching you something of which you are ignorant but reminding you of what you know already. Our Lord and savior Jesus Christ is the head of his body. He, the one mediator between God and humanity, the human Jesus,[6] was born of a virgin in a solitary place, as we learn from the Book of Revelation. I think this mention of solitude is a way of saying that he alone was born of a virgin. The woman bore him to rule his people with an iron rod.[7]

But this woman is the ancient city of God, of which a psalm sings, *Glorious things are spoken of you, city of God* (Ps 86:4(87:3)). This city originates from Abel, as the wicked city derives from Cain.[8] This city of God is therefore very ancient. Tolerating the earth, its hope is fixed on heaven. It is called both Jerusalem and Zion. A psalm says of him who was born in Zion yet is also Zion's founder, *Zion, my mother, a man will say.* Who is this man? *He who was made man in her; the Most High himself established her.* (Ps 86(87):5) He was indeed made man in Zion. As man he was made lowly, yet all the

---

5. See Jn 6:71.
6. See 1 Tm 2:5.
7. See Rv 12:5–6.
8. See Gn 4:17, and all the story in Gn 4. Compare Exposition of Psalm 86, which has affinities with the present Exposition; see note 1 above.

while he was the Most High who established the city in which he was himself made man.

This is why the woman who bore him is said to have been clothed with the sun,[9] the very sun of righteousness[10] unknown to the godless, who will lament at the end, *No doubt of it, we strayed from the path of truth. On us the light of righteousness did not shine, nor did the sun rise for us.* (Wis 5:6) Evidently there is a sun of righteousness that does not dawn upon the godless, though scripture also tells us that God makes his sun rise over good and evil alike.[11] This woman who was clothed with the sun was pregnant with a male child and about to give birth. Her child was he who had founded Zion, and the woman was the city of God, protected by the radiant light of him whom she was bearing in the flesh. With good reason, too, was she depicted with the moon under her feet, because in her strength and holiness she trampled on the mortality of flesh which, moonlike, waxes and wanes.

Our Lord Jesus Christ is both head and body, and, having deigned to die for us, he has also willed to speak in us, for he has made us his members. Sometimes he speaks in the person of his members and at other times in his own person, as our head. He has some things to say without us, things which can come only from him, but without him we cannot say anything. The apostle desires *to fill up what is lacking to the sufferings of Christ in my own flesh* (Col 1:24). He speaks of *what is lacking* not to his own sufferings but *to the sufferings of Christ*, yet he prays that he may fill up this deficit not in the flesh of Christ but *in my own flesh*. He says that Christ is still suffering; but Christ cannot suffer in his own flesh, now glorified in heaven. Christ therefore suffers in my flesh, as it still struggles on earth. This is exactly what the apostle is telling us: Christ suffers in my flesh. *Now I live my own life no longer; it is Christ who lives in me* (Gal 2:20). If Christ himself were not truly suffering in his members, his faithful disciples, Saul could not possibly have been persecuting on earth the Christ who was enthroned in heaven. The former persecutor explains the matter clearly in another passage: *As your body is a unit and has many members, and yet all the members of the body, many though they be, are one body, so too is Christ* (1 Cor 12:12). Note that he

---

9. See Rv 12:1.
10. See Ml 4:2.
11. See Mt 5:45.

does not say, "That is how it is with Christ and his body," but, *So too is Christ*. He says, *The body is a unit and has many members; so too is Christ*. All of it is simply Christ, and because the whole is Christ, the head shouted from heaven, *Saul, Saul, why are you persecuting me?* (Acts 9:4).

Hold onto this truth and imprint it indelibly on your minds like well-educated members of the Church, soundly instructed in the Catholic faith. Then you will understand that the Christ who is both head and body is the same Christ who is the only-begotten Word of God, equal to the Father. And then too you will see how wondrous is the grace that has brought you so close to God that he who is one with his Father has willed to be one with us. How do we know he is one with the Father? Because he said, *I and the Father are one* (Jn 10:30). And how do we know he is one with us? Because *scripture does not say, To his descendants, as though indicating many, but as to one only, And to your seed, which is Christ* (Gal 3:16). Perhaps someone may raise an objection: "Well, yes, Christ is the descendant of Abraham. But that doesn't prove that we too are Abraham's offspring, does it?" Yes it does. Remember that Christ is Abraham's descendant, and, if we too are, that would mean that we are Christ. But we are Christ, for Paul has told us, *As the body is a unit and has many members; so too is Christ*, and he tells us elsewhere, *As many of you as have been baptized in Christ, have clothed yourselves in Christ* (Gal 3:27). Now we know for certain that Christ is from the stock of Abraham, for the apostle's plain words cannot be gainsaid: *And to your seed, which is Christ*. Look what he is telling us: *If you belong to Christ, you are the descendants of Abraham* (Gal 3:29).

That *they shall be two in one flesh* (Gn 2:24) is deeply mysterious, and so the apostle tells us, *This is a great mystery, but I am referring it to Christ and the Church* (Eph 5:32). Christ and the Church, two in one flesh. The fact that they are *two* points to the distance between us and the majesty of God. They are two, undeniably, for we are not the Word, we were not with God in the beginning, not through us were all things made.[12] But when we consider the flesh, there we find Christ, and in Christ we find both him and ourselves. Small wonder that we find this mystery in the psalms. There he says many things in his own name as head and many others in the name of his members, yet all

---

12. See Jn 1:1–3.

of it is said as though one single individual were speaking. Wonder not that there are two with one voice, if there are two in one flesh.[13]

The enemies among our nearest and dearest

4. Now Judas was and is a "son of the bridegroom" who nonetheless persecutes the bridegroom.[14] It happened then, in Christ's time, but was that perhaps also a foreshadowing of future events? Surely it was, for the Church was destined to suffer many false brethren, so that even today the bridegroom's own son persecutes him and will do so until the end of time. *If an enemy had slandered me, I could have borne it; or if someone who hated me had talked arrogantly against me, I could surely have hidden from him* (Ps 54:13(55:12)). Who is the enemy? Who is the one who hates me? The person who sneers, "Who is this Christ? Christ was just a man who wanted to stay alive and couldn't. He died in the end, however hard he tried not to. He was an outcast, crucified and killed." This is what our enemies say. Such people are my open enemies, Christ is saying. They swear open hostility to me, and it is easy to put up with them or avoid them altogether. But what am I to do about Absalom? What am I to do about Judas? What about false brethren? What about my wicked children, who are yet my children? What about people who do not contradict us by blaspheming Christ but worship Christ along with us, yet persecute Christ in us? The psalm just quoted goes on to point it out: it would have been easy enough to endure someone who plainly hated me, and anyway I could have hidden from him. You hide from a pagan when you come into a church. But what if you find the foe you fear even here? What is the use of looking for a place where you can hide from him? The apostle, groaning amid false brethren, complained of *fighting without, and fears within* (2 Cor 7:5). And the psalm speaks similarly: *If someone who hated me had talked arrogantly against me, I could surely have hidden from him. But it was you, a like-minded person.* (Ps 54:13–14(55:12–13)) The psalmist called that covert enemy *a like-minded person* because he had seemed to be one with us in Christ. The Church has to contend with sufferings without and pain within, but it is forced to recognize that both those without and those

---

13. The foregoing paragraphs are a key to Augustine's understanding of the psalms.
14. The argument begun in section 2 is resumed here, after Augustine has established in section 3 the identification of Christ with the Church.

within are enemies. The ones outside can be avoided more easily; those within are much harder to bear.

5. So then let our Lord say, let everyone say this who together with us constitutes the whole Christ, *Hear my prayer, O Lord, let your ears be open to my petition.* The idea contained in *hear* is echoed in *let your ears be open*; the repetition reinforces the plea. *In your truth hear me, in your justice.* Be very careful how you interpret that phrase, *in your justice*, brothers and sisters, for it includes the idea of grace, to prevent any of us imagining that our justice is our own achievement. Any justice or righteousness you have belongs to God; God gave it to you so that it might be yours. Remember what the apostle said about people who wanted to boast of their own righteousness: *I bear this witness against them: they have zeal for God.* He means the Jews. *They have zeal for God*, he says, *but it is not informed by knowledge.* (Rom 10:2) What does he mean by *not informed by knowledge*? What kind of knowledge do you regard as valuable? Not, I hope, the knowledge which, on its own, merely puffs us up? That kind of knowledge does not build us up if it is not accompanied by charity.[15] No, not that, but the knowledge that is allied with charity, the teacher of humility. Let us see if that was what the Jews had. *They have zeal for God*, said Paul, *but it is not informed by knowledge.* Let him tell us what kind of knowledge it was that they lacked. *They failed to recognize the righteousness that comes from God and, by seeking to set up a righteousness of their own, they did not submit to God's righteousness* (Rom 10:3).

What kind of people are anxious to set up a righteousness of their own? Those who, when they have done well, ascribe it to themselves but, when they have done badly, impute it to God. They are thoroughly twisted. They will get themselves straightened out only if they turn their conviction on its head. You are twisted because you attribute the wrong you have done to God and the good to yourself. You will be straight if you ascribe your wrongdoing to yourself and any good you have done to God. You, who were once godless, would not be living justly unless you had been made just by him who justifies the godless.[16] And so the psalmist prays, *In your truth hear me, in your justice.* Not in any justice of mine; rather, *may I be found in him, not having any righteousness of my own, derived from the law, but that*

---

15. See 1 Cor 8:1.
16. See Rom 4:5.

which comes through faith (Phil 3:9). This is what the psalm means when it says, *In your justice, give me a hearing*, for, when I look at myself, I find nothing that is my own except sin.

Verse 2. In this life not one of us is just in God's sight

6. *Do not contend in judgment with your servant.* Who would ever want to go to law against God, except those who aspire to set up a justice of their own? *Why have we fasted and you did not notice, stinted our souls and you ignored it?* (Is 58:3) This is as good as saying, "We have done what you ordered. Why don't you give us the reward you promised?" God replies, "When you receive what I promised, it will be by my gift, just as I have already given you the means to deserve it."[17] It is undoubtedly to people as proud as these that a prophet addresses the Lord's question: *Why do you want to dispute your case at law with me? You have all abandoned me, says the Lord.* (Jer 2:29) What are you doing, planning to take me to court and enumerating your own just actions? List everything that might justify you, if you like; I know your misdeeds. How can I approve any righteousness in you, where all I find is pride that I must condemn?

Very different is the plea of our psalmist, a humble suppliant in the body of Christ, who has learned from the head, from him who is meek and humble of heart.[18] *Do not contend in judgment with your servant*, he prays. "Let us not go to law; I want no dispute with you, for, if I try to vindicate my justice, you convict me of iniquity. *Do not contend in judgment with your servant.*" Why does he say this? Why is he fearful? Because *no living person will be found righteous in your sight*. By *no living person* he obviously means no one living here, living in the flesh, living a life that must end in death: no one who is born human and lives a life derived from other humans and initially from Adam, no living person who is Adam over again. A person living this life may possibly be justified in his own eyes but not in yours. How could he be justified in his own estimation? He might find himself pleasing, but he would be displeasing to you, for *no living person will be found righteous in your sight*. Do not contend in judgment with your servant, then, O Lord, my God. However straight

---

17. *Ut accipias quod promisi, ego dabo; ut faceres quare acciperes, ego dedi.* A terse, compact statement of Augustine's doctrine of grace.
18. See Mt 11:29.

I think I am, you have only to draw out a ruler from your storehouse and measure me against it, and I am shown up as crooked.

Do not contend in judgment with your servant. The psalm significantly says, *with your servant*. It is beneath your dignity to conduct a lawsuit against your servant and even more against your friend. We are indeed your friends, for you would not have said, *I tell you, my friends* (Lk 12:4), if you had not yourself raised us from servants to friends.[19] Yet though you call me friend, I confess that I am your servant. I need your mercy, I return to you like a runaway slave, I am not worthy to be called your son.[20] *Do not contend in judgment with your servant, for no living person will be found righteous in your sight.* Scripture warns us, *Praise no one before his death* (Sir 11:30), no living person at all. But what about those rams of the flock, the apostles, of whose young lambs another psalm cries, *Bring to the Lord the offspring of rams* (Ps 28(29):1)? Paul was one of these rams, yet even he acknowledges his imperfection: *Not that I have gained it already, or am already perfect* (Phil 3:12). Furthermore, brothers and sisters, there is a clinching argument by which you can grasp the point quickly: the apostles themselves learned to pray as we pray. The rule to be followed in presenting petitions was given them by the heavenly expert in law: *Pray like this* (Mt 6:9), he said. After indicating the earlier phrases of the prayer, he gave them a specific instruction—yes, even them, our foremost rams, the leaders of the sheep, the principal members of the chief shepherd and gatherer of the one flock.[21] They were taught to say, *Forgive us our debts, as we forgive those who are in debt to us* (Mt 6:12). Not even the apostles presumed to pray, "Thanks be to you, who have forgiven us our debts, as we too forgive those who are in debt to us." No, they simply prayed, *Forgive us as we forgive*. And when they used these words in their prayer they were certainly believers already; indeed, they were already apostles. The Lord's prayer is prescribed principally for believers. If the reference were to sins forgiven in baptism, it would be more fitting for catechumens only to pray, *Forgive us our debts*. But no; the apostles needed to say it. They too had to pray, *Forgive us our debts, as we forgive those who are in debt to us*. And if anyone had asked them, "Why do you make that petition? What debts

---

19. Compare Jn 15:15.
20. See Lk 15:19,21.
21. Variant: "members of the chief shepherd, the gatherers of the one flock."

have you?" they would have replied, *No living person will be found righteous* in God's sight.

Verses 3–4. The downward pull, the upward call

7. *The enemy has persecuted my soul, and grounded my life on the earth.* Refer this to ourselves, certainly, but look also to the head who speaks on our behalf. *The enemy has persecuted my soul.* The devil quite obviously did persecute Christ's soul, as Judas too persecuted the soul of his master, and still today the devil is busy persecuting Christ's body, for one Judas has been succeeded by another. The prayer is still apposite today, for the Church can say, *The enemy has persecuted my soul, and grounded my life on the earth.* Notice that last phrase, *He has grounded my life on the earth.* In another passage the psalmist laments, *They bent my soul down* (Ps 56:7(57:6)), for, when anyone persecutes us, what else is he trying to do but persuade us to abandon our hope of heaven and savor only this earth, as we yield to our pursuer and love earthly things? That is undoubtedly their purpose, and they put their whole strength into achieving it. But, please God, it will not happen to us, for to us scripture says, *If you have risen with Christ, have a taste for what is above, where Christ is seated at the right hand of God. Seek the things that are above, not the things on earth; for you are dead.* (Col 3:1–3) No living person will be found righteous in God's sight. Our enemies strive by open savagery or by subterfuge to bend our life downward to the earth. Let us be on the watch against them, so that we may truly say, *Our way of life is in heaven* (Ph 3:20). But remember the psalm's warning: the enemy has tried to ground my life on the earth.

Christ, free among the dead

8. *They assigned me a place in dark regions, like the dead of this world.* You more readily hear the voice of the head in this verse and more readily understand its meaning in him. He indeed died for us, but he was not one of the *dead of this world.* Who are *the dead of this world*, and why can we say that he was not one of them? *The dead of this world* are those deservedly dead, who are receiving the due recompense for their iniquity. They have inherited death from the rootstock of sin, from the race that must confess, *Lo, I was conceived in iniquity, and in sins did my mother nourish me in the womb* (Ps 50:7(51:5)). But when Christ came he took flesh from a virgin, taking to himself not the iniquity inherent in our flesh but clean flesh with

power to cleanse ours. People who believed him to be a sinner naturally reckoned him to be one of *the dead of this world*. But in another psalm he declared, *I was paying the price, though I had committed no robbery* (Ps 68:5(69:4)), and in the gospel he claimed, *Now the prince of this world is coming*—the sovereign over death, the prompter to evil, the exactor of punishment—*now he is coming, and he will find nothing in me* (Jn 14:30). What did he mean by *he will find nothing in me*? He will find no guilt in me, nothing for which I ought to die. Yet, he continued, *So that the world may know that I am doing my Father's will, rise, let us leave here* (Jn 14:31). In dying, I am doing my Father's will. I do not deserve to die; I have done nothing to merit death. But I am going to meet death so that those who by their sins deserved to die may be freed through the death of one who is innocent.

They assigned me a place in dark regions, like the darkness of the underworld, the darkness of the tomb, the darkness of the passion itself. There they placed him *like the dead of this world*; there they left him who asserts, *I have become like a man bereft of help, free among the dead* (Ps 87:5–6(88:4–5)). Free? Why free? Because *whoever commits sin is the slave of sin* (Jn 8:34). Clearly he could not free others from their fetters if he were not free himself. Being free, he slew death, broke bonds, and captured captivity when they assigned him a place in dark regions, like *the dead of this world*.

We were there

9. *My spirit was dismayed within me*. Remember his cry, *My soul is sorrowful to the point of death* (Mk 14:34). Hearken to a single voice here. Is it not obvious that there[22] is movement between head and members, members and head? *My spirit was dismayed within me*, he says, and we cannot but be reminded of the words: *My soul is sorrowful to the point of death*. Yet we too were there. He took over

---

22. Some witnesses, by omitting the *non*, convey the sense, "to a single voice, though it is not obvious, is it, that there...."

into himself our lowly body and transformed it, configuring it to his own glorious body.[23] Our old self was nailed to the cross with him.[24]

Within me my heart was distressed. He says *within me*; the distress was not in others, for they all abandoned me. All who had been close to me ran away and changed their minds about what I was, because they saw me dying. The robber did better than they did: he believed[25] when they defected.

Verse 5. All is grace

10. Now it is the turn of the members to speak. *I called to mind the days of old.* Could Christ, through whom every day has been created, be said to call to mind the days of old? No, this is the body speaking, this is everyone who, having been justified by his grace, clings to him in charity and dedicated humility: "*I called to mind the days of old, and meditated on all your works*, for you have made everything good, and nothing could have existed had you not created it. I surveyed your creation; I sought the artist in his work, the creator in all his creatures." Why did he do this? To what purpose? Surely in order to understand that whatever good there was in himself was created by God, lest, being ignorant of God's justice and trying to establish his own, he might fail to acknowledge himself as subject to the justice of God?[26] And having understood this, would he not have taken as his own the opening verse of our psalm, confessing that *in your truth and in your justice* all this was done? In all the works of God, and in his meditation on all these divine works, he instills into our minds the truth about God's grace. He reminds us about grace, and he glories in having found grace, that grace whereby we have been saved gratis.

---

23. See Phil 3:21. The expression, *transfiguravit in se* ("he took [us] over into himself and transformed us"), is a key phrase in Augustine's theology of the *totus Christus*. Compare *nos transfiguravit in se* (Exposition of Psalm 60,3); *transfiguravit in se suos* (Exposition 2 of Psalm 32,2); *praefigurans... et transformans in se nos ipsos* (Exposition 1 of Psalm 68,3). Christ "took us over into himself" or "incorporated us into his own person." The ideas of intercession and exemplary causality are certainly included, but Augustine goes further. His conviction is that "we were there" when Christ prayed, suffered, struggled, was tempted, and obeyed the Father's will. So, in the present section, *illic nos eramus*. There are other examples of the same assertion; compare Exposition 2 of Psalm 21,3 and Exposition 2 of Psalm 30,3.
24. See Rom 6:6.
25. See Lk 23:40–43.
26. See Rom 10:3.

For indeed, *by grace* we *have been saved* (Eph 2:8). How can you boast about any justice of your own? How can you extol yourself and ignore the justice of God? Perhaps you did make some contribution to your own salvation, but did you have any hand in your coming to be human in the first place? Turn your eyes toward him who created your very life, the author of your being, your righteousness and your salvation. Meditate on the works of his hands, because then you will discover that even the justice that is in you is part of his handiwork. Listen to the apostle inculcating this lesson: *It does not come from works, lest anyone boast* (Eph 2:9). Have we nothing to show, then? To be sure we have, but notice how the apostle continues: *We are his own handiwork*, he says. *We are his own handiwork*— but was he perhaps referring only to our human nature and calling that God's handiwork? By no means. He was speaking about our works: *Not from works, lest anyone boast*. But let us not trust to guesswork, let the apostle make the point himself: *We are his own handiwork, created in Christ Jesus for good works* (Eph 2:10).

Do not claim any work as your own, then, except insofar as you are a bad worker. Turn away from your own work and look to the work of him who made you. He forms you; now let him reform what he formed and you marred. He acted to bring you into being; now he acts to make you good, if good you are. *Work out your own salvation in trembling and fear* (Phil 2:12), scripture enjoins. But if we work out our own salvation, why in fear and why in trembling if the work is within our own power? Read on, and you will see why you must act in fear and trembling: *For it is God who is at work in you, inspiring both will and work, for his own good purpose* (Phil 2:13). Keep yourself in fear and trembling, so that our artificer may enjoy working in a deep valley,[27] for he who executes judgment among the nations and rebuilds the ruins[28] works too in us when we are cast down. *I pondered on the works of your hands*. As I contemplated your works, what I saw was this: that there can be nothing good in us, unless it comes from you who made us.

---

27. See Exposition of Psalm 126,6.
28. See Ps 109(110):6.

Verses 6–7. Thirsting for God, the psalmist begs for grace and for God's benign regard

11. What did I do next, when I had seen that every good gift, every perfect endowment, comes from above, that it comes down from the Father of lights, with whom there is no variation, no play of changing shadow?[29] When I had seen this I turned away from the botched work for which I was responsible in myself, and *to you I stretched out my hands*. He says, *To you have I stretched out my hands; my soul is like waterless earth to you*. Rain on me, he prays, that I may yield good fruit, for *the Lord will give sweetness* (Ps 84:13(85:12)) so that our earth may produce its expected harvest. *To you have I stretched out my hands; my soul is like waterless earth to you*—not to me but *to you*. I can thirst for you, but I cannot irrigate myself. *My soul is like waterless earth to you*, for it thirsts for the living God.[30] *When shall I come?* (Ps 41:3(42:2)) Only when he comes first to me. My soul thirsts for the living God, for it is *like waterless earth to you*. The sea rises and floods the land; it is immense and its waters roar, but it is salt and bitter.[31] Then the waters were confined to their place and my dry soul was exposed.[32] Irrigate it, I beg, for it is *like waterless earth to you*.

12. *Make haste to hear me, O Lord*. Why this delay when I am so thirsty? Is it because you mean to inflame my thirst still more? Are you withholding your rain so that when it comes I may gulp it eagerly and not spit out anything you pour into me? If that is your reason for delaying, give it to me now, I beg, for *my soul is like waterless earth to you. Make haste to hear me, O Lord, for my spirit has fainted away*. Let your Spirit fill me, for my own spirit has fainted away; this is why you must hear me quickly: *My spirit has fainted away*. I have already been made poor in spirit; make me blessed in the kingdom of heaven.[33] If anyone's own spirit is alive in him, that person is likely to be proud, because he will use his own spirit to exalt himself against God. It will be very good for such persons if a prophecy elsewhere in scripture is verified in them: *When you withdraw their breath, they faint, and return to the dust whence they came* (Ps 103(104):29), for

---

29. See Jas 1:17.
30. See Ps 41:3(42:2).
31. An image of the world without grace.
32. See Gn 1:9.
33. See Mt 5:3.

then they will confess, *Remember that we are dust* (Ps 102(103):14). Once they have made that confession, *that we are dust*, they will be disposed to pray, *My soul is like waterless earth to you*. What is more truly waterless earth than dust? But *make haste to hear me, O Lord, rain upon me, give me strength*, so that I may not be *dust which the wind sweeps away from the face of the earth* (Ps 1:4). *Make haste to hear me, O Lord, for my spirit has fainted away.* So urgent is my need that I cannot wait. You have taken my own spirit away to leave me faint, reduced to my native dust, and pleading that *my soul is like waterless earth to you*. Deal with me now as that other psalm goes on to prophesy: *You will breathe forth your Spirit and they will be created, and you will make the face of the earth new* (Ps 103(104):30). If a new creation is brought about in Christ, all that belongs to the old has passed away.[34] In your Spirit all old things have passed; in your Spirit all are made new.

13. *Do not turn your face away from me.* When I was proud, you did turn away. Time was when I was affluent, and in my affluence I was high and mighty. *I said in the midst of my plenty, I shall be unmoved for ever* (Ps 29:7(30:6)). That was my belief, and I boasted *in the midst of my plenty, I shall be unmoved for ever*, because I was unaware of your righteousness and was trying to establish my own.[35] *In your kindly will* you, Lord, *added strength to my beauty* (Ps 29:8(30:7)). *In the midst of my plenty I said, I shall be unmoved*, yet whatever wealth I had was your gift to me. And to prove that it had come to me from you, *you turned your face away from me, and I became distraught* (Ps 29:8(30:7)). After that distraught condition in which I found myself because you had turned away your face, after the dismay of my spirit and the distress of my heart within me, I became like waterless earth to you. *Do not turn your face away.* You turned away from me when I was proud; turn your gaze back now upon one who is humble. *Do not turn your face away from me, or I shall be like those who go down into the lake of the dead.* What does this mean, *like those who go down into the lake of the dead*? Scripture warns, *A person devoid of reverence goes deep into sin and is defiant* (Prv 18:3). The ones who go down into the lake of the dead are those who lose even the will to confess. Against such a fate the psalmist prays, *Do not let the pit close its mouth over me* (Ps 68:16(69:15)). A depth

---

34. See 2 Cor 5:17.
35. See Rom 10:3.

like this is often called a lake in scripture. When a sinner has plumbed such depths, he is defiant. In what sense? He no longer believes in any divine providence; or, if he does believe in it, he does not think it extends to himself. He gives himself unrestrained license to sin; having lost hope of pardon, he gives free rein to iniquity. He does not say, "I will return to God, so that he may turn back to me." He does not hear the prophetic words, *Turn back to me, and I will turn back to you* (Ml 3:7), for he has plunged into the depths of evil and can show nothing but contempt. As scripture warns us, *No confession can be made by a dead person: he is as though nonexistent* (Sir 17:26). Let this not be my fate. *Do not turn your face away from me, or I shall be like those who go down into the lake of the dead.*

Verse 8. Mercy in the morning; while night lasts, walk toward the lamp of the divine scriptures

14. *Make your mercy known to me in the morning, for I have hoped in you.* See, I am still in the night, but I have hoped in you, and I will go on hoping until the sin that belongs to night has passed away.[36] As Peter reminds us, *We have the trusty message of the prophets to rely on, and you will do well to attend to it, for it is like a lamp burning in a dark place until day breaks and the morning star rises in your hearts* (2 Pt 1:19). By *morning* the psalmist means the era after the end of the world, when we shall see what in this world we believe. *In the morning you will hear my voice. In the morning I will stand before you, and contemplate* (Ps 5:4–5(3)). *Make your mercy known to me in the morning, for I have hoped in you,* because *if we hope for what we do not see, we wait for it in patience* (Rom 8:25). The night demands patience, the day will give us joy. *Make your mercy known to me in the morning, for I have hoped in you.*

15. But what about our time here, before morning breaks? It is not enough to hope for morning;[37] we have work to do. Why need we do anything? Another psalm tells us, *On my day of trouble I searched for God; during my sojourn in the night I sought him. How did you search for him? With outstretched hands at night in his presence, and I was not disappointed.* (Ps 76:3(77:2)) We must seek God in the night by using our hands, then. But how can we seek with our hands? By performing good works. Significantly, the psalm says,

---

36. See Ps 56:2(57:1).
37. Many codices omit "for morning."

In his presence, for *when you give alms, be careful not to blow a trumpet before you, and then your Father, who sees in secret, will reward you* (Mt 6:2.4). If we must hope so firmly for the morning and endure the present night and persevere in it patiently until daybreak, what must we do while we are waiting? Beware! You do not imagine, do you, that you are going to do anything by your own powers that could earn you the right to be brought through until morning? *Show me, Lord, the way in which I must walk*. For this very reason did he light the lamp of prophecy; for this same reason did he send the Lord himself clothed in flesh as though in an earthenware covering,[38] a comparison he would use himself in his passion: *My strength was dried up like an earthenware pot* (Ps 21:16(22:15)). Walk toward the prophecies, walk toward the lamp of those predictions of the future, walk toward the words of God. You do not yet behold the Word who was in the beginning, God with God,[39] but walk toward the form of a servant[40] and you will be led to the divine nature of the Lord. *Show me, Lord, the way in which I must walk, for to you have I lifted up my soul*. To you, not against you. *For with you is the fount of life* (Ps 35:10(36:9)), and *to you have I lifted up my soul*. I have brought it like an empty vessel to the fountain. Fill me, *for to you have I lifted up my soul*.

Verse 9. Fleeing to God from invisible enemies

16. *Deliver me from my enemies, O Lord, for I have fled to you.* Once I fled away from you, but now *I have fled to you*. Adam fled away from the face of God and hid among the trees of paradise[41] *like a slave fleeing from his master and grasping at a shadow* (Job 7:2, LXX). He fled from the face of his Lord and found shadow, for into that shadow among the trees of paradise his flight took him. Woe betide any of his descendants who have persisted in hugging the shadow, for later they may say, *All things have passed away like a shadow* (Wis 5:9).

Deliver me from my enemies. I am not thinking now of human foes, for *it is not against flesh and blood that we have to struggle*. Against whom, then? *Against principalities and powers and the rulers of this*

---

38. The earthenware lamp carried the light.
39. See Jn 1:1.
40. See Ph 2:7.
41. See Gn 3:8.

world. This world? Do they rule this world? They certainly do not rule the heavens and the earth, for they cannot hold sway over what they did not make. Scripture says, *the rulers of this world*, but what does it mean? *This world of darkness* (Eph 6:12). But what darkness is it referring to? The world of godless people, undoubtedly, for we are reminded in the sacred writings, *You were darkness once, but now you are light in the Lord* (Eph 5:8). The rulers of *this world of darkness* are those who dominate wicked people, and against them we are bound to wrestle. A formidable battle is ahead of you, for you must defeat an invisible foe. You must contend *against the rulers of this world of darkness*, the devil and his angels. Your opponents do not rule the world of which the gospel says, *The world was made by him*, but the world of which it says, *The world did not know him* (Jn 1:10).[42]

Deliver me from my enemies, O Lord, for I have fled to you. In saying, *my enemies*, the psalmist envisages not Judas but the enemy who instigated Judas. I have to endure the visible enemy, but I must do battle with an enemy I cannot see. Judas received the morsel he was offered, and Satan entered him,[43] because our David was destined to suffer persecution stirred up by his own son.[44] How many other Judases there are whom Satan has filled! They receive a certain morsel unworthily to their own condemnation, for whoever eats and drinks unworthily eats and drinks judgment on himself.[45] What he or she is given is not evil, but a good thing given to a bad person turns to that person's condemnation. A good gift cannot benefit anyone who receives it in a bad way.

Deliver me from my enemies, O Lord, for I have fled to you. Where else could I flee? *Whither shall I go from your spirit? If I mount to heaven, you are there; if I sink down to hell, even there you are present*. What is left to me? *If I take wings like a dove, and fly to the uttermost parts of the sea*—if I dwell in hope at the end of the present age, he means—*even there your hand will lead me, your right hand bring me through*. (Ps 138(139):7–10) *Deliver me from my enemies, O Lord, for I have fled to you*.

---

42. Compare similar remarks in Exposition of Psalm 141:14–15.
43. See Jn 13:27.
44. See section 2 above.
45. See 1 Cor 11:29.

Verse 10. God is all things to me

17. *Teach me, that I may do your will, for you are my God.* What a magnificent confession! What a comprehensive rule of life! *For you are my God*, he says. Let me run to someone else, if it was anyone other than you who made me. You are everything to me, because *you are my God*. Shall I look for a father, in hope of an inheritance? *You are my God* and not only the giver of an inheritance: you are yourself my inheritance, for *the Lord is my portion and my inheritance* (Ps 15(16):5). Shall I look for a master who can redeem me? *You are my God*. And most of all, am I, a creature, longing to be created anew? *You are my God*, you are my creator. You created me through your Word and recreated me through your Word. You created me through the Word abiding in yourself, and you recreated me through the Word who was made flesh for us.

Teach me, that I may do your will, for you are my God. If you do not teach me, I shall do my own will, and my God will abandon me. *Teach me, that I may do your will, for you are my God*, he prays. *Teach me*, for it is not that you are my God and that I shall be my own teacher. Notice how the psalmist emphasizes our need of grace. Hold onto this truth, drink it in, take it to heart, and let no one dislodge it from your hearts, for otherwise you might have zeal for God but not a zeal well informed. You might be ignorant of God's justice and, in striving to establish your own, fail to submit to the justice of God.[46] You know what the apostle had to say about that. Pray, then, *Teach me, that I may do your will, for you are my God*.

Verses 10–12. A hurried conclusion

18. *Your good Spirit*—not my own bad spirit—*your good Spirit will lead me straight forward into the right country.* My own bad spirit has led me[47] in a crooked way, into the wrong place. What have I deserved? Have I any good works to my account, performed without your help, which I could adduce to plead that I am worthy to be led straight forward by your Spirit? What works can I claim, what merits? Yet *for the glory of your name, O Lord, you will give me life.* Listen hard, brothers and sisters, and observe the stress he puts on grace, the grace which saves us gratis. *For the glory of your name, O Lord, you will give me life.* Another psalm prays, *Not to us,*

---

46. See Rom 10:2–3.
47. Variant: "will lead me."

Lord, not to us, but to your name give the glory (Ps 113(115):1). *For the glory of your name, O Lord, you will give me life, in accordance with your justice.* Not in response to any justice of mine, not because I have deserved life, but because you show mercy. If I were to put forward any merits of my own, I would be proved to deserve nothing from you except punishment. But you have torn out my demerits and engrafted your gifts. *For the glory of your name, O Lord, you will give me life in accordance with your justice. You will lead my soul out of its distress, and in your mercy you will steer my enemies toward their destruction. You will do away with all who trouble my soul, because I am your servant.*

Exposition of Psalm 143

A Sermon to the People

Verse 1. The title: David and Goliath

1. The title of today's psalm consists of very few words, but it carries weighty mysteries. It runs, *For David himself, when he went forth against Goliath.* You, like me, beloved, recall the story told in the holy scriptures; you remember the contest that was waged in the days of our ancestors. Foreigners were attacking God's people, and one of the enemy challenged one of the Israelites to single combat: Goliath against David.[1] It was proposed that the will of God concerning the outcome of the war should be sought by this one-to-one fight. But why should we go to any trouble to determine who would be victorious? All we need do is consider who provoked the contest and who was provoked. Impiety challenged devotion, pride provoked humility, and in the end the devil provoked Christ. Why wonder that the devil was defeated? One fighter was of huge bodily size; the other was small of stature but great in faith. At first holy David donned armor and weapons with which to go and engage Goliath, but he was too young and, as we have said, too small of stature, and not strong enough to bear them. So he threw away these accouterments, which were no help to him but only a burden. He took five stones from the brook and put them into his shepherd's milk pitcher.[2] Armed outwardly with these, but spiritually with the name of God, he went forth and conquered.

All these things are related of David, the David of old. But let us look deeper for the mysteries they contain. We pointed out to you just now that the title is only a few words long but pregnant with deep mysteries. Recall the apostle's wise saying, *All these things happened to them with symbolic import* (1 Cor 10:11). This assures us that we cannot be accused of shameless curiosity if we seek hidden meanings where perhaps it might have been said that the story is simple and straightforward and conceals no mysterious depths.

---

1. See 1 Sm 17:4–54.
2. The word in the Septuagint can mean either a purse or wallet, or a small pitcher. Augustine takes it in the latter sense, as emerges in section 2.

In the apostle's statement we have an authorization which makes us eager to search, vigilant in our investigation, devoutly ready to listen, faithful to believe what we hear, and zealous in acting on it. Christ was present in David, but you who are well instructed in his school are used to understanding that Christ comprises head and body. You must therefore not assume that anything you hear spoken in reference to Christ himself is no concern of yours. It does concern you, because you are members of Christ.

We have laid the foundation, so now consider what follows.

2. You know that the first people of God were burdened with a multitude of sacred observances[3] of a visible, material kind. There were, for example, circumcision, a priesthood with multifarious duties, a temple rich in symbols, and a great variety of holocausts and sacrifices. Our David laid all these aside, like arms that did not help him but only weighed him down. For *if a law capable of giving life had been granted to us, then of course righteousness would have been obtainable through the law.* But it was not capable, so what purpose did the law serve? *Scripture has included all things under sin, so that through faith in Jesus Christ the promise might be given to believers.* (Gal 3:21-22) In the fullness of time the new David set forth—Christ, who is both head and members—at the time when the new covenant was to be revealed, the time when God's grace was to be made known and imparted to us. How did this new David act? He laid aside all his armor and chose five stones instead. The burdensome armor was, as we have explained, the mysterious observances of the law. They were not imposed on the gentiles, and we do not keep them. You will recall how many injunctions found in the old law are not binding on us, yet we must understand that they were laid down in an earlier age because they were fraught with significance. We do not simply throw off God's law, but we no longer celebrate mysterious rites which held a promise, because that promise is now fulfilled. What they promised has come to pass for us. The grace of the new covenant was veiled in the law but is revealed in the gospel. We have removed the veil and recognized what was hidden beneath it. We have recognized the truth, thanks to the grace of our Lord Jesus Christ, our head and our

---

3. *Sacramentis*, a word with wide meaning in Augustine. Here it denotes Old Testament observances which could not be fully understood in themselves but pointed to a greater reality. See the notes on Expositions of Psalms 73,2; 67,16; 126,2.

savior who was crucified for us, just as at his crucifixion the veil of the temple was torn apart.

Yet, although Christ laid aside the armor which symbolized the onerous observances of the old law, he did not discard the law itself. This he suggested by taking the five stones from the river. The stones stand for the five books of Moses, and you know what a river signifies. This death-ridden era glides past, and whatever arrives in this world flows out of it again. The stones were in God's ancient people as though in a river: they were no use there; they did nothing and helped no one. They were swept along by the current. What did David do to render the law useful? He applied grace. The law cannot achieve its purpose without grace, for *the fullness of the law is charity* (Rm 13:10). And where does charity come from? You will find, I think, that it is born of grace, for scripture says, *The charity of God has been poured out into our hearts through the Holy Spirit who has been given us* (Rm 5:5).

Now since grace, bestowed gratis, enables us to keep the law, grace is aptly symbolized by milk. Milk is in a sense gratuitous in the body, for a mother does not need it herself but seeks to give it. She gives it freely and is distressed if there is no one to receive it. How, then, did our David suggest that the law cannot be kept without grace? He took those five stones, which represented the law with its five books, and associated them with grace by putting them into his shepherd's pitcher, which he had been accustomed to use for milking. Equipped with these he was armed with grace, and therefore he placed no reliance on himself but only on his Lord. And so he went forth against Goliath, his proud, boastful, self-reliant foe. David selected one stone, slung it, and struck Goliath on the forehead. The enemy fell, wounded in that very part of his body where the sign of Christ was missing.

Notice another point: he carried five stones but cast only one. Five books were read,[4] but unity won the victory, for *the fullness of the law is charity*, as we have just reminded you; and the apostle urges us, *Bear with each other in love, careful to maintain the unity forged by the Spirit in the bond of peace* (Eph 4:2–3). David struck Goliath and felled him, took his sword, and used it to cut off his enemy's head. And our David acted likewise: he overthrew the devil through the agency of the devil's own followers. Certain great men

---

4. Or "selected."

formerly lay in the devil's power, and he used them to slaughter the souls of others, but when these great ones come to believe, they turn their eloquent tongues against the devil. Thus Goliath's head is cut off with his own sword.

We have explained the title as well as our limited time permits. Let us now see what the psalm itself has to tell us.

The whole body of Christ, armed by the Spirit, fights Goliath

3. *Blessed be the Lord my God, who trains my hands for battle, and my fingers for war.* This is our voice speaking, if we are the body of Christ. Let us bless the Lord our God, who trains our hands for battle and our fingers for war. There seems to be repetition here, for to say that he trains our hands for battle is much the same as saying that he trains our fingers for war. Or does the psalm intend to make a distinction between hands and fingers? Obviously the hands work through their fingers, so we can quite reasonably take the fingers to represent the hands. All the same, there is a difference, because we can see in the fingers a specialization of action, yet a radical unity. The same is true of grace; look what the apostle says about it: *To one is given wise utterance through the Spirit, to another knowledgeable speech according to the same Spirit, to another faith, to another gifts of healing in the same Spirit, to another various tongues, to another prophecy, to another discernment between true spirits and false. But the one same Spirit is at work in all these operations, distributing appropriate gifts to each one as he wills.* (1 Cor 12:8-11) By saying *to one, to another* he suggests the diversity of works, but by affirming that *the one same Spirit is at work in all these operations* he points to the root of unity. The body of Christ sets out to fight armed with these fingers. It sallies forth to warfare, ready for battle.

4. It would probably take too long to enumerate the different types of battles and wars; in fact it would almost be easier to wage them than to describe them. But we have one war to fight about which the apostle warns us, *It is not against flesh and blood that you have to struggle.* It is not against human enemies that you are pitted, not against men and women who seem to be giving you trouble, *but against principalities and powers and the rulers of this world of darkness* (Eph 6:12). If he had not added those last two words, you might have thought that by *world* he meant the heavens and the earth, so he made his meaning clear by adding *of darkness*. Not the world made through the Word, then, not that of which scripture says, *The world was made through*

him, but the world that failed to recognize him, of which the gospel goes on to say, *The world did not know him* (Jn 1:10). The darkness of which the apostle speaks is not a natural darkness but a condition of the will. The soul does not derive light from itself. Humbly and truthfully it sings, *You, Lord, will light my lamp; my God, you will enlighten my darkness* (Ps 17:29(18:28)), and, *With you is the fountain of life, and in your light we will see light* (Ps 35:10(36:9)): not in our own light but *in your light*. This is exactly true, for, though our eyes are sometimes called lights, they need light from an outside source; if this is lacking they will remain in darkness even though they are healthy and open.

We must engage in warfare, then, against the rulers of this dark world, the captains of unbelievers. By these I mean the devil and his angels, who use unbelievers as a sword to wield against the faithful. But just as when Goliath was felled his sword was seized, and Goliath's head cut off with his own sword, so too, when unbelievers come to faith, the apostle says to them, *You were darkness once, but now you are light in the Lord* (Eph 5:8). You were once a sword wielded in the fight by Goliath, but now you are in Christ's hand. Cut off Goliath's head.

The interior warfare of each Christian

5. That is one battle, but another awaits each one of us within ourselves. You heard about this kind of warfare when the apostle's letter was read just now: *The flesh lusts against the spirit, and the spirit against the flesh, so that you do not act as you want to* (Gal 5:17).[5] This is a perilous war, and all the worse for being interior. If anyone is victorious in this struggle, he or she will immediately defeat our invisible enemies as well, for the devil and his angels tempt you only insofar as your carnal desires are powerful in you. How are we ever going to defeat enemies we cannot see? Only by resisting the carnal impulses we are aware of within ourselves. As we fight against these,

---

5. In the Pauline context, *spirit* should probably be capitalized, because it refers there to the whole human person, body as well as mental and spiritual faculties, as indwelt by the Spirit of God, whereas *flesh* means the whole human person, mental as well as physical, bereft of the Holy Spirit. Compare Exposition of Psalm 114,8 and the note there. But in the present Exposition Augustine, especially in section 6, seems to take *spirit* in the sense of the spiritual dimension of human nature, struggling against the flesh, so lower case for *spirit* has been preferred.

we strike our invisible, spiritual foes. If you are in love with money, avarice dominates in you, and then from without the devil suggests to the avarice that rules within some way of making money dishonestly. In most cases you cannot win the profits unless you consent to the fraud, and so he puts his proposal from the outside to the avarice within you that you have not conquered or subdued, or subjected to your control. Like a wicked superintendent of the games[6] he dangles before his athlete the fraud and the prize. "Do this, and the prize is yours." If you trample your greed underfoot, if you do not allow it to hold the mastery within you, you will be victorious over a palpable enemy. The devil who is trying to trap you is not palpable, but if you have overcome your avarice, you are attentive to another who also has suggestions to make, one who offers you a work to do and a prize to win. What did the devil propose? Fraud and profits. And what does this other propose? Innocence and a crown. Each of them says to you, "Do this, and the prize is yours." You are a warrior in the inner battle. If you are not conquered by avarice but have won the victory over it, you are listening to the one and defeating the other. You make a realistic judgment about the choice confronting you. You say to yourself, "On the one hand I see a challenge and a prize, on the other a bait and a snare." There is nothing that you say within yourself for which you can disclaim responsibility, for it is you who are divided against yourself as a result of sin. You draw along with you the vigorous shoots of concupiscence and the rooting branches of death. You have within you the foe you must fight, the inner enemies you must rout. But you have an ally on whom you can call. Ask him who made you when you did not exist to help you as you fight and crown you when you win.

If you are first subject to God, your carnal impulses will be subject to you

6. "How will I win the victory?" you ask. "The apostle is challenging us to a very daunting combat, and if I did not understand how laborious or even unwinnable it is, he makes it clear. *The flesh lusts against the spirit, and the spirit against the flesh, so that you do not act as you want to* (5:17). How can you urge me on to victory when the apostle tells me that I am unable to act as I want to?"

---

6. *Agonotheta.*

You are asking me how? Remember the grace stored in the shepherd's vessel. Drop the pebble into the milk pitcher. I am giving you this advice, but it is truth itself that speaks to you. Well now, you do not do what you really want to, because your flesh rebels against your spirit. If you are relying on your own resources in the struggle, you need a warning. Perhaps you were not listening attentively when you heard a psalm bid you, *Shout for joy to God our helper* (Ps 80:2(81:1)), for, if you were expected to do it all by yourself, you would not need a helper. On the other hand, if you did nothing at all by your own will, God could not be called your helper, for a helper comes to the aid of someone who is making an effort. But, in any case, the apostle himself directs your attention to the helper. After saying, *The flesh lusts against the spirit, and the spirit against the flesh, so that you do not act as you want to*, after thus pitting you against yourself, he promptly refers you to your helper, as though to show you that your own strength will inevitably fail you. *If you are led by the Spirit, you are no longer under the law* (Gal 5:18). Anyone who is under the law does not fulfill the law but is weighed down by it, as David was by the armor. If you are led by the Spirit, realize who it is who will help you to accomplish what you want to do: it is your helper, your supporter, your hope, the one who trains your hands for battle and your fingers for war. The apostle goes on to warn you, *The works of the flesh are plain to see: fornication, uncleanness, idol-worship, self-indulgence, sorcery, strife, enmity, drunkenness, gluttony, and the like. I tell you now, as I have told you before, that those who do these things will not possess the kingdom of God.* (Gal 5:19–21) Observe that he does not say "those who struggle against these things" but *those who do these things*. When you are fighting, that is one situation; when you overcome the temptation, that is another; and when you have peace and rest, that is another again.

Please give me your attention while I briefly explain this matter. Some dishonest procedure is suggested to you, and you find it attractive. It involves fraud, but the gain will be significant. You feel the lure, but you do not consent. A fight is in progress, you see: the suggestion is still there, the pressure is still on, and you have not yet made up your mind. Our warrior is fighting still and is in danger. So much for the fight; now let us look at another scene. The person in question has rejected the righteous choice and chosen to act dishonestly. He has been overcome. Or perhaps the opposite has happened: he has refused the fraudulent course and chosen to serve the cause of justice; he has conquered. Three different situations, then. I mourn over the person who has been defeated; I am fearful for the one still fighting; I rejoice with the conqueror.

But what about this last one, the conqueror? Has he been so totally victorious within himself that money will never tempt him again, that it will never arouse any desire in him, not even a desire he can overcome, not even a desire he scorns, not even a desire which he disdains so much as to fight, let alone entertain? I do not think so. Some pleasurable feelings still tickle him. This tickling is no longer an enemy within challenging him to fight, nor is it dominant, but it is still there. It is within him, and though it will not be there for ever, it lodges in his mortal flesh for the time being. His whole nature will eventually be brought to its triumph, but that is for later. For the present, *the body is a dead thing by reason of sin* (Rom 8:10), and therefore sin still dwells in this body, even though it does not reign there. But *the spirit is life through righteousness. If he who raised Jesus Christ from the dead lives in you, he who raised Jesus Christ from the dead will bring life to your mortal bodies too, through his Spirit who dwells in you.* (Rom 8:10–11) Then there will be no enemy to fight us and no temptation to solicit us; everything will proceed in peace.[7]

This does not mean that there are two opposed natures at war within you;[8] it is more like the case of a husband and wife sharing their home. If they are at loggerheads there is misery, trouble, and danger. If the husband is subservient and the wife dominates him there is peace of a perverse kind. If the wife submits to her husband's rule there is a rightly ordered peace, yet there is no question of her being subdued by some alien nature, for woman was made for man, from his own essence. Now your flesh is like your wife or your servant: call it what you like, but bring it under your control and, if you have to fight it, make sure the fight turns out well for you. Your advantage lies in the subordination of the lower to the higher, and this means that if you want what is inferior to yourself to be subject to you, you must in your turn subject yourself to one who is higher.

Recognize the due order and seek peace. You are to be subject to God, and your flesh to you. What could be more just? What more seemly? You submit to one greater than yourself, and what is less than you submits to you. Serve him who made you, so that what

---

7. Variant: "will be brought to peace."
8. As the Manichees taught.

was made for your sake may serve you. But notice that what we are recognizing and recommending is not this order of things: that first your flesh must be subject to you, and then you to God. No, this is what we are saying: you must be subject to God, and then your flesh will submit to you. If you disdain to submit to God, you will never succeed in bringing your flesh under your control. If you do not obey the Lord, you will be tormented by your servant. If you have not first submitted to God and thereby ensured that your flesh is submissive to you, will you ever be able to say, *Blessed be the Lord my God, who trains my hands for battle, and my fingers for war*? If you attempt to go into action untrained, you will be beaten and condemned for it. Put yourself under God's command first, and then, under his training and with his help, you may say of him, *He trains my hands for battle, and my fingers for war.*

Verse 2. The condition for God's mercy to us: we must forgive

7. So you are to engage in battle, and while you are in the thick of the fight you will be in danger. This is when you must say, "*My mercy*, don't let me be overcome." But what does it mean to say *My mercy* to God? Does it mean, "You grant your mercy to me, you show yourself merciful in my regard"? Or does it mean, "You have given me the grace to be merciful myself, as you are merciful to me"? There is nothing that so surely trounces the enemy than our acting mercifully toward others. He bends all his efforts to find accusations he can make against us in the presence of our judge. He cannot lay false charges, for there is no one whom he could deceive. If he were haling us before a human tribunal he might be able to deceive the judge by lying and incriminate us with false charges, but, since our case is to be tried by a judge who cannot be hoodwinked, the enemy tries every stratagem to lead us into sin, so that he may have true allegations to bring forward. But when, perhaps, human weakness has succumbed to his deceits, humility has immediate work to do in making confession, and must then employ itself in works of mercy and devotion. All sins are blotted out when with sincere hearts and total confidence we say to him who sees us, *Forgive us as we forgive.* Say it with all your heart, with faith and unwavering trust, say it with the certainty of being heard: *Forgive us as we forgive.* What you imply is, "Do not forgive us unless we forgive." You do not actually say, "Do not forgive us if we do not forgive," but obviously God does not forgive us if we withhold forgiveness from each other.

Does this mean that God will be untrue to his promises in letting you off without punishment, you who are a sinner? No. He himself lays down the condition: "Do you want me to forgive you? Then forgive." There is another work of mercy: "Do you want me to give you something? Then give." The two injunctions occur together in the gospel: *Forgive, and you will be forgiven; give, and gifts will be given to you* (Lk 6:37-38). "I have something against you," the Lord says, "and you have something against someone else. Forgive your neighbor, and I forgive you. You are asking a favor of me, while someone else is asking a favor of you. Give it, and I will give you yours." What is it that God forgives? What does he give? What else but charity? And how does he give us charity if not through the Holy Spirit who has been given to us?[9] If, then, our enemy is defeated by our works of mercy, and if we could not perform works of mercy without having charity, and if there would be no charity in us unless we received it through the Holy Spirit,[10] we can be sure that the Lord is training our hands for battle and our fingers for war. We rightly call him *My mercy*, for it is only by his gift to us that we can be merciful. *Merciless judgment will be passed on anyone who has not shown mercy* (Jas 2:13).

8. Do you think it a small thing to perform works of mercy? I would like to say more on this subject, but first consider the passage of holy scripture from which I quoted just now, *Merciless judgment will be passed on anyone who has not shown mercy*. A person who, before being judged, has not shown mercy to others will be judged without mercy. But what follows? What is the next line? *Mercy reigns supreme over judgment* (Jas 2:13). What does that mean, brothers and sisters—*Mercy reigns supreme over judgment*? It means that mercy is given a higher place, that it takes precedence. If some act of mercy is found in a person who also has, perhaps, some sin that deserves to be punished at the judgment, the fire of sin is extinguished by the flood of mercy. *Mercy reigns supreme over judgment*. What are we to think of this? Is God unjust because he comes to the aid of such persons and sets them free and pardons them? Not at all. In this too he is just. His mercy does not exclude his justice nor his justice his mercy. Consider carefully, and see if he is not just: "Forgive, and I forgive. Give, and I give." See if he is not just: *The measure that you*

---

9. See Rom 5:5.
10. Some codices read, "unless we received the Holy Spirit," more closely identifying the gift of charity with the Spirit himself.

have dealt out to others will be dealt out to you in return (Lk 6:38). In saying this the Lord does not mean that the two measures are equal, but the same terms apply to both: "Forgive, and I forgive. You have within your power a measure of pardon that you need to grant, and you will find in me a measure of pardon that you need to receive. It lies within your power to measure out as gift what you have, and you will find that it lies with me to measure out to you what you do not have."

The prospect of peace after strife

9. *My mercy and my refuge, my support and my deliverer.* The warrior is having a hard time, he is struggling to hold his flesh in check as it lusts against his spirit. Continue to hold it. You will receive in fullness all you long for when death is swallowed up in victory,[11] when this mortal body of ours has risen from the dead, when it passes over into an angelic state and flies up to share in a heavenly mode of life. *Those who have died in Christ will be the first to rise*, scripture tells us. *Then we who are still alive will be snatched up together with them in the clouds to meet Christ in the air; and thus we shall always be with the Lord.*(1 Thes 4:16–17) Then, when death has been swallowed up into victory, the challenge will be flung at it, *Where is your strife, O death? Where, O death, is your sting?* (1 Cor 15:55). Neither in our minds nor in our bodies will there be anything left to rebel against the love of God. That will be total victory, unshakable peace.

Some foretaste of this peace is given to us, even now while we are still engaged in battle, when scripture invites us, *Come, children, and hear me; I will teach you the fear of the Lord* (Ps 33:12(34:11)). You are in the thick of battle, you are caught in conflict, yet you are longing for rest. *Is there anyone who wants life, and loves to see good days?* (Ps 33:13(34:12)) Who would not respond, "I do"? That is real life, those are good days, when nothing lusts against our spirit, where we no longer hear the order, "Into battle!" but only the summons, "Rejoice!" Who aspires to days like this? Unquestionably everyone will reply, "I do!" Listen, then, to the next lines. I see how hard the struggle is for you, I see that while you are fighting you are exposed to danger. Listen to the Lord's instructions, then, for he is training your hands for battle and your fingers for war: *Restrain your tongue from evil, and your lips from guileful speech. Turn away from evil and do good.* (Ps 33:14–15(34:13–14)) How will you ever be able to

---

11. See 1 Cor 15:54.

do good if you have not first turned away from evil? What is the use of my urging you to clothe the poor if you are still despoiling them? What point is there in telling you to give alms if you are still seizing what does not belong to you? *Turn away from evil and do good.* Let the poor man cease to groan under your oppression and begin to rejoice at your kindness. *Turn away from evil and do good.* Even now, while you are still engaged in the contest, you ask what the prize will be. *Seek peace and pursue it* (Ps 33:15(34:14)). Learn the lesson. Say to God, *My mercy and my refuge, my support and my deliverer, you are my protector.* You are *my support,* to keep me from falling; *my deliverer,* that I may not become trapped; *my protector,* that I be not stricken. The Lord is *my deliverer, and in him have I hoped.* In all these vicissitudes, in all my struggles, in all my battles, in all my difficulties, *in him have I hoped,* in him *who brings my people into subjection to me.* Listen there to our head joining his voice to ours.

Verses 3–4. The glory and humiliation of human beings

10. *Lord, what are humans, that you should make yourself known to them?* All that a human being is, he is only because you have made yourself known to him. *Lord, what are humans, that you should make yourself known to them, or their children, that you value them so highly?* You value men and women so highly, make so much of them, deem them so precious; you give them their due place in your creation, knowing well to what you subordinate them and what you put under their authority. A valuation placed on anything is a decision about its worth. What valuation did God place on human beings, when he poured out for them the blood of his only Son? *What are humans, that you should make yourself known to them?* Who are you, who made yourself known? And to whom? What are *their children, that you value them so highly?* In making so much of us, in setting so high a value on us, you show that we are precious to you. God does not assess a man or woman's value in the way human beings reckon the worth of one another, for when a buyer finds a slave on sale he is often willing to pay more for a horse that for a man. Yet consider what a price God puts on you, if you can ask, *If God is for us, who can stand against us?* How highly did he value you, he who *did not spare even his own Son, but delivered him up for us all*? And *how can he fail to give us everything else along with that gift?* (Rom 8:31–32) If God gave such rations to his soldier during the campaign, what is he reserving for the victorious warrior? *I am the living bread which*

has come down from heaven (Jn 6:41), the Lord declared; this is the rations for fighting forces, provisions brought out from the Lord's barns, the very food of angels. *Mortals ate the bread of angels* (Ps 77(78):25). But will he still dole out these rations when the battles are over? What will he give the victors? Another psalm suggests the answer: *One thing have I begged of the Lord, and that will I seek after: to live in the Lord's house all the days of my life, that I may contemplate the Lord's delight, and I, his temple, may be protected* (Ps 26(27):4). *What are humans, that you should make yourself known to them, or their children, that you value them so highly?*

11. *Men and women have come to resemble emptiness*, yet you have made yourself known to them and value them so highly. *Men and women have come to resemble emptiness*. What kind of emptiness, what kind of vanity, is meant? Times and seasons, which slip away and flow past, for human beings are vanity and emptiness in comparison with the truth that abides for ever, unfailing. Yet even this transience has its place in God's creation, for, as scripture testifies, *God filled the earth with his good things* (Sir 16:30). His good things? That seems to imply that they are akin to God himself, yet all these earthly things are fleeting and ephemeral compared with truth himself, who says, *I AM WHO AM* (Ex 3:14). Everything transitory is rightly called vanity. It fades away with time, like smoke wafted off by the breeze. Need I say any more than the apostle James said about this, when he wished to guide proud people back to proper humility? *What does your life amount to?* he asked. *It is a mist, seen for a little while, and then dispersed.* (Jas 4:15)

Indeed, *men and women have come to resemble emptiness*. But they *have come to resemble emptiness* through sin, for when human beings were first created they were akin to the truth,[12] but when they sinned they suffered condign punishment and came to resemble vanity. As another psalm acknowledges, *You chastise human beings for their sin; you brush their souls away like a spider* (Ps 38:12(39:11)). Our present psalm echoes this with the words, *Men and women have come to resemble emptiness*. What else does the earlier psalm say? *Lo, how old you have made my days!* (Ps 38:6(39:5)) And our psalm? *Their days pass away like a shadow.* Men and women must bestir

---

12. Or "were like the truth." In the background is Gn 1:26–27. Human beings, created in the image of God, distorted the image by sin and came to resemble vanity, emptiness, foolishness.

themselves in their shadowed days to do something worthy of the light they long for. If they are still in nocturnal shadow they must seek the light of day. For anyone of good sense the day of vanity is a day of tribulation. Whether the world afflicts us with sundry troubles and disadvantages or favors us with prosperity, it is all a matter for fear and grief, because human life on earth is nothing but temptation.[13] That is why the psalmist says, *All day long I was walking about in sorrow* (Ps 37:7(38:6)). We need solace, but whatever God provides for us now when things go well is only a consolation for the wretched, not the joy of the blessed.

Men and women need to do something now that is worthy of the light they long for. They need to do it now, I tell you, in their days of shadow. They must seek God in the night, as the psalmist says he did. *On my day of trouble I searched for God. With outstretched hands at night in his presence I sought him, and I was not disappointed.* (Ps 76:3(77:2)) He calls his time of distress both a *day of trouble* and a *night*, doesn't he? *With outstretched hands at night in his presence I sought him*: we are still in the night, and we keep watch by the lamp of prophecy. Something has been promised to us for which we are still waiting, but what does the apostle Peter tell us? *We have the trusty message of the prophets to rely on, and you will do well to attend to it, for it is like a lantern burning in a dark place until day breaks and the morning star rises in your hearts* (2 Pt 1:19). The Lord himself is the day that we shall receive as our reward.[14] *In the morning you will hear my voice. In the morning I will stand before you, and contemplate you.* (Ps 5:4–5(3)) Work hard with your hands, then, though the night is still upon you; that is to say, seek God with good works before the dawn of the day that will gladden you, for, if you do not, that day may dawn to bring you only grief. And see how free from anxiety you can be as you do your work, for he whom you seek will not abandon you. *With outstretched hands at night in his presence I sought him*, says the psalmist. He emphasizes *in his presence* because you want to receive your reward from your Father, who sees what is done in secret.[15] Your mercy and your charity must be

---

13. See Jb 7:1.
14. The sentence is a little obscure in Latin: *Ipse dies praemium nostrum ibi est*. The translation assumes that *ipse* refers back to *dies* and *lucifer* in the preceding quotation, both being messianic titles.
15. See Mt 6:4.

within you, not paraded so that other people can see and admire. The psalmist says, *With outstretched hands.* "I work with them in shadow, in this life," he says, "and I work where God sees, not attempting to curry favor with other people." And what was the outcome? *I was not disappointed.*

Men and women have come to resemble emptiness; their days pass away like a shadow. Yet still you have made yourself known to them and set a high value upon them.

Verses 5–8. The Church prays for deliverance from pride, conspiracy, and foolish talkers

12. *Bow down your heavens, O Lord, and descend; touch the mountains, and they will send forth smoke. Flash your lightning and you will scatter them, shoot your arrows, and you will dismay them. Stretch out your hand from on high to deliver me, and rescue me from surging waters.* This is the body of Christ speaking, our humble David, full of grace, relying on God, fighting its battles in this world and calling upon divine help. *Bow down your heavens, and descend.* Who are these bent heavens? The apostles, humbled under God, for they are the *heavens* who *proclaim God's glory* (Ps 18:2(19:1)). As they tell forth his glory it is said of them that *there is no speech, no language, in which their voices are not heard; their sound has gone forth throughout the world, their words to the ends of the earth* (Ps 18:4–5(19:3–4)). Thus it came about that, when these heavens were trumpeting their words through all the lands and working wonders, when the Lord was thundering through them with his miracles and commands, the apostles were mistaken for gods who had come down from heaven to visit human beings. Some of the gentiles who made this mistake even tried to offer sacrifice to them. But, when the apostles saw that they were being paid inappropriate honors, they were horrified and denounced such attempts as blasphemous; they were so determined to put their would-be worshipers right that they tore their garments to express their detestation. *What are you doing?* they demanded. *We are frail human beings, like yourselves!* (Acts 14:14) And after this protest they began to extol the surpassing glory of our Lord Jesus Christ, humbling themselves so that all homage would redound to the honor of God. The heavens had been lowered only so that God might descend.

The psalm prays, *Bow down your heavens, and descend*: this has been done. It continues, *Touch the mountains, and they will send forth smoke*. Mountains represent proud people, earthly pretensions, and those swollen with self-importance. *Touch them*, prays the psalmist. Touch those mountains, give them your grace, and grant that they may *send forth smoke* as they acknowledge their sins. The smoke from sinners confessing will wring tears from all other proud persons brought low. *Touch the mountains, and they will send forth smoke*: as long as they remain untouched, they will go on thinking how lofty they are. But, once touched, they will confess, "How great you are, O Lord." The mountains will say, *You alone are the Most High over all the earth* (Ps 82:19(83:18)).

13. But there were some people who conspired for evil ends, who came together to make common cause against the Lord and his anointed.[16] They gathered, they hatched their plots. *Flash your lightning, and you will scatter them*; intensify your miracles and their conspiracy will collapse. *Flash your lightning, and you will scatter them*. If your prodigies scare them off, they will not dare to attempt anything against you; their terror at your miracles will give them pause. "Who is this, who can do such mighty deeds?" they will ask. "Who is this, who is so sublime, whose name is so powerful?" When they begin to ask, "Who is this?" they will be ready to believe. You have flashed forth your resplendent miracles and dispersed their evil plots.

Shoot your arrows, and you will dismay them, the psalm continues. Your commandments are *sharp arrows of the mighty one* (Ps 119(120):4), and your utterances have power to strike at their hearts. *Shoot your arrows, and you will dismay them*. Let those of the wicked who enjoy good health be wounded for their own good and so be healed. Then let them from within the Church, incorporated into Christ's body, say with the rest of the Church, *I am wounded by love* (Sg 2:5, LXX). *Shoot your arrows, and you will dismay them*.

14. *Stretch out your hand from on high*. And then what? What will happen at the end? How can Christ's body prove victorious? Only with help from heaven, for the Lord will come again in person, *the Lord himself will descend from heaven, to the shout of an archangel and the blast of God's trumpet* (1 Thes 4:16), he who is the savior of his body, he who is the hand of God. *Stretch out your hand from on high to deliver me, and rescue me from surging waters*. What tumultuous waters are these? The crowds of peoples. Which peoples? Foreigners and unbelievers, whether they attack us from outside or try to entrap

---

16. See Ps 2:2; Acts 4:26–27.

us within. *Deliver me from surging waters.* You were training me as I contended with them, and you rolled me in them to wash off my stains. They were for me like the water of contradiction, where your people strove long ago.[17] *Deliver me, and rescue me from surging waters.*

15. Let us listen a little longer to what the psalm suggests about these tumultuous waters from which God will rescue the body of his Christ, from which he will pluck his humble David. What does it mean to speak of *surging waters*? What else have you to say about them, to make sure we do not think it is some other waters you have in mind? Why did you speak of many waters?

Listen, says the Lord, and I will explain why I said that. *From the hand of alien sons*, the psalm continues. Understand from those words, brothers and sisters, among whom we find ourselves, among whom we have to live, and from whom we long to be delivered. They are the ones *whose mouths have spoken empty words.* Suppose all of you here today had not gathered to contemplate the divine panorama of God's word.[18] At this very hour you would have been rubbing shoulders with all those people, and what a foolish din you would have been listening to! *Their mouths have spoken empty words,* silly rubbish. If they are all the time talking rubbish, how are they to hear you when you speak the truth? *Their mouths have spoken empty words, and their right hand is a hand that deals unjustly.*

Verses 9–10. The new song; the sword of division

16. What were you doing among them, with your shepherd's pitcher and its five pebbles? To put my query otherwise, can you make me understand the law, which you symbolized by the five stones?

O God, to you will I sing a new song. The new song is the hymn to grace; the new song belongs to the new person; the new song belongs to the New Covenant. The song I will sing to you is new, says the psalmist. But you must not think that grace annuls the law; rather is the law brought to its fulfillment through grace. *On a ten-stringed psaltery I will play psalms to you.* By the words, *on a ten-stringed*

---

17. See Nb 20:13.
18. Compare Exposition of 39,9, where Augustine, aware of the addictive power of popular shows and the difficulty any new convert experienced in staying away from them, points to the greater wonders on display in Christianity. See also the Exposition of Psalm 96,1; and the Exposition of Psalm 39,8, with the note there. Today's congregation might have been at the games or the theater instead.

psaltery, he indicates the law with its ten commandments. On these ten strings I will play psalms to you. On these strings let me rejoice in your presence, on them let me sing a new song, for the fullness of the law is charity (Rom 13:10). Those who lack charity may carry the psaltery, but they cannot sing. But as for me, while I am still floundering in the waters of contradiction I will sing a new song to you. Never shall the din of those waters drown the music of my psaltery. *On a ten-stringed psaltery I will play psalms to you.*

17. *The Lord grants salvation to rulers*—to mountains already issuing smoke. *He redeems*[19] *David, his servant.* You recognize David by now; just make sure you are David.

From what does he redeem his servant, David? From what does he redeem Christ? From what does he redeem Christ's body? *Redeem me from the baleful sword.* It would not suffice to say simply "from the sword"; he needed to specify *the baleful sword*, because there is undoubtedly a benign sword too. What is the benign sword? The one of which the Lord said, *I have come to bring not peace on earth, but a sword* (Mt 10:34), for he had come to divide believers from unbelievers and children from parents and to cut through other ties that hampered his followers. His sword sliced away diseased tissue and brought healing to the members of Christ. Clearly, then, there is a benign double-edged sword, powerful on each of its keen edges: these represent the Old and the New Testaments, sharp in their story of the past and sharp in their promise of the future. This is a beneficial sword whereby God speaks truth, and it is contrasted here with the baleful sword whereby unbelievers speak their empty foolishness. And so the psalmist prays, *Redeem me from the baleful sword*, for indeed *the teeth of human beings are weapons and arrows, their tongue a sharp sword* (Ps 56:5(57:4)). From that vindictive sword deliver me. What he now calls a sword he earlier designated tumultuous waters: *Deliver me from surging waters*, he said. Yes, says the psalmist, I called them surging waters, but now I call them a baleful sword.

In that earlier verse, after speaking of the surging waters, he elaborated, *From the hand of alien sons, whose mouths have spoken empty words*. And now he wants to make it clear that he still has the same people in mind, because after praying this verse, *Redeem me from the baleful sword*, he continues with the same words he has used already: *Deliver me from the hand of alien sons, whose mouths*

---

19. Variants: "has redeemed"; "you have redeemed."

have spoken empty words. And then the repetition of earlier words is prolonged, for he adds, *Their right hand is a hand that deals unjustly,* which was an accusation he made concerning the people he called *surging waters.* You might have thought until now that surging waters were a good thing, but the psalmist indicates their character by calling them by this other name, a *baleful sword.*

Now he has some more explaining to do. He said of these people, *Their mouths have spoken empty words, and their right hand is a hand that deals unjustly.* What are the vain things they talk of, and in what sense are their right hands given to dealing unjustly?

Verses 12–14. The aliens are known by their desires. What is happiness?

18. *Their sons in youth are like well-set saplings.* The psalmist means to enumerate for us the things that make these people happy. Listen carefully, you children of light, children of peace; listen, you sons and daughters of the Church, you members of Christ. Notice who these people are, the ones he calls foreigners, alien sons, the ones he calls waters of contradiction, and a baleful sword. Listen most carefully, I beg you, for it is among these people that you are imperiled. Amid their tongues you wage your warfare against the desires of your flesh, amid their tongues which the devil has taken in his hand and uses as his weapons. That is where your battle is pitched. You are contending *not against flesh and blood, but against principalities and powers and the rulers of this world of darkness* (Eph 6:12), against the wicked. Listen most attentively, that you may understand what distinguishes you from them. Listen and consider, for, if you do not, you may be deceived into thinking that the things weak and malicious people crave constitute true happiness.

You are well aware, brothers and sisters, that the psalmist called them alien sons and surging waters and a baleful sword. You know this, certainly. But take a look at the foolish nonsense they talk, and beware of falling into the same habits of speech yourselves. Beware of imitating the way they talk lest you imitate their deeds too. *Their mouths have spoken empty words, and their right hand is a hand that deals unjustly.* What kind of vain things have their mouths spoken? To what sort of right-handed wickedness are their right hands accustomed? Listen: *Their sons in youth are like well-set saplings, their daughters are adorned and gathered round them like the pillars of the temple, their store-rooms are full to overflowing, their ewes are fruitful, increasing at every lambing-time, and their oxen are sturdy. Never is their hedge broken down or an opening forced, nor is there rioting in their streets.* Well, that sounds like happiness, doesn't it?

Or does it? I am asking you as the heirs of the kingdom of heaven; I am putting my question to the children of the resurrection that will last for ever; I am interrogating Christ's body, Christ's members, the temple of God. So is this not happiness, to have healthy sons, daughters beautifully attired, full storehouses, teeming herds, and no damage even to your hedge, let alone your wall? Is it not happiness to have no rioting or shouting in your streets but only tranquility, peace, abundance, a plethora of goods both in your houses and in your cities? Is this not happiness? Is there any reason for the just to shun such good fortune? Do you not find the home of many a good man, too, overflowing with all these things and full of such prosperity? Did Abraham's household not abound in gold, silver, children, servants, and livestock?[20] And what of the holy patriarch Jacob? He fled from his brother Esau into Mesopotamia and worked there and grew rich, and when he returned did he not give thanks to the Lord his God because, though he had crossed the river with nothing but his staff, he came back with such a great company of children and animals?[21] What are we to say, then? Is this not happiness?

In a sense, yes, it is, but it is the happiness of the left hand. What does that mean—"happiness of the left hand"? It is temporal, mortal, material happiness. I do not want you to shun it, but neither do I want you to think it belongs to your right hand. The people mentioned by the psalmist are not baleful or stupid or empty because they enjoy an abundance of good things but because they regard as their right hand what ought to be their left. That is why *their right hand is a hand that deals unjustly*, and that is why *their mouths have spoken empty words*. What ought they to have set at their right hand? God, eternity, God's years that never end, of which it is said, *Your years will not fail* (Ps 101:28(102:27)). That is the place for our right hand; there must our desire be fixed. Let us make use of the left hand for a time, but let us long for the happiness of the right hand that will last for ever. If wealth flows all around you, do not let your heart become attached to it.[22] Riches may flow freely but they also flow away, and, if you fix

---

20. See Gn 13:2.6; 24:35.
21. See Gn 32:7–10.
22. See Ps 61:11(62:10).

your heart on them, you will be making them into the wealth of your right hand when they really belong to the left. Get your priorities right and recognize the wisdom that embraces you, the wisdom of whom it was said, *His left hand is beneath my head, and his right hand will embrace me* (Sg 2:6). Study those holy hymns of love; read the Song of Songs which celebrates the heavenly nuptials of Christ with his Church. What does the bride say of the bridegroom? *His left hand is beneath my head, and his right hand will embrace me.* His left hand, notice, is under her head, his right hand above her head. The arm stretched over her head is the arm of a lover embracing her, while the left supports her head from below. *His left hand is beneath my head,* she tells us.[23] "He will not leave me forlorn in my temporal needs, but his left hand will be under my head, supporting my head from beneath. It must not be given any place of honor above my head but must remain subordinate, so that only his right hand may embrace me, the hand that promises eternal life." The left hand will keep its proper place below her head if his right hand is above, and then the apostle's words to Timothy will have full value. Godliness, he says, *holds the promise of life, both in the present and in the future* (1 Tm 4:8). Dwell on these words, *the promise of life, both in the present and in the future.* What are we promised for the present life? The Lord's left hand beneath our head. And what for the future? His right hand embracing us. Are you pursuing things you need for this present time? *Seek first the kingdom of God*—that is, look first to the right hand—*and all these things will be given you as well* (Mt 6:33). You will have wealth and honor here, the Lord implies, and in the world to come eternal life. With my left hand I will support your weakness, and with my right hand I will crown your perfect maturity. The apostles abandoned all they had, or distributed it all to the poor, and were they left penniless in this world? If they had been, what would the promise have been worth, the Lord's promise that referred even to the left hand, the promise that one who leaves everything for his sake *shall receive seven times*[24] *as much even in this world* (Mk 10:30)? He promised them that their goods would be multiplied.

And indeed, dear friends, in your experience does a person who belongs to God lack anything? If someone is an unbeliever, he has

---

23. This development on the right hand and the left, relying on the text from the Song of Songs, recalls Exposition of Psalm 120, 8–10.
24. Variant: *a hundred times.*

one house or perhaps a few. But *there is a whole world of riches for a believer* (Prv 17:6, LXX). The Lord's left hand is beneath the head of the just, as he promised: they will *receive seven times as much, even in this world*. But look how the Lord's right hand embraces them: *and in the world to come, eternal life* (Mk 10:30). With good reason does scripture testify in another place concerning wisdom, *Years of life are in her right hand, but in her left are riches and fame* (Prv 3:16, LXX).

Verse 15. God's children know their right hand from their left

19. Why, then, are some people who value these things condemned for talking foolishly? Why is it said that their mouths speak empty words? Because *their right hand is a hand that deals unjustly.* I have no quarrel with them because their young sons are like well-set saplings, nor because their daughters are adorned and gathered round them like the pillars of the temple, nor because all that other prosperity enfolds them in earthly well-being and peace. Why then do I find fault? Because *they have called blessed people who have these things.* What nonsense they are talking! *They have called blessed people who have these things.* In their ill-will they have lost the real treasure of the right hand, these perverted people. They have arrayed themselves in the good things God gave them, but put them on upside down. Truly you are malicious and full of foolish talk, you alien sons! *They have called blessed people who have these things.* What belonged to the left hand they have switched to the right. *They have called blessed people who have these things.*

But what about you, David? What about you, body of Christ? What about you, who are Christ's members? What have you to say, you who are no alien sons but sons and daughters of God? The alien sons have spoken empty words in declaring, *Blessed are the people who have these things.* What do you say? *Blessed rather is the people whose God is the Lord.* Possess those left-hand commodities, by all means, but keep them for your left hand. Set your longing upon the right hand, that you may win a place at Christ's right. The people who found him hungry and fed him, who saw him thirsting and gave him a drink, who encountered him as a stranger and gave him hospitality, who met him naked and clothed him[25]—all these regarded their left-hand goods as proper to their left hands. But they used all these

---

25. See Mt 25:35–36.

things from the left to do right-handed works, so that they might find a place at Christ's right hand.

Alien sons, with their empty talk, *have called blessed people who have these things.* But you must say, in union with us, *Blessed rather is the people whose God is the Lord.*

Let us turn to the Lord now.[26] Amen. Thanks be to God always.

---

26. *Conversi ad Dominum*, perhaps an invitation to the people to pray by reciting the whole psalm. Compare Expositions of Psalms 80, 22; 86, 9; 128, 13.

Exposition of Psalm 144

A Sermon[1]

Introduction: to show us how to praise him rightly, God has praised himself

1. It was our wish to praise the Lord together with you, and he has granted us this privilege. We must take care that the praise we offer him proceeds in good order, with no kind of excess creeping in which could offend the one whom we praise. We therefore think it best to follow the path of praise marked out in God's scriptures, not declining from the way either to the right hand or to the left. I would go so far as to say to you, beloved,[2] that God has praised himself in order to give human beings a pattern by which they can praise him in a seemly fashion. Because God has kindly praised himself, men and women know how to praise him. It cannot, of course, be said to God, as it is to humans, *Let not your own mouth praise you* (Prv 27:2). If a human being praises himself, it is arrogance, but if God praises himself, he does so out of his mercy. It is to our advantage to love him whom we praise because, by loving the good, we become better. Knowing that it is good for us to love him, God has made himself lovable by praising himself, and in making himself lovable he has our good at heart. He therefore stirs up our hearts to praise him, and he has filled his servants with his own Spirit, to enable them to offer him praise. And if it is his own Spirit, present in his servants, who is praising him, what else can we conclude but that God is praising himself?

Verse 1. The honor of the Jewish people

2. Today's psalm begins like this: *I will exalt you, my God and my king, and I will bless your name throughout the age, and for ages of ages.* You hear how the note of praise has been struck already,

---

1. Probably preached at Utica, on 18 August 417, the feast of the martyrs known collectively as the *Massa Candida* ("White Multitude"), in the basilica dedicated in their name.
2. *Caritati vestrae.*

and praise will be prolonged to the end of the psalm. What is more, the psalm's title is, *Praise for David himself.* Christ, who came to us from the seed of David,[3] is called David, and he is our king, the king who rules us and leads us into his kingdom. The dedication, *Praise for David himself,* is therefore to be understood as meaning, "Praise to Christ himself." But though according to fleshly descent Christ is called Son of David, according to his divinity he is David's creator and David's Lord.

Paul emphasized the dignity of God's primal people, from whom the apostles had emerged, they who were the first to believe. From this same Jewish people many of the early churches sprang, and among those first believers were many thousands who obeyed an invitation that one rich man in the gospel heard, only to depart sadly. You remember the story in the gospel just read.[4] But great numbers of the first Jewish Christians sold all their property and distributed the proceeds to the poor, seeking to be perfect in the Lord.[5] This honorable race was deemed worthy of special commendation by the apostle, who said of God's first chosen people, *The patriarchs belong to them; and from them Christ was born according to the flesh, he who is sovereign over all, God, blessed for ever* (Rom 9:5). Because Christ in his bodily nature sprang from this race, he is called David. But because he is sovereign over all, God, blessed for ever, the psalmist prays to him, *I will exalt you, my God and my king, and I will bless your name throughout the age, and for ages of ages.* Possibly by *throughout the age* he means here and now, and by *for ages of ages* he indicates eternity. If you are going to praise God for eternity, you may as well begin now. Anyone who refuses to praise him in this transitory world will be mute in the world that lasts for ever. This same thought is reiterated in the following lines.

Verse 2. Praising God in good fortune and in calamity

3. Someone might possibly misunderstand the words, *I will praise your name throughout the age,* by taking them as a resolve on the psalmist's part to praise God in some age other than the present one.

---

3. See Rom 1:3.
4. See Mt 19:21–22. There are other indications in the sermon that this passage of Mt 19 was the gospel of the day. Compare section 3 below (Mt 19:17), and section 6 (Mt 19:28).
5. See Acts 2:44–45; 4:32–35.

To exclude this misconception the psalm continues, *During every single day I will bless you*. Praise and bless the Lord your God through every single day so that, when these single days are over and the one unending day has arrived, you may pass from many praises to one endless act of praise, as you will also pass from many virtues to one virtue.[6] *During every single day I will bless you*.

There is nothing remarkable about it if you bless your God when you are enjoying a happy day. But what about when a sad day dawns for you? It is, after all, a matter of common human experience: plenty of things can go wrong; trials and temptations multiply. So will you give up praising God when something sad happens? Will you stop praising your creator? If you do stop, you must have been lying when you said, *During every single day I will bless you, O Lord*. But if on a sad day, when things seem to be going badly for you, you do not slacken in your praise of him, things will turn out well for you in your God. Even when your affairs are proceeding badly, the possibility of their going well for you is still there, for if some calamitous event means that they go badly, it is equally certain that something good can mean that they go well. And what is as good as your God, of whom the gospel says, *No one is good, except the one God* (Mt 19:17)? You can infer from the nature of this unique good how free from anxiety your praise may be and how securely you may trust that all is indeed well with you. Think about this. If you rejoice in some good thing that happens to you and lasts all day, this good thing that brought you joy may perhaps have vanished when the next day dawns. "Things went well for me yesterday," you reflect. "I had a good day." Perhaps profits flowed in, or you received a special invitation, or you were a guest at a lengthy banquet. Do you think yourself lucky because you ate for such a long time? Another day teaches you a lesson, since you felt no shame on the day before.

In any case, whatever good thing of this kind brings you enjoyment, it is without doubt transitory. But, if you rejoice in the Lord your God, you will hear scripture encouraging you, *Delight in the Lord* (Ps 36(37):4). You will rejoice with all the more confidence because he in whom you rejoice is so much more dependable. If you rejoice

---

6. See Ps 83:8(84:7). In his Exposition of Psalm 83,11 Augustine plays on different meanings of *virtus*: it can signify many "powers" leading us to the one Power, Christ, or many "virtues" of action leading us to the one virtue of contemplation. See the notes in that place.

over money, you need to fear a thief, but if your joy is in God, what is there to be afraid of? That someone may steal God from you? No one will steal God from you unless you choose to reject him, for God is not like that bright object shining on us from the sky. We cannot always have access to sunshine because the sun is not always shining everywhere. So weak are we that though we enjoy being in sunlight during the winter, now in the summer we have sought a place to stand where we can be away from the direct rays of the sun.[7] God is not like that. If you stand in your God and delight in the radiance of his truth, you have no need to look for a place where you can enjoy his light; it is your conscience that brings you near to him and your conscience that takes you further away. The invitation, *Draw near to him and receive his light* (Ps 33:6(34:5)), was addressed to your soul, not to your vehicle; to your loving intentions, not to your feet. And when you have taken your stand in him, you will not suffer from the heat. The Holy Spirit will breathe upon you, and under his wings you will be confident.[8]

4. You must see, then, that you have a reason for delight throughout every day that passes, for God will not reject you, even if some sad event has occurred. Think what sad misfortunes befell the holy man Job. How suddenly it all happened, how many and how grievous were his woes! There had been so many things in which people supposed him to have rejoiced (though these were not the real source of his joy), and when the devil began to tempt him they were all taken away. Even his children died. What he was storing up perished, and those for whom he was storing it up perished likewise; but God, who had given both the former and the latter, did not perish. As for Job's children, though they were lost to this present world, they were ready to be recognized and welcomed in the next. Throughout these trials the holy man had a quite different spring of joy, so that the promise on which we were reflecting was kept in his case: *During every single day I will bless you.* That day when everything had perished dawned sadly for him, but did the inner light fail in his heart? Not at all. He stood in that light and said, *The Lord gave, and the Lord has taken away. This has happened as the Lord willed: may the Lord's name be blessed.* (Jb 1:21) Clearly it must have been true of him that

---

7. These words lend credibility to the conjectural dating, 18 August.
8. See Ps 90(91): 4.

during every passing day he praised God, for even on such a sad day he offered praise.

This story is a brief lesson: you must always praise God and praise him with a sincere heart, not making a false claim when you profess, *I will bless the Lord at all times; his praise shall be in my mouth always* (Ps 33:2(34:1)). It is a brief, simple lesson, which shows you that, when God gives, he gives in mercy, and when he takes away, he takes away in mercy. You must believe that his mercy never leaves you, whether he caresses you with his giving, lest you grow discouraged, or tempers your glee when you are jubilant, lest you perish. Your business is to praise him for his gifts and for his chastisements. To praise the one who whips you is a remedy for your wound.

During every single day I will bless you, says the psalm. Make up your minds, brothers and sisters, to bless God in all that happens, whatever it may be. Bless God. He takes care that nothing will happen to you that you cannot bear; of this you can be quite sure. When things are going well for you, remain cautious and do not assume that you will never be tested. If you are never assayed, you will never be proved genuine. Is it not better to be tested and proved than to escape testing and be reproved?[9] *I will praise your name throughout the age, and for ages of ages.*

Verse 3. *Your praise of God will not be interrupted by your death*

5. *The Lord is great and exceedingly worthy of praise.* How great was the reality of which the psalm was attempting to speak? What words could it choose? What an immensity it enfolded in that word *exceedingly!* Think all round the idea, as far as you are able. But will God, who cannot be contained, ever be captured in our thought? He is *great and exceedingly worthy of praise; there is no limit to his greatness.* This is why the psalm said *exceedingly:* because *there is no limit to his greatness.* If it had not said this, perhaps you might have wanted to praise God and thought you could make an end of the work of praising him. No, you could not, because his greatness can have no end. Do not imagine that you are equal to the task of praising him whose greatness is endless. Is it not better then, that, as he has no end, his praise should never end either? His greatness is endless, and your praise of him should likewise be endless. What does the psalm

---

9. An Augustinian pun: *Nonne melius est tentari et probari, quam non tentatum reprobari?*

say of his greatness? *There is no limit to his greatness.* And of your praise? *I will praise your name throughout the age, and for ages of ages.* This suggests that, since his greatness is unending, your praise will be unending too, for you will not cease to praise the Lord when you undergo bodily death. It is true that scripture says, *The dead will not praise you, O Lord* (Ps 113(115):17). But that refers to the kind of person of whom it says elsewhere, *No confession can be made by someone who is dead: he is as though nonexistent* (Sir 17:26), not to those of whom the Lord said, *Any who believe in me, though they die, shall yet live* (Jn 11:25), for *the God of Abraham, the God of Isaac, and the God of Jacob is the God not of the dead, but of the living* (Lk 20:37–38). If you never belong to anyone but God, your praise of him will never fall silent. Can you really be afraid that, while you are alive here, you belong to him, yet, once you have died, you will belong to him no more? Don't worry: listen to the apostle promising you safety in this matter. *If we live, we live for the Lord,* he says, *and if we die, we die to the Lord, so whether we live or die, we belong to the Lord* (Rom 14:8). How does it come about that you belong to him even when you are dead? Because Christ too died and redeemed you at the cost of his blood.[10] How could he let go of his dead servant, when his own death is your ransom? After saying, *Whether we live or die, we belong to the Lord,* the apostle points to the price paid: *This is why Christ died and rose again: so that he might be Lord of both the dead and the living* (Rom 14:9).

Verse 4. Praising God for his wonderful works

6. *There is no limit to his greatness,* and we are bidden to praise him whom we cannot comprehend. If we could comprehend him, there would be a limit to his greatness; but because his greatness is without limit, we can comprehend something of God, but never the whole. Since this is so, since we are weak and fall far short of his grandeur, let us look to what he has made, so that we may be strengthened by his goodness. As we contemplate his works let us praise the worker, the maker for what is made, the creator for his creation, passing in review all the things known to us, things plain to see. Yet how many other works have his immense goodness and boundless power accomplished, works beyond our ken? If we lift our eyes and focus

---

10. Variant: "because Christ redeemed you at the cost of his blood, even though you were dead."

on the uttermost point of the sky and then, leaving sun and moon and stars, lower our gaze to earth, our eyes will have wandered over a vast expanse. But who can stretch even the power of the mind, much less bodily sight, to what towers beyond the heavens? Let us at least praise God for his works insofar as they are known to us, for ever since the world began his invisible wonders have been understood through the things that are made.[11]

Generation after generation will praise your works. Every succeeding generation will praise them, and perhaps this is all the psalm means to suggest by *generation after generation,* for it is quicker to use this phrase than to enumerate all of them; the repetition of the word by the speaker directs our minds forward across the long succession. This generation that is alive today will pass on even as it came, but while it lives it praises the works of God. When it has made way for another, the new generation will likewise extol God's works, and after that another again, and so on until the end of the world. How many generations! This may well be what the psalm indicates by saying, *Generation after generation will praise your works.*

Alternatively, we could take the repetition of the word to signify two kinds of generation. In this present generation we are children of God, but in another generation we shall be children of the resurrection. Scripture has given us this name, *children of the resurrection,* and has called the resurrection itself a *new-born world. In the new-born world, when the Son of Man has taken his seat upon his glorious throne* (Mt 19:28), said the Lord; and in another place, *They will not marry or take wives, for they will be children of the resurrection* (Lk 20:35–36). Therefore the psalm declares, *Generation after generation will praise your works.* We praise the works of the Lord now, in this mortal life, and, if we glorify him in our chains, how gladly we shall praise him when we are crowned! We must contemplate the Lord's works now, in this generation: as the psalm says, extolling him, *Generation after generation will praise your works,* for *there is no limit to his greatness.* We are allowed to gaze on your works, Lord, so that you, the worker, may be glorified for them.

7. *They will proclaim your power.* Their only object in praising your works is to proclaim your power. Children are taught praise and admiration at school, and everything commended to them as praiseworthy is made by God. Similarly adults are encouraged to admire

---

11. See Rom 1:20.

and praise the sun, the sky, and the earth, and even—to turn to lesser things—a rose or a laurel. All these things held up to their admiration are God's work; all of them are affirmed, praised, celebrated; the works are magnified. But no mention is made of the worker. I want the creator to be glorified in all he has made. I am not fond of anyone who, though mouthing praises, is ungrateful. How can you commend what God has made and say nothing of him who made it? Were he not so great, you would not have found anything worthy of your admiration. You look at these things, and what do you find in them to evoke your song of praise? Their beauty, perhaps, their usefulness, some virtue or power. If you are delighted with their beauty, what is more beautiful than their maker? If they attract you because they are useful, ask yourself if anything could be more useful than the creator of the universe. If it is their mighty potential that you admire, what is more powerful than he who not only made all things but did not leave them to their own devices, for he rules and guides them all?

Generation after generation of your servants praises your works, but not as do those eloquent talkers who might as well be dumb, for they praise the creature and forget the creator. How, then, do your servants glorify you? *They will proclaim your power*. In praising your works they will proclaim your power. These are the true praise-singers, holy, good, and faithful. They are not ungrateful for grace as they praise all the varied works of God, the highest and the lowest, heavenly things and things on earth. And among his works they find themselves, for he who made all things made us among them. It seems to follow, then, that if you praise God's works you will have to praise yourself, since you are a work of God. And then what becomes of scripture's warning, *Let not your own mouth praise you* (Prv 27:2)? Don't worry; you have found a way in which you can praise yourself without being pretentious. Direct your praise not to yourself but to God in you; express your admiration not because you are so wonderful but because he made you so; glorify him not because you can do anything but because, in you and through you, he can. In this spirit they will give you glory, Lord, and *they will proclaim your power*, commending not their own power but yours. Contemplate his works, brothers and sisters, and wonder at the artificer. Give thanks to him and do not be arrogant. Praise him because he made you, because he designed you as he did, because he has endowed you with such gifts.

Verses 5–7. Telling the story of God's greatness and his abundant sweetness

8. Now look at the next verses. *They will proclaim your power*, the psalm has predicted. *They will tell of your magnificent, glorious holiness, and they will recount your wonders. They will speak of the power of your dread acts, and will tell the tale of your greatness. They will belch forth the memory of the abundance of your sweetness*: yours and no other. Study this observer of God's doings and see whether he is ever diverted from the worker to the work. See whether he ever falls away from the maker to what is made. Rather he has used created things as a means of mounting to the creator and never fallen back from him, for, if you love these things more than God, you will not possess God. And then what will be the use of any amount of created goods, if the creator has abandoned you? Love them too, by all means, but love him more, and love them only for his sake. Proclaim his power; tell of his magnificent, glorious holiness; recount his wonders; speak of the power of his dread acts, for he is both lovable and terrible. Do not tell yourself that he treats us tenderly but does not threaten. If he did not treat us tenderly, there would be nothing to cheer us on, but if he never threatened, we would not be corrected. Those who praise you, Lord, will also speak of the power of your dread acts, not passing over in silence the power latent in your creation to punish and chastise us. They will not proclaim your eternal kingdom while keeping quiet about eternal fire. The praise you offer to God sets you on the right path, brothers and sisters, and it must show you both what to love and what to fear, what to seek and what to avoid, what to choose and what to reject. The time for choosing is now; the time for receiving our reward will come later. We need to hear now about the power of God's dread acts.

They will tell the tale of your greatness, says the psalm. But your greatness is infinite, for we heard in another verse that it has no limit. At least they will not be silent about it. That greatness of yours, Lord, of which we have been told that *there is no limit to his greatness*, of this they will tell the tale. How can they, if it has no boundaries? They will tell the tale of it as they praise it, and, just as your greatness has no end, so will their praise of it be unending. We can prove that God's praise will never end, for another psalm says, *Blessed are they who dwell in your house; they will praise you for ever and ever* (Ps 83:5(84:4)). *They will tell the tale of your greatness*, even of that infinite greatness.

Verse 7. The sweetness of grace

9. *They will belch forth the memory of the abundance of your sweetness.* What happy banquets this evokes! What are they going to eat, if they are to belch like that? *The memory of the abundance of your sweetness.* What does that mean—the memory of the abundance of your sweetness? It means that you did not forget us, even though we forgot you. The whole of fleshly humanity had forgotten God, but he did not forget his works. Because he did not forget us, his abiding mindfulness of us is a matter for proclamation, a truth to be told and told again. And because it is very delicious, it is to be eaten and then belched forth. So eat, that you may belch; so receive, that you may give. When you learn, you are eating it; when you teach, you are belching it forth; when you listen, you are eating; and when you preach, you are belching it forth. But make sure that what you belch forth is what you have eaten.

Think of an exceptionally eager guest at the banquet, the apostle John. It was not enough for him to share the Lord's table; he even had to recline on the Lord's breast[12] and drink in divine secrets from that hidden source. What did he belch forth? *In the beginning was the Word, and the Word was with God* (Jn 1:1).

They will belch forth the memory of the abundance of your sweetness. Would it not have been enough to say "the memory of you" or "the memory of your abundance" or "the memory of your sweetness"? No, the psalm had to say *the memory of the abundance of your sweetness.* What use would mere abundance have been if it had been sour? But it would have been just as disappointing if it had been sweet, but scanty.

10. *They will belch forth the memory of the abundance of your sweetness,* because you did not forget us, and, being mindful of us, you admonished us to bring us back to mindfulness of you. *All the ends of the earth will be reminded and will turn to the Lord* (Ps 21:28(22:27)). As they *belch forth the memory of the abundance of your sweetness* they will understand that there is nothing good in them except by your gift, that they could not have turned to you unless you had admonished them, and that they could not have been brought back to any remembrance of you if you had forgotten them. Reflecting by your grace on all these things, *they will rejoice in your holiness.*

---

12. See Jn 13:23.

I will say it again: reflecting by your grace on all these things, *they will rejoice in your holiness*, not their own.

Brothers and sisters, if you want to belch forth grace, drink grace. What do I mean by that—"drink grace"? Learn grace, understand grace. Before we came to be, we had no existence whatsoever. Then we, who had been nothing at all, were made human. So now we were people, human beings, but because we were offshoots from an ancient sinner we were ill-disposed, by nature children of wrath like everyone else.[13] Let us consider what God's grace was in our regard, not only the grace by which he made us but also that by which he made us anew. We are indebted to him for our existence and equally indebted to him for the fact that we are justified.[14] No one has any right to give God credit for his existence while attributing his justification to himself. If you do that, you are giving more credit to yourself than to God, for to be justified is a nobler state than to be human. You are allowing God the lesser achievement and claiming the greater for yourself. Give him the entire credit, praise him for all that you are, take care not to fall out of the hand of him who shaped you. Who brought you into being? Is it not written that God took mud from the earth and formed man?[15] Before you existed as a human being you were mud, you were nothing. But it is not only for this work of shaping you that you should give thanks to the artificer; there is another work of art that went into the making of you. *It is no work of yours, so let no one boast* (Eph 2:9), says scripture. But the apostle who said, *It is no work of yours, so let no one boast*, had reminded us of something else just before this. What was it? *By grace you have been saved, through faith, and this is not your own doing* (Eph 2:8). These are the apostle's words, not mine: *By grace you have been saved, through faith, and this*—namely, the fact that you were saved through faith—*is not your own doing*. That it was not your own doing was implied already by the word "grace," but he was kind enough to spell out the meaning more plainly, in case anyone understood him otherwise. For anyone of good insight the matter had been stated in its entirety by the words, *By grace you have been saved*. Whenever you hear the word "grace," understand that we are talking about something gratuitous. If salva-

---

13. See Eph 2:3.
14. This anti-Pelagian remark is for some commentators a further indication that the dating of the sermon in 416 or 417 is correct.
15. See Gn 2:7.

tion is given to you gratis, that means you contributed nothing and deserved nothing, for, if something is a recompense for merits, it is a just payment, not grace. But scripture insists, *By grace you have been saved, through faith.*

Explain it to us more clearly, please. There are arrogant people about, men and women who are complacent, who are ignorant of God's righteousness and try to establish their own.[16] Explain the point further, for their sake. "Very well," says the apostle. "Listen while I spell it out. Even this, that *you have been saved by grace*, is *not your own doing but the gift of God*" (Eph 2:8). But perhaps we did do something to deserve God's gifts? No, *it does not come from works, lest anyone boast.* How can this be true? Do we not do anything good? Yes, certainly we do. But how? Only because God acts in us, because by faith we make room in our hearts for him who does good works in us and through us. Listen again while scripture tells you the source of the good actions you perform: *We are his own handiwork, created in Christ Jesus for the good works which God has prepared in advance for us to walk in* (Eph 2:10).

This is the abundant sweetness of God's memory of us. When they belch this forth his preachers will *rejoice in his holiness*, not their own. What have you done for us, Lord? You have granted us existence and enabled us to praise you and to exult in your holiness and to belch forth the memory of the abundance of your sweetness. All this you have done for us, Lord, you whom we praise. Let us tell of it and praise you in the telling.

Verses 8–9. The generosity and forbearance of God

11. *The Lord is merciful and compassionate, forbearing and full of mercy. The Lord is kind to all, and his mercies extend over all his works.* If the Lord were not like this, he would not have sought to recover us. Scrutinize yourself. You were a sinner: what did you deserve? You had scorned God: what was due to you? Consider whether you could expect anything except punishment and torture. You see, then, what was owing to you, and you see what God, who gave gratis, has in fact given you. To a sinner pardon has been given, and the justifying Spirit. Charity and love have been given to you, the love in which you can perform all good works, and over and above these he will give you eternal life and fellowship with the angels. All

---

16. See Rom 10:3, though the Pelagians may be the target.

this flows from his mercy. There is no room whatever for you to vaunt your merits, because they are themselves God's gift to you.[17] *They will rejoice in your holiness.* You are *merciful and compassionate, O Lord, for you have given us all these things freely and for nothing.*

He is *forbearing.* What heinous sinners does he bear with! *The Lord is merciful and compassionate* to those whom he has already forgiven, and *forbearing* toward others to whom he has not yet granted pardon. He does not immediately condemn these but waits for them, and as he waits he calls to them, *Turn to me, and I shall turn to you* (Zech 1:3; Ml 3:7). In his extreme forbearance he declares, *I do not will the death of a sinner, but that he come back, and live* (Ezk 33:11). He is forbearing, but *you with your hard and impenitent heart are storing up against yourself anger that will be manifest on the day of God's just judgment, for he will render to each and all as their deeds deserve* (Rom 2:5–6). Do not delude yourself that his forbearance in putting up with sinners means that he will never prove himself just in punishing them. He has assigned his actions to appropriate seasons: at present he calls you, at present he exhorts you; he waits for you to come to a better mind, but you delay. It is a great mercy on his part that he has kept you from knowing the span of your life, so that you are uncertain when you will leave this world. If you are in daily expectation of departing, surely you will be converted sooner or later. This is a mark of his tender mercy.

Suppose, on the contrary, he had notified everyone of his or her appointed day. It would have led to an increase of sins, because they would all feel safe. He chose rather to give you the hope of pardon, so that you may not plunge deeper into sin out of desperation. Both presumption and despair are pitfalls for sinners. Listen to the voice of a desperate person whose despair is driving him to multiply sins, and to the voice of a presumptuous person who is lured into multiplying sins by rash hope, and then see how the mercy of God counters both errors. Listen first to the voice of a person in despair: "I am damned already, so why shouldn't I do whatever I like?" Now listen to the voice of the presumptuous: "The Lord's mercy is great. When I am converted later on, he will forgive me everything, so why shouldn't I do whatever I like?" The one sins because he despairs, the other because he is presumptuously confident. Either extreme is to be feared, both

---

17. Compare similar statements in *Confessions* IX,13,34; Letter 194,19; Exposition 2 of Psalm 70,5; Expositions of Psalms 98,8 and 102,7.

are perilous. Beware of desperation! Beware of misplaced hope! How does God's mercy counter both dangers, both evils? Let us see. What did you say, you who out of sheer despair decided to go on sinning? "I am damned already, so why shouldn't I do whatever I like?" But listen to the Lord's assurance in scripture: *I do not will the death of a sinner, only that he come back, and live* (Ezk 33:11). By this word from God a sinner is brought back to hope. But then there is another snare, for he or she might be encouraged by hope itself to go on sinning. What was it you were saying, you other sinner, you who were prompted to sin by your rash hope? "When, later on, I am converted, he will forgive me everything; so I will do whatever I like." You too need to listen to scripture: *Do not delay in turning back to the Lord, do not put it off from one day to another, for his anger will overtake you suddenly, and he will destroy you when the time comes for punishment* (Sir 5:8–9). Do not say, "Tomorrow I will be converted, tomorrow I will make myself pleasing to God, and then everything I did today and yesterday will be forgiven." It is true that God has promised you that he will forgive you on your conversion, but he has not promised to your tardiness that there will be any tomorrow.

12. *The Lord is kind to all, and his mercies extend over all his works.* If that is so, why does he condemn anyone? Why does his scourge fall upon any? Are they not also his works, the people whom he condemns or whips? To be sure they are. Do you want a demonstration that *his mercies extend over all his works*? Why does he cause his sun to rise over both the good and the wicked if not because of his patient forbearance? If he sends his rain on the just and the unjust alike,[18] does it not show that *his mercies extend over all his works*? In his forbearance he waits for a sinner, saying, *Turn to me, and I shall turn to you.* Is that not a sign that *his mercies extend over all his works*?

When he says, *Depart from me into the eternal fire which was prepared for the devil and his angels* (Mt 25:41), that is an exercise not of mercy but of severity; but while his mercy is bestowed on his own works, his severity is meted out not to his own works but to yours. If, however, you get rid of your bad works and nothing remains in you except his work, his mercy will not forsake you. If you do not forsake your own works, his severity will fall not on his works but on yours.

---

18. See Mt 5:45.

Verse 10. The very earth confesses to God's glory

13. *Let all your works confess to you, O Lord, and let your saints bless you.* The psalmist prays, *Let all your works confess to you.* What does he have in mind? What about the earth? Is it not God's work? And are not the trees his work? And all the animals, tame and wild, the fishes, the birds? Are not all of them works of the Lord? Most certainly they are. But then how can they all confess to him? It is not difficult to see that his works confess to him if I consider the angels, who are obviously God's works. So are human beings, and, when humans offer their confession, this too is the confession voiced by his works. But what about trees and stones? They surely lack the voice to confess to the Lord? By no means: all his works are summoned to confess to him; all, without exception. What are you saying? Earth and trees too? Yes, all his works. If all of them can be said to praise him, why can we not say that they all offer him their confession? The word "confession" covers not only confession of sins but the offering of praise too. You should not think that, whenever confession is mentioned, the reference is always to sin. This misconception is so prevalent that, whenever the word occurs during the proclamation of the divine scriptures, people beat their breasts from force of habit. But I can prove to you that confession may equally mean an utterance of praise. Did the Lord Jesus Christ have any sins to confess? Of course not; but he said, *I confess to you, Father, Lord of heaven and earth* (Mt 11:25). Confession can therefore mean praise.

How, then, are we to understand the psalm's prayer, *Let all your works confess to you, O Lord*? It means, "Let all your works praise you." But to say that is only to raise again in connection with praise the same question that we encountered with reference to confession. If the earth, the trees, and all other creatures that lack understanding are to be judged incapable of confession because they have no voice to confess with, they must be equally incapable of praising God, because they have no voice to proclaim him. But then what about all the creatures that the three youths enumerated as they walked about amid flames that did not hurt them? They enjoyed not only freedom from being burnt but also freedom to praise God, and they exhorted all creatures, from the highest heaven down to the earth, *Bless him, sing a hymn and exalt him above all for ever* (Dn 3:57–90).

Let us consider how such things can indeed sing hymns of praise. No one should suppose that a dumb stone or a dumb animal has a rational mind wherewith to understand God. People who have entertained that fancy have been adrift from the truth. God disposed all things and made all things. To some he gave feeling and intellect and immortality, as to the angels. To others, as to human beings, he gave feeling and intellect but also a mortal nature. To others again he gave bodily sensation but neither intellect nor immortality; these are the animals. To others he gave neither sensation nor intellect nor immortality, and among these are plants, trees, and stones;[19] yet in their own way of being not even these can fail,[20] for God has ordained[21] the whole creation in its proper hierarchies, from earth even to heaven, from visible things to invisible, from mortals to immortal beings. This intricate creation, this supremely ordered elegance, sweeping up from lowest to highest, flowing down from highest to lowest, nowhere interrupted but duly proportioned among dissimilar beings—the whole praises God. How does it all praise him? Because when you contemplate it and perceive its beauty, you praise God through it. The dumb earth sings with the voice of its beauty. You gaze upon the earth and you behold its loveliness, you observe its fecundity, you marvel at its secret powers, how it conceives its seed and how it may bring forth offspring different from what was sown. As you reflect on these things you long to question the earth. Your research is an asking of the questions. Wondering and awed, you search for the truth, you probe it patiently. You discover the earth's springing energy, its amazing beauty, its most excellent potency. But because it could not have such virtue in itself or of itself, swiftly there flashes into your mind the conviction that not by any possibility of its own can the earth have come to be, but only from the hands of its creator. This very truth that you have discovered is the earth's cry of confession, and to praise your creator you make the earth's cry your own. When you question the vast loveliness of this fair world, does it not reply to you, "I did not make myself. God made me"?[22]

---

19. He seems to assign living vegetation to the same level as rocks, perhaps for the sake of brevity.
20. Perhaps he means "fail in their praise."
21. Variant: "ordained and adorned."
22. This beautiful passage recalls Augustine's *Confessions* X,6,9.

Verses 11–13. The glorious beauty of the coming kingdom

14. *Let all your works confess to you, O Lord, and let your saints bless you.* Let your holy ones observe your creation as it sings its confession, so that they too may bless you by confessing your glorious works. Hear now the voices of your saints as they bless you, for when they hymn their benedictions, what do they say? *They will announce the glory of your kingdom, and will tell of your power.* How powerful is God, who made the earth! How powerful is God, who filled it with good things, who gave their several lives to all its living creatures, who sowed various seeds in the womb of the earth that it might bear so many different shrubs and such beautiful trees! How powerful is God, and how great! It is your calling, you saint of God, to question, and creation's part to respond to you. Its response is creation's song of confession, and as you hear it, you bless God and tell of his power.

15. *To make your power known to all people, and proclaim how glorious is the greatness of the beauty of your kingdom.* It is the saints who bring to our minds the glory of the magnificent beauty of your kingdom, reminding us of its immense loveliness. There is a special grandeur in its beauty, says the psalm; your kingdom has its own loveliness, a loveliness that is very great indeed. To be sure, everything that is beautiful derives its fair quality from you, but what must the beauty of your own kingdom be like? That kingdom should not crush us with fear, because it is lovely as well as terrifying, and full of delight for us. Think what dignity the saints will enjoy when they are invited, *Come, you who are blessed by my Father, take possession of the kingdom* (Mt 25:34)! What will they have left behind? And whither will they proceed? Try to envisage it, brothers and sisters and, if you can, or rather as best you can, think what the seemly loveliness of that coming kingdom must be like, for which we pray, *Thy kingdom come.* This is the kingdom for whose coming we long, the future kingdom that the saints proclaim. Cast your eyes over this world; it has its own decorous beauty. What beauty clothes earth, sea, air, sky, and stars! Do not all these fill the beholder with awe? Does not their beauty seem so outstanding that nothing more beautiful could ever be found? Yet amid this seemliness, amid this almost unutterable beauty, little worms and mice are your neighbors, and all the creatures that creep on the ground. All of them live with you amid this beauty. What, then, will be the dignity and loveliness of that kingdom where your only companions will be angels?

This is why the psalmist could not be content to speak of its glorious beauty. He could have used those words of any beautiful form created even in this world, whether growing from the earth or beaming from the sky. He spoke, rather, of *the greatness of the beauty of your kingdom,* hinting at a reality we do not yet see but believe in without seeing: a reality which, as we believe in it, we ardently desire and for the sake of which we are prepared to suffer anything. There is a certain beauty so great that it must be loved before it is seen, so that once seen it may be held fast.

16. *Your kingdom*: what kingdom do I mean? *Your kingdom is a kingdom that endures through all ages.* Even the kingdom of this present age has its own dignity, but it falls far short of that immense dignity inherent in the kingdom that lasts through all ages. *Your sovereignty abides in generation after generation.* This is the customary repetition that may refer either to each successive generation here or to the new generation that will follow the passing of the present era.[23]

Verse 13. The scriptures are a record of God's promises to us, and nearly all are fulfilled already

17. *The Lord is faithful in all his words, and holy in all his deeds,* the psalm continues. *The Lord is faithful in all his words, and holy in all his deeds.* For has he ever promised us anything and not given it? *The Lord is faithful in all his words, and holy in all his deeds.* Well, yes, there are certain things he has promised which are not yet given, but we have good reason to believe him on the strength of what he has given already. *The Lord is faithful in all his words, and holy in all his deeds.* We might well have believed him if he had chosen only to speak to us, but he wanted us to have his scriptures to hold onto; it is like promising something to a friend and saying to him, "Don't rely on word of mouth; I'll put it in writing for you." It was necessary for God's written guarantee to endure as each generation comes and goes, as the centuries roll by and mortals give way to their successors. God's own handwriting would be there for all the passers-by to read, so that they would keep to the way of his promise.

What great pledges he gave in that written guarantee, and how many he has kept already! Can men and women hesitate to believe him about the resurrection and the world to come—the only promise that remains unfulfilled—when the unbelievers must even now be

---

23. See above, section 6.

put to shame if he goes through his accounts with them? What if God says to you, "You have my written statement. I have promised that there will be a separation between[24] the good and the wicked and that an everlasting kingdom will be conferred on the faithful. Do you refuse to believe me? Read there in my own handwriting all the things I have promised, and then draw up an account with me. Even by reckoning what I have discharged already you can be certain that I will pay you what I still owe. In my written document you will find that I promised you my only Son, and indeed I did not withhold him but delivered him up for all of you,[25] so count that as paid. Consult my written statement again; I promised in it that through my Son I would give you the Holy Spirit as a pledge;[26] mark that item as paid. I promised the blood-shedding and the crowning of very glorious martyrs; reckon that promise as kept, and let the Massa Candida[27] confirm the discharge of my debt in this matter. The glory promised to the martyrs was alluded to in my document, where I wrote in their name, *For your sake we are done to death all day long* (Ps 43(44):22), but it would never have come to them without the fulfilment of another prophecy: *The nations raged, and the peoples devised futile schemes. The kings of the earth have arisen, and the rulers conspired together against the Lord and against his Christ.* (Ps 2:1–2) Rulers certainly did conspire together against Christians. But what else happened? Did I not also give you a promise in writing that the kings themselves would believe, and have I not kept my promise? Look at the passage where I guaranteed it: *All the kings of the earth will worship him, and all nations will serve him* (Ps 71(72):11). Ungrateful scoffer, when you read the record of my debt, and see that I have paid it, can you still doubt my promise?

"Read further in the document I wrote for you. Read how *the nations raged*; read how *my enemies*—Christ's enemies, that is—*reviled me, saying, When will he die, and his name disappear?* (Ps 40:6(41:5)) You know that all these things have happened and that people acted and spoke as I foretold. So now read the pledge I gave,

---

24. Variant: "I have promised concerning the recompense for."
25. See Rom 8:32.
26. See Acts 1:8; 2:24; and on *pignus* ("pledge") see Exposition of Psalm 122,5 and the note there.
27. On these martyrs see the note at Exposition of Psalm 49,9. The present Exposition was preached at Utica, near the place where they had died some 160 years earlier.

and to what I committed myself: *The Lord will prevail against them. He will exterminate all the gods of the gentiles throughout the earth. They will worship him from their own homes."* (Zeph 2:11)

Undeniably he has prevailed; he has exterminated all the gods of the gentiles throughout the earth. Does he not act as his written prophecy indicated, does he not keep his promise? He has posted up the discharge of his debts before the eyes of everyone. Some of his promises he kept in the time of our ancestors, when we were not there to see it; others he has kept in our own days, when our forebears are not here to watch. But throughout all generations he has discharged the debts he recorded in writing. How much is still outstanding? You have reckoned it all up, haven't you? If he has paid so much, is he to be regarded as untrustworthy because a few items still remain? That is an absurd suspicion. Why? Because *the Lord is faithful in all his words, and holy in all his deeds.*

Verses 14–17. The Lord sustains those who lose worldly status but remain faithful; he gives or withholds favors for our good

18. *The Lord strengthens all who are falling.* Whom does the psalm mean by *all who are falling*? All who fall away? No; probably only those who fall in a particular sense, because many fall away from God, and these cannot be the ones envisaged here. Others, many others, fall away from their own ideas about themselves.[28] If they were accustomed to entertain bad thoughts, they fall away from them, and then *the Lord strengthens all who are falling.* But some people, holy people, lose their worldly goods and are dishonored in the world's estimation. Once rich, they are impoverished; once of high rank, they are reduced to servility; and yet they are God's saints. They seem to be falling, but *the Lord strengthens all who are falling.* A righteous person falls seven times and gets up again, whereas the godless are weakened in their misfortunes.[29] When disasters overtake godless persons, the effect is to weaken them, but, when similar disasters

---

28. *Multi... decidunt a cogitationibus suis*; see Ps 5:11(10). The phrase is slightly ambiguous, as Augustine admitted in his Exposition of Psalm 5,13. He said there that it could mean either "Let them fall away from their own thoughts," in the sense of thinking evil no longer, or "Let them fall by their own thoughts," a bad fate. The context in Psalm 5 seemed to him to demand the latter meaning. Here, in Psalm 144, a different context demands a slightly modified version of the former.
29. See Prv 24:16.

befall the just, *the Lord strengthens all who are falling.* Job had fallen from his earlier high estate, from the bright fortune of temporal riches with which he had shone for a time; he had fallen away from his brilliant home. Are you wondering how far he had fallen? Right into the dunghill where he sat, and the Lord strengthened him in his fall. How much strength was he given? So much that, even though serious ulcers covered his entire body, he was able to reply to the wife who tempted him—the wife left to him by the devil to be the devil's own ally, *You have spoken like the silly woman you are. If we have received good things from the Lord's hands, should we not endure the bad too?* (Jb 2:10) How effectively the Lord had strengthened Job as he fell! *The Lord strengthens all who are falling.* Scripture says elsewhere, *When the just falls he will suffer no harm, for the Lord strengthens his hand* (Ps 36(37):24.

And he raises up all who have been struck down, all those who belong to him, for God thwarts the proud.[30]

19. *The eyes of all hope in you, and you give them their food in due time.* You, Lord, are like someone giving refreshment to a sick person at the right moment by giving him what he ought to have at the time he ought to have it, and giving him only what is good for him. Sometimes, when a request is made to God, he does not give us what we ask for, because he who cares for us in our infirmity knows the right time to give it.

Why am I making these remarks, brothers and sisters? So that, if perhaps one of you has asked God for some reasonable thing and the prayer has not been heard, the petitioner may not be discouraged or put off. I am not talking about an instance where someone asks God for something bad, of course, for in that case to grant it would harm the petitioner. No, in the case where what people ask for is something good and right, their eyes must hope for the food that God gives in due time. If he does not grant a request, this is so that the granting of it may not be for the suppliant's harm.

It was not some bad or unreasonable favor that the apostle sought when he kept on begging that the sting of the flesh, that messenger of Satan that belabored him, might be taken away. He asked, and he did not get what he asked for, because it was still the time for experiencing weakness, not the right time for food. *My grace is sufficient for you,* the Lord assured him, *for my power finds complete scope in*

---

30. See Jas 4:6; 1 Pt 5:5.

weakness (2 Cor 12). Yet the devil asked for Job, in order to tempt him, and was given what he asked.[31] Pay attention to this great mystery, my brothers and sisters; learn from it, ponder it frequently, lay it up in your minds and never forget it, for temptations come thick and fast in this world. What am I saying? Am I really comparing the apostle with the devil? The apostle asks God for something and does not get it; the devil asks and immediately gets what he wants. Yes, but the apostle is refused so that he may grow more perfect; the devil is granted his wish for his own condemnation. In any case, Job was restored to health when the time was right. Restoration was delayed only to test him. He sat there in his ulcerous condition for a long time and talked a great deal and begged God to take away his misfortunes, but God went on not taking them away. God had heard the devil's prayer more quickly when he asked permission to tempt Job than he heard Job himself when he begged for healing.

Learn from these examples not to murmur against God, even when your prayers are not heard. If you murmur, a verse we heard earlier in the psalm will cease to be true in your case: *During every single day I will bless you.* God's only Son himself exemplified this. He had come to suffer, undoubtedly. He had come to pay a debt for which he was not liable, to die at the hands of sinners, and to cancel the bond[32] that decreed our death by blotting it out with his blood. He had come for this purpose. Yet, to give you an example of patience, he prayed—he who transfigured our lowly body to conform it to his glorious body[33] prayed, *Father, if it is possible, let this cup pass from me.* He did not get what he seemed to be asking. But, to give full meaning to that verse, *during every single day I will bless you,* he continued, *Yet not what I will, but what you will be done, Father* (Mt 26:39). *The eyes of all hope in you, and you give them their food in due time.*

20. *You open your hand, and fill every living creature with blessing.* There are times when you do not give, but you give when it is opportune. You delay but do not deny us,[34] and you decide when the time is right.

---

31. See Jb 1:9–12; 2:4–6.
32. See Col 2:14.
33. See Phil 3:21.
34. *Differs, non aufers.*

21. *The Lord is just in all his ways.* He is just both when he strikes and when he heals; there is no inequity in him. In point of fact all the saints took care, when they prayed in their troubles, to praise his justice first and beg favors afterwards. The first thing they always said was, "What you are doing is just." This was how Daniel made his petitions, as did all the saints: "Your judgments are just, we have deserved to suffer, it is right that this suffering should come upon us."[35] They did not accuse God of injustice, nor did they attribute to him any lack of equity or wisdom. First they praised him as he chastised them, and thus they experienced him as the one who fed them. *The Lord is just in all his ways.* Let no one who has to endure some calamity think that God is unjust; rather let him praise God's justice and admit his own injustice. *The Lord is just in all his ways, and holy in all his actions.*

Verses 18–19. The right way to pray for things, and God's way of answering

22. *The Lord is close to all who call upon him.* If the psalmist had stopped there, he would have seemed to contradict another saying of scripture: *They will call upon me, but I will not listen to them* (Prv 1:28). But look how he continues: *to all who call upon him in truth.* There are many who invoke him, but not in truth; they seek something from him but do not seek God himself. Why do you love God? "Because he has given me good health," someone says. It is quite obvious that he has given it, for there is no health, no salvation,[36] except from him. Or: "Because though I used to be penniless he has given me a rich wife, and she waits on me," someone else replies. She too is God's gift to you; you speak truly. "He has given me lots of fine children, and a staff of servants. He has given me all the good things I could want." And is that why you love him? Do you seek nothing further? Be hungry and knock on the householder's door; he still has more to give you. In spite of all the things you have received, you are a pauper, and you don't even know it. You are still wearing the tattered flesh of your mortality; you have not yet been arrayed in the robe of immortal glory. Have you stopped praying for it, as though you were full-fed and needed nothing? *Blessed are those who hunger and thirst for righteousness, for they shall be satisfied*

---

35. See Dn 3:27–31; 9:5–19.
36. The same word, *salus*, can cover both.

(Mt 5:6). If you know God is good because he gave you those things, how much more blessed will you be when he has given you himself? You desired so much from him; but, I beg you, desire himself. Those other things are not really more delightful than he is. They cannot bear comparison with him.

When a person has received good things from God and finds joy in them, yet puts God before all he has received, that person calls upon God in truth. Ask yourself what you would do if God wished to take away from you everything that gives you joy. Will he be loved no longer, will there be no one to say, *The Lord gave, and the Lord has taken away. This has happened as the Lord willed: may the Lord's name be blessed* (Jb 1:21)? Perhaps the one from whom God has taken it all may protest, "O God, what have I done to you? Why have you taken things away from me, yet given them to others? You shower gifts on the ungodly and deprive your own followers." You are accusing God of being unjust and lauding your own justice. Turn it around the other way: accuse yourself and praise him. You will be on the right lines if you find God pleasing in all the good things he does and do not find him displeasing in any of the bad things you suffer. This is what it means to call upon God in truth. When people invoke him like this, he hears them. *He is close* to you, for although he has not yet given you what you want, he is there for you nonetheless. He is close in the way that a physician stays near a patient when he applies some painful remedy to an eye or the internal organs, intending to heal through some caustic procedure. The patient begs him to remove it, but the doctor waits for the appropriate time; he does not do what the sick person demands, but neither does he go away. He stays near and abstains from action; in fact it is because he is so near and attentive that he does not act. He has applied the remedy for the purpose of healing the sick person, and it is equally for the sake of healing that he refuses to do what the sick person asks. He does not grant your immediate request, because he is hearing you with a view to your future health. His decision is undeniably in accord with your true desire, because a patient certainly wants to get well, even if he does not want to be seared by the treatment.

The Lord too is in this sense *close to all who call upon him*. All, without distinction? No, *to all who call upon him in truth*. And he has always strengthened such people when they were falling, all those *who call upon him in truth*.

23. *He will fulfill the desires of those who fear him.* He will fulfill them; he truly will. Even though he seems not to do so at once, he will. There is no doubt at all that, if you have such reverent fear of God that you do what he wants, he in turn will almost make himself your servant and do what you want. *He will hear their prayers and save them.* The doctor hears them, you see, in order to save his patients. When will he act? The apostle tells you: *In hope we have been saved. But if hope is seen, it is hope no longer, for when someone sees what he hopes for, why should he hope for it? But if we hope for what we do not see, we wait for it in patience.* (Rom 8:24–25) What we hope for is the salvation which, according to Peter, *is ready to be revealed at the end-time* (1 Pt 1:5).

Verse 20. Gentleness and severity in God

24. *The Lord guards all who love him, but he will destroy all sinners.* From this verse you can see that in God there is not only immense sweetness but also severity. He will save all who hope in him, all who believe, all who fear him, and all who call upon him in truth, but *he will destroy all sinners.* Who are covered by this phrase, *all sinners*? Surely those who continue obstinately in their sins, those who presume to rebuke God instead of themselves, and those who argue against God every day. It must also mean those who despair of forgiveness for their offences, and for very despair pile up offences more and more. But it also means people who delude themselves with the promise of forgiveness, making that promise an excuse for not renouncing their sins and for despising God. The time will come for all these to be weeded out. Two groups will be formed, one at Christ's right hand and the other at his left. The just will receive an eternal kingdom, but the others will depart into everlasting fire.[37]

Verse 21. Conclusion: universal praise

25. We have heard about the blessing that the Lord imparts, about the words of the Lord, the wonders of the Lord, the mercies of the Lord, the severity of the Lord, and his providential care for all he has made. We have heard the confession sung to him by all his works. Now, with all these things in mind, hear how the psalm concludes by praising him: *My mouth will tell forth the praise of the Lord. May all flesh bless his holy name throughout the age, and for ages of ages.*

---

37. See Mt 25:33–34.46.

Exposition of Psalm 145

A Sermon to the People

While dwelling on earth, we are called heavenward by God's word

1. The songs God has inspired are the delight of our spirit, and we cannot weep over them except with tears of joy. For every faithful person on pilgrimage in this world there is nothing more agreeable than the thought of the city which is the goal of our journey; yet while we are still exiled from it our memory of that city cannot be altogether free from pain and sighs.[1] Nonetheless the certainty that we shall reach it one day consoles and encourages us while we are still wayfarers. Allow the words of God to seize your heart,[2] and let him who owns you claim your minds as his rightful possession, so that they may not turn aside to any other end. Each one of you should be wholly present here, yet in such a way that you are also not here. What I mean is this: we must be so entirely present to the word of God which sounds here on earth that we are exalted by it, and are no longer held by the earth. God is with us in order that we may be with him; he who came down to us in order to be with us is at work now to draw us up to himself, so that we may be in his company. Until this should be finally accomplished he did not disdain to share our exile, though he who created all things is nowhere an exile himself.[3]

Verse 2. Rejoice in hope

2. Listen now to what this psalm is singing. We hear the voice of someone inviting his soul to praise God, and, if you are willing, it is your voice too. *Praise the Lord, my soul*, he says. Your soul is sometimes troubled by the calamities and trials of the present life, whether you consent or not. In another psalm the speaker addresses his gloomy soul, demanding, *O my soul, why are you sorrowful?* (Ps 41:6.12; 42:5(42:5.11; 43:5)) But he wants to relieve his soul of its

---

1. The sermon opens, as it also ends, with one of Augustine's favorite themes, our longing for Zion.
2. Variant: "your heart to seize the words of God."
3. Augustine does not discuss the title of the psalm, which forms verse 1.

distress, so he suggests to it a motive for joy, though a joy that depends on hope, not on reality already achieved. To his troubled, anxious soul in its discouragement and grief he says, *Hope in the Lord, for I will still confess to him* (Ps 42(43):5). What filled him with hope and enabled him to rise above sadness was his confession. We can imagine his sad soul telling him the reason for its dejection: "How can you say to me, *Hope in the Lord*? I am brought up short by the memory of my sins. I know the sins I have committed, and do you tell me to *hope in the Lord*?" He replies, "Yes, it is true that you committed all those sins, but where does your hope lie? In confession, so *I will still confess to him*."

As God hates a sinner who defends his misdeeds, so does he raise up the sinner who confesses. The soul that has been given this hope can arise, for such hope necessarily implies joy. Even though we are beset with difficulties as far as this life is concerned, and tossed by storms and tempests, our soul can arise and stand up straight because it is joyful in its hope. As the apostle says, we must be *joyful in hope, and patient in anguish* (Rom 12:12). The soul has been uplifted by God that it may praise God, and so it is bidden, *Praise the Lord, my soul*.

Who is the speaker, if the soul is addressed? Not the body, for the soul is nobler than the body

3. But who is this speaking, and to whom is the advice being given? It surely cannot be the flesh that counsels, *Praise the Lord, my soul*? Is the flesh capable of giving good advice to the soul? We should be thankful if the flesh even remains submissive, if through the strength imparted by the Lord we can keep it in subjection and serving our good purposes, subordinate to us like a slave taken on only under certain stipulations. It is enough for us if the flesh does not get in our way. In any case, dearly beloved, advice is customarily sought from those better than ourselves.

It is true, of course, that, while our soul is good, our flesh is also good, because both were created by him who made all things exceedingly good.[4] Both are good, each according to its kind, yet the apostle says, *The body is a dead thing by reason of sin* (Rom 8:10). It is also true that a different kind of body is promised to us, one that we do not possess as yet, over the redemption of which we rejoice in hope. As the apostle teaches, *We groan inwardly as we await our*

---

4. See Gn 1:31.

adoption as God's children, the redemption of our bodies. For in hope we have been saved. But if hope is seen, it is hope no longer, for when someone sees what he hopes for, why should he hope for it? But if we hope for what we do not see, we wait for it in patience. (Rom 8:23-25) So, although our bodies are indeed good, as long as they are mortal because of sin, as long as they are needy, as long as they are prone to decay, as long as they are so changeable that they cannot remain self-consistent for a moment, it is undeniable that we must long for an ultimate redemption that will transform them into something unlike their present state. What will they be like in the future? Something like what the apostle describes in another place: *This corruptible body must put on incorruptibility, and this mortal body be clothed in immortality* (1 Cor 15:53). But even when our body has undergone that change, when it has become a heavenly, spiritual body, an angelic body fit for companionship with angels, even then it will not be giving advice to the soul. The body, simply in virtue of being a body, will always be inferior to the soul. Any soul, however abject, is more excellent than the most excellent body.

4. What I have just said should not seem strange to you: that even a disreputable, sinful soul is nobler than a fine, outstandingly beautiful body. The soul is better not by its merits but by its nature, and this is true even of a sinful soul, defiled by the stains of its lusts. Gold, even tarnished gold, is better than the purest lead. Let your minds rove over all created beings and you will see that what we are saying is quite credible: even a soul in disgrace is more worthy of praise than a laudable body.

Think of two realities, a soul and a body. I blame the soul, and I praise the body. I blame the soul because it is sinful, but I praise the body because it is healthy. But if we consider the nature of each, then within its nature I either praise the soul or find fault with the soul; and similarly within its own nature I either praise the body or find fault with the body. If you ask me which of the two is better—the one I blamed or the one I praised—you will receive a puzzling answer. To be sure, I condemned one and praised the other, yet, when you ask me which is better, I reply that the one I condemned is better than the one I praised. If you find this baffling when we are talking about the soul and the body, think instead of the other pair we used as an example just now: gold and lead. Remember, I found fault with the gold. It is not fine gold, there is dross in it, it does not gleam as it should, it is not sufficiently purified. But the lead is of the best quality, more thoroughly purified than any other. I have condemned the former and praised the latter; I have put them both before you with contempt for the one and approval for the other. After listening to the condemnation and the praise, ask me which is better. I will answer, "Gold is nobler, even if it contains impurities, than purified lead." "But," you ask, "in what way is it better? And if it is better, why did you condemn it?" Why did I condemn it? Because the gold is not yet what it has the potential to be. What can it become? Purified, and thus of higher worth. Because it has not yet been purified it deserved to be disparaged. Why was the lead commended? Because it is already so well purified that it is not capable of further improvement. Similarly you could compare a very fine horse with a very wicked human being, and you would have to admit that you rate the person you censure higher than the horse you admire. If someone asks you which of the two is higher in dignity, you will answer, "The man," not because of his merits but because of his nature. So too where skills are in question. You may, for instance, recognize the excellence of a cobbler but denounce some lawyer because of his ignorance of many of the laws. You have praised the cobbler and condemned the lawyer, but ask yourself which of the two ranks higher. An unskilled lawyer takes precedence over a perfect cobbler.

Try to grasp the point, beloved ones. We praise many things and condemn many others, but when questioned we often regard the things we condemn more highly than those we praise. In this sense the nature of the soul is nobler than the nature of the body. The soul is an excellent creature, a spiritual entity, an incorporeal reality akin to the substance of God himself. It is invisible, but it rules the body, moves the limbs, directs the senses, gives birth to thoughts, implements actions, and makes room in itself for the images of infinite realities. In the end we have to ask, brothers and sisters, if anyone is capable of adequately praising the human soul. And if we flag in praising the soul, what kind of praise do we owe him who created it? Yet so powerful is his grace that the psalmist is driven to say, *Praise the Lord, my soul.* Who is sufficient to praise God? If anyone were bidden, "Praise yourself," he might well fall short; yet the psalmist says, "Praise God!" Try with all the loving devotion you can muster: you will flag in praising him, but it is better to fail in praising God than to succeed in praising yourself. When you praise God but cannot express what you want to, your thoughts seek the larger space within you,[5] and this very stretching makes yet more room within you for him whom you are praising.

The soul admonishes itself: the rational mind counsels the lower faculties

5. To return now to the question I began to propose: Who is saying, *Praise the Lord, my soul*? It cannot be the flesh speaking. Even an angelic body is lower than the soul, and the lower cannot give advice to the higher. The soul is in a bad state if it looks to the body for advice. Properly obedient flesh is the servant of the soul; the soul rules and the flesh is ruled; the one gives orders and the other carries them out. How can the body ever be in a position to give an admonition like that to the soul?

Who is it, then, who counsels, *Praise the Lord, my soul*? We cannot find anything in a human being other than flesh and soul; the whole human person is comprised of spirit and flesh. Can it be, then, that the soul is speaking to itself, somehow commanding itself, exhorting and arousing itself? Perhaps some disturbances were causing it to waver in some dimension of its being, but then another part realized what was happening? The part we call the rational mind, the faculty that thinks about wisdom, that even now cleaves to the Lord and longs for him—this faculty has become aware that some of its lower powers are being seriously perturbed by worldly impulses, that they are being lured toward external things by earthly cravings and forsaking God, who dwells within the soul. The soul then recalls itself from exterior to interior, from lower things to higher, and admonishes itself, "*Praise the Lord, my soul*. What satisfaction can the world afford you? What is it that you want to praise? What is it that you want to love? In whatever direction you turn with the senses of the body, you will see only the sky or the earth. Whatever you love on earth is earthly, and whatever you love even in the sky is still corporeal. Everywhere you find things to love and things to praise: yes, but how much more worthy of praise is he who made these things which evoke your praise? You have lived under their spell for too long, buffeted by conflicting desires. You bear the marks of the wounds they have dealt you. You are torn apart by these many loves, restless everywhere and nowhere at peace. Gather yourself together into your real self. If anything outside you has been giving you joy,

---

5. Variant: "seek earlier things."

ask who is its author. You may think that there is nothing better on earth than this thing or that: gold or silver, for instance, animals, trees, pleasing landscapes—cast your mind over the whole earth. Or what is better in the sky than sun, moon, and stars? Cast your mind right across the heavens. All these things individually, and all of them together, are exceedingly good, because God made all things exceedingly good. All around you is the beauty of his work, and it all speaks to you of the beauty of the artist. If you admire the edifice, love the builder. Do not be so bewitched by what he has made that you stray from him who made it. He has subordinated these captivating creatures to you, because he has subordinated you to himself. If you cling to him who is above you, you will tread underfoot what is beneath you; but if you desert him who is above you, those lower things will become your torment."

This is how matters have been arranged, my brothers and sisters. Human beings have been given their bodies as servants. We have God as our master and the body as our servant; we have our creator over us and under us what has been created. The rational soul is, so to speak, stationed between the two. It has been given a law: it must cleave to what is higher and control what is below. If it is not itself ruled by the higher, it cannot take command of the lower. It is then dragged along by what is inferior to itself, and so it forsakes him who is better. It can no longer rule what it used to rule, because it has refused to be ruled by him who used to rule it.

Illuminated by God, the soul gives itself counsel through the medium of its rational mind. Through its reason it is open to the truth established in the eternity of its maker. There, in its rational mind, the soul can communicate with an awe-inspiring reality, a reality it is drawn to praise, to love, to desire, and to seek. It does not yet grasp this reality or possess it, but a gleam of that light has brushed against it, though the soul is not yet strong enough to stay there. This is why it recalls itself to some kind of sanity, saying, *Praise the Lord, my soul.*

Imperfect praise on earth will give way to perfect praise in heaven

6. But do we need that admonition, brothers and sisters? We do praise the Lord, don't we? Don't we sing a hymn[6] every day? Don't our lips sing and our hearts bring forth praise to God, as far as our puny strength allows? He whom we praise is very great, but our

---

6. Variant: "hymns."

competence to praise him is still inadequate. Will the praise-singer ever match the excellence of the one who is praised?

A person stands there praising God, perhaps for quite a long time. And often enough, while his lips are moving in song, his thoughts are flitting to and fro among all kinds of desires. So what has happened? Our reason was standing there, so to speak, intent on praising God, but our soul was vacillating, wavering hither and thither between various desires or worries about its business. The mind looked down from above upon this flighty soul and rebuked its anxieties about its troubles: *"Praise the Lord, my soul.* Why are you so preoccupied about other matters? Why does care about earthly, perishable things engross you? Stand here with me and praise the Lord." But the soul is heavily burdened and lacks the strength to stand as steadily as it should, so it replies to the mind, *I will praise the Lord throughout my life.* What does *throughout my life* mean? The implication is, "At present I am still in my dead state."

You then, you who are listening, first exhort yourself, *Praise the Lord, my soul.* Your soul will respond to you, "I am praising him as best I can, in my frail, puny, feeble way." Why do you say that? Because as long as we are in the body we are exiled from the Lord.[7] Why is it that you praise the Lord so imperfectly, so unsteadily? Put your question to scripture, and it will tell you: because *the corruptible body weighs down the soul, and this earthly dwelling oppresses a mind that considers many things* (Wis 9:15). Relieve me of this body that weighs down the soul, and then I will praise the Lord. Dismantle this earthly dwelling that clogs the mind as it considers many things, and then I will withdraw from the many and flow with all my being toward the one.[8] Then I will praise the Lord. But, as long as I am in this state, I cannot, because I am too heavily burdened.

Will you remain silent, then, and render no perfect praise to the Lord? No, *I will praise the Lord throughout my life.*

---

7. See 2 Cor 5:6.
8. *Tolle mihi terrenam habitationem deprimentem sensum multa cogitantem, ut a multis in unum confluam.* In the preceding quotation from Wisdom it is clearly the mind that *considers many things*, though its operations are hampered by its earthly habitation. In the sentence that follows the quotation Augustine, by adjusting the grammar, appears to leave open the possibility that the multiple thoughts belong to the earthly habitation, and the mind's job is to summon the earth-bound soul back to unity.

7. What is meant by *throughout my life*? Here on earth, Lord, *you are my hope*. We say to him, *You are my hope* here, but you will be *my portion* not here but *in the land of the living* (Ps 141:6(142:5)), for here below we are in the land of the dying. We are on our way out of it, but it makes a great difference which route we take. A bad person is in exile here, and a good person too is in exile here. It is not as though the good one were on the way out and the bad one staying here, nor as though the bad one were departing and the good one staying. Both are on their way, but not to the same destination.

There were two men: a pauper lying at a rich man's gate and a rich man clad in purple and fine linen who banqueted splendidly every day. Both were in this world and both passed out of it, but not to the same place. Different places received them because their different routes corresponded to their different merits. The poor man crossed over into Abraham's embrace, while the rich man crossed over into the torments of the underworld. They had been near neighbors on earth, one in the house and the other outside the gate, but after death they were so far apart that Abraham could say, *There is a great chasm fixed between us and you* (Lk 16:26).

So then, brothers and sisters, we feed on hope now, but there is no real life for us other than the life that is promised us in the future. Here our experience is of groaning, temptations, miseries, and dangers; but in the world to come our soul will praise the Lord as he deserves to be praised, as suggested in another psalm: *Blessed are they who dwell in your house; they will praise you for ever and ever* (Ps 83:5(84:4)). Our whole occupation then will be praise. But when will I praise him like that? *Throughout my life*. What is your existence now? The answer might be, "My death." How is that? Because I am exiled from the Lord. If it is life to cling to him, it is death to be far away. Have you any consolation, then? Yes, hope. In this world you are already living in hope; praise him from your hope, sing to him in hope. Do not sing from that position which spells death to you, but sing to him from the place where you are truly alive. From the grief of this world comes your death, but you live in hope of the world to come. *I will praise the Lord throughout my life*.

8. How will you praise your Lord? *I will sing psalms to him as long as I exist*. What will that offering of praise be like, if the psalmist can say of it, *I will sing psalms to him as long as I exist*? Consider what it must be, brothers and sisters. If there is to be everlasting praise, there must be an everlasting mode of being. You exist now, but are

the psalms you sing to God as uninterrupted as your existence? Obviously not, for just now you were singing psalms then you turned aside to attend to some business, and now you are not singing. Yet you go on existing. You exist, but you are not singing psalms. It may be that you were swayed by some disorderly craving, and so you are not only not singing psalms but you are even making some noise that offends God's ears. All the same, you still exist. What will your offering of praise be like when it is coterminous with your very being? But it is not enough to say that, not enough to say, *as long as I exist*, for will there ever come a time when the speaker will not exist? That *as long as* will be eternal, and so it truly merits the epithet *long*. Anything that comes to an end within the span of time, however extensive it seems, is not really long. *I will sing psalms to him as long as I exist.*

Verses 3–4. Do not trust in powerful men, or regard the minister of baptism as the source of salvation

9. Still, for the time being you will praise the Lord throughout your life and sing psalms to him who will be your God for as long as you exist. This is quite right. Whatever you anticipate as necessary for you here, hope for from God. Hope must never leave us on this pilgrimage. This is our time of trial, during which we are exposed to the shameless tricks of the enemy. The temptations of the world beset us on all sides, and we are embroiled in struggles and vexations. What are we to do? Listen to the next verse: *Put not your trust in princes.* Brothers and sisters, this is a very serious matter, a command issued from on high by the divine voice that sounds in our ears. I do not know what kind of infirmity it is that makes a soul in trouble despair of the Lord in this world and want to look for human aid. You have only to say to someone in distress, "There is a powerful man who will help you out," and the sufferer smiles and rejoices and picks himself up. But if instead you say to him, "God will deliver you," he freezes in despair. How can you be happy when the help of a mortal man is promised you and sad when you are promised the help of one who is immortal? If you are offered deliverance by someone who needs deliverance along with you, you cheer up as though some mighty aid were at hand, yet, if you are promised a deliverer who himself needs no deliverance, you despair as though it were no more than an idle tale. Away with such thoughts! They are[9] far astray, but a real and

---

9. Variant: "He is."

dreadful death lurks in them. Come near, kindle your desire, begin to seek and recognize him by whom you were made. He will not forsake his handiwork unless his handiwork forsakes him. Turn back to him of whom you declare, *I will praise the Lord throughout my life, I will sing psalms to him as long as I exist.* The psalmist, already filled with the might of the Spirit, is warning us. To people still far off, to distant exiles, to those who are not only unwilling to praise God but are even reluctant to hope for anything from God, the psalmist says, *Put not your trust in princes, or in the sons of men, for in them you will find no salvation.*

In one Son of Man alone is there salvation, and in him not because he is a son of man but because he is the Son of God; not because of the nature he took from you but because of that which he retained in himself. It is rightly said that there is no salvation in any human being, because even in him there is salvation for us only inasmuch as he is God, *he who is sovereign over all, God, blessed for ever.* Of Christ scripture says, *From them Christ was born according to the flesh* (Rom 9:5). From whom? From the Jews. From the patriarchs *Christ was born according to the flesh.* But was that all there was in Christ, the nature that came to birth according to the flesh? No, for in that nature whereby he is *sovereign over all, God, blessed for ever*, he was not born according to the flesh. We find salvation in him because *salvation is from the Lord.* Another psalm affirms this: *Salvation is from the Lord, and may your blessing be upon your people* (Ps 3:9(8)).

Human agents speak falsely if they arrogate to themselves the power to grant salvation. Let them grant it to themselves. Your reply to such a proud person should be, "You are boasting when you say that you are conferring salvation on me. Give it to yourself. Ask yourself whether you have it; consider carefully your own frailty and you will see that it is not yet yours. Do not invite me to look for salvation from you, then. Rather wait for it along with me."

Put not your trust in princes, or in the sons of men, for in them you will find no salvation. All sorts of princes spring up nowadays from I know not where, saying, "I baptize people, and what I give is holy. If you have received baptism from anyone else, you have nothing, but if you received it from me, you have what matters."[10] So this is your

---

10. He obviously has the Donatists in view. On their practice of rebaptizing Catholics who joined them, see Expositions of Psalms 39,1 and 131,14. That the validity of a sacrament did not depend on the holiness of the minister was

ambition, you who pose as a prince, to be among those sons of men in whom we cannot find salvation? Am I going to qualify for salvation because you give it to me? Does what you give belong to you? In fact, do you even give it? Is it even correct to say you give it? If a pipe has the right to say that it gives water of itself, if a conduit can claim that it gushes from its own resources, then a preacher can rightly claim that he sets people free. But as for me, when I see the water I think of the spring, and in the tones of the preacher I recognize the judge.

You will in no way be the author of my salvation. He alone will be that, he of whom I am certain, whereas about you I have no certainty. If you forsake your arrogance, I will not be the only one who is uncertain about you: you will be uncertain of yourself. My salvation comes from him *who is sovereign over all,* because *salvation is from the Lord.* You are among the sons of men, you are among the princes, but I am listening to the psalm that warns me, *Put not your trust in princes, or in the sons of men, for in them you will find no salvation.*

10. What are these *sons of men* anyway? Are they any different from the great crowd of human beings? Of one who makes high claims the psalm predicts, *His spirit will go forth and return to its own country.* Such a person talks a lot, but he does not know how long he will be able to go on talking; he threatens us, but he does not know how long he will live. His spirit goes forth suddenly, to return to its own land. Does he choose the time of its going? It will go forth and its departure will not wait upon his wishes; when he is not expecting it, his spirit will go forth to its own country. And when his spirit departs, his flesh will go back to the earth. But it was the flesh that proudly proclaimed, "Trust me, and I will give you what you want," for the only people who would speak so are those of whom scripture says, *They are only flesh* (Gn 6:3). *His spirit will go forth and return to its own country, and on that day all his*[11] *plans will come to nothing.* Where is his conceit now? Where is his pride? What has become of his boasting?

But, you may say, perhaps he has passed over to a good place, into the company of the just? Well, perhaps, if he has passed at all, for I do not know what kind of place a fellow who talked like that will have passed to. He spoke in pride, and I do not know whither such

---

a vital point in Augustine's opposition to the Donatists. Compare the note at Exposition of Psalm 10,1.

11. Variant: *their.*

people are bound, unless I look into another psalm and discover that their passage is a bad one. *I saw the godless exalting himself very high, overtopping the cedars of Lebanon. But I passed further on, and look! He was not there. I searched for him, but his place was not to be seen.* (Ps 36(37):35-36) That devout person, who passed by and did not find the godless, himself reached a place where no godless people are to be found.

Let us all listen carefully to this, brothers and sisters. I beg you, you who are beloved by God, let us all hear the message. Whatever trouble we may be in, or however keen our desire for God's gifts, let us not put our hope *in princes, or in the sons of men, for in them we will find no salvation.* The whole lot of them are mortal, transient, ephemeral. Of each of them the psalm predicts, *His spirit will go forth and return to its own country, and on that day all his plans will come to nothing.*

Verse 5. God will be your possession, and you will be his

11. What are we to do, then, if we cannot put our trust in mere mortals or in powerful men? Where are we to turn? *Blessed is everyone whose helper is the God of Jacob.* Not this or that human ally, not this or that angel; rather, *blessed is everyone whose helper is the God of Jacob,* for so powerful a helper was he to Jacob that he turned Jacob into Israel.[12] That was a mighty act of help, for "Israel" means "one who already contemplates God." While you are here below, still a wayfarer, you do not yet see God, but if you have the God of Jacob as your helper you are the one who will see God. All your toil, all your groaning, will be over and done with, all your gnawing cares will pass and joyful praises will take their place. *Blessed is everyone whose helper is the God of Jacob,* for such a person is like Jacob.

But how can he or she be called blessed while still sighing in the present life? *His hope is in the Lord, his God.* That is the reason for his beatitude: *His hope is in the Lord, his God.* The God in whom his hope is lodged is his possession, his property. Was I wrong to say that, brothers and sisters—that God will be our property? But suppose I put it a little differently and say that God will be our inheritance? *You are my hope, my portion in the land of the living* (Ps 141:6(142:5)). You, Lord, will be my portion. It is true, brothers and sisters. You will be both possessed and possessors: you will be God's possession and

---

12. See Gn 32:28.

God will be your possession. You will be his possession so that you may be cultivated and cared for[13] by him, and he will be your possession so that you may devote yourself to his worship. You cultivate God, and you are yourself cultivated by God. It is quite correct to say, "I cultivate God." But how am I cultivated by God? We find the apostle saying as much: *You are God's cultivated field, and God's building* (1 Cor 3:9). And the Lord likewise: *I am the vine, you are the branches, and my Father is the vine-dresser* (Jn 15:1.5). God tends and cultivates you so that you may be fruitful, and you cultivate and worship God—so that you may be fruitful! It is good for you to be cultivated by God, and it is also good for you to cultivate God. If our farmer-God withdraws from anyone, that person degenerates into a desert; and if we, the farmers, withdraw from God, it is still we who become a desert. God does not grow because you give him your services, nor does he dwindle if you leave him. He will be our possession so that he may feed and tend us, and we shall be his possession so that he may rule us.

Verse 6. The glory of God in creation

12. *His hope is in the Lord, his God.* Who is this Lord, his God? Give me your attention now, brothers and sisters. Many people worship a multiplicity of gods, and they call these their lords and their gods. But the apostle reminds us, *Even if there are beings called gods in the sky or on earth (as in fact there are gods and lords aplenty), still, for us there is one God from whom all things come; and one Lord, our Lord Jesus Christ, through whom all things come* (1 Cor 8:5–6). Let him be your hope then, the Lord, your God; let your hope be lodged in him. When someone pays cult to Saturn, his hope is in that lord, his god; when someone pays cult to Mars or Neptune or Mercury, the worshiper's hope is in that lord, his god. I will go further: the same can be said of one who pays cult to the belly, for scripture mentions some *whose god is their belly* (Phil 3:19). So one god is god to one client, another is god to someone else. But who is god to the one called blessed, that one who is blessed because *his hope is in the Lord, his God*? Who is he? He is the God *who made heaven and earth, the sea, and all the creatures in them.*

---

13. In these lines Augustine plays on different meanings of the verb *colere*: "to care for" in the agricultural sense of cultivation, and "to care for" in the sense of devoting oneself to, and hence "to worship." The English words "cultivate" and "cult" retain something of the dual meaning.

What a great God we have, brothers and sisters! Let us bless his holy name, because he has deigned to make us his possession. You do not yet see God, and you cannot fully love him whom you do not yet see. But the things you do see are of his making. If you are wonderstruck at the world, why not at[14] the world's architect? You gaze up at the sky and are filled with awe. You think about the whole vast earth and tremble at its grandeur. And when will your mind ever compass the immensity of the sea? Contemplate the unnumbered multitude of the stars, consider the endless variety of seeding plants, the huge diversity of animal species, all those that swim in the waters or slither along the ground or fly in the air or circle in the heavens: how great all these things are, how magnificent, how beautiful, how amazing! And he who made them all is your God. Fix your hope in him that you may be blessed, and that of you it may be said, *His hope is in the Lord his God.* Who is God? He *who made heaven and earth, the sea, and all the creatures in them.* We have a great God, indeed!

God's providential care encompasses all he has made

13. Focus your minds, brothers and sisters, on this great God, this good God who fashioned such creatures. What was God meaning to do (if we may use this expression of God)—what was God meaning to do when he *made heaven and earth, the sea, and all the creatures in them*? Perhaps someone may say, "I see all these great things, to be sure: God made sky and earth and sea. But does God regard me as one of the things he made? Does he really care about me among all these? Is God even aware of me now? Does he know whether I am alive?" What are you saying? Do not let such wicked ideas creep into your heart. Align yourself rather with the praise-singers of whom we were speaking not long since, the ones who say, *I will praise the Lord throughout my life, I will sing psalms to him as long as I exist.* But the psalmist is addressing people of a different type, lukewarm doubters whom he exhorts because he seems to be afraid that they may despair and stop believing that God takes account of them. There are many who think like this. The reason why they abandon God and stray into all kinds of sin is that they do not believe God cares what they do. But listen to God's own words and do not despair about yourself. If God took the trouble to create you, will he not take the trouble to re-create you? Is not he who made heaven and earth and sea your God?

---

14. Variant: "seek."

But, if the psalmist had stopped there, you might perhaps have retorted, "The God who made heaven and earth and sea is a great God, but does he bother about me?" But he made you! "How can that be? Am I heaven? Am I the earth? Am I the sea? It is quite obvious that I am neither heaven nor earth nor sea. I am only on the earth." So you grant me that much, that you are on the earth. Very well, listen to the psalm, for it is telling you that God's creative work was not confined to setting up sky and earth and sea. He *made heaven and earth, the sea, and all the creatures in them.* So, if he made *all the creatures in them*, that includes you. But it is not enough to say "you"; he made the sparrow and the locust and the tiny worm. There is not one among these creatures that he did not make, and he takes care of them all. His care for them is not conditional on their obeying his commands, for only to human beings did he give commandments. Another psalm says of him, *Men and beasts you will save, Lord, as your mercy has been multiplied, O God* (Ps 35:7–8(36:6–7)). It praises the multiplication of his mercy, and in accordance with this is says, *Men and beasts you will save, Lord.*

Yet the apostle asks, *Does God care about oxen?* (1 Cor 9:9) So we have, on the one hand, *God does not care about oxen*, and, on the other, *Men and beasts you will save, Lord.* Is there a contradiction here? No. What does the apostle say? *Does God care about oxen?* But then, what becomes of the prohibition in the law, *You shall not muzzle an ox while it is threshing* (Dt 25:4; 1 Cor 9:9; 1 Tm 5:18)? This hardly suggests that God gives no thought to oxen. He must have meant some particular oxen,[15] for God does not bother to give you special instructions as to how to treat your livestock; human nature itself suffices for that. Human beings are so made that they know how to look after their animals. This is not a subject on which men and women have been given commands by God; rather, God has instilled understanding into their minds so that they act properly without a commandment. This is how God has made them. Just as a man rules his beast, so must he be ruled by another, and it is from this other that he receives his orders.

Evidently, then, if we are looking for a direct instruction about animal husbandry, we can say, *God does not care about oxen.* But if

---

15. In his Exposition of Psalm 65,20 Augustine says that these oxen symbolize preachers of truth. In his Exposition of Psalm 8,12 he says they stand for angels as messengers of truth and, by extension, evangelists.

we consider the universal providence of God, who created all things and rules the world, we can say, *Men and beasts you will save, Lord.*

14. Now think hard, beloved ones. It could happen that someone might challenge me about what I have just said. The statement, *God does not care about oxen,* comes from the New Testament, the objector might say, whereas the text, *Men and beasts you will save, Lord,* comes from the Old. Basing themselves on this observation, there are some who falsely allege that the two testaments are out of tune with each other. What am I to do, if I want to deny that one thing is said in the Old Testament and something contrary in the New, while the objector is challenging me to find something in the New that matches the statement, *Men and beasts you will save, Lord?*

Well, within the New Testament nothing is more authoritative than the gospel. In the gospel I find that all created things belong to God. No one can contradict that. But can the apostle be opposing the gospel? Of course not. Let us listen to the Lord himself, the master and teacher of the apostles. *Study the birds in the sky,* he bade them. *See how they neither sow, nor reap, nor garner produce into barns, yet your heavenly Father feeds them.* (Mt 6:26) This shows that not only human beings but animals too fall within the scope of God's providence—but to be fed, not to receive any law. As far as the imposition of a law goes, God does not concern himself with oxen; but with regard to creation, feeding, guiding, and ruling, all things belong to God. *Are not two sparrows sold for a penny?* asked Jesus Christ. *Yet not one of them will fall to the ground unless your Father wills it. How much more valuable are you than they?* (Mt 10:29.31) Do not say, then, "I am no concern of God's." Your soul is God's concern and your body is God's concern, because God made both your soul and your body. Perhaps you are tempted to reply, "But God cannot keep track of me in so great a crowd." A wonderful saying in the gospel refutes you: *The very hairs on your head are numbered* (Mt 10:30).

Verse 7. Not all suffering is injury; God sees justice done for those who suffer injustice

15. He, then, is my God, and my hope is lodged in him *who made heaven and earth, the sea, and all the creatures in them.* But what about me? How does he act in my regard? *He keeps faith for ever.* The psalm has portrayed for us a God who is to be both loved and feared, a God who *keeps faith for ever.* What is this faith that he keeps for ever, and for whom does he keep it? He *sees justice done for those*

who suffer injury. He avenges those who suffer wrong, my brothers and sisters, and sees justice done in their cause. But notice on whose behalf he so acts. He avenges those who suffer injury by punishing all injurious persons. Well now, if he intends to champion those who suffer injury and to punish those who inflict it, make up your mind now in which group you wish to be. Look carefully at the difference and decide whether you wish to join those who suffer injury or those who injure them. The apostle's words immediately confront you, for he says to you, as well as to those whom he addressed, *This is very wrong of you, to have any lawsuits at all between you. Why do you not rather suffer injury?* (1 Cor 6:7) He rebukes people for not putting up with it when they are injured. But notice that he is not saying you must put up with affliction in general; he refers only to injury, for not all affliction is injury.[16] Anything that you lawfully suffer is not injury.[17] You might be tempted to say, "I belong to the company of those who suffer injury, for I had to put up with hardship in this place or that; I suffered for this or that reason." But consider carefully whether what you endured was indeed an injury. Robbers suffer many punishments but not injury. Criminals, rogues, burglars, adulterers, and seducers all suffer many harsh penalties, but no injury is involved.[18] It is one thing to suffer injury and something different to suffer distress or punishment or harassment or torture. Consider, then, where you belong; reflect on what you have done; reflect on the reason for your suffering, and then you will discern its nature. Law and injury[19] are mutually opposed, for law is what is just.[20] Of course, not everything that is called law is truly law. What if someone passes an inequitable law? It has no right to be called law if it is unjust. Only what is also just is truly law. Ask yourself what you have done, not what you are suffering. If you have acted justly, your suffering is injury; if you have inflicted injury, you are suffering under the law of justice.

16. Why have I said all this, brothers and sisters? So that the heretics may not give themselves airs if they happen to suffer under

---

16. Throughout this section Augustine uses the word *iniuria* in its strict sense, that which is unjust. He goes on to point out the connection between *ius* "law" and that which is *iustum*, and the corresponding connection between *iniuria* and what is *iniustum*.
17. *Quidquid... iure pateris, non est iniuria.*
18. In the next section he will apply this principle to the Donatists.
19. *Ius et iniuria.*
20. *Ius enim est quod iustum est.*

the decrees of earthly rulers. They have no business to count themselves among those who suffer injury or to say, "Look, the psalm is my consolation, for I worship the God who will see justice done for those who suffer injury." But I claim the right to ask whether you are in fact suffering injury. If you have dealt justly, what you suffer is an injury. But is it just to blow out the light of Christ? Is it just to raise an altar in rebellious pride? Is it just to rend Christ's Church asunder, when even his executioners forbore to tear his tunic?[21] Clearly, if such behavior is not just, whatever you suffer for it is just. You do not therefore belong in the company of those who suffer injury.

In the gospel I read something even plainer: *Blessed are those who suffer persecution* (Mt 5:10). Wait a minute! Don't be in too much of a hurry. How dare you interrupt, "That's me!" Wait, I tell you, let me read the whole verse. As soon as you heard the words, *Blessed are those who suffer persecution*, you began to make all sorts of arrogant assumptions. If you will only bear with me, I will read it all. See what the next words are: *Blessed are those who suffer persecution for the sake of justice*. Now say, "That's me!" If you dare say that, we will withdraw what I have been saying.

Or, to clinch the matter, I will put this one question to you: If you were to condemn a single individual without knowing the facts of the case, would you dare to say that you were pursuing the path of justice? Or, if you had to suffer for so acting, would you call it injury? You climb high into the presumptuous tribunal of your own heart, but you will be hurled down. You have the temerity to pass sentence on someone of whose case you are ignorant! If you acted like this with regard to a single individual, you would be unjust. When you act like this with regard to the whole world, do you think you are just?

Dearest brothers and sisters, who is it who is suffering injury? Who else but the Catholic Church, which is subjected to these outrages? The Church groans amid all the offences occasioned by heretics; it sees its weak members torn from its lap by their evil persuasions and deceits. It has to watch its little ones dragged away through the dark recesses of wicked dens and being baptized over again. It watches Christ's flame being blown out in them and the slaying not of the mortal life that makes them human but of that life by which they are destined to live for ever. A person is persuaded to say, "I am not a Christian," and that is called justice! "When you go before the

---

21. See Jn 19:24.

bishop," they instruct him, "be careful not to say you are a Christian. If you say you are, you will not receive baptism from us. If you want to receive it, you must say you are not a Christian."[22]

What are you telling him—you who are a Christian yourself? What are you teaching? Suffering persecution, are you? Would it not be much truer to say that you are the persecutor? When the emperors were persecuting Christians, they coerced with threats, but you obtain the same results by deceitful persuasion. You coax a Christian into denying that he or she is a Christian, and you succeed by your wiles where a persecutor failed by slaughter. Someone who denies that he is a Christian lives under your authority. But if he denies his faith, does he still live? No, he has already lost his life; it is only a corpse that is answering you. One who was struck by the persecutor's sword fell and still lives, but the one to whom you are talking has fallen, even though he is still on his feet.

If you do these things, will any suffering that comes to you be an injury? Do not flatter yourself. If all this conduct of yours is unjust, whatever you suffer will be just. In whose cause will he who *keeps faith for ever* see justice done? In the cause of *those who suffer injury*.

Verse 8. The Lord's saving work

17. Go on arguing and trying to prove by your specious, clever, and so subtle reasoning that you are truly a shepherd to the faithful. You ask, "Can a starving person feed others?" You mean, "Can a sinner give anything holy?[23] Can a starving person feed others? Can a sick man heal others? Can one who is bound loose the bonds of anyone else?"

These are powerful, subtle arguments, with which they deceive the poorly instructed. But our psalm silences them. It is the Lord who *gives food to the hungry*. From you, heretic, I expect nothing; it is God who *gives food to the hungry*. Which hungry people are meant? All who are hungry. What does that mean—all? To all living creatures, and to all human beings, he gives food. And does he not keep something special for his loved ones? If they feel a different hunger,

---

22. On these Donatist practices see Exposition of Psalm 39,1 and the note there.
23. The Donatists, claiming to be the pure, as contrasted with the discredited Catholic Church, disputed the validity of sacraments conferred by unworthy ministers. Augustine always insisted that it is Christ who baptizes. See the note at Exposition of Psalm 10,1.

they have also a different food. Let us inquire first about their hunger and then we shall discover their food. *Blessed are those who hunger and thirst for justice, for they shall be satisfied* (Mt 5:6). We must be God's starving clients. Let us take our place as beggars at the gate of his presence, for he *gives food to the hungry*. How can you boast, you heretic, that you set anyone free, lift anyone up, or illumine anyone's blindness? Because you have been set free yourself, because you are standing upright, because you are the light? You are much mistaken. Go back to the earlier words of the psalm: *Put not your trust in princes, or in the sons of men, for in them you will find no salvation*. They do not give salvation. Let the heretics get out of our way.

The Lord sets the bound free; the Lord lifts up those who have been thrown down; the Lord makes blind people wise; that is to say, he turns those who were blind into wise people. That last phrase deftly explains all the preceding ones for us. Without it, we might have thought that the words, *The Lord sets the bound free*, referred to slaves who are shackled by their masters for some misdeed, and that the words, *The Lord lifts up those who have been thrown down*, was a promise to anyone who had tripped over something and fallen, or been thrown from his horse. There is a different kind of falling and there are other fetters, just as there is a different darkness and a different light. The psalm avoided saying, "He enlightens the blind," in case you might take that in a carnal sense. It preferred to say, *The Lord makes blind people wise*. Without this clarification you would have thought of the man whose blindness was cured by the Lord, the one whose eyes he anointed with clay mixed with saliva, in order to heal him.[24] The psalmist does not want you to entertain hopes of that kind when he is speaking of spiritual illumination, so he points to the light of wisdom as the means by which blind people are illumined. Taking our cue from this we can understand that, as the blind are illumined by the light of wisdom, so too are the bound set free and those who are cast down lifted up.

How did we become bound? How were we cast down? Our body was given to us as a beautiful adornment, but when we sinned it became the source of our bondage. What are our shackles? Mortality itself. Listen to what the apostle Paul had to say, remembering that during this earthly pilgrimage he was bound like the rest of us. Yet even in his fettered condition, what a long way he traveled! His

---

24. See Jn 9:6.

fetters cannot have seemed heavy to him if, even hampered by them, he preached the gospel all around the world. The Spirit of charity seized his fetters, and Paul traveled around as far as he could. Yet what did he say? *I long to be released and to be with Christ.* What did he mean by being released? To be freed from the fetters of mortality. Nonetheless, out of charity he was willing to stay fettered for the sake of others similarly bound, the people to whom he could still minister: *But it is necessary for you that I remain in the flesh* (Phil 1:23-24), he said. The Lord in this sense *sets the bound free*; he makes mortal men and women immortal. *The Lord lifts up those who have been thrown down.* Why were they thrown down? Because they raised themselves up. And why are they now lifted up? Because they have been humbled. Adam fell and was thrown down; he fell, but Christ descended. Why did he who had not fallen descend? So that Adam, who *did* fall, might be lifted up. *The Lord makes blind people wise; the Lord loves the just*, and therefore he sees justice done for those who suffer unjustly.

Verse 9. The Church is a foreigner, an orphan, and a widow

18. But who are these just ones? Or, rather, to what extent are they just in this present era? To the extent that the psalm suggests by saying, *The Lord protects foreigners.* Foreigners[25] are strangers, and the entire Church of the gentiles is a foreigner. She came as a new arrival to the race of the patriarchs, a daughter born from them not carnally but by imitating their faith. All the same, it is the Lord who protects her, not any man.

He will welcome the orphan and the widow. It is not like when someone welcomes an orphan with an eye to the inheritance, or a widow for any personal gain. To be sure, God does help people in these circumstances, and, in all the services human beings render to each other, one who takes care of an orphan or does not desert a widow is performing a good work. But in another sense we are all orphans, for our Father is absent, though not dead. In ordinary human terms someone becomes an orphan when his or her father dies. Yet, if you look for the truth of the matter, brothers and sisters, our parents are still alive, because the soul does not die. Those whom we regard as orphans are called so only because their parents are away. If those who have left us were wicked, they are alive and undergoing punishment;

---

25. *Proselyti.*

if good, they are alive and enjoying rest. All things remain whole and unimpaired to their creator. But, if we look at it from our own point of view, as long as we are in the body and dwell in this place of exile, our Father is absent; that is why we cry to him, *Our Father, who art in heaven.* And so too the Church is a widow, because her bridegroom is away. He will come back, and even now he protects her, though she cannot see him but can only long for him. We are possessed by an intense longing, and, out of love for him whom we cannot see, we yearn for him. When we do see him, we shall be enfolded tightly in his embrace, as even now when we do not see him we are held fast by our faith in him.

Well then, brothers and sisters, what did the psalmist mean us to understand by *the orphan and the widow*? Those, surely, who are bereft of all resources and all help. Let every soul that is destitute in this world hope for help from God. Suppose you have possessions here—gold or whatever: do you rely on them? If so, you are not a foreigner, nor an orphan, nor can you count as a widow. Or have you a friend? If you put your trust in him and neglect God, you are not destitute. But if you have all these things, but do not rely on them and are not made proud by them, you are God's orphan and God's widow. He welcomes those who are destitute: the psalm has said so in telling us that he welcomes the orphan and welcomes the widow.

19. *And he will destroy the way of sinners.* What is *the way of sinners*? The attitude that mocks what we say. "Who is an orphan? Who is a widow? What is the kingdom of heaven? What are the pains of hell? All these are fables invented by Christians. I live for what I can see. *Let us eat and drink, for tomorrow we shall die* (1 Cor 15:32)." Take care that people like this do not influence you or make their way into your heart through your ears. Let them find thorns in your ears, so that anyone who has tried to get in that way may be stabbed and repulsed. *Evil conversations corrupt good morals* (1 Cor 15:33).

But perhaps you will ask me, "Why then are they so prosperous? They do not worship God, and they commit all kinds of wicked deeds every day, yet they have plenty of the things that I lack, things that I have to work hard to earn." Do not envy sinners.[26] You see what they are getting now, but can you not also see what is being stored up for them? "How can I?" replies the objector. "How can I see what is not visible?" You forget that faith has eyes of its own, better and more

---

26. See Ps 36(37):1.

powerful eyes, eyes with longer range. These eyes have never deceived anyone; they are fixed always on the Lord, so that he may pluck your feet clear from such snares.[27] The way of sinners looks attractive to you because it is wide and many people are walking along it. You see its breadth, but you do not see its end. Where it comes to an end there is a precipice; where it ends there is a deep chasm. People who are now enjoying themselves and wandering along that way at their ease will plunge to ruin at the end of it. But if you cannot see far enough to glimpse the end, believe one who does see it. What mere human can? None, perhaps; but your Lord came to you that you might believe God. Are you not even prepared to believe the Lord your God when he says to you, *How broad and spacious is the road that leads to perdition, and how many there are who walk along it* (Mt 7:13)? This is the way that the Lord will destroy, because it is the way of sinners.

Verse 10. The prospect of eternity

20. And when the way of sinners has been destroyed, what is left for us? *Come, you who are blessed by my Father, take possession of the kingdom prepared for you since the creation of the world* (Mt 25:34). On this note the psalm ends. *The Lord will destroy the way of sinners*; but what about you? *The Lord will reign for ever.* Rejoice, because he will reign for you; rejoice, because you yourself will be his kingdom. Look too at what is said next. You are, quite certainly, a citizen of Zion, not of Babylon. I mean that you do not belong to the city of this world, the city doomed to perish, but to Zion, the city which is struggling and exiled at present but destined to reign for eternity.[28] And since you belong to this city, you have been told about its destiny, which concerns you: *The Lord will reign for ever, your God, O Zion*. O Zion, your God will reign for all eternity, and your God will not reign without you, will he? *Generation after generation*: the psalm says it twice, being unable to go on saying it unceasingly. But do not imagine that when the words are ended, eternity will end. By no means. "Eternity"—just four syllables, and it's over: the word, that is. But eternity itself will never be over. The reality of it could

---

27. See Ps 24(25):15.
28. A brief statement of one of Augustine's favorite themes, referred to several times in the Expositions (see, for example, Expositions of Psalms 61,6; 64,2; 86,6; 136,1.6.20–21) and developed at length in one of his greatest works, *The City of God*.

not be conveyed to you in any other way than by saying, *Your God will reign, generation after generation.* To say that is not enough, but, even if the psalmist went on saying it all day, it would still not suffice. Even if the psalmist said it all his life, he would still have to fall silent sooner or later, wouldn't he?

Love eternity. You will reign without end, if Christ is your end. With him you will reign for ages upon ages. Amen.

Exposition of Psalm 146

A Sermon

Verse 1. Why praise God?

1. We were all listening attentively when this psalm was sung, but not all of us who listened understood it. But now my hope and dearest wish is that anything obscure in the psalm will be clarified by God's grace, if all of you here present help me with your prayers. How much more attentively, then, should each one of us listen now, so that our listening may be fruitful? It would be sad if anyone who had listened carefully were to depart without having gained anything.

How does it begin? We are bidden, *Praise the Lord*. This exhortation is addressed to all peoples, not only to us. The voice of the reader proclaims it in each separate place, and all the churches hear it individually, but the one voice of God rings out unceasingly over all the churches, never falling silent in its invitation to us to praise him. Perhaps we might wonder why we ought to praise God, and the psalm seems to anticipate our question by giving us a motive: *Praise the Lord, because a psalm is good*. Is that all the reward that those who praise him are to expect? "Let us praise the Lord." "Why?" *Because a psalm is good*. Someone might reply, "I would be prepared to praise the Lord if he were to give me something in return for the praise I offer." Does anyone praise even a human being disinterestedly? If, then, those who sing the praises of other men or women look for some kind of reward, should not one who praises God expect or ask or at least hope for some recompense? A weak human being is praised, and something is hoped for from him. Is the Almighty to be praised, with no reward to follow?

"But perhaps what I desire is something he cannot give?" That is impossible. Is there anything we can covet that it is not in God's power to bestow? If it is a fellow human that you praise, you may well desire something he cannot grant, but you need have no such misgivings when you praise God. No one can say that he lacks the power to give anything that you have the power to long for.

We are certainly right to look for some reward when we are told that we must praise God, but it does not follow that he will give us whatever we desire, for he is our Father, and a father does not give his children what they want if it is bad for them. Let us praise him and hope and desire, but let us not desire this or that particular thing. Let us desire only what he whom we praise judges it suitable to give us. He knows what it is expedient to give, and we should direct our intention to what it is good for us to receive. The apostle reminds us that *we do not know how to pray as we ought* (Rom 8:26). Moreover this same apostle, Paul, went on hoping that it would be to his profit if he were relieved of the sting of the flesh, that envoy of Satan by which he was constantly belabored. He confesses this, saying, *Three times I begged the Lord to take it away from me, but he said to me, My grace is sufficient for you, for my power is fully deployed in weakness* (2 Cor 12:8–9). He longed for something, but his wish went unsatisfied in order that his true interests might be served with a view to his healing.

So what is now recommended to us? *Praise the Lord.* Why should we praise the Lord? *Because a psalm is good.* But the psalm itself is an expression of praise to the Lord, so the verse is tantamount to saying, "Praise the Lord because it is good to praise the Lord." But let us not dismiss so lightly this matter of praising the Lord. The word "praise" is spoken, and it has died away; the job is finished and our duty done; we have praised him, and now we are quiet again; we have sung and now fallen silent. We are off to see to the other business we have in hand, and other activities demand our concentration. Does this mean that divine praise has ceased within us? No, certainly not, for, though your tongue praises him for only an hour or so, your life should praise him all the time.[1] On this basis a psalm is good.

Let the whole of your life be a psalm of praise to God

2. A psalm is not a song like any other; it is sung to the accompaniment of a psaltery. A psaltery is an instrument associated with singing, like the lyre, the harp, and others of the same kind, designed to accompany song. Anyone who sings psalms does not therefore use the voice alone; he takes up the instrument known as a psaltery and, with the aid of his hands, harmonizes it with his voice.

---

1. Compare Exposition of Psalm 97,5.

What about you? Do you too want to sing and play psalms? Then not only must your voice sing God's praises but your actions must keep in tune with your voice. After you have been singing with your voice you will have to be quiet for a while, but sing with your life in such a way that you never fall silent. Suppose you are engaged in business and you are contemplating some dishonest deal: you have allowed your praise of God to be silenced and, worse still, you have not only smothered your praise but have committed blasphemy; for since God is praised by your good works you are praising him simply by performing them, whereas your evil deeds are a blasphemy, and so you blaspheme him as you commit them.

Sing with your voice, then, to edify and encourage yourself and others by the sounds that appeal to the ears, but do not let your heart be dumb or your life be silent. If you have no truck with fraud in your business, you are singing and playing psalms to God. When you are eating and drinking play psalms to him, not by punctuating your meals with sweet music to charm the ear but by eating and drinking moderately, frugally, and temperately. This is what the apostle enjoins: *Whether you eat, whether you drink, whatever you do, do everything for the glory of God* (1 Cor 10:31). If you act reasonably, all the while thanking God who has provided these supports to sustain your mortal, frail nature, even your food and drink are praise offered to God. But if you exceed the measure owed to nature by your immoderate greed, or gorge yourself with wine to the point of intoxication, your life is a blasphemy against God, however lustily your tongue may be singing his praises.

After you have eaten and drunk, you retire to sleep. Do not do anything unseemly in bed or go beyond what God's law permits you. Let the couch you share with your spouse be chaste. If you are trying to procreate children, keep your sexual pleasure within bounds. Be considerate toward your spouse in bed, for both of you are members of Christ,[2] both are created by him, and both re-created by his blood. If you conduct yourself like this you are praising God and there is no question of the praise you offer him being interrupted. What about when sleep comes? Even when you are asleep, let no uneasy conscience disturb your rest, and then even your innocent slumbers praise God.

If you want to praise God, do not sing with your tongue alone but take up the psaltery of good actions as well, *because a psalm is good.*

---

2. See 1 Cor 6:15.

You are praising God when you transact your business, praising him when you take food and drink, praising him when you rest in bed, praising him while you are asleep. Is there ever a moment when you are not praising him? Yet our praise of God will be made perfect only when we arrive at the eternal city, when we have been made equal to the angels,[3] when no bodily need assails us from any quarter, when neither hunger nor thirst makes its demands, when heat does not tire us or cold freeze us, when fever does not lay us low or death finish us off. Let us get into practice for that most perfect praise by exercising ourselves now in the praise we offer through good actions.

3. Accordingly, after his exhortation, *Praise the Lord, because a psalm is good*, the psalmist adds, *Let your praise sound delightful to our God*. How will our praise be delightful to our God? It will be, if he is praised by our good lives. Listen, and I will show you that this is what delightful praise implies. In another passage scripture says, *Praise is not seemly in a sinner's mouth* (Sir 15:9). If, then, praise in a sinner's mouth is not seemly, it cannot be delightful either, for only what is seemly can give delight. Do you want your praise to be delightful to God? Do not allow your good singing to be drowned by the din of your bad morals. *Let your praise sound delightful to our God*. What has the psalmist told you? Live good lives, you who praise him. Praise offered by those who do not reverence him is offensive to God. He takes more notice of how you live than of the quality of your voice. Obviously you want to be at peace with him whom you praise, but how can you seek peace with him if you are out of tune with yourself? "How can I be out of tune with myself?" you will ask. Ah, but you can, if your tongue is singing one tune and your life is pitched to something different. *Let your praise sound delightful to our God*. A man or woman can find praise delightful when listening to someone offering it in elegant, finely honed phrases and with a well modulated voice, but praise must be delightful to our God, whose ears are sensitive not to the mouth but to the heart, not to the tongue but to the life of the one who praises him.

Verse 2. The building of Jerusalem, whose citizens see God

4. Who is this God of ours, to whom our praise must sound delightful? He is for ever showing himself gentle and proving his love for us. Thanks be to him for the gracious kindness that makes

---

3. See Lk 20:36.

him want to prove his love. It is not as though we were going to give him anything, for we are the ones who stand to gain and to receive a great deal from him. How does God give us proof of his benevolence? Listen to the apostle Paul: *God displays his love for us*, he says. How? Concentrate now, and let the apostle himself tell us, so that we can compare what he says with the psalm. *God displays his love for us*. How does he display it? *In that while we were still sinners Christ died for us.* (Rom 5:8–9) If he gives a proof like that to sinners, what must he be reserving for those who praise him?

Well now, the apostle has told us that God has conclusively proved his love in that Christ died for the wicked. He did not intend that they should remain wicked but that, by the death of a righteous man, they might be healed of their unrighteousness. In the light of what he has said, what does the psalm suggest to you after saying, *Let your praise sound delightful to our God*? Let us see whether the psalm goes on to speak of a comparable demonstration of love, something like the love the apostle mentioned, the love proved by Christ's dying for the wicked. *The Lord is building up Jerusalem, and gathering in the dispersed of Israel*, says the psalm. We know that in building up Jerusalem the Lord is gathering in the scattered members of his people, because the people of Israel is the people of Jerusalem. There is an eternal Jerusalem in heaven, where the angels too are citizens. But how can we say that Israel has a place there? If we focus only on Abraham's grandson, the man who was also called Jacob, how can we regard the angels as Israel? But if, on the contrary, we consider the interpretation of the name Israel—for even Jacob's name was changed, remember, and he became Israel[4]—then it is evident that the name Israel is even more appropriate to the citizens of heaven. And indeed, let us hope that we too may follow and become Israel in our turn. How is the name interpreted? "One who sees God." All the denizens of that city rejoice in seeing God. They rejoice in that great, spacious, heavenly city, for God gives himself to them for their contemplation.

We, though, are exiled from the city, expelled by sin and forbidden to remain there and further burdened by the mortality that prevents us from returning. Yet God has looked down on our pilgrim path, and he who is at work building up Jerusalem has restored the part which had fallen away. How has he restored it? By *gathering in*

---

4. See Gn 32:28.

the dispersed of Israel. Part of it fell away and was exiled, but God looked mercifully upon it and sought those who did not seek him. What did he do to seek them? Whom did he send to search for us in our captivity? He sent a redeemer, as the apostle has been explaining: *God displays his love for us in that while we were still sinners Christ died for us*. To us captives he sent his own Son as redeemer. "Take a purse," he told him, "and carry in it the ransom-price for the captives." So the Son clothed himself in mortal flesh, in which was the blood that he would shed to redeem us. With that blood he gathered[5] the dispersed of Israel.

If he gathered in the dispersed long ago, how zealous should we be now in gathering those who are scattered? If the dispersed were gathered in to be formed into a building by the architect's hand, how much more should those be gathered who have fallen out of his hand by their restlessness? *The Lord is building up Jerusalem*. This is the God whom we praise, the God to whom we owe praise all our life long. *The Lord is building up Jerusalem, and gathering in the dispersed of Israel*.

Verse 3. Broken, contrite hearts will be healed

5. How does he gather them? How does he go about his work of gathering them in? *He heals the bruised of heart.*[6] Now you see how the dispersed of Israel are gathered so that the bruised of heart may be healed. People who do not bruise their hearts are not healed either. What does it mean to bruise one's heart? Be very clear about this, dearly beloved: may it happen in you, that you too may be able to receive healing. The same truth is reiterated in many scriptural passages and especially in that text where someone, singing with our voice, says to God, *If you had wanted a sacrifice I would certainly have offered it*. Yes, this is what he says to God: *If you had wanted a sacrifice I would certainly have offered it; but you take no pleasure in holocausts* (Ps 50:18(51:16)). But what does he mean? Are we to stand empty-handed, with no sacrifice to offer? No, but listen to what God wants you to bring him. That psalm continues, *A sacrifice to God is a troubled spirit. A contrite and humbled heart God does not scorn.* (Ps 50:19(51:17)) We are assured, then, that *he heals the bruised of heart* and that he comes close to them in order to do his

---

5. Variant: "gathers."
6. The verb *conterere* has given us the English word "contrition."

healing work; as another psalm says, *The Lord is close to those who have bruised their hearts* (Ps 33:19(34:18)).

Who are the people who have bruised their hearts? The humble ones. And who are the ones who have not bruised their hearts? The proud. The bruised heart will be healed, the arrogant one struck. But perhaps the proud heart is struck down only that it may be bruised and so healed. Let not our hearts stand up straight before they truly are straight, brothers and sisters. Nothing has the right to stand erect unless it is first corrected.

6. *He heals the bruised of heart, and binds up their bruises.* The psalm assures us that he *heals the bruised of heart*, he heals those whose hearts are humbled, he heals those who confess, he heals those who punish themselves and judge themselves severely, so that they may also be the people who experience his mercy. God heals people of this sort, but their perfect healing will be achieved only when their mortality is done away with, when this perishable nature has put on imperishability and our mortality has been clothed in immortality.[7] Then there will be no more solicitation from our fallen flesh, and I do not mean only none that we consent to, but no suggestion whatever arising from the flesh. In our present state, my brothers and sisters, how many unlawful pleasures brush against our minds! It may be that we do not consent to them, being resolved that our members shall serve the cause of righteousness, not the demands of iniquity,[8] but even to experience pleasure without consenting is a sign that we do not yet have perfect health. But you will be healed. If your heart is bruised and contrite, you will be healed. Do not be ashamed: bruise your heart, for God heals people who do.

But, you ask, what about now? What am I to do now? *I take great delight in God's law as far as my inner self is concerned, but I am aware of a different law in my members that opposes the law of my mind, and imprisons me under the law of sin.* What are you to do about this? Bruise your heart and confess. Go ahead and say, as the rest of this text goes on to say, *Who will deliver me from this death-ridden body, wretch that I am?* And then you will hear the answer: *Only the grace of God, through Jesus Christ our Lord.* (Rom 7:23–25)

But how will it happen? How will this grace of God, of which we have received a pledge, set us free? Listen to the same apostle:

---

7. See 1 Cor 15:53–54.
8. See Rom 6:13.

The body indeed is a dead thing by reason of sin, but the spirit is life through righteousness. If the Spirit of him who raised Jesus Christ from the dead lives in you, he who raised Jesus Christ from the dead will bring life to your mortal bodies too, through his Spirit who dwells in you. (Rom 8:10–11) Our spirits have received the Spirit as a pledge[9] so that we may begin to serve God by faith and, on the ground of our faith, deserve to be called just, for *the one who lives by faith is just* (Hb 2:4; Rom 1:17). Whatever distaste or resistance there may still be in us results from the mortality of our flesh and will be healed; as scripture promises, *He will bring life to your mortal bodies too, through his Spirit who dwells in you.* His reason for giving us this pledge is to give us certainty that he will complete what he has promised.

However, what about now, in this life, while we still confess and do not yet possess?[10] How will it work out for us in this life? *He heals the bruised of heart*, but perfect healing is not to be expected yet, as we have explained. What is there for us now? *He binds up their bruises.* He takes care of those whose hearts are bruised, those who must wait for the resurrection of the just to find perfect healing, and he takes care of them, says the psalm, by bandaging their injuries now.

A badly set fracture may need to be broken and re-set

7. What kind of splints are applied? The bruises are treated as doctors treat fractures. It is sometimes necessary—you must understand this, beloved; those of you who have watched the procedure, or have heard about it from doctors, will know—it is sometimes necessary for doctors to break anew a limb that has set in a crooked, deformed position. They make a new wound because the distorted healing was bad. Similarly scripture testifies that *the Lord's ways are straight, but anyone with a crooked heart will stumble in them* (Hos 14:10). What does *anyone with a crooked heart* mean? A person with a twisted, perverted heart. Such a person thinks that everything God says is twisted and that all God does is crooked; all God's judgments are reprehensible to him, particularly those by which he himself is rebuked. He sits down and argues about how wrongly God acts, because God's actions do not accord with his wishes. His heart is distorted, but it

---

9. *Pignus.* See the note on *pignus* and *arrha* at Exposition of Psalm 122,5, though the present passage seems not to observe the distinction between them which Augustine explains elsewhere.
10. *Adhuc confessores sumus, nondum possessores.*

is not enough for him to refuse to correct his depravity by aligning himself with the ruler-straightness of God: he even tries to twist God out of shape to fit himself. What says God from on high? "You are twisted, I am level. If you were straight yourself, you would feel how level I am." If you laid a twisted plank on a level floor it would not lie true; it would rock and wobble to and fro not because of any unevenness in the floor but because of the distortion in the plank. As scripture says, *How good God is to Israel, to those of straightforward hearts!* (Ps 72(73):1)

What are we to do, then? How is a twisted heart to be straightened? It is not only twisted but hard as well, so the twisted, hard heart must be broken and bruised if it is to be straightened. You cannot straighten your own heart: you must break it so that God may straighten it. How do you break it? How do you bruise it? By confessing and punishing your sins. What else but this does the beating of our breasts signify? You do not suppose, surely, that our bones have sinned and that we strike our breasts to punish them? No, we signify that we are bruising our hearts, so that they may be straightened by the Lord.

The Church's sacraments and rites are bandages for our temporal condition

8. The Lord *heals the bruised of heart*, the people whose hearts are contrite. The healing of our hearts will be perfect when our bodies are perfectly re-created, as we have been promised, but meanwhile what does the doctor do? He binds up your bruises to enable you to attain the greatest possible strength: this is necessary until what has been broken and bandaged grows firm. What are the bandages? The holy signs proper to our temporal state.[11] These temporal sacred signs that comfort us in this in-between time are the medicinal dressings suited to our condition. All the sermons we preach to you, the words that are heard and then fade away, all the temporal actions performed in the Church, are dressings applied to our bruises. And just as the doctor removes the bandage when healing is complete, so it will be in the holy city, Jerusalem, when we have been made equal to the

---

11. *Temporalia sacramenta.* Not only the "seven sacraments" but all the rites, actions, and symbols which signify and convey the grace of salvation. How widely Augustine understood the term is evident from the few examples he goes on to mention. Compare Expositions of Psalms 73,2 and 67,16 and the notes in those places.

angels. You do not suppose, do you, that we shall receive there what we receive here? Or that we shall need to have the gospel proclaimed to us to sustain our faith? Or that any bishop will need to lay hands on us? All these are splints for our fractures, and when our healing is perfect they will be removed. But we would never attain perfect healing without them, and so the Lord *heals the bruised of heart, and binds up their bruises.*

Verse 4. Being numbered among the stars, through charity

9. *He counts the great host of the stars, calling all of them by their names.* Is it any great thing for God to number the multitude of the stars? Even human beings have attempted to do that. It is for them to say whether they have managed it, but they would not have tried if they had not hoped to succeed. Let us leave it to them to judge how successful their attempts have been and what progress they have made. But I do not think it any great matter for God to count all the stars. Would he need to keep a note of the number, in case he forgets? Is it anything special for God to number the stars, if he has counted all the hairs on our heads?[12]

It is evident, brothers and sisters, that God means us to understand something else when the psalm says, *He counts the great host of the stars, calling all of them by their names.* There are luminaries in the Church who console us in our night; there are stars, and to some of them the apostle says, *You appear like luminaries in this world.* He explains, *Amid a crooked and perverse race you appear like luminaries in this world, holding fast the word of life* (Phil 2:15-16). These are the stars God counts; they are the people destined to reign with him. He keeps a tally of those who are to be built into the body of his only-begotten Son. He numbers them, but anyone who is unworthy is not counted. Many have come to faith, or at any rate have joined themselves to his people with some faint semblance of faith, but God knows whom he will count and whom he will sift out. So noble is the excellence of the gospel that the prediction of another psalm has been verified: *I announced the news and spoke the message, and they were multiplied, in numbers beyond reckoning* (Ps 39:6(40:5)). Among the crowds there are some supernumeraries, so to speak. What do I mean by that? There are more people here than there will be there;

---

12. See Mt 10:30.

within these walls there are more than will be found in the kingdom of God, in the heavenly Jerusalem. These are the supernumeraries.

Let each one determine whether he or she is shining in the darkness, and is not led astray by the dark iniquity of this world. Anyone who is neither led astray nor extinguished will be like a star, counted already as such by God.

10. *Calling all of them by their names,* says the psalm, and in that lies their whole reward. We have our own special names with God, and we must long for God to know our names, and lead our lives so that he will. We must do all we can to ensure it, not seeking enjoyment in anything else, not even in any spiritual gifts we may have. You must try to see this point, beloved: there are many gifts in the Church, as the apostle observes: *To one is given wise utterance through the Spirit, to another knowledgeable speech according to the same Spirit, to another faith through the same Spirit, to another gifts of healing, to another discernment between spirits*—that is, between true spirits and false—*to another various tongues, and to another prophecy* (1 Cor 12:8–10). What great gifts he has mentioned! And what a wealth of them! Yet many people who have exercised such gifts will hear at the end, *I never knew you.* And how will they protest at the end, these people who have heard the Lord say, *I never knew you? Lord, did we not prophesy in your name, and in your name cast out demons, and in your name work many prodigies?* (Mt 7:22) In your name we did all this! And what will he say to them? *I never knew you; depart from me, all you who act unjustly* (Mt 7:23).

What can it mean to be a light in the sky even now, alleviating the night and not being extinguished by it? *Now I will point out to you a way that surpasses all others,* the apostle continues. *If I speak with human tongue or angel's tongue, but have no love, I have become like a booming gong or a clashing cymbal.* (1 Cor 12:31–13:1) What a gift that is, to speak with all the tongues known to angels and human beings! Nevertheless, *if I have no love, I have become like a booming gong or a clashing cymbal.* He goes on, *If I have cognizance of all mysteries and all knowledge; if I have the gift of prophecy, and if I have such perfect faith that I can move mountains*—and what mighty gifts these are!—*but have no love, I am nothing.* But what about the grace of martyrdom, and the grace to give away one's goods? No, *if I distribute all my resources to feed the poor, and deliver my body to be burnt, yet have no love, it profits me nothing.* (1 Cor 13:2–3) If someone lacks charity, even though he has these gifts for a time, they will be taken away from him. What he has will be taken from him because he lacks a certain something, and that something is the means whereby all the others could have been retained and he himself not have perished. What was it that we heard the Lord saying just now? *Anyone who has will be given more, but if anyone has not, even what he does have will be taken away from him* (Mt 13:12). If someone does not have this important thing, even what he does have will be taken away. He has the grace of possessing these powers but not the charity needed to use them aright, and, because he lacks it, what he does have will be taken from him.

He who *counts the great host of the stars, calling all of them by their names*, ensured that those whom he wanted to make stars in his sky would have charity and walk in the way that surpasses all others. When, therefore, the disciples returned to the place from which they had been sent out, exulting, *Lord, even unclean spirits submitted to us in your name!* (Lk 10:17) he who *counts the great host of the stars, calling all of them by their names*, tempered their glee. He knew that many people will demand of him one day, *Did we not cast out demons in your name?* and that he will have to say to them at the end, *I never knew you*, because he will not have counted them among the host of stars or called them by their names. So he warned his disciples, *Do not rejoice because the spirits were subject to you; rejoice because your names have been written in heaven* (Lk 10:20). *He counts the great host of the stars, calling all of them by their names.*

Verse 5. *God's understanding is infinite, and it baffles us*

11. *Great is our Lord*. The psalmist is filled with joy; he blurts this out because he could not find the right words. He has no power to say whatever it was. Indeed, how could he even think it? *Great is our Lord, and great is his power; his understanding cannot be reckoned*. He who counts the great host of the stars is himself uncountable. *Great is our Lord, and great is his power; his understanding cannot be reckoned*. Who could explain that statement? Who could even think worthily about what has been said, *His understanding cannot be reckoned*? I wish the Lord would pour himself into you. We are unequal to the task of explaining, but he is powerful. Would that he would himself illumine your minds to grasp what that phrase means, *His understanding cannot be reckoned*! Think of it, brothers and sisters: Could we possibly count grains of sand? We could not, but God can. He to whom the number of hairs on our heads is known

has also counted the sand. Any infinite[13] thing this world embraces, though innumerable to human beings, is not innumerable to God. We could go further and say that it is not innumerable to the angels either.

His understanding cannot be reckoned. His understanding defeats all mathematicians, for it is incalculable. Who can count number itself? Whatever is to be counted is counted by means of numbers, but number itself cannot be numbered; there is no way whatever of numbering number. What is there in God, then, what power wherewith he made all things, what place where he made them all, if scripture can say to him, *You have disposed all things in measure, and number, and weight* (Wis 11:21)? Who could ever count or measure or weigh that very measure, the very number or the very weight in which God has disposed all things?

And so, *his understanding cannot be reckoned.* Let human voices fall silent and human thoughts be still. Let them not stretch out toward what is incomprehensible as though they could comprehend, but only as seeking to participate in it. For we shall indeed participate. We shall not ourselves be that reality which we attempt to grasp, nor shall we grasp it totally, but we shall be participants in it. Something great was said about Jerusalem—the Jerusalem whose dispersed citizens God is collecting—*Jerusalem is being built like a city; it shares in the Selfsame* (Ps 121(122):3). What does that phrase, *the Selfsame,* signify, if not a reality that cannot change?[14] Created things can exist in a variety of ways, but the creator cannot exist in this way or that, variably. He is the Selfsame, and to him another psalm sings, *You will discard them, and they will be changed, but you are the Selfsame, and your years will not fail* (Ps 101:27-28(102:26-27)). If, then, he is the Selfsame, incapable of any change, we who participate in his divinity shall ourselves be immortal and shaped for eternal life. As I have explained to you already, holy brethren, God gave us a pledge in the person of his Son: before we could become participants in his immortality, he had to become a participant in our mortality. But as he became mortal not because of anything in his own nature but by sharing in ours, so do we become immortal not in the power of our own nature but through his. We shall truly participate in it; let no one be in any doubt of this, for scripture has said so.[15]

---

13. Variant: "finite."
14. See the note at Exposition of Psalm 121,5.
15. See 2 Pt 1:4.

But in what can we participate? Are there any parts in God? Is he parceled out? If not, is it possible for many to be participants in one simple being? No one can explain this, so do not demand a plain statement about things that cannot be adequately put into words, as I think you see,[16] but turn back to the healing power of our savior. Bruise your hearts. Let your obdurate hearts be bruised and your stubborn attitudes worn down. Let your heart be condemned for its bad deeds and be reborn into a new, good life. Let God straighten you. He will bind up your fractures and consolidate your health. Things that at present are impossible for us will then be possible. Those who aspire to reach divinity will do well to confess their weakness. God's *understanding cannot be reckoned.*

Verse 6. If scripture at first seems obscure, do not be impatient like the Manichees

12. The psalm indicates to you what you must do if you have difficulty in understanding, for it goes on to say, *The Lord welcomes the meek.* Suppose you do not understand some passage, or understand only a little of it, or at any rate cannot master it: hold God's scripture in honor, respect God's word even when it is not clear to you, maintain a reverent attitude while you wait for understanding to come. Do not be over-bold and find fault with the obscurity of scripture or even allege that it is self-contradictory. There is no contradiction here. Some obscurity there may be, not in order that insight may be denied you, but so that your mind may be stretched until you can receive it. When some text seems dark to you, be sure that the physician has made it so; he is inviting you to knock. He wanted it to puzzle you so that you may be put through your paces as you keep on knocking; he wants it to be so, that he may open to you when you knock.[17] As you persevere in knocking you will be stretched; as you are stretched, your capacity will be enlarged; as your capacity grows, you will receive what comes to you as gift. Do not be angry, then, when you find the door closed. Be gentle, be meek. Do not lash out against the obscure passage, saying, "That thought would have been better expressed if it had been put like this...." When will you ever be qualified to say it, or even to judge how it ought to be said? It has been said in the right

---

16. Variant: "do not demand what I think cannot be more plainly stated than you see."
17. See Mt 7:7.

way. The patient has no business to alter his treatment; the doctor knows when to modify it. Trust him who is working on your cure.

What does the next line say? *The Lord welcomes the meek.* Do not rage against God's closed doors; be meek so that he may welcome you in. If you are rebellious, watch out for the warning that follows: *But he humbles sinners right down to the ground.* There are many kinds of sinners, but when the psalm says of the Lord that he *humbles sinners right down to the ground*, what sinners can it mean if not those who are the opposite of meek? By saying, *The Lord welcomes the meek, but he humbles sinners right down to the ground*, the psalm indicates the species of sin by contrasting it with the meekness mentioned alongside it. We can therefore identify the sinners in this passage as those who are not meek, those who are anything but meek. Why does the Lord humble them right down to the ground? Because, when they carp at intelligible realities, they are reduced to discerning only the earthly.

13. This is how the Lord dealt with people who were bent on deriding the law[18] before they had come to know it. No meekness for them! I want you to understand this, beloved. A certain corrupt sect arose, called the Manichees.[19] Having received and read the scriptures, this sect mocked them. It was determined to censure what it did not understand, and, by insulting and railing at what it had not understood, it ensnared many. But the people who chose to act in that way were humbled right down to the ground. They were not allowed to understand the things of heaven but savored only those of earth. Everything you hear in their fanciful tales is blasphemy, images dreamed up from material things. When they did want to understand God, they arrived only at contemplation of the light we can see; they could not get any further. And so they believed that there were fields of light in God's kingdom similar to our visible sun and that these were the product of God's light.

But everything that is accessible to our earthly flesh is earth to God. We have senses with which we see and hear and smell and taste and touch. Our flesh perceives things through these five messengers we call our senses, but it perceives bodily things only; intelligible and spiritual realities are grasped only by the mind. When, therefore, the Manichees derided obscure passages in the scriptures—scriptures

---

18. That is, the Old Testament.
19. See Expositions of Psalms 10,3; 67,39; 80,13–14; 140,10–12 and the notes at these places.

that were closed only that those who knocked might be tested, not that their contents might be withheld from little ones—they were humbled right down to the ground and rendered incapable of thinking anything thereafter except what is perceived by earth. Perceived by earth—what am I saying? Yes, perceived by the flesh. Our flesh is earth, made from the earth. Whatever you take in through your eyes belongs to the earth; whatever you take in through your ears, your nostrils, your sense of taste or touch—all of it belongs to the earth, because it is perceived by earth. The Manichees were therefore unable to understand understanding itself, which cannot be reckoned because God's *understanding cannot be reckoned*. Instead they carped at the scriptures, which conceal true understanding beneath certain mysterious figures for good reason, so that little ones may thereby be put to the test and trained. By thus finding fault the Manichees became anything but meek—became, in fact, the very opposite of meek. And they were accordingly humbled right down to the ground, becoming incapable of any perception of our incorporeal God. Whatever they thought about God, they could think only in bodily fashion.

Verse 7. Begin with confession if you wish to attain to the contemplation of wisdom

14. If God *humbles sinners right down to the ground*, what must we do if we do not want to be humbled right down to the ground? It is a great thing to advance to intelligible realities, a great thing to advance to what is spiritual, and it is a great thing for the heart to reach the point where it knows that something exists that is neither extended in space nor subject to variations with time. After all, what does wisdom look like? Who can think about it? Is it long? Or square? Or round? Is it now here, now there? Suppose someone in the east thinks about wisdom, and someone in the west too. If they think well about it, then, even though they are far apart, wisdom is wholly present to both of them. How can this be? Does anyone understand it? Does anyone comprehend that substance, that divine, unchangeable nature? No, but do not be in too much of a hurry, for you will be able to understand later. Listen to the next verse: *Let your first song to the Lord be one of confession*. This must be your point of departure if you want to attain to clear understanding of truth. If you wish to be led from the way of faith to the possession of God in vision, begin from confession. Accuse yourself first. Accuse yourself and praise God. Call upon him whom you do not yet know, that he

may come and make himself known to you:[20] I do not mean that he comes by a change of place but call upon him so that he may lead you to himself. How can he come to a place he never leaves? This is an aspect of wisdom's perfection: it is everywhere, yet far away from the wicked. It is everywhere, I tell you, yet far away from wicked people who are to be found everywhere! From whom can it be far away, I ask you, if it is everywhere? Where else can it be distant, do you think, except in the place where people who have effaced God's likeness in themselves are lying in their state of unlikeness? When they became unlike him they went far off, but let them be reformed and return. "By what means can we be reformed?" someone may ask. "When shall we be reformed?" *Let your first song to the Lord be one of confession.* And what happens after our confession? Let good works follow. *Play psalms to our God upon the lyre.* Why on the lyre? As I have explained already,[21] just as a psalm is played on the psaltery, so is it also on the lyre, not with the voice alone but with the action of the hands. *Play psalms to our God upon the lyre.*

Verse 8. The sky of scripture is providentially obscured so that, when the clouds expound it, we may enjoy rain

15. Go on, then, confess to him and employ yourselves in works of mercy: *Play psalms to our God upon the lyre.* Who is this God of ours? *He who covers the sky with clouds.* What does it mean by saying, *He who covers the sky with clouds?* It means that he conceals his scripture behind figures and holy signs.[22] He who humbles sinners right down to the ground, he who welcomes the meek, *covers the sky with clouds.*

But then who can see the sky, if clouds are hiding it? Don't worry, listen to the next words. *He covers the sky with clouds, he who prepares rain for the earth.* You were anxious when you heard that he *covers the sky with clouds*, because that seemed to mean you could not see the sky. But when it has rained[23] you will yield your fruit and gaze up at a clear sky. *He covers the sky with clouds, he who prepares rain for the earth*; perhaps this is just what the Lord our God has done. If there were no obscure passages in the scriptures we should

---

20. Variant: "you may come to know him."
21. See section 2 above.
22. *Sacramenta*, see note at section 8 above.
23. Variant: "when you [God] have rained."

have no occasion to speak to you, telling you things that give you joy. So perhaps these things you find enjoyable are the rain? The truth could not have been expounded to you through our tongue if God had not covered the sky of his scriptures with the clouds of figurative words and events. His purpose in covering the sky with clouds is therefore to prepare rain for the earth. He willed the prophets[24] to express themselves obscurely, so that later God's servants would, by interpreting the texts, pour true teaching into the ears and hearts of their hearers. These hearers would thus receive from God's clouds[25] a rich feast of spiritual joy. *He covers the sky with clouds, he who prepares rain for the earth.*

Almsgiving to the poor and contributions to your pastors are your duty

16. *He makes grass spring up on the mountains, and verdure for the service of human beings.* There you see the effects of the rain. Notice that the psalm says, *He makes grass spring up on the mountains.* Surely on lower ground too? But mountains are mentioned because this is a remarkable event. The psalm calls persons who are important in the world's eyes *mountains*; you must understand mountains in this text to represent people endowed with high dignity. There was nothing particularly wonderful about a widow dropping two tiny coins into the temple chest,[26] for in that case it was the earth, the lowly earth, that sprouted grass. But a mountain did so too. Zacchaeus was a leading man among the tax collectors,[27] and it was more remarkable that a mountain like him brought forth grass, for the more elevated people's rank, the more avaricious they tend to be, and the greater they are in this world, the more they love their wealth. This is why another man, the one who sought advice from the Lord about attaining eternal life, went away sad. He had called the Lord *Good master*, and asked him, *What must I do to gain eternal life?* The Lord replied, *Keep the commandments. Which ones?* he asked. Then the Lord listed the commandments of the law. *I have kept all these since my youth*, the man answered. The Lord told him, *If you want to be perfect, go and sell all you possess and give the money to the poor:*

---

24. A wide term for Augustine, including all sacred writers.
25. Preachers now, as often in Augustine.
26. See Mk 12:42.
27. See Lk 19:2–8.

you will have treasure in heaven. Then come, follow me. (Mt 19:16–21) What did the Lord say to him? "Look, you are a mountain. Receive the rain and sprout grass. After all, what are you going to give up? It's only grass, isn't it?"

Indeed, all the donations made by rich people to the Church to provide for the needs of God's servants are only grass, aren't they? They are material resources that appear only for a time. Yet what is won by the donors is no material reward. Think what you can purchase with your base riches. When speaking of these offerings and showing that they were no more than grass, the apostle said, *If we have sown spiritual seeds for your benefit, is it too much to ask that we reap a carnal harvest from you?* (1 Cor 9:11) And carnal goods are indeed grass, as a prophet says: *All flesh is but grass, and human glory like the flowering of grass* (Is 40:6).

So the questioner went away sad, and the Lord reflected, *How difficult it is for a rich person to get into the kingdom of heaven!* (Mt 19:23) This is why it is a great achievement when the Lord *makes grass spring up on the mountains*. But how can it be said that he *makes grass spring up on the mountains* when the rich man, on hearing that he was invited to give his goods to the poor, went off sad? How did the Lord subsequently reply to the apostles in their dismay? *What is difficult for human beings is easy for God* (Mt 19:26). This is why he can make grass spring up on the mountains; everything is easy for him, even though nothing is more sterile than very hard mountains.

He sends rain, he who *makes grass spring up on the mountains, and verdure for the service of human beings*. What *service* does the psalm refer to here? Listen to what Paul has to say. *We are your slaves, through Jesus Christ* (2 Cor 4:5), he declared. He had demanded of them, *If we have sown spiritual seeds for your benefit, is it too much to ask that we reap a carnal harvest from you?* but now he called himself their slave. We are indeed your servants, your slaves, brothers and sisters. No one among us should make any pretence of being superior to you; we will be greater than you only if we are humbler. *Whoever wishes to be greater among you will be your servant* (Mt 20:27): this is the Lord's view of the matter. The Lord *makes grass spring up on the mountains, and verdure for the service of human beings*. It is true that the apostle Paul lived by the work of his own hands and would not accept the grass provided by the mountains.[28] He preferred to

---

28. See 1 Cor 9:15.

be[29] in want, but, all the same, the mountains did provide grass. His unwillingness to accept it would not have justified the mountains in refusing to give and in remaining barren, would it? Fruitfulness is the due response to rain, and food is the due recompense to a servant, as the Lord ordained: *Eat what they provide for you.* And then, in case they might think they were giving something that was truly their own, he added, *The laborer deserves his pay.* (Lk 10:7)

17. When we address you on this subject, brothers and sisters, we speak the more freely inasmuch as we are not seeking such contributions from you, even though, if we did seek them, it would be fruitfulness on your part, righteous conduct from you, and not your wealth, that we would be concerned to see.[30] However, we have taken the opportunity to speak to you before on this matter, and at some length,[31] so we will keep our admonitions brief; this sermon must end sometime. What we wish to emphasize is this: if you do not want to remain barren, if you want to prove fertile out of gratitude for the rain, if you do not wish to be condemned in the end for your sterility, you must make demands on yourselves. You must become debt-collectors, requiring due payment from your own resources. Remember that God threatens barren, thorny ground with fire but opens his storehouse to fruitful earth.[32] Christ makes his demands silently, but the voice of the silent Christ is the more powerful because in the gospel he is by no means silent. He is not silent when he counsels us, *Make yourselves friends from sinful mammon, so that they may welcome you into the tents of eternity* (Lk 16:9). Christ himself is not silent: listen and you will hear his voice.

No one can make direct demands on you, except perhaps in a situation where those who serve you in the gospel are forced to beg from you. If it comes to that, and they have no choice but to beg, take care that you do not beg in vain when you beg some favor from God. But it must not come to that: you are the ones who must make demands on yourselves. Otherwise it may not even happen that those who serve you in the gospel do beg from you; they may not ask even in their need. But in that case their silence will be your condemnation.

---

29. Variant: "was not willing to be."
30. Compare Phil 4:17.
31. See Exposition 3 of Psalm 103,9–12, where the mention of grass—*the earth brings forth grass for cattle, and plants for the service of human beings*—inspired ideas similar to those developed here.
32. See Heb 6:7–8.

It is written, *Blessed is everyone who understands about the poor and needy person* (Ps 40:2(41:1)). One who does understand is not content to wait for the poor to ask. Try to understand a poor person's need. If one needy person seeks you out, you must go and look for another. Both kinds of readiness are enjoined on us, brothers and sisters. You heard one injunction just now: *Give to everyone who asks you* (Lk 6:30); and in another place scripture says, "Let your alms sweat in your hand until you find a deserving person to whom you can deliver it."[33] If one petitioner is seeking you out, you must go and seek another. This does not mean leaving the first one destitute, for scripture has told you, *Give to everyone who asks you*, but you must still go searching for another, for you are also instructed, "Let your alms sweat in your hand until you find a deserving person to whom you can deliver it."

You will never be in a position to do this unless you put aside some part of your resources for the purpose. Each person must decide for himself what this is to be, taking into account the needs of his own household. You should regard what you put aside as a tax that you owe. Does Christ not have his own commonwealth? Then he can also levy taxes. Do you know what a *fiscus* is?[34] A *fiscus* is a purse, and from *fiscus* we get the diminutive forms *fiscellae* and *fiscinae*.[35] You should not think of it as a dreadful monster, as do people who are afraid when they hear the taxman coming. The *fiscus* is a purse for the public good. The Lord himself had one here on earth; we hear of his having receptacles for money and that they were entrusted to Judas. The Lord bore with Judas, who was both a traitor and a thief,[36] and dealt patiently with him on all occasions. Nonetheless, people who offered contributions were helping to defray the Lord's own expenses. You do not imagine, surely, that when the Lord was traveling about he was accustomed to beg or else go hungry—he whom angels served, and who fed thousands of people on five loaves? Why

---

33. Augustine cited this maxim before—in a slightly different version—in his Exposition of Psalm 102,12 and Exposition 3 of Psalm 103,10. The words are quoted as scriptural for the first time in Christian literature in *Didache* 1,6.
34. *Fiscus*, originally a basket woven of rushes or twigs; then a money-basket or money-bag, a purse. By extension it came to mean the treasury or imperial revenue or the emperor's privy purse. By further extension, the *fiscus iudaicus* was the tax paid by Jews into the imperial treasury.
35. Small baskets for fruit, cheese, etc.
36. See Jn 12:6.

did he will to need money? Why else than to give an example to the mountains whose duty it was to sprout grass and not defy the rain by remaining barren?

Your duty, then, is to set something aside and reserve a fixed sum[37] either from your annual income or from your daily trading. This is the best way because, if you stretch out your hand to take anything from the money you have not saved for this purpose, it will seem like taking from your own livelihood, and then your hand may well tremble. Earmark some portion of your revenues. Have you decided on a tenth? Very well, put a tenth aside, though this is not much. The Pharisees are said to have given a tenth: *I give tithes from everything I own* (Lk 18:12), boasted one of them. And what does the Lord say? *If your righteousness does not exceed that of the scribes and Pharisees, you will not get into the kingdom of heaven* (Mt 5:20). The Pharisee, whose righteousness yours must outstrip, gives a tenth, yet you do not give even a thousandth part! How are you to go one better if you are not even keeping up with him?

The Lord *covers the sky with clouds, and prepares rain for the earth. He makes grass spring upon the mountains, and verdure for the service of human beings.*

Verse 9. Raven chicks cry to the Lord for food

18. *He provides the cattle with their food.* He calls God's flocks *cattle.* God does not deny his flock its food but supplies it through human pastors, for whose service he makes grass spring up. With this in mind the apostle asks, *Does anyone ever tend a flock without drinking its milk?* (1 Cor 9:7) *He provides the cattle with their food and feeds the ravens' squabs that call upon him.* Are we meant to think that raven squabs really do cry out to God to feed them? No, you should not assume that irrational beings invoke God; no soul knows how to invoke God except a rational soul. You must take the psalm's statement in a figurative sense or you may fall into the error of some unbelievers who say that human souls are reincarnated in cattle, dogs, pigs, or ravens. Banish such a notion from your hearts and from your faith. The human soul is made in the image of God,[38] but God does not grant that image of himself to a dog or a pig.

---

37. *Aliquid fixum.* Many codices read *aliquid fisco* ("something for the tax/treasury").
38. See Gn 1:26.

What does the psalm mean, then, when it says, *He feeds the ravens' squabs that call upon him*? Who are these young ravens? The Israelites claimed that they alone were righteous because they had received the law, and they reckoned as sinners the rest of the human race, all the gentiles. And indeed it was true that all the gentiles were abandoned to sin, to idolatry, and to the worship of stones and trees. But did they remain in that state? By no means. Even if those ravens, our parents, did not call upon God, still we, the raven squabs, do ourselves call upon him. *He provides the cattle with their food and feeds the ravens' squabs that call upon him.* To raven squabs like these Peter said, *It was not with the corruptible currency of gold or silver that you were ransomed from the worthless ways of life you inherited from your ancestors* (1 Pt 1:18). Young ravens seemed to be worshiping their parents' idols, but as they grew up they turned toward God instead, and now you hear a raven squab calling upon the one God. "What is this?" you ask him. "Have you left your father?" "I certainly have," he replies. "He was a raven, and he did not call upon God, but I, a raven squab, call upon him." *The ravens' squabs call upon God.*

Verses 10–11. Not human strength, but hope in his mercy, finds favor with the Lord

19. *He will take no pleasure in the power of the horse.* The power of the horse represents pride, for a horse seems almost designed to lift up a human being that he may travel in a more dominant position. And a horse has a strong neck too, suggestive of a certain arrogance. Men and women are ill-advised to mount high in their dignity and think themselves elevated by the honors they receive. They should beware lest an unbroken horse throw them. Notice what another psalm says on this theme: *Some trust in chariots and some in horses, but as for us, we will triumph in the name of the Lord our God.* It is saying that while those others look for glory in temporal honors, we shall find our true excellence in the name of the Lord our God. And what was the outcome? What happened to those others? Look at the next verse: *They were shackled and they fell, but we have arisen and we stand upright* (Ps 19:8–9(20:7–8)).

He will take no pleasure in the power of the horse, nor will he look favorably on the tents of a man. The psalm speaks of *the tents of a man,*[39] for there is also a tent of the Lord, which is holy Church,

---

39. *Viri.*

spread throughout the world. Heretics have departed from the Church's tents and pitched tents of their own, but God does not look favorably on these man-made tents. Hear the different cry of a raven's squab: *I would rather be degraded in the Lord's house than dwell in the tents of sinners* (Ps 83:11(84:10)). If some good, devout raven chick in the Church, some squab that confesses its weakness and calls upon God, finds itself denied temporal honor, it does not leave the Church, or pitch a tent for itself outside the Church, for on such a tent God will not look with favor. What does the chick say? *I would rather be degraded in the Lord's house than dwell in the tents of sinners.* The Lord *will not look favorably on the tents of a man.*

20. But what does the psalmist add? *The Lord will look favorably on those who fear him, and on those who hope in his mercy.* The Lord looks favorably on those who fear him. But God is not feared in the same way that a robber is feared, is he? Certainly a robber is feared too, and a wild animal is feared, and an unjust man in power is feared greatly. *The Lord will look favorably on those who fear him*, but how are they to fear him if they are to win his favor? The psalm explains: *on those who hope in his mercy.* Think of Judas, who betrayed Christ: he feared the Lord but did not hope in his mercy, for afterwards he felt remorse at having betrayed the Lord and said, *I have sinned, for I have betrayed righteous blood* (Mt 27:4). You were right to be afraid, Judas, but your fear ought to have been accompanied by hope in the mercy of him whom you feared. Instead he despaired and hanged himself.

You, then, must fear the Lord in such wise that you hope in his mercy. If you are afraid of a robber, you hope for help from someone else, not from the one you fear. You beg someone of whom you are not afraid to help you against the one who threatens you. But if you fear God like that, if you fear God because you are a sinner, whom will you ask for help against him? Where will you go? What will you do? Is it any use trying to flee from God? Rather, flee to him. Are you trying to flee from him in his anger? Flee to him in his appeasement. You will appease him if you hope in his mercy, and, as you have besought him to forgive you for your past sins, so will you beware of sin in the future. To him belong all honor and majesty, together with the Father and the Holy Spirit, for endless ages. Amen.

Exposition of Psalm 147

A Sermon to the People[1]

Sunday's sermon on the last judgment did not leave time for any exposition of the psalm, which has been deferred until today

1. You remember, beloved, that we were obliged to postpone until today a sermon on the psalm which we have just sung. This was the psalm which was read last Sunday, the one on which we began to comment; but, since on that occasion we were deeply moved by the gospel reading, we spent a long time on it, prompted by fear on our own part and the desire to help you. In the gospel the Lord warned us about the last day and bade us be wary and vigilant as we await his coming. He does not want to condemn us when he comes to judge, and so he also drew our attention to a frightening example. The future coming of the Son of Man, he said, will be like the cataclysm in Noah's day. People were eating and drinking, buying and selling, marrying and taking wives, until Noah entered the ark. Then came the flood and wiped out all of them.[2] What believer could hear this warning without being terrified? Terrified we were, certainly, and full of concern, and so we lingered over this passage as long as time allowed, hoping so to speak about your conduct, about the way you live your lives, and about the lives of all of us, that we may not only await that final day without foreboding but even desire it. If we love Christ, we inevitably must desire his coming. It would be altogether illogical to be afraid that someone you love may come; indeed, I do not know whether you really could do that. Is it possible to pray, *Thy kingdom come* (Mt 6:10), and at the same time be afraid that your prayer may be heard? What are you frightened of? That the judge will come? Yes, but he is not unjust, is he? Or malevolent or ill-disposed toward you? Clearly not. Furthermore, you surely do not think you could do better for yourself by entrusting your case to some other advocate, lest the one you have briefed be dishonest and deceive you

---

1. Tentatively dated December 403; see the notes at section 16 below. Certainly earlier than Exposition 1 of Psalm 103; see Exposition 1 of Psalm 103,12.
2. See Mt 24:37–42.

or let you down by his lack of eloquence or skill or fail to make a good case for your innocence? None of this can be true.

Who is it, then, who is coming? Why are you not rejoicing at the prospect? Who is coming to judge you? Who else but he who came to be judged for your sake? You have no need to fear the accuser concerning whom Christ himself testified, *The ruler of this world has been cast out* (Jn 12:31). Neither need you be anxious about your advocate, for he who is your advocate now is none other than he who will then be your judge. There will be only he and you and your case, and the only evidence to be alleged will be the testimony of your own conscience.

Well then, if you—any of you—are afraid of the judge you will have to face in the future, correct your conscience now, in its present state. Is it not enough for you that he will not inquire into your life before today? When he judges you, no time will be left to you; but what a lot of time he is giving you now, while he admonishes you with his commandments! You will not be allowed to correct yourself then, but is anyone stopping you now?

Last Sunday we put these thoughts before you very earnestly, because they almost seemed the only things that needed to be said. The result was that no little time sped by. Although we had begun to discuss the psalm, therefore, we were forced to put off the rest until today. But now here we are, ready to tackle it. Let us give it our full attention, or, rather, let us give our attention to God, who has mercifully deigned to entrust us with these scriptural words through his Spirit, knowing as he does how to treat our infirmity. Does any sick person presume to give advice to his doctor?

If some parts of scripture are initially obscure, knock humbly

2. I suspect that, while the psalm was being sung, all or most of you noticed that it included verses which demand that we knock, so that they may be opened. This is especially true of the following passage: *He gives snow like wool, spreads mist like ashes, and sends his ice like bread crumbs. Who shall withstand his cold?* (Verses 16–17) When you heard these words, anyone who took them literally would have thought about the works of God, for who except God gives the snow? Who except God spreads the mist? Who, if not he, hardens the ice? And these three comparisons work in the inverse direction too,

for wool is not unlike snow, and ash not unlike mist,[3] and crumbs of white bread do resemble the shining whiteness of ice or crystal, for crystal is a kind of glass, but white. This description is passed on to us by people who know about it, and we should not be in any doubt that scripture is entirely trustworthy in the witness it gives. We are told by the experts that when snow stays unmelted over the course of many years it freezes so hard into ice that it cannot be melted easily. Ordinarily the advent of summer melts the snows of the previous winter without difficulty, for there has been no long lapse of time to harden them. But when successive snowfalls have piled up on each other, and their compacted mass has defied the onslaught of summer (not one summer but many, and especially in those parts of the world like the northern shores, where even in summer the sun is not very hot), that long, year-upon-year hardening produces ice which can be compared to crystal. Try to focus on this, beloved. What is ice? It is snow, frozen and solidified, and so hardened by the passing of years that it cannot easily be melted by the sun or fire.

We have explained this matter at some length because many people have no experience of it. But even those who perhaps are familiar with these things should not reckon it tedious to listen to a discourse about something they know already, because it is provided not for them but for others who were ignorant. When the reader's voice rang out, and you listened to those verses, I feel sure that there were different reactions among you. Some probably said, "How great are the works of the Lord! One little part of them is celebrated here, and that an earthly part, familiar to nearly everyone: how God sends the snow, how he spreads the mist, and how he solidifies the ice." And they would be right to say this. But others will have said to themselves, "Can these things have been mentioned in scripture without some special purpose? Is there perhaps more to these verses than their obvious meaning? Did not the pairing of snow and wool, mist and ash, ice and bread, suggest something else to our minds? But why did scripture deliberately speak in cloudy similes? Could not the truths it contains have been much better expressed otherwise? Why do I have to cast about to discover what the words demand, and often admit that I am uncertain? Why do I have to work so hard even to

---

3. The resemblance is not immediately obvious, except for the greyness of both. But *nebula*, here translated "mist," can mean a smoky exhalation, and this may be what Augustine had in mind.

listen to them? Why do I often have to go away none the wiser, even after hearing the psalm?"

If you reacted like that, you are demonstrating the truth of what I said to you not long since:[4] allow yourself to be cured. Only in this way can you be healed. A sick person is very proud and headstrong if he presumes to tell the doctor what to do, even though the doctor is only human. Will the patient dare to give him advice? But, in the case we are considering, though the patient is human, it is God who heals, and you will make an excellent first step toward piety and health if, before you understand why something was said in scripture, you believe that it was said as it ought to have been. Through this reverent approach you will be able to inquire into the meaning of what was said, so that having inquired you may find, and having found you may rejoice.

Let your loving prayers to the Lord our God support us, then. If not for our sake, at any rate for yours, may he graciously enable us to find what lies hidden here. We promised you that today would be a day for something worth looking at, for a divine exhibition, so to say.[5] Think of it this way: the verses of the psalm which have been proclaimed but not yet expounded are like tightly-wrapped parcels that we have brought along from the divine giver. They are presented to us wrapped up in order that your eagerness may be aroused as the wrappings are being removed. But you must prepare yourselves not merely to look on but also to clothe yourselves in the contents.

If our faith is wide awake, we shall long for eternal life

3. Last Sunday, beloved, we told you—those of you who were present will remember this—that the passage of the gospel read that day, which detained us so long that our explanation of the psalm had to be postponed, was well matched with the psalm that accompanied it. We told you this but could not explain why for lack of time; we had to put off the psalm until today. Now, therefore, we must also demonstrate how well the gospel and the psalm go together.

---

4. See the end of section 1, and perhaps also Exposition of Psalm 146,12.15.
5. Augustine is fond of the idea that the Christian mysteries are a better spectacle than the shows or games that lure many people away. The day of this sermon may have been also that of a notable entertainment in the amphitheater; see section 3. Compare Expositions of Psalms 39,8 and 143,15 and the notes at both places.

When that gospel was read we were terrified by the thought of the last day. Intense fear like this gives birth to security, because if we are frightened we take precautions, and if we have taken precautions we shall be safe. Just as premature carelessness drives us into the arms of danger and fear, so does due care issue in freedom from foreboding. We need to be frightened so that we may not love the present failing, fleeting, transient life as though there were no other life for us. If indeed there is no other, let us all fall in love with this one. If there is no other life, those who have stayed awake today to go to the amphitheater are better off than we are. What does the apostle say? *If our hope in Christ is a matter for this present life only, we are in a more wretched state than all the rest of humankind* (1 Cor 15:19). So there is another life. Let each one of you question Christ, through his faith. But you can't, can you, because your faith is asleep? No wonder you are tossed about, if Christ is asleep in your boat. The gospel describes such a situation: Jesus was asleep in the boat, and the boat was being tossed about by waves and high winds.[6] So too is the heart battered when Christ is asleep. But surely Christ is always awake, so what can it mean to say that he is asleep? I mean that your faith has gone to sleep. Why are you still flung about by the storm of doubt? Wake Christ up, arouse your faith. Fix the eye of your faith on the future life, for love of which you came to believe, and for love of which you are sealed with Christ's sign. He led this life of yours in order to show you how contemptible was the kind of life you earlier made your own, and how worthy of hope is that other life in which you had not until then believed.

So now, if you have awakened your faith and directed its gaze toward what will come at the end; if you have set your sights on the world of the future, where we shall rejoice after the second coming of the Lord, after his judgment has been accomplished and the kingdom of heaven has been delivered to the saints; if you have begun to ponder on that life, my dearest ones, and on its well-filled leisure, of which we have often spoken: then, beloved, you know that our occupation will then be subject to no storms. Our leisurely occupation[7] will be filled with nothing but sweetness, assailed by no harassment, spoiled

---

6. See Mk 4:37–40.
7. *Otiosum negotium*, not an oxymoron for the ancients, whose idea of *otium* was richer than that conveyed by "leisure"; see the note on Exposition 1 of Psalm 36,2.

by no fatigue, disturbed by no cloud. What will our occupation be? To praise God, to love him and praise him, to praise him out of love, and to love him as we praise. *Blessed are they who dwell in your house; they will praise you for ever and ever* (Ps 83:5(84:4)). And why, if not because for all eternity they will love you? Why, if not because they will contemplate you for ever and ever?

What kind of spectacle will that be, my brothers and sisters, when we behold God in direct vision? Men and women watch a gladiator, and they enjoy it. Wretched folk, it will be the worse for them if they do not come to a better mind! These fans of the games, who watch a fighter and enjoy the spectacle, will see the savior and find only gloom. What can be more wretched than the fate of those for whom the savior does not mean salvation? If for them a man fighting represents pleasure, small wonder that a God who liberates will not for them represent salvation.

But for our part, brothers and sisters, if we bear in mind that we are among his members, if we long for him, if we persevere, we shall see him and rejoice. We shall find our place in that city where all the citizens have been made pure, where there is no trace of sedition or rioting, where the envious foe who tries to stop us from reaching our homeland can lie in wait for no one because he is not permitted even to set foot there. If even now he is shut out from the hearts of believers, how much more definitively will he be shut out from the city of the living? What will it be, brothers and sisters, what will it be, I ask you, to be within that city, if even to speak of it is such a joy? We must prepare our hearts for that future life. Those who have prepared their hearts for it hold all this present life cheap, and contempt for this life makes them await peacefully the day of which the Lord's warnings made us so fearful.

How to be prepared for the last day

4. We have seen that, while the psalm sings to us about the prospect of future life, the gospel has struck fear into us about the present. We could say that the psalm makes us love the life to come but the gospel instills fear about the life we have now. But other parts of the New Testament are not silent about the delights that await us in the future, and this is still more the case in passages where the truths they teach are not presented under wraps but quite openly. Thus what we find obscure in the psalm can be understood in the light of what is openly taught elsewhere. The gospel warned us, "Be on the watch

for the last day, the day when the Son of Man will come,"[8] because it will spell disaster for those it finds secure as they are now—secure for the wrong reasons, I mean, secure in the pleasures of this world, when they ought to be secure only when they have dominated this world's lusts. The apostle certainly prepares us for that future life in words of which I also reminded you on that occasion: *This is what I mean, brethren: time is short. What remains for us is that those who have wives should live as though they were unmarried, those who buy things hold to them lightly, those who rejoice be as though they were not rejoicing, those who weep be as though they wept not, and those who use the world do so as though they made no use of it; for the form of this world is passing away, and I want you to be free from preoccupation.* (1 Cor 7:29–32) If someone locates his entire joy, his total happiness, in eating, drinking, marrying a wife, buying, selling, and making use of this world, such a person may well be free from preoccupation, but he is outside the ark. Woe betide him when the flood sweeps in! But another person does everything for the glory of God, whether he eats or drinks or whatever he does.[9] If something sad happens connected with his worldly business he weeps, but he weeps only while still rejoicing in hope within himself. If some joyful development occurs in his worldly business he rejoices, certainly, but in such fashion that he is spiritually fearful within. He takes care not so to abandon himself to happiness as to be corrupted by it, nor to sink under adversity and be crushed. This is what it means to weep as though one wept not and rejoice as though one were not rejoicing. If a man is married, he is so compassionate for his wife's weakness that he renders her the marital debt but does not demand it of her; or, if he marries because he is himself weak in this respect, he is more inclined to bewail his inability to manage without a wife than to rejoice because he has one. Anyone who sells things does so in the knowledge that what he is getting rid of could not make him happy if he kept it. If another buys, he knows that what he is acquiring will pass away. He places no reliance on his possessions, even if they are plentiful, even if he is awash with them, but he uses what he has to relieve the needs of others who lack them, hoping to receive what he himself lacks from the one who owns all things.

---

8. See Mt 24:44; Lk 21:36.
9. See 1 Cor 10:31.

People who so order their lives await the last day without anxiety, for they are not outside the ark. Already they are reckoned among the imperishable timbers from which the ark is built.[10] They have no reason to fear the future coming of the Lord, but they hope for it and long for it, because for them he will come not to impose punishment but to put an end to troubles. But such hope is possible only where there is longing for the holy city. Thus desire for that city is a fitting response to the warnings in this gospel. Remember, I told you that this gospel and this canticle are well matched.

Verse 12.[11] The prophets Haggai and Zechariah stir us to love and longing for the holy city

5. Now let us hear what city it is of which the psalm sings. Let us hear and sing about it ourselves, for the joy we feel in hearing is already a song to our God. It is not only when we frame a song with our voice and our lips that we are singing; there is also a song that is sung within, because we also have interior ears. We sing with our voices to stir up our own devotion, but we sing with our hearts to please God.

This is said to be a psalm of Haggai and Zechariah. These two men were prophets, and they prophesied during the captivity of that earthly Jerusalem which was a shadow of the heavenly city. While in Babylon, during the earthly city's captivity, these two prophets foretold the restoration of Jerusalem and the new city that would arise out of the ruins of the old, once the people had been freed from captivity.[12] If we have a true sense of our own exile, we shall understand what that captivity signifies for us. Placed as we are in this world, amid worldly troubles, beset by every kind of obstacle and offence, we are like prisoners groaning in captivity. But we shall be raised up; our new city, the peer of the old, is proclaimed to us in advance. After the prophecies of these two men of God a restoration occurred even visibly, for events unfolded in such a way that everything necessary to perfect the earthly image of our city was carried through. Jerusalem

---

10. See Gn 6:14.
11. The numbering of the verses is continued from the preceding psalm, with which the present one forms a single whole in the Massoretic text.
12. Whether or not Haggai and Zechariah exercised some prophetic ministry in Babylon before 538 B.C., as Augustine suggests, their main activity is associated with efforts at restoration in Judah itself in the years 520–518 B.C. See Ezr 5:1; 6:14; Hg 1:1; 2:1; Zec 1:1.7; 7:1.

was rebuilt after seventy years of captivity. The prophet Jeremiah had spoken of seventy years,[13] using this hallowed number to symbolize the whirling mutability of the whole present era. As you well know, our days come and go, rolling past in periods of seven. After the lapse of these seventy years, which Jeremiah had prophesied must intervene, Jerusalem was indeed restored, so that even there, in that earthly city, an image might be established of what is to come. We have been given a sign that after the whirl of time, which rolls on now in seven after seven, our future city will be built in the one unending day of eternity. In that dwelling there is no revolving time, because no one who dwells there declines or grows old. The prophets beheld the heavenly city in spirit, but they spoke of the city on earth. Yet what they said of the earthly was designed to lead us toward the celestial Jerusalem, and all the developments that occurred in time, through material changes and human activity, were signs and foreshadowings of things to come.

6. Let us listen now to how this city is celebrated in song, and let us lift up our eyes and hearts to it. The Spirit of God gives us a magnificent description, infusing into us such love for the city that we sigh for it, beginning to groan even while we are still exiles, and longing to reach it. Let us love it, for even to love it is to be already walking toward it. Come, let us express our love in the words of those holy, prophetic lips that cry out under the prompting of the Spirit of God, *Sing united praise to the Lord, O Jerusalem.* Our prophets are still enduring captivity, and they gaze upon the scattered flocks; or, rather, they behold one single flock comprised of all the citizens gathered at last into the city. They see the joy of the harvested grain, safely stored in the barn after all the threshing and winnowing, afraid of nothing any more, no longer laboring or harassed. The prophets are still on earth, still involved in the beating out of the grain; but even now, before they see it, they gasp for joy and hope for the city, seeming to join their hearts with the angels of God and with the people who will one day be with them in abiding joy. *Sing united praise to the Lord, O Jerusalem.*

What will you be doing, Jerusalem, when that day comes? Hard work and complaining will have passed away: no doubt of that. What will you find to do, then? Will you plough or sow or set out young plants? Will you sail the seas or trade? No? Then what will you do?

---

13. See Jer 25:11–12; 29:10.

Will you still need even to devote yourself to good works, to the duties prompted by compassion? Look round at the great multitude that fills you, look at the company thronging you on every side. See whether there is any hungry person to whom you should hand out bread, whether any thirsty person needs you to offer a cup of cold water. See whether any stranger is applying to you now for hospitality, whether there is any sick person whom you might visit, whether any are engaged in litigation whom you might reconcile, whether anyone is dying whom you might bury.[14] If none of these works will occupy you, what will you do? *Sing united praise to the Lord, O Jerusalem.* That will be your business. You sometimes read on a label, "Enjoy using this!"[15] In the same way: *Sing united praise to the Lord, O Jerusalem.*

We have better things to watch than pagan shows

7. Be Jerusalem, all you who are here today. Remember who it is of whom scripture said, *In your city, O Lord, you will reduce their image to nothing* (Ps 72(73):20). They are the same people who now enjoy frivolous displays, and among them are Christians who have not come here today because there is a show[16] on offer elsewhere. A gift to whom? And a loss to whom? Or turn it round the other way and ask, Who makes the gift? And who sustains the loss? Not only do those who put on these shows suffer financial loss; an even greater loss afflicts those who freely watch them. The donors empty their treasure chests of gold, but the spectators find their hearts emptied of righteousness. Those who stage the shows often lament the need to sell their estates. How much more should sinners bewail the loss of their souls! The Lord cried his warning last Sunday: *Watch!* Do you think he meant that today anyone should be watching that?

I implore you, citizens of Jerusalem, I charge you by the peace of Jerusalem, by her redeemer, by Jerusalem's builder and ruler: direct your prayers to God on their behalf. Make them see and feel that they are playing the fool. However intent they may be on watching the spectacles that please them, let them spare a glance for the spectacle they make of themselves, and find it displeasing. We are

---

14. See Mt 25:35–36; 5:9; Tb 1:20; 2:4–10.
15. *Utere felix*, possibly attached to cups or other utensils, especially if given as presents.
16. *Munus* can mean a show, or a gift. Augustine plays on both meanings.

glad to say that this is indeed what has happened in many cases. We ourselves have sat there and joined in the madness;[17] and how many may we suppose are sitting there now who in the future will be not only Christians but even bishops? We surmise the future on the basis of the past; from what has happened before, we predict what God will do. Keep watch in prayer, then, brothers and sisters; you are not sighing in vain. People who have escaped are precisely the ones most likely to be heard when they pray for those in peril, because they have been among the imperiled themselves. God will draw his people out from captivity in Babylon; he will ransom them and deliver them completely, and the full complement of saints who bear God's image will be reached. Among them will none of those be found whose image God will spurn and reduce to nothing in his city, because they in their own city, Babylon, have reduced his image to nothing. In the holy city will be the people that praises God. The Spirit of prophecy foresees this people now, bids us exult in hope, and invites us to long for the same destiny. *Sing united praise to the Lord, O Jerusalem; praise your God, O Zion.* The psalm says, *Sing united praise*,[18] because you, Jerusalem, are comprised of many; but it adds, *Praise him*,[19] because you have become one. *We, though many, are one in Christ* (Rom 12:5), says the apostle. Because there are many of us, we praise him all together, and because we are one, we praise him as one. The many are the same as the one, because he in whom we are one is himself always one, undivided.

8. "But why should I praise the Lord, all of us together in unison?" asks Jerusalem. "Why should I praise my God?" inquires Zion. Zion and Jerusalem are the same city: there are different reasons for the duplication of the name. Jerusalem is said to mean "vision of peace," and Zion means "lookout post."[20] Now observe that both these names suggest something worth looking at. The pagans must not think that, while they have shows, we have none. It sometimes happens that, when the performance in theater or amphitheater comes to an end and the spectators' benches begin to spew out the dissolute crowd, these dissipated folk retain the fantasies of their empty pleasure in

---

17. See *Confessions* III,2,2–4 of Augustine himself and VI,7,11–12 of Alypius, Augustine's close friend who also became a bishop.
18. *Collauda.*
19. *Lauda.*
20. Compare the Exposition of Psalm 50,22.

their minds and continue to feed on the memory of things that are not merely useless but positively harmful, enjoying impressions that seem pleasant but are in fact baleful. Then it often happens that they see some of God's servants passing by and recognize them from their style of dress or headgear, or because their faces are familiar. So the theatergoers say in their own minds, or to one another, "Poor fellows, what they are missing!"

My brothers and sisters, let us beg God to take their good will into account, for it is a kindly thought. They wish us well, but whoever loves iniquity hates his own soul.[21] And if he hates his own soul, how can he love mine? Yet in their perverse, futile benevolence—if benevolence it can be called—they are grieved that we are missing what they love. Let us pray that they do not lose what we love.

See then, what this Jerusalem is, the city urged to sing praise, or rather, see what the city is that will sing praise in the future, as the psalm foretells. In that future life when we shall see and love and praise God, the praises of the city will not need to be evoked and aroused by any prophetic voice. But the prophets speak in this way now because they long to drink the future joys of the blessed insofar as they can while still living in the flesh, and then, by belching into our ears, arouse in us a love for that city. Let us burn with desire and not be slothful of spirit.

Verse 13. The reinforced gates

9. Now consider the nature of the Jerusalem which, according to the psalm, will praise God. Consider also the reason she will have for praising him: the very perfection of beatitude. *Sing united praise to the Lord, O Jerusalem; praise your God, O Zion.* Then, as though she had asked, "How can I be safe as I praise him?" the psalm continues, *For he has strengthened the bars of your gates.* Take note of this, brothers and sisters: *He has strengthened the bars of your gates.* The strengthening of the bars is not something you do when gates are open but only when they are closed, which is why several codices have: *He has strengthened the bars now in place*[22] *on your gates.* Concentrate on this statement, beloved; the psalm is telling us

---

21. See Ps 10:6(11:5).
22. *Seras,* as opposed to *vectes* in the earlier occurrence. There is little difference, except that a *vectis* was usually a bar attached to the gate and a *sera* a removable bar.

that the Jerusalem which praises the Lord is a locked city. *Sing united praise to the Lord, O Jerusalem; praise your God, O Zion.* We do sing united praise to him, all of us together, even now; we do praise him now, but amid scandals. Many people get in who are unwelcome to us, and many leave, though we do not want them to go. Scandalous problems result. *With iniquity increasing mightily, the love of many grows cold* (Mt 24:12), as truth himself warns us. Scandalous problems are raised by people who join us, whose character we cannot discern, and by those who leave us, whom we cannot restrain. Why does this happen? Because we are not perfect yet and that beatitude is not yet ours. Why do we have these troubles? Because this is still the threshing-floor, and we are not yet in the barn. When we get there, what will it be like? Certainly there will be nothing to fear. *Sing united praise to the Lord, O Jerusalem*, the psalm invites us. *Praise your God, O Zion, for he has strengthened the bars of your gates.* It says that *he has strengthened* them, not that he has simply attached them.[23] Let no one go out and no one enter. Let no one go out: let us be glad of that. But that no one may enter should frighten us. But no, do not fear even this, for once you have entered you will be told, "Just be one of the group of virgins who have brought oil with them."[24]

The whole Church is a virgin

10. These virgins represent souls. There are not just the five, for thousands of others are included with them under this symbolic number. Within this five-strong group we are to think of many thousands, and not of women only but of men as well. Both sexes are represented as feminine because both make up the Church. And both sexes together, being the Church, are called virgins. *I have betrothed you to your one husband, Christ, as a chaste virgin* (2 Cor 11:2), says the apostle. Few people preserve bodily virginity, but all must be virgins at heart. Virginity of the flesh means an untouched body; virginity of heart means uncorrupted faith. This is why the whole Church is called a virgin but is also called the people of God, which is a masculine title.[25] The people of God is comprised of both sexes, and it is one people, a unique people. The Church is one Church,

---

23. By altering the punctuation we could translate, "It does not say that he has attached them, only that he has strengthened them."
24. See Mt 25:4.
25. *Populus* ("people") being masculine.

a unique dove,[26] and within this virginity thousands of saints are included. Five virgins therefore aptly symbolize all the souls that will enter the kingdom of God, but it is significant that five are mentioned, because the body has five senses, well known to all of us. Through these five gates anything perceived by the body gains entrance to the soul. Anything you covet inordinately makes its way in either through your eyes or through your ears or through your sense of smell or through your taste or through your sense of touch. A person who has not granted admittance to corruptive influences through any of these five gates is reckoned among the five virgins. But corruptive influences do get in through unlawful desire. The books of scripture are full of teaching about what is lawful and what unlawful.

It is essential, therefore, that you should be among these five virgins. You must not be alarmed by what I said just now, "No one shall enter." That is the rule indeed, and it will be enforced, but only after you have entered. No one will shut you out, but, once you have stepped inside, the gates of Jerusalem will be closed and the bars made firm. If you have not resolved to be a virgin at heart, or if, though a virgin, you are one of the foolish set, you will be left outside, and you will hammer on the door in vain.

Make sure you have the oil of a good conscience in God's sight

11. Who are the foolish virgins? They too are five in number, so whom can they represent but souls that achieve chastity of body, resisting the corruptive influences which seek admission through the five senses I have enumerated? They seem to avoid the corruption that assails them from all sides, but they do not stand in God's presence in the truth of their consciences, holding their good lives before him. Instead they try to seem good in the eyes of men and women, conforming to the judgment of others. They chase after the favors of the crowd; they want to be highly valued by all who observe them, because they hold themselves cheap. The testimony of their own consciences is not enough for them. It is aptly said that such people do not bring oil with them, for on account of its power to burn and shine brightly oil represents a glowing reputation. But what do the apostle's words suggest about this? Think back for a moment to the wise virgins who brought oil with them. *Let each of us examine our own work, and then it is only within ourselves that we will have*

---

26. See Sg 6:8.

credit, not in the eyes of others (Gal 6:4), says Paul. Such were the wise virgins. The foolish, however, do indeed light their lamps, and so their deeds seem to shine. But their flames will gutter and go out, because they are not fed with oil from within.

All of them fall asleep when the bridegroom's return is delayed, because this is the fate of both classes of human beings. All, both foolish and wise, sleep in death when the Lord is slow in coming; they sink into the bodily, visible death which scripture calls sleep, as all Christians are aware. When speaking of sick persons, for example, the apostle said, *This is why many among you are infirm or sick, and quite a few have fallen asleep* (1 Cor 11:30). When he says they fall asleep, he means that they die. When the moment comes, and the bridegroom is almost here, they will arise, but not all of them will gain entry with him. The good conduct of the foolish virgins will have petered out, for oil in their consciences will be lacking, and they will not find anyone to sell them what they used to obtain from their flatterers. The taunt, *Go and buy some for yourselves,* is uttered not in hatred but in mockery, because the foolish had tried to beg from the wise: *Give us some oil, for our torches are going out* (Mt 25:8). How did the wise respond? *There may not be enough for both us and you. Better that you go to the sellers, and buy some for yourselves.* (Mt 25:9) This amounted to a warning: "What use are they to you now, those people from whom you are accustomed to purchase adulation?"

But then, says scripture, *while they were on their way there, the others entered, and the door was shut* (Mt 25:10). Their hearts have turned aside as they go searching and are preoccupied about it. While they are distracted, looking back and recalling the good opinion of others that they used to enjoy, they are going to find the people who sold them oil. But they do not find those who once held them in high esteem; they cannot find those who used to praise them; nowhere to be found now are the flatterers to whom they were accustomed to look for praise. They used to depend on such praise as an incentive to good deeds, but it fails them now. Never have they been strengthened by a good conscience; all that motivated them was the sycophantic talk of others.

Merciful generosity toward the needy will secure a merciful judgment on ourselves, in spite of our shortcomings

12. The saying, *There may not be enough for us*, proceeds from deep, enlightened humility, for the oil we carry in our conscience is the judgment we make on ourselves, the assessment we make of what kind of people we are. And it is difficult for anyone to judge perfectly in his own case. However much progress a person makes, my brothers and sisters, however strenuously he reaches out to what lies ahead, forgetting what lies behind,[27] if he says to himself, "Now I'm all right," immediately there issues from the secret counsels of God the standard which judges us with absolute clarity. And then, who dare boast of having a chaste heart? But what does scripture say? *Merciless judgment will be passed on anyone who has not shown mercy* (Jas 2:13). Advance as far as you may, you will still have to hope for God's mercy; for, if judgment is pronounced without mercy, it will find matter for condemnation in everyone.

But is there any other passage in scripture to comfort us? Yes, for scripture exhorts us to engage in works of mercy and to grow increasingly generous in giving away whatever we have to spare. If we hold onto only what we need, we shall find that there are many superfluous things in our possession; although, if we seek worthless trifles, we shall never have enough. My brothers and sisters, seek what is necessary for God's work, not what gratifies your own greed. Your greed is not the work of God. Your whole being, your body, your soul—all this is God's work. Seek only what you need, and you will see how few things that is. Two little coins were all a widow needed to do a deed of mercy;[28] two small coins to buy the kingdom of God! Yet how much does the one who puts on the games need in order to clothe those who time and again are to fight the beasts?

Take stock then: not only can you manage on a few things only, but God himself asks very few from you. Ask yourself how much he has given you and then pick out what you need; all the rest of your things lie there as superfluities, but for other people they are necessities. The superfluity of the rich is necessary to the poor. If you hold onto superfluous items, then, you are keeping what belongs to someone else.

---

27. See Phil 3:13.
28. See Mk 12:42.

13. There is therefore a way for you to face the prospect of judgment without apprehension. If you deal mercifully in the ways we have mentioned, if you especially practice the kind of giving that costs you nothing: *Forgive us as we forgive* (Mt 6:12)—for by doing that you are giving away nothing but charity, and charity increases as you give it—you need not be anxious about the judgment to come. If you are fervent and assiduous in these merciful good works, works which, as we have pointed out already, will not be necessary in the next world because there will be no wretched person there to need your compassionate aid, you can face the judgment without terror, secure not so much in any justice of your own as in the mercy of God, because you yourself have shown mercy to others. *Merciless judgment will be passed on anyone who has not shown mercy, but mercy reigns supreme over judgment* (Jas 2:13), says scripture. You must not think, brothers and sisters, that God is not just when he denies us mercy,[29] or that he is departing from his own rule of justice. He is just when he condemns, and he is just when he treats us with mercy. What is more just than to show mercy to one who has shown mercy first? What is more just than that you should receive in the measure that you yourself have measured out to others?[30] Give to your needy brother. Who is this brother? Christ. If, then, you are giving to Christ in giving to your own brother or sister and giving to God because you give to Christ, it means that God—who is blessed above all things for ever[31]—has willed to be in need of your gift. And are you going to withdraw your hand? You are certainly ready to stretch it out when you ask God for a favor, so remember that scripture bids you, *Let not your hand be outstretched to receive, but tucked away when it is time to give* (Sir 4:36). God wants you to give to him out of what he has given to you. What do you ever give that he did not give you first? *What have you that you did not receive?* (1 Cor 4:7) And not only when you give to God, but even when you give to someone else, do you give anything that is truly your own? You are only giving something that belongs to God, who commands you to give. Be the person who hands out goods before you are asked, not the one who usurps them.

---

29. Variant: "when he shows us mercy."
30. See Mt 7:2.
31. See Rom 9:5.

If you make this your custom, and if in genuine humility you say about your oil, *There may not be enough for us*, you enter the city, and the gate is shut behind you. Listen to the apostle making this same point: *It matters very little to me that I am judged by you* (1 Cor 4:3). When will you ever be in a position to judge my conscience? When can you discern my motive in acting, whatever I do? How far can human beings judge each other? A person can judge better concerning himself, but God judges us even better than we can judge in our own case.

Well then, if you conduct yourself in the way I have outlined, you will gain entry. You will be among the five virgins who enter while the others, the foolish ones, are shut out. The gospel tells us this: the door will be closed and those others will stand outside crying, *Open the door to us!* (Mt 25:11) But it will not be opened, *because he has strengthened the bars of your gates*. You must stand there without fear, praise him without fear, praise him without end. Your gates are strongly shut: no friend of yours goes out and no enemy comes in. *He has strengthened the bars of your gates.*

14. *He has blessed your children within you.* They do not wander abroad or go into exile; they rejoice within the city and praise God within it and are blessed[32] within it. In that city no one is in travail, for no longer do they give birth. They are God's children, they are saints, these holy sons and daughters who are now praising him and giving him glory. The mother who was in labor with them and brought them forth was charity, and charity gathered them and brought them into the secure city. Listen to an example of charity in travail with her children. The apostle Paul was imbued with it and bore within him not a fatherly heart only, but a motherly heart too, toward his children. *My little children*, he says, *I am in travail with you over again* (Gal 4:19). When Paul was in travail with them, charity was in travail, for *the charity of God has been poured out into our hearts through the Holy Spirit who has been given us* (Rom 5:5). May charity gather in those for whom it has labored and whom it has brought to birth. Even now they are inwardly God's children and they are free from anxiety. They have flown away from the nest of fear and taken wing toward heavenly realms; they have taken flight to eternal things and no longer dread anything temporal.

---

32. Variant: "they bless [God]."

Verse 14. Love for the peace of Jerusalem

15. *He has blessed your children within you.* Who has blessed them? *He who has established peace on your frontiers.* You all leapt for joy when I said that! Love this peace, my brothers and sisters. We are absolutely delighted when love of peace shouts from your hearts, so how delighted you must be yourselves! I had not yet said anything about it, I had not explained; all I did was read out the verse, and you shouted your joy. What was it that cried out in you? Love of peace. But who displayed peace before your eyes? Why did you shout? Why else if not because you love it? But how do you love something you can't see? Peace is invisible. What kind of eye equips you so to see it that you love it? If you did not love it, you would not acclaim it so joyfully as soon as it is mentioned. Such are the displays of invisible realities which God puts on for us.[33] How intensely beautiful must that peace be, if your understanding of it has pierced you to the heart! What am I to say now about peace and in praise of peace? Your delight in it has run ahead of any words of mine; I cannot fulfil your expectations, I am unequal to the task, I am too weak.

Let us all agree, then, to postpone our praise of peace until we reach the native country of peace, where we shall praise it more fully because we shall possess it fully. If we are so much in love with it when it is only initiated in us, how shall we praise it when it is brought to perfection? What I am saying is this, O beloved sons and daughters, children of the kingdom, citizens of Jerusalem: in Jerusalem we shall find the vision of peace. All those who love peace are blessed in that city; they enter it and then the gates are closed, the bars fixed firm. Pursue this peace, long for this peace of which even the name so swiftly arouses your love and wins your hearts. Love peace in your homes, love it in your business; love peace with your wives, your children, your slaves. Love peace with your friends, and love peace with your enemies.[34]

---

33. See note on shows at section 2 above.
34. This lyrical passage on peace introduces an ample, carefully constructed anti-Donatist polemic in sections 16–18.

The law (Genesis), the prophets (Psalm 21), and the gospel foretell the universality of the Church

16. This is the peace which the heretics lack. What is the work of peace amid the uncertainties of the land where we still live in our mortal, pilgrim condition, where no one is clearly known by anyone else, and no one sees another's heart? What is the work of peace? It passes no judgment on uncertain matters, it does not assert what it does not know. It is more inclined to think the best of any man or woman than to suspect the worst. It is not very grieved over its mistake if it gives even a bad person the benefit of the doubt. What really hurts is a chance misapprehension that leads it to hold a bad opinion of someone who is good. "I don't really know what he is like," it will say, "so what have I to lose if I think he is good?" If the matter is unclear you must be careful, for someone's bad reputation may be deserved, but you must not condemn him as though it were deserved. This is what peace commands. *Seek peace and pursue it* (Ps 33:15(34:14)), says another psalm.

But what advice does heresy offer?[35] It condemns people it does not know; indeed, it condemns the whole world. "The entire world has perished," it alleges. "Africa alone stands firm; there are no Christians anywhere else." What a fine judgment that is! From what tribunal do you presume to give your verdict on the whole earth? In what forum did the world stand before you? I don't want anyone to take my word for it, but neither do I want anyone to rely on yours. Let Christ be believed, let the Spirit of God be believed, let the law of Moses be believed.[36] What did Moses say about the future, about our own era? To Abraham it was foretold, *In your seed shall all the nations of the*

---

35. The Donatists are clearly his target.
36. Augustine here announces the three headings of his argument: the law (i.e. the Pentateuch), the prophets (by which, as often, he understands the psalms), and the gospel. He will deal with these three points in this section and the following. The three epochs provide him with a bridge to the consideration of the dialogue between Abraham and Dives (Lk 16:29–31). This pattern of ideas is paralleled in *A Letter to Catholics on the Donatist Sect* and other works dated to 400–406. In addition there is a parallel between the present section of the Exposition of Psalm 147 and Dolbeau Sermon 21,16–17 in the use of Ps 21:28–29, joined with Gn 22:18, and the association of these with the idea of Christ on the cross buying the whole world with his blood. This Dolbeau sermon is dated to the winter of 403–404. These indications suggest that the Exposition of Psalm 147 may belong to December 403.

earth be blessed (Gn 22:18). Have you any doubt as to who is the seed of Abraham? I do not think you will go on doubting if the apostle tells you, but if you disbelieve even the apostle, how can you say, *Peace, peace, when there is no peace* (Jer 6:14)? Well then, what does the apostle have to say? *To Abraham were the promises made, and to his seed. Scripture does not say, To his descendants, as though indicating many, but as to one only: And to your seed, which is Christ.* (Gal 3:16) Think about it: that promise was made thousands of years ago to Abraham: *In your seed shall all the nations of the earth be blessed.* A prophecy uttered thousands of years ago and believed by one man we see fulfilled today. In peace we read of it, in peace we behold it, yet you come at us head-on and contradict us. What have you to say? "Don't believe that." Don't believe whom? The Spirit of God? Don't believe God, speaking to Abraham? Whom, then, am I to believe? You? "That is not what I am saying," you will reply. Not what you are saying? Isn't it? Are you not saying in effect, "Believe me rather than God's Spirit, rather than God addressing Abraham"? What else are you telling me? "So-and-so handed over the sacred books, and another did the same."[37] But is this a charge you level against the gospel or the apostle or the prophets? Examine all the scriptures and read me out a proof of your allegation from these writings in which I believe, for I do not believe you. Where will you find any such passage to read to me? "That is what my father told me, and my grandfather and my brother and my bishop. They all told me about it," you retort. So they told you, did they? But it was God who told Abraham, *In your seed shall all the nations of the earth be blessed.* One man hears that and believes it, and it comes true centuries later. If the promise is believed when it is given, is it to be doubted now that it has been fulfilled?

So then, Moses testified to the promise; let the prophets add their testimony. Look at what they said of the business deal by which we were purchased. Christ hangs on the cross. Consider the price he is paying, and then you will see what he is buying. He obviously intends to buy something, though you do not yet know what it is. Look, look hard at the cost, and you will identify his purchase. He poured out his blood. With his blood he bought it, with the blood of the stainless lamb he bought it, with the blood of God's only Son he bought it. What was purchased with the blood of the only Son of God? But wait, look

---

37. A reference to the original dispute which provoked the Donatist schism. See the note at Exposition of Psalm 10,1.

further at the cost. Long before the Lord's passion a prophet said, *They dug holes in my hands and my feet, and numbered all my bones* (Ps 21:17–18(22:16–17)). This is a huge payment that I see, O Christ; now let us see what you bought with it. *All the ends of the earth will be reminded and will turn to the Lord* (Ps 21:28(22:27)). In one and the same psalm I find the purchaser, the price, and the possession. The purchaser is Christ, the price is his blood, and his possession is the whole round earth. Let us listen to the prophetic voices, refuting the argumentative heretics. See, this is my Lord's property. I read his entitlement in the same psalm: *All the ends of the earth will be reminded and will turn to the Lord, and all the families of the nations will worship in his presence.* Listen to him disputing with his opponents and defending his right to it: *The kingship is the Lord's, and he will hold sway over the nations.* (Ps 21:29(22:28)) The purchaser was Christ himself, not the apostate Donatus. *All the families of the earth will worship in his presence,* it says. They will worship, and with good reason. Why do I say "with good reason"? *Because the kingship is the Lord's, and he will hold sway over the nations.*

Moses has taught us this, the prophets have testified to the same truth, and so have thousands of other texts. Can anyone count the testimonies to the worldwide spread of the Church? Who shall count them? The heresies that attack the Church are far outnumbered by the testimonies borne to the Church in the law.[38] What page of scripture does not proclaim it? What verse is silent about it? They all shout in support of the unity given us by the Lord, for he has established peace on Jerusalem's frontiers. And you yap against these, you heretic! It is rightly said of this city, as the Book of Revelation records, *Outside are dogs* (Rv 22:15). You yap against all this evidence. As I began to ask you earlier, what right have you to judge the whole earth? Over what tribunal do you preside? Obviously your only title is the presumption in your own heart. That is a lofty judgment-seat but a very shaky one. Moses taught the truth, the prophets taught it, yet people who wish to be regarded as Christians do not believe it!

---

38. That is, scripture as a whole.

The rich man's request—but someone has risen from the dead to tell us

17. A certain rich man was suffering torments in the underworld.[39] Roasting in the flames, he longed for a drop of water from a poor man who used to lie despised at his gate.[40] It was not granted to him because *merciless judgment will be passed on anyone who has not shown mercy* (Jas 2:13). Being denied it, he besought Abraham, *Father Abraham, send Lazarus. I have five brothers; let him tell them what I am suffering, so that they may not come to this place of torment too.* (Lk 16:24.28) And how did Abraham reply? *They have Moses and the prophets there.* But he protested, *No, Father Abraham, but if someone rises from the dead, they will believe.* Abraham refused. *If they do not listen to Moses and the prophets, neither will they believe even if someone rises from the dead.* (Lk 16:29–31)

Now of whom did he say, *They have Moses and the prophets there*? Obviously of people who were still alive and had ample time for amending their lives, people who had not yet come to the places of torment. *They have Moses and the prophets there*, he said, *let them listen to them.* No, they do not believe these, *but if someone rises from the dead, they will believe.* But Abraham will not have it: *If they do not listen to Moses and the prophets, neither will they believe even if someone rises from the dead.* This is Abraham's view of the matter. Abraham's verdict, but where and whence did he give it? From a lofty place, a place of perfect peace and happiness, a place the man tortured in flames could see if he raised his eyes. In Abraham's embrace—in his innermost counsels, that is—he also saw the poor man in transports of happiness. From that place was the decision announced. What an august tribunal it was! There dwelt God himself, for God dwells in his saints; this is why the apostle admits his longing: *I long to die and to be with Christ, for that is much the best* (Phil 1:23). And the robber was promised, *Today you will be with me in paradise* (Lk 23:43). Thus it was the Lord himself, dwelling with Abraham and in Abraham, who delivered the decision: *They have Moses and the prophets there; if they do not listen to them, then even if someone rises from the dead, they will not believe him.*

---

39. The witness of Moses (in Genesis) and that of "the prophets" (in Psalm 21(22)) give Augustine a convenient transition to the gospel parable where this same witness is an important theme.
40. 40. See Lk 16:19–31.

O you heretics, you have Moses and the prophets here with you. You are still alive, you can still listen to them, you still have the chance to correct yourselves and restrain your animosity. The opportunity is still open to you to embrace the truth. Discuss among yourselves whether Moses is worth a hearing, and the prophets too, men who provided such weighty testimonies to their faith; decide now, when we see human history unfolding as they predicted. Why do you still hesitate to believe Moses and the prophets? Why are you so unready to listen? Are you perhaps looking for someone to rise from the dead, to find out whether he, at least, might tell you something about his Church? The rich man in the underworld sought precisely that; he asked for someone to be sent from the dead to his brothers. But he was rebuked for asking, because Moses and the prophets ought to have been enough to convince his brothers. He begged in vain so that you might be warned by his example, lest making the same request too late and to no purpose you might be similarly tormented. You must listen to Moses and the prophets. What did Moses say? *In your seed shall all the nations of the earth be blessed* (Gn 22:18). And what did the prophets say? *All the ends of the earth will be reminded and will turn to the Lord* (Ps 21:28(22:27)).

Will you[41] still object to me, "Let someone rise from the dead. I will not believe unless someone comes from there to persuade me"? O Lord, thanks be to you for your mercy! You willed to die so that someone might indeed rise from the underworld. And that someone was no ordinary mortal. Truth himself rose from the underworld. Even if he had never been there himself he would have told us the truth about it, but to silence the objections of ignorant and wicked people he himself died, and he himself rose from the world below. What have you to say now, you heretic? What did you say? Speak up, I can't hear you! All your excuses are demolished. Even if you choose to make your own the words of that rich man in hell, the fact remains that Christ has risen from the dead. Will you deign to believe him? Surely you must. Even if, still alive as you are, you want to take the same line that the rich man took after his death, the fact remains that Christ has risen from the world below. It is not your father who has arisen, nor your grandfather, nor those who branded other people with infamy on the charge of surrendering holy books. All right, the

---

41. Augustine reverts to the singular here, after the plural address to "you heretics" in the preceding paragraph.

infamy was deserved. Your people told the truth; I grant you that much. But do you think I care? Let us listen together to the one who has risen from the dead.

Need I prolong this argument? Let us listen, let the gospel be opened, let the happenings of the past be read as though they were happening now, let past events be put before our eyes so that we may be warned about the future. See, then: Christ, on rising from the dead, shows himself to his disciples. This is his wedding: he is the bridegroom and the Church is his bride. The bridegroom was considered dead, destroyed, done away with; but see, he has risen again, whole and perfect. Look and see: he makes himself visible to the eyes of his disciples; see, he is presented to their hands to be felt; behold, they touch as scars what were hopeless wounds. He has shown himself to their eyes to be seen and to their hands to be handled, but they think he is a ghost, so despairing have they become of their salvation. He encourages them and strengthens them in faith: *Handle me and see: a ghost does not have flesh and bones, as you see I have* (Lk 24:39). They touch him, they rejoice, yet they are confused and frightened. *And as they were still confused for joy:* that is how scripture puts it. It is difficult to believe in very joyful events, even if they are quite certain. If someone has been slow to believe, the doubt he felt adds piquancy and intensity to the pleasure he feels[42] on embracing the truth. We inevitably rejoice all the more when something arrives after we had despaired of its coming.

To season and increase the disciples' joy, Christ willed to be unrecognized at first. He controlled the eyes of two of them, the two whom he found talking together on the road. They told him, *We had been hoping that he was the one to redeem Israel* (Lk 24:21), but they had given up hope by now. They had thought this of him, but they thought so no longer. Although Christ was there with them, hope was not. But when he gave himself to them once more, he brought hope back too. Later, after they had recognized him in the breaking of bread, and after he had offered himself to the rest of the disciples, the ones who thought him a ghost, he said to them, *Handle me and see: a ghost does not have flesh and bones, as you see I have. And as they were still confused for joy, he asked them, Have you anything here to eat?* (Lk 24:39.41) He took it, blessed it, ate some and gave some to them. The reality of his body was demonstrated and all

---

42. Variant: "to his determination."

suspicion of falsehood dispelled. And what did he say next? *Did you not know that all that is written about me in the law of Moses, and the prophets, and the psalms, had to be fulfilled?* (Lk 24:44) They did believe Moses and the prophets. Abraham's judgment had been right when he said, *If they do not listen to Moses and the prophets, neither will they believe even if someone rises from the dead* (Lk 16:31). But because these disciples did believe Moses and the prophets, and there were none among them upon whom Abraham's rebuke could fall, they heard the Lord's words, *Did you not know that all that is written about me in the law of Moses, and the prophets, and the psalms, had to be fulfilled?* They believed Moses and the prophets; and see how, on the basis of their testimony, these men now believe him who has risen from the dead: *Then he opened their minds to understand the scriptures, and he said to them, Thus it was written, and thus it was necessary for Christ to suffer, and to rise from the dead on the third day.* (Lk 24:45-46)

The risen one not only revealed himself as the bridegroom; he also pointed to his bride, the universal Church

18. So there you have the Church's bridegroom. Moses was not silent about him and neither were the prophets; they foretold that Christ would rise from the dead on the third day, that he would suffer and rise again. We were given a picture of the bridegroom, to save us from going astray. But there are some people, people who appear to hold the same faith about the bridegroom as we do, who, on seeing that we do not stray from him, try to draw us away from the bridegroom's members. They say to us, "Yes, he in whom you believe is indeed the bridegroom; we too believe in him. But the bride is not the Church to which you belong." So who is? "The Donatist party." So you say, but does the bridegroom back you up? You tell us this, but is this what God tells us through Moses? It is because of the witness borne by Moses that I hold fast to the Church, for through Moses we have God's promise, *In your seed shall all the nations of the earth be blessed* (Gn 22:18). You tell us that the Donatist party is the bride, but is that what the Spirit of God tells us through the prophets? The Church to which I hold is guaranteed by the prophets, for through a prophet it was foretold that *all the ends of the earth will be reminded and will turn to the Lord* (Ps 21:28(22:27)).

You see, then, that I hold to the witness of the law and the witness of the prophets. Now let us listen also to him who rose from the dead. He showed himself to be the bridegroom, and we hold fast to him. He confirmed it by demonstrations, he provided proofs. Just as Moses had foretold, just as the prophets had foretold, *it was necessary for Christ to suffer, and to rise from the dead on the third day* (Lk 24:46). So far, then, we both hold fast to the bridegroom on the basis of his words, and I think you are even beginning to agree with me in believing in the words of Moses and the prophets. So let us believe also in what he said, he who rose from the dead.

Take the next step. The prayer of a believer must be, "O Lord, I already see that Christ is the bridegroom. That much is done. But let no one entice me away from the members of your bride. Do not be the head for me, unless I am among your members. Tell me something about the Church, for I am no longer in any doubt about her bridegroom." Listen, then, to what he says about the Church. He continues, *And for repentance and forgiveness of sins to be preached in his name* (Lk 24:47). Nothing can be truer than that: *For repentance and forgiveness of sins to be preached in his name.* But where? Some say, *Here, look!* or *Look, there!* But what does Christ say? *Do not believe them. False Christs and false prophets will arise and say, Here he is! There he is!* (Mt 24:23–24) They do not say now about the head himself, *Here he is! There he is!* for everyone knows that Christ is in heaven. They say it about the Church where Christ is, the Church to which he promised, *Lo, I am with you throughout all days, even to the end of the ages* (Mt 28:20). But the Lord insists, "Do not believe them. Anyone who says, *Here, look!* or *Look, there!* is pointing to parts. I purchased[43] the whole." Let the gospel tell me this. But, Lord, tell me the same yourself from the gospel, because you are now risen from the dead, so that those who believe Moses and the prophets may believe you as well. Tell me this yourself. I am listening. *It was necessary for Christ to suffer, and to rise from the dead on the third day, and for repentance and forgiveness of sins to be preached in his name throughout all nations, beginning from Jerusalem* (Lk 24:46–47).

So now where do we stand, heretic? When I was reading from Moses, and when I was reading from the prophets, you wanted to put off a decision until you heard from one who was to rise from the dead. Very well: he has risen and he has spoken. There is no more room for doubt now about the Church of Christ and the wife of Christ than

---

43. In the sense of "redeemed."

there is about the body of Christ, displayed to the eyes of the disciples and felt by their hands. He who rose from the dead manifested both: he showed the head and he showed the members; he pointed to the bridegroom and he pointed to the bride. Either join me in believing in both, or believe in one only to your own condemnation. What use is it to believe that he rose from the dead, that he rose again in the same body? You believe that he displayed his scars and that, as he had been crucified and buried, so he returned to them alive and proved that it was truly he. Fine: you do well to believe this. But he in whom you believe is speaking, so you had better listen: *For repentance and forgiveness of sins to be preached in his name.* Where? Throughout the whole wide world. If I wanted to make this point, I who am wrestling with heretics, I who am in the thick of the fight with them and am even now in dispute with them about this vital question, I could not put it as effectively against heretics in the present as he put it against those who would arise in the future. What more do you ask? Forgiveness of sins is being preached in Christ's name. Where? *Throughout all nations.* Whence? *Beginning from Jerusalem.* You need to be in communion with this Church. Why should we quarrel? This Church began from the earthly Jerusalem, so that it might come to rejoice in God in the heavenly Jerusalem. It begins from the earthly city and ends in the heavenly city. In the heavenly Jerusalem will be the whole Church that drew the beginning of its faith from the earthly Jerusalem.

Another argument: the Church of the Holy Spirit speaks in all languages

19. If you think I am lying, read the Acts of the Apostles. There you find that the disciples were gathered together when the Holy Spirit came, and this shows you what the Lord meant when he said that their preaching was to begin from Jerusalem. You will also read that those on whom the Holy Spirit came spoke in the languages of all peoples.[44] Why are you unwilling to speak in the languages of all? Every tongue resounded there. How is it that today a person to whom the Holy Spirit has been given does not speak in the tongues of all? At that date it was a sign that the Holy Spirit had come upon people when they spoke in all languages. What are you going to say now, you heretic? That the Holy Spirit is not given? "I am not saying

---

44. See Acts 2:1–11.

that." Where, then? Is the Spirit given or not?[45] If he is not given, what are you doing when you preach and baptize and bless? What are you about? Your celebrations are pointless and empty.

So the Spirit must be given. But if he is given, why do those to whom he is given not speak in the tongues of all peoples? Has God's gift lost its strength or become less fruitful? The weeds have grown up, to be sure, but so has the wheat. *Let them both grow together until harvest time* (Mt 13:30).[46] The Lord did not say, "Let the weeds grow, but the wheat must shrink." No, both have grown. Why then does the Holy Spirit not manifest himself today in the multiplicity of languages?

But he does; he is manifest today in all tongues. At the beginning the Church was not yet spread throughout the entire world, making it possible for Christ's members to speak among all nations, and therefore the miracle happened in each person as a presage of what would later be true of all. Today the whole body of Christ does speak in the languages of all peoples, or, rather, if there are any tongues in which it does not yet speak, it will. The Church will grow until it claims all languages as its own. How much it has grown, Christ's body that you have abandoned! Hold on with us to the territories it has reached, so that you, together with us, may spread into those it has not reached yet. I dare to say to you, "I speak in the tongues of all men and women. I am in Christ's body, I am in Christ's Church. If Christ's body today speaks in the languages of all, I too speak in all languages. Greek is mine, Syriac is mine, Hebrew is mine. Mine is the tongue of every nation, because I am within the unity that embraces all nations."

---

45. Doubtful punctuation. It could also be translated, "That the Holy Spirit is not given? I am not asking where; I am just asking, Is the Spirit given or not?"
46. Although Augustine does not dwell on it here, this question of the wheat and the weeds was a sore point in his controversy with the Donatists. He is intent in the present context on demonstrating the geographical universality of Christ's Church as opposed to the narrowness and parochialism of the Donatists, but in the background is his conception of the Church as the field where Christ wills wheat and weeds to grow together until the final sorting, as opposed to the Donatists' conception of the Church as a society of the pure.

Hunger for perfect peace

20. We know then, brothers and sisters, that the Church set out from Jerusalem and spread through all nations. The testimony of the law, the prophets, and finally the Lord himself makes this quite clear. The voices of the apostles resound everywhere, rendering their witness to what we hope to attain within the unity of the body of Christ. Rejoice in the plentiful crop, tolerate the weeds, groan during the threshing process, and sigh with longing for the barn. The time will come when, after the gates of Jerusalem have been securely barred, we shall simply rejoice. Let everyone enter who is destined to enter. Any man or woman who will enter that city in all honesty does not enter the Church here on false pretences; for anyone who does enter here with us under false pretences is really still outside. He or she is outside and does not know it, but the winnowing will reveal the truth, and so will the barring of the gates. Anyone who is now truly within, with no pretence, will be firmly within the heavenly city, and anyone who is within now, enduring the company of sinners, will be within that city in perfect joy.

How can we know this? Because the frontiers of Jerusalem are peace. So says the psalm: *He has established peace on your frontiers.* We yearn for peace now, but we have it here only in hope, for what kind of peace is there for us, even within ourselves? *The flesh lusts against the spirit, and the spirit against the flesh* (Gal 5:17). Where does perfect peace reign, even within one individual? When it is full and perfect in one man or woman, then it will be fully realized in all the citizens of Jerusalem. But when will this perfect state of peace come about? Only when our corruptibility has put on incorruptibility and our mortality has been clothed in immortality[47] will there be complete peace, unshakable peace. Nothing within any human being will contend with the soul, nor will the soul be at war with itself by reason of being wounded in any of its faculties. Nothing will oppose or hinder it: no bodily need, no hunger or thirst or cold or heat or weariness or any kind of poverty or any provocation to quarreling, and certainly no need for constant, careful watchfulness both to avoid an enemy and to love him. All these things strive against us now, my brothers and sisters; we do not yet enjoy full and perfect peace. When I mentioned peace earlier in this sermon you shouted in response, but it was a shout of desire. Your shouting sprang from thirst, not from

---

47. See 1 Cor 15:53.

satiety, because only where there is perfect righteousness will there be perfect peace. All we can do now is hunger and thirst for righteousness. *Blessed are those who hunger and thirst for righteousness, for they shall be satisfied* (Mt 5:6). How, when, will they be satisfied? When we attain to peace. This is why the psalm, after saying, *He has established peace on your frontiers,* promptly adds, *He satisfies you with the choicest wheat*; for there we shall find total satisfaction, and no one will lack anything.

21. This peace of which we are speaking is not in all of us, brothers and sisters; or perhaps I should say that it is not whole in any one of us. It may well be that to go on listening while it is talked about is a spiritual delight for you, but, if no bodily problems get in our way, we must try to finish the psalm. I never see you looking tired, and yet, as God knows, I do worry that I may be burdening you or be demanding too much of at least some of our brothers and sisters. On the other hand I see the eagerness of many of you who demand of me this toil and sweat, and I hope in the Lord that it will not be without fruit. What makes me very joyful is this: you take such intense pleasure in the truth of God's word that your good zeal, your delight in the good, and your keen concern for what is good, far outstrip the zeal of those crazy folk who frequent the amphitheater. They would never stay on their feet as long as you do and still watch the shows, would they?

So then, brothers and sisters, let us listen to the rest of the psalm, since this is what you want. May the Lord be with us, and may he support our strength and our minds. *He has established peace on your frontiers*, the psalm says to Jerusalem, *he satisfies you with the choicest wheat*. Hunger and thirst for righteousness pass away and satisfaction takes their place. What will that choicest wheat be which awaits us there? What else but the bread which came down to us from heaven?[48] If he fed us like this during our pilgrimage, how will he satisfy us in our homeland?

Verse 15. The swiftness of the Word

22. The psalmist is going to speak now about this pilgrimage of ours, the journey that will bring us to Jerusalem. There we shall sing united praise to the Lord and extol the Lord our God, for there we shall be Jerusalem, we shall be Zion, when the bars of our gates are made firm. But while we are still on the journey, what does he do

---

48. See Jn 6:41.

for us, he who will then satisfy us totally with the choicest wheat? This is what he does, as the psalm goes on to say: *He sends forth his word to the earth.* Think of our earthly condition, and how worn out, faint, slow, and cold we are. When would we ever aspire to that choice wheat, that totally satisfying wheat, if God had not sent his word to this earth that weighs us down, to the earth that hinders us from returning to him? But he sent his word, for even in the desert he did not forsake his people but rained down manna from heaven. *He sends forth his word to the earth,* and at last his Word came to the earth. How did he come? What is his Word?

Very swiftly runs his Word, with the speed of speed itself. The psalm did not content itself with saying, "His Word is very swift." It says, *Very swiftly runs his Word, with the speed of speed itself.*[49] Let us try to take this in, brothers and sisters, for the psalmist could not have chosen a better expression. A hot body grows hot by means of heat, a cold object grows cold through cold, a swift mover is swift because of its swiftness. What is hotter than heat itself, whereby anything that heats up grows hot? What is colder than cold itself, by which anything that cools down grows cold? So then, what is speedier than speed itself, whereby anything that runs speedily increases its speed?[50] Many things can be called speedy, some more so, some less; any object is speedy to the degree that it participates in speed. This or that object participates more fully in speed, and it therefore moves faster; another participates to a lesser degree in speed, and therefore it is slower. What, then, can be speedier than speed itself? How fast does God's Word run? *With the speed of speed itself.* You may go on asserting the swiftness of the Word as much as you like; you may say, "The Word is swifter than this fast mover or that, swifter than a bird's flight, than the winds, than the angels." But however wonderful the speed of any of these, does it reach the speed of speed itself?

What is speed itself, brothers and sisters? It is present everywhere, not divided or distributed in parts. But this is true of the Word of God, for the Word is present not here or there in a partial way but everywhere through himself, because from eternity, before his incarnation, he is the power of God and the wisdom of God.[51] If

---

49. *Usque in velocitatem.*
50. Augustine is thinking in Platonic terms.
51. See 1 Cor 1:24.

we are thinking of him as God, in the form of God,[52] as the Word equal to the Father, he is identified with the wisdom of God, of whom scripture says, *Wisdom reaches strongly from end to end* (Wis 8:1). What speed that evokes! *Wisdom reaches strongly from end to end.* But perhaps wisdom reaches so far only by being immobile? If it were by immobility, in the way that a mass of rock fills a place, wisdom could be said to reach from end to end of that area, but only by inertia. But what are we saying? Is God's Word static, his wisdom dully motionless? If that were so, what would become of the texts that describe the spirit of wisdom? Although many things are said of her, this is plain: she is *acute, mobile, clear, undefiled* (Wis 7:22). We know for certain, then, that God's wisdom is mobile. If she is mobile, does it mean that wisdom touches one thing but not another? That she touches one thing and abandons something else? If that were so, what of her swiftness? Her very speed causes her to be everywhere all the time and be held prisoner nowhere.

But we cannot grasp this; we are too sluggish. Could anyone think it through clearly? Truly, my brothers and sisters, I have stated it as my ability allowed (if I had any ability at all, that is, if I have really understood it), and you have understood as far as your ability permitted. But what does the apostle say? *He has power to do all things far more abundantly than we ask or understand* (Eph 3:20). What is scripture indicating here? That, every time we think we have understood, we have not understood the reality as it is. Why not? Because *the corruptible body weighs down the soul* (Wis 9:15).

Thus it happens that we on earth are cold. Speed is burning hot. All burning objects move fast, and cold ones are slower. We are slow, and so we are cold. But wisdom runs with the very speed of speed itself. Wisdom burns with supreme intensity, and no one can hide from her heat.[53]

Verse 16. We are cold and unresponsive, but God calls us to repentance through his beneficial mist

23. What about us? We are slow because of the weight of the body, and therefore we are cold; we are weighed down by the fetters of this decaying, earthly life. Does this mean that we have no hope of comprehending the Word, who runs with the speed of speed itself?

---

52. See Phil 2:6.
53. See Ps 18:7(19:6).

Or that the Word has abandoned us? No, he has not, even though we are pressed down into the depths by our body. Did he not predestine us, even before we were born in this mortal, sluggish body? He who predestined us gave snow to the earth, and the snow represents ourselves.

Let us get on now with the rather obscure verses of the psalm. They are rolled up tightly, but let us hope that they will begin to unroll, because God's word finds you more and more eager the more we proclaim it to you. Listen now: we slow, sluggish creatures have, so to speak, frozen in this world. When snow falls it is because water has frozen higher up and then fallen down to our world. Similarly, when charity grew cold, human nature fell onto the earth and, being wrapped up in a slow, unresponsive body, it became like snow. But, even when immersed in snow, men and women were predestined to be children of God, for he *gives snow like wool*.

Why *like wool*? Although these creatures whom he has predestined are still cold and dull of spirit, the psalm hints that out of them God intends to make something. Wool is the raw material of a garment: when you see wool, you know you are seeing a garment in its early stages. God has predestined people who, for the time being, are coldly creeping on the earth and not yet afire with the spirit of charity, though they will be later, for he is telling us about predestination. He has put them here because he means to knit a garment out of them. It was significant that on the mountain Christ's vesture shone like snow.[54] Christ's garment gleamed, to signify that a tunic had already been made out of that wool, but the predestined, represented by the snow like wool that he sent down, were still coldly unresponsive. But wait awhile. Because the snow he sent is like wool, a garment is fashioned from it, for just as the Church is called the body of Christ, the Church is also called Christ's apparel. The apostle refers to this when he writes that Christ willed *to present the Church to himself as his bride, free from stain or wrinkle* (Eph 5:27). Let him do this, let him present to himself a glorious Church, *free from stain or wrinkle*; let him make for himself a garment out of the wool which he predestined while it was still snow. Even where people are still cold and unbelieving and inert, let him use them as wool to make his vesture. It needs to be cleansed of stains, but let it be cleansed by faith. It must have no wrinkle, so let it be stretched on the cross. *He gives snow like wool*.

---

54. See Mk 9:2.

24. If they have been predestined, they need to be called, for *those whom he predestined, he also called* (Rom 8:30). How are they called from the sickly condition of this body of ours, in order to be healed? How are they called? Listen to the Lord's answer in the gospel: *I did not come to call the righteous but sinners to repentance* (Lk 5:32). In consequence of the snow's predestination, a person begins to recognize his torpor and to acknowledge his sin; in response to the Lord's call he begins to come to repentance. We can therefore see why he who *gives snow like wool*, with his eye on the making of a garment in the future, also *spreads mist like ashes* in order to call us to repentance. *He spreads mist like ashes*, says the psalm. Who does this? None other than the Lord who *gives snow like wool*, for *those whom he predestined, he also called*. Ashes properly belong to repentance. Listen to how the Lord, rebuking certain cities, summoned them to repent: *Woe to you, Chorazin! Woe to you, Bethsaida! If the mighty works done in you had been done in Tyre and Sidon, they would long ago have done penance in sackcloth and ashes.* (Mt 11:21) This is why he *spreads mist like ashes.*

What does the psalm mean, though, by saying that *he spreads mist like ashes*? Why the mist? When someone is called to know God, and an instructor says to him, "Take this truth in," he begins to want to take in the truth, but he cannot do it, and he thinks that he is lost in some kind of fog of which he was not conscious before. This is the function of the mist: it helps you to know that you do not know, and to know what you ought to know; and at the same time it helps you to see that you lack the strength to know what ought to be known. If you have already begun to presume that you do know, you will hear the apostle's correction: *If anyone considers that he knows something, he does not yet know in the way he ought to know* (1 Cor 8:2). You have not yet understood, you are still struggling in the mist. But the Lord has not abandoned you, for he has lighted for you the lamp of his own flesh.

You will not get lost in the mist. Follow the Lord by faith. But when you try to see and find that you cannot, you are sorry for your sins, because the mist has been spread like ashes. Begin to be sorry that you have been so obstinately set against God; be sorry now that you followed your own evil ways. You are discovering for yourself how hard it is to reach the blessed vision of God, and this mist which he has spread like ashes will do you good. You are yourself a mist still, but a mist that is like ashes.

Still today penitents roll in ashes, my brothers and sisters, as though they were thereby testifying that they are kin to ashes. They say to their God, *I am ashes.* That is the confession made in a text of scripture: *I despise myself and waste away, I reckon myself earth and ashes* (Jb 30:19; compare 42:6). This is the humble avowal of a penitent. When Abraham talks to his God, wanting God to open to him the mystery of Sodom's destruction by fire, he says, *I am but dust and ashes* (Gn 18:27).

How persistent was such humility in great and holy men! God *spreads mist like ashes.* To what purpose? Because *those whom he predestined, he also called,* for he *did not come to call the righteous but sinners to repentance.*

Verse 17. The significance of ice

25. *He sends his ice like bread crumbs.* There is no need to spend time explaining over again what ice is. We have already spoken about it,[55] and I do not think it will have slipped your memories, beloved. But what is meant by saying, *He sends his ice like bread crumbs*? As the snow is his, because it symbolizes the predestined, and the mist we spoke of is his, because those who have been predestined to salvation are called to repentance, so too the ice in a sense belongs to him. What is ice? It is a substance that has frozen very hard and is tightly compacted; it can no longer be melted easily, as snow can. Snow which has hardened over many years or through the passage of centuries is called ice, and God sends it like bread crumbs. What does this mean?

There have been people who were so hard that they were compared to ice more aptly than to snow, yet even they were predestined and called, and some of them were even called to feed others and to be useful to people other than themselves. Need we enumerate them? We have probably known many like this. Any one of you who thinks about examples he or she has known will recall how intensely hard and obstinate they were and how they fought against the truth, but now they are preaching the truth and have become like bread crumbs. Who is the one loaf of bread? The apostle tells us: *We, though many, are one body in Christ* (Rom 12:5), and again, *Because there is but one bread, we, though many, are one body* (1 Cor 10:17). It follows, then, that if the whole body of Christ is one loaf, the individual members of

---

55. See section 2 above.

Christ are crumbs of bread. Christ makes certain hard people members of his body, and they become useful for feeding others. Why need we look through a list of examples? Let us consider one whom we know very well, the apostle Paul. Nothing is better known to us than this man, nothing sweeter, nothing in the scriptures more familiar. Even if there have been others converted from an obstinacy as hard as his to become bread,[56] still, let us all concentrate on this example that is set before us, so that the verse, *He sends his ice like bread crumbs*, may disclose its meaning. Think about Paul. He was hard, he fought against the truth, he shouted down the gospel, he seemed to be hardened against the sun. How hard he was, growing up according to the law, educated at the feet of a doctor of the law, Gamaliel![57] Did he not hear Moses and the prophets proclaiming Christ? What inveterate obduracy! It was quite different for the gentiles: they had never heard of Moses, so they were cold, but they were not ice, whereas a man like Paul, who believed in[58] the words that preached Christ, yet did not believe in Christ when he came, must have hardened exceedingly. Since he was icy, he looked white and glittering, but he was hard and frosty. In what sense was he gleaming white? He was *a Hebrew of Hebrew stock, and as to the law, a Pharisee* (Phil 3:5). There you see the shining surface of the ice. But notice how hard it was: *As for zeal, I was a persecutor of the Church of Christ* (Phil 3:6). This hard man was among those who stoned the holy martyr Stephen; indeed, he could be thought harder than all the others, for, since he guarded the clothes of the men who threw the stones, he was doing the stoning through the hands of them all.[59]

Verse 18. God's word and God's breath melt even ice

26. We observe snow, mist, and ice. What a good thing it would be if God were to breathe and melt them! If he does not breathe on them, if he does not himself dissolve this ice-bound hardness, *who shall withstand his cold?* Whose cold does the psalm mean when it asks, *Who shall withstand his cold?* God's, obviously. But in what sense is it his cold? Well, think. He abandons a sinner and no longer

---

56. Variant: "Even if there are others who, when converted from an obstinacy like his, will become bread."
57. See Acts 22:3.
58. Variant: "had grown up with."
59. See Acts 7:58.

calls him; suppose he ceases to open the sinner's mind and no longer infuses grace. Now let this person release himself, if he can, from his frozen foolishness. He cannot do it. Why not? *Who shall withstand his cold?* Look at this helpless, hopelessly frozen person, who laments, *I am aware of a different law in my members that opposes the law of my mind, and imprisons me under the law of sin inherent in my members. Who will deliver me from this death-ridden body?* (Rom 7:23–24) Look at me! I'm getting cold, I'm freezing over. Where can I find the warmth to melt me, so that I can run? *Who will deliver me from this death-ridden body?* Who indeed? *Who shall withstand his cold?* Who will ever free himself if God has abandoned him?

Who liberates us? *Only the grace of God, through Jesus Christ our Lord* (Rom 7:25). Listen to the psalm, for here again we find a mention of God's grace. *He sends his ice like bread crumbs: who shall withstand his cold?* Are we to despair? By no means, for the psalm continues, *He will send forth his word, and melt them.* Let not the snow despair, let not the mist despair, let not the ice despair, for, out of the snow which is so much like wool, a tunic is woven, and the mist finds salvation through repentance, because *those whom he predestined, he also called* (Rom 8:30). And even if among those who are predestined there are some very hard characters who have frozen progressively over a very long period and become solid ice, they will not be too hard for the mercy of God. *He will send forth his word, and melt them.* What does the psalmist mean by *melt them*? You must not take it in a pejorative sense when the psalm says that God melts or dissolves them, for their hardness is due to pride. Pride is rightly called numbness, and a numb, insensitive thing is cold. In everyday speech, when people are suffering from stiffness, they say, "I have gone numb." So pride is a kind of numbness.

But God *will send forth his word, and melt them.* The mounds of snow are warmed and they dissolve in humility. We could think of a heap of snow as maintained in its upright position by cold rigidity, and similarly pride raises up fools. But *he will send forth his word, and melt them.* Remember that block of ice who arose after the murderous stoning of Stephen, the block called Saul. He was hard and rigid in his opposition to Christ. He begged the priests to furnish him with letters, empowering him to track down Christians wherever they might be. He was breathing out murderous threats.[60] If ever there

---

60. See Acts 9:1.

was a man hardened and icy against the fire of God, it was he. But, although Saul was hard and frozen, the Lord, who *will send forth his word, and melt them*, uttered a burning cry from heaven, *Saul, Saul, why are you persecuting me?* (Acts 9:4) At that one question all the hard ice in Saul dissolved. *He will send forth his word, and melt them.* We have no need to despair even of ice, so how much less of snow or mist? Despair not, even where there is ice. *I was originally a persecutor and a blasphemer, and harmed people* (1 Tm 1:13), Paul tells us. Why did God choose to melt that ice? So that snow might not lose hope in its own case, for Paul continues, *I received mercy so that Christ Jesus might give proof in me of his long forbearance, for the instruction of those who will believe in him unto eternal life* (1 Tm 1:16). God is shouting to the gentiles, "I have melted the ice; come to me, all you who are snow."

He will send forth his word, and melt them, he will blow with his wind, and the waters will gush forth. See how the ice and the snow are melting: they dissolve into water. Let all who are thirsty come and drink. Saul was as hard as ice and hounded Stephen to death, but, having been transformed into Paul, he is living water, and he calls the gentiles to the fountain. *He will blow with his wind, and the waters will gush forth.* God's breath[61] is a scorching fire, which is why another psalm prays, *Turn our captivity around, O Lord, like a torrent in the south wind* (Ps 125(126):4). Captive Jerusalem seemed to have frozen in Babylon, but the south wind blows, the rigidity of her imprisonment melts away, and her burning love brings her running toward God. *He will blow with his wind, and the waters will gush forth.* That water will be for them a spring leaping up to eternal life.[62]

Verse 19. Only Christ suffered in total innocence

27. *He announces his word to Jacob, his just decrees and judgments to Israel.* What just decrees are they? What are his judgments? They are so called because, whatever the human race suffered in this world during the time when it was snow and mist and ice, it suffered as a punishment for its pride and self-exaltation against God. Let us look back at the origins of our misfortunes and see how right another psalm

---

61. *Spiritus*, God's breath or wind or Spirit. The thought of the Holy Spirit is just below the surface in this paragraph, but Augustine does not make the reference explicit. Lower case has therefore been preferred.
62. See Jn 4:14.

was when it sang, *Before I was humiliated, I sinned* (Ps 118(119):67). But the psalmist who acknowledged that *before I was humiliated, I sinned* also recognized that *it is good for me that you have humbled me, so that I may learn your ways of justice* (Ps 118(119):71).[63] Jacob learned these ways of justice from God, who made him wrestle with an angel, though in truth it was the Lord himself, in the guise of an angel, who had been Jacob's adversary.[64] Jacob held on; he exerted all his strength to hold on; he proved the stronger and maintained his hold. But the Lord let himself be held out of mercy, not weakness. Thus Jacob prevailed in the struggle and held his opponent, and, though he seemed to be the winner, he begged his opponent to bless him. How did he understand who this wrestler was, whom he had fought and held fast? Why did he wrestle so violently and hang on? Because *the kingdom of heaven is subjected to violence, and the violent snatch it away* (Mt 11:12). Why the struggle? Because much effort is required of us. Why do we find it so difficult to hold onto what we lost so easily? This is necessary, because, if we easily regain what we have lost, we may become accustomed to letting go of what we have. It is good for a person to work hard in order to get hold of something, for he will hold onto it very firmly if it cost him so much labor. God manifested his judgments to Jacob in this way—to Jacob who became Israel.

Let me put the point more plainly. The same lesson is apposite for all the righteous in this world who justly suffer labors, dangers, distress, and pain in accordance with the just judgment of God. One alone can say that he suffered here without cause—although it was not without cause, because he suffered for us. He alone can say, *I was paying the price, though I had committed no robbery* (Ps 68:5(69:4)). He alone could say, *Now the prince of this world is coming, and he will find nothing in me* (Jn 14:30). But then, as though someone had asked him, "In that case, why do you suffer?" he continued, *But so that the world may know that I am doing my Father's will, rise, let us leave here* (Jn 14:31). No others who suffer because they have deserved it, by God's judgment, or even in the cause of justice, have any right to claim that theirs is innocent suffering like Christ's. Listen

---

63. These two verses of Psalm 118(119) occur in close association throughout Dolbeau Sermon 21, dated to early in 404. This may be another clue to the dating of the present Exposition. Compare the note at section 16, above.
64. See Gn 32:24-29.

to what the apostle Peter tells us: *It is time for judgment to take place, beginning from the house of the Lord* (1 Pt 4:17). He is encouraging the martyrs and all who bear witness to God, exhorting them to endure with the utmost patience all the threats of a raging world. *It is time for judgment to take place, beginning from the house of the Lord*, he says, *and if it originates with us, what will be the outcome for those who do not believe in the gospel of God? What will become of the wicked and the sinner if the righteous will scarcely be saved?* (1 Pt 4:17–18) *He announces his word to Jacob, his just decrees and judgments to Israel.*

Verse 20. The true Israel

28. **He has not dealt so with any other nation.** Let no one beguile you: not to every nation has this judgment of God been made known. Not to all has it been demonstrated that both the just and the unjust suffer, all according to their deserts, and that the just are set free not by their own merits but by the grace of God. This was not revealed to every nation but only to Jacob, only to Israel. Where do we come in, then, if God did not announce it to every nation but only to Jacob, only to Israel? Where shall we find ourselves in this dispensation?

Exactly there: in Jacob and in Israel. *He has not revealed his judgments to them.* To whom? To the nations in general. But then how was it that the snows were called, once their ice had been melted? How were the gentiles called, after Paul had been justified? How indeed, unless they were destined to belong to Jacob and be found within it? A branch of the oleaster was cut off to be engrafted into the olive.[65] They should not be called "the nations" any longer but one single nation in Christ, the nation of Jacob, the nation of Israel. Why can we say "the nation of Jacob and the nation of Israel"? Because Jacob was the son of Isaac, and Isaac the son of Abraham. And what promise was made to Abraham? *In your seed shall all the nations of the earth be blessed* (Gn 22:18). The same promise was repeated to Isaac and to Jacob.[66] We belong to Jacob, therefore, because we belong to Isaac and to Abraham, for the seed of Abraham is Christ. It is not I who assert this, nor any upstart speaker. The holy apostle himself teaches, *Scripture does not say, To his descendants, as though indicating many, but as to one only: And to your seed, which is Christ*

---

65. See Rom 11:17.
66. See Gn 26:4; 28:14.

(Gal 3:16). If there is one seed only, and one Jacob and one Israel, it means that all nations are one person in Christ.

It follows that what was revealed to Jacob, to Israel, applies to all nations. The only ones not included and to be reckoned as gentiles still are those who refuse to believe in Christ and are unwilling to forsake the oleaster and be engrafted into the olive. They will be left as sterile, bitter branches among the forest trees. But Jacob must rejoice. What does the name Jacob mean? "Supplanter," for he supplanted his brother.[67] *Blindness fell upon part of Israel, until the full tally of the gentiles should come in* (Rom 11:25).

And Jacob was transformed into Israel. What does the name Israel mean? Let us all listen to the answer, and let us all be Israel, both you, members of Christ here present, and those also who are outside—yet not truly outside, because I am thinking of those who are dispersed everywhere throughout all nations yet are everywhere within. Let this Israel listen, this Jacob who has become Israel. What is Israel? One who sees God. Where will Israel see God? In peace. In what peace? In the peace of Jerusalem, for the psalm says, *He has established peace on your frontiers.* There we shall praise him. All of us will be one in the one Christ, and all of us will be intent upon him who is one, for nevermore shall we be a crowd of scattered individuals.

---

67. See Gn 25:31–34; 27:36.

Exposition of Psalm 148

A Sermon to the People

Lent and Eastertime signify our present life and the life to come

1. Our thoughts in this present life ought to be centered on the praise of God, because to praise God will be our everlasting joy in the life to come, and no one will be fit for that future life unless he or she is well practiced in the art of praising God now. In our present state we praise him, but we also make our requests to him, and, though our praise is joyful, our petitions are accompanied by groans. We have been promised a happiness we do not yet possess, and therefore, while we rejoice in hope because he who promised is trustworthy, we also groan with longing, because we do not yet see the fulfillment. Our good lies in persevering in our desire until what we are promised has come; then groaning will pass away and praise alone will take its place.

Since we must live through these two periods of time—the present era with its temptations and all life's troubles, and the future life with its freedom from danger and its perpetual joy—the Church has likewise appointed for us a celebration of two distinct periods, the time before Easter and the time after it. The time before Easter represents the afflictions we experience in our present life, but the time after Easter, which we are keeping now, is a sign of the beatitude in which we shall live hereafter. So, you see, what we celebrate before Easter corresponds to our actual experience, but in our celebrations after Easter we signify realities not yet within our grasp. This is why in the former period we train ourselves with fasting and prayer, but in this post-Easter season the regime of fasting is relaxed and we devote ourselves to praise. Accordingly we sing *Alleluia*, which, as you know, means in our language, "Praise the Lord!"

The earlier period represented the time before the Lord's resurrection, and the period we are in now is the time after his resurrection. This latter period is a sign of the future life which we do not hold as yet, but what we celebrate through signs after the resurrection of the Lord we shall hold in reality after our own resurrection. In the person of our head both phases were prefigured, and both were demonstrated in fact. His passion manifested to us the conditions of our present life, in which we are bound to labor and suffer hardship and eventually die. But the resurrection and glorification of the Lord manifest to us the life we shall receive when he comes again to mete out just retribution to all, an evil fate to evil people and good things to the good. It is true that for the time being all wicked people can sing *Alleluia* with us, but, if they persist in their malice, this song proper to our future life will be no more than a sound on their lips. They cannot win that life itself, the life celebrated in signs now but waiting for us in reality, because they have refused to orient themselves toward it now, before the time, and to hold fast to it before it comes.

Praise God with all your thoughts and actions

2. With this in mind, brothers and sisters, we exhort you to praise God, and it is this exhortation that we all address to each other when we say *Alleluia*. "Praise the Lord!" you say to someone, and he says the same to you. Thus, when people are all saying it to each other, they are all doing exactly what they are inviting one another to do.

But you must praise him with the whole of yourselves.[1] Not only must your tongue and your voice praise God, but your conscience must praise him too, and your life and your deeds. What I mean is this: now, while we are gathered in church, we praise God, but when each of you goes off home it looks as though you cease to praise him. But let each one of you not cease to live a good life, and then he or she will be praising God all the time. You only stop praising God when you swerve from just conduct and from what pleases him. If you never turn aside from what is right your tongue is silent, but your life is shouting, and God's ears are attuned to your heart. Just as our ears are sensitive to our voices, so are God's ears sensitive to our thoughts.

But it is impossible for anyone who entertains good thoughts to commit bad deeds, for deeds proceed from thoughts. A person cannot do anything, or move his limbs to perform any action, unless his thoughts first issue the order. Think how it is in the Roman Empire: any order issued by the emperor proceeds from inside his palace and travels through the empire, so that you see its effects throughout the

---

1. *De totis vobis.* Some manuscripts read *totis votis,* "with full desire" or "with all-embracing prayers."

provinces. What a flurry of activity follows one command from an emperor sitting still indoors! He moves only his lips when he speaks, but a whole province is astir when the order is carried out. Similarly there is an emperor within each of us, enthroned in our hearts. If he is good and issues good commands, good deeds follow. If he is bad and gives bad commands, bad deeds are the result. If Christ is enthroned there, what else but good can he command? If the devil is in possession, what can he order but bad deeds? God has willed that it shall be left to your own decision whether to prepare a place for God or one for the devil. When you have prepared it, whoever takes possession will give the orders.

So then, brothers and sisters, do not confine your attention to the sound you make. When you praise God, praise him with your whole selves: let your voice sing, let your life sing, let your actions sing. Even though you are still beset with groaning, troubles, and temptation, you must hope that all these will pass and that the day will dawn when we shall praise God without fainting or failing.

This psalm is so straightforward that we can run through it easily. It envisages all creation singing praise to God and addresses all creatures, category by category, exhorting the whole universe to praise him, as if it had fallen silent.

Verse 1. All creatures praise the Lord in their own way

3. *Praise the Lord from the heavens.* Indeed, one might almost suppose that the psalmist had found some heavenly beings fallen silent in their praise of the Lord, since he exhorts them to bestir themselves and extol him. But heavenly creatures have never fallen silent in their praise of their creator, any more than earthly creatures have ever ceased to praise God. Among them are some whose will to praise him springs from their delight in God, for an intelligent being praises only what is recognized as lovable. Other creatures there are which lack spiritual life and intelligence wherewith to praise God, but they too are good, and, being assigned their places within an ordered whole, they contribute to the beauty of the universe that God has created. These creatures do not praise him with their own voices and hearts, but, when they are contemplated by intelligent observers, God is praised through them. And, if God is praised through them, it can be said that in a way they too praise God.

Let us look at some examples. Praise is offered to God *from the heavens* by all those of his creatures who have spiritual life and pure intelligence, which enable them to contemplate him and to love him without weakness or weariness. But God is praised on earth by beings who possess the intelligence to distinguish between good and evil and to know both creation and its creator. Such are human beings who can ponder these things, for the Lord has endowed them with discerning minds and the faculty to take delight in him and praise him. Human beings can do this, but what about animals? Do they have this kind of understanding? If beasts had intellects like ours, God would not have admonished us, *Do not be like a horse or a mule, devoid of understanding* (Ps 31(32):9). By exhorting us not to be like irrational beasts, God reminds us that he has given us understanding so that we may praise him. What about trees? Do they even have the kind of sentient life that animals enjoy? Animals lack the interior rationality, the intelligent and discerning mind that humans have, with which to praise God. They do manifest a life of their own, however, as we all know, a life that prompts them to seek food, eating what is good for them and rejecting what is harmful. They have senses that enable them to distinguish between material things: eyesight for colors, hearing for voices, a faculty of smell, a palate for tasting; and they have the power of movement that draws them toward what gives them pleasure and makes them shun what hurts. We understand all this and see it demonstrated before our eyes. Animals do not have rational intelligence, but they have their own spirit that animates their bodies, and they obviously have life. Trees do not have even this kind of life, but they all praise God nonetheless. Why can we say that they praise God? Because when we see these things and ponder on the creator who made them, it means that all of them praise God.

The psalmist begins with heaven. All things are singing praise, yet he says, *Praise the Lord*. Why does he invite them, *Praise the Lord*, when they are praising him already? Because he is delighted to find that they are singing praises, and he wants to give them further encouragement. You may feel like that if you come across people joyfully engaged in some good work—in the vineyard, perhaps, or in the grain harvest or in any kind of agriculture. You are pleased about what they are doing, and you say, "Good work! Get at it!" not because they will only begin when you speak to them but because you are so pleased about the work you have found them doing that you want to congratulate them and spur them on to further efforts. By calling out, "Get at it!" you are expressing your desire to share the work yourself. And in the same way the prophet, full of the Spirit, voices his encouragement.

The prophets promise future freedom

4. The psalm bears the title, *Of Haggai and Zechariah*. During the time when their people was being held captive in Babylon, these two prophets foretold that the captivity would end, making possible the rebuilding of the city of Jerusalem, which had been overthrown in war.[2] In a mysterious way they directed our attention toward that future life in which we shall praise God, when the captivity of our life here is ended. We are captives still, burdened by the luggage of our mortal bodies as we walk our pilgrim way and sigh for the great city, Jerusalem. When she is finally made new, we shall be at home in her, exulting in the city we sighed for on our pilgrimage. Anyone who does not sigh as a pilgrim will never rejoice as a citizen, for there cannot be any desire in him. The two holy prophets gave powerful comfort to a people still prisoners physically, a people exiled in Babylon and subject to foreign kings. They prophetically evoked a time to come, a time of liberation from captivity and of the restoration of Jerusalem. But all these events prefigured something else,[3] and their full meaning was yet to be disclosed. They happened with symbolic import to people in antiquity, but their fulfillment is revealed among us. What does the apostle say about our present condition? *As long as we are in the body we are on pilgrimage and away from the Lord* (2 Cor 5:6). We are not yet in our homeland. When shall we reach it? When our enemy, the devil, has been defeated and we shout over him in triumph, when *death, the last enemy, is destroyed. Then the saying will come true: Death is swallowed up into victory. O death, where is your strife? Where, O death, is your sting?* (1 Cor 15:26.54–55) Death is ever striving against us now, making us grieve over the unreliability and changeable nature of things and the fragility of our human flesh. When will death's striving no longer trouble us? Every day temptations strive against us, every day we feel the striving of illicit pleasures, and even if we do not consent we suffer under their onslaughts. We have to strive, and anyone engaged in strife is in serious danger of being worsted. If we win and do not consent, we

---

2. On the ministry of Haggai and Zechariah, see the note at Exposition of Psalm 147,5.
3. See 1 Cor 10:6.

still endure pain and battering as we resist these alluring pleasures. Our enemy never gives up the fight and never dies; there will be no security for us until the resurrection of the dead.

But let us take courage and be confident, for Haggai and Zechariah arouse our hope. They sing of our future liberation. If they sang of liberation to their own people, and their predictions came true, is it likely that predictions made to the Christian people will go unverified? Do not worry; simply be watchful as to how you must bear yourselves during life's pilgrimage. Do not let love of Babylon steal your hearts, lest you forget your own city, Jerusalem. Even though your body is still held prisoner in Babylon, let your heart race ahead to Jerusalem.

Let every creature praise the Lord,[4] therefore, because what fills our thoughts here will be our whole occupation when we arrive home.

5. *Praise the Lord from the heavens, praise him in the heights.* The psalm speaks first of the heavens and afterwards of the earth, for God is praised as maker of both heaven and earth. The heavens are tranquil, for peace reigns there. All is joy without end; there is no death, no illness, no pain. The blessed praise God eternally. We are still here below, but when we reflect on how God is praised there, our hearts are on high. With good reason are we invited, "Lift up your hearts!"[5] Let us raise our hearts on high lest they grow moldy on the ground: what angels are doing up there is delightful to us as well. Let us join in now, in hope, as we shall later in fact when we arrive in their company. *Praise him in the heights.*

Verses 2–5. The summons addressed to all creation

6. *Praise him, all you his angels; praise him, all you his powers. Praise him, sun and moon; praise him, all you stars and light. You heavens of heavens, praise him, and let the waters that are above the heavens praise the name of the Lord.* How can the psalmist hope to unfurl them all? By enumerating them? No, that is impossible, but he summarizes and binds them all together into a tight bundle which contains all the heavenly beings that praise their creator.

7. And then, perhaps, he thought someone might ask him, "Why do they praise God? What do they owe him? What has he bestowed on them to deserve their praise?" The psalmist responds, *He spoke, and they were made; he gave the command, and they were created.* There

---

4. Variant: "Every creature praises the Lord."
5. See the note at Exposition of Psalm 10,3.

is nothing remarkable about the works praising the artificer, nothing remarkable in things that are made praising their maker, nothing to surprise us if a creature praises its creator. Christ is mentioned here, though perhaps some of us did not catch his name. Who is Christ? *In the beginning was the Word, and the Word was with God; he was God. He was with God in the beginning. Everything was made through him; nothing came to be without him.* (Jn 1:1–3) Through whom were they made? Through the Word. But how does the psalm teach this same truth, that they were made through the Word? By telling us that *he spoke, and they were made; he gave the command, and they were created.* No one speaks and no one commands except with a word.

Verse 6. The guarantee of the promise that we shall live for ever

8. *He established them for ever, for age after age.* All heavenly beings did he establish, all beings on high, all powers and angels, and a celestial city, an excellent, holy, blessed city. We are still wretched because we are exiled from it, but because we shall return there one day we are blessed in our hope, and when we reach it we shall be blessed in reality.

He established them for ever, for age after age; he issued his decree, and it will not pass away. What kind of decree could be imposed on heavenly beings and holy angels, do you think? What kind of decree did God issue for them? Surely none other than that they should praise him. Blessed are those who have no other duties than to praise God! They do not plough or sow or grind wheat or cook, for all these are works dictated by necessity, and no necessity exists there. They do not steal or pillage or commit adultery, for these are the works of iniquity, and there no iniquity is to be found. They do not break bread for the hungry or clothe the naked or welcome strangers or visit the sick or reconcile the quarrelling or bury the dead, for all these are works of mercy, and there no misery exists to call forth mercy. How blessed are those who dwell there! Do you think we too shall be like them? Let us long ardently for that blessed life and groan in our longing.

But what are we, that we should aspire to it? Mortals, reprobates, outcasts, dust and ashes. Yet he who made the promise is almighty. If we look to ourselves, what are we? But if we look to him, he is God, and he is omnipotent. Is he not capable of making an angel out of a human being, he who made a human being out of nothing? Or do you think that God sets little store by human beings, when he willed that his only Son should die for them? Let us fix our eyes on the proof of his love that he has already given. We have received peerless pledges[6] of God's promise: we hold Christ's death, we hold Christ's blood. Who died? God's only Son. For whom did he die? We would like to say that it was for good, righteous people, wouldn't we, but was it? *Christ died for the wicked* (Rom 5:6), says the apostle. If he made a gift of his death to the wicked, what can he be reserving for the righteous, except his life?

Let human weakness raise itself from despair; let it not knock itself down, let it not turn away, saying, "One day I shall no longer exist." It is God who has promised. He came to us in order to deliver his promise. He appeared to men and women. He came to take our death upon himself and to promise us his life. He came to the far-off country of our exile to take on himself things of which we have plenty: insults, scourgings, punches, spittle in the face, humiliations, a crown of thorns, nailing to a tree, crucifixion, and death. There are plentiful supplies of all these in our country, and he came to strike a bargain. What did he pay, and what did he buy? He handed over exhortation, teaching, the forgiveness of sins, and in return he received insults, death, and the cross. He brought us good things from his homeland and endured evil things in ours, and yet he promised us that we shall one day be in that country from which he had come. He prayed, *Father, I will that where I am, those also whom you have given me may be with me* (Jn 17:24). He has forestalled all our doubts with his great love. Where we were, he came to be with us, and where he is, we shall be with him.

What has God promised you, mortal creature? That you are to live for ever. Do you not believe it? Believe it, I beg you, believe it. What God has done already is greater than what he has promised. What has he done? He has died for you. What has he promised? That you will live with him. It is more incredible that the eternal has died than that mortal creatures will live eternally. And yet the more incredible fact is that of which we have proof already. If God has died for the sake of human beings, is it so hard to believe that human beings will live with God? Is a mortal not to live for all eternity, when, for that mortal, he who lives for all eternity has died?

But how can it be that God has died? How did God die? Can God die? He took from you the means of dying for you. Only flesh could

---

6. *Arrhas*. See the notes at Expositions of Psalms 122,5 and 127,8.

die; only a mortal body could die. And so he clothed himself in the mortality that made it possible for him to die for you, and he will clothe you in the immortality in which you can live with him. Where did he don the vesture of death? Within the virginity of his mother. Where will he clothe you in life? In his equality with his Father. Here on earth he chose for himself a nuptial chamber, where bridegroom was joined to bride. *The Word was made flesh* (Jn 1:14) in order to become the head of the Church. In his own nature the Word is not part of the Church, but in order to be the Church's head he took flesh. Something of ours is already on high, something he assumed as his own here, where he died, where he was crucified. The first-fruits of yourself has gone ahead already. Can you doubt that you will follow?

Verse 7. Weather systems and dragons praise God

9. Now let the psalmist turn his attention to earthly creatures, since he has finished considering those in the heavens. *Praise the Lord from the earth.* How did he begin when he was addressing creatures above? *Praise the Lord from the heavens,* he said, and then he enumerated them. Listen now to what he has to say to creatures on earth. *You dragons and all the depths.* The depths he means are the deep places of the ocean. Associated with them are all the seas and cloudy atmospheric conditions. Whatever kinds of weather God wishes to prevail on the earth—clouds, winds, storms, rain, lightning, thunder, hail, snow—all of them are generated by this damp, foggy air. The psalm calls all of it *earth* because it is very changeable and short-lived (though you may, of course, think that God sends rain down from the stars).[7] All these weather systems operate close to the earth. It sometimes happens that people on high mountains see clouds below them, and often such clouds are producing rain lower down. All these events are well known to those who observe them carefully. They are stirred up when the atmosphere is turbulent, and they are characteristic of this lower part of the world.

We can see why, when the devil and his angels fell from the glory of the angels on high, he was condemned to inhabit this cloudy region, this air of ours. The apostle refers to him as *the prince of the power of the air, who is now at work in the children of unbelief* (Eph 2:2), and another apostle spoke of their condemnation like this: *If God did not spare the sinful angels, but thrust them down into the dark prisons of*

---

7. Variant: "that God rains down stars."

the underworld, it was because in his judgment he handed them over to be detained for punishment (2 Pt 2:4). He called our regions *the underworld* because they represented a fall from heaven. Disregard what the devil gained and consider what he lost.

When you look at all these things in our lower world you are struck by how changeable they are, how turbulent and terrifying and prone to decay. Yet they too have their place, for they keep their appointed order and contribute in their own way to the beauty of the whole, and therefore they praise the Lord. This is why the psalmist, turning to them and addressing his invitation to these lowly things too, began by saying, *Praise the Lord from the earth, you dragons and all the depths.* He wanted us to praise the Lord through our study of them, for, when they move us to praise God, they themselves are praising him.

Now dragons favor watery habitats. They emerge from caves and take to the air. They create major atmospheric disturbance, for dragons are very large creatures, the largest of all on earth.[8] This is probably why the psalm began its consideration of earthly creatures with them. There are caves in which hidden waters rise, and from them spring the fountains that issue in rivers. Some of these flow above ground, but others make their way below the surface, hidden from our gaze. All of them, together with the entire watery world, the sea, and our damp atmosphere here below, are called *the depths* in our psalm, they and the great deeps in which dragons live and praise God. What? Are we to imagine dragons forming a choir to praise God? Of course not, but when you think about dragons you are reminded of the dragons' designer, the dragons' creator. When they fill you with amazement you reflect, "How great must be the God who made them!" In this way dragons praise God through your voices, and so the psalm invites them, *Praise the Lord, you dragons and all the depths.*

Verse 8. God's providence extends to all his works

10. *Fire, hail, snow, ice, stormy winds, all these that do his bidding.* Why does the psalm add those last words, noting that they *do his bidding*? Because there are plenty of stupid people who are incapable

---

8. Or possibly "the largest of all land animals." *Draco* can also mean a snake or some kind of serpent, but it is evident from Augustine's remarks that he is thinking of the huge mythical beasts that pervade the folklore of many cultures.

of contemplating them and discerning the diversity in a creation where all things function in their own places and their own order, pursuing their activities under God's authority and at his command. To such foolish persons it looks as though God controls all higher beings but despises, ignores, and abandons lower creatures, taking no care of them and leaving them without governance or guidance. Such creatures, on this view, are ruled only by chance and act haphazardly, however and wherever they can. People who think like this sometimes say to themselves, and convince themselves as they say it, "If it were God who sent the rain, he would not let it fall on the sea, would he? What kind of providence would that be? Getulia[9] is parched, yet rain is plentiful over the sea!" They think this an acute piece of reasoning, but I hope they will not talk to you like that; or at any rate I hope you will not listen and agree, for such talk is blasphemous and hateful to God. We should answer them as follows: Getulia may well be thirsty, but you are not.[10] It would do you good to say to God, *My soul is like waterless earth to you* (Ps 142(143):6), or, as another psalm puts it even more plainly, *my soul thirsts for you, and for you my flesh is athirst, in how many ways!* (Ps 62:2(63:1)) And the Lord suggests the same in the gospel: *Blessed are those who hunger and thirst for righteousness, for they shall be satisfied* (Mt 5:6). A person who argues on the lines we have mentioned is satisfied already. He esteems himself knowledgeable and has no wish to learn, and so he is not thirsty. If he were athirst he would long to learn, and he would discover that everything happens on earth by God's providence. Then he would be filled with wonder even by the arrangement of the parts of a flea. Let me have your attention, please, beloved. Who was it who so arranged the bodily parts of a flea or a gnat that they would enjoy coordination, life, and movement? Study any tiny creature, any one you choose. I want you simply to consider the disposition of its organs and the life that animates it: look how it avoids death, loves life, seeks pleasures, avoids painful conditions, deploys its various senses, and flourishes in the mode proper to itself. Who gave the flea a sting with which to suck blood? How tiny is the pipe through which it drinks! Who arranged matters so? Who made these things?

If you tremble with awe at these minute creatures, praise him who is so great. Be very determined, brothers and sisters, that no one

---

9. A region in north-west Africa, within modern Morocco.
10. Variant: "Getulia may well be thirsty so that you may not be."

dislodge you from your faith or from sound teaching.[11] He who made an angel in heaven also made a little worm on earth, but he designed the angel for a heavenly habitation and the worm for an earthly habitat. He did not design the angel to crawl in the mud or the worm to move in heaven, did he? He assigned the dwellers to their respective homes, settling creatures of incorruptible nature in incorrupt abodes and corruptible creatures into corruptible places. Study his whole plan and praise the whole. If God disposed the organs of a flea, does he not control the clouds? Why, then, does he cause rain to fall on the sea? Well, are there not creatures in the sea that are nourished by the rain? Did God not create fish there, and other living creatures? And you know how fish hasten toward fresh water.

"But then," someone objects, "why does he send rain for a fish but sometimes sends no rain for me?" Perhaps this is so that you may realize that you are in the desert, trudging along on life's pilgrimage, and so that this present life may grow bitter for you and the future life arouse your desire. Or perhaps so that you may be chastised and rebuked and corrected.

But think how God has distributed to various regions the resources suited to each. We spoke just now of Getulia. Where we live, here, it rains almost every year, and every year our soil yields grain. But our grain cannot be kept for long because it quickly goes bad, and this is right for us, since it is given us anew every year. In Getulia, on the contrary, grain can be harvested only rarely, but, when it is, there is plenty, and it can be stored for a long time. You surely do not think that God abandons the people who live there? Do you not think that they cheerfully praise and glorify God in their own fashion? Pluck a Getulian from his own country and put him here among our shady trees: he will want to run away and go back to his barren Getulia! To all places, all regions, and all seasons God has assigned and ordered the appropriate conditions.

It would take too long to consider all these things in detail. Who would be equal to explaining the whole? But anyone who has eyes will study many of this world's creatures, and in studying them find delight in them. When these things delight us we praise them, but not for themselves. We praise God who made them, and thus all creatures praise God.

---

11. Variant: "that no one dislodge sound teaching from your faith."

11. The spirit of the prophet was aware of these truths as he said, *Fire, hail, snow, ice, and stormy winds*. All these seem to some foolish people to be chaotic and random in their changes, moved only by chance. But the psalmist added, *All these do his bidding*. You must not believe that creatures which serve God through all the changes they undergo are moved by mere chance. Fire spreads[12] to the place which God determines. To the place he appoints a cloud drifts, whether it bears rain or snow or hail. Why does lightning sometimes strike a mountain but not a robber? I will answer this question as far as my mental capacity allows and in the measure that God empowers me, but better people know better than I and understand more. May God grant you more wisdom than I can put into words, but may your wisdom be exercised with temperance and without pride. Well then, as far as my[13] small understanding permits, I can say this about why lightning strikes a mountain but not a robber. Perhaps God is still looking for the robber's conversion, and therefore the mountain, which cannot feel fear, is struck so that the frightened man may be changed. You sometimes act similarly yourself, don't you? When you are imposing discipline you strike the ground to frighten your child. God goes further: sometimes he strikes a man or woman, at his own choice. You will say to me, "Look, he is striking an innocent person and letting the more guilty one off scot-free!" Do not be surprised: death is a boon to a devout person, whencesoever it may come. How do you know what hidden punishment may be in store for that more guilty offender if he refuses to change? Will not those who at the end hear the sentence, *Depart from me into the eternal fire* (Mt 25:41), wish that they had been burnt up by lightning instead? What matters is that you be found innocent. In any case, is it a calamity to die by shipwreck and a blessing to die of fever? Whatever the cause of someone's death, the questions you should ask are what kind of person he is and where he will go after death, not how he will make his exit from this life. We may take a variety of routes out of life when our time comes to depart. What kind of deaths did the martyrs deserve to die? Were they carried off by fever, as many people hope to be? Some were killed at a single stroke of the sword, others by fire, others by wild animals. Beasts devoured the martyrs' bodies, to be sure, but God's servants were not afraid that their bodies would

---

12. Variant: "gives light."
13. Variant: "Without pride, then, and as far as my."

perish, for God, to whom even the number of hairs on our heads is known,[14] will bring the bodies of his saints from every place where they are scattered. He delivered the three youths from the fire when he willed,[15] but does that mean that he deserted the Maccabees in their fiery ordeal?[16] He openly delivered the former but secretly crowned the latter. God knows what he is doing. Your job is to be wary and to be good. Whatever the means by which he wills you to depart this life, let him find you ready. You are only a sojourner,[17] not the owner of your house. The house is let to you, not given, and, whether you will it or no, you will have to leave. Moreover you did not rent it on condition that the duration of your lease was fixed. What did your Lord say to you? "When I decide, when I say to you, 'Move on,' you are to be ready. I shall expel you from your temporary lodging, but I will give you a home. You are a sojourner on earth, but you will possess your own home in heaven."

12. Whatever happens here that is not to our liking, recognize that it happens only in accordance with God's will, by his providence, as part of his design, by his permission, and in conformity with his laws. Even if we do not understand why something happens, let us ascribe it to his providence, certain that it does not happen without a good reason, and then we do not[18] blaspheme. If, on the contrary, we begin to argue about God's dispositions, "Why this? Why that?" or say, "He should not have acted so, he was unfair in what he did," what becomes of God's praise? You have lost your Alleluia.[19] Look at everything that happens with a desire to please God and praise his artistry. If you went into a blacksmith's forge, you would not presume to criticize the bellows, the anvils, the hammers. But suppose some ignorant fellow goes in, one who does not know the purpose of any of it; he will find fault with everything. However, if he lacks the craftsman's knowledge but still surveys the scene from the angle of common sense, what does he say to himself? "There must be a good reason for placing the bellows there; the smith knows it, though I do not." The visitor does not presume to insult an artisan in his workshop, yet a fool dares to rebuke God in this world!

---

14. See Mt 10:30.
15. See Dn 3:24.93.
16. See 2 Mc 7.
17. See Ps 118(119):19.
18. Variant: "shall not."
19. See sections 1–2 above.

Be sure, then, that as *fire, hail, snow, ice, and stormy winds do his bidding,* so do all things in nature do his bidding because they act only at his command, even though to empty-headed persons they appear ill-considered.

Verses 9–13. The litany concludes

13. Finally the psalmist enumerates the rest of earth's creatures, exhorting them to praise the Lord: *Mountains and all hills, fruit-bearing trees and all cedars, wild beasts and tame,*[20] *reptiles and winged birds.* Then he turns to human beings: *Kings of the earth and all peoples, rulers and all the world's judges, young men and maidens, old and young, let them praise the name of the Lord.* The praise offered in heaven was set forth in order, and now the praise of the earth has been ordered too.

14. *For his name alone is exalted.* No human being may seek the exaltation of his own name. Do you aspire to be exalted? Submit to him who cannot be brought low, for *his name alone is exalted.*

Verse 14. Universal confession

15. *His confession fills earth and heaven.* What does that mean—*His confession fills earth and heaven*? The confession God makes? No, that by which all things confess him, and all things cry out his praise. The very beauty of all these things is like a voice that they raise to confess God. The sky cries to God, "You made me, I did not make myself." The earth cries out, "You founded me, I did not establish myself." How do these things cry out in worship? Whenever men and women observe them and discover the truth of them, all creatures cry out through your appreciation of them; they shout with your voice. *His confession fills earth and heaven.* Gaze up at the sky: how beautiful it is! Look to the earth: it is lovely. Each in its own way is beautiful, and together they are very beautiful. He made them and he rules them, by his pleasure they are directed. He orders their seasons, he restores their movements and restores them through his own will, through himself.[21] Therefore all these things praise him,

---

20. Literally *cattle,* which stood for all tame animals. Old Testament writers (e.g. Gn 1:25) thought of some species as having been created tame, unlike their wild cousins.
21. Variant: "he restores all things through himself."

whether they are at rest or in motion, whether on earth below or in heaven above, whether they grow old or are made new again.

When you see all these things and rejoice over them you are drawn up toward their maker; through the things that have been made you understand and contemplate something of his invisible nature.[22] *His confession fills earth and heaven,* for you confess to him through contemplating things of earth, and you confess to him through contemplating the things of heaven. And because he made all things, and nothing whatever is better than he is, whatever he has made is within[23] him. Whatever among all these gives you pleasure is less than God himself. Do not allow your pleasure in what he has made, therefore, to lure you away from him who made it; rather, if you love what he has made, love the maker far more. If the things he has made are so beautiful, how much more beautiful must he be who made them? *His confession fills earth and heaven.*

In winter life is hidden, but summer will reveal it

16. *He will exalt the strength[24] of his people.* This was what Haggai and Zechariah were predicting. At present the strength of his people is brought low, ground down in distress, in temptations, in the beating of our breasts. When will he *exalt the strength of his people*? Only when the Lord himself comes and our sun has risen—not the sun our eyes can see, the sun that rises over good and bad alike,[25] but that of which scripture says, *For you who fear God the sun of righteousness will arise, with healing in his wings* (Mal 4:2). This is the same sun of which the proud and impious will say, *On us the light of righteousness did not shine, nor did the sun rise for us* (Wis 5:6). Then it will be summer for us. In winter a plant is rooted in the soil but no fruit appears on it; as you look at trees in winter time they seem to have dried up. Anyone who does not know how to look will think a vine has shriveled, and perhaps there is another alongside this one that really is shriveled and dead. Throughout the winter the two can scarcely be distinguished, yet one is alive and the other is dead. The life of the one and the death of the other are still concealed, but when summer comes both life and death are manifested. The glory

---

22. See Rom 1:20.
23. Variant: "below."
24. Literally, *the horn.*
25. See Mt 5:45.

of leaves and the abundance of fruit adorn the living vine. What was present all the time in its root now clothes it visibly.

It is the same with us, brothers and sisters. For the time being we are just like everybody else. As other people are born, eat, drink, wear clothes, and lead their lives, so too do the saints. This fact sometimes disconcerts onlookers. They say, "Now that So-and-So has become a Christian, he won't suffer from headaches any more, will he?" or, "What has he got from being a Christian that I don't have?" What you see beside you, you shriveled vine, is a fellow vine naked in winter but not dried up or dead. Summer is on its way, the Lord who is our glory will come; at present he is hidden in the root. Then, after the captivity in which we pass our mortal lives, *he will exalt the strength of his people*. Reflecting on this, the apostle warns, *Pass no judgment prematurely, until the Lord comes; for he will light up the dark, hidden places, and then there will be praise for everyone from God* (1 Cor 4:5). But you ask me, "Where is my root? Is there any fruit on me?" If you are a believer, you know where your root is. It is where your faith is, where your hope is, and your charity. Listen to the apostle: *You are dead*, he says, for his disciples looked dead enough in their wintertime. But they are alive, for *your life is hidden with Christ in God*. So you see where your root is. But Paul has more to say: *When Christ appears, Christ who is your life, then you too will appear with him in glory.* (Col 3:3–4) Then *he will exalt the strength of his people*.

The Israel that is close to God

17. *A hymn for all his saints.* Do you know what a hymn is? It is a song in praise of God. If you praise God without singing, you are not offering a hymn. If you sing but do not praise God, that is not a hymn either. If you praise something else, something unconnected with the praise of God, then, even though you are singing praise, you are not singing a hymn. A hymn implies three things: it must be sung, it must consist of praise, and the praise must be offered to God. The praise of God, when sung, is called a hymn.

What does the psalm mean when it says, *A hymn for all his saints*? Let God's saints claim a hymn as their own, let them sing a hymn, because that is what will be their own for ever, an everlasting hymn will be theirs. In another psalm the Lord tells us, *By a sacrifice of praise I shall be honored, and there is the way where I will show him the salvation of God* (Ps 49(50):23), and elsewhere scripture declares, *Blessed are they who dwell in your house; they will praise you for ever and ever* (Ps 83:5(84:4)). This is what our psalm is referring to when it says, *A hymn for all his saints.*

But who are his saints? *The children of Israel, the people that draws close to him.* No one must say, "I am not a child of Israel." In case you are inclined to think like that, in case you are tempted to assume that, while the Jews are children of Israel, we are not, I will say something daring to you, my brothers and sisters: they are not, but we are. I will tell you why. The son born according to the Spirit ranks before the one born according to the flesh. From whom did Israel spring? From Abraham, for Isaac was the son of Abraham and Israel the son of Isaac. How did Abraham become pleasing to God? *Abraham believed God, and it was reckoned to him as righteousness* (Gn 15:6; Rom 4:3; Gal 3:6). Anyone who imitates Abraham is a descendant of Abraham, but those who degenerate from Abraham's faith have lost their pedigree. The Jews degenerated and lost it; we imitated Abraham's faith and have found it. Listen to how scripture demonstrates that they lost their pedigree. What did the Lord reply when the Jews claimed, *We are Abraham's descendants* (Jn 8:33)? They presumed to flaunt themselves and held their heads high, conscious of their nobility as scions of a righteous race. But what did the Lord say to them? *If you were Abraham's children, you would have acted as Abraham did* (Jn 8:39). If they lost their title to be Abraham's children, we have found it. By believing we have found what they lost by not believing, for *Abraham believed God, and it was reckoned to him as righteousness.*

Moreover, Abraham's seed is Christ,[26] and we are in Christ. A people sprang from Israel, and from that people Mary was born, and from Mary was born Christ. But we are in Christ, and therefore we are children of Israel.

Did the psalm add anything further, any distinguishing mark to be looked for in us? Yes, it points to *the children of Israel, the people that draws close to him.* Observe the Jews: if they are close to him, the reference must be to them. "But they are close to him," someone may say to me. "Every day they too sing a psalm, and they too sing hymns in praise of God." Yes, but do you not hear what God said of them through a prophet? *This people honors me with its lips, but its heart is far from me* (Is 29:13). Their heart may be far away, but our heart is very close to him, because we believe, we hope, and we love

---

26. See Gal 3:16.

him; because we are joined to Christ; because we have been made his members. Can the members of a body be distant from their head? If they were distant, if they were cut off from him, he could not have said, *Lo, I am with you even to the end of the ages* (Mt 28:20). If they were separated from him, he would not have cried from heaven, *Saul, Saul, why are you persecuting me?* (Acts 9:4) If he were not present in us, he would not be able to say, *I was hungry, and you fed me*, and when they reply, *When did we see you hungry?* he could not say, *When you did it for even the least of those who are mine, you did it for me.* (Mt 25:35.37.40)

Look around: this is the Israel that is close to him, in hope now, but later in all reality.

Exposition of Psalm 149

A Sermon to the People

Verse 1. The new song of grace, charity, and unity

1. Let us praise the Lord with our voices, our minds, and our good works, and let us sing him a new song, as this psalm bids us. It opens by urging us, *Sing to the Lord a new song.* The old song belongs to our old selves, the new song is proper to persons made new. The old covenant sings an old song, the new covenant demands a new song. Under the old covenant the promises dealt with temporal, earthly benefits, and therefore anyone who is in love with earthly goods is still singing the old song, but anyone who wants to sing a new song must love the things of eternity. Such love is itself new and eternal; it is always new because it never grows old. If you think about this carefully you will see that what we are talking about is something ancient. So how can it be new? We can scarcely regard eternal life as something lately born, can we, brothers and sisters? Eternal life is Christ himself,[1] and in respect of his divine nature Christ is certainly not lately born, for *in the beginning was the Word, and the Word was with God; he was God. He was with God in the beginning. Everything was made through him; nothing came to be without him.* (Jn 1:1–3) If the things that were created through him are ancient, what can we say of him through whom they were made? What else but that he is eternal and co-eternal with the Father?

As for ourselves, we fell into sin and thereby into a process of growing old. When another psalm laments, *I have grown old among all my enemies* (Ps 6:8(7)), we hear the threnody of our own voice. Humankind has aged in sin but is made new through grace. It is right, then, that all who are renewed in Christ, all those in whom eternal life has begun, should sing a new song.

2. And this song is a song of peace, a song of charity. People who separate themselves from the fellowship of the saints are not singing the new song; they are following the score of old animosity, not

---

1. See Jn 17:3.

the new music of charity. What is the melody of this new charity? Peace, the bond of holy society, spiritual union, a building made of living stones. And where is it found? Not in a single place only but throughout the whole world. The point is made clearly when another psalm invites us, *Sing a new song to the Lord, sing to the Lord, all the earth* (Ps 95(96):1). From these words we can be sure that anyone who is not in tune with all the earth is still stuck in the old song, whatever the words that come out of his mouth. Why should I bother about the sounds he makes, when I can read his thoughts?

"But you can't see what he is thinking, can you?" someone objects. Not exactly, but his deeds indicate it. The eye cannot penetrate anyone else's conscience, but if I observe a person's actions I can guess what he is thinking. If I discover someone committing theft, or homicide, or adultery, I cannot discern the thoughts in the offender's heart, but I infer them from his deeds. Some thoughts, admittedly, do remain hidden within, but there are also many that issue in actions, and so become obvious to other people. Take the case of those who have cut themselves loose from the bonds of Christ's charity and from the society of holy Church. As long as their malice was contained within themselves, no one knew about it except God. Then temptation struck. It cut them off[2] and laid bare to human eyes what had been known only to God.

The fruit borne by a person's life is evident only in his actions. This is why we are warned, *By their fruits you will know them* (Mt 7:16). The Lord said this with reference to certain people who clothe themselves in sheepskin but are savage wolves within. He knew that human weakness might be unable to detect the wolf that lurks beneath the sheep's fleece, so he said, *By their fruits you will know them.* We look for the fruits of charity, and we find the thorns of discord. *By their fruits you will know them.*

Their song is an old song, but let our song be a song that is new. As we have already pointed out, brothers and sisters, it is the whole earth that sings this new song.[3] Anyone who refuses to join in this new song with all the rest of the world may use whatever words he chooses, but it will make no difference. He may shout "Alleluia" all day long and all night, but I am not inclined to listen to the singer's

---

2. Variant: "overcame them."
3. As often, Augustine is contrasting the universality of the Catholic Church with the parochial narrowness of the Donatists.

voice; I am looking for the agent's deeds. I ask him, "What are you singing?" and he replies, "Alleluia." But what does Alleluia mean? "Praise the Lord." Fine: let us praise the Lord together. If you praise the Lord and I praise the Lord, why aren't we in tune? Charity praises the Lord, but discord blasphemes him.

The new song is sung worldwide

3. Now would you like to know where you are to sing the new song? Observe, then, how and where the events that are to be described in the psalm will take place: whether they will occur throughout all nations or in some particular region of the world only. If you are clear about this, you will understand much better who has the right to sing the new song. The implication of another psalm which I have already quoted is unmistakable: *Sing a new song to the Lord*. Then, to show that the fruits of charity and unity are present in the new song, it added, *Sing to the Lord, all the earth* (Ps 95(96):1).

Let none cut themselves off from the rest; let no one break away from our unity. If you are wheat, you must tolerate the chaff until winnowing time. Are you longing to be shaken free from the threshing floor? Good grain you may be, but the birds would find you if you were outside the threshing area, and they would gobble you up. What is more, your very decision to depart and fly away would prove that you were only straw: the wind blew, and because you were so light it swept you away from under the feet of the oxen. The people who are real wheat endure the trampling. They rejoice to be grain, they moan amid the straw, they look forward to the winnower whom they know to be their redeemer. *Sing to the Lord a new song, his praise in the assembly[4] of the saints*. This is the Church of the saints, the Church of the grains dispersed over all the earth. It is the Church sown throughout the Lord's field, which is this world. The Lord explained this himself when he spoke of a farmer sowing: *A man sowed good seed in his field, but an enemy came and over-sowed the field with tares. And when the shoots had grown up and come into ear, then the tares became apparent. The servants said to the owner, Was it not clean seed that you sowed in your field? Where have the tares come from? He replied, An enemy has done this.* (Mt 13:24–25. 27–28) They

---

4. *Ecclesia*, which also means "church." In the following lines it will sometimes be translated as "assembly" and sometimes as "Church," depending on the context.

wanted to take out the tares, but he restrained them, saying, *Let them both grow together until harvest time. At harvest time I will instruct the harvesters, Collect the tares first, and tie them up in bundles for burning; but store my wheat in the barn.* (Mt 13:30) Later the Lord's disciples questioned him, saying, *Explain the parable about the tares to us* (Mt 13:36). He then explained it in detail so that no one would give credit to his own heart if he understood some part of it, but only to our heavenly teacher, who made it plain. Nor must anyone say, "But he just made it mean whatever he liked!" No: if the Lord had expounded a parable told by a prophet (for, after all, it was he who had spoken through the prophet), would anyone have the temerity to assert that he ought not to have expounded it in the way he did? How much less, then, should anyone presume to gainsay the plain truth when the Lord expounded a parable he had himself proposed? Well then, the Lord explained it like this: *The sower is the Son of Man* (obviously he meant himself). *The good seed represents the children of the kingdom* (and this is *the assembly of the saints*). *The tares are the children of the evil one, and the field is this world.* (Mt 13:37–38)

Now you can see, brothers and sisters, that the good seed is sown all over the world, and the tares are scattered worldwide too. We do not find a patch of wheat here and a patch of tares there, do we? Wheat and tares are intermingled throughout. It is the world that constitutes the Lord's field, not just Africa. It is not as we might say with regard to our own countries, "Getulia[5] yields sixty-fold or a hundredfold, but Numidia[6] yields tenfold." No, God does not see his fields like that. Harvests are yielded to him everywhere: a hundredfold, sixtyfold, and thirtyfold. All that matters is that you make up your mind what you want to be, if you are thinking of being part of the Lord's crop.[7]

Clearly, then, *the assembly of the saints* is the Catholic Church. The church of the heretics is not an assembly of saints. The true Church of the saints is the one which God caused to be prefigured before it became visible, and then displayed that it might be seen by all. *The Church of the saints* was present from of old in the sacred

---

5. See the note at Exposition of Psalm 148,10.
6. A territory between Mauretania and Carthage, in modern Algeria. Few Donatist bishops from Numidia supported the more moderate Maximianists at the Council of Cebarsussa in 393. See Exposition 2 of Psalm 36,20 and the notes there. Possibly this fact influenced Augustine's attribution of a low yield to Numidia.
7. Variant: "thinking to belong to the Lord of the crops."

books, but now among the gentiles. *The Church of the saints* was at first only read about but is now both read about and seen. When it was only read about, it was believed in, yet now that it is seen, it is denied! *His praise is in the assembly of the saints.*

Verse 2. Israel sees God through charity

4. *Let Israel rejoice in him who made it.* What is Israel? The one who sees God; this is the interpretation of the name. The psalm is saying that all who see God must rejoice in the God who made them. What can it mean, brothers and sisters? We have said that we belong to the Church of the saints, but that does not imply that we already see God, does it? Yet how can we be Israel if we do not see him?

There is a seeing that is proper to this present time and a different seeing in the age to come. Our present seeing is by faith; the seeing we shall have in the future will be face-to-face vision. If we believe, we see; if we love, we see. What do we see? God. Where is God? Ask John: *God is charity* (1 Jn 4:16). Let us bless his holy name and, if we rejoice in charity, let us rejoice in God. If someone has charity, why should we send him far afield to see God? Let him only look into his own soul,[8] and there he sees God. If charity does not dwell there, God does not either, but, if charity dwells there, God dwells there too. Perhaps such a person aspires to see God enthroned in heaven; let him have charity, and God dwells in him as truly as in heaven.

Let us then be Israel and be glad in him who made us: *Let Israel rejoice in him who made it*, rejoice in the one who created Israel, not in Arius[9] or in Donatus or in Caecilian[10] or in Proculian[11] or in Augustine; *let Israel rejoice in him who made it.* We are not commending ourselves to you, brothers and sisters. Rather do we commend God to you, because we commend you to God. How do we commend God to you? By urging you to love him for your own benefit, not his, because, if you do not love him, it will be to your detriment, not God's. God will have not a whit less divinity if a man or woman has no love for him. You grow by loving God; he gains nothing from your love, and yet he took the initiative in loving us so much, before ever we loved

---

8. Literally "conscience."
9. See the notes at Expositions of Psalms 35,9 and 54,22.
10. On Donatus and Caecilian see the notes at Expositions of Psalms 10,1 and 85,14.
11. A Donatist bishop at Hippo early in the fifth century.

him,[12] that he sent his only Son to die for us.[13] He who made us was himself made one of us. How did he make us? *Everything was made through him; no part of created being was made without him* (Jn 1:3). How was he made one of us? *The Word was made flesh, and dwelt among us* (Jn 1:14). It is in him therefore that we must find our joy. No human being may claim for himself what belongs to God;[14] from him comes the joy that makes us happy. *Let Israel rejoice in him who made it.*

5. *And let the children of Zion exult in their king.* Israel and the children of the Church: these two titles denote the same people. Zion was a historical city which fell to its enemies. Some holy people did live in its ruins for a time, but the true Zion, the true Jerusalem (Zion and Jerusalem are the same city), is eternal in heaven, and she is our mother.[15] She is *the assembly of the saints*; she brought us to birth and nourished us. Part of her is still in exile, but the greater part abides unshakably in heaven. In that abiding heavenly part of her she is the beatitude of angels; in her pilgrim part in this world she is the hope of the just. Of the one scripture sings, *Glory to God in the highest*, and of the other, *Peace on earth to men of good will* (Lk 2:14).

All of us who sigh in this life and long for that homeland must run toward it, not by swift feet but by love. Such travelers look not for ships but for wings; let them seize the twin wings of charity. What are charity's paired wings? Love of God and love of our neighbor. So we are pilgrims, we sing and groan with desire. But letters from home have reached us,[16] and those letters we read out to you.

Christ is our creator, our king, our priest, and our pure sacrifice

6. *Let Israel rejoice in him who made it, and the children of Zion exult in their king.* The phrase, *him who made it*, means the same as *their king*. Just as you heard two expressions, *Israel* and *children of Zion*, and knew that the same thing was being said, though in different words, so also do these two expressions mean the same: *him who made it* and *their king*. The Son of God who made us was made one of us, and he rules us as our king because as our creator he made

---

12. See 1 Jn 4:19.
13. See Jn 3:16.
14. *Nemo... sibi arroget partes ipsius*: this could also mean "regions that are his."
15. See Gal 4:26.
16. On the Bible as a collection of letters from God, see Exposition of Psalm 73,5 and the note there.

us. He through whom we are ruled is none other than he through whom we were made, and we are called Christians because he is the Christ. The title "Christ" is derived from chrism, which is used in anointing. Kings and priests used to be anointed,[17] and Christ was anointed as both king and priest. As king he fought for us, and as priest he offered himself for us. When he fought for us he was to all appearances overcome, but in truth he was the victor. He was crucified, and from the cross to which he was fastened he slew the devil, and thus he proved himself our king. But in what sense is he a priest? Because he offered himself for us. Give your priest something he can offer. But what could human beings have found that would serve as a clean victim? What shall your victim be? What clean sacrifice can a sinner offer? Wicked, impious pretender, whatever you bring is tainted, yet something clean is needed to be offered for you. Look for something fit within yourself: you will find nothing. Look among your possessions for an acceptable offering: but God takes no pleasure in rams or he-goats or bulls. They all belong to him anyway, even if you do not offer them. Go on, then, offer him a clean sacrifice. But you are a sinner, a wicked person, and your conscience is defiled. If you were purified first you would, perhaps, be in a position to make a clean offering, but, if you are to be purified, something must be offered on your behalf.

What are you going to offer for yourself, to effect your cleansing? Only if you have first been cleansed will you be able to offer anything clean.

Let a clean priest offer himself, then, and cleanse you. That is what Christ did. He found nothing clean in human beings that he could offer on behalf of human beings, so he offered himself as a clean victim. How auspicious a victim, how genuine; and how spotless a sacrifice! What he offered was not something we had given him; rather did he offer what he took from us, but he offered it in a clean condition. He took flesh from us, and that was what he offered, but whence did he take it? From the womb of his virgin mother,[18] so that he might offer it clean for us who were unclean. He is our king and he is our priest. Let us rejoice in him.

---

17. See 1 Sm 10:1; 16:13; Ex 30:30.
18. Compare Exposition of Psalm 142,8.

Verse 3. Christ's worldwide choir

7. *Let them praise his name with choral singing.*[19] What is a choir? Many know what a choir is, and, since we are speaking in a city,[20] almost everyone here knows. A choir is a group of people singing in harmony. If we sing in a choir, we must sing in tune with the others. If one voice in a choir is off-key it jars on the ear and upsets the choir.

But now, if the voice of an inept performer disrupts the harmony of the singers, how badly does a discordant heresy disrupt the harmony of those who are praising God! The whole world is by now Christ's choir, and as Christ's choir it sings harmoniously from east to west. Let us check that statement: does Christ's choir extend so far? Yes, for another psalm says, *From the rising of the sun to its setting, let them praise the name of the Lord* (Ps 112(113):3).

8. *Let them play psalms to him on drum*[21] *and psaltery.* Why does anyone take up a drum or a psaltery? In order to praise God not only with the voice but with actions as well. When we take up a drum or a psaltery our hands keep time with our voices. It is the same for you if, when you sing "Alleluia," you also hand out bread to the hungry, clothe the naked, and welcome the traveler; then it is not only your voice that makes a sweet sound but your hands too are joining in, because your deeds are in tune with your words. You took up a musical instrument, and your fingers are in accord with your tongue.

We should not pass over in silence the mysterious symbolism of the drum and the psaltery. A drum is made by stretching skin out tightly, and in a psaltery the gut is stretched. In both instruments there is a kind of crucifixion of the flesh. There was once a certain expert player, very skilled on drum and psaltery, who testified, *The world has been crucified to me, and I to the world* (Gal 6:14). The Lord, who loves to hear your new song, wants you to pick up your psaltery and your drum,[22] for he it is who teaches you, *If anyone wants to be my disciple, let him renounce himself, take up his cross, and follow me* (Mt 16:24). Let a disciple not lay aside his psaltery, let him not discard his drum; let him be stretched upon wood, so that the concupiscence of the flesh may be dried out of him. The further

---

19. *In choro.* The primary meaning of *chorus* is a dance, accompanied by singing. But Augustine does not dwell on the aspect of dance.
20. This sermon is thought to have been preached in Carthage.
21. *Tympanum* can mean a drum or a tambourine.
22. Variant: "wants to pick you up as his psaltery or drum."

the strings are stretched, the purer the sound. How did the apostle Paul ensure that his psaltery would give a pure note? *Forgetting what lies behind and stretching out to what lies ahead, I bend my whole effort to follow after the prize of God's heavenly call* (Phil 3:13–14). He stretched forward, Christ touched him, and the sweet sound of truth rang out. *Let them play psalms to him on drum and psaltery.*

Verses 4–5. True and false glory

9. *For the Lord has conferred benefits on his people.* What greater benefit could he bestow than to die for the impious? What greater kindness than to blot out with his own blood the decree that stood against a sinner?[23] What greater favor than to say, "I do not care what you have been. Become now what you were not"? *The Lord has conferred benefits on his people* by forgiving sins and promising eternal life. He is beneficent in turning back to himself one who is turned away, in aiding one who does battle, in crowning one who conquers. *The Lord has conferred benefits on his people.*

And he will lift up the gentle to salvation. The proud are uplifted too, but not to salvation. The gentle are raised up to salvation, but the proud in death, for, while the proud exalt themselves, the Lord humbles them, but the gentle humble themselves, and the Lord exalts them. *He will lift up the gentle to salvation.*

10. *The saints will exult in their glory.* I want to say something about this, and I hope you will listen while I speak about the glory of the saints. There is no one who does not love glory. But the glory of fools, that which passes for glory in popular estimation, though tempting, is deceptive. One who is lured toward it feels that somehow, in the eyes of some at least, he must become famous. This drives people into madness: they are puffed up with self-importance, empty within and pretentious in their bearing. They even want to waste their money by hiring players, actors, gladiators,[24] charioteers. What fortunes they squander! What sums they spend! They pour out all their resources, not only those they inherited but also those of mind and spirit. They care nothing for a poor person, because the populace is not shouting to be given a pauper but is yelling that it wants a gladiator. Celebrity-seekers are unwilling to hand out money where they will not be acclaimed for it, but where they are acclaimed by frantic

---

23. See Col 2:14.
24. A *venator* could be a huntsman, or, as here, a gladiator.

crowds they become crazed themselves. All of them together go crazy: the performer, the spectators, and the donor of the games.[25]

This insane glory is censured by the Lord and merits rebuke in the eyes of the Almighty, and yet, brothers and sisters, there is a special reproof that Christ issues to his own. He tells them, "You did not give as much to me as you gave to the gladiators, and, in order to give to them, you took what rightfully belonged to me. *I was naked and you did not clothe me.*" And when they protest, *Lord, when did we see you naked, and not clothe you?* he will reply, *As long as you did not do it for one of the least of those who are mine, you did not do it for me either.* (Mt 25:43–45) You want to give fine clothes to someone you like, don't you? But how has Christ earned your dislike? You are eager to bedeck the gladiator, yet if he is beaten you may feel ashamed. Christ is never beaten, but he beat the devil, and beat him in your cause, for you and in you. You are reluctant to clothe such a victor. Why? Because there is less shouting for him, less frantic enthusiasm. And in consequence people who crave this kind of glory have nothing left in their souls.[26] As they ransack their wardrobes for clothes they can send,[27] they are emptying their very souls, leaving nothing of any value there.

11. There is no need for us to describe the manner in which the saints exult in their glory; you need only listen to the next words of the psalm: *The saints will exult in their glory, they will rejoice on their couches.* Not in theaters or amphitheaters or circuses or idle jesting or in public places but *on their couches.* What does this mean—*on their couches?* In their hearts. Listen to the apostle Paul exulting on his couch: *Our glory is this: the witness of our own conscience* (2 Cor 1:12).

On the other hand there is the opposite danger that a person may become self-complacent, proud of his state of conscience and satisfied about it. Each of us must exult with fear,[28] because what each is exulting over is the gift of God, not something he has merited. There are many self-satisfied people who congratulate themselves on their righteousness, but another page of scripture should give them pause:

---

25. On Augustine's vehemence on this subject, see the notes at Expositions of Psalms 39,8 and 93,20.
26. Literally "conscience" here and in the following sentence.
27. Variants: "clothes they can change"; "clothes that will look bright."
28. See Ps 2:11.

Who will boast of having a pure heart? Or who will claim to be clean of sin? (Prv 20:9, LXX)

There is a temperate way of glorying in your good conscience. You need to know that your faith is sincere, you need to know that your hope is determined, you need to know that your charity is unfeigned. But there are many things in you which still, perhaps, offend God's eyes. Therefore you must praise God for what he has given you, and then he will bring his gifts to perfection in you.

Verse 6. The saints praise God for his gifts

After saying, *They will rejoice on their couches*, the psalm accordingly guards us against any self-complacency by adding, *The worship of God is in their mouths*. They will rejoice on their couches, but in such fashion that they praise him who gave them the gifts that made them what they are and who called them to become what they have not become yet. To him they give thanks for the work he has begun. *The worship of God is in their mouths*. Now look at the saints. Look at their glory, and see how it is present throughout the world. Listen to how *the worship of God is in their mouths, and double-edged swords in their hands*.

The double-edged sword of God's word

12. *And double-edged swords in their hands*. What is called a *spatha* in common parlance[29] is called a *framea* here.[30] There are swords which are sharpened on one side only; these are known as *machaerae*. In our psalm, whether it is called *framea* or *rompaea*[31] or *spatha*, a sword is meant. But a mystery is latent in the description of this weapon as sharpened on both sides, or double-edged. *Double-edged swords are in their hands*, says the psalm. By double-edged swords we understand the word of the Lord. This is one single sword, but it is mentioned in the plural because of the many mouths and tongues of the saints where it is found. God's word is a sword[32] sharpened on both sides.[33] Why on both sides? Because it speaks of

---

29. A broad, blunt sword.
30. Originally a spear or javelin, *framea* meant a sword in late Latin. See the notes at Exposition of Psalm 9,8 and Exposition 2 of Psalm 36,3.
31. Also spelt *rhompaea* or *rumpia*, this was a long missile used by certain non-Roman peoples, a long Thracian spear.
32. Another word again, *gladius*.
33. See Heb 4:12; Rv 1:16.

temporal matters, and it speaks of the things of eternity. It vindicates its statements about both, and it cuts free from the world everyone whom it smites. Is not this the sword of which the Lord said, *I have come to bring not peace, but a sword* (Mt 10:34)? Consider how it came to divide, to sever. It parts the saints from the wicked, and it separates you from anything that holds you back. A son wants to serve God, but his father is not agreeable: the sword comes, God's word comes, and it divides son from father. Or a daughter wants to and her mother does not, and they are severed from each other by the sword. A daughter-in-law wants it and her mother-in-law refuses: let the double-edged sword intervene, let it come with its promise concerning both the present and the future life, a promise of the consolation of temporal things and the blissful enjoyment of those of eternity.

This is the sword sharpened on both sides, bearing temporal and eternal promises. Has it ever deceived us in any matter? Can we not see that there was once a time when the Church of God had not spread all over the world? Look, it has now. In former days it was read about but not seen; now it is plain to see, even as it is read about. Whatever is promised to us in the temporal sphere belongs to one edge of the blade; whatever is promised for eternity pertains to the other. You thus have hope for future happiness and you have the consolation of present blessings. Do not be dragged away by anyone who attempts it, be it father, mother, sister, wife, or friend. Make up your mind that no one will succeed in pulling you away, and then the double-edged sword will be useful to you. It separates you effectively, for it would be bad for you to glue yourself to these people. Our Lord came bearing this double-edged sword, promising eternal goods and fulfilling temporal promises. This is why we speak of two covenants or testaments. What were the *double-edged swords in their hands*? Both covenants belong to this double-edged sword, for the old covenant promised earthly rewards and the new covenant those of eternity. In both cases God's word has been proved true, like a twice-sharpened sword.

If it symbolizes the word of God, why is the sword said to be in the hands of the saints and not on their tongues? That is what the psalm says, *Double-edged swords in their hands.* By *in their hands* it means "in their power." They received God's word as a weapon under their own control so that they might speak it where and to whom they chose, without fear of human grandeur or contempt for poverty. They held the sword in their hands, they brandished it, turned it, and struck out with it wherever they willed. All this was within their power when they preached. If the word had not been in their hands like this, someone might have objected, "How can the word be a double-edged sword, and how can it be in their hands?" But if the word is not in their hands, how could scripture say, *The word of the Lord was committed to the hand of Haggai* (Hag 1:1)? Are we meant to think, brothers and sisters, that God inserted his word between the prophet's fingers? Why then does scripture say that it was committed to his hand? Because the preaching of the Lord's word was put into his power.

There is, finally, another way of understanding this reference to their hands. Those who spoke had God's word on their tongues, but those who wrote had it in their hands. *Double-edged swords are in their hands.*

Verse 7. The sword is wielded

13. Now you see how the saints are armed, brothers and sisters. Expect slaughter, expect glorious battles. If there is a supreme commander, there must be a soldier; if there is a soldier, there must be an enemy; if there is warfare, there will also be victory. What was their job, the job of these holy people with double-edged swords in their hands? *To wreak vengeance upon the nations.* Look around you. Has vengeance not been wreaked upon the nations? It happens every day; indeed we too share in it by speaking out. Consider how the citizens of Babylon were massacred. Double punishment is meted out to Babylon, for we find in scripture the petition, *Repay her twice over for what she has done* (Rv 18:6). Twice over—in what sense? The saints wage war, unsheathing their double-edged swords; slaughter, killings, and separations follow. But how is there a twofold punishment? When Babylon[34] had the power to persecute Christians, she was accustomed to killing bodies but did not destroy God. And now she is receiving her double punishment, for the pagans are being stamped out and the idols smashed. "How are the pagans being killed?" you will ask. How? How else but by becoming Christians? I look for a pagan and I can't find him, because he is now a Christian. That means that the pagan has died! If it is not true that pagans are killed in this way, how could Peter have been ordered, *Slay and eat* (Acts 10:13)? How else was Saul the persecutor killed and Paul the preacher raised up? I look for Saul the persecutor and I do not find him: he has been

---

34. Which symbolizes pagan, persecuting Rome.

killed. How? With a two-edged sword. But though he was slain in himself he was also brought to life in Christ. Full of confidence he tells us, *Now I live my own life no longer; it is Christ who lives in me* (Gal 2:20). And then the slaying that took place in him is carried on through him, for, having become a preacher, he took into his hand the double-edged sword *to wreak vengeance upon the nations*.

But you must not think of people being literally struck with swords or of blood being spilt or of wounds in the flesh. So, to exclude these notions the psalm continues, *And to issue reproofs among the peoples*. What is a reproof? A correction. Let the double-edged sword be active in your hands too. Do not sit idle; God gave it to you to use insofar as your strength allows. Say to your friend, "What sort of person are you, to be worshipping idols?" Say it, if there is anyone left to whom you can issue such a reproof. "What sort of person are you, to be abandoning him who made you and adoring what you have made yourself? The craftsman is nobler than what he fashions. If you would be ashamed to worship a craftsman, are you not ashamed to worship what a craftsman made?" When your friend begins to blush, when he begins to feel compunction, you have wounded him with your sword. You have pierced his heart; he is about to die, so that he may live. *Double-edged swords in their hands, to wreak vengeance upon the nations and to issue reproofs among the peoples*.

Verse 8. The fetters of restraint, of fear, of love, and of marriage

14. *To bind their kings in fetters, and their nobles in iron shackles, to enforce upon them the judgment already written*. We found it quite easy to explain how they fall under the sword in order to rise again, how people are divided from one another in order to be gathered into one, how they are wounded in order to be healed, how they die in order to live. But what are we to do with the next verse? How shall we interpret *to bind their kings in fetters*? The kings of the nations are to be fettered, and *their nobles* put into *iron shackles*.

Apply your minds, and then you will recognize in this verse something you already know. The lines which we have begun to expound are certainly obscure, but what I am going to say as I explain them is not new. It is familiar to you already, so you have no need to learn it, only to be reminded. God willed to include some obscurity in certain of his lines, not because anything new is to be dug out of them but so that what is already well known may seem fresh and be understood anew as the obscure lines are expounded. Now we know that kings have become Christians, and that nobles from gentile races have also become Christians. They do so today, they did in the past, and they will in the future; the double-edged swords do not sleep idle in the hands of the saints. How then are we to understand the fettered kings, the iron-shackled nobles?

Dearly beloved, well-instructed friends,[35] you know a relevant scriptural passage, for you have been brought up in the Church and are used to hearing readings from the divine books. You know that *God has chosen the weak things of this world to confound the strong, and the foolish things of this world to confound the wise, even the nonentities, to bring to nothing things that are.* So speaks the apostle: *Look at your own vocation, brethren; not many of you are wise in a worldly way, not many are powerful, not many noble. But it is the foolish things of this world that God has chosen, and the weak things of this world, to confound the strong; it is the lowly and contemptible things of the world that God has chosen, even the nonentities, to bring to nothing things that are.* (1 Cor 1:26–28) Christ our God came to save all, but he chose to save the emperor through a fisherman, not a fisherman through the emperor; he chose instruments that were of no importance in the world. He filled his chosen ones with his Spirit, gave them double-edged swords, and ordered them to preach the gospel throughout the whole earth. The world raged and the lion was aroused against the lamb, but the lamb proved mightier than the lion. The lion was conquered even as it roared; the lamb conquered by suffering. The hearts of men and women were turned toward reverence for Christ; kings and nobles began to be moved by the miracles they witnessed. They were taken aback by the fulfillment of prophecy, and they watched the whole human race gathering into unity under one name.

What were they to do? Many chose to embrace lowly, ignoble status. Forsaking their palaces and distributing their wealth to the poor, they ran toward perfection. To such a man, as yet imperfect, the Lord said, *If you want to be perfect, go and sell all you possess and give the money to the poor. Then come, follow me, and you will have treasure in heaven.* (Mt 19:21) Many persons of noble birth followed this call, but in so doing they ceased to be nobles of the gentiles. They chose poverty in the world but nobility in Christ. Many others hold

---

35. *Caritas vestra et eruditio,* an expansion of Augustine's frequent address to the people, "Your charity" or "Dearly beloved."

onto their noble status and retain their royal power, yet still become Christians; these are in a way fettered and iron-bound. How is that the case? Because they have accepted fetters to hold them back from unlawful deeds. The fetters are those of wisdom, the fetters of God's word.[36]

15. In that case, why are they called iron shackles? Should they not be called shackles of gold? They are iron as long as fear dominates the wearers. Let them love, and their shackles will turn to gold. Try to understand what I am saying, beloved. Just now you heard the apostle John telling us, *There is no room for fear in charity, for charity made perfect casts out fear, because fear is concerned with punishment* (1 Jn 4:18). This is the shackle made of iron. Yet if we do not begin to worship God out of fear, we shall never attain to love. Fear of the Lord is the beginning of wisdom.[37] We begin from the iron shackle but end with a golden collar, for of wisdom scripture says, *Her collar will be for you a gold adornment* (Sir 6:30, LXX).[38] Wisdom would not adorn you with a golden collar unless she had first bound you with shackles of iron. You began from fear, but you are made perfect by approaching wisdom.

How many people are there who abstain from wrongdoing only because they are afraid of hell and fear torment? They do not yet love righteousness. If they were guaranteed impunity, if they were told, "Do what you like, don't worry, you will not be punished for it," they would give free rein to their lusts to the point of indulging in the most wicked deeds. This is especially true of kings and nobles, my brothers and sisters, because no one can easily say to them, "What have you done?" If a poor man strays he soon halts his wrongdoing out of fear of other people, even if he has no fear of God, for being weak and without resources he is afraid of being dragged off to the torture. Very different is the behavior of people who are powerful in this world. If they do not fear God, of what are they afraid? But the word is preached to them, and they are smitten with the double-edged sword. They are told that there is one who will place some people at his right hand and others at his left and will say to those at his left, *Depart from me into the eternal fire which was prepared for the devil*

---

36. See Sir 6:30.
37. See Ps 110(111):10.
38. The quotation is loosely based on the Septuagint of Sirach. The Greek word here rendered "collar" can also mean "fetters."

and his angels (Mt 25:41). Such nobles do not yet love righteousness, but they are afraid of punishment; fearing punishment they have accepted fetters, and in their iron shackles they are being trained.

Some powerful man of the world comes to us. His wife has offended him, or perhaps he has cast his eyes on someone else's wife because she is more beautiful or richer than his own. He wants to divorce the wife he has, but he does not do it.[39] He listens to a servant of God, he listens to a prophet, he listens to the apostle, and he does not do it. He hears someone in whose hands is the double-edged sword telling him, "You must not do this. It is not lawful for you; God does not allow anyone to divorce his wife, apart from the case of fornication."[40] He listens to this, he is afraid, and he refrains from doing it. His nimble feet were already hastening toward a fall, but they are hindered by his fetters. He wears iron shackles, for he fears God. He is warned, "God will condemn you if you do this. He is judge over us all, he hears the sighs of your wife, and you will be held guilty in his sight." On one side concupiscence is dandling him, on the other punishment is deterring him. He was well on the way to consenting to his base desire, but his iron shackles held him back.

What is more, he may say, "I mean to practice continence henceforth, I don't want a wife any longer." You can't[41] do it. What if you want to but she doesn't? Is she to be driven to fornication by your continence? If she marries someone else during your lifetime she will be an adulteress. God does not want your gain to be balanced against such a loss. Render the marital debt. Even if you do not demand it for yourself, render it to her. God will account it perfect holiness in you if you do not demand of her what she owes you but you render to your wife what you owe to her. You are afraid, and you do not do it. Your chains are rattling. From what you hear, you understand that you are restrained by iron shackles: *Are you bound to a wife? Then do not seek to be unbound.* (1 Cor 7:27) That is hard, iron-hard. When the Lord said, *What God has joined together, no one may divide* (Mt 19:6), he showed that it is an iron bond.

In passing I want to say something about this to you who are young. Those shackles are iron-hard, so do not put your feet into them. Once you have, you will be very tightly constrained by your

---

39. Variant: "you do not do it."
40. See Mt 5:32.
41. Variant: "He can't."

fetters. The hands of your bishop consolidate them and fasten them onto you. Men come running to this place seeking to divorce their wives, only to find that they are bound more tightly. No one loosens those fetters.

What God has joined together, no one may divide. The bonds are hard: who is in any doubt about that? The apostles lamented this inflexible hardness and complained, *If things stand thus between husband and wife, it is better not to marry* (Mt 19:10). If the bonds are made of iron, you need not put your feet into them. But the Lord replied, *Not everyone can accept that. But let anyone accept it who can.* (Mt 19:11–12) *Are you bound to a wife? Then do not seek to be unbound,* for you are bound with iron fetters. *Are you free of a wife? Do not seek one* (1 Cor 7:27), do not tie yourself up in iron shackles.

Verse 9. The fulfillment of prophecy, the glory of the saints

16. *To enforce upon them the judgment already written.* This is the judgment which the saints enforce throughout the nations. Why *already written*? Because these events were described in writing long ago but are being fulfilled now. Look at what is happening today: these things were once read in prophecies, but were not happening then.

The psalm concludes, *This is the glory shared by all his saints.* Throughout the whole world, throughout all nations, this is what the saints are doing. This is how they are glorified, this is how the worship of God is in their mouths, this is how they rejoice on their couches, this is how they exult in their glory, this is how they are lifted up to salvation, this is how they sing their new song, this is how they shout "Alleluia" with their hearts, their mouths, and their lives. Amen.

Exposition of Psalm 150

A Sermon

Why are there 150 psalms?

1. The order of the psalms seems to me to be a very holy mystery,[1] and its content has not yet been revealed to me. However, since the psalms number one hundred and fifty in all, this total suggests something even to us whose minds are not keen enough to penetrate the depths of mystery concealed in their order. It does not seem presumptuous, therefore, to discuss this number, a hundred and fifty, insofar as the Lord enables us.

Let us first consider the number fifteen, which is a factor of a hundred and fifty. What fifteen represents if we count in units is a hundred and fifty if we count in tens, because ten times fifteen makes a hundred and fifty. If we count in hundreds, 1,500 is again a multiple of fifteen, because a hundred times fifteen makes 1,500. If we count in thousands, we get 15,000, again a multiple of fifteen, because a thousand times fifteen is 15,000. Well now, the number fifteen symbolizes the agreement between the two testaments. In the Old Testament we find prescriptions concerning the observance of the Sabbath, which signifies rest;[2] under the New Covenant we celebrate Sunday, the Lord's day, which stands for the resurrection. Now the Sabbath is the seventh day, but since Sunday comes after the Sabbath, what is it but the eighth day, as well as the first?[3] But it is also called the first day of the week, from which the others are numbered successively: the second, third, fourth, and so on, until the seventh, which is the Sabbath. Counting from Sunday at the beginning of the week, the following Sunday is the eighth day, the day on which the New Covenant is fully revealed, for, while the Old Covenant was in force, the New had been disguised under earthly promises.

---

1. *Magni sacramenti... secretum.* On the wide sense of the term *sacramentum* by Augustine, see the notes at Expositions of Psalms 67,16; 73,2; 126,2; 143,2.
2. See Ex 20:10–11.
3. See a note on Christian awareness of the mystique of eight at Augustine's Exposition of Psalm 6,1.

And, obviously, seven plus eight makes fifteen. The canticles which are called *Songs of Steps*[4] also number fifteen, because this was the number of the steps leading up to the temple.

Furthermore, the number fifty is pregnant with mystery, for it is made up of a week of weeks, as it were, with one extra day added to complete the number fifty. Seven times seven makes forty-nine, and then we add one to make fifty. Now the number fifty is so significant that when fifty days had passed since the Lord's resurrection, the Holy Spirit came on the fiftieth day upon those who had been gathered together in Christ.[5] Now the Holy Spirit is specially associated with the number seven in the scriptures, both in Isaiah and in the Book of Revelation. In the latter place[6] seven spirits of God are expressly mentioned, because of the sevenfold activity of the one Spirit of God. This sevenfold action is described by the prophet as follows: *The Spirit of God shall rest upon him: a spirit of wisdom and understanding, a spirit of counsel and strength, a spirit of knowledge and piety, and the spirit of fear of the Lord* (Is 11:2–3). This fear must be recognized as the chaste fear of the Lord that abides for ever and ever.[7] It must be distinguished from the servile fear which is driven out by charity made perfect,[8] for such charity makes us children of God,[9] so that we do not engage in the servile works forbidden on the Sabbath. But this same charity is given with the Spirit, for *the charity of God has been poured out into our hearts through the Holy Spirit who has been given us* (Rom 5:5), so here again the Holy Spirit is linked with the number seven.

Another point is this: the Lord divided the fifty into forty plus ten, because on the fortieth day after his resurrection he ascended into heaven, and then after ten more days had elapsed he sent the Holy Spirit, thus suggesting that the number forty signifies our temporal sojourn in this world. Now the number four is an important factor in the number forty. But both the world itself and our year are divided into four quarters, and if we add ten to forty—ten, which symbolizes our reward for fulfilling the law by good works—the resulting number, fifty, is a symbol of eternity.

---

4. That is, Psalms 119–133(120–134). See the note at Exposition of Psalm 119,1.
5. See Acts 2:1–4.
6. See Rv 4:5; 5:6.
7. See Ps 18:10(19:9).
8. See 1 Jn 4:18.
9. Or "free persons"; Latin uses *liberi* for both "free persons" and "children."

Fifty is therefore a significant number, and if we multiply it by three we get a hundred and fifty, as though the Holy Trinity had multiplied it. We can thus quite reasonably conclude that this is the reason why there are a hundred and fifty psalms.

On a certain occasion after Christ's resurrection a hundred and fifty-three fish were caught in the apostles' nets,[10] which means that three were added to our special number, one hundred and fifty. This seems to be a hint to us that three is the number into which it is thought of as divided: three times fifty. But there is another explanation for the number one hundred and fifty-three, a much more subtle and attractive explanation. If all the numbers from one to seventeen are arranged in a column and added together we arrive at the same number, one hundred and fifty-three.[11] But ten represents the law, and seven represents grace. Nothing fulfils the law except the charity which is poured out in our hearts through the Holy Spirit, who is symbolized by the number seven.

Is there only one book of Psalms or five?

2. Some people have held that the psalms constitute five books, basing their opinion on the recurrence of the words, *Amen, amen*.[12] I have tried to fathom the reason behind these divisions, but I have not found any satisfactory explanation, first, because there is no equality between the parts, either as to the length of text or as to the number of psalms in each division, as though each were to contain thirty; and, secondly, because, if these words, *Amen, amen*, mark the end of each book, surely we must ask why the fifth book, the last of all, does not end in this way.

For our part we prefer to follow the authority of the canonical scriptures, where we read, *It is written in the Book of Psalms* (Acts 1:20). This makes it clear that there is only one Book of Psalms. However, while I see that this is true, I also see that if the other opinion is sound it cannot ultimately conflict with this. It is quite possible that by some convention in Hebrew literature several books which form a single entity may be referred to as one book, even as

---

10. See Jn 21:11.
11. See Augustine's Exposition of Psalm 49,9, where he makes the same calculation, and the note there.
12. *Fiat, fiat*. These words occur at the end of Psalms 40(41), 71(72), 88(89), and 105(106).

there is one Church consisting of many churches, and one heaven of many heavens. For he who said, *My help is from the Lord, who made heaven and earth* (Ps 120(121):2), cannot have intended to exclude any part of the heavens from the Lord's creative act. Moreover, scripture tells us that *God called the firmament heaven* (Gn 1:8) and that the waters were placed above this firmament, that is, above heaven, and yet scripture cannot have been lying when it said elsewhere, *Let the waters that are above the heavens praise the name of the Lord* (Ps 148:4–5), rather than "above heaven" in the singular. Then again, we speak of the land, but in reality it consists of many lands; in everyday parlance we speak of "the whole land" and of "all the lands."

Someone might object that, although in the light of common usage the writer could be thought to have meant that there is only one book of psalms when he said, *It is written in the Book of Psalms*, it is also possible that by this expression he meant "in *a* book of psalms," that is, in one of the books among the five books of psalms. Such usage is not found elsewhere, or so rarely that we can only envisage it because a parallel text says, *As it is written in the Book of the Prophets* (Acts 7:42), which we would then have to understand as meaning that the twelve prophets are only a single book.

There are in fact people who regard all the books of the canonical scriptures as one single book because of the wonderful concord between them, a unity that can have come only from God. They accordingly interpret the statement, *At the foremost place in the book it is written of me that I should do your will* (Ps 39:8–9(40:7–8)), as a reference to the Father's creation of the world through his Son, since the account of creation in the Book of Genesis stands at the foremost place of all the scriptures. Or, perhaps better, since this text seems to be a prophecy (it says, *that I should do your will*, not "because I have done your will"), it could refer to another prophecy which also occurs in the opening chapters of Genesis: *They will be two in one flesh* (Gn 2:24). The apostle declares this to be a great mystery, understanding it of Christ and the Church.[13]

Another way of interpreting the text, *At the foremost place in the book it is written of me that I should do your will*, is to assume that the book referred to is the Book of Psalms itself, for the text continues, *O my God, this is what I want, and your law is in the midst of my heart* (Ps 39:8–9(40:7–8)). The first psalm is generally agreed to

---

13. See Eph 5:32.

have prophesied about Christ *at the foremost place in the book* when it said, *Blessed is the person who has not gone astray in the council of the ungodly, and has not stood in the way of sinners, and has not sat in the seat of pestilence, but in the law of the Lord was his will, and on his law will he reflect day and night* (Ps 1:1–2), for this comes to the same thing as the declaration, *O my God, this is what I want, and your law is in the midst of my heart.*

The next phrase, *I have freely proclaimed your righteousness in the great Church* (Ps 39:10(40:9)), is more fittingly referred to the other words of Genesis already cited, *They will be two in one flesh.*

There is special significance in the conclusion of each set of fifty psalms

3. We may interpret the phrase, *at the foremost place in the book*, in either way. But if we put our question to the Book of Psalms itself and do so by considering the psalms in sets of fifty, we receive a profound answer, one that deserves careful thought. I do not think it is an accident that the fiftieth psalm is concerned with repentance, the hundredth with mercy and judgment, and the one hundred and fiftieth with the praise of God offered by his saints; for this is the route by which we travel toward the blessed life of eternity. We begin by condemning our sins and continue by leading good lives, so that after repudiating our bad life and persevering in a good one we may deserve a life that is eternal. According to the determination of God's most secret justice and goodness, *those whom he predestined, he also called; those whom he called, he also justified; and those whom he justified, he glorified as well* (Rom 8:30). Our predestination is not something that has happened in us; it takes place secretly in God, within his foreknowledge. But in us three things happen: calling, justification, and glorification. We are called through the preaching of repentance, for the Lord began to proclaim the good news by saying, *Repent, for the kingdom of heaven has drawn near* (Mt 4:17). Then we are justified by God's merciful calling and by fear of his judgment; this is why another psalm prays, *O God, save me by your name, and judge me in your power* (Ps 53:3(54:1)), for one who has first begged to be saved does not fear being judged afterwards. Once called, we renounce the devil through repentance, so as not to remain under his yoke; once justified we are healed through God's mercy, so that we may not be afraid of his judgment; and being glorified, we make the passage to eternal life, where we praise God without end.

I think this pattern is also found in the Lord's saying, *Take note of this: I cast out demons and bring healing and wholeness today and tomorrow, and on the third day I am consummated* (Lk 13:32). Moreover, he enacted the same sequence in the three days of his passion, his rest, and his awakening; for he was crucified, he was buried, and he rose again. On the cross he triumphed over the principalities and powers,[14] in the grave he rested, in the resurrection he was filled with joy. So too in our own case: repentance crucifies us, justification brings us peace, and eternal life glorifies us. We hear the cry of repentance in the psalm, *Have mercy on me, God, according to your great mercy, and in your manifold pity blot out my iniquity* (Ps 50:3(51:1)). This same psalm offers as a sacrifice to God a troubled spirit, a heart broken and humbled.[15] But in the one hundredth psalm the song of Christ's righteousness is sung by his elect when it begins, *I will sing to you of your mercy and judgment, O Lord. I will play a psalm, and I shall find understanding in a stainless path when you come to me* (Ps 100(101):1–2), for it is by God's mercy that we are helped to do deeds of justice and to come without anxiety to his judgment. At that divine judgment all sinners are expelled from the Lord's city.[16] With that verse the one hundredth psalm ends, for this is the proclamation of eternal life.

Verses 1–2. The attributes of God which the psalm bids us praise are found in the saints themselves

4. *Praise the Lord in his saints*: this obviously means in those whom he has glorified. *Praise him in the firmament of his strength. Praise him in his mighty exploits*,[17] or, as other translators have it, *in his powerful ones*.[18] *Praise him according to the vast extent of his greatness*. All these expressions mean the same: they refer to God's saints. Remember how the apostle says that God has enabled us *to become* in Christ *the righteousness of God* (2 Cor 5:21). If God's saints are identified with his own righteousness, a righteousness he has wrought in them, why should we not also say that they are the strength of God, they are the mighty deed which he wrought in them,

---

14. See Col 2:15.
15. See Ps 50:19(51:17).
16. See Ps 100(101):8.
17. *In virtutibus eius.*
18. *In potentatibus eius.*

so that they might rise from the dead? In the resurrection of Christ himself what strikes us most of all is his power, just as his passion exhibited his weakness. As the apostle says, *Though he was crucified in weakness, he is alive by the power of God* (2 Cor 13:4), and elsewhere, *That I may know him, and the power of his resurrection* (Phil 3:10). The psalm aptly speaks of *the firmament of his strength*, for it is a manifestation of the firmament of his strength that he will never die again and that death has no more dominion over him.[19] The saints are indeed his acts of power, just as scripture says that in Christ we are the righteousness of God, for what could more plainly demonstrate the power of God in them than that they reign everlastingly, with all their enemies trampled underfoot? And again, why should we not say that they are also the vast extent of God's greatness? Not, of course, the greatness by which God himself is great, but that by which he has made them great, and so many of them, thousands upon thousands. The distinction is the same as that between the righteousness by which God himself is righteous and that which he creates in us, so that we may be his righteousness.[20]

Verses 3–4. The diversity of musical instruments represents the diversity of holiness

5. These saints are symbolized by a variety of musical instruments employed in the praise of God. The psalm has already bidden us, *Praise the Lord in his saints*, and now it proceeds to do so, indicating the saints themselves by the diverse instruments.

6. *Praise him with sound of trumpet.* This is mentioned first because of the excellent clarity of its sound. *Praise him with psaltery and lyre.* The psaltery represents someone who praises God from above, the lyre someone who offers him praise from below. Together they praise him from heavenly places and from places on earth, for he it is who made heaven and earth. As we have already explained in connection with another psalm,[21] the psaltery has its wooden sounding-chamber at the top, and to it the series of strings is attached, which gives better resonance. A lyre has its wooden sounding-chamber at the base.

---

19. See Rom 6:9. Some codices refer the sentence not to Christ but to the saints: "that they will never die again... no more dominion over them."
20. A distinction echoed by the Council of Trent, Session VI, chapter 7.
21. See Exposition of Psalm 56,16 and the note there.

7. *Praise him on the drum and with choral singing.*[22] A drum praises God when our flesh has undergone a change, and no trace of earthly corruption remains in it, for a drum is made from skin dried out and stretched firm.[23] A choir praises God when a society at peace with itself offers him praise. *Praise him with strings and organ.* The psaltery and the lyre have strings, as we have pointed out already. Strictly speaking, *organ* is a general term for any musical instrument, but a custom has become established of using the term "organ" only for those instruments that are inflated by bellows. I do not think this later usage is present in the psalm, because while "organ" is, as I have said, a Greek word common to all instruments, the kind which is inflated with bellows is given a different name by the Greeks. To call this latter an organ is more a Latin custom and found only in popular speech. When, therefore, the psalm says, *with strings and organ,* I think that *organ* must mean some musical instrument equipped with strings, for psalteries and lyres are not the only stringed instruments. Now we have already discovered an intelligible distinction between psalteries and lyres: whether the sound proceeds from below or from above. The psalm must be prompting us to look for some further meaning in this mention of strings, for strings are made from gut, which represents flesh, but flesh set free from corruption. To these strings the psalm perhaps adds *organ* to suggest that the individual strings do not sound separately but harmonize with each other in their melodious diversity, tuned to one another as they are in an organ. Even God's saints will play their different notes, different but harmonious, not clashing with each other but sweetly harmonized. This is the effect produced when many play different notes, but not in disagreement, for *star differs from star in brilliance, and so will it be at the resurrection of the dead* (1 Cor 15:41–42).

Verses 5–6. Every type of sound is included, every spirit invited to praise God

8. *Praise him on sweet-sounding cymbals, praise him with the cymbals of jubilation.* Cymbals touch each other to produce their sound, and for this reason some people have compared them to our lips. But a better way of understanding cymbals is, I think, to refer them to a particular mode of praising God whereby each person is honored not

---

22. *Choro*: see Exposition of Psalm 149,7 and the note.
23. On the symbolism of "crucified flesh" see Exposition of Psalm 149,8.

by himself but by his neighbor, so that by their mutual respect they give praise to God. The psalm rules out any idea of cymbals as mere inanimate objects by adding, *with the cymbals of jubilation.* Jubilation is wordless praise[24] that proceeds only from the soul.

There is another point that I do not think we should pass over in silence. Musicians tell us—and indeed it is obvious if we think about it—that there are three kinds of sounds: those made respectively by the voice, by the passage of air, and by percussion. Sound is produced by the voice alone when someone sings unaccompanied, using only the mouth and the windpipe. It is produced by blowing and the passage of air when a person plays the flute or some similar instrument. And it is produced by percussion in the playing of the lyre and other instruments of the same type. Our psalm has not left out any kind of sound, for it has indicated the voice by speaking of choral song, the breath or air in its mention of the trumpet, and percussion in the lyre. It seems as though the psalmist intended to suggest the mind, the spirit, and the body, though by analogy only, not in the proper sense of the words.

When, at the beginning of the psalm, he invited us to *praise the Lord in his saints,* to whom was he speaking, if not to the saints themselves? And in whom were they to praise God, if not in themselves? The psalm is as good as saying, "You are his saints, for you are his strength, but only because he deploys his strength in you. You are his powerful ones, you are the vast extent of his greatness, because of the great deeds he has wrought in you. You are the trumpet, the psaltery, the lyre, the drum, the choir, the strings, the organ, and the cymbals that sound so splendid because they are attuned to each other." You are all these instruments, and when you listen to the psalm do not think of anything in this orchestra as worthless or transitory or lacking in dignity. And since it is death to judge by the standards of the flesh, *let every spirit praise the Lord.*

Concluding prayer[25]

Let us turn to the Lord our God, our almighty Father, and from pure hearts render to him the highest and most sincere thanks that our puny strength allows. Let us entreat him with our whole hearts

---

24. Compare Expositions of Psalms 94,3 and 99,3–4.
25. Some codices prefix the words, "The prayer of Saint Aurelius Augustine, which he was accustomed to say after each sermon or exposition." Indications

so that in his unique gentleness he may accord a favorable hearing to our prayers. May he in his power cast out the enemy from our actions and thoughts, increase our faith, guide our minds, grant us to think spiritually, and bring us at last to his own beatitude. We ask this through his Son, Jesus Christ our Lord, who lives and reigns with him in the unity of the Holy Spirit, God for ever and ever. Amen.

---

of a concluding prayer are found at the Expositions of Psalms 80,22; 86,9; 128,13; 143,19.

Index of Scripture

(prepared by Michael Dolan)

(The numbers after the scriptural reference refer to the section of the work)

Old Testament

Genesis
1:8	150, 2
1:9-10	135, 7
1:22	127, 15
1:28	137, 8
2:24	138, 2; 140, 3; 142, 3; 150, 2
3:19	121, 9
3:20	126, 8
6:3	145, 10
15:6	148, 17
18:27	147, 24
22:18	147, 16; 147, 17; 147, 18; 147, 28
25:23	134, 8; 136, 18

Exodus
3:6	137, 6
3:13	121, 5
3:14	121, 5; 127, 15; 130, 12; 134, 4; 134, 6; 143, 11
3:15	121, 5; 134, 6
7:15	135, 7
33:13	138, 8
33:20.22-23	138, 8

Deuteronomy
25:4	145, 13
32:35	137, 15

Judges
6:37	137, 9
6:39	137, 9

1 Samuel
15:29	131, 18

Job
1:21	138, 17; 144, 4; 144, 22
2:9-10	133, 2
2:10	144, 18
7:1	122, 7
7:2, LXX	142, 16
28:28	135, 8
30:19	147, 24

Psalms
1:1	123, 7
1:1-2	150, 2
1:4	142, 12
1:6	141, 6; 141, 9
2:1-2	144, 17
2:8	122, 2; 126, 8; 126, 13
3:6(5)	131, 15; 138, 2
3:9(8)	145, 9
4:3(2)	139, 13
5:4-5(3)	142, 14; 143, 11
6:6(5)	138, 11
6:8(7)	149, 1
7:4-5(3-4)	130, 9
7:15(14)	139, 13
9B(10):13	123, 9
10:2(11:1)	124, 5
10:6(11:5)	134, 16; 140, 2
11:9(12:8)	139, 13
12:5(13:4)	139, 12
14(15):5	128, 6

607

15(16):5	142, 17	36(37):4	144, 3
15(16):11	139, 18	36(37):24	144, 18
17:6(18:5)	136, 5	36(37):35-36	145, 10
17:11(18:10)	137, 4	37:7(38:6)	143, 11
17:29(18:28)	138, 15; 143, 4	38:6(39:5)	127, 15; 143, 11
17:30(18:29)	134, 20	38:12(39:11)	122, 6; 122, 7; 143, 11
18:2(19:1)	121, 9; 134, 16; 143, 12	39:6(40:5)	128, 2; 146, 9
18:4-5(19:3-4)	143, 12	39:8-9(40:7-8)	150, 2
18:5(19:4)	121, 9; 134, 17	39:10(40:9)	150, 2
18:10(19:9)	127, 7	39:15(40:14)	141, 11
19:8-9(20:7-8)	146, 19	40:2(41:1)	146, 19
21:2(22:1)	140, 5; 140, 6	40:5(41:4)	128, 9; 140, 9; 140, 11
21:4(22:3)	122, 4	40:6(41:5)	137, 14; 144, 17
21:16(22:15)	142, 15	40:11(41:10)	131, 17
21:17-18 (22:16-17)	125, 10; 147, 16	41:2(42:1)	126, 12
21:17-19 (22:16-18)	140, 6	41:3(42:2)	142, 11
		41:4(42:3)	126, 6; 127, 10; 130, 12; 138, 4
21:27(22:28)	131, 24	41:4-5(42:3-4)	130, 12
21:28(22:27)	144, 10; 147, 16; 147, 17; 147, 18	41:6.12 (42:5.11)	145, 2
		42:5 (43:5)	145, 2
21:29(22:28)	147, 16	43(44):22	144, 17
21:30(22:29)	131, 24	44:3(45:2)	127, 8
24(25):1	130, 12	49(50):23	134, 11; 148, 17
24:4(25:3)	123, 9	49(50):23.16-17	134, 2
24(25):9	141, 8	50:10(51:8)	139, 15
24(25):10	137, 5; 137, 10	50:11(51:9)	122, 3
24(25):18	130, 4	50:18(51:16)	130, 4; 146, 5
26(27):4	127, 9; 143, 10	50:18-19 (51:16-17)	140, 14
26(27):9	122, 3		
27(28):3	139, 6	50:19(51:17)	130, 4; 146, 5
28(29):1	142, 6	50:3(51:1)	150, 3
29:7(30:6)	142, 13	50:5(51:3)	122, 3
29:8(30:7)	142, 13	50:7(51:5)	142, 8
31(32):4	138, 8	53:3(54:1)	150, 3
31(32):9	141, 8; 148, 3	53:8(54:6)	134, 11
32(33):1	134, 2	54:7(55:6)	121, 1
33:2(34:1)	132, 5; 138, 16; 144, 4	54:13(55:12)	142, 4
33:6(34:5)	144, 3	54:13-14 (55:12-13)	142, 4
33:12(34:11)	143, 9		
33:13(34:12)	143, 9	55(56):12	134, 11
33:14-15 (34:13-14)	143, 9	56:5(57:4)	131, 15; 143, 17
		56:7(57:6)	142, 7
33:15(34:14)	143, 9; 147, 16	60:3(61:2)	122, 2
33:16(34:15)	137, 11	61:5(62:4)	132, 13
33:17(34:16)	137, 11	61:6(62:5)	138, 20
33:19(34:18)	137, 11; 146, 5	62:2(63:1)	148, 10
35:7(36:6)	124, 6	64:2(65:1)	136, 1
35:7-8(36:6-7)	145, 13	64:4(65:3)	136, 21
35:9(36:8)	122, 11	67:10(68:9)	132, 10
35:10(36:9)	137, 13; 142, 15; 143, 4	68:5(69:4)	142, 8; 147, 27
35:10.12-13 (36:9.11-12)	121, 3	68:16(69:15)	142, 13
		68:30(69:29)	122, 11
35:12-13 (36:11-12)	131, 14	71(72):3	124, 4
		71(72):11	144, 17

72(73):1	146, 7	121(122):2	123, 4; 124, 3; 136, 4
72(73):1-3	124, 2	121(122):3	124, 3; 146, 11
72(73):11-13	124, 1	122(123):4	131, 24
72(73):16	138, 9	125(126):4	147, 26
72(73):20	131, 8; 147, 7	125(126):6	127, 10
74:4(75:3)	140, 25	126(127):2	127, 10; 138, 4
74:7-8(75:6-7)	141, 4	126(127):4	127, 2; 132, 2
75:5(76:4)	124, 4	129(130):3	128, 9
75:6(76:5)	131, 8	132(133):1	133, 3
75:12(76:11)	132, 2	132(133):3	133, 2
76:3(77:2)	137, 18; 142, 15; 143, 11	138(139):2	126, 5
77(78):25	143, 10	138(139):7-10	142, 16
79:8(7)	127, 9	139:6(140:5)	141, 9
80:2(81:1)	143, 6	140(141):10	141, 19
81(82):1.6	134, 9	141:6(142:5)	145, 7; 145, 11
81(82):1.6-7	135, 2	142(143):6	148, 10
81(82):2	135, 2	143(144):11-14	136, 16
82:19(83:18)	143, 12	143(144):15	136, 16
83:3(84:2)	126, 12	148:4-5	150, 2
83:5(84:4)	121, 3; 131, 10; 133, 1; 141, 19; 144, 8; 145, 7; 147, 3; 148, 17		

Proverbs

83:6(84:5)	126, 6
83:7(84:6)	126, 6
83:11(84:10)	146, 19
84:13(85:12)	142, 11
86:4(87:3)	142, 3
86(87):5	142, 3
87:5-6(88:4-5)	142, 8
95(96):1	149, 2; 149, 3
95(96):4-5	135, 3
100(101):1-2	150, 3
101:27-28 (102:26-27)	121, 6; 138, 8; 146, 11
101:28(102:27)	143, 18
102(103):14	142, 12
103(104):24	135, 6; 142, 12
103(104):30	142, 12
109(110):4	131, 18
109(110):7	123, 7
111(112):10	137, 14
112(113):3	149, 7
112(113):7-8	140, 21
113(115):1	142, 18
113(115):17	144, 5
114(116):3-4	136, 5; 137, 12
115(116):15	140, 21
118(119):67	147, 27
118(119):71	147, 27
119(120):2	123, 6
119(120):3-4	139, 14
119(120):4	143, 13
120(121):1	124, 4
120(121):1-2	124, 4
120(121):2	150, 2
120(121):4	126, 3

1:28	144, 22
3:16, LXX	143, 18
5:22	130, 2; 139, 9
8:3, LXX	126, 13
8:27-28, LXX	137, 4
8:30, LXX	137, 4
9:8	140, 13
12:23, LXX	121, 9
17:6, LXX	143, 18
18:3	129, 1; 142, 13
20:9, LXX	149, 11
21:20, LXX	141, 1
27:2	144, 1; 144, 7

Ecclesiastes

1:2-3	141, 17
1:18	122, 6
6:9	141, 17

Song of Songs

2:5, LXX	139, 14; 143, 13
2:6	143, 18
4:8, LXX	134, 18
6:8	141, 7
8:6	121, 12

Wisdom

1:5	138, 26
1:9	134, 16
5:3	122, 9

5:3-5	122, 9	58:9, LXX	137, 7
5:6	142, 3; 148, 16	64:4	127, 16
5:6-8	122, 9	65:24	137, 7
5:8	134, 20	66:1	121, 9
5:9	142, 16	66:1-2	131, 4
7:22	147, 22		
7:24-25	141, 15		
7:27	138, 8		

Jeremiah

2:29	142, 6
6:14	147, 16
9:5	139, 13
16:19	136, 21
17:16	137, 17; 140, 23

8:1	141, 4; 141, 15; 147, 22
9:15	127, 16; 141, 19; 145, 6; 147, 22
11:21	146, 11

Sirach

3:17	125, 10
3:20	130, 7; 130, 12
3:22	130, 13
4:36	147, 13
5:8-9	144, 11
6:30, LXX	149, 15
9:20	141, 9
11:30	142, 6
15:9	134, 2; 146, 3
16:30	143, 11
17:26	138, 26; 142, 13; 144, 5
23:25	138, 11
33:5	132, 12
39:15-16(20-21)	141, 19

Ezekiel

14:17.14.16	132, 5
33:11	144, 11

Daniel

3:57-90	144, 13
10:11.19	132, 5

Hosea

14:10	146, 7

Joel

2:32	140, 3

Isaiah

1:3	126, 11
2:5.6	134, 22
3:14	121, 9
5:6	134, 17
5:18	130, 2; 139, 9
6:10	138, 8
10:22	131, 17
11:2-3	150, 1
22:13	128, 4; 128, 8
25:13, LXX	131, 3
29:13	148, 17
40:6	131, 28; 146, 16
48:22, LXX	137, 3
52:7	140, 8
52:15	132, 2
53:1	135, 9
53:2	127, 8
54:1	134, 26
54:13	134, 22
56:7	130, 3
57:21, LXX	137, 3
58:3	142, 6

Habakkuk

2:4	124, 4; 131, 16; 146, 6

Zephaniah

2:11	134, 24; 144, 17

Haggai

1:1	149, 12

Zechariah

1:3	144, 11

Malachi

1:2-3	126, 8; 136, 18
3:7	142, 13; 144, 11
4:2	148, 16

New Testament

Matthew

3:2	137, 6
3:7-9	131, 13
3:12	128, 7
4:17	150, 3
5:3	141, 5
5:5	122, 6
5:6	122, 12; 125, 6; 131, 24; 139, 17; 144, 22; 145, 17; 147, 20; 148, 10
5:8	123, 2; 130, 8; 139, 18
5:9	124, 10; 127, 13
5:10	145, 16
5:20	146, 17
5:22	129, 5; 140, 18
5:25	128, 4
5:44	132, 8; 132, 13; 138, 27
6:2.4	142, 15
6:3	136, 15
6:5-6	141, 3
6:9	142, 6
6:10	147, 1
6:12	129, 3; 129, 4; 140, 18; 142, 6; 147, 13
6:26	145, 14
6:33	143, 18
7:7	139, 17
7:13	145, 19
7:16	149, 2
7:21	128, 13
7:22	146, 10
7:23	138, 26; 141, 6; 146, 10
8:11-12	134, 7
8:29	130, 1
9:15	127, 12; 142, 2
10:16.28	140, 20
10:19-20	141, 5
10:22	141, 6
10:23	139, 16; 141, 11
10:24	126, 4
10:28	130, 10; 141, 4; 141, 13
10:29.31	145, 14
10:30	145, 14
10:32	141, 4
10:33	141, 9
10:34	143, 17; 149, 12
10:42	125, 12; 140, 8
11:11	140, 26
11:12	147, 27
11:15	134, 24
11:17	128, 1
11:21	147, 24
11:25	137, 2; 141, 19; 144, 13
11:28	139, 13
11:30	125, 6
12:48	127, 12
12:48-50	127, 12
13:12	146, 10
13:24-25.27-28	149, 3
13:25.26-27	139, 4
13:26	128, 8
13:30	147, 19; 149, 3
13:36	149, 3
13:37-38	149, 3
13:39	128, 7; 128, 12; 128, 13
15:10-11	125, 6
15:11	125, 7
15:19-20	125, 7
16:16-17	138, 22
16:22	126, 4; 138, 22
16:23	126, 4; 138, 22
16:24	149, 8
17:23-26	137, 16
19:6	138, 2; 140, 3; 149, 15
19:10	149, 15
19:11-12	149, 15
19:16	136, 13
19:16-21	146, 16
19:17	136, 13; 144, 3
19:20	136, 13
19:21	136, 13; 149, 14
19:23	146, 16
19:24	132, 4
19:26	146, 16
19:28	121, 9; 126, 5; 144, 6
20:22	123, 7; 126, 4
20:22-23	126, 5
20:27	146, 16
20:28	137, 4
22:13	130, 2; 139, 15
22:40	125, 15; 140, 2
23:3	128, 6
23:9	127, 12
23:26	125, 5
23:37	121, 3
24:12	131, 13; 138, 14; 141, 16; 147, 9
24:12.13	139, 11
24:13	131, 13; 138, 14
24:14	134, 17
24:23-24	147, 18
24:35	122, 4
24:40	132, 12
24:40-41	132, 4
25:8	147, 11
25:9	147, 11
25:10	147, 11
25:11	147, 13

25:21.23	139, 15	16:9	121, 9; 146, 17
25:30	139, 15	16:10.12	136, 2
25:34	141, 4; 141, 10; 144, 15; 145, 20	16:19	132, 4
		16:24.28	147, 17
25:34-35.37.40	121, 9	16:26	145, 7
25:35.37.40	140, 7; 148, 17	16:29-31	147, 17
25:41	138, 7; 141, 10; 144, 12; 148, 11; 149, 15	16:31	147, 17
		17:34	132, 4
25:41.34	129, 10	18:3	131, 23
25:43-45	149, 10	18:4-5	131, 23
26:34	138, 21	18:11	140, 8
26:39	144, 19	18:12	146, 17
27:4	146, 20	18:13	128, 9
27:40:42	134, 22	18:14	134, 20
28:20	125, 2; 140, 7; 147, 18; 148, 17	18:27	132, 4
		20:35-36	144, 6
		20:37-38	144, 5
		21:18	141, 13
Mark		22:33	138, 21; 138, 22
6:11	126, 10	22:44	140, 4
6:18	140, 26	22:62	138, 21; 140, 24
9:47	127, 7	23:34	124, 7; 132, 8; 134, 22
10:18	134, 3; 134, 4	23:43	147, 17
10:26-27	136, 13	24:21	147, 17
10:30	143, 18	24:39	147, 17
11:17	130, 3	24:39.41	147, 17
12:30	140, 2	24:44	147, 17
12:31	140, 2	24:45-46	147, 17
14:34	142, 9	24:46	147, 18
		24:46-47	147, 18
		24:47	147, 18
Luke			
2:14	125, 11; 134, 11; 139, 8; 149, 5	**John**	
5:32	147, 24	1:1	123, 2; 124, 4; 130, 10; 144, 9
6:25.21	137, 12		
6:30	146, 17	1:1-3	130, 9; 148, 7; 149, 1
6:37-38	143, 7	1:1.3.14	134, 5
6:38	143, 8	1:3	139, 3; 149, 4
6:45	134, 4	1:10	141, 15; 142, 16; 143, 4
7:39	125, 5; 140, 8	1:14	121, 5; 123, 2; 129, 7; 130, 9; 148, 8; 149, 4
7:41-47	140, 8		
9:26	141, 9	1:17	123, 14
10:7	146, 16	1:21	132, 5; 133, 2
10:17	130, 8; 146, 10	1:33	131, 14; 131, 27
10:20	130, 8; 146, 10	1:47	121, 8
10:33	125, 15	2:19	126, 2
10:35	125, 15	3:13	122, 1
11:41	125, 5	3:29	131, 14; 133, 1; 139, 15
12:4	142, 6	3:30	132, 11
13:32	150, 3	4:6	126, 5; 135, 7
14:11	134, 20	5:5.7	132, 6
15:12	123, 9; 131, 12; 138, 9	5:35	131, 27
15:18	138, 5	6:41	131, 24; 143, 10
15:20	138, 5	6:44	134, 22

Index of Scripture

6:45	134, 22	10:13	123, 5; 149, 13
6:51	138, 1	14:14	143, 12
6:56	135, 9	15:9	123, 2
8:31-32	123, 2	17:27-28	137, 2
8:33	148, 17		
8:34	142, 8		
8:39	131, 20; 148, 17	## Romans	
8:44	121, 3; 131, 14; 133, 1	1:1	122, 5
8:48	136, 7	1:3	139, 3
8:48.49	125, 15	1:17	124, 4; 131, 16; 146, 6
8:49	136, 7	2:5-6	144, 11
8:50	137, 15	2:8-9	133, 1
9:39	134, 22	3:1-2	137, 9
10:9	126, 13	3:23	134, 22
10:11-12	141, 11	4:3	148, 17
10:18	138, 21	4:17	140, 21
10:30	138, 3; 142, 3	5:3	136, 5; 138, 20
10:34-35	135, 2	5:3-5	138, 20; 139, 14
11:25	144, 5	5:5	133, 1; 143, 2; 147, 14; 150, 1
12:24-25	140, 25		
12:31	147, 1	5:8-9	146, 4
12:32	140, 25	5:14	138, 2
12:35	138, 22	6:6	140, 5; 140, 6
13:1	138, 8; 140, 25	6:9	126, 7; 130, 4; 131, 15
13:36	140, 24	6:21	125, 3
14:6	123, 2; 138, 30	7:14	125, 2
14:8	134, 11	7:22	140, 15
14:9	127, 8	7:22-23	134, 12
14:21	139, 18	7:23	140, 15; 141, 17
14:28	138, 3	7:23-24	147, 26
14:30	140, 3; 142, 8; 147, 27	7:23-25	139, 11; 146, 6
14:30.31	137, 16	7:24	134, 12; 140, 16
14:31	142, 8; 147, 27	7:24-25	140, 15
15:1.5	145, 11	7:25	134, 12; 147, 26
15:5	130, 6	8:10	143, 6; 145, 3
15:15	122, 5	8:10-11	127, 16; 143, 6; 146, 6
16:32	138, 22	8:22.20	125, 2
16:33	123, 6	8:23	134, 18; 140, 16
17:24	126, 4; 148, 8	8:23-24	125, 2
		8:23-25	145, 3
		8:24	122, 1
## Acts of the Apostles		8:24-25	125, 2; 127, 5; 129, 10; 144, 23
1:20	150, 2		
2:21	140, 3	8:25	142, 14
2:28	139, 18	8:26	146, 1
2:37	138, 8	8:28	124, 9
2:38	131, 17; 138, 8	8:30	147, 24; 147, 26; 150, 3
2:45	132, 2	8:31-32	143, 10
4:32	131, 5; 132, 2; 132, 6; 132, 12	9:5	144, 2; 145, 9
7:42	150, 2	9:12	134, 8; 136, 18
7:49	121, 9	9:13	126, 8; 136, 18
7:51	132, 8	9:27	131, 17
7:60	132, 8	10:2	142, 5
9:4	122, 1; 123, 1; 138, 2; 140, 3; 140, 7; 141, 11; 142, 3; 147, 26; 148, 17	10:3	124, 6; 142, 5
		10:4	139, 3
		10:8	123, 2

613

10:13	140, 3	10:31	146, 2
10:15	140, 8	10:32	141, 7
11:2.1	134, 22	10:33	121, 12
11:17-18	134, 7	11:30	147, 11
11:25	147, 28	12:8-10	135, 8; 146, 10
11:25-26	138, 8	12:8-11	143, 3
11:32	138, 9	12:12	142, 3
11:33-36	138, 8	12:21.17	130, 6
12:5	147, 7; 147, 25	12:27	127, 3; 138, 2; 140, 3
12:12	127, 5; 127, 10; 131, 16; 145, 2	12:31	141, 7
		12:31-13:1	146, 10
12:19	137, 15	13:1.3	121, 10
13:10	140, 2; 143, 2; 143, 16	13:1-3	141, 7
14:8	144, 5	13:2-3	146, 10
14:9	144, 5	13:12	130, 14
		14:20	130, 12
		15:19	127, 16; 147, 3

1 Corinthians

		15:26	127, 16
1:13	124, 6	15:26.54-55	148, 4
1:23-24	122, 5	15:28	124, 8
1:25	126, 5	15:32	128, 4; 128, 8; 145, 19
1:26-28	149, 14	15:33	145, 19
1:28	140, 21	15:33-34	128, 4
2:2	130, 10	15:41-42	150, 7
2:9	127, 16	15:46	136, 18
2:13-14	127, 1	15:47-49	136, 18
3:2	130, 9	15:50	136, 18
3:6	124, 6; 132, 4; 134, 16	15:51	126, 7
3:9	145, 11	15:53	140, 16; 145, 3
3:9-10	134, 16	15:55	123, 4; 125, 14; 127, 16; 143, 9
3:11	121, 4		
3:17	121, 4; 122, 4; 126, 3; 130, 1; 137, 4		

2 Corinthians

4:3	147, 13	1:12	140, 13; 149, 11
4:3-4	141, 8	2:13	141, 19
4:5	148, 16	2:15	134, 24
4:7	147, 13	2:16	139, 14
6:7	145, 15	4:5	146, 16
7:3	121, 10	4:7	141, 1
7:7	121, 10	4:16	131, 1; 134, 18
7:27	121, 10; 149, 15	5:1	121, 3
7:29-32	147, 4	5:6	148, 4
7:31-32	132, 4	5:6.7	123, 2
8:2	147, 24	5:21	150, 4
8:4	135, 3	6:10	127, 5; 138, 20
8:5-6	134, 9; 135, 3; 135, 9; 145, 12	7:5	142, 4
9:7	134, 16; 146, 18	8:14	121, 9
9:9	145, 13	8:15	121, 9
9:9-10	126, 11	9:6	125, 11
9:11	121, 9; 146, 16	10:3	141, 15
9:26-27	140, 16	11:2	147, 10
10:4	136, 21; 140, 19	11:3	126, 3
10:11	134, 21; 143, 1	11:14	134, 20
10:17	147, 25	11:29	141, 19
10:20	135, 3		

12	144, 19	6:5-7	124, 7
12:7	130, 7	6:12	136, 8; 139, 4; 141, 14; 142, 16; 143, 4; 143, 18
12:7-9	130, 7		
12:8-9	146, 1		
13:4	150, 4		

Philippians

1:21	121, 13
1:23	121, 13; 141, 18; 147, 17
1:23-24	145, 17
1:24	141, 18
2:6	121, 5; 126, 5; 130, 9; 138, 3
2:7	138, 3
2:7-9	126, 5
2:12	142, 10
2:13	142, 10
2:15-16	146, 9
3:5	147, 25
3:6	147, 25
3:9	124, 6; 142, 5
3:10	150, 4
3:12	142, 6
3:13-14	149, 8
3:13	130, 14
3:13-14	130, 14
3:15	130, 14
3:19	145, 12
3:20	141, 15; 142, 7
4:7	131, 10

Galatians

1:10	121, 12
1:15-16	138, 18
1:22-24	141, 7
2:20	142, 3; 149, 13
3:6	148, 17
3:16	142, 3; 147, 28
3:21	129, 3
3:21-22	143, 2
3:27	131, 27; 142, 3
3:29	134, 7; 142, 3
4:7	122, 5
4:10-11	126, 2
4:19	126, 8; 147, 14
4:27	134, 26
5:17	134, 12; 140, 16; 143, 5; 143, 6; 147, 20
5:18	143, 6
5:19-21	143, 6
6:1	129, 4
6:2	129, 4; 132, 9
6:4	140, 13; 147, 11
6:9-10	125, 11
6:14	121, 12; 149, 8

Colossians

1:24	142, 3
2:3	135, 8
3:1-3	122, 1; 142, 7
3:3	121, 12; 122, 8; 139, 17; 141, 15; 141, 17
3:3-4	148, 16
3:4	122, 9
4:2-4	140, 1

Ephesians

2:1-3	136, 8
2:2	141, 14; 148, 9
2:8	142, 10; 144, 10
2:8-10	137, 18
2:9	142, 10; 144, 10
2:10	142, 10; 144, 10
2:14	124, 10; 126, 2
3:17	122, 4
3:20	147, 22
4:2-3	143, 2
4:27	141, 3
5:8	136, 8; 139, 4; 139, 14; 139, 18; 141, 14; 142, 16; 143, 4
5:14	131, 8
5:27	132, 9; 147, 23
5:29	140, 16
5:30	127, 3
5:31-32	138, 2
5:32	142, 3
6:5	124, 7

1 Thessalonians

4:16	143, 14
4:16-17	143, 9
5:6-7	131, 8

2 Thessalonians

3:2	139, 1

1 Timothy

1:5	140, 2
1:13	147, 26

1:16	147, 26	4:6	130, 14
4:4	125, 6; 141, 1	4:15	143, 11
4:8	143, 18		
5:5	131, 23	**1 Peter**	
5:6	131, 23		
5:18	145, 13	1:5	144, 23
6:7-10	136, 14	1:18	146, 18
6:17	132, 4; 136, 13	2:5	121, 4
6:17-19	131, 26; 132, 4	2:21	127, 8
6:18-19	136, 13	2:22-23	137, 15
		4:17	147, 27
2 Timothy		4:17-18	147, 27
		5:5	130, 14
2:19	123, 5; 126, 3		
3:12	127, 16	**2 Peter**	
4:7	132, 6		
4:8	141, 19	1:19	142, 14; 143, 11
		2:4	148, 9
Titus			
1:15	125, 6; 141, 1	**1 John**	
		2:1-2	138, 30
		3:2	122, 8; 139, 18
Hebrews		3:4	129, 5
5:12	130, 12	3:15	138, 26; 141, 11
12:6	122, 10	4:16	149, 4
		4:18	127, 7; 149, 15
James			
1:19	139, 15	**Revelation**	
2:13	143, 7; 143, 8; 147, 12; 147, 13; 147, 17	18:6	149, 13
		22:15	147, 16

Index

(prepared by Joseph Sprug)

The first number in the Index is the Psalm number.
The number after the colon is a paragraph number.
Different expositions in the same heading are separated by a semicolon.
Biblical texts/words are in italics.

Aaron, 132:7
Abel, 128:2; 142:3
Abraham, 121:5; 128:2; 131:13,20; 134:6,7,25; 137:6; 139:3; 142:3; 143:18; 147:16,17,28; 148:17
Absalom, 142:2
actions, *See* human acts.
Adam and Eve, 122:6; 125:15; 126:7; 133:2; 132:10; 137:13; 142:6,16
   Christ and his Church, 127:11
   Christ foreshadowed by Adam, 138:2
   Church prefigured by Eve, 126:8; 138:2
   Eve: *curse God, and die*, 133:2
adoption, 136:1; 137:13
advice as gift, 125:13
affections, 121:11; 123:1; 138:18; 134:18,19; 145:15
affluence, *See* wealth.
agonistici, 132:6
Alleluia, 148:2; 149:2
almsgiving, 125:5,12,13; 136:13; 146:17; 147:13
Amorites, 134:20; 135:9
amphitheatre, 147:21
angel(-s), 122:4; 126:3; 128:12,13; 130:9; 134:5,8,9; 135:3; 137:3,4; 141:14; 146:2; 148:10
anguish: *I have found anguish...*, 137:12
animals, 144:13; 145:13; 148:3
anthropomorphism, 130:12
Antichrist, 128:13
apocrypha, 130:7
apostasy: persecutions and, 140:23
apostles, 121:9; 122:4; 126:2,9,10,11,12; 132:2; 138:20; 142:6; 143:18; 144:2
   born from the prophets, 126:11; 127:2
   bridegroom's children, 142:2
   Church and, 127:12
   friends become exceedingly honorable, 138:23

heavens, 143:12
   powers; miracles, 130:5
Aristotle, 140:19
Arius, 124:5; 149:4
ark, 127:13; 128:2; 130:1; 131:15; 147:4
arrows, 126:9,13; 127:2; 139:14
ashes, 147:24
ass: symbol of God's people, 126:11
astrology, 128:9; 140:9
authority, 124:7
avarice, 128:4,5; 136:9; 143:5

baby(-ies), 130:9,13
Babylon, 121:4; 125:3; 136:1-14,20,21,22; 138:18; 147:5,7,26; 148:4; 149:13
baptism, 131:14,27,28; 134:21; 135:8,9; 138:8; 142:3; 145:9,16
barren woman, 127:2
Bashan, 134:20
Bathsheba, 126:2
beard, 132:7,8,9,12
beasts, 134:18
beatific vision, 147:3,24
beatitude, 135:1; 139:2; 150:8
beauty, 138:29; 144:13,15; 148:15
bed, 132:4
beggars, 125:12; 140:12
being: absolute, 121:6
Being-Itself, 121:5; 134:4
bellows, 150:7
Bible: all books as one book, 150:2
   double-edged sword, 143:17
   letters from home, 149:5
   obscure passages in, 146:12,13
   two testaments (number 15), 150:1
   See also psalms; words of God
birds, 127:15
bishops, 126:3; 128:4
blessing, 128:13; 132:1,2; 133:3
brothers who live in unity, 132:13

Come now ..., 133:1
blindness, 145:17
body and soul, 141:19; 145:3,4,5
   See also human body; soul
bone: *not hidden from you* [God], 138:20,21
   strength, 138:20
bread: nourishment from milk, 130:9,11
bread of sorrow, 127:10
breadcrumbs, 147:25
bride and bridegroom, 122:5; 147:18
brood of vipers, 131:13
brothers: *dwell together in unity*, 132:1,5,7,10; 133:3
   like oil flowing down upon the beard, 132:7,9
burden: law to *bear one another's burdens*, 129:4,5; 132:9

Caecilian, 149:4
Cain, 142:3
calling, 150:3
Canaan, 134:20
captivity, 125:10; 147:5; 148:4
carnally-minded, 136:18
cartwheel, 132:12
Catholic Church, 130:9; 140:18; 145:16; 149:3
cattle, 146:18
cave, 141:17
centurion, faith of, 134:7
chaff, 121:8; 130:13
change, 121:6; 131:18
charity, 121:10,12,13; 125:12; 127:13; 128:13; 131:13,26; 132:12; 138:14; 140:2; 141:18; 142:5; 143:7; 147:13,14,23; 149:2,11
   blessing God, 133:1
   dwell together in unity, 132:1,2
   fullness of the law, 140:2; 141:7; 143:2,16
   if I have no love..., 146:10
   law: *bear one another's burdens*, 129:4; 132:9
   one with Christ, 140:3
   unconquered, 132:8
   See also love
chastity, 147:11
children, 127:15; 131:19
   children's children, 127:16
   increase and multiply, 137:8
   inheritance of the Lord, 126:9
   of God, 135:8; 139:18; 147:14,23; 150:1
choir, 149:7; 150:7
chrism, 149:6
Christian life, 121:12
   contempt, 122:8
   daily closer to Christ, 138:21
   early Church: common ownership, 131:5
   focus on gifts *entrusted to you*, 130:13
   hear Christ speaking in our voices, 140:3
   I live my own life no longer..., 142:3

lead me in the eternal way, 138:30
   long for Christ's friendship, 131:6
   nailed to cross with Christ, 140:5
   pilgrimage, 122:2
   rise before the light, 126:4,5
   sadness and, 138:20
   show me the way..., 142:15
   sides of your house, 127:11
   straining to what lies ahead, 130:14
   temptation; trial, 122:7
   union with the Word, 130:10
   worldly happiness and, 126:7
   See also Church; spiritual life
Christians, 134:18; 136:17; 149:6
   Christ's mother, 127:12
   confession of Christ's name, 140:26
   Jews as elders, 136:18
Church, 121:5; 122:1,5; 123:5; 125:9; 131:15,21; 132:12; 136:20; 137:1; 146:19; 147:16,18,20; 149:3,4; 150:2
   body joined to Christ the head, 139:2
   body, temple, house, city, 131:3
   born from side of Christ, 126:7
   both below and on high, 137:4
   bride and bridegroom, 147:18
   choice: member or enemy, 139:2
   Christ builds his own house, 126:2
   Christ prays when members pray, 140:7
   Christ the head of, 132:7
   Christ's apparel, 147:23
   Christ's body is holy, 138:2
   Christ's brothers, sisters, mother, 127:12
   commingling of the wicked and the good, 128:8
   Eve as type of, 126:8
   God's house, 131:10,13
   heart of the, 140:7
   Jesus, head of his body, 142:3
   labor pains for her children, 126:8
   members as feminine, 147:10
   members of his body, 127:3
   mixture of good and bad members, 138:29,31
   mother of heretics, 130:11
   numbers beyond reckoning, 128:2
   persons from O.T. and, 128:2
   rulers, 132:4
   sinners in the midst of, 138:26
   symbol: priestly garments, 132:9
   tongues of every nation, 147:19
   two in one flesh, 138:2
   two types in, 134:16
   two will be in the field, 132:4
   unity, 121:9,13; 141:7
   unity: tearing apart bond of, 138:26,27
   very often have they attacked me, 128:2,3,6,7
   whole personified, 134:7

widowed state, 131:23; 145:18
wife and children as identical, 127:12
wife of Christ, 127:11
Zion, 128:10
Church year, 148:1
Circumcellions (Circellions), 132:3,6
city, 121:4,12; 126:13; 138:26
clouds, 134:13,17; 146:15
coals, burning, 139:14,15
cold, 125:10; 147:22,26
comfort, 125:4
commandments, 146:16
  God's paths, 139:9; 141:6,7
  love in keeping, 139:18
  reward for keeping, 131:19
  ten-stringed psaltery, 143:16
common life, 131:5
communion of saints, 126:3; 147:10
  compassion, 121:11; 122:1
concupiscence, 149:15
conduct of life, 122:9; 133:2
confession, 121:8; 138:26; 140:9; 142:12; 146:14
  door to restrain my lips, 140:6
  fills earth and heaven, 148:15
  God's mercy and truth, 137:5
  goodness of the creation, 135:4
  mercy and, 135:4
  not made by dead person, 142:13
  sins or praise, 135:1; 137:2; 139:9; 141:19; 144:13
  works of the Lord, 144:13
conscience, 125:8; 129:2; 140:13,14; 147:11,12; 149:11
consent, 128:4,7,8; 129:4; 139:12; 146:6
consolation, 125:4
constancy, 138:20; 139:14
contempt, 122:8,10; 125:1
continence, 149:15
conversion of life, 125:2; 139:10,14; 144:11
  from evil to good, 124:10
converts, 134:22,25; 149:13,14
cords: symbol of sin, 130:2; 139:9
correction, 140:13,14,17; 149:13
couches, 149:11
courage, 137:12; 138:21
covenant, 131:20
  old and new, 149:1,12
coveting, 147:10
craftsman, 149:13
creation, 134:13,14,15; 140:10; 142:10; 144:6,7,8; 145:12,14; 148:7,8; 149:4,6; 150:2
  confession: goodness of God, 135:4
  do not despise works of your hands, 137:18
  everything is good, 125:6
  everything made through him, 139:3
  exceedingly good, 134:3
  God *alone does wonderful deeds*, 135:4,5
  groaning in travail, 125:2

  he made whatever he wanted, 134:10
  heavens made by God's intelligence, 135:6,8
  intricate; supremely ordered, 144:13
  love God's work; hate sinful work of men, 139:2
  praising God, 128:5
  works of the Lord, 144:13
creatures, 122:5; 145:5,13; 148:9,13
  minute, 148:10
  real existence, 134:4
  sing hymns of praise, 144:13
Crispina, Saint, 137:3,7,14,17
crucifixion, 149:8
  See also under Jesus Christ.
curia, 121:7
curse, 132:13; 133:2
cymbals, 150:8

dance: refusing to, 128:1
Daniel, 132:5
darkness, 136:8; 138:15,16,17,18; 139:4; 140:10,11; 141:14; 142:8,16; 143:4
David, King, 128:13; 131:2-4,18,19,27; 139:3; 142:2,16; 143:1,2; 144:2
daytime, 133:2
dead, 138:26
  miracle: raising the dead, 130:6
death, 123:4,5,13; 125:4,14; 129:1,8; 141:18; 143:9; 145:7; 148:4,11
  abolished in Christ, 130:11
  fallen asleep, 147:11
  fear of, 138:21; 140:20,21
  last enemy, 127:16
  power of love, 121:12
  soul cannot be killed, 130:10
  See also immortality; resurrection of the body; soul
debt: *You will repay my debt, Lord*, 137:16
debt-collectors, 146:17
deer: crossing a strait, 129:4
delight, 138:14; 140:15; 146:3
demons, 130:1; 135:3
Deo gratias, 132:6
depths, 129:1; 148:9
desire, 121:1; 122:1,4,12; 134:12; 137:9; 143:6; 146:1; 147:10
  betrayed by, 139:12
  devil's door, 141:4
  earthly, 141:17
despair, 144:11,24
detachment, 138:18
devil, 121:8; 125:2; 126:2; 127:16; 128:13; 130:7; 131:3,14; 132:6; 133:1; 134:20; 135:9; 136:7,8,9,10; 139:4,7,8,11,12; 140:20; 141:3,4,14,15; 142:7,16; 143:1,2,4,5; 144:19; 148:2,9; 149:6,10; 150:3
dew of Hermon, 132:11

disappointment: God's special love, 127:1
disasters, 136:7
disciples, 149:8
    multitude of, 138:24
    terrified during Christ's passion, 138:22
    thought of Christ as man only, 138:22
discipline, 124:7; 140:16; 148:11
disgrace, 122:9,10
divinization, 130:10
divorce, 149:15
Donatists, 131:14; 145:16; 147:18
Donatus, 124:5; 132:6; 149:4
dove, 127:13; 130:5; 138:15
drachma, 138:14
dragons, 148:9
draught-horses, 132:12
drum, 149:8; 150:7
dust, 142:12
duty: vicarious fulfillment of, 121:10
dwelling, 122:4

ear, 130:6
early Church, 131:5
    unity, 132:2,12
earth, 144:13; 147:22; 148:9
    established upon the waters, 135:7
    waterless, 142:11
Easter: time before and after, 148:1
eating, 125:7; 146:2
Edom, 136:18,19
Egypt, 134:14,18,19; 135:8
Egyptians, 123:6; 128:2
elect, 140:8,9,10,12,24
Elijah, 129:9
Elisha, 129:9
embarrassment, 141:9
Emmaus, 147:17
emotions, 135:3
emperor, 148:2
emptiness, 143:11
encouragement, 121:2
end of the world, 142:14; 147:3,4
endurance, 138:20; 139:14
enemy(-ies), 133:1,13; 137:14; 139:7,10; 141:14; 142:4,16; 143:5
    body of Christ (Church), 139:2
    charity not conquered by, 132:8
    God's hand is worse than anger of, 137:13
    love them; hate their sins, 138:27,28
Enoch, 128:2
envy, 124:2; 139:8
Ephrathah, 131:11
episcopus, 126:3
Esau, 136:18
escape, 123:3,4,8
eternal life, 121:11; 122:8; 123:4; 127:7,15; 129:6; 130:1,15; 134:6; 136:9,15; 138:30; 143:18; 149:1; 150:3

desire for Jerusalem, 136:22
    present life given precedence, 140:24
    seeing God face to face, 130:14
    sell all you possess..., 136:13
    See also heaven
eternal punishment, 138:7; 141:4
eternity, 121:6; 137:16; 143:18; 144:2; 145:20; 148:8; 149:12
Eucharist: Christ as nourishment, 130:11
Eve, *See* Adam and Eve.
    example, harmful, 139:4
Exodus, 135:9
eye, 130:6,8
eye of a needle, 132:4

faith, 122:4; 124:2,4; 136:10; 139:1; 144:10; 145:19; 146:6; 149:4,11
    asleep, 147:3
    believing in Jesus means loving, 130:1
    guarded; growth, 134:18
    health in Christ's body, 130:8
    hearts cleansed by, 123:2
    milky diet of, 130:11
    riches for a believer, 143:18
    salvation; grace, 137:18
false accusation, 128:4; 138:26
fathers, 127:12
fear, 129:3; 135:3; 141:4; 147:4
    charity casts out fear, 127:7; 149:15
    devil's door, 141:4
    motivated by, 127:7
    second coming of Christ, 147:1
fear of God, 127:1,8-9,15; 138:19; 144:23; 146:20; 150:1
feet, 140:8
Felix (martyr), 127:6
fidelity: may I be struck dumb..., 136:17
fingers, 143:3,6,9
fire, 128:8; 148:10,11,12
fiscus, 146:17
fish (153 caught), 150:1
fishing, 138:27
flattery, 140:13,17; 147:11
flautist, 121:8
flea, 148:10
flesh: versus spirit, *See under* law
food, 145:17
fool, 122:3,8; 129:5
forbearance, 144:11
forgiveness, 143:7; 147:13
forgiveness of sin, 129:3,6,12; 136:1; 144:24; 147:18
    woman drying Christ's feet, 140:8
fortune, illusory, 129:1
foundation, 121:4
fraud, 143:5
free will, 134:11
fruit of the womb, 126:8

fruit: *eat the labors of*, 127:4,10
fullers, 132:9
future: God and, 125:10
future life, 147:4; 148:1
　See also heaven; hell; immortality

garment, 147:23
gate: Christ as, 126:13
　bars strengthened, 147:9,20
generation, 144:6
generosity, 125:12
gentiles, 126:11; 134:8,22,24; 145:18
Getulia, 148:10; 149:3
Gideon, 137:9
gifts, 130:8; 144:22; 146:10
giving: motivation, 125:11-12
gladiator, 147:3; 149:10
glorification, 150:3
glory, 131:28; 138:20; 142:18; 146:19; 149:10,11
gnat, 148:10
God: abiding in himself, 122:4
　abundance of your sweetness, 144:9,10
　all-powerful, 134:12
　alone does wonderful deeds, 135:4,5
　being of, 121:5,6,12
　blamed; praised, 128:5
　caring, 145:13,14
　change and, 131:18
　cursed by one's life, 133:2
　death of, 148:8
　disciplinary scourge of, 138:15
　early deeds as "face" of, 138:8
　earthly kin, 127:12
　fleeing from, 138:12,13
　forbearing toward sinners, 144:11
　future acts and, 125:10
　glory, 137:6,10
　God of gods, 135:2,9
　goodness, 134:3,4,5; 144:3,5,6,8
　greatness of, 150:4
　humans find riches in, 124:2
　I AM WHO AM, 121:5; 127:15; 130:12; 134:4,6; 143:11
　joy: prospect of seeing God, 130:8
　justice, 144:21
　keeps faith for ever, 145:15
　knowledge of, 141:6
　knowledge too wonderful for me, 138:9
　lovable and terrible, 144:8
　love shown in Christ's death, 146:4
　Manichee teaching, 140:10
　master and mistress, 122:5
　Moses and, 138:8
　my mercy, 143:7
　my rest for ever and ever, 131:22
　my support and deliverer, 143:9
　name of, 121:5
　omnipresence, 138:10-13; 142:16

　peace, 124:10
　personal, 139:10
　possession, 145:11
　power of, 144:8; 146:11
　promises, 148:8
　repenting, 131:18
　seeing Him Who Is, 121:8
　speaks in his own substance, 138:8
　speaks through his scriptures, 127:9
　submission to, 143:6
　taunt, where is your God, 127:10; 130:12
　understanding cannot be reckoned, 146:11,13
　wonderful and terrible, 138:19
　works of, 144:7,9; 147:2
　you have stretched out your hand..., 137:13
　See also creation; Holy Spirit; Jesus Christ; Trinity
godless, 142:5; 145:10
godliness, 143:18
gods, 134:9; 135:2; 144:17; 145:12
gold, 123:9,10; 145:4
Goliath, 143:1,2
good and evil, 121:14; 134:16; 142:4,10; 145:19; 148:2
　conversion of life, 124:10
　good cannot separate from the wicked, 138:26,27,31
　members of the Church, 128:8
　rejoicing over evil, 139:12
　roots of all evils, 139:1
　unrighteous persons, 139:4
good example, 123:6
good people: *luminaries in this world*, 146:9
good Samaritan, 136:7
good works, 125:13; 131:20; 132:4; 142:10,15; 143:9,11; 146:2; 147:6
　children's children as, 127:16
　credit God for, 137:18
　rich in, 136:13
grace, 130:14; 132:10; 133:2; 140:15; 142:5,10,18; 143:2,3; 144:10; 146:6; 147:26; 150:1
　new song, 143:16
　pride in gifts from God, 130:7
　saved, through faith, 137:18
grass, 128:11,12; 146:16
greed, 123:10; 131:26; 136:9; 147:12
groaning, 131:10
guardian: bishop as, 126:3
guile, 121:8; 123:6; 138:6
gyration, 139:13

Haggai, 147:5; 148:4; 149:12
hail, 148:10,11,12
handicapped, 125:12
hands, 143:3,6,9
　good works, 142:15

Index

left and right, 136:15,16,17; 137:14; 143:18
    power, 149:12
happiness, 122:2,8; 126:7; 127:9; 136:5,16,22; 137:14; 143:18; 147:4
harmony (music), 150:7
harps, 136:6,10
harvests, 149:3
harvesters: angels, 128:12,13
hate, 139:2; 140:14
    men of blood, 138:26
    perfect hatred, 138:28
healing, 144:22; 146:7,8
health, 122:11,12; 143:13
    coordination of all members, 130:6
    seeking, in body of Christ, 130:8
hearers (parable of the seed), 128:1
heart, 123:9; 128:1; 129:2; 130:4; 131:4; 132:6; 134:4,16; 138:18; 139:15; 142:9; 143:18; 145:1; 148:17; 149:11; 150:8
    ascents in, 122:3; 126:6
    bruised, 146:5,6,7,8
    crooked; perverted, 146:7
    cursing in, 132:13
    inner mouth, 125:5,7,8
    lift up your hearts, 132:13; 141:15
    purified by faith, 130:8
    spiritual holocaust, 137:2
    straightforward hearts, 124:2,9,10
    striking (bruising) our breasts, 146:7
    test me, O God, 138:29
    unrighteous thoughts, 139:5
    virgin at heart, 147:10
    wrung with pain, 122:2
heat, 147:22
heaven, 121:3,4; 122:1,3,4,6; 124:3; 130:8; 132:13; 136:9; 141:4; 142:7,12; 147:27; 149:5
    praising/loving God, 147:3
    see, love, and praise God, 147:8
heavens, 135:5; 148:3,5; 150:2
    apostles as, 143:12
    just persons, 121:9
    saints, 135:3
hell, 123:12; 127:8,15
heresies, 124:5; 130:9,10; 138:26; 141:9; 145:16
Hermon, Mount, 132:11
hills, 124:4,10; 126:6
holiness, 130:13; 131:28; 144:10
holocaust, 130:4; 137:2
holy of holies, 132:7
Holy Spirit, 125:10; 126:2; 127:8; 130:5; 132:7,8; 135:3; 139:14; 141:5; 142:18; 143:7; 144:1; 146:6
    gifts of, 143:3
    helper, 143:6
    new creation, 142:12
    seven-fold action, 150:1
home, 141:17

honesty, 123:9
honor, 123:9
hope, 122:1; 123:2,3,10; 124:4,6; 125:2,4; 126:7; 127:5,10; 129:2,3,6,8,9,10,11,12; 130:15; 131:16,19,24; 138:12,20; 139:14; 141:12; 142:14; 144:11,19,23; 145:2,3,7,9; 146:20; 147:3; 148:1; 149:11
horn: symbol of exaltation, 131:27
horse, 145:4; 146:19
hospitality, 140:8
house, 141:15
house of the Lord, 121:3,14; 126:3,13
human acts: *by their fruits...*, 149:2
    God's *eyes are upon the righteous*, 137:11
human beings
    benefits conferred by Christ, 136:9
    bodies as servants, 145:5
    both foolish and wise, 147:11
    do not despise works of your hands, 137:18
    God's care for, 148:8
    goodness of humankind, 134:4
    value of, 143:10
human body, 121:6; 147:23
    animal; spiritual, 136:18
    corruptibility, 141:18
    flesh is from earth, 146:13
    See also immortality; resurrection of the body; soul
human condition, 122:6,11,12; 125:3; 129:1; 138:16; 140:15; 146:8; 148:4
    emptiness, 143:11
    fashioned by God in the womb, 138:7
humiliation, 134:20; 138:4; 141:13; 146:14; 147:27
humility, 121:8; 123:13; 126:4,5; 130:7; 137:10
    bruised hearts, 146:5
    false, re learning, 130:12,14
    God *looks on the lowly*, 137:11
    pursuit of wisdom, 130:12
    rise after sitting down, 127:10; 138:4
    sacrifice; heart, 130:4
    true perfection, 130:14
    truly poor, 131:24
hunger: *Blessed are those who hunger...*, 131:24; 145:17
husband and wife, 143:6; 149:15
    chaste fear, 127:8
hymn, 148:17
hypostatic union, 130:10

I AM WHO AM, 121:5; 127:15; 130:12; 134:4,6; 143:11
ice, 147:2,25,26; 148:10,11,12
idipsum, 121:5

idolatry, 123:5
idols, 134:23,24; 135:3
image of God, 129:1; 147:7
immortality, 122:1; 127:16; 140:16; 146:6; 148:8
imperfection: beheld by God, 138:21,23
Incarnation: *Word made flesh...*, 130:9
incorruptibility, 141:18; 147:20
increase: kinds and modes, 137:8
iniquity, 124:10; 147:8
   increasing mightily, 138:14
   love of, 140:2
   night as, 131:8
   See also good and evil; sin
injury, 145:15,16
innocence, 125:8; 139:4
insult, 122:9,10
intelligence, 148:3
intention, 125:5,7
interior life: affection of heart, 141:2
   enter within, 139:15
irreligion, 136:6,15
Isaac, 134:6,7; 137:6; 147:28; 148:17
Israel, 126:3; 128:2,3; 129:12; 134:7,22,25;
   145:11; 146:4; 147:28; 148:17; 149:4,6
   meaning of the word, 124:10
   name, 121:8
   testimony to, 121:8
   tribes of, 121:7,8

Jacob, 126:8; 134:6,7,8,9,22; 136:18; 137:6;
   143:18; 145:11; 146:4; 147:27,28
Jeremiah, 147:5
Jerusalem, 121:2,3,4,9,11; 122:4; 124:3;
   125:1,3,9; 126:3; 127:3,15; 134:26;
   136:1,2,7,12,15,19,20,21; 138:18,29;
   142:3; 146:4,8,9,11; 147:6,7,8,9,15,18,20,
   22, 26,28; 148:4; 149:5
   built like a city, 121:4,5
   goal of ascent, 121:7
   meaning: vision of peace, 124:10; 127:16
   restoration in prophecy, 147:5
Jesus Christ, 125:1,5,6; 126:3,11; 129:1,2,3;
   130:2,7; 132:9; 134:4; 135:9; 136:22;
   137:9; 139:2,7; 141:4; 143:1,12; 144:5;
   145:9; 146:17; 147:3,13; 148:7,16;
   149:1,10,14
   Abraham's seed, 148:17
   anointed, 131:28; 149:6
   beautiful, 127:8
   believing in, means loving, 130:1
   bread for us to eat, 138:1
   bride and bridegroom, 122:5
   called to mind days of old, 142:10
   cornerstone, 126:2
   crucifixion, 121:8; 130:7; 131:17; 134:22;
      138:8; 140:5,6; 141:9; 148:8
   David and, 143:2; 144:2
   died as man; rose as God, 130:10
   disciples: he is only a man, 138:22

divinity, 138:2,3
divinity invisible to human eyes, 138:8
end of the law, 139:3
equal to the Father, 126:5
eternal way, 138:30
Father, forgive them..., 124:7; 132:8
feet (place of worship), 131:13,14
figures (Solomon's temple), 126:2
firmament of his strength, 150:4
form of God, 121:5
foundation stone, 121:4
gate, 126:13
get behind me, Satan, 126:4; 138:22
God is Father and Lord, 138:3
heavenly bread, 130:9
humanity, 134:5; 139:18
I confess to you, Father..., 137:2;
   141:19; 144:13
I was hungry, and you fed me, 140:7
I will that where I am..., 126:4
left hand; right hand, 143:18,19
light, 132:11
living bread come down from heaven,
   131:24
master and slave, 124:7
mediator, 134:5
My grace is sufficient for you, 130:7
not peace but a sword, 143:17
one with the Father, 142:3
passion, 126:4; 129:7; 138:4; 146:4;
   147:16; 148:8; 150:3
   agony in the garden, 140:4
   disciples terrified by, 138:22
   doing my Father's will, 142:8
   I am all alone ..., 140:25,26
   let this cup pass from me, 144:19
   my soul is sorrowful..., 142:9
peace, 124:10
post-resurrection appearances, 138:8,25;
   147:17
power to lay down my life, 138:21
prays in the Church, 140:7
prefigured by David, 142:2
priest and victim, 130:4; 132:7; 149:6
prophesied about (psalm 1), 150:2
psalms: his words in all, 131:2
resurrection, 129:6,7,9; 131:15;
   138:4,21,23,25; 140:25; 147:17,18;
   148:1; 150:4
rock, 140:19
Samaritan, 125:15
sanctifying power, 131:28
Saul, why are you persecuting me?
   122:1; 130:6; 138:2; 140:3; 141:11;
   142:3; 148:17
second coming, 143:14; 147:1,3
sinless, 137:16; 140:3
Son of God; son of man, 138:22
spiritual generation of, 139:3

suffering still, in the Church, 142:3
transfiguration, 147:23
victim, 149:6
washing of his feet, 125:5
way, truth, and life, 123:2; 125:4; 141:9
Who is my mother..., 127:12
wisdom's lamp, 138:14
Without me you can do nothing, 130:6
woman drying his feet, 140:8
world did not know him, 141:15
See also Christian life; Church; Mystical Body of Christ; Son of Man; Word of God
Jews, 134:7,22; 138:18; 148:17
blinded for their pride, 138:8
book-bearers for Christians, 136:18
captivity; exile, 125:3; 136:1,4
law as yoke, 125:6
laws, 143:2
remnant saved, 131:17
See also Israel
Job, 132:5; 133:2; 138:17; 144:4,18,19
John, Apostle, Saint, 144:9
John the Baptist, 131:14,27; 132:11; 139:15; 140:26
Jonah, 129:1
joy, 121:3; 123:3; 125:5,6,11,14; 127:5,10; 130:8; 136:17; 139:18; 145:2; 149:4
jubilation, 150:8
Judas, 130:7; 136:9; 142:2,4,7,16; 146:17,20
judgment, 134:22; 142:6; 150:3
merciless, 143:8; 147:12
sitting in, 121:9,10
judgment day, 121:9; 128:7; 129:10; 134:20; 135:1; 138:26,27,29; 139:2; 141:4,10; 144:17; 147:1,3,13; 148:1; 149:15
Julian, emperor, 124:7
justice, 124:6; 139:18; 140:14; 142:5,18; 143:17; 145:15,16; 150:3
justification, 144:10; 150:3

kindness, 125:15
kingdom (of God), 144:15,16; 147:10
kings, 149:14
knocking, 146:12
knowledge: wisdom and, 135:8

laity, 132:4
lamb, 141:1
land, 150:2
languages, multiplicity of, 147:19
Latin language, 123:8
latria, 135:3
law, 123:14; 147:16; 150:1
bear one another's burdens, 129:4
charity, fear, mercy, 129:3
flesh opposes law of mind, 140:16; 143:5,6,9; 146:6; 147:26

just, 145:15
mysteries; significance, 143:2
lawgiver, 129:3
Lazarus, 126:7; 129:9
lead, 145:4
learning: false humility, 130:12
lies; lying: root of every bad action, 139:13
life, 143:11
anguish, 137:12
confusion, 125:3
hours, days, years, 121:6
shouting, 148:2
sojourner on earth, 148:11
sought by persecutors or by lovers, 141:11
stages, 127:15
temporal and eternal, 136:15
light, 124:4,5; 126:4,7; 138:16,17; 139:4,14; 141:11,14; 143:4,11; 144:3
lightning, 134:13; 143:13
listening, 139:15
longing, 123:2; 126:1,12; 136:2,22; 143:19; 145:1,18; 147:4,17; 148:1
Lord's Prayer
Forgive us our debts [trespasses]..., 129:3,4,5,12; 140:18,19; 142:6; 143:7
Thy kingdom come, 147:1
Lot, 128:2
love, 123:2; 124:6; 134:11; 136:2; 137:2; 141:15; 144:1; 145:5,20; 147:3,15; 148:15; 149:5
ascending / descending, 122:1
believing in Jesus means loving, 130:1
charity casts out fear, 127:7; 149:15
city's strength, 121:12
commandments and, 139:18
commending God to you, 149:4
death suggests power of, 121:12
disappointments and, 127:1
experience of anguish, 137:12
fear and, 149:15
God is charity, 149:4
holy / impure, 121:1
interior life, 139:15
powerful; duty, 121:10
suffering for, 141:7
true and false, 140:2
two commandments, 121:1; 125:15; 140:2
See also charity
lust, 134:12
lyre, 146:14; 150:6

Maccabees, 137:14; 148:11
maid: God our mistress, 122:5
Manichees, 123:14; 140:10,12; 146:13
manna, 130:9

marriage, 127:1; 138:2
martyrs, 123:3,7,13; 125:2; 127:2,5,16; 129:11;
    132:9; 134:24; 137:14,17; 139:12,16;
    140:20,21; 141:4,5; 147:27; 148:11
  precious in sight of the Lord, 140:21
  prophets as, 140:26
  rich crop (early martyrs), 140:21
Mary, Blessed Virgin, 131:15; 148:17
  city of God, 142:3
  righteousness, 142:3
Massa Candida, 144:17
master: slave and, 124:7,8
Maximianus, 124:5
meek, 146:12
melt, 147:26
mercy, 125:14; 129:12; 134:21; 137:5,16,17;
    139:18; 140:13; 143:7; 144:4,11,12;
    147:12; 150:3
  corporal / spiritual works of, 121:9, 10
  eternal; every verse in this psalm, 135:1
  God's law, 129:3
  merit and, 123:14
  motive for confession, 135:4,9
  peace and, 125:11
  supreme over judgment, 143:8
  works of mercy, 125:11; 130:13; 147:12,13
merit, 123:14; 134:8; 139:18
milk, 130:9,11,13,14; 143:2
mind, 121:6; 145:5
miracles, 130:5,6; 143:13
  pride in, 130:8
  raising the dead, 130:6
miser: blames God, 128:5
misfortune : God *strengthens all who are falling*,
    144:18
mist, 147:24,25,26
mockery, 145:19; 147:11
monasteries: *brothers dwell together in unity*,
    132:2
money, 131:25; 146:17
moneylenders, 128:6; 140:12
monks: *agonistici*, 132:6
  Circumcellions, 132:3
  spurious, bogus, 132:4
moon, 135:8; 142:3
morning, 142:14,15
mortality, 145:17
Moses, 121:5; 123:14; 128:2,6; 134:14; 138:8;
    147:16,17,18,25
    See also law; Pentateuch
mother: baby in arms of, 130:13
mountains, 124:4-5; 143:12; 146:17
  love; hope, 124:6
  represent great persons, 124:5; 132:12;
    146:16
mouth, 149:11
  defiled by what comes from, 125:7
  filled with joy, 125:6
  heart, 125:5,7,8; 137:2

murder, 125:7
murmuring, 144:19
musical instruments, 150:5-8
mysteries, 126:2; 147:2
  Christ and the Church, 142:3
  in holy scripture, 140:1
Mystical Body of Christ, 122:1; 123:1;
    125:13; 127:3; 130:1,3; 140:3; 142:3;
    148:17
  faith and health of, 130:8
  gifts given to each member, 130:6
  perfect man, 138:2
  two speak with one voice, 138:21
  unity, 147:25
  See also Church

names, 130:8; 146:10; 148:14
Nathaniel, 121:8
nations, 147:28
need, 125:13; 141:19; 147:12
New Covenant, 123:14; 138:28; 143:16; 150:1
night, 131:8; 138:14,16,17,19; 142:15; 143:11
Noah, 128:2; 132:5; 147:1
nonbelievers, 134:16
numbers (symbolism)
    3, 4, 7, 10, 15, 40, 50, 150, 153,
    150:1
    5, 147:10
    70, 147:5
Numidia, 149:3

Og, king of Bashan, 135:9
oil, 127:13; 132:7,8; 140:13; 147:11,13
Old Testament: hidden meanings in, 143:1
oleaster, 134:7; 147:28
olive, 127:13
olive-press, 136:9
olive tree, 134:7,8
one alone (*monos*), 132:6
organ, 150:7
original sin, 132:10
orphans, 145:18
ossum, 138:20
ownership: common; early Christians, 131:5
ox(-en), 126:11; 145:13,14

pagans: killed by conversion, 149:13
pain, 122:6
parables (of sown seed), 128:1; 139:4; 149:3
pardon, 144:11
parents: children and, 136:21
Pasch, 138:8; 140:25
past, 125:10
patience, 138:27
patients, 147:2
Paul, Saint, apostle, 126:2; 140:21; 142:6;
    147:14,25; 149:8,13
  greatness of, 124:6
  inner strength, 138:20

livelihood, 146:16
manual labor, 125:15
mysteries revealed to, 130:14
shipwrecked, 123:9
sting of the flesh, 130:7; 144:19; 146:1
synagogue as mother of, 138:18
weak and on fire, 141:19
peace, 121:11,12,13; 124:5,10; 126:2; 127:16; 130:14; 134:26; 136:2; 143:9,18; 147:15,20,28; 149:2
   blessed are the peacemakers, 127:13
   mercy and, 125:11
   work of, 147:16
Pentateuch: five stones, 143:2
Pentecost, 132:2; 138:8; 147:19
people of God, 147:10
perdition, 139:16; 145:19
perfection, 130:14; 132:9
persecution, 123:5,7; 127:16; 128:2,3; 132:7,8; 136:19; 137:14; 138:20,27; 139:16; 140:22-24; 141:5,6,11,14,16; 142:7; 145:16
perseverance, 131:13; 133:1; 134:2; 138:14; 139:11; 141:6
Peter, Saint, apostle, 126:4; 130:6; 138:8,21,22; 140:21,24,26; 141:8
Pharaoh, 134:18; 136:17
Pharisees, 140:8
Photinus, 124:5
physician, 144:22
pig(-s), 130:1; 141:1
pilgrim(-age), 122:2; 123:2,3; 126:3,6; 131:10,21; 138:5; 145:1,9; 147:22; 148:4,10
pleasure, 124:10; 126:12; 127:16; 131:8; 136:6,9; 138:15; 147:4; 148:15
pledge, 122:5; 127:8; 146:6,11
poor person[s], 121:11; 125:13; 136:14; 146:17
   humility: the truly poor, 131:24
   justice for, 139:17
   pride and, 131:26; 132:4
   rebuking God, 124:2
possessions, 122:8; 123:9; 131:6; 145:18; 147:4,12
poverty, 121:11
powers in the night, 135:8
praise, 128:5; 131:10; 134:5,6,8,9,11; 139:2; 140:11; 142:6; 144:1-7,10,22,25; 145:2,4,5,6,7,8; 146:1,2,3,4; 147:3,6-9, 13,15; 148:1,3,5-10,12,17; 149:11; 150:3,4,7,8
   beneficial for us, not for God, 134:1,2,4,5
   bless God at all times, 138:16
   confession of, 137:2; 141:19
   during every single day, 144:3
   generation after generation, 144:6
   whole of yourselves, 148:2
prayer, 147:7

all one in Christ, 122:2
call upon him in truth, 144:22
Church's prayer, 139:2
concluding prayer, 150:8
God's *ears are open to*, 137:11
good and right things asked for, 144:19
hear me quickly, 137:7,8,12
I have cried to you ..., 140:4
let your ears be open, 142:5
out of the depths..., 129:1,2
pour out, before him, 141:3,5
rise like incense before you, 140:5
secret, 141:3
soon to be *very popular*, 140:18,19,20
supplication, 141:2
temple, 130:1,3
to you I have stretched out my hands, 142:11
whole life is entreaty, 139:10,11
with outstretched hands..., 143:11
You know my paths, 141:8
preachers: clouds as, 134:17
preaching, 134:16
preaching at the gate, 126:13
predestination, 136:21; 147:23; 150:3
presumption, 138:21; 144:11
pretense, 121:8
pride, 121:3,11; 122:3,9,10; 128:9,11; 130:5,8,12,14; 131:14; 136:13; 137:11; 138:19,27; 139:8,15; 140:18; 141:9; 142:6; 146:19; 147:26
   do not turn your face away, 142:13
   gifts from God, 130:7
   private ownership and, 131:7
   rich and poor, 131:26
   Starting point of every sin, 139:13
   temptation re wisdom, 130:12
priests, 130:4
prison: *lead my soul out...*, 141:17,18,19
Proculian, 149:4
Prodigal Son, 123:9; 131:12; 138:5,7,9
promises: God *is faithful in all his words*, 144:17
   temporal and eternal, 149:12
property (ownership), 131:3,5,7
prophecy: future as though it were past, 125:10
   speaking in tongues, 130:5
prophets, 147:16,17,18
   apostles born from, 126:11; 127:2
   Christ speaks through, 138:2
   full of Christ, 142:2
   martyrs, 140:26
propitiation, 129:3,5
prosperity, 138:16
Providence, 131:4; 138:1; 142:13; 145:14; 148:12
   all creatures do God's bidding, 148:10
   submission to, 124:2

Index

prudence: avoiding evil, 135:8
   seek not what is above you..., 130:13
psalms, 134:5,8; 145:8; 146:1,2; 147:2; 148:2
   150 (symbolism), 150:1
   find Christ and self in, 142:3
   five books, 150:2
   hear Christ's words in, 131:2
   sets of fifty, 150:3
   See also Song(-s) of Ascents
psaltery, 146:2,14; 149:8; 150:6
punishment, 141:18
   fear of, 127:8; 149:15
purity, 125:5
   blessed are the pure of heart, 130:8; 139:18
   commandment of charity, 140:2

rain, 132:10; 134:17; 146:16; 148:10
ravens, 146:18
Rebecca, 126:8
Red Sea, 135:9
redemption, 125:1,2; 129:12; 134:18; 136:7; 138:2; 143:17; 147:16,18,24; 149:9
reincarnation, 146:18
repentance, 136:3; 147:24; 150:3
reproof, 149:13
respect, 124:7; 136:3
resurrection of the body, 125:14; 126:7; 129:6,7,9; 131:16; 141:13
retribution: bargaining with God, 130:9,13
revenge: *You will vindicate me*, 137:15
reverence, 135:8; 142:13
reward, 126:8; 131:19; 134:11; 135:1; 138:18; 141:3; 142:6; 143:11; 146:1
rich: difficult to get into heaven, 146:16
   humility and, 131:26; 132:4
   liable for many sins, 132:4
   sell all you possess..., 136:13
   tested by attitude towards the poor, 124:2
rich and poor, 125:13; 127:16; 131:7,24; 136:14; 139:17; 145:7; 147:12,17
   See also poor; rich; wealth
righteousness, 121:8; 122:11,12; 124:6; 125:8; 129:2; 139:8,17; 140:18; 142:3,5,13; 144:22; 146:17; 147:20; 148:16; 150:3,4
rivers, 125:10
robber, 128:6,8; 130:3; 146:20
roots, 139:4
rulers, 124:7
ruminating, 141:1
running, 121:2; 130:14

Sabbath, 150:1
sacraments, 127:11
sacrifice, 134:11; 140:14; 146:5; 147:12,17; 149:6
   humility of heart, 130:4
sadness, 136:3; 138:20
saints, 122:4; 123:3; 124:5; 134:11; 135:3; 144:14,15,18; 147:14; 148:17; 149:3,4, 10-12,16; 150:4,5,8

   See also martyrs
salvation, 124:5; 131:27; 136:13; 144:23; 145:9; 149:9
   fear and trembling, 142:10
   grace, through faith, 144:10
   name written in heaven, 130:8
   temporal and eternal, 137:14
Samaritan, 125:15
Satan, 130:7,14
Saturn, 145:12
Saul, King, 131:2,18
Saul (later Paul), 149:13
scandals, 147:9
schism, 124:10; 138:29,31
scourging, 122:10
sea, 135:7; 138:12
   nonbelievers represented by, 134:16
seats sat in judgment, 121:9
seeds, 125:11,14; 128:1; 149:3
self, 122:3
self-discipline, 140:16
self-image, 129:2
self-love, 131:6; 139:18; 140:2
self-righteousness, 140:9
Selfsame, 121:5,6,8; 146:11
senses, 146:13; 147:10,1
   bodily unity, 130:6
Septuagint, 135:3
servant, 134:1,2; 142:6; 146:16
   God as our master, 122:5,6
sexual pleasure, 146:2
shackles, 149:15
shadow, 142:16; 143:11
shaker / shaken, 126:10,11; 127:2
shame, 141:9
shipwreck, 123:9
Sihon, 134:20; 135:9
silence, 139:15
Simon (magician), 130:5
sin, 125:9; 127:7,9; 136:7; 138:15,16; 140:6,11,13; 143:11; 145:2; 146:20; 149:1
   many small, daily sins, 129:5
   confessing and punishing, 146:7
   cords as symbol of, 130:2; 139:9
   dwells but does not reign, 143:6
   excuses sought for, 140:3,11,24
   hating, 139:2
   loving the world, 141:15
   melting away, 125:10
   slave of, 142:8
   turn your face away..., 122:3
   uncovered, 129:5
   works of the flesh, 143:6
   See also confession; repentance; sinners
singing, 123:2; 146:2; 147:5; 148:17
   love for this world, 136:17
   presence of angels, 137:3

sinners, 124:2,8; 127:11; 128:7,8; 129:1; 139:4; 140:9,13,14,18; 144:11; 145:19; 146:3,12,18; 147:7,26
  add sins to sins, 139:9
  break the necks of..., 128:9
  confessing, 143:12
  dead of this world, 142:8
  God will destroy all, 144:24
  loss of will to confess, 142:13
  presumption or despair, 144:11
  scourged by their own sins, 130:2
  slain: alienated from God, 138:26
sitting, 126:5; 138:4
sky, 146:15
slave: master and, 124:7,8
sleep, 131:8,9
snake, 139:6
snow, 147:2,23,24,25,26; 148:10,11,12
Sodomites, 128:2
soldiers, 131:10; 136:3
  monks as, 132:6
Solomon, 126:1-2
Son of Man, 145:9; 149:3
song(-s), 136:8,11; 137:10
  new song, 149:1,2,3
  singing *in a foreign land*, 136:13
Song[s] of Ascents (or *Steps*) (psalms), 121:2; 122:1,3; 123:1; 124:1,3; 125:1,15; 126:1,6; 129:1; 131:1; 150:1
Song of Songs, 143:18
sons: hope for the future, 131:19,20
sorrow, 126:6; 127:10
soul, 146:18
  bird escaped from net, 123:12
  inner strength, 138:20
  mind counsels, 145:5
  persecutors and, 141:11,14; 142:7
  suffering when flesh is killed, 130:10
  thirsts for the living God, 142:11,12
  transcending itself, 130:12
  wind as, 137:4
sounds, 150:8
sowing and reaping, 125:11,14
sparrow, 123:12; 124:5
speaking: demanded by duty, 139:15
  quick to hear, slow to speak, 139:15
speaking in tongues, 130:5
"speed of speed," 147:22
spirit, 141:5,6; 142:12; 145:10
  lusts against the flesh, See under law
spiritual life
  affections; riches, 121:11
  enemy *plotted to trip me up*, 139:7
  flesh under control, 143:6,9
  goal of our ascent, 121:7
  good faith, 123:9
  growth in, 131:1
  growth: milk to solid food, 130:12

heaven as foundation of, 121:4
horn: symbol of exaltation, 131:27
imperfection and fear, 138:21
possession of my inmost parts, 138:18
straightforward people, 139:18
test me, O God, 138:29
transcend self to reach God, 130:12
unspiritual persons and the Spirit of God, 127:1
spiritual warfare, 127:16; 136:8; 139:5,11,14; 143:3,4,5,9,10,18; 147:20
standing, 134:2
stars (heavenly bodies), 121:6; 135:8; 146:9,10
stealing, 125:7
Stephen, Saint, 132:8; 147:25
stones, 121:4
strength, 144:18; 148:16
substance, 123:9
suffering, 140:25; 147:27,28
  fill up what is lacking..., 142:3
  fruits of, 138:20; 139:14
  life hidden with Christ, 139:17
summer, 148:16
sun, 135:8; 142:3; 144:3; 148:16
Sunday, 150:1
superfluities, 147:12
Susanna, 125:8; 137:2
swallowed alive, 123:5,6
sword: *baleful*, 143:17
  double-edged, 149:12
synagogue, 127:12

tabernacle: Church as, 131:10,12
talkative person, 139:15
tares, 149:3
teaching, 139:15
tears: *bread to me day and night*, 127:10
temperance, 146:2
temple: buyers and sellers in, 130:2,5
  Christ prefigured (Solomon's temple), 126:2
  early Church, 131:5
  God's temple is yourselves, 126:3; 130:1; 137:4
  holy; yourselves as, 122:4; 137:4
  living stones, 121:4
  protected by God, 127:9
temporal goods, 123:5; 124:1; 127:1,2,9,15, 16; 129:8,11; 131:24,26; 136:3,5,9,16; 138:18; 140:24; 142:7; 143:18,19; 146:19; 147:3; 149:1,12
temptation, 124:1; 129:4; 134:20; 136:21,22; 141:17; 143:6,11
  weakness of soul, 122:6
tents (*tabernaculum*), 131:10
thanksgiving, 134:2
theater, 147:8
thief, 125:7

thirst, 142:12
thoughts, 148:2; 149:2
threshing-floor, 137:9
throne, 137:4
time, 147:5
    creation, 122:4
    seven-day rhythm, 125:3
    years failing, 121:6
tithes, 146:17
tongue, 140:18
    gladness, 125:6
    heart's, 125:8
    vipers' venom, 139:6
torrents: winter rivers, 125:10
trap, 123:12,13; 141:9
treasure: *earthen vessels*, 141:1
trees, 148:3
tribes, 121:7
tribulation, 136:5
tribute: *earthly kings exact*, 137:16
Trinity, 130:11; 135:6; 139:18; 150:1
triumph, 123:4
troubles, 122:7; 123:2; 139:16; 147:9
trumpet, 150:8
trust, 145:9,11,18
truth, 123:2; 130:1; 136:11; 137:5; 139:15; 140:19,20,26; 143:17; 144:22; 147:21
tunic, border of, 132:9

unbelievers, 143:4,17
understanding, 146:11,12; 147:22; 148:3
    underworld, 148:9
unity, 122:1,2; 123:1; 124:10; 127:13,14; 130:6; 132:1,2,6,10,12; 133:3; 138:26,27; 147:7,19,28; 149:3
usury, 128:6; 140:12

valleys, 126:6
value, 143:10
vanity, 141:17; 143:11,18
Venus, 140:9
vice, 138:28
victim, 123:10
vine, 148:16
virginity, 147:10
virgins: both sexes in the Church, 147:10
    five foolish virgins, 147:11
virtue: *increase in my soul*, 137:8
vocation: set apart in mother's womb, 138:18
vows, 131:3; 132:2

watchtower, 126:3
water: *insubstantial*, 123:7-9,11
    sinful nations as, 123:6
    surging waters, 143:15,17
wealth, 122:9-12; 123:9; 131:8,24; 132:4; 136:13,14,16; 138:17; 142:13; 143:18; 146:16

weather, 148:9
weeping, 126:6
    sowing seed, 125:14
weight, 121:4
wheat, 149:3
whipping, 122:6,7
wickedness, 134:4
    lowly in mind..., 130:12
widow, 145:18
    offering two tiny coins, 125:11; 128:1; 147:12
    truly desolate, 131:23,25
wife, *See* husband and wife.
will, 125:11,12
will (of God), 140:2; 142:17
willows, 136:6
wind, 134:13,17; 148:10,11,12
    soul, 137:4
wings, 138:13
winter, 148:16
wisdom, 121:9; 126:4; 130:14; 135:6,8; 136:7; 138:8; 141:4,15; 146:14; 147:22; 149:14,15
    false humility, 130:12
    light for the blind, 145:17
witnesses: not afraid, 140:20,21
womb, 138:18
woodland pastures, 131:11
wool, 147:23,24
Word of God, 138:8; 142:2; 147:22
    In the beginning..., 123:2; 130:9,10
words, 125:7
words of God (Holy Scripture) 123:6; 127:9; 128:1,4; 138:18; 143:15; 145:1
    double-edged sword, 149:12
    he continues to speak to us, 130:14
    hidden meanings in, 143:1
    my words have prevailed, 140:20
work, 125:3; 142:10; 148:3
    eat the labors of your fruits, 127:4,10
    joy in, 127:10
world, 131:24; 147:4
    cave or prison, 141:17
    creator of, 141:15
    threshing-floor representing, 137:9
    wicked persons called, 141:14,15
worm, 148:10
worship, 130:1; 137:4; 145:11
worth, 143:10

years, 121:6

Zacchaeus, 125:11,12; 128:1; 146:16
zeal, 138:27; 142:5; 147:21
Zebedee, sons of, 126:5
Zechariah, 147:5; 148:4
Zion, 125:3; 127:15; 128:10,13; 131:21,22; 132:12; 134:26; 136:1,2,4,5,14,17,20, 22; 142:3; 145:20; 149:5,6,8

THE COMPLETE WORKS OF ST. AUGUSTINE
A Translation for the 21st Century

Part I — Books

Autobiographical Works

The Confessions (I/1)
   cloth, 978-1-56548-468-9
   paper, 978-1-56548-445-0
   pocket, 978-1-56548-154-1
   Mobile App for iOS & Android available

Revisions (I/2)
   cloth, 978-1-56548-360-6

Dialogues I (I/3) forthcoming

Dialogues II (I/4) forthcoming.

Philosophical-Dogmatic Works

The Trinity (I/5)
   cloth, 978-1-56548-610-2
   paper, 978-1-56548-446-7

The City of God-Abridged Study Edition
   paper, 978-1-56548-660-7

The City of God 1-10 (I/6)
   cloth, 978-1-56548-454-2
   paper, 978-1-56548-455-9

The City of God 11-22 (I/7)
   cloth, 978-1-56548-479-5
   paper, 978-1-56548-481-8

On Christian Belief
   cloth, 978-1-56548-233-3
   paper, 978-1-56548-234-0

Pastoral Works

Marriage and Virginity (I/9)
   cloth, 978-1-56548-104-6
   paper, 978-1-56548-222-7

Morality and Christian Asceticism (I/10) forthcoming

Exegetical Works

Teaching Christianity (I/11) (On Christian Doctrine)
   cloth, 978-1-56548-048-3
   paper, 978-1-56548-049-0

Responses to Miscellaneous Questions (I/12)
   cloth, 978-1-56548-277-7

On Genesis (I/13)
   cloth, 978-1-56548-175-6
   paper, 978-1-56548-201-2

Writings on the Old Testament (I/14)
   cloth, 978-1-56548-557-0

New Testament I and II (I/15 and I/16)
   cloth, 978-1-56548-529-7
   paper, 978-1-56548-531-0

The New Testament III (I/17) forthcoming

Polemical Works

Arianism and Other Heresies (I/18)
   cloth, 978-1-56548-038-4

Manichean Debate (I/19)
   cloth, 978-1-56548-247-0

Answer to Faustus, a Manichean (I/20)
   cloth, 978-1-56548-264-7

Donatist Controversy I (I/21) forthcoming

Donatist Controversy II (I/22) forthcoming

Answer to the Pelagians (I/23)
   cloth, 978-1-56548-092-6

Answer to the Pelagians (I/24)
   cloth, 978-1-56548-107-7

Answer to the Pelagians (I/25)
   cloth, 978-1-56548-129-9

Answer to the Pelagians (I/26)
   cloth, 978-1-56548-136-7

Part II — Letters

Letters 1-99 (II/1)
   cloth, 978-1-56548-163-3

Letters 100-155 (II/2)
   cloth, 978-1-56548-186-2

Letters 156-210 (II/3)
   cloth, 978-1-56548-200-5

Letters 211-270 (II/4)
   cloth, 978-1-56548-209-8

Part III — Homilies

Sermons 1-19 (III/1)
   cloth, 978-0-911782-75-2

Sermons 20-50 (III/2)
   cloth, 978-0-911782-78-3

Sermons 51-94 (III/3)
   cloth, 978-0-911782-85-1

Sermons 94A-150 (III/4)
   cloth, 978-1-56548-000-1

Sermons 151-183 (III/5)
   cloth, 978-1-56548-007-0

Sermons 184-229 (III/6)
  cloth, 978-1-56548-050-6
Sermons 230-272 (III/7)
  cloth, 978-1-56548-059-9
Sermons 273-305A (III/8)
  cloth, 978-1-56548-060-5
Sermons 306-340A (III/9)
  cloth, 978-1-56548-068-1
Sermons 341-400 (III/10)
  cloth, 978-1-56548-028-5
Sermons Newly Discovered Since 1990 (III/11)
  cloth, 978-1-56548-103-9
Homilies on the Gospel of John 1-40 (III/12)
  cloth, 978-1-56548-319-4
  paper, 978-1-56548-318-7
Homilies on the Gospel of John (41-124) (III/13) forthcoming
Homilies on the First Letter of John (III/14)
  cloth, 978-1-56548-288-3
  paper, 978-1-56548-289-0
Expositions of the Psalms 1-32 (III/15)
  cloth, 978-1-56548-126-8
  paper, 978-1-56548-140-4
Expositions of the Psalms 33-50 (III/16)
  cloth, 978-1-56548-147-3
  paper, 978-1-56548-146-6
Expositions of the Psalms 51-72 (III/17)
  cloth, 978-1-56548-156-5
  paper, 978-1-56548-155-8
Expositions of the Psalms 73-98 (III/18)
  cloth, 978-1-56548-167-1
  paper, 978-1-56548-166-4
Expositions of the Psalms 99-120 (III/19)
  cloth, 978-1-56548-197-8
  paper, 978-1-56548-196-1
Expositions of the Psalms 121-150 (III/20)
  cloth, 978-1-56548-211-1
  paper, 978-1-56548-210-4

Essential Texts Created for Classroom Use

Augustine Catechism: Enchiridion on Faith Hope and Love
  paper, 978-1-56548-298-2
Essential Expositions of the Psalms
  paper, 978-1-56548-510-5
Essential Sermons
  paper, 978-1-56548-276-0
Instructing Beginners in Faith
  paper, 978-1-56548-239-5
Monastic Rules
  paper, 978-1-56548-130-5
Prayers from The Confessions
  paper, 978-1-56548-188-6
Selected Writings on Grace and Pelagianism
  paper, 978-1-56548-372-9
Soliloquies: Augustine's Inner Dialogue
  paper, 978-1-56548-142-8
Trilogy on Faith and Happiness
  paper, 978-1-56548-359-0

E-books Available

Essential Sermons, Homilies on the First Letter of John, Revisions, The Confessions, Trilogy on Faith and Happiness, The Trinity, The Augustine Catechism: The Enchiridion on Faith, Hope and Love.

Custom Syllabus

Universities that wish to create a resource that matches their specific needs using selections from any of the above titles should contact New City Press.

Free Index

A free PDF containing all of the **Indexes** from *The Works of Saint Augustine, A Translation for the 21st Century* published by NCP is available for download at www.newcitypress.com.

New City Press — The Works of Saint Augustine Catalog

For a complete interactive catalog of *The Works of Saint Augustine, A Translation for the 21st Century* go to New City Press website at: www.newcitypress.com

Electronic Editions

InteLex Corporation's Past Masters series encompasses the largest collection of full-text electronic editions in philosophy in the world. The Past Masters series, which includes *The Works of Saint Augustine, A Translation for the 21st Century*, published by New City Press, supports scholarly research around the world and is now being utilized at numerous research libraries and academic institutions. The Works of Saint Augustine (Fourth release), full-text electronic edition, is available for subscription from InteLex. The Fourth release includes all 41 of the published volumes as of May 2016. For more information, visit: http://www.nlx.com/home.

About the Augustinian Heritage Institute

In 1990, the Augustinian Heritage Institute was founded by John E. Rotelle, OSA to oversee the English translation of *The Works of Saint Augustine, A Translation for the 21st Century*. This project was started in conjunction with New City Press. At that time, English was the only major Western language into which the Works of Saint Augustine in their entirety had not yet been attempted. Existing translations were often archaic or faulty and the scholarship was outdated. These new translations offer detailed introductions, extensive critical notes, both a general index and scriptural index for each work as well as the best translations in the world.

The Works of Saint Augustine, A Translation for the 21st Century in its complete form will be published in 49 volumes. To date, 42 volumes have been published.

About New City Press of the Focolare

New City Press is one of more than 20 publishing houses sponsored by the Focolare, a movement founded by Chiara Lubich to help bring about the realization of Jesus' prayer: "That all may be one" (John 17:21). In view of that goal, New City Press publishes books and resources that enrich the lives of people and help all to strive toward the unity of the entire human family. We are a member of the Association of Catholic Publishers.

Free Index to *The Works of Saint Augustine*

Download a PDF file that provides the ability to search all of the available indexes from each volume published by New City Press.

Visit http://www.newcitypress.com/index-to-the-works-of-saint-augustine-a-translation-for-the-21st-century.html for more details.